Kenyon S. Tweedell

Recent Results in Cancer Research
Special Supplement

Biology of Amphibian
Tumors

Edited by
Merle Mizell

with 186 Figures

Springer-Verlag
New York-Heidelberg-Berlin
1969

Symposium: Biology of Amphibian Tumors

Sponsored by:
Tulane University; Cancer Association of
Greater New Orleans, Inc.; National Cancer Institute
October 28, 29, 30, 1968

To the memory of

Dr. Gladys M. Mateyko
(August 22, 1922–October 11, 1968)

Dr. Mateyko, the first woman to receive a Fellowship from the Damon Runyon Memorial Fund for Cancer Research, was an active investigator in the field of cancer research, and especially amphibian tumor studies. Her friends and colleagues dedicate this volume to her memory.

Contents

Preface . . . . **xi**

Introduction . . . . **xiii**

List of Participants . . . . **xv**

Introduction

State of the Art: Lucké Renal Adenocarcinoma. MERLE MIZELL . . . 1

Biology of Amphibians

Interrelations of the Populations of the *Rana pipiens* Complex. JOHN A. MOORE   26

Spontaneous and Experimental Mutations in the Newt *Pleurodeles Waltlii* Michah. LOUIS GALLIEN 35

Nucleo-Cortical Interactions During Amphibian Development. PHILIP GRANT   43

Amphibian Cells *in vitro*

Mass Culture of Amphibian Cells: Methods and Observations Concerning Stability of Cell Type. KEEN A. RAFFERTY, JR. 52

Dependence of Tumor Formation in Frogs on Abnormal Nucleolar Function. WILLIAM R. DURYEE 82

Characteristics of Cell Lines from Haploid and Diploid Anuran Embryos. JEROME J. FREED, LISELOTTE MEZGER-FREED *and* SUSAN A. SCHATZ . . 101

Species Identification of Poikilothermic Tissue Culture Cells. ARTHUR E. GREENE, LEWIS L. CORIELL *and* JESSE CHARNEY . . 112

Amino Acid and Nucleoside Incorporation in Frog Kidney Cells: An Autoradiographic Study. DANIEL MALAMUD *and* JOHN TINKER 121

Immunity and Tolerance in Amphibia

Immunity and Tolerance in Amphibia. EDWIN COOPER 130

Immunologic Tolerance and Blood Cell Chimerism in Experimentally Produced Parabiotic Frogs. E. PETER VOLPE, BRYAN M. GEBHARDT, SHERILL CURTIS, *and* ELIZABETH M. EARLEY 137

Immunogenetic and Developmental Aspects of Tissue Transplantation Immunity in Urodele Amphibians. NICHOLAS COHEN 153

Immunoglobulin and Complement Systems of Amphibian Serum. DONALD W. LEGLER, E. EDWARD EVANS, PETER F. WEINHEIMER, RONALD T. ACTON and MARIE H. ATTLEBERGER 169

The Amphibian as a Key Step in the Evolution of Lymphoid Tissue and Diverse Immunoglobulin Classes. B. POLLARA, W. A. CAIN, J. FINSTAD and R. A. GOOD 177

Tumors and Related Pathology in Amphibia

Some Morphological and Biological Characteristics of a Tumor of the Newt, *Triturus cristatus* Laur. VINCENZO G. LEONE and TERESA ZAVANELLA . 184

Skin Carcinogenesis, Mammals Versus Amphibia. BEPPINO C. GIOVANELLA . 195

Plasmacytoma in a *Rana pipiens*. SYDNEY S. SCHOCHET, JR. and PETER W. LAMPERT 204

Structures of Spontaneous and Transplanted Tumors in the Axolotl (*Siredon mexicanum*). VICTOR V. BRUNST 215

Tumors of the Testis in the Mexican Axolotl (*Ambystoma or Siredon mexicanum*). R. R. HUMPHREY 220

Distribution and Transmission of the Lucké Renal Adenocarcinoma

Simulated Transmission of Renal Tumors in Oocytes and Embryos of *Rana pipiens*. KENYON S. TWEEDELL 229

Non-Specific Transmission of the Lucké Tumor. DONALD J. MULCARE . . 240

Lucké Renal Adenocarcinoma: Epidemiological Aspects. ROBERT GILMORE McKINNELL 254

Chromosome Studies of Primary Renal Carcinoma from Vermont *Rana pipiens*. MARIE A. DiBERARDINO and NANCY HOFFNER 261

Viruses of Amphibia

Studies on the Viral Etiology of the Renal Adenocarcinoma of *Rana pipiens* (Lucké Tumor). ALLAN GRANOFF, MANETH GRAVELL and R. W. DARLINGTON . . . 279

Fine Structure Studies of Cytoplasmic Viruses Associated with Frog Tumors.
PHILIP D. LUNGER 296

Comparative Studies of Amphibian Cytoplasmic Virus Strains Isolated from the
Leopard Frog, Bullfrog, and Newt. H. FRED CLARK, CLAUDIA GRAY,
FRANCES FABIAN, ROBERT F. ZEIGEL *and* DAVID T. KARZON . . . 310

Tadpole Edema Virus: Pathogenesis and Growth Studies and Additional Sites
of Virus Infected Bullfrog Tadpoles.
KEN WOLF, G. L. BULLOCK, C. E. DUNBAR *and* M. C. QUIMBY . . . 327

The Herpestype Virus of the Lucké Renal Adenocarcinoma

Herpestype Virus Latency in the Lucké Tumor.
MERLE MIZELL, CHRISTOPHER W. STACKPOLE *and* J. JOYCE ISAACS . . 337

Density Gradient Centrifugation Studies on the Herpes-type Virus of the Lucké
Tumor. IRV TOPLIN, PHILLIP M. BRANDT *and* PETER SOTTONG . . . 348

Reactivity of Serum from Frogs and Other Species with a Herpesvirus Antigen
Extracted from a Burkitt Lymphoma Cultured Cell Line.
MARY A. FINK, GLADYS KING *and* MERLE MIZELL 358

A Preliminary Report on the Serology of Lucké and Burkitt Herpes-type Viruses:
A Shared Antigen. JOHN M. KIRKWOOD, GAYLA GEERING, LLOYD J. OLD,
MERLE MIZELL *and* JOHN WALLACE 365

Lymphoid Diseases in Amphibia

Possible Immunological Factors in Amphibian Lymphosarcoma Development.
LAURENS N. RUBEN 368

Organ Cultures of Normal and Neoplastic Amphibian Tissues.
MICHAEL BALLS, JOHN D. SIMNETT *and* ELIZABETH ARTHUR . . . 385

Acceptance and Regression of a Strain-specific Lymphosarcoma in Mexican
Axolotls. LOUIS E. DeLANNEY *and* KATE BLACKLER 399

Biologically Defined Strains of Amphibia

Development of Biologically Defined Strains of Amphibians.
GEORGE W. NACE *and* CHRISTINA M. RICHARDS 409

Diseases in an Amphibian Colony. GERALD D. ABRAMS 419

Neoplasia in Higher Vertebrates: Relevance to Amphibian Tumors

A. INVESTIGATIONAL APPROACHES

Some Comparative Morphological Aspects of Renal Neoplasms in *Rana pipiens*
and of Lymphosarcomas in Amphibia. CLYDE J. DAWE, JR. .   .   .   429

Immunological Approaches to the Study of Viral Antigens Associated with
Neoplasms. PAUL GERBER   441

Nucleic Acid Homology as Applied to Investigations on the Relationship of
Viruses to Neoplastic Diseases. MAURICE GREEN   445

B. TUMORS AND ASSOCIATED HERPES VIRUSES

Viruses Associated with Burkitt's Lymphoma. ROBERT A. MANAKER   .   .   455

A Herpes Virus as a Cause of Marek's Disease in Chickens.
B. R. BURMESTER, R. L. WITTER, K. NAZERIAN *and* H. G. PURCHASE .   .   460

Studies on the Viral Etiology of Marek's Disease of Fowl. DALE J. RICHEY   .   469

Herpes Simplex Viruses and Human Cancer: Current Status of the Problem.
BERNARD ROIZMAN   478

Summation and Perspectives

Summation and Perspectives. KARL HABEL   482

Preface

New Orleans has a distinguished history as a center for medical and biological learning, a history shared by Tulane University, its School of Medicine, and its Biological and Medical Sciences departments. This background made it especially fitting that the University, in conjunction with the Cancer Association of Greater New Orleans, Inc. and the National Cancer Institute, should sponsor the "Symposium: Biology of Amphibian Tumors" held October 28, 29, 30, 1968. The University wishes to express its appreciation to the Cancer Association for its assistance in making the Symposium possible and to acknowledge the support made available through the Biomedical Sciences Support Grant program of the National Institutes of Health.

As the title of this volume indicates, the Symposium yielded valuable results in the area of cancer research and it stands to stimulate further efforts in this most important field. Some notion of the impact of this symposium is suggested by the broad range of the 200 participants it attracted. They came not only from the breadth and length of the U.S., but from abroad, from France, England, Austria, and Italy.

No international convocation can reach any measure of success without the aid of a great many individuals. For the grand concept of the Symposium, credit must go to the members of the *ad hoc* organizational committee; and for the many local arrangements which provided the proper atmosphere for the exchange of information, we are indebted to all of the members of the New Orleans Host Committee.

It was Tulane's privilege to play a part in the presentation of the Symposium.

DAVID R. DEENER, Ph.D.
Provost and Dean of the Graduate School
Tulane University

The Cancer Association of Greater New Orleans and its parent organization, The United Fund of Greater New Orleans, are proud to have had the opportunity to co-sponsor the symposium in which these papers were presented. It was an exciting experience for our group to be involved in a meeting which brought together tumor researchers from such a variety of disciplines and geographical locations. The exchange of ideas fostered by such a gathering is a valuable goal in itself; however, it is particularly satisfying to realize that the effects of the symposium will extend far beyond the meeting itself because of this monograph, which will make the ideas available to cancer researchers throughout the world. We are most happy that we could extend the goal of our organization by contributing to such an endeavor.

SAMUEL LOGAN, M.D.
President, Cancer Association of
Greater New Orleans, Inc.

Introduction

Knowledge of major advances in amphibian tumor biology is of obvious value to amphibian oncologists and developmental biologists, but ironically the impetus for the compilation of this information had its origin with mammalian and avian investigators at the 1966 Gordon Research Conference on Cancer and was reinforced by similar comments made by mammalian colleagues at the IXth International Cancer Congress in Tokyo.

As originally conceived, the purpose of the Symposium was to promote the exchange of ideas between researchers working in various fields related to the study of amphibian tumors and to collate the current information into a single volume so that it would be readily available to *all* investigators in the field of tumor biology.

In an attempt to compile a comprehensive survey of current knowledge in the area of amphibian tumor biology, experts from an assortment of disciplines were invited to participate in the symposium and to present their latest results along with a general review of their area of interest. Population geneticists, immunologists, embryologists, virologists, epidemiologists, molecular biologists, biochemists and pathologists, as well as oncologists, contributed to the meeting and to this volume. As a result, a variety of approaches to the study of amphibian neoplasia were utilized, and the problem was examined on various levels, including subcellular, cellular, organismal and populational levels.

The fact that the renal adenocarcinoma (Lucké tumor) of the leopard frog, *Rana pipiens*, is the best understood amphibian tumor system and one in which many significant recent advances have occurred, is reflected by the attention it receives in this volume. However, the lymphosarcoma of the African clawed toad, *Xenopus*, as well as a number of other spontaneous amphibian neoplasms are also discussed.

To further the dialogue between mammalian, avian and amphibian tumor researchers, a panel of investigators working with tumors of higher vertebrates were invited to participate in a round table discussion. A significant feature of this session was the fact that it brought together for the first time investigators studying the suspected role of herpesviruses in several tumors: the Burkitt lymphoma and cancer of the cervix in humans, Marek's disease of fowl, and the Lucké tumor of frogs.

Highlights of the meeting were found in each of the in-depth sessions: the biology of amphibians; the culture of amphibian cells *in vitro*; immunity and tolerance in amphibia; distribution and transmission of the Lucké tumor; viruses of amphibia; the herpestype virus of the Lucké tumor; lymphoid diseases in amphibia; and biologically defined strains of amphibians. The difficult task of summation was handled with such clarity and acumen by Dr. Karl Habel that his presentation in itself became one of the highlights of the meeting.

The organization and assemblage of these topics was the result of a great deal of effort and imagination of a diligent and hard-working *ad hoc* organizational committee, which included: Dr. Allan Granoff, Dr. George W. Nace, Dr. Keen A. Rafferty, Jr., Dr. Laurens N. Ruben, Dr. Harry G. Steinman and Dr. Kenyon S. Tweedell. In addition, the organizational talents of Dr. Michael Balls, Dr. Robert G. McKinnell and Dr. E. Peter Volpe were called upon to make this a complete coverage of the biology of amphibian tumors. Dr. Robert A. Manaker arranged for the panel discussion, which provided an effective means of relating amphibian neoplasia to neoplasia in higher vertebrates. The panel elicited lively discussion, and the members of the panel were asked to prepare manuscripts, which are included in this volume.

Funding for the Symposium was provided by the National Cancer Institute, Tulane University and the Cancer Association of Greater New Orleans, Inc. Local support for the meeting was especially gratifying. Provost David R. Deener was instrumental in recognizing the value of this endeavor and in arranging for Tulane's support. Nor was the support of the Cancer Association of Greater New Orleans limited to financial assistance; the enthusiastic cooperation of Dr. Joseph V. Schlosser (Chairman of the Special Projects Committee) and Mrs. Ruth A. Sherwood (Executive Director) added immeasurably to our undertaking. The success of the meeting was assured by the tireless efforts of members of the New Orleans Host Committee. Compilation and production of this volume were simplified by the cooperation and assistance of the symposium organizers, each of whom read carefully the session he organized. The editorial assistance of Dr. Harold A. Dundee, Grace Bannatyne and Deborah Ramsey aided in ferreting out errors. I particularly want to thank Joyce Isaacs, who read literally every word and went over every manuscript with me. The publication of this type of book is a rather formidable undertaking which can involve many unforeseen problems; this volume was no exception. However, the staff of Springer-Verlag New York worked diligently to resolve the difficulties that arose and to enhance this volume with the fine quality of production that is the hallmark of Springer-Verlag.

An important, perhaps *the* important, result of the collation of information into this monograph is that it clearly indicates the prospective value of the study of amphibian tumors as a source of insight into neoplasms in higher forms. The spontaneous tumors of outbred populations of amphibians are potentially excellent model systems for the spontaneous tumors of man, who also represents an outbred population. To date, however, only a small portion of the knowledge to be gained from studies of amphibian tumors has been utilized; if this volume can provide the stimulus for investigations which will further tap this source of information, then the efforts of all involved will be amply rewarded.

MERLE MIZELL

New Orleans
June, 1969

List of Participants

ABRAMS, GERALD D.
Department of Pathology
The University of Michigan
Ann Arbor, Michigan

BALLS, MICHAEL
School of Biological Sciences
University of East Anglia
Norwich, England

BRUNST, VICTOR V.
Department of Experimental Biology
Roswell Park Memorial Institute
Buffalo, New York

BURMESTER, BEN R.†
Regional Poultry Research Laboratory
East Lansing, Michigan

BURNS, KENNETH *
Department of Vivarial Science
Tulane University School of Medicine
New Orleans, Louisiana

CLARK, H. FRED
Wistar Institute of Anatomy and
   Biology
Philadelphia, Pennsylvania

COHEN, NICHOLAS
Department of Microbiology
University of Rochester School of
   Medicine and Dentistry
Rochester, New York

COOPER, EDWIN L.*
Department of Anatomy
University of California School of
   Medicine
Los Angeles, California

DALTON, ALBERT J.†
Viral Oncology
National Cancer Institute
Bethesda, Maryland

DAWE, CLYDE J.* †
Laboratory of Pathology
National Cancer Institute
Bethesda, Maryland

DELANNEY, LOUIS E.
Department of Biology
Ithaca College
Ithaca, New York

DIBERARDINO, MARIE A.
Department of Anatomy
Women's Medical College of Pennsyl-
   vania
Philadelphia, Pennsylvania

DURYEE, WILLIAM R.
Department of Pathology
The George Washington University
   School of Medicine
Washington, D.C.

FINK, MARY A.*
Immunology Section
Viral Leukemia and Lymphoma Branch
National Cancer Institute
Bethesda, Maryland

FREED, JEROME J.
The Institute for Cancer Research
Philadelphia, Pennsylvania

FRIEDEN, EARL *
Department of Chemistry
Florida State University
Tallahassee, Florida

---

† Panel Discussant.
* Session Moderator.

GALLIEN, LOUIS
Laboratoire d'Embryologie
Faculté des Sciences de Paris
Paris, France

GERBER, PAUL †
Laboratory of Viral Immunology
Division of Biologics Standards
National Institutes of Health
Bethesda, Maryland

GIOVANELLA, BEPPINO C.
McArdle Laboratory for Cancer Research
University of Wisconsin
Madison, Wisconsin

GRANOFF, ALLAN ‡
Laboratory of Virology
St. Jude Children's Research Hospital
Memphis, Tennessee

GRANT, PHILIP
Department of Biology
University of Oregon
Eugene, Oregon

GREEN, MAURICE †
Institute for Molecular Virology
Saint Louis University School of Medicine
Saint Louis, Missouri

GREENE, ARTHUR
Institute for Medical Research
Camden, New Jersey

HABEL, KARL
Department of Experimental Pathology
Scripps Clinic and Research Foundation
La Jolla, California

HALPEREN, SIDNEY *
Dupont Central Research Department
Experimental Station
Wilmington, Delaware

HUMPHREY, R. R.
Department of Zoology
Indiana University
Bloomington, Indiana

KAPLAN, ALBERT *
Department of Microbiology
Albert Einstein Medical Center
Philadelphia, Pennsylvania

KING, THOMAS J.*
Department of Biology
Georgetown University
Washington, D.C.

KIRKWOOD, JOHN M.
Division of Immunology
Sloan-Kettering Institute for Cancer Research
New York, New York

LEGLER, DONALD W.
Department of Microbiology
University of Alabama Medical Center
Birmingham, Alabama

LEONE, VINCENZO G.
Laboratory of Embryology and Experimental Morphology
University of Milan
Milan, Italy

LUNGER, PHILIP D.
Department of Biological Sciences
University of Delaware
Newark, Delaware

MALAMUD, DANIEL
Fels Research Institute
Temple University School of Medicine
Philadelphia, Pennsylvania

MANAKER, ROBERT A.* †
Microbiology Section
Viral Biology Branch
National Cancer Institute
Bethesda, Maryland

‡ *Ad Hoc* Organizational Committee.

McKinnell, Robert G.
Department of Biology
Newcomb College of Tulane University
New Orleans, Louisiana

Mizell, Merle ‡
Department of Biology
Tulane University
New Orleans, Louisiana

Moloney, John B.†
Special Animal Leukemia Ecology Segment
National Cancer Institute
Bethesda, Maryland

Moore, John A.
Department of Life Sciences
University of California
Riverside, California

Mulcare, Donald J.
Department of Zoology
The University of Michigan
Ann Arbor, Michigan

Nace, George W.‡
Department of Zoology
The University of Michigan
Ann Arbor, Michigan

Pollara, Bernard
Pediatric Research Laboratories
University of Minnesota Hospitals
Minneapolis, Minnesota

Rafferty, Keen A., Jr.‡
Department of Anatomy
The Johns Hopkins University School of Medicine
Baltimore, Maryland

Richey, Dale J.†
Poultry Disease Research Center
University of Georgia
Athens, Georgia

Roizman, Bernard †
Department of Microbiology
University of Chicago
Chicago, Illinois

Rose, S. Meryl *
Department of Anatomy
Tulane University School of Medicine
New Orleans, Louisiana

Ruben, Laurens N.‡
Department of Biology
Reed College
Portland, Oregon

Schochet, Sydney S., Jr.
Neuropathology Branch
Armed Forces Institute of Pathology
Washington, D.C.

Steinman, Harry G.‡
Viral Oncology
National Cancer Institute
Bethesda, Maryland

Toplin, Irving
The John L. Smith Memorial for Cancer Research
Chas. Pfizer and Co., Inc.
Maywood, New Jersey

Tweedell, Kenyon S.‡
Department of Biology
University of Notre Dame
Notre Dame, Indiana

Volpe, E. Peter
Department of Biology
Tulane University
New Orleans, Louisiana

Wolf, Ken
Bureau of Sport Fisheries and Wildlife
Eastern Fish Disease Laboratory
Kearneysville, West Virginia

Zambernard, Joseph E. *
Department of Anatomy
University of Colorado Medical Center
Denver, Colorado

State of the Art: Lucké Renal Adenocarcinoma[1]

Merle Mizell

Department of Biology [2]
Tulane University
New Orleans, Louisiana

Amphibians are subject to the same range of neoplasms found in higher vertebrates; renal adenocarcinomas, lymphomas, lymphosarcomas, plasmacytomas and melanomas are among those which have been described. The Lucké tumor, a renal adenocarcinoma of the leopard frog, *Rana pipiens*, is undoubtedly the best understood of these cold-blooded tumors. This transmissable tumor has become the subject of increasingly intensified interest because of recent significant contributions to an understanding of its suspected viral etiology.

The Lucké tumor occurs spontaneously in feral populations of northern *Rana pipiens*. Although the gross external appearance of the tumor remains relatively unchanged, there are significant seasonal differences in the tumor's microscopic appearance. "Winter" tumors display cytopathic characteristics associated with the presence of virus, whereas "summer" tumors lack virus.

The Lucké tumor pictured in Fig. 1a developed in a laboratory housed frog which had received a 1 mm^3 tumor implant into its anterior eyechamber. Four months after implantation a small primary kidney tumor was detected by palpation and the frog was retained at laboratory temperature for an additional four months to allow growth of the tumor. The animal was then transferred to a low temperature cabinet ($7.5 \pm 0.5\,°C$) to induce virus production. After four months at low temperature the nine gram tumor (Fig. 1a) was removed, fractionated, and herpestype virus (HTV) was harvested (Figs. 1b, 1c). [The virus yield was greater than 10^{11} virus particles per gram of tumor (35).]

The two forms of the Lucké tumor—summer ("virus-free") and winter (virus-containing)—are temperature related states of the same tumor and evidence indicates that the viral genome is present in a masked or latent state in the "virus-free" form (21, 22). Because of the latitude of temperature demands in poikilotherms, this cold-blooded tumor system may provide basic information regarding tumor cell-virus interaction which avian and mammalian systems have been unable to supply.

Routine Propagation Techniques

Lucké and coworkers originally propagated this tumor by growing small pieces of tumor in the privileged immunological site [3] of the anterior chamber of the eye

---

[1] Aided by grant #E-494 from the American Cancer Society.

[2] The Chapman H. Hyams III Laboratory of Tumor Cell Biology.

[3] It should be noted that there is no experimental evidence to prove that the frog eyechamber is, in fact, a privileged immunological site.

1

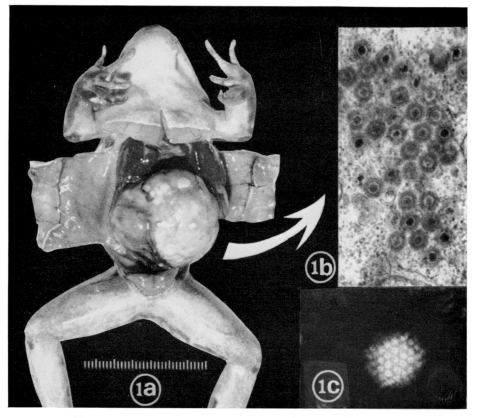

PLATE 1

Fig. 1a. Lucké renal adenocarcinoma which developed and was grown to nine grams at room temperature; the frog was then subjected to prolonged low temperature to induce virus production. Scale in millimeters.

Fig. 1b. Electron micrograph of frog HTV in the cytoplasm. $\times 37,000$.

Fig. 1c. Electron micrograph of negatively stained frog HTV, showing capsomere detail. $\times 140,000$.

(16, 31). Once established in the eye the tumors could then be serially passaged (31). Because efforts to propagate the Lucké tumor in tissue culture have been unsuccessful (9), eyechamber culture has remained a valuable *in vivo* "tissue culture" system and has been employed for a variety of studies (5, 11, 16, 17, 21, 22, 42).

Fig. 2 illustrates an eyechamber growth which began as a 1 mm³ implant and now covers most of the pupil. Dense cords of tubular growth can be seen in the central region surrounded by fluid-filled vesicular outgrowths. A more advanced eyechamber growth is pictured in Fig. 3. In this case, the rapidly growing tumor has filled the anterior chamber, ruptured the cornea, and is continuing to grow on the external surface of the cornea accompanied by a vascular supply from the host iris. Once a tumor becomes vascularized, the anterior chamber cannot be a privileged immunological site; nevertheless, if growth is vigorous, as shown in Fig. 3, it continues, apparently unaffected by any host immune reaction. (Perhaps the phenomena

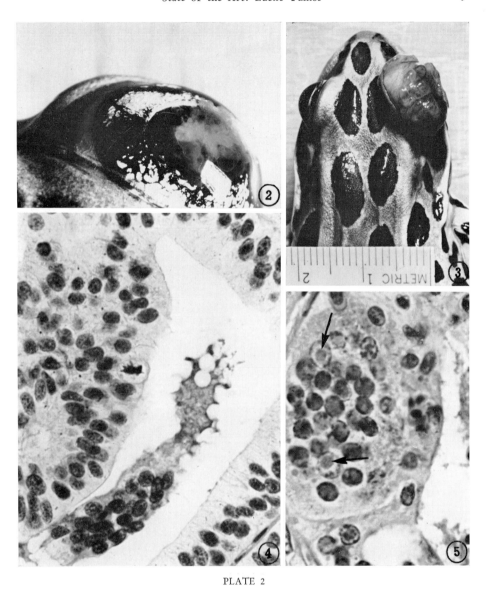

PLATE 2

Fig. 2. Lucké tumor growing in anterior eyechamber of *Rana pipiens*. Vesicular outgrowths can be seen originating from a central region of tubular tumor growth. ×6.5.

Fig. 3. Advanced eyechamber growth, which has completely filled the eye socket and ruptured the cornea. Scale in millimeters.

Fig. 4. Histological section of "summer" primary tumor biopsy. Note evenly dispersed chromatin; also note mitotic figure in center of photograph. (H & E) ×400.

Fig. 5. Histological section of tumor shown in Fig. 4 after 4 months of low temperature treatment. Several cells now display typical "winter" tumor characteristics: enlarged nuclei containing Cowdry Type A intranuclear inclusions (arrows) with chromatin margination along the nuclear membrane. (H & E) ×400.

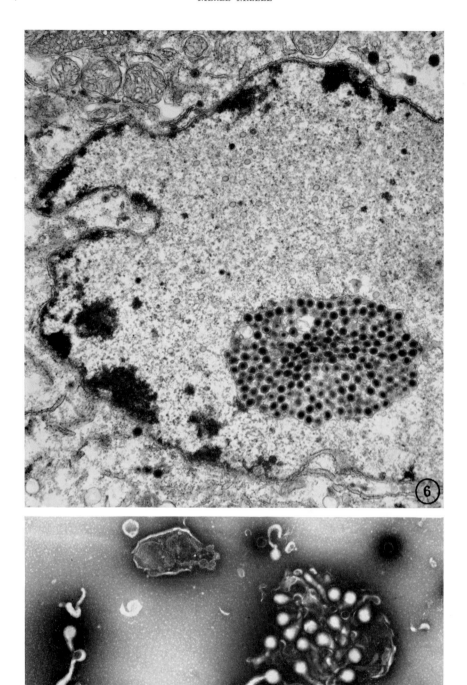

of dosage and acquired tolerance are operative under these conditions.) Regression of this type of growth seems to occur because of secondary infection, hemorrhage, or lack of suitable substrate.

Although there is significant variation in the growth rate of *primary tumors*, most tumors grow at a relatively rapid rate when housed at laboratory temperature. The typical histology of a "summer" renal adenocarcinoma (in this case, a tumor which developed at laboratory temperature) is shown in Fig. 4. This tissue was obtained by biopsy before the frog was placed at low temperature for virus induction. Fig. 5 illustrates the nuclear alterations within cells of the same tumor after four months of low temperature treatment. Although the general pattern of multi-layered tumor tubules is similar to the "summer" tumor pattern, several cells display nuclear alterations characteristic of "winter" tumor cells: (a) enlarged nucleus, (b) margination of chromatin, and (c) eosinophilic Cowdry Type A inclusions. These nuclear characteristics are also evident in the electron micrograph of the tumor cell shown in Fig. 6.

The Suspected Viral Etiology

Lucké suggested a viral etiology because he noted that some tumor cells contained nuclear inclusions similar to those found in herpetic infections, and also because he could increase the incidence of tumors if he inoculated leopard frogs with glycerinated or desiccated tumor material (13, 14, 15).

The viral etiology of the frog carcinoma was accepted as a working hypothesis by later investigators and in 1956 Fawcett described "virus-like" particles in epithelial cells of *some* tumors (6). Fawcett's work represented the first electron microscope study of the tumor and he remarked upon the similarity of the frog virus and herpes simplex virus. Thus, herpesvirus remained a prime suspect.

Nevertheless, many investigators rightly cautioned that the herpestype particle might merely be a passenger virus, for it was known that: intranuclear inclusions were not present in all tumors; Fawcett's study was the only electron microscope study that demonstrated virus; and definitive infectivity studies had not been performed.

In 1964, Rafferty reviewed the Lucké tumor literature and called attention to the observations that inclusion-containing nuclei occurred only in tumors of hibernating ("winter") frogs; they were lacking in "summer" frog tumors as well as in tumors that developed at normal laboratory temperature (29). Thus, 30 years after Lucké first described this tumor the importance of this pattern was fully recognized.

During the period from 1963 through 1965 Fawcett's electron microscopic demonstration of herpestype virus in the inclusions of tumor parenchymal cells was corroborated by other investigators (18, 20, 41, 42)—"winter" tumors contained virus and

---

PLATE 3

Fig. 6. Electron micrograph of "winter" tumor cell. A large intranuclear sac containing a cluster of nucleated virus particles can be seen. Chromatin is marginated and the nuclear membrane continuity is interrupted in several places in this virus-infected cell. $\times 15,000$.

Fig. 7. Electron micrograph of negatively stained mitochondrial fraction (250-2) of tumor shown in Fig. 6. After 20 hours of hypotonic buffer treatment, the nuclear sac has ruptured and the enclosed virus particles are being released. $\times 23,000$.

"summer" tumors lacked virus. Thus, the existing morphological evidence and the limited immunological evidence noted in 1965 *supported* the contention that the herpestype virus was indeed the Lucké tumor agent (24).

Although it is difficult to apply bacterial disease criteria to viral caused disease, it became apparent that *conclusive* evidence for a viral etiology would have to await the fulfillment of conditions similar to Koch's postulates (24).

Two different approaches have been employed in an attempt to identify the Lucké tumor agent(s): (a) the cultivation of virus isolates in pure culture with the subsequent inoculation of frogs in attempts to produce tumors, and (b) fractionation of virus-containing tumors and the injection of frog embryos with these cell-free fractions.

Cultivation of Virus Isolates

The first coordinated endeavors to isolate, grow and characterize frog viruses in tissue culture were performed in the laboratories of Granoff and Rafferty.

These two investigators agreed to designate their frog virus isolates as FV-1 (Frog Virus-1), FV-2, FV-3, etc.

FV-1 and FV-2 were isolated in Granoff's laboratory from cultured normal *Rana pipiens* kidneys; FV-3 was derived by Granoff from an inclusion-containing Wisconsin Lucké tumor; and FV-4 and FV-5 were obtained by Rafferty from Vermont frogs with inclusion-containing Lucké tumors.

A variety of mammalian, fish and reptilian cell lines, as well as amphibian cells, were employed in attempts to find a suitable tissue culture system that would support growth of the various frog isolates. Some of the early isolates were readily propagated in several of these cell lines, and some even displayed cytopathogenic effects, but none caused transformation.

The first isolates, FV-1 and FV-2 (isolated from normal frog kidney cell culture) and FV-3 (isolated from a frog kidney tumor), were indistinguishable in ether sensitivity, filterability, cytopathology and temperature stability (10). Unfortunately, it was erroneously thought that these viruses were indistinguishable from the frog herpesvirus found in the epithelial cells of the Lucké tumor [(10) page 253].[1]

It was soon learned that FV-1, FV-2 and FV-3 are polyhedral cytoplasmic viruses, quite distinct from the frog herpestype virus. However, the original error has caused a great deal of confusion, especially for interested investigators who do not usually work with the Lucké tumor system. [It even resulted in the polyhedral cytoplasmic virus being mistaken as an aberrant herpestype virus (25).][2]

The information is now quite clear. Only one of these viruses, a *herpestype virus*, has been found in nuclei of frog tumor *parenchymal cells*. The *polyhedral cytoplasmic virus* has been isolated from a variety of amphibian tissues and is always restricted to the cytoplasm. In the few cases where polyhedral virus has been found in tumor

---

[1] In this same paper it was pointed out that FV-4 and FV-5, isolated from tumor-bearing frogs by Rafferty (30), differed from the FV-1, FV-2 and FV-3 isolates. FV-4 has since been identified and recognized as a herpesvirus.

[2] It seems unwise to continue the use of the FV nomenclature; herpestype virus should be identified as *herpestype virus*.

tissue, it is limited to the *stromal cells* and has never been reported in parenchymal (epithelial) cells of the tumor (3, 19). Furthermore, numerous morphological characteristics are now recognized which readily distinguish the polyhedral cytoplasmic virus. Although polyhedral cytoplasmic viruses have been isolated from a number of different amphibians, as well as a variety of amphibian tissues, all of these isolates (e.g., FV-1, FV-3, FV-15, LT-1, LT-3, L-4b, and TEV) are antigenically indistinguishable by virus neutralization, complement fixation, and agar gel immunodiffusion tests and therefore probably represent a *single* agent (2, 4).

All attempts to induce tumors by the frog tissue culture isolates were negative. Culture supernatants of FV-1, FV-2 and FV-4 were injected into adult frogs, but tumor induction never resulted from this procedure (30). Furthermore, the recent inoculation of FV-3 into *Rana pipiens* embryos and larvae was also negative (40).

There is *no* evidence that the polyhedral cytoplasmic viruses have any etiologic relationship to the Lucké tumor.

Fractionation of "Winter" Tumor—Differential Centrifugation

Instead of attempting to grow the agent in pure culture, in 1965 Tweedell fractionated virus-containing "winter" tumors and injected various fractions into embryos and larvae of *Rana pipiens* (37, 38). The tumors were homogenized and fractionated by differential centrifugation to yield nuclear, mitochondrial, and microsomal fractions. Inoculation of mitochondrial and microsomal fractions into embryos induced typical renal carcinomas which appeared during, or soon after, metamorphosis. The microsomal fraction was oncogenic, but the greatest oncogenic activity was noted in the mitochondrial precipitate ($5090 \times G$). These results were somewhat unexpected since the diameter of the frog herpestype virus capsid is approximately 100 mμ and therefore all of the various forms of HTV should remain in solution under the centrifugal forces used *if* the virus exists as discrete, individual particles. However, electron microscopic examination revealed that the different developmental stages of the frog herpestype virus *were* present in both the mitochondrial and microsomal pellets. The oncogenic activity of these fractions was attributed to clumping and absorption of the virus on heavier components of cellular debris (38). Electron microscopy of the mitochondrial fraction also revealed the presence of sacs enclosing a cluster of virus particles. It was suggested that these viral sacs might also have contributed to the enhanced oncogenicity of the mitochondrial fraction.

Tweedell also passed the mitochondrial supernatant through a 0.45 μ filter and found that the filtrate retained oncogenic activity, but at a reduced incidence; the demonstration of oncogenic activity in this filtrate represented conclusive evidence for a subcellular or viral agent. Control experiments demonstrated that fractions of non-inclusion ("summer") tumors were *not* oncogenic.

Fractionation of "Winter" Tumor—Zonal Centrifugation

Two questions were raised by the results of Tweedell's enlightening experiments: (1) what was responsible for the oncogenic activity displayed by the mitochondrial fraction; and (2) if the herpestype virus was the oncogenic agent, which of the various morphological forms of the herpestype virus were oncogenic?

With these questions in mind, we undertook an investigation aimed at obtaining purified fractions of frog herpestype virus. If successful, this study would enable us to determine which of the variety of forms of the herpestype virus found in the Lucké tumor was (were) the oncogenic agent(s). Furthermore, these HTV fractions could be used as antigen in immunological experiments.

Preliminary Differential Centrifugation and Treatment of Mitochondrial Pellet

In collaboration with I. Toplin, low-temperature induced inclusion tumors were homogenized and differentially centrifuged to obtain fractions similar to those prepared by Tweedell. These fractions were further purified by sucrose gradient differential rate zonal centrifugation. Before the mitochondrial pellet was placed on the zonal gradient, it was resuspended in *hypotonic* buffer solution to prevent clumping of virus particles. It was noted that the sacs of virus found in the mitochondrial pellet were identical to those found in the nucleus; therefore, these sacs of virus particles originated in the nucleus (see Fig. 6). In the virus infected cells, the nuclear membrane appears weakened and even interrupted in several places (see Fig. 6). Apparently in the homogenization procedure many of these nuclear membranes rupture and release intact nuclear sacs. It was further noted that the hypotonic buffer treatment disrupted the nuclear sacs and resulted in the release of virus particles enclosed within the sacs (see Fig. 7). The fractionation procedure is diagramed in Fig. 8.

Two Types of Enveloped Herpesvirus

Higher resolution and closer inspection of the nuclear sacs [1] by thin-section electron microscopy disclosed that the virus particles within these sacs were enveloped by a thick membrane which was closely applied to the capsid (Fig. 9). These thick envelopes were seen to be continuous with the sac membrane (see arrows, Fig. 9). When examined by negative staining these particles appeared as lucent spheres because of the inability of the phosphotungstic acid to penetrate the closely applied, thick membrane (Fig. 10). In the first electron microscope study of the Lucké tumor, Fawcett (6) noted the occurrence of this nuclear enveloped form; and tightly enveloped forms have also been reported for other herpesviruses, e.g., varicellazoster (36), cytomegalovirus (27) and herpes simplex (26).

The more commonly described enveloped form of frog herpesvirus is found in the cytoplasm or the extracellular spaces and is distinguished by a thin, loosely applied envelope [see Figs. 11 and 12 and refer to Fawcett (6) and Lunger (20)]. Thus, it should be emphasized that one can recognize *two* types of enveloped herpesvirus in the Lucké renal adenocarcinoma—one, a nuclear form, with a thick envelope closely

---

[1] The term "intranuclear sac" was used by Lunger *et al.* (20), who noted that the sac membrane was fused with the inner nuclear membrane. Virus particles within these intranuclear sacs probably lie between the inner and outer nuclear membranes. In the present paper the use of the term "nuclear sac" merely implies that in thin section these sacs of virus are surrounded by nucleoplasm rather than cytoplasm; and the term "nuclear enveloped form" refers to particles which are morphologically similar to the enveloped form found within these intranuclear sacs, i.e., they are invested with a thick envelope which is closely applied to the capsid.

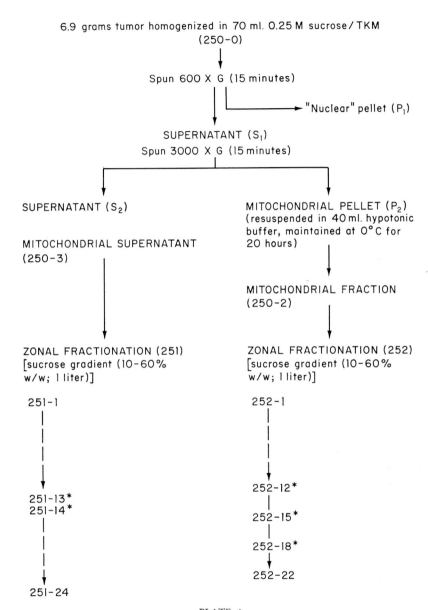

6.9 grams tumor homogenized in 70 ml. 0.25 M sucrose/TKM
(250-0)

Spun 600 X G (15 minutes)

"Nuclear" pellet (P₁)

SUPERNATANT (S₁)
Spun 3000 X G (15 minutes)

SUPERNATANT (S₂)

MITOCHONDRIAL SUPERNATANT
(250-3)

MITOCHONDRIAL PELLET (P₂)
(resuspended in 40 ml. hypotonic
buffer, maintained at 0°C for
20 hours)

MITOCHONDRIAL FRACTION
(250-2)

ZONAL FRACTIONATION (251)
[sucrose gradient (10-60%
w/w; 1 liter)]

ZONAL FRACTIONATION (252)
[sucrose gradient (10-60%
w/w; 1 liter)]

251-1

252-1

252-12*

251-13*
251-14*

252-15*

252-18*

252-22

251-24

PLATE 4

Fig. 8. FRACTIONATION PROCEDURE. Both the mitochondrial supernatant (S₂) and the mitochondrial pellet (P₂) were subjected to zonal fractionation (251 and 252, respectively). *Zonal fractions 251-13 and 251-14 from the mitochondrial supernatant and zonal fractions 252-12, 252-15, and 252-18 from the mitochondrial pellet were tested for oncogenicity by injection into embryos. See text for details. In the present paper, discussion has been limited to injection of the mitochondrial pellet and derived fractions. However, it should be noted that the homogenate (250-0) and the mitochondrial supernatant (250-3) were also injected and found to be oncogenic. Of the two mitochondrial supernatant zonal fractions which were injected, only one, 251-13, was oncogenic.

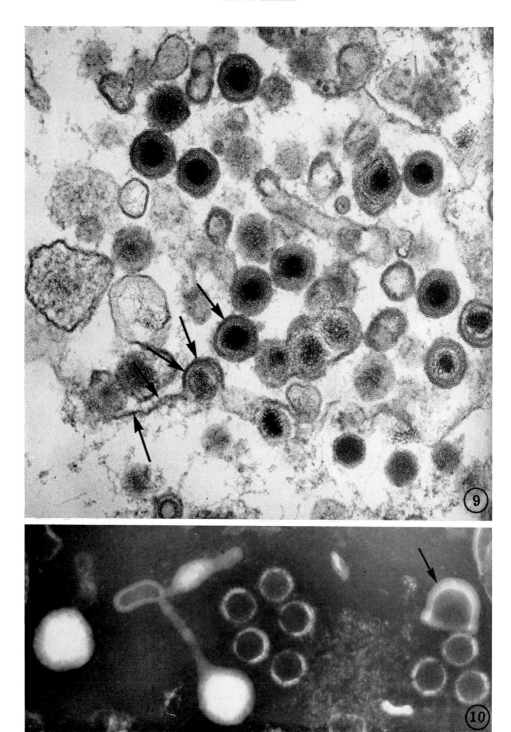

applied to the capsid, and the other, an extranuclear form, with a thin envelope separated from the capsid by a zone of low electron density. These envelopes may, in fact, be the same; the above mentioned variation may merely reflect a response to different milieus and/or treatment. This variation, however, appears to have functional significance.

We call attention to these two types of enveloped HTV because the herpes virion or infectious particle is believed to be enveloped, and also because of the results of our zonal fractionation and embryo injection experiments (23).

Zonal Centrifugation

Since it was known that fractions obtained from differential centrifugation lost their oncogenic activity upon standing for short periods of time at 0°C (Tweedell, personal communication), small samples from each fraction obtained by differential centrifugation were divided into two portions. One portion was immediately frozen at −70°C; the other was maintained at 0°C and injected into test embryos within 24 hours after fractionation. The major portion of each fraction was further purified by zonal centrifugation.

The B-XV zonal centrifuge system (1), with a one-liter sucrose gradient ranging from 10 to 60% (w/w) sucrose in 0.002M Tris, 0.002M EDTA, pH 7, was utilized for further fractionation of the mitochondrial pellet. The gradient was cushioned with potassium citrate, density 1.35. The samples were overlayed with 190 ml. hypotonic buffer. Centrifugation was at 24,000 rpm for 60 minutes ($w^2t + 23 \times 10^9$ radians^2/sec). The 50 ml. fractions were collected through the flow cell of a recording spectrophotometer set at 265 mμ. The sucrose content of each fraction was determined by refractometry. Protein assays were carried out by the Lowry method. Twenty-two fractions were collected. The fractions of interest were diluted to 70 ml. with hypotonic buffer and subjected to high-speed centrifugation at 80,000 × G for 90 minutes. The pellets from each fraction were suspended in 2 ml. phosphate buffered saline by aspiration. [See Toplin et al., this volume (35), for additional details.] Immediately after collection a small portion of each fraction was prepared for negative staining (1:5 dilutions of the sample in 2% potassium phosphotungstate, pH 4.5, were placed on 200-mesh carbon/Formvar-coated ionized copper grids) and viewed in a Siemens Elmiskop 1A.

Zonal fractionation partially purified and separated the various types of HTV particles. Most of the empty capsids were distributed in the lighter portions of the gradient, whereas most of the nucleated particles came down in the heavier portions of the gradient.

PLATE 5 NUCLEAR ENVELOPED FORM OF HTV

Fig. 9. High resolution electron micrograph of nuclear sac and its enclosed viral cluster. Note that most viruses are enclosed by a thick envelope (single arrow), which is closely applied to the capsid. One virus is pictured as it is acquiring its thick envelope; continuity between the sac unit membrane and the envelope of this virus is apparent (arrows). ×71,000.

Fig. 10. Electron micrograph of negatively stained nuclear enveloped form of HTV from zonal fraction 15. Because the phosphotungstic acid cannot penetrate the closely applied, thick envelope, this enveloped form of HTV appears as lucent spheres. Two of these spheres can be seen in the lower left-hand corner. An empty, thick envelope which has ruptured can be seen in the upper righthand corner (arrow). ×75,000.

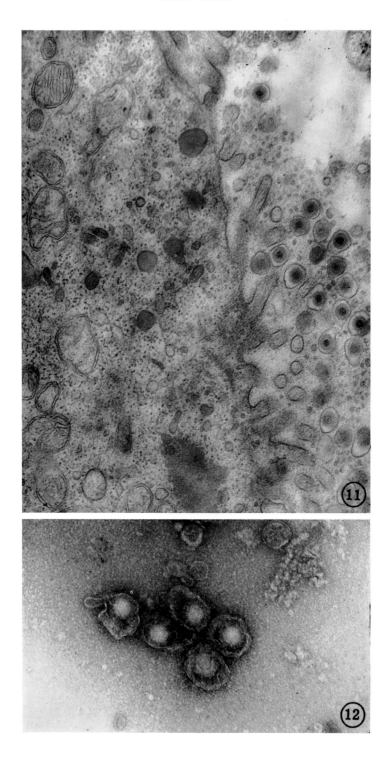

Injection of Embryos—Tumor Induction

Mitochondrial fractions maintained at $0°C$ and $-70°C$ as well as selected zonal fractions (fractions 12, 15 and 18—maintained at $0°C$ and injected less than 6 hours after zonal separation) were tested for oncogenic activity by inoculation into Shumway stage 19–20 (33) *Rana pipiens* embryos. Watchmaker's forceps were used to remove the egg membranes enclosing the 5 mm. embryos, prior to injection. A 10 μl syringe fitted with a repeating dispenser and a specially-adapted 31-gauge needle was used to inject 0.2 μl into the region of the developing pronephric kidney of each embryo (see Fig. 13, arrow).

Both uninjected controls and injected controls (phosphate-buffered saline injected and sucrose buffer injected) were employed. All animals were maintained at room temperature and fed parboiled lettuce; segregation of animals injected with different fractions was maintained throughout the experiment.

Some of the developing embryos, both control and experimental, died before the onset of metamorphosis; autopsies revealed that tumors had not developed in these young animals. When the tadpoles reached the early stages of metamorphosis (3 months after injection), a selected number of animals from each group was sacrificed and examined for tumors.

Mitochondrial Fractions

The first tumors were found 3 months after injection in animals which had been injected with the frozen ($-70°C$) mitochondrial fraction. Two animals from this group are shown in Figs. 14 and 15. The tadpole in Fig. 14 [Taylor-Kollros stage VIII (34)] had developed a right pronephric kidney tumor (arrow), measuring approximately $1 \times 1 \times 0.75$ mm. In the normal process of development, the pronephric kidneys are transitory structures which function only in early larval life. They are soon replaced by the mesonephric kidneys, which are functional in late larval stages and remain as the definitive kidneys of the adult frog. At the stage of development attained by the animal shown in Fig. 14 it is unusual for a pronephros to persist. Undoubtedly it persisted because the pronephros was tumorous. The left pronephric kidney had atrophied in a normal manner and was no longer present; the mesonephric kidneys (small arrows) were well developed and normal.

Fig. 15 shows another animal injected with the same fraction. This animal had reached metamorphic stage X at the time of sacrifice and had developed a right pronephric tumor similar in size to that of the previous tadpole.

Within the next few weeks, many animals from this group developed externally visible protuberances in the region of the pronephros (Fig. 16) which on autopsy were verified to be pronephric tumors (Fig. 17). A tally of the number of animals which had developed tumors was made 5 months after injection of the various frac-

---

PLATE 6 EXTRANUCLEAR ENVELOPED FORM OF HTV

Fig. 11. Electron micrograph showing loosely enveloped HTV in the lumen of a tumor tubule. $\times 37,500$.

Fig. 12. Electron micrograph of negatively stained extranuclear form of HTV with its thin, loose envelope, separated from the capsid by a zone of low electron density. $\times 46,500$.

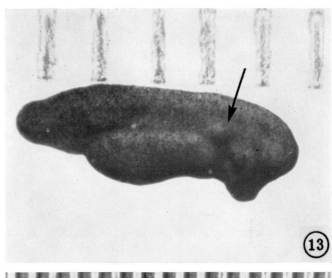

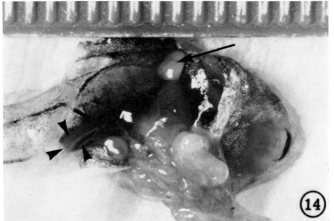

TABLE 1

FRACTIONATION AND TUMOR INCIDENCE

Fraction	# Injected (May 22)	# Sacrificed or died @ early stage (stage X or less)	# With tumor @ early stage	Survivors (Aug. 15)	# Died or sacrificed @ later stage	# With tumor	%	Survivors (Oct. 22)
Mitochondrial Differential Centrifugation Fractions								
250–2 dry ice (−70°C)	70	26	5	44	22	12	55%	22
250–2 1:1000 dry ice (−70°C)	30	16	1	14	7	5	71%	7
250–2 wet ice (0°C)	54	29	0	25	11	7	64%	14
Mitochondrial Zonal Centrifugation Fractions								
252–12	50	35	0	15	8	0	0%	7
252–15	50	25	0	25	15	8	53%	10
252–18	70	47	0	23	11	0	0%	12
Buffer control	101	41	0	60	37	0	0%	23

tions. Only animals which died or were sacrificed at a "late" stage were considered in this calculation of tumor incidence (see Table 1). In the group injected with the mitochondrial fraction which was maintained in the frozen state prior to injection, 12 out of 22, or 55%, of the animals developed tumors. In the group which was injected with the unfrozen (0°C) mitochondrial fraction, 7 out of 11, or 64%, developed tumors. Figs. 18 and 19 show an animal from the latter group. This animal had bilateral pronephric tumors and large, multiple tumors of the right mesonephros. The

---

PLATE 7

Fig. 13. Stage 19 embryo removed from egg membranes. The longitudinal bulge (arrow) indicates the region of the developing pronephric kidney into which virus fractions were injected. (Scale for Plate 7 in millimeters.)

Fig. 14. Stage VIII tadpole (11 weeks after injection) with right pronephric kidney tumor (arrow). Intestine and other organs reflected to the left in order to show the normal mesonephric kidneys (small arrows). Animal was injected with frozen mitochondrial fraction.

Fig. 15. Stage X tadpole (11 weeks after injection), also injected with frozen mitochondrial fraction. Arrow indicates right pronephric tumor.

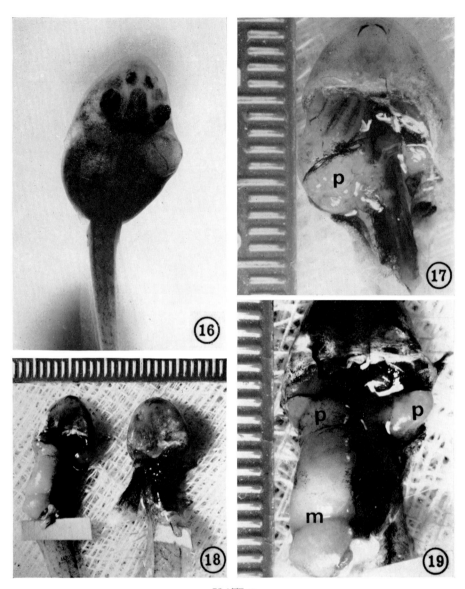

PLATE 8

Fig. 16. Dorsal view of an animal fifteen weeks after injection with frozen mitochondrial fraction. Large right pronephric tumor is visible. ×4.

Fig. 17. Ventral view of above animal dissected to show large right pronephric tumor (p). (Scale for Figs. 17–19 in millimeters.)

Fig. 18. Animal on left, injected with unfrozen mitochondrial fraction, had developed bilateral pronephric tumors and large, multiple tumors of the right mesonephros. Control animal on right, injected with phosphate buffered saline, shows normal kidney development: pronephric kidneys have atrophied and mesonephric kidneys have developed in normal manner. (Both animals stage XII, pictured 14 weeks after injection.)

Fig. 19. Closeup of animal in Fig. 18, showing bilateral pronephric tumors (p) and right mesonephric tumor (m). Left mesonephric kidney (not clearly seen in photo) is normal.

left mesonephros was normal. Since freezing at $-70°C$ apparently does not impair the oncogenicity of the fraction, this practice may prove to be an effective means of preserving the infectivity for extended periods of time.[1]

The animal in Figs. 20 and 21 developed bilateral pronephric and mesonephric tumors after having received a thousandfold dilution of the frozen mitochondrial fraction. Tumors developed in 5 of 7, or 71%, of the animals (see Table 1). Thus, the oncogenic activity of the frozen mitochondrial fraction did not diminish after a *thousandfold dilution*.

Zonal Fractions

As stated previously, 22 fractions were obtained from the zonal centrifuge. Since the empty capsids (which would not be expected to display oncogenic activity) accumulated in the lighter portion of the gradient, our attention was focused on the heavier zone, which contained the highest concentrations of nucleated particles. On the basis of absorption peaks, protein concentration, and concentration of nucleated virus particles [see Toplin *et al.*, Fig. 6, this volume (35)] three fractions (fractions 12, 15 and 18) were deemed likely candidates and were injected into embryos to test for oncogenic activity. However, when tested, only zonal fraction 15 produced tumors (see Table 1). Tumors developed in 8 of 15, or 53%, of the animals.

The external view of an animal which was injected with zonal fraction 15 can be seen in Fig. 22. The bilateral pronephric tumors are evident even externally. Fig. 23 is a ventral view of this animal's pronephric tumors at autopsy.

When tumors developed in animals injected with fraction 15 but not in those injected with fraction 12 or 18, a careful evaluation of the electron microscopic photographs of these three fractions was undertaken. It was immediately apparent that the difference between these three fractions was the presence of a high concentration of the nuclear form of enveloped HTV particle in fraction 15 (Fig. 24) and the lack of this tightly enveloped particle in fractions 12 and 18. Zonal fraction 14 (Fig. 25) contained an even higher concentration of the nuclear enveloped form of HTV than fraction 15. A low power view of a negatively stained preparation of fraction 14 is shown in Fig. 26; the relative homogeneity of this fraction and the high concentration of the nuclear enveloped particle are evident. A thin section of a pellet prepared from the same zonal fraction confirmed the abundance of this particle (Fig. 27).

It should be noted that, although remarkably "clean," the zonal fractions which contained high concentrations of these tightly enveloped, nuclear forms of HTV also contained some sub-cellular debris. Furthermore, these fractions were not completely devoid of other types of HTV particles. Nevertheless, these experiments have demonstrated that oncogenic mitochondrial fractions can be further purified by zonal centrifugation to yield a zonal fraction which retains oncogenicity. In these experiments the oncogenic zonal fraction, fraction 15, contained a high concentration of the nuclear enveloped form of HTV, whereas fractions above (fraction 12) and below (fraction 18) lacked this form and lacked oncogenic activity when injected into embryos.

---

[1] We have recently obtained tumor induction with fractions stored for 6 months.

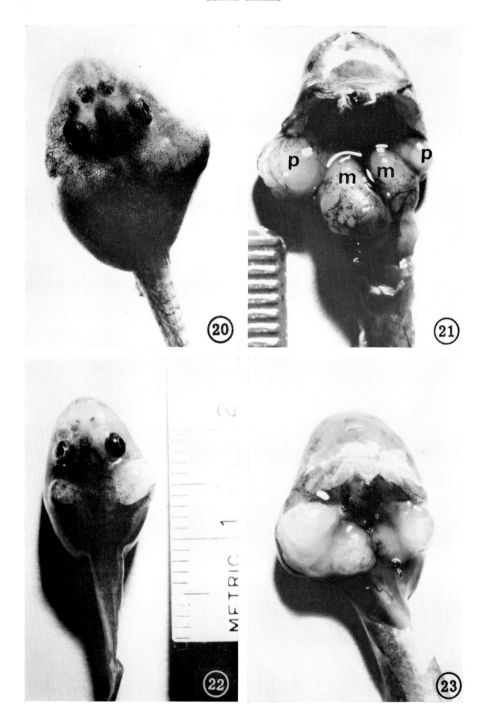

In his differential centrifugation of HTV-containing Lucké tumors, Tweedell obtained the greatest oncogenic activity in his mitochondrial fraction. This unexpected result raised two questions for which provisional answers can now be proposed: (1) the nuclear sacs of virus were apparently responsible for the oncogenic activity displayed by the mitochondrial fraction; and, (2) embryo injection with zonal fractions has provided persuasive evidence that the nuclear enveloped HTV particle is the oncogenic agent of the Lucké tumor.

The Lucké kidney tumor-embryo injection studies have indicated that the agent has a preferential affinity for *differentiating* kidney tissue. Since the pronephros was differentiating at the time of injection, the unusually high incidence of pronephric tumors indicates that the target cell of the Lucké tumor virus is, in all probability, the differentiating kidney cell—*not* a differentiated cell, but a cell in the process of differentiation. These observations are in accord with the findings that the target cells of Rauscher leukemia virus are cells in an early stage of differentiation (28).

Recent investigations and the major advances in our knowledge of the frog carcinoma now point the way to experiments which will provide conclusive identification of the Lucké tumor agent. The results of our zonal fractionation-embryo injection study suggest that the nuclear enveloped form of HTV plays a role in the genesis of the Lucké tumor. Oncogenic zonal fractions have recently been used to obtain purified isopycnic separation of the nuclear enveloped form of HTV, which banded at density 1.20–1.21; the oncogenicity of this isopycnic preparation is currently being tested. Even if these tests are negative, further examination of oncogenic zonal fractions should result in identification of the oncogenic agent(s).

In virus studies, immunological evidence has been accepted as reasonably adequate to satisfy Koch's second and fourth postulates. Since zonal fractionation of "winter" tumors has yielded high titers of frog HTV antigen, it is now possible to employ immunological tools in Lucké tumor etiology studies and also to relate these studies to other tumor-virus systems. Indeed, the recent immunodiffusion tests which revealed a common antigen shared by the frog HTV and the EB virus of Burkitt's lymphoma (7, 8, 12) are undoubtedly the forerunners of many future immunological investigations utilizing Lucké tumor system information. These initial immunological studies have already provided the basis for meaningful comparisons of the Lucké tumor with avian and mammalian tumors which have similar suspected viral agents (see pp. 358–367, this volume).

PLATE 9

Fig. 20. Dorsal view of animal injected with thousandfold dilution of frozen mitochondrial fraction, pictured at stage IX, 17 weeks after injection. Large pronephric tumors are externally visible. (Scale for Plate 9 in millimeters.)

Fig. 21. Ventral view of animal in Fig. 20, dissected to show bilateral pronephric (p) and mesonephric (m) tumors.

Fig. 22. Dorsal view of animal injected with zonal fraction 15, shown at stage V, 20 weeks after injection. Bilateral pronephric tumors are externally visible.

Fig. 23. Ventral view of animal in Fig. 22, dissected to show bilateral tumors.

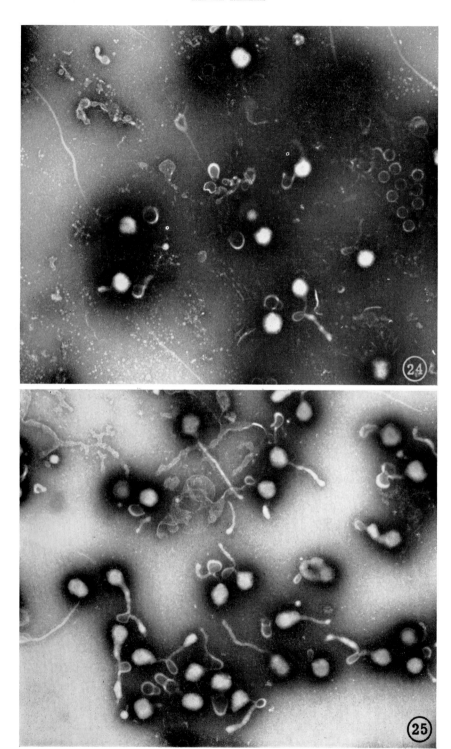

The Lucké Tumor—Unique Attributes and Future Investigations

This poikilothermic solid tumor system has many unique attributes which make it especially well suited for virus-tumor studies:

(1) External fertilization and the ability to work at egg and embryo level make this an excellent system to investigate vertical transmission (24, 39).

(2) Microsurgical and embryological manipulations are well developed for Amphibia. Nuclear transplantation is a routine procedure in *Rana pipiens*. Since the haploid number of chromosomes is merely 13 and frog cells are unusually large, transplantation of individual chromosomes to enucleated egg cytoplasm will become feasible. Eventually, one should be able to localize the insertion site of viral genetic information.

(3) Temperature related effects determine whether this solid tumor contains or lacks herpesvirus. Low temperature treatment apparently activates the production of herpesvirus in "summer" tumors which indicates that the complete viral genome is present in a masked, or latent, state in the "virus-free" form. This apparent relationship between temperature and virus-cell interaction and the ease of manipulating temperature in this poikilotherm should provide the means for an adequate investigation of gene repression-derepression phenomena.

One of the vexing problems encountered in rodent DNA virus-tumor systems has been the inability to routinely recover virus from tumors which had been induced by virus. A similar enigma is represented by the current inability to demonstrate virus in human neoplasms. Many investigators believe that a viral genome may exist in human tumors in a masked state and ultimately can be "rescued." The Lucké tumor evidence (21) and the recent induction of infectious Shope papilloma virus in rabbit tissue culture cells which were "virus-free" (by lowering the incubation temperature) (32) lend additional support to this belief.

Thus, the Lucké tumor system, per se, is interesting and warrants attention. The frog kidney tumor system also has promise of yielding valuable information about the mechanism of tumorigenesis—information which may provide insight into some of the provocative problems encountered in mammalian tumor-virus systems.

Acknowledgments

I am indebted to Joyce Isaacs for unexcelled assistance in this study. Without her dedicated aid much of the reported work from our laboratory could not have been accomplished. I. Toplin of the John L. Smith Memorial for Cancer Research, Charles Pfizer and Co., Maywood, New Jersey, performed all fractionations; I wish to express

---

PLATE 10

Fig. 24. Electron micrograph of negatively stained preparation of zonal fraction 15. The nuclear enveloped form of HTV, which appears as lucent spheres, is present in a relatively high concentration. $\times 28,500$.

Fig. 25. Electron micrograph of negatively stained preparation of zonal fraction 14, which contains an even higher concentration of the nuclear enveloped form of HTV. $\times 28,500$.

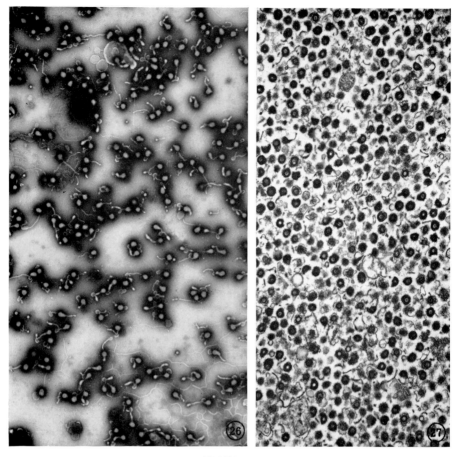

PLATE 11

Fig. 26. Low power view of negatively stained preparation of zonal fraction 14, soon after removal from the zonal centrifuge. The homogeneity and high concentration of the nuclear enveloped particle are evident. ×9,000.

Fig. 27. Electron micrograph of sectioned pellet prepared from zonal fraction 14 after 2 months storage at −70°C, during which time it was thawed and refrozen 3 times. Even after this harsh treatment it is still possible to recognize the nuclear enveloped form of the frog HTV with its thick envelope. ×14,000.

my appreciation to him for his expertise and enthusiasm. The author wishes to thank Christopher W. Stackpole for the electron micrographs of Figs. 1, 11, and 12, and Philip M. Brandt of the John L. Smith Memorial for Cancer Research for all other electron micrographs. The cooperation of Dr. J. J. Oleson and his staff at the J. L. Smith Memorial for Cancer Research is gratefully acknowledged. The author would also like to thank Hawley Martin, Beverly Williams, Rebecca Scarbrough, Howard Grenier, John Butler, Janet Everitt, Jan Draper, and Ken Fontenot for patient care of the animals. I wish to express my appreciation to Lorraine Mizell for invaluable assistance in the preparation of the manuscript. Portions of plates 3, 5, and 11 are reprinted with permission from *Science*, Vol. 165 (3898) (Copyright 1969 by the American Association for the Advancement of Science).

References

1. ANDERSON, N. G.: The development of zonal centrifuges and ancillary systems for tissue fractionation and analysis. Monograph 21, Natl. Cancer Inst., Bethesda, 1966, 526 pp.

2. CAME, P. E., G. GEERING, L. J. OLD and E. A. BOYSE: A serological study of polyhedral cytoplasmic viruses isolated from Amphibia. Virology 36:392–400, 1968.

3. CAME, P. E. and P. D. LUNGER: Viruses isolated from frogs and their relationship to the the Lucké tumor. Arch. f. ges. Virusforschung 19:464–468, 1966.

4. CLARK, H. F., C. GRAY, F. FABIAN, R. ZEIGEL and D. T. KARZON: Comparative studies of amphibian cytoplasmic virus strains isolated from the leopard frog, bullfrog and newt. In Biology of Amphibian Tumors (M. Mizell, ed.), Springer-Verlag New York Inc., 1969, pp. 310–326.

5. DiBERARDINO, M. A., T. J. KING and R. G. McKINNELL: Chromosome studies of a frog renal adenocarcinoma line carried by serial intraocular transplantation. J. Natl. Cancer Inst. 31:769–789, 1963.

6. FAWCETT, D. W.: Electron microscope observations on intracellular virus-like particles associated with the cells of the Lucké renal adenocarcinoma. J. Biophys. Biochem. Cytol. 2:725–742, 1956.

7. FINK, M. A., G. S. KING and M. MIZELL: Preliminary note: identity of a herpesvirus antigen from Burkitt lymphoma of man and the Lucké adenocarcinoma of frogs. J. Natl. Cancer Inst. 41:1477–1478, 1968.

8. FINK, M. A., G. S. KING and M. MIZELL: Reactivity of serum from frogs and other species with a herpesvirus antigen extracted from a Burkitt lymphoma cultured cell line. In Biology of Amphibian Tumors (M. Mizell, ed.), Springer-Verlag New York Inc., 1969, pp. 358–364.

9. FREED, J. J. and S. J. ROSENFELD: Frog renal adenocarcinoma: cytological studies in situ and in vitro. Ann. N.Y. Acad. Sci. 126:99–114, 1965.

10. GRANOFF, A., P. E. CAME and K. A. RAFFERTY, JR.: The isolation and properties of viruses from Rana pipiens: their possible relationship to the renal adenocarcinoma of the leopard frog. Ann. N.Y. Acad. Sci. 126:237–255, 1965.

11. KING, T. J. and M. A. DiBERARDINO: Transplantation of nuclei from the frog renal adenocarcinoma I. Development of tumor nuclear-transplant embryos. Ann. N.Y. Acad. Sci. 126:115–126, 1965.

12. KIRKWOOD, J. M., G. GEERING, L. J. OLD, M. MIZELL and J. WALLACE: A preliminary report on the serology of Lucké and Burkitt herpestype viruses: a shared antigen. In Biology of Amphibian Tumors (M. Mizell, ed.), Springer-Verlag New York Inc., 1969, pp. 365–367.

13. LUCKÉ, B.: A neoplastic disease of the kidney of the frog, Rana pipiens. Am. J. Cancer 20:352–379, 1934.

14. LUCKÉ, B.: Carcinoma in the leopard frog: its probable causation by a virus. J. Exptl. Med. 68:457–468, 1938.

15. LUCKÉ, B.: Kidney carcinoma in the leopard frog: a virus tumor. Ann. N.Y. Acad. Sci. 54:1093–1109, 1952.

16. LUCKÉ, B. and H. G. SCHLUMBERGER: The manner of growth of frog carcinoma, studied by direct microscopic examination of living intraocular transplants. J. Exper. Med. 70:257–268, 1939.

17. LUCKÉ, B. and H. G. SCHLUMBERGER: Effects of roentgen rays on cancer. Direct microscopic observations on living intraocular transplants of frog carcinoma. J. Natl. Cancer Inst. 11:511–543, 1950.

18. LUNGER, P. D.: The isolation and morphology of the Lucké frog kidney tumor virus. Virology 24:138–145, 1964.

19. LUNGER, P. D.: Fine structure studies of cytoplasmic viruses associated with frog tumors. In Biology of Amphibian Tumors (M. Mizell, ed.), Springer-Verlag New York Inc., 1969, pp. 296–309.

20. LUNGER, P. D., R. W. DARLINGTON and A. GRANOFF: Cell-virus relationships in the Lucké renal adenocarcinoma: an ultrastructural study. Ann. N.Y. Acad. Sci. 126:289–314, 1965.

21. MIZELL, M., C. W. STACKPOLE and S. HALPEREN: Herpes-type virus recovery from "virus-free" frog kidney tumors. Proc. Soc. Exp. Biol. and Med. 127:808–814, 1968.

22. MIZELL, M., C. W. STACKPOLE and J. J. ISAACS: Herpestype virus latency in the Lucké tumor. In Biology of Amphibian Tumors (M. Mizell, ed.), Springer-Verlag New York Inc., 1969, pp. 337–347.

23. MIZELL, M., I. TOPLIN and J. J. ISAACS: Tumor induction in developing frog kidneys by a zonal centrifuge purified fraction of the frog herpes-type virus. Science, 165:1134–1137, 1969.

24. MIZELL, M. and J. ZAMBERNARD: Viral particles of the frog renal adenocarcinoma: causative agent or passenger virus? II. A promising model system for the demonstration of a "lysogenic" state in a metazoan tumor. Ann. N.Y. Acad. Sci. 126:146–169, 1965.

25. MORRIS, V. L., P. G. SPEAR and B. ROIZMAN: Some biophysical properties of frog viruses and their DNA. Proc. Nat. Acad. Sci., USA. 56:1155–1157, 1966.

26. NII, S., C. MORGAN and H. M. ROSE: Electron microscopy of herpes simplex virus. II. Sequence of development. J. Virol. 2:517–536, 1968.

27. PATRIZI, G., J. N. MIDDELKAMP, J. C. HERWEG and H. K. THORNTON: Human cytomegalovirus: election microscopy of a primary viral isolate. J. Lab. Clin. Med. 65:825–838, 1965.

28. PLUZNIK, D. H., L. SACHS and P. RESNITZKY: The mechanism of leukemogenesis by the Rauscher leukemia virus. In Conference on Murine Leukemia (M. A. Rich and J. B. Moloney, eds.), Monograph 22, Natl. Cancer Inst., Bethesda, 1966, pp. 3–14.

29. RAFFERTY, K. A., JR.: Kidney tumors of the leopard frog: a review. Cancer Res. 24:169–185, 1964.

30. RAFFERTY, K. A., JR.: The cultivation of inclusion-associated viruses from Lucké tumor frogs. Ann. N.Y. Acad. Sci. 126:3–21, 1965.

31. SCHLUMBERGER, H. and B. LUCKÉ: Serial intraocular transplantation of frog carcinoma for fourteen generations. Cancer Res. 9:52–60, 1949.

32. SHIRATORI, O., T. OSATO and Y. ITO: "Induction" of viral antigen in established cell line (SP-8) derived from Shope virus-induced cutaneous papilloma of rabbits. Proc. Soc. Exp. Biol. and Med. 130:115–121, 1969.

33. SHUMWAY, W.: Stages in the normal development of Rana pipiens. Anat. Rec. 78:139–148, 1940.

34. TAYLOR, A. C. and J. J. KOLLROS: Stages in the normal development of Rana pipiens larvae. Anat. Rec. 94:7–23, 1946.

35. TOPLIN, I., P. BRANDT and P. SOTTONG: Density gradient centrifugation studies on the herpes-type virus of the Lucké tumor. In Biology of Amphibian Tumors (M. Mizell, ed.), Springer-Verlag New York Inc., 1969, pp. 348–357.

36. TOURNIER, P., F. CATHALA and W. BERNHARD: Ultrastructure et developpement intracellulaire du virus de la varicelle observé au microscope electronique. Press Med. 52:1230–1235, 1957.

37. TWEEDELL, K. S.: Renal tumor transmission in frog embryos by subcellular fractions. Am. Zool. 5:171–172, 1965.

38. TWEEDELL, K. S.: Induced oncogenesis in developing frog kidney cells. Cancer Res. *27*: 2042–2052, 1967.

39. TWEEDELL, K. S.: Simulated transmission of renal tumors in oocytes and embryos of *Rana pipiens*. *In* Biology of Amphibian Tumors (M. Mizell, ed.), Springer-Verlag New York Inc., 1969, pp. 229–239.

40. TWEEDELL, K. S. and A. GRANOFF: Viruses and renal carcinoma of *Rana pipiens*. V. Effect of frog virus 3 on developing frog embryos and larvae. J. Natl. Cancer Inst. *40*:407– 410, 1968.

41. ZAMBERNARD, J. and M. MIZELL: The fine structure of the frog renal adenocarcinoma before and during intraocular transplantation. Am. Zool. *3*:511, 1963.

42. ZAMBERNARD, J. and M. MIZELL: Viral particles of the frog renal adenocarcinoma: causative agent or passenger virus? I. Fine structure of primary tumors and subsequent intraocular transplants. Ann. N.Y. Acad. Sci. *126*:127–145, 1965.

Interrelations of the Populations of the *Rana pipiens* Complex[1]

JOHN A. MOORE [2]

Department of Biological Sciences
Columbia University,
and the Department of Herpetology
American Museum of Natural History
New York, New York

Measures of similarities and differences among organisms are basic to many branches of biology. Systematics is the codification of such information. Lewontin (4) has stated recently that "the major unsolved problem of descriptive population genetics is an adequate specification of the genetic difference between two closely related species as compared to the genetic difference between populations of the same species." A reasonable solution to this problem cannot be expected until it becomes possible to state the problem more precisely. For example, one cannot expect "an adequate specification of the genetic difference between two closely related species . . ." unless there is an adequate specification of specific and intraspecific categories. Then again, biologists have never agreed on what they have meant by genetic differences, genetic relatedness, etc. Usually some measure of total difference is implied though, of necessity, only a minute and unknown fraction of the total difference is actually dealt with.

There are two general categories of genetic differences: genotypic and phenotypic. A population geneticist is most concerned with genotypic differences. A general evolutionist is more concerned with phenotypic differences, though admittedly with those phenotypic differences that are under genetic control.

It is not unduly optimistic to maintain that useful measures of total genotypic differences will soon be available. McCarthy and Bolton (6) have shown how it may be possible to detect the degree of homology between the DNA molecules of two species or between the DNA of one species and the messenger RNA of another. The method consists of determining the extent to which the DNA of one species will bind ("hybridize") to the DNA (or RNA) of the species to which it is being compared. When the procedures become more reliable, it should be possible to measure the percentage of DNA in one species that is homologous to the DNA of another. Such data would reveal the percentage of genes shared by the species but it would not indicate the degree to which the *organization* of the two genomes is identical. Nevertheless this

---

[1] The work reported in this paper was supported by the National Science Foundation (Grant G 9001).

[2] Present address: Department of Life Sciences, University of California, Riverside, California.

information will be of enormous usefulness in biological classification: it will provide a molecular numerical taxonomy.

But many systematicists and evolutionists will be as unhappy with numerical taxonomy at the molecular level as they are with numerical taxonomy at more complex levels. Mere summing is an uncertain measure of the differences that are of importance in evolution. The alleles that control the sickle cell and normal hemoglobins are far more important than the alleles that contribute to the blue eye and brown eye phenotypes. Yet each results from single allelic differences.

It is the final product of the action of genes, the phenotype, that is the effective unit of evolutionary change and, for this reason, both systematics and evolutionary biology must consider the entire organism. Not unexpectedly, studies at this level are beset with difficulties and uncertainties. One would like to have measures of adaptation, yet there is not even a useful definition of the term. One would like to know the evolutionary significance of the characters that differentiate species, yet usually all that can be said is that the characters must be a consequence of natural selection and, hence, be adaptive. One would like to possess some overall measure of evolutionary divergence and relatedness but this problem is so vaguely characterized that it has hardly been studied.

Probably the most useful measure of overall adaptation is that employed long ago by Turesson (17, 18) and more recently by Clausen, Keck, and Heisey [see Clausen, (1)]. These workers grew plants of the same population, or even portions of the same individual, in various experimental gardens having markedly different environments. Comparisons were made of the extent of growth, production of seeds, and many other biological features of the same genotype living under a variety of environmental conditions. Comparisons could also be made among plants from different habitats growing in the same garden. The ability of the plants to live and produce seeds could be used as a measure of their overall adaptation in the garden where they were growing. One should not be disappointed that the answer related to a specific garden and to a specific period of time. Adaptation has meaning only in relation to a specific environment.

Not only do these procedures tell us a good deal about adaptation but, in some cases, they reveal hereditary differences between seemingly identical populations. If individuals of these populations are transplanted to an experimental garden with an environment different from that of either population, or if the individuals of one population are transplanted to an experimental garden where the other population lives, differences may be revealed. Observations of this sort indicate that apparently identical phenotypes may have a very different genetic basis. The similarity is a case of parallel evolution.

These are extraordinary experiments and it is unfortunate that they remain almost unique. A few less extensive observations have been made by others on plants but no one has obtained similar information for any animal species.

I would like to introduce some of the problems and indicate some of the tentative answers of studies of relatedness and evolutionary divergence in animal species. My example will be the leopard frog, *Rana pipiens*. Markedly different populations of this frog occur over most of North America, with the exceptions of the extreme north and the west coast of the United States and Canada. Many different taxonomic

arrangements have been suggested to deal with the very extensive geographic variability that is encountered. Several examples will be mentioned.

In 1889 Cope (2) recognized four subspecies of *Rana virescens* (an old name for
Rana pipiens) largely on the basis of the shape of the head, the pigmentation, and the
presence or absence of external vocal sacs. The subspecies *virescens* (which would now
be *pipiens*) was said to occur throughout eastern America from Maine and southern
Illinois south to the Gulf of Mexico. The area to the north, as well as that extending
from the eastern edge of the Great Plains to the Sierra Nevada, was occupied by
brachycephala (which earlier he had named *berlandieri*). Some individuals from Florida, Georgia, and Louisiana were called *sphenocephala*. The subspecies *austricola* was
restricted to Mexico. There were difficulties, however. *Sphenocephala* was recorded
from Minnesota, which was in the range of *brachycephala;* both *virescens* and *sphenocephala* were listed for Florida, Georgia, and Louisiana; and *virescens* was listed from
the Athabasca River, Canada, within the range of *brachycephala*. In Cope's day, of
course, it was not customary to think of subspecies as being strictly allopatric.

Nearly half a century later Kauffeld (3) suggested that it was best to recognize
three species of leopard frogs in the United States and Canada: *Rana brachycephala*
in New England, Canada, and west to the Pacific Coast States; *Rana sphenocephala*
in the southeastern and Gulf region of the United States; and *Rana pipiens* in the
area between *brachycephala* and *sphenocephala*.

Several years later I studied the material then available in the American Museum
of Natural History (8), as well as live frogs from a few localities. It seemed to me
that the geographic variation was so extensive that one would have to recognize
literally dozens of subspecies or none at all. I chose the second course.

Schmidt (16) in the Sixth Edition of the authoritative "A Check List of North
American Amphibians and Reptiles" returned to the subspecies categories. He recognized *pipiens* as occurring in eastern North America south to New Jersey and the
Ohio River; *sphenocephala* in the southeast states and west to eastern Texas and
Oklahoma; *brachycephala* in the area to the west of *pipiens* and *sphenocephala;* berlandieri in the Rio Grande Basin, Mexico, and throughout Central America; and
fischeri in the Vegas Valley of Nevada. It is difficult to see how this taxonomic solution of the *pipiens* problem served any useful purpose. Possibly the most homogeneous
populations of the *pipiens* complex occur in the glaciated areas of the United States
and Canada, yet they were divided into *pipiens* in the east and *brachycephala* in the
west. The populations in the United States south of New Jersey and the Ohio Valley,
designated as *sphenocephala*, are extremely heterogeneous. Similarly the populations
of the Rio Grande Basin, Mexico, and Central America, lumped as *berlandieri*, show
great differences and, as we now know, some show extreme genetic incompatibility.
Their most distinctive feature, and so far as I know their only diagnostic one, is that
they occur in the area delimited for the subspecies.

In the years since Cope there has been a progressive shift from purely morphological to "biological" criteria for recognizing species and, to a lesser extent, subspecies. When Schmidt made his proposals there were some data on hybridization of
local populations, but none on male calls, no detailed observations on the behavior
of populations in areas of possible overlap, and no biochemical data. In the last few

years there have been many new studies of local populations, using a variety of methods, and the next decade should see a markedly improved understanding of the interrelations of the local populations of the *Rana pipiens* complex.

Many years ago I crossed individuals from various localities in the United States (9), Mexico (10), and Costa Rica (11). Data of this sort were obtained: when Vermont eggs were fertilized with sperm of Wisconsin males, the embryos were entirely normal; if the males were from New Jersey, Oklahoma, or Louisiana, there were moderate defects in the hybrids; when the males were from Florida, the defects were pronounced; when the males were from western Texas or the lowlands of northeast Mexico, the embryos were extremely abnormal and the mortality usually 100 percent. Considering these data alone, one might conclude that there is a marked change in the populations somewhere between Oklahoma and Texas. However, the embryos of a cross of Texas females and males from Florida or New Jersey were only slightly abnormal. The general conclusion for the eastern U.S. was that the degree of defectiveness in the hybrids increased fairly regularly (except for the Oklahoma-Texas area) with the increase in north-south distance between the populations. There was no evidence of any barrier in nature but this conclusion was based on data from a relatively few localities.

Recently I have returned to the *pipiens* problem and, most happily, so have some other workers. My own experiments have involved the technique of haploid hybridization, which promises to be a very sensitive method for detecting differences among geographic populations (12, 13, 14).

Haploid hybrids are formed by removing the female pronucleus from an egg fertilized with sperm of a male from a different locality. The haploid embryo then develops as a combination of egg cytoplasm and a set of chromosomes from the male. Haploid development is not normal, even when the parents are from the same locality (the controls) but, by using these controls as a standard, one can compare the development of haploid embryos formed by parents of different geographic origins.

Fig. 1 shows some of the data for *diploid hybrids* involving Vermont females. The letters A–F are measures of defectiveness. Embryos scored A are normal. B and C are progressively more abnormal but there is little or no embryonic mortality. D embryos are very abnormal and the mortality is 50 per cent or greater. F are the most abnormal [for detailed criteria, see (13)]. The dotted areas in the figure show the regions from which the males are derived that give normal or reasonably normal embryos. One might conclude that the populations of the *pipiens* complex from a vast portion of North America are a fairly homogeneous assemblage, as tested by diploid hybridization. Included in this area are populations with pronounced differences in size, coloration, body proportions, and physiological characteristics. Nevertheless these very different looking frogs seem to be genetically compatible.

Fig. 2 shows the data for *haploid hybrids* and the conclusions are very different. Here the range of defectiveness extends from 1 (typical haploid development) to 6 (the most defective). The dotted area encloses the populations having values of 1, 2, or 3. One should note especially the values for Mexican frogs: all of these haploid hybrids are extremely abnormal in contrast to the data for the diploids, which showed essentially normal development for the populations from the central plateau and the west coast lowlands. The data for haploids suggest, therefore, that there are great

Fig. 1. The type of development shown by diploid hybrids involving eggs of *Rana pipiens* from Vermont and sperm from other localities. The degree of abnormality is shown by the letters A–F, as described in Moore (13). The dotted area shows the known extent of populations that can be crossed and the hybrids show no or only slight defects.

Fig. 2. The type of development shown by haploid hybrids involving enucleated eggs of *Rana pipiens* from Vermont and sperm from other localities. The degree of abnormality is shown by the numbers 1–6. The dotted area shows the known extent of populations that can form haploid hybrids that show typical haploid development or only mild defects.

differences among these populations that are not detected by the techniques of diploid hybridization.

In a haploid embryo one measures the ability of the male genome to function in a maternally determined, though enucleate, cytoplasm. A New Jersey or Oklahoma male genome can function in an enucleated Vermont egg almost as well as a Vermont male genome. Other male genomes, for example from western Texas and nearly all parts of Mexico, do far less well—in fact, the combinations scored 5 and 6 are unable to even reach the end of gastrulation normally.

I am suggesting that the compatibility between male genome and maternally determined, enucleate, female cytoplasm can be used as a general measure of genetic relatedness. If development is essentially of the typical haploid type, it is assumed that the parent populations are genetically close. Increasing defectiveness of haploid development is taken as evidence of increasing genetic differences between the parent populations. So far this is a wholly empirical procedure: there is no independent check of how the results might compare with other measures of genetic relatedness (except for the data on the diploid hybrids).

The data suggest strongly that there has been a complex genetic differentiation of local populations. In some areas there seem to be clines in the degrees of genetic relatedness. In others, for example Oklahoma-Texas, the Isthmus of Tehuantepec, and the Florida peninsula, there is evidence for much greater differences between the local populations.

These data may be measures of genetic relatedness but they tell little about the behavior of frogs in nature. If frogs cannot be crossed and produce normal embryos in the laboratory, there is little likelihood that they can in nature. Yet the ability of two frogs to be crossed and to produce normal embryos in the laboratory does not assure that they will in nature, even if they are sympatric.

In the last few years there have been several most important studies on natural populations. For the most part the critical data are unpublished but their general nature can be indicated.

Margaret B. Parr has found that the chromosomes in haploid hybrids of different geographic populations show a high frequency of visible defects. Post and Pettus are finding evidence of two distinctive populations of frogs in Colorado, one in the mountains and the other in the plains [some of their earlier observations were published in 1966 (15)]. Stanley N. Salthe[1] is studying the geographic variation of the lactic dehydrogenases. Mecham[1] (7) has found two quite different populations in eastern Arizona that may be behaving as full species. M. J. Littlejohn and R. S. Oldham,[1] following the earlier work of McAlister (5), are finding that some populations have different male calls, differences of the magnitude that usually characterize full species. Most of these studies point to the southwest as an area of critical importance.

---

[1] These investigations, mentioned in the text as unpublished, have now appeared:

Littlejohn, M. J. and R. S. Oldham: *Rana pipiens* complex: Mating call structure and taxonomy. Science *162*:1003–1005, 1968.

Mecham, John S.: New information from experimental crosses on genetic relationships within the *Rana pipiens* species group. Journal of Experimental Zoology *170*:169–180, 1969.

Salthe, Stanley N.: Geographic variation of the lactate dehydrogenases of *Rana pipiens* and *Rana palustris*. Biochemical Genetics *2*:271–303, 1969.

In conclusion it can be said that the more the local populations of the *Rana pipiens* complex are studied the greater the differences become. It seems quite probable that some of the local populations, or groups of local populations, may have complex relations with other local populations. In some areas of contact there may be potential panmixia, in others slight barriers to gene exchange and, in still others, sympatry with no evidence of gene interchange. If this spectrum of relations is observed, then the local populations of the *Rana pipiens* complex will exhibit all of the critical stages in speciation. It remains a species worthy of intensive study.

Summary

It has long been known that *Rana pipiens* is a highly variable species and that some of its populations have diverged to the extent that, if crossed, they behave as different species. For the most part, however, such populations are widely separated from one another. Adjacent populations seem to be wholly compatible. This picture is now changing.

In recent years there have been many new studies of the *Rana pipiens* complex that have employed a variety of techniques: morphological and behavioral studies, androgenetic hybridization, analysis of male calls, comparisons of enzymes, and field studies. Evidence is now available for a few localities, such as southern Mexico, Colorado, Arizona, and Texas-Oklahoma, suggesting that different populations may be closely allopatric or even sympatric and not cross in nature.

Rana pipiens seems to have a diversity of interpopulational relations that, when studied further, should throw much light on the relation between evolutionary divergence and systematic position.

References

1. CLAUSEN, JENS: Stages in the evolution of plant species. Ithaca: Cornell University Press, 1951.
2. COPE, E. D.: The Batrachia of North America. Bulletin of the United States National Museum 34:397–406, 1889.
3. KAUFFELD, CARL F.: The status of the leopard frogs, *Rana brachycephala* and *Rana pipiens*. Herpetologica 1:84–87, 1937.
4. LEWONTIN, R. C.: Population genetics. Annual Review of Genetics 1:37–70, 1967.
5. McALISTER, WAYNE H.: Variation in *Rana pipiens* Schreber in Texas. American Midland Naturalist 67:334–363, 1962.
6. McCARTHY, B. J. and E. T. BOLTON: An approach to the measurement of genetic relatedness among organisms. Proceedings of the National Academy of Sciences 50:156–164, 1963.
7. MECHAM, JOHN S.: Evidence of reproductive isolation between two populations of the frog, *Rana pipiens*, in Arizona. Southwestern Naturalist 13:35–43, 1968.
8. MOORE, JOHN A.: Geographic variation in *Rana pipiens* Schreber of eastern North America. Bulletin of the American Museum of Natural History 82:345–370, 1944.
9. MOORE, JOHN A.: Incipient intraspecific isolating mechanisms in *Rana pipiens*. Genetics 31:304–326, 1946.
10. MOORE, JOHN A.: Hybridization between *Rana pipiens* from Vermont and eastern Mexico. Proceedings of the National Academy of Sciences 33:72–75, 1947.

11. MOORE, JOHN A.: Further studies on *Rana pipiens* racial hybrids. American Naturalist *84*:247–254, 1950.

12. MOORE, JOHN A.: Diploid and haploid interracial hybrids in *Rana pipiens*. Genetics Today. Proceedings of the XI International Congress of Genetics *2*:431–436, 1964.

13. MOORE, JOHN A.: Diploid and haploid hybridization of different populations of the *Rana pipiens* complex. I. Experiments with females from Mexico. Journal of Experimental Zoology *165*:1–20, 1967.

14. MOORE, JOHN A.: Diploid and haploid hybridization of different populations of the *Rana pipiens* complex. II. Experiments with females from Oklahoma. Journal of Experimental Zoology *165*:461–474, 1967.

15. POST, DOUGLAS D. and DAVID PETTUS: Variation in *Rana pipiens* (Anura: Ranidae) of eastern Colorado. Southwestern Naturalist *11*:476–482, 1966.

16. SCHMIDT, KARL P.: A check list of North American amphibians and reptiles. Sixth Edition. American Society of Ichthyologists and Herpetologists, 1953.

17. TURESSON, GÖTE: The species and the variety as ecological units. Hereditas *3*:100–113, 1922.

18. TURESSON, GÖTE: The genotypical response of the plant species to the habitat. Hereditas *3*:211–350, 1922.

Spontaneous and Experimental Mutations in the Newt *Pleurodeles waltlii* Michah.

L. GALLIEN

Laboratoire d'Embryologie
Faculté des Sciences de Paris
Paris, France

Introduction

Among Urodeles, the newt *Pleurodeles waltlii* Michah. (also known as *Pleurodeles waltl* Michah.) is of particular interest. This newt can be bred in the laboratory at almost any time of the year, and the larvae are easy to rear and maintain (1). A stock culture was established in our laboratory in 1945, from which several different lines have been obtained. The eggs survive a wide variety of microsurgical manipulations, and considerable success has been attained in the now familiar technique of nuclear transplantation (2, 3).

P. waltlii Michah. is widespread in Spain, Portugal, and Morocco. A closely related species, *P. poireti* Gervais, occurs in North Africa, principally Tunisia and Algeria. Although the two species are geographically isolated and differ both morphologically and immunologically (4), they can produce viable hybrids. Karyotype analyses of mitotic chromosomes reveal no differences in chromosome morphology between the two species (5). Differences, however, have been detected in lampbrush chromosomes of the two species (6).

Genetic and cytogenetic studies have been carried out at three levels: (a) point mutations, (b) chromosomal aberrations, and (c) heteroploidy. Initially the analysis was confined to mitotic chromosomes of somatic cells from the caudal epithelium of larvae. The study has now been extended to the lampbrush chromosomes in viable animals that have survived to the adult stage.

Mutations

Since the establishment of the original strain in 1945, three different mutations have been uncovered. The three mutant conditions have been designated "lethal mitotic," "ulcer," and "caudal edema," respectively.

Lethal Mitotic (l.m.)

This is a recessive autosomal mutant, first reported in 1964 by Gallien and Collenot (7). The defective gene is lethal in the homozygous state. Lethality occurs at the time of hatching. It is manifested by the appearance of large numbers of mitoses, followed by the development of pycnotic nuclei in all organs. The tissues subsequently

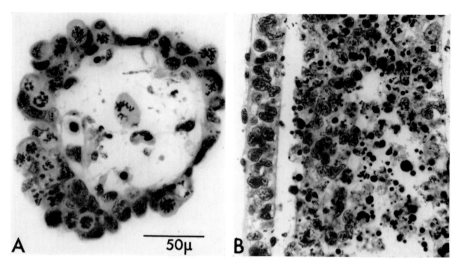

Fig. 1. The effects of the "lethal mitotic" mutation. (A) Transverse section through the gills, showing numerous mitoses in epidermal and mesenchymal cells. (B) Longitudinal section through spinal cord, revealing pycnosis and degenerating cells. [From Gallien and Collenot (7).]

become necrotic (Fig. 1). Prolonged, but limited, survival of the mutant form may be attained by joining the affected embryo in parabiotic union with a normal embryo.

Ulcer (ul)

This is a recessive autosomal mutant, also lethal when homozygous. The mutant trait was first detected by Signoret et al. (8). Lethality is expressed at the start of larval life by the characteristic appearance of ulcerations in the intestine and in the ventral integument (Fig. 2).

Caudal Edema (a.c.)

This is a recessive autosomal mutant, semilethal in the homozygous state. The deformity has been described by Beetschen and Jaylet (9). The abnormality is characterized by the formation of blisters and a massive edema of the tail, which is typically shortened and twisted.

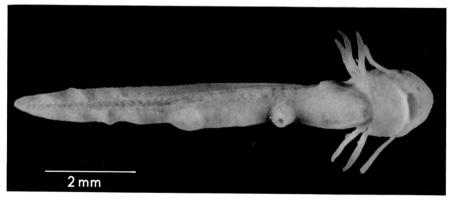

Fig. 2. The recessive autosomal mutant, termed "ulcer." [From Signoret et al. (8).]

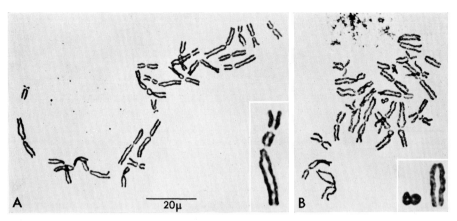

Fig. 3. Chromosomal aberrations induced by γ rays. (A) Karyotype with one dicentric chromosome. (B) Karyotype with minute chromosome and telocentric chromosome. Enlarged aberrant chromosomes are represented at the right of (A) and (B). [From Labrousse (11).]

Chromosomal Aberrations

Mishaps in the chromosomes have been induced by two experimental means: (a) exposure of eggs to γ rays (10, 11) and (b) accidental occurrences in the course of nuclear transplantation (3). Only the radiation experiments will be considered here.

The freshly laid and fertilized eggs are exposed to radiation by γ rays during various stages of fertilization which extends over a period of six hours. Characteristic radiation-induced chromosomal aberrations are breakages and deletions, as well as translocations (Fig. 3B). Breaks in chromosomes are evidenced by the presence of fragments: minute, ring, and telocentric (Fig. 3B). Chromosomal accidents also result in the loss of entire chromosomes, generally one or two. Translocations are associated with the breakage of chromosomes. The fragments produced by a breakage may become attached secondarily to another chromosome. In this event, a dicentric chromosome is formed (Fig. 3A).

Three doses of radiation have been utilized: 280, 140, and 70 r. These doses correspond to three classes of results (A, B, and C) indicated in Table 1. Attention will be directed to the classes of abnormalities designated B and C. These constitute embryos

TABLE 1

Radiation-induced Abnormalities in the Newt, *Pleurodeles waltlii*
(from M. Labrousse, unpublished data)

Number of eggs irradiated 280/140/70 r	Lethality produced before the tailbud stage (b.c.); st. 24 [1] (A)	Hypomorphic lethals st. 24–34 [1] (B)	Viable animals (C)	
			Abnormal	Normal or subnormal
1,194	676	239	43	236

[1] Stages of Gallien and Durocher (18). St. 24 = b.c.; st. 34 = hatching, 12 days old.

that die at hatching (class B) and those that are less afflicted and survive beyond hatching (class C).

Lethality at Hatching (Class B)

These embryos are either anencephalic or microcephalic. They are edematous, have twisted bodies, and underdeveloped gills. The syndrome of malformations is general, and it is not possible to relate a given hypomorphic characteristic to a specific chromosomal deficiency (Fig. 4).

Viable Individuals (Class C)

The class includes primarily those eggs exposed to 70 r, although some eggs from the 140 r group are also included. The majority of exposed eggs appear to develop normally through the larval period. Approximately 20 percent of the embryos are lethal. Anomalies among these embryos include microphthalmia, cephalic dissymmetry, and abnormal limbs.

In some individuals which attain the adult state, development, size, and fertility are impaired. Chromosomal aberrations in such individuals are relatively slight in comparison to those inviable forms of class B. It is of interest to treat in some detail three representative cases of viable animals of class C. These animals have been designated 23/S-II-10 (Fig. 5A), 17/S-II-11 (Fig. 7), and 23/S-II-11 (Fig. 5C).

Animal 23/S-II-10. The animal has a deficiency of the long arm of one chromosome (No. 7). The breakage was followed by the elimination of the acentric fragment.

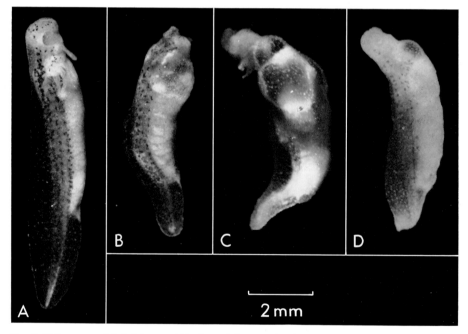

Fig. 4. Major types of lethal larvae. (A) Control larva at hatching. (B) Anencephaly. (C and D) Microcephaly. [From Labrousse (11).]

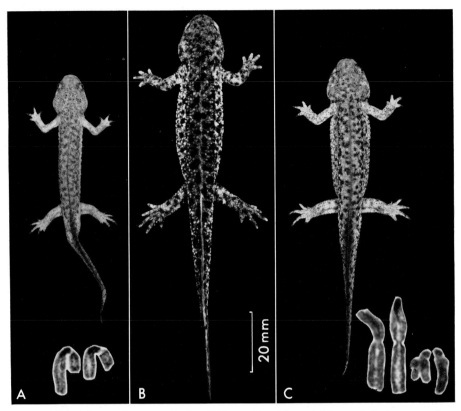

Fig. 5. Viable adult animals. (A) Animal 23/S-II-10, affected by a deficiency of the long arm of one chromosome (No. 7). Compare with Fig. 6. (B) Normal Pleurodele, two years old. (C) Animal 23/S-II-11, affected by a reciprocal translocation between chromosomes No. 1 and No. 12. [From Labrousse (11).]

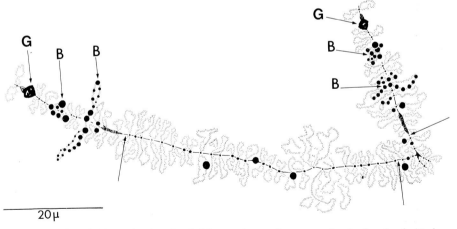

Fig. 6. Animal 23/S-II-10, showing the deficiency of one chromosome in the lampbrush bivalent. *Single* arrow on chromosome segment at right signifies the deficient region. The area between arrows on left chromosome segment indicates the region that is lacking on the right segment. The characteristic markers of this chromosome are designated G, B, B. [From Lacroix (12).]

Growth was retarded such that at the age of two years, the animal, a sterile female, was dwarfed (Figs. 5A and B). Mitotic chromosomes of cells of the caudal epithelium of the larva, as well as chromosomes of cells of the gut of the adult, displayed the aberration (11). Analyses of lampbrush chromosomes (Fig. 6) revealed that the deficiency corresponded to an interstitial segment of chromosome No. 7. In addition, the ovocytes presented a trisomy of the same chromosome (12).

Animal 17/S-II-11. The examination of 17 metaphases from the caudal epithelium revealed that the animal is a genetic mosaic (Figs. 7B and C). Two metaphases were normal, while 15 others showed a deletion in the long arm of one chromosome (No. 8). Among these metaphases one dicentric chromosome was found. The dicentric was formed by the attachment of the broken long arm of chromosome No. 8 to the

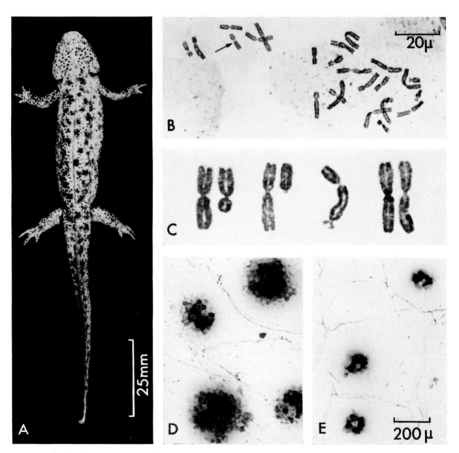

Fig. 7. Animal 17/S-II-11. (A) Black keratinized cells around the pores of the skin are well-marked on the head. Compare with Fig. 5. (B) Metaphase with the No. 8 chromosome showing the deletion (arrow). (C) Enlarged chromosomes of pair No. 8 in different metaphases. From left to right: deletion, telocentric, dicentric, and normal. (D) Shedding of the skin of the aberrant animal, 17/S-II-11. (E) Shedding of the skin of a control (normal) animal, at same magnification as in (D). (A, B, and C from Labrousse; D and E from Gallien.)

telomeric region of the long arm of chromosome No. 12. The adult, at the age of 30 months, is subnormal in size (Fig. 7A). The skin is exceedingly rough, containing strongly keratinized blocks of epidermal cells around the pores of the skin glands (Figs. 7D and E). The animal is a fertile female whose germ cell line apparently has not been affected by the deletion.

Animal 23/S-II-11. Karyotypic analyses have been made both on mitotic chromosomes from caudal epidermal cells at the larval stage and from lampbrush chromosomes of the ovocytes (12, 13). A reciprocal translocation had occurred between chromosome No. 1 and chromosome No. 12. The animal, although small, was a well-proportioned female. When mated, she provided a small spawn of 52 eggs. All eggs perished before or slightly after first cleavage.

Thus, eggs which received weak doses of irradiation, and in which chromosomal damage did not impair chromosome replication, were able to survive and develop to adulthood. In contrast, eggs exposed to intermediate doses (140 r) or strong doses (280 r) experienced such severe chromosomal damage as to result in lethality at hatching or earlier.

Heteroploidy

Refrigeration of fertilized eggs tends to produce triploid individuals; some of the refrigerated eggs are androgenetic haploids (14, 15). Haploid embryos typically die soon after hatching. The parabiotic union of a haploid and normal diploid embryo promotes better development of the haploid. Indeed, the haploid partner has been maintained to an age of two and three years. The prolonged survival of haploid parabionts has permitted the elucidation of the haploid syndrome. Among other features, it has been shown that spermatogenesis in haploids is abortive (16).

The technique of nuclear transplantation has led to the identification of tetrasomic embryos, described by Gallien *et al.* (3). Trisomy has been found among the progeny of a fertile aneuploid obtained originally from the cross of a diploid female and a triploid male (17). Trisomy was detected by karyotypic analyses of both mitotic and lampbrush chromosomes.

It is evident, then, that the newt *Pleurodeles waltlii* is suitable for genetic and cytogenetic studies. The newt is as equally subject to changes at the gene and chromosome levels as other vertebrates. The types of induced genic and chromosomal abnormalities are strongly reminiscent of the kinds of deformities in mammals and especially in man.

Summary

The newt *Pleurodeles waltlii* has special advantages for genetic and cytogenetic studies. Investigations on point mutations, chromosomal aberrations, and heteroploidy in this favorable organism are reviewed and discussed. The types of induced chromosomal abnormalities bear a strong resemblance to the kinds of deformities which occur spontaneously in higher vertebrates, including man.

References

1. GALLIEN, L.: Elevage et comportement du Pleurodèle au Laboratoire. Bull. Soc. Zool. France 77:456–461, 1952.

2. SIGNORET, J., et PICHERAL, B.: Transplantation de noyaux chez *Pleurodeles waltlii* Michah. C. R. Acad. Sc. 254:1150–1151, 1962.

3. GALLIEN, L., LABROUSSE, M., PICHERAL, B., et LACROIX, J. C.: Modifications expérimentales du caryotype chez un Amphibien Urodèle (*Pleurodeles waltlii* Michah.) par irradiation de l'oeuf et la greffe nucléaire. Rev. Suisse Zool. 72:59–85, 1965.

4. CHALUMEAU-LE FOULGOC, M. TH., et GALLIEN, C. L.: Recherches comparatives sur les protéines sériques dans le genre *Pleurodeles* (Amphibien, Urodèle). Comp. Biochem. Physiol. 23:679–689, 1967.

5. GALLIEN, C. L.: Le caryotype de l'Urodèle *Pleurodeles poireti* Gervais. Etude comparative des caryotypes dans le genre *Pleurodeles*. C. R. Acad. Sc. 262:122–125, 1966.

6. LACROIX, J. C.: Etude descriptive des chromosomes en écouvillon dans le genre *Pleurodeles* (Amphibien, Urodèle). Ann. Embr. Morph. 1:179–202, 1968a.

7. GALLIEN, L., et COLLENOT, A.: Sur un mutant récessif léthal, dont le syndrome est associé à des perturbations mitotiques chez le Triton *Pleurodeles waltlii*. C. R. Acad. Sc. 259:4847–4849, 1964.

8. SIGNORET, J., COLLENOT, A., et GALLIEN, L.: Description d'un nouveau mutant récessif léthal (u) et de son syndrome chez le Triton *Pleurodeles waltlii*. C. R. Acad. Sc. 262: 699–701, 1966.

9. BEETSCHEN, J. C., et JAYLET, A.: Sur un facteur récessif semi-léthal déterminant l'apparition d'ascite caudale (a.c.) chez le Triton *Pleurodeles waltlii*. C. R. Acad. Sc. 261:5675–5678, 1966.

10. GALLIEN, L., LABROUSSE, M., et LACROIX, J. C.: Aberrations chromosomiques associées à des hypomorphoses, consécutives à l'irradiation de l'oeuf par les rayons γ, chez l'Amphibien Urodèle, *Pleurodeles waltlii* Michah. C. R. Acad. Sc. 256:5413–5415, 1963.

11. LABROUSSE, M.: Analyse des effets des rayonnements appliqués à l'oeuf sur les structures caryologiques et sur le développement embryonnaire de l'Amphibien Urodèle *Pleurodeles waltlii* Michah. Bull. Soc. Zool. France 91:491–588, 1966.

12. LACROIX, J. C.: Variations expérimentales ou spontanées de la morphologie et de l'organisation des chromosomes en écouvillon dans le genre *Pleurodeles* (Amphibien, Urodèle). Ann. Embr. Morph. 1:205–248, 1968b.

13. GALLIEN, L., LABROUSSE, M., et LACROIX, J. C.: Détection sur les chromosomes mitotiques et sur les chromosomes en écouvillon (lampbrush) d'anomalies, provoquées par l'irradiation de l'oeuf, chez l'Amphibien Urodèle *Pleurodeles waltlii* Michah. C. R. Acad. Sc. 263:1984–1987, 1966.

14. GALLIEN, L.: Recherches sur quelques aspects de l'hétéroploidie expérimentale chez le Triton *Pleurodeles waltlii* Michah. J. Embr. Exp. Morph. 7:380–393, 1959.

15. BEETSCHEN, J. C.: Recherches sur l'hétéroploidie expérimentale chez un Amphibien Urodèle, *Pleurodeles waltlii* Michah. Bull. Biol. France et Belgique 94:12–127, 1960.

16. GALLIEN, L.: Développement d'individus haploides adultes éléves en parabiose chez le Triton *Pleurodeles waltlii* Michah. Syndrome de l'haploidie et différenciation sexuelle. J. Embr. Exp. Morph. 18:401–426, 1967.

17. LACROIX, J. C.: Obtention de femelles trisomiques fertiles chez l'Amphibien Urodèle *Pleurodeles waltlii* Michah. C. R. Acad. Sc. 264:85–88, 1967.

18. GALLIEN, L., et DUROCHER, M.: Table chronologique du développement chez *Pleurodeles waltlii* Michah. Bull. Biol. France et Belgique 91:97–114, 1957.

Nucleo-Cortical Interactions
During Amphibian Development*

PHILIP GRANT

Department of Biology
University of Oregon
Eugene, Oregon

The egg cortex, though poorly defined (11), is often implicated as an important determinant of morphogenesis in amphibian and mollusc development (13, 14). Recently, for example, Arnold (1) has demonstrated that irradiation of the squid egg cortex with a UV microbeam specifically inhibits development of embryonic eyes and arms. The grey crescent cortical region of the amphibian egg is well known as the organization center for the primary neural axis of the embryo. Pasteels (13), reviewing experiments on amphibian eggs, postulates a yolk-cortex interaction system as a causal factor in establishing the axial organization in the embryo, a view formulated earlier by Dalcq and Pasteels in 1936. Curtis (4, 5) reported the induction of a secondary embryonic axis after transplantation of the grey crescent cortex at the fertilized egg stage in *Xenopus*. Although his experiments were few in number and have not been repeated, the results support the view of the grey crescent cortex as a site for organization and storage of developmental information.

If the egg cortex contributes developmental information, we want to know how this information is organized and how it is utilized. We also want to know whether cortical information interacts with genetic information in the nucleus. It is to this latter question that these experiments are addressed.

The nuclear transplantation technique developed by Briggs and King (2) has already been used to assess developmental capacities of nuclei after interaction with nitrogen mustard-treated egg cytoplasm (8). Similar techniques may be used to evaluate nucleo-cortical interactions. Our plan is to focus on the gray crescent of the fertilized egg. Irradiation of this region with a UV microbeam should yield specific developmental abnormalities related to formation of the primary embryonic axis. If specific developmental patterns are induced, then we can ask whether cortical lesions are irreversibly transmitted to nuclei. The design of the experiment is relatively simple. Nuclear transfers, made from cells occupying irradiated cortical regions, are compared to control transfers taken from similar, but unirradiated, regions. If the cortex normally interacts irreversibly with nuclei during cleavage and blastulation, irradiated cortex should also transmit developmental lesions to nuclei. Such nuclear lesions may be demonstrable after nuclear transfer. Reported here are some initial attempts to explore this question.

---

* This research was supported by AEC contract AT(45-1)-2011.

Materials and Methods

The eggs of *Rana pipiens,* obtained by the usual procedures of induced ovulation, were fertilized and prepared for irradiation by removing jelly with watchmaker's forceps.

After several trials, it was realized that grey crescents are not easily identified in *Rana pipiens* eggs, nor do they form in any predictable manner. Consequently, it was decided to irradiate the entire vegetal-marginal region to insure inclusion of the grey crescent region. Groups of ten eggs each were irradiated at different times after fertilization, usually at 1–1½ hours. The eggs were grouped together on a quartz slide supported over a small UV source (Pen-Ray lamp 22 SC-35, Ultraviolet Products Inc.) as shown in Fig. 1 and irradiated for one minute. The lamp was positioned approximately two millimeters from the egg surface; UV dose was not measured. After irradiation the eggs were placed in small Stender dishes and allowed to develop at 18°C. Embryos were examined daily, normal and abnormal embryos were recorded, and developmental patterns to hatching noted.

Activated, enucleated eggs were the recipients of nuclear transfers from irradiated and control blastulae. Donor St. 9-9+ blastulae were de-jellied and vitelline membranes were removed. Blastulae were separated into small pieces in Ca and Mg-free Steinberg's (15) solution containing 10^{-3}M versene. After 10–15 minutes, the partially disaggregated pieces were transferred to Steinberg's solution in an operating dish for nuclear transplantation. Cells on the surface usually adhered firmly to one another in spite of the versene treatment while cells just below the surface coat layer were easily disaggregated. Donor cortical transfers were taken from vegetal or marginal surface layers in both experimentals and controls. Some control transfers were completed with donor cells from the inner layer of the animal and vegetal halves. Transfers were also made with early St. 10 gastrula donors, cells taken from the cortical region immediately above the dorsal lip.

Eggs were placed in individual Stender dishes and allowed to develop at 18°C. They were examined daily and developmental patterns were recorded.

The data are presented as percentages of total eggs and blastulae which show normal development. The percentages of embryos reaching gastrula, neurula, tailbud

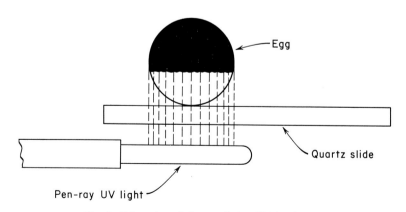

Fig. 1. Orientation of the egg during UV irradiation.

and hatched stages were determined, based on the total number of normal blastulae taken as one hundred percent.

Results

With the geometry indicated in Fig. 1, the irradiated area covers the entire vegetal region including marginal zones at the equator. Maximum UV absorption is probably concentrated in the cortex since the energy falls off rapidly after absorption at the surface. We assume, therefore, that the maximum effect is at the plasma membrane, the underlying cortical region and possibly a thin layer of cytoplasm beneath.

The Acephalic Syndrome

The effect of irradiation of the vegetal region is shown in Table 1 and in Figs. 2 and 3. Irradiation of the vegetal region significantly inhibits normal blastula formation. Only 50% of the eggs develop as normal blastulae compared to 74–84% for controls. About 75% exhibit a gastrulation delay, sometimes forming an abnormal dorsal lip and blastopore. Twenty-five percent of the blastulae gastrulate normally, however, forming a typical late yolk plug stage (Stage 12-12+). A developmental crisis occurs at neurulation for all irradiated gastrulae. Virtually all embryos (97%) do not neurulate, arresting at the very beginning of neurulation (Fig. 2a). No neural plate or folds are formed (Fig. 2c). Embryos survive for several days in this arrested condition until controls have become hatched larvae. During this time they become edematous and gradually develop a short wrinkled tail stump and form a characteristic severe acephalic syndrome (Figs. 2e, 3a). Control embryos, irradiated through a glass slide or irradiated at the animal pole show either no effect (Figs. 2b, d, f), or develop as haploid embryos.

At lower doses, a milder form of the syndrome is manifested. First, many more

TABLE 1

EFFECT OF UV IRRADIATION OF VEGETAL REGION OF EGGS
UP TO ONE HOUR BEFORE FERTILIZATION

Eggs	No. of eggs	Percent normal development				
		S8-9	S11-12	S13-14	S17	S20
Unirradiated controls	777	74	96	92	89	85
Glass controls	37	84	100	84	84	84
Irradiated eggs	236	49	25	3	3	3

Percentages for St. 8-9 are based on total number of eggs. Percentages of normal development of later stages based on the total number of complete St. 8-9 blastulae.

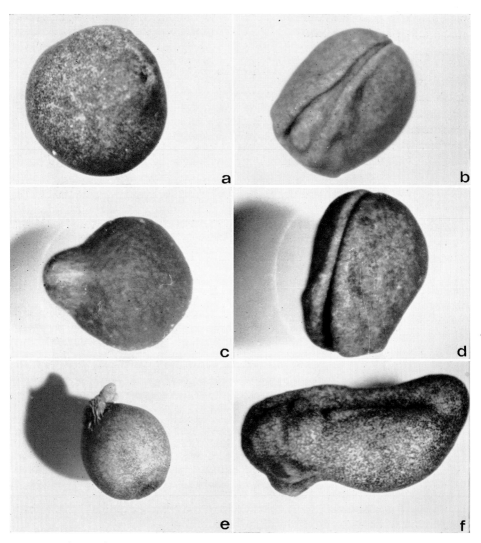

Fig. 2. Developmental pattern of irradiated eggs. Figs. 2a, c, e represent characteristic morphology of the severe acephalic syndrome, comparable to the controls shown in Figs. 2b, d, f. Fig. 2e is at a lower magnification. Note the irregular tail.

blastulae gastrulate normally. During neurulation only narrow, abnormal folds appear, and cephalic folds fail to develop (Fig. 3b). Neurulation is completed but acephalic embryos develop with a well formed trunk and tail (Fig. 3c). The irradiation syndrome suggests that factors essential for head formation and axial organization are destroyed. These are properties of the grey crescent region and suggest that the grey crescent is the primary site of irradiation damage.

Post Fertilization Sensitivity

Irradiation of the egg at various times after fertilization results in different developmental patterns. A progressive change in UV sensitivity is observed as the egg

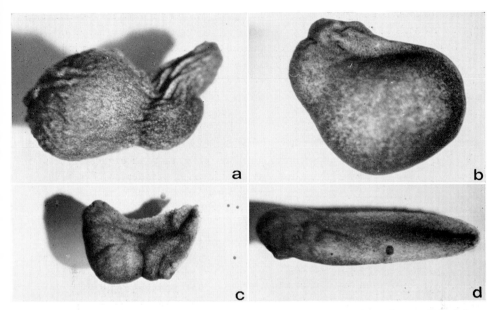

Fig. 3. Developmental pattern of irradiated eggs. Fig. 3a represents a more advanced stage of acephalic syndrome. Fig. 3b and c are stages in the less severe syndrome with well developed trunk and tail forming a headless tadpole. Fig. 3d is a control tadpole.

proceeds towards first cleavage. In Fig. 4, a plot is shown of the percentages of blastulae developing normally to hatching after irradiation at $\frac{1}{2}$–1 hour, $1\frac{1}{2}$–2 hours, and $2\frac{1}{2}$–3 hours after fertilization. The curves show a change in sensitivity with time of irradiation. Abnormalities are most severe after irradiation within the first hour (Figs. 2e, 3a) whereas the less severe syndrome (Fig. 3c) is typical of eggs

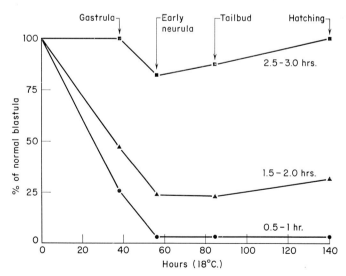

Fig. 4. A plot of percentage of normal development of eggs irradiated at different intervals after insemination.

irradiated later. At 2½–3 hours most embryos develop normally. These results suggest a reduction in UV sensitivity of the cortex or membrane or perhaps a displacement of some sensitive cytoplasmic component towards the egg interior as it prepares for first cleavage.

Irradiation of ventral regions of St. 9 blastulae produces completely different abnormal patterns. Irradiated blastulae usually gastrulate abnormally, produce spina bifida embryos which develop into hatched larvae with tail and trunk abnormalities. No irradiated blastulae become acephalic nor do they exhibit abnormalities of the axial organization except for minor tail modifications. The pattern of blastula sensitivity is totally different from that of the egg. This means that the egg cortex is most vulnerable to irradiation damage during a short interval after fertilization.

Nuclear Transfers

Only a limited number of control nuclear transfers were completed with St. 9-9+ donor blastulae. Donor transfers from marginal and vegetal cortical regions were compared to transfers from inner cell layers. The results in Table 2 indicate a difference in the developmental capacity of cortical nuclear transfers. Only 12%, or two out of a total of 17 completed blastulae develop as normal tadpoles, compared to 38% or 9 out of 24 inner layer donor cells. Cortical cells, held together by the surface coat, are difficult to isolate and are probably more easily damaged during transplantation.

Transfers of irradiated cortical cells show no significant difference in developmental pattern. In fact, the results are better than controls. In the case of vegetal and unpigmented marginal zone cells, 43% of normal blastulae develop to hatching. The

TABLE 2

BLASTULA NUCLEAR TRANSFERS FROM IRRADIATED
AND NON-IRRADIATED CORTICAL CELLS

Cell type	No.	Percent normal development				
		S8-9	S11-12	S13-14	S17	S20
Cortex control	51	33	29	12	12	12
Inner layer (animal and vegetal)	52	46	54	42	42	38
Irradiated:						
vegetal cortex	25	28	43	43	43	43
marginal zone (unpig.)	75	35	58	46	42	42
marginal zone (pig.)	30	27	38	0	0	0

See footnote to Table 1.

pattern of abnormalities is identical to those obtained from normal controls. No pattern typical of the acephalic syndrome of irradiated donor embryos was observed. Differences obtained with pigmented marginal zone cells are too few to be interpreted as significant. Only 8 normal blastulae out of 30 eggs resulted and these developed abnormally. Abnormalities in no way resembled any irradiated syndrome but were typical of abnormalities derived from controls. One can conclude, therefore, that irradiated cortical transfer embryos develop as do the controls. The UV lesion responsible for inhibition of neurulation in irradiated embryos is apparently not communicated irreversibly to nuclei by a late blastula stage.

Early stage 10 gastrulae were also used as donors. Presumptive chorda-mesoderm is easily identified at this stage and cells can be taken from this region for nuclear transfer. Above all others, these cells should be most critical if inductive properties have been altered. Cells from the surface layer just above and around the dorsal lip were used as donors in irradiated and control embryos. The results of these few experiments are shown in Table 3. Although the number of transfers is low, the developmental pattern is similar in experimentals and controls. None of the abnormalities resembled those obtained from irradiated donor embryos, which suggests that even at the early gastrula stage, presumptive chorda-mesoderm nuclei have not been irreversibly modified by interacting with an irradiated cortex. In spite of a loss of inductive properties, the nuclei of these cells exhibit no change in their developmental capacities after transplantation.

Discussion

These results permit only a few tentative conclusions. Irradiation of the entire vegetal region of the egg elicits a reproducible acephalic syndrome. Gastrulation occurs, but formation of a neural plate and an axial organization are completely inhibited. The absence of induction and the specificity of the syndrome point to the grey crescent region of the fertilized egg as the likely site for UV damage. Progressive changes in UV sensitivity of the egg after fertilization support the hypothesis that the grey crescent cortex is a principal target for UV absorption. Hebard and Herold (11) report a progressive change in the thickness and distribution of the so-called "electron

TABLE 3

Early Gastrula (St. 10) Nuclear Transfers
From Irradiated Cortical Cells (Above Dorsal Lip)

Cell type	No.	Percent normal development				
		S8-9	S11-12	S13-14	S17	S20
Unirradiated control	32	25	13	13	25	25
Irradiated	38	39	27	13	13	13

See footnote to Table 1.

dense layer" or cortex in fertilized eggs of *Xenopus* prior to first cleavage. Displacement of cortical regions prior to cleavage can explain a progressive loss in UV sensitivity. This hypothesis is being tested further with a UV microbeam apparatus which permits highly localized irradiation of cortical regions.

The nature of the UV lesion is unknown. We assume that the bulk of the radiation is absorbed at the plasma membrane and underlying cortex. The properties of the surface coat, so important during gastrulation (12), are probably modified as a result of irradiation.

The nuclear transfer experiments indicate that irreversible lesions are not induced in nuclei by an irradiated cortex. Several explanations are possible for these negative results: (1) nuclei do not normally interact with the cortex during blastulation or during early St. 10 gastrula, or (2) nuclei, in fact, interact with the cortex but do so reversibly. Cortical lesions leading to minor nuclear changes may be reversed after nuclei are transplanted to egg cytoplasm. The present experiments do not distinguish between these alternatives. Gurdon and Woodland (10) review the evidence for nucleo-cytoplasmic interactions in the amphibian egg and conclude that egg cytoplasm can profoundly modify nuclear behavior. Transfer of nuclei actively synthesizing ribosomes into egg cytoplasm, for example, is followed by an immediate shutting off of ribosomal RNA synthesis (9). Similarly, adult brain cell nuclei can be stimulated to DNA synthesis after transfer to egg cytoplasm (7). Transformations of nuclear function in egg cytoplasm may restore induced cortical changes which would go undetected in the transplantation technique.

Other explanations are possible for failure to detect any nuclear changes. Perhaps the wrong cells were sampled for transfer. Donor cells were taken from the marginal zone surface since these cells were assumed to incorporate part of the irradiated cortex during cleavage. During invagination these cells come to occupy the roof of the archenteron but are not immediately opposed to the presumptive neural ectoderm. The cells just beneath the surface layer come closest to the presumptive neural ectoderm during invagination and it is these cells and not the surface coat cells that merit further investigation.

Finally, timing may be an important factor. The data show that an irreversible interaction has not taken place between nuclei and cortex by the early gastrula stage. Are interactions during or after gastrulation more important? To answer this question, transfers of invaginated irradiated cells from mid and late gastrulae are necessary. Such experiments are more difficult to interpret since normal gastrula transfers yield a greater proportion of abnormal embryos (3). Unique differences in developmental patterns between normal and irradiated nuclear transfers must be obtained before any conclusions can be made about specific nucleo-cortical interactions. Ideally, of course, irreversible changes perpetuating the typical acephalic syndrome would be the most promising sign of developmentally significant nucleo-cortical interactions.

Summary

The grey crescent region of the amphibian egg represents a morphogenetically significant cortical differentiation. UV irradiation of the vegetal region of the *Rana pipiens* egg results in characteristic acephalic developmental abnormalities suggesting that lesions have been induced in the grey crescent region. Nuclear transplantations were carried out with irradiated cortical cells to determine whether UV induced cortical lesions are irreversibly communicated to nuclei. The results indicate that no significant interaction between cortex and nuclei take place during cleavage through blastulation. The significance of these results are discussed.

References

1. ARNOLD, J. M.: The role of the egg cortex in cephalopod development. Develop. Biol. *18*:180–197, 1968.

2. BRIGGS, R. and KING, T. J.: Factors affecting the transplantability of nuclei of frog embryonic cells. J. Exp. Zool. *122*:485, 1953.

3. BRIGGS, R. and KING, T. J.: Nuclear transplantation studies on the early gastrula. Develop. Biol. *2*:252–270, 1960.

4. CURTIS, A. S. G.: Cortical grafting in *Xenopus laevis*. J. Emb. Exptl. Morph. *8*:163–173, 1960.

5. CURTIS, A. S. G.: Morphogenetic interactions before gastrulation in the amphibian *Xenopus laevis*—the cortical field. J. Emb. Exptl. Morph. *10*:410–424, 1962.

6. DALCQ, A. and PASTEELS, J.: Une conception nouvelle des bases physiologiques de la morphogénèse. Arch. Biol. *48*:669–710, 1936.

7. GRAHAM, C. F., ARMS, K. and GURDON, J. B.: The induction of DNA synthesis by egg cytoplasm. Develop. Biol. *14*:349, 1966.

8. GRANT, P. and STOTT, P.: Effect of nitrogen mustard on nucleocytoplasmic interaction. *In* Biological Interactions in Normal and Neoplastic Growth (M. J. Brennan and W. L. Simpson, eds.), 47–74. Little, Brown and Co., Boston, 1962.

9. GURDON, J. B. and BROWN, D. D.: Cytoplasmic regulation of RNA synthesis and nucleolus formation in developing embryos of *Xenopus laevis*. J. Molec. Biol. *12*:27–35, 1965.

10. GURDON, J. B. and WOODLAND, H. R.: The cytoplasmic control of nuclear activity in animal development. Biol. Rev. *43*:233–267, 1968.

11. HEBARD, C. N. and HEROLD, R. C.: The ultrastructure of the cortical cytoplasm in the unfertilized egg and first cleavage zygote of *Xenopus laevis*. Exp. Cell Res. *46*:553–570, 1967.

12. HOLTFRETER, J.: Properties and functions of the surface coat in amphibian embryos. J. Exp. Zool. *93*:251, 1943.

13. PASTEELS, J. J.: The morphogenetic role of the cortex of the amphibian egg. Adv. Morph. *3*:363–388, 1964.

14. RAVEN, C. P.: *Oogenesis: The Storage of Developmental Information*. Pergamon Press, New York, 1961.

15. STEINBERG, M.: Carnegie Inst. Wash. Year Book, *56*:347, 1957.

Mass Culture of Amphibian Cells: Methods and Observations Concerning Stability of Cell Type[1]

Keen A. Rafferty, Jr.

Department of Anatomy
The Johns Hopkins University School of Medicine
Baltimore, Maryland

A large number of workers have reported the culture of amphibian cells, but most of the accounts are found in older literature and few of them report success in maintaining monolayer strains through serial subculture. The first permanent amphibian line is that of Wolfe and Quimby (27), derived from bullfrog tongue. This line subsequently proved to be fibroblastic in morphology and subtetraploid in chromosome number. To date, it has passed through hundreds of cell generations in culture. Freed *et al.* (13, 14) and Seto (26) have also reported extended serial subculture of amphibian cell lines.

The present writer has used the basic methods of Wolfe *et al.*, and of Auclair (1) to establish a number of additional strains, of which sixteen, representing six species of anurans, are reported here. The methodology and some findings resulting from study of the derived strains are being reported because of features which are unusual among vertebrates, and which render cultured amphibian cells useful members of the armamentarium of cells which can be propagated *in vitro*. Several amphibian lines show unusual ability to persist in diploid form, in comparison with piscine and mammalian cell lines. Further, unlike the cells of other vertebrate classes, cells of epithelioid morphology often predominate in cultures derived from amphibian tissues. Because there is reason to believe that these cells may be of bona fide epithelial origin, the prospect arises that organ parenchymal cells may be grown in quantity and studied in the diploid condition in terms of specific cell products. Additionally, because Lucké tumor cells and cell lines which support replication of the suspected etiological agent (FV-4) both tend to remain diploid, there is the possibility that such systems may be used to study malignant transformation in the absence of chromosomal transformation.

A final feature concerns the utility of amphibian cells in studies of aging, since particular lines of cells remain euploid for many more cell generations than expected from consideration of *in vivo* longevity, while cultured cells of other vertebrate classes show a marked propensity for the development of chromosomal abnormalities and establishment as permanent cell lines.

---

[1] This investigation was supported by PHS research grant CA-06008 from the National Cancer Institute.

Materials and Methods

Adults and Large Embryos

Many amphibian cells respond well to handling procedures in use for mammalian and avian cells, provided the incubation temperature and medium tonicity are lowered. In general, results have not been satisfactory with cells of adult *Rana*, but adult tissues of some other species, notably *Xenopus*, often give rise to vigorous cultures and permanent lines. The usual protease digestion methods do not seem to work well with tissues composed of large cells, as in the case of Urodeles or of early anuran embryos. In these cases, cultures may be started from small teased fragments. Lines established from embryo cells tend to be more vigorous than do those of adult origin.

Digests of minced tissues from adults or from large embryos are made using a buffered isotonic saline free of divalent cations (wash medium: method of preparation is given in appendix for this and other solutions) containing pronase or trypsin with penicillin (50–100 U/ml) and streptomycin (50 μg/ml). Tissues are removed aseptically and minced with scissors to give fragments of about 1 mm^3. The fragments, consisting of 500 mg or more of tissue, are transferred to a fluted 125 ml trypsinization flask containing a Teflon-covered stirring magnet. About 25 ml of enzyme solution is added and the fragments agitated slowly at room temperature, using a magnetic stirrer, with care to ensure that the suspension is not heated above about 25°C. After 5–10 minutes, the enzyme solution is discarded and the process repeated. Subsequent cell suspensions are harvested and planted in culture flasks at intervals of 30–60 minutes, the process being continued for as long as four hours. Immediately after decanting, each harvest is centrifuged at 350 × G for five minutes, the supernate discarded and the pellet suspended in nutrient medium by gentle pipetting. Each pellet is planted in a culture flask of 75 cm^2 surface area, in 15–20 ml of medium. Pellets should contain at least 10^5 cells per cm^2 of culture vessel area, since attachment efficiency is low. The flasks are gassed with a 4% or 5% mixture of CO_2 in air, sealed and incubated at 25°C. The first few subcultures are made at high cell density (1:1 or 1:2) until strain vigor is determined. The derived strains vary considerably, however, in their vigor and growth rates, and some cannot safely be subcultured at ratios exceeding 1:2 even when considered established.

An alternative method consists of overnight trypsinization (18 hours) at 4–5°C following a brief preliminary wash in the enzyme solution.

Small Embryos

Despite several attempts, mechanical agitation in protease solutions has not given long-term cultures in the case of the cells of early embryos or from urodele donors, which have unusually large cells. Since tissues of older anuran embryos can be cultured by conventional dissociation methods, and since cultures of dividing cells have been established by others from explanted urodele tissue fragments, the suggestion is that some amphibian cells are too fragile to withstand dissociation. Cultures of newly hatched anuran embryos may be started by crudely mincing or teasing apart whole embryos in 5 ml of nutrient medium contained in flasks of 25 cm^2 surface area. When these are gassed and incubated directly, small tissue fragments often attach after a few days and cell outgrowth may be well advanced in one or two weeks. Such cultures may subsequently be transferred in the usual manner.

Sepsis during the removal of tissues is more likely to become a problem in the case of aquatic or amphibious animals than is the case with terrestrial forms. Good results have been obtained, however, by the following procedure. Donor carcasses of adults and large embryos are immersed for one minute each in 1% Lysol solution and then in 70% ethyl alcohol before removal of tissue with sterile instruments. Newly hatched embryos are a lesser problem because the mouth and cloaca remain closed for about 25 hours post-hatching. Hence, they can often be "sterilized" by transfer to 5 successive dishes containing wash medium with 500 units of penicillin and 100 μg of streptomycin/ml.

Preparation of Tissue Culture Chromosomes

Methods for preparing chromosomes for study have been adapted from Moorhead *et al.* (23) and others. Colcemid in a small volume of nutrient medium is added to actively growing cultures in 250 ml Falcon flasks to give a final concentration of 0.5 μg/ml. After 2–5 hours of additional incubation, the cells are harvested enzymatically, and dispersed by gentle pipetting. Fetal bovine serum is added to 20%, and the suspension is pelleted by slow speed centrifugation in a conical-tipped glass centrifuge tube. The supernate is aspirated and the pellet resuspended in 0.3 ml of Hanks' Solution diluted to 70% and made up with 10% fetal bovine serum. Distilled water is added rapidly to 1.0 ml and the suspension allowed to stand undisturbed at room temperature for ten minutes. After recentrifugation and aspiration of the hypotonic medium, the pellet is fixed for 5 minutes by the addition of 0.5 ml of fresh methanol-glacial acetic acid mixture (3:1) at room temperature, allowing the fixative to run down the slanted wall of the tube so that the pellet is not disturbed. Resuspension of the pellet is accomplished by gently "eroding" it, through squirting the fixative against it with a Pasteur pipette. After the cells are dispersed in the fixative, the suspension is then further diluted to 5.0 ml by the addition of more fixative and centrifuged. The cells are centrifuged and resuspended in fixative 2 or 3 times, in order to remove water. When chromosome preparations are to be made, the final pellet is resuspended in 0.5 to 1.0 ml of fixative, and slides made by the ignition-air dry method (23).

Preparation of Chromosomes from Tissues

Lymphocytes may be cultured by anesthetising the frog with MS 222 (Sandoz) and removing blood from the heart in a heparinized syringe. To a 30 ml culture flask containing 5 ml of nutrient medium with 20% fetal calf serum and 1% phytohemagglutinin (Difco M type), 0.1 ml of whole blood is added. Cultures are gassed with 5% CO_2 and incubated for 3 days or more at 25 °C. Hypotonic treatment and chromosome preparation are carried out as for tissue culture cells.

For the preparation of marrow chromosomes, colchicine is injected at the level of 0.5 ml of an 0.025% solution per 30 grams. The long bones of the caudal extremities are removed, the ends cut off, and the marrow extruded by flushing the medullary cavity with 1.5% sodium citrate solution contained in a syringe equipped with a 25 ga. needle. The pelletized cells are resuspended in 0.5 ml of the citrate solution and further diluted to 1.1 ml by the addition of distilled water. Hypotonic treatment is continued for 18 minutes, after which the cells are centrifuged, fixed and prepared as for tissue culture cells. Teased suspensions of testis cells may be treated in the same way. *Xenopus* sp. lack marrow hematopoeisis, but chromosome preparations may be obtained from spleen of frogs weighing more than 25 grams.

All chromosome preparations were made by the ignition air dry method; most were stained with Giemsa stain according to Schmid's method for autoradiography (25). In practice, a phase contrast microscope is convenient for examining trial preparations during the washing process.

Frozen Storage of Cells

Cells are harvested enzymatically from 250 ml Falcon flasks containing nearly confluent cultures in the logarithmic growth phase. The pellet from each flask is suspended in 1.0 ml of freezing solution consisting of nutrient medium to which are added dimethyl sulfoxide and additional fetal bovine serum to give final concentrations of 10% and 15%, respectively (3). The suspensions are sealed in 1.0 ml ampules, and these are frozen slowly by embedding them in a bag of insulated packing material and depositing the bag in a mechanical freezer at $-63\,°C$ for 2 hours. The frozen ampules are then plunged into liquid nitrogen for permanent storage. Thawing is done rapidly, by immersing the ampules in water at room temperature. The suspension is centrifuged, washed once in nutrient medium, and the final suspension seeded in 1 or 2 250 ml Falcon flasks. Usually about 50% of the cells attach, and these may be subcultured in the usual manner when confluent. Care must be taken to avoid contacting concentrated DMSO with plastic.

Results

All strains observed to date grow within a broad pH range, estimated at extremes of 6.5 to 7.6. The optimal growth temperature seems to be rather uniformly at about $25\,°C$, but some growth may occur at temperatures as high as $30\,°C$, and at least one line (A-8) can tolerate $37\,°C$ for one hour. Temperatures lower than $25\,°C$ lead to a slowing of growth, and lines vary greatly in their ability to survive refrigerator temperatures for more than a few days.

Antibiotic Tolerance

Tests for mycoplasmas have been conducted with all reported strains except A-21–A-24, and were negative.[1] Casual bacterial and mold contamination may be managed with the usual antibiotics, but if test plates are made to determine antibiotic sensitivity of a contaminant, bacterial cultures should be made in duplicate and incubated at $25°$ and $37°C$. Many contaminants show striking differences in antibiotic sensitivities at the two temperatures. All strains tested tolerate amphotericin B and mycostatin at least to levels of 2 $\mu g/ml$ and 50 U/ml, respectively. Penicillin G is not toxic, at least to levels of 200 U/ml, but some slowing of growth may result from the use of streptomycin at concentrations higher than 100 $\mu g/ml$. Kanamycin

---

[1] Kindly performed by Dr. Theodore Carski of the Baltimore Biological Laboratories.

and erythromycin are tolerated well by at least some lines at the level of 2 μg/ml and 50 μg/ml, respectively. Tylosin does not appear to cause slowing of growth when a commercial solution (GIBCO) is used to 1%.

Medium and Medium Components

The water used in making medium is quite important: best results have been obtained using freshly distilled water with resistivity of 9×10^5 ohms or higher. Fetal bovine serum is stored frozen, and heated to 56°C for 30 minutes before use. Serum may be added shortly before the medium is used, but complete medium has been successfully stored at 5°C for several weeks. Nevertheless, cultures sometimes wax and wane without adequate explanation. Since most lines receiving a particular lot of medium often behave similarly, the medium itself seems to be incriminated but decline in growth has usually not been identified with particular sources or lots of components. Diploid lines usually require more care, but vigorous heteroploid lines seem to be about as hardy as comparable mammalian lines.

In our experience, the most effective medium for general use in amphibian cell culture is a modified batch of dry powder NCTC-109, in which NaCl and KCl are reduced to 4.380 and 0.216 grams/liter, respectively, and in which uridine and thymidine are omitted, and bicarbonate reduced to 1.0 gm/l. This medium is improved somewhat by the addition of an aliquot of MEM amino acids. Nearly as effective, however, is medium made up with diluted commercial NCTC-109 (see appendix) or Leibowitz's medium L-15 (2). Waymouth's MB-752/1 is next best, followed by BME, Medium 199 and Eagle's Minimal Essential Medium, in that order. The *Xenopus* lines do well in all of the media; A-1 did poorly in any but NCTC-109, and A-5 grows well in either NCTC-109 or MB-752/1. Other supplements, such as whole egg ultrafiltrate or yeast extract, have been of doubtful benefit. These lines were not tested with L-15, which, however, has proven very convenient and generally excellent.

Characteristics of Cell Lines

Table 1 gives the principle characteristics of 16 cell lines. Eleven are distinctly epithelioid in morphology, 2 regarded as mixed or intermediate, and 3 as fibroblastic. Of the 11 lines for which chromosome counts have been completed and for which the diploid number of the donor is known, 4 are either diploid and of epithelioid morphology (3 cases) or of mixed morphology (1 case). This is strikingly different from experience with mammalian cells, in which all diploid lines are fibroblastic and all epithelioid lines are heteroploid. Line A-1 persisted for at least 90 cell generations in diploid form, a much longer period than expected on the basis of donor longevity (see below). When lost due to bacterial contamination, it had been growing vigorously.

At least 2 lines (A-6 and A-8) have far exceeded 100 cell generations *in vitro* and are therefore regarded as established or permanent. A third, A-11, is approaching the 100 generation mark and grows quite vigorously; and a fourth, A-24, has recently become very vigorous, in the manner heretofore associated with permanency.

Lines A-3 and A-24 have both derived from tumors, in *Rana pipiens* and *Xenopus laevis*, respectively. The first of these, although chromosomally abnormal, was maintained only with difficulty and was not tested, by injection into the donor species, for continued malignancy. Cell line 24 was derived from a spontaneous lymphoma-

TABLE 1

SOURCES AND CHARACTERISTICS OF SIXTEEN AMPHIBIAN CELL LINES

| | Cell Line | | | | | Species | Donor | | |
Desig-nation	Primary culture (date)	Current sub-culture no. (10/3/68)	No. chromo-somes: No. cell generations	No. cell generations in vitro	Cell type		Tissue	Devel. stage and sex	2n number
A-1	5/8/63	90[1]	26:79	90	E[2]	R. sylvatica	Kidney	Large embryo	26
A-2	5/1/63	50[1]	25:40	50	E	R. pipiens	Whole	Hatching embryo	26
A-3	10/8/63	44[1]	28:27	44	E	R. pipiens	Lucké tumor	Adult ♀	26
A-4	4/14/65	16[1]	26:5	16	M[4]	Pseudacris t.f.	Whole	Hatching embryo	U[3]
A-5	7/19/65	25[1]	26:6	25	F[5]	R. clamitans	Whole	Hatching embryo	26
A-6	7/23/65	98[6]	45:116	495	E	Xenopus l.	Kidney	Adult ♂	36
A-7	11/19/65	26[7]	>60:26	26	E	Xenopus l.	Kidney	Adult ♂	36
A-8	11/19/65	108[6]	37–38:166	487	E	Xenopus l.	Liver	Adult ♀	36
A-11	3/31/66	51	23:50	70	M	Hyla c.	Whole	Hatching embryo	24?[8]
A-19	7/14/67	22	—	22	F	R. clamitans?	Whole	Hatching embryo	26
A-20	7/14/67	30	—	30	F	R. clamitans?	Whole	Hatching embryo	26
A-21	3/23/68	18	54–55:21	22	E	R. sylvatica	Whole	Hatching embryo	26
A-22	3/23/68	16	26:16	16	E	R. sylvatica	Whole	Hatching embryo	26
A-23F	3/23/68	13	52:13	15	E	R. sylvatica	Whole	Hatching embryo	26
A-23R	3/23/68	14	26:14	14	E	R. sylvatica	Whole	Hatching embryo	26
A-24	12/14/67	16	—	31	E	Xenopus l.	Tumor	Adult ♀	36

[1] Lost from bacterial contamination.   [2] Epithelioid.   [3] Unknown.   [4] Mixed.   [5] Fibroblastic.   [6] Less 14 wks frozen storage.
[7] Discontinued June, 1967.   [8] Diploid no. for 5 other species of Hyla.

like ovarian growth in an adult female of *Xenopus*. A large intracellular bacillus was associated with the donor cells and with early passage cells of the derived line, which was of poor vigor. After a few slow passages, vigor of the line suddenly increased and ultrastructural examination of the latter cells indicated that they were free of the bacterium.[1] Earlier experiments (unpublished) had shown that the tumor was readily transmitted *via* cells but not filtrates. Following "transformation" of the derived cell line, 10^6 cells from culture were injected intramuscularly into adult *Xenopus*. No tumor resulted.

Line A-6, a vigorous established strain derived from *Xenopus,* was also tested for malignancy by injecting 10^6 cells in individuals of *Rana pipiens*, but no tumor resulted from this heterologous combination.

Clonal Analysis

The most rapidly growing heteroploid lines (A-6 and A-8) compare with mammalian cells in hardiness and vigor, and are cloned readily by harvesting colonies derived from single cells after low density plating in unconditioned medium, using Konigsberg's method (19). Culture dishes of 100 mm diameter are seeded with 2×10^2 to 4×10^2 cells and the location of single attached cells is marked the next day, using an inverted phase contrast microscope. A week or so later, the colonies derived from the marked cells are harvested after placing Penicylinders over them (Fisher). Colony counts in such dishes indicate a plating efficiency of 44% (A-8) and 23% (A-6). Harvesting efficiency is about 80%. Line A-8 has also been cloned by Regan (24).

In the case of Line A-8, colony production following low density plating varied considerably in morphology, about 12 recognizable types being identified. Since 15% of the cells of the parent line had the 2n chromosome number, an attempt was made to derive one or more diploid lines by cloning. Twelve clones were derived for analysis, representing 11 distinct morphological types. In several of these, diploid cells were predominant. However, during further culturing and subcloning all of these strains reverted to the parental morphology and chromosomal type. For this reason, Line A-8 is considered to be thoroughly stabilized and aneuploid.

Attempts to clone diploid lines have not succeeded to date in this laboratory, but Freed *et al.* (14) have derived clones from diploid or pseudodiploid lines of *R. pipiens* cells.

Growth Rates

Lines which remained diploid proved the least vigorous in most instances. In practice, diploid lines cannot be serially subcultured at split ratios much higher than 1:2 or 1:3 since even when cultures survive such treatment they require an abnormally long time to achieve confluency. In a growth rate determination the doubling times of Line A-1 cells (diploid) and a heteroploid line (A-6) were compared (Fig. 1). The minimum doubling time in the case of the former was 30 hours; in the latter, it was 22 hours. However, in practice the disparity in terms of vigor is much

---

[1] Guy de Thé, Centre International de Recherche sur le Cancer, Lyon. Personal communication.

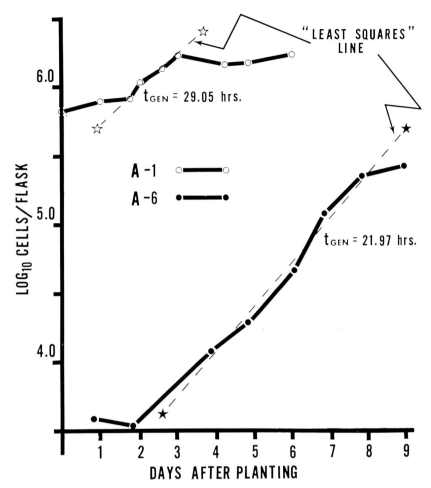

Fig. 1. Growth rates of a euploid cell line from *Rana sylvatica* (A-1) and a heteroploid line from *Xenopus laevis* (A-6).

greater than the doubling times alone suggest, since the diploid line shows pronounced contact inhibition of mitosis, the rate of cell division showing a sharp decline several days before confluency is achieved. The heteroploid line, on the other hand, remains continuously in the logarithmic phase of growth until the culture is confluent; in fact, cell growth continues beyond the point of confluency provided the medium is changed frequently, and the cells then accumulate in layers. Lines A-6 and A-8 are subcultured weekly, by seeding 10^4 cells in dishes, and produce 7.67 cell generations in that time, compared with 1–2 generations in the case of the diploid lines.

Cell Morphology

A curious feature of avian and mammalian cell lines is that those derived as mass cultures from dissociated organs almost always are fibroblastic in their morphology. Permanent epithelioid lines of mammalian cells are available, but are all heteroploid

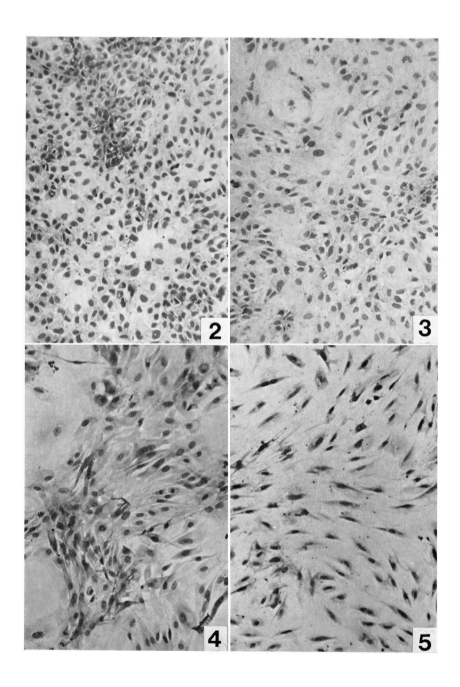

and there is now some reason to suspect that all originated from malignancies, possibly through contamination of early passage cultures by HeLa cells (15). In any case, it is generally recognized that the establishment of long-term fibroblastic lines from avian or mammalian sources is routine, while establishment of epithelioid lines occurs only very rarely, and the establishment of diploid epithelioid lines apparently never occurs. In anuran amphibians, however, lines may be fibroblastic and diploid (14), fibroblastic and aneuploid [(27); see Table 1], or epithelioid and either diploid or aneuploid (Table 1). Thus, all combinations have been derived. Experience seems to suggest that the selection of subcutaneous anuran tissue (27) or the removal of epithelium before culturing (14) leads to development of fibroblastic lines, while epithelioid cells tend to predominate when the tissues contain a normal proportion of epithelium.

As previously noted, 12 of the 16 lines reported in Table 1 are epithelioid, and 3 of the 12 are diploid. Four epithelioid lines are illustrated in Figs. 2, 3, 6, 7 and 8 (A-1, A-6, A-7, and A-8). Line A-5 (Fig. 4) is considered intermediate on the basis of average characteristics, and A-11 (Fig. 5) is regarded as fibroblastic. Although classification of cell lines by morphological type is subjective, there is seldom any difficulty in making a decision, provided cultures are classified when confluent: cells of obvious epithelioid characteristics are often quite elongated when seen in isolation. Cells are classified as epithelioid if polygonal, rounded or stellate when confluent. They are regarded as fibroblastic if they remain spindled after confluency occurs.

Fig. 9 is a photograph of mouse L-929 cells at the same magnification as Figs. 2–8. It is included to illustrate the fact that all of the amphibian lines consist of much larger cells. Most L-cell nuclei range between 5 and 10μ; those of Line A-1, for example, range between 12 and 18μ.

Chromosomal Analysis

Chromosome counts of the cultured lines and the diploid number reported for the donor are given in Table 1. In two cases where karyotype analysis has been completed (A-1 and A-5), the strains have proven to be euploid; in two others (Lines 4 and 11) the diploid number is not known with certainty. Line A-4 may be diploid, but Line 11 probably is not since the culture mode is 23. Other species of this genus (*Hyla*) have 24 chromosomes (21, 22). The line derived from kidneys of two large tadpoles of *Rana sylvatica* (Line A-1) was lost in the 90th subculture from bacterial

Fig. 2. Line A-1, derived from pooled kidneys of two large embryos of *Rana sylvatica*; third subculture. Most nuclei range between 12μ and 18μ in diameter. Cells are epithelioid in morphology. Giemsa stain for this and all subsequent photomicrographs. Figs. 2–8 are reproduced at the same magnification.

Fig. 3. The same cell line, in the 30th subculture. Little morphological transformation is evident, and the line continued to be euploid in chromosomal constitution.

Fig. 4. Line A-5, from a whole hatching embryo of *Rana clamitans*; 25th subculture. The line was euploid at the 6th subculture, and chromosome counts at the 17th subculture indicated persistent diploidy at that time. The line was considered to be fibroblastic in morphology.

Fig. 5. Line A-11, from a whole hatching embryo of *Hyla crucifer*; 11th subculture. Mixed in morphology. In the 16th subculture the major chromosomal mode (48%) was one less than the reported diploid number of 24, with a second mode (22%) at 22 and a diploid mode of 12%.

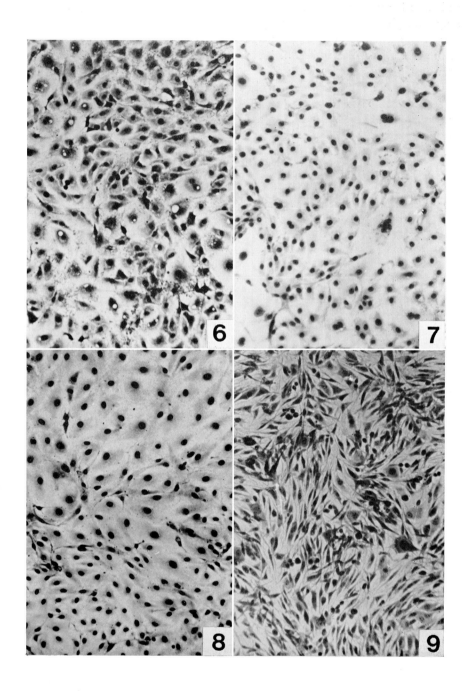

contamination, but was euploid when last examined (see below) at the 79th subculture. As indicated in Fig. 10, there was a tendency for abnormal nuclei to disappear with progressive subculture, with the exception of a seemingly constant fraction of subtetraploid cells at the level of about 10%. The proportion of diploid nuclei at subcultures 62 and 79 (representing somewhat more than that number of cell doublings) was 88%.

Chromosome counts of a line of embryonic *Rana pipiens* cells (A-2) are given in Fig. 11 for three subcultures. At the 34th subculture, this line showed no sharp major mode. During the next six cell generations, however, distinct modes developed at 25 (one less than the diploid number) and at approximately the tetraploid level. Together these modes accounted for 78% of the nuclei, that is 46% and 32%, respectively. Idiogram analysis of a few nuclei did not reveal a characteristic pattern of loss or rearrangement in nuclei with 25 chromosomes. It is probably significant that this line was unusually difficult to maintain: its "fastidiousness" may be related to the fact that it could not become chromosomally stabilized.

A similar analysis of chromosome number was carried out for the line derived from a Lucké renal adenocarcinoma (A-3, see Fig. 11). Although this line passed through periods of rapid growth, it was generally difficult to propagate. As Fig. 11 indicates, the chromosome number shifted from the diploid mode of 26, seen at the 4th subculture, to a roughly bimodal distribution at the 27th subculture, with most nuclei containing 26 or 28 chromosomes. Again, idiogram analysis of these chromosomes showed no characteristic stable pattern in cells with 27 or 28 chromosomes. This line was also lost in an episode of bacterial contamination, but had been apparently senescent for several preceding subcultures, and it seems doubtful that it could have been maintained. It is of interest to note that the Lucké tumor seems to remain euploid for as many as 14 serial transplantations *in vivo*. (9, 10).

As in the case of A-1, a cell line derived from a *Rana clamitans* embryo (A-5, Fig. 12) showed both moderate chromosomal constancy at the diploid mode and relatively vigorous growth in culture. The 6th and 17th subcultures (Fig. 11) seem to have remained constant at about 62%, while the number of subtetraploid cells may have been decreasing. This line was lost from contamination in the 25th subculture, while still vigorous. The line proved euploid (see below) at the 6th subculture, but later subcultures were not analyzed karyotypically.

Fig. 6. Line A-6, 23rd subculture, derived from kidneys of an adult male of *Xenopus*. The line had gradually transformed to a more compact epithelioid cell type, accompanied by an increase in vigor. The major mode at the 17th subculture was 45, compared with the diploid number of 36.

Fig. 7. Line A-7, 25th subculture, also derived from kidneys of an adult male of *Xenopus*. The line showed an epithelioid morphology of quite different type from that of Line 6, however, and chromosome counts in the 10th subculture showed a high degree of instability, with a tendency toward the subtetraploid number (28%). The line was not particularly vigorous.

Fig. 8. Line A-8, 21st subculture. Derived from the liver of an adult male of *Xenopus*. In early subcultures, the line was of a different epithelioid type, but small colonies of different character rapidly dominated. At the 15th subculture, the line showed major modes at 37 and 38 (2n = 36). This is the most rapidly growing amphibian cell line in our experience.

Fig. 9. A culture of mouse L-929 cells at the same magnification as the other figures for comparison of nuclear and cell size. Most of the mouse cell nuclei are about 5μ in diameter, while the nuclei of the amphibian lines are about $12-18\mu$.

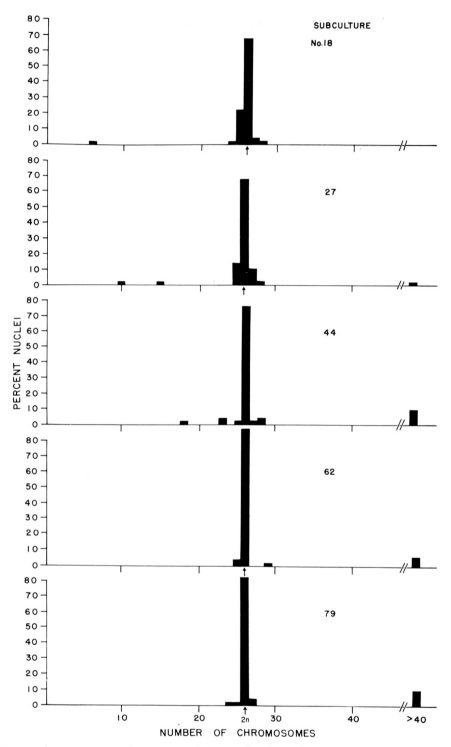

Fig. 10. Chromosome counts for Line A-1 (kidneys of larval *R. sylvatica*). Subculture numbers also represent minimum numbers of cell generations. The line has shown a strong tendency to remain diploid, with perhaps some tendency toward an increase in subtetraploid nuclei. Each count based upon 50 nuclei chosen at random.

64

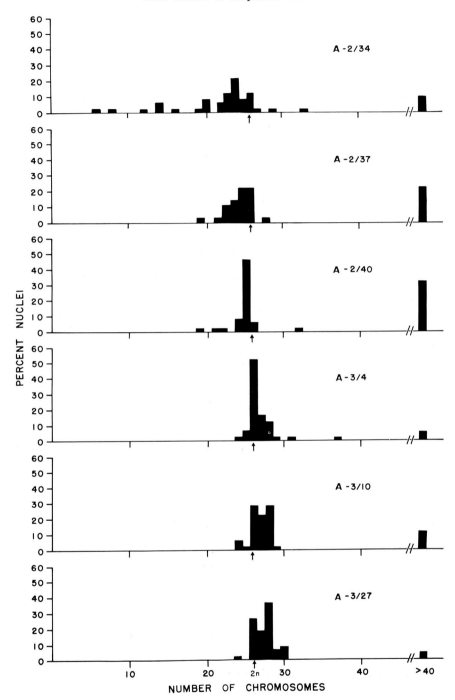

Fig. 11. Chromosome counts for Lines A-2 (derived from a hatching embryo of *R. pipiens*) and A-3 (Lucké renal adenocarcinoma). Line A-2 showed a progressive stabilization of the major mode at one less than the diploid number of 26, with development of a secondary subtetraploid mode. The carcinoma line showed a moderate tendency toward heteroploidy. Both lines were epithelioid, but slow growing and difficult to maintain.

Fig. 13 illustrates the distribution of chromosome counts in three lines derived from *Xenopus laevis* adults. Two of the lines, A-6 and A-8, are extremely vigorous: both can be subcultured at split ratios of at least 1:50 in unconditioned medium, and a cell generation time of 22 hours was determined (Fig. 1) for A-6. In spite of the vigor of the line, the principle distributional mode of 45 chromosomes accounts for only 36% of the nuclei, with the remainder being quite scattered. However, this determination was made at the 17th subculture, while the line is currently in its 98th subculture (after three months of frozen storage) and has passed through 495 cell generations. Further analysis is planned. It may be significant that this line was long characterized by rather extreme variation in cell morphology (Fig. 6) but in recent subcultures has become more homogeneous, and possibly more vigorous. Although the line is more than a year old, it was quite slow growing for the first nine months, when the growth rate rapidly increased.

As indicated in Fig. 13, Line A-8 (Fig. 8) appears to be shifting away from the diploid mode with a tendency toward an increased chromosome number. Further analysis is planned.

A-7 (Fig. 13) is characterized by a comparative lack of vigor and extreme variation in the number of chromosomes per cell: at the 10th subculture 28% of the nuclei were in the tetraploid-subtetraploid range. Most of the nuclei were sub-diploid, but no significant modes could be identified in this range. Although the chromosome distribution fits well with the line's comparative lack of vigor, its cell morphology, as seen in Fig. 7, is fairly homogeneous.

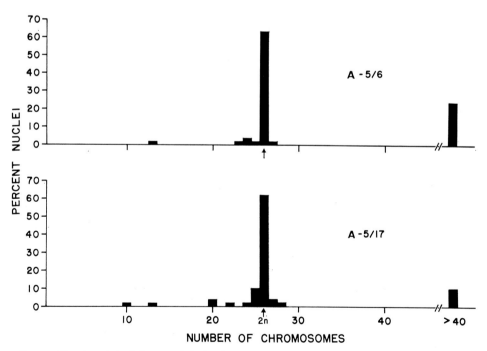

Fig. 12. Line A-5, derived from a whole hatching embryo of *R. clamitans*. The line was fibroblastic in morphology. It demonstrated a pronounced tendency toward persistent diploidy, but it was quite vigorous in culture.

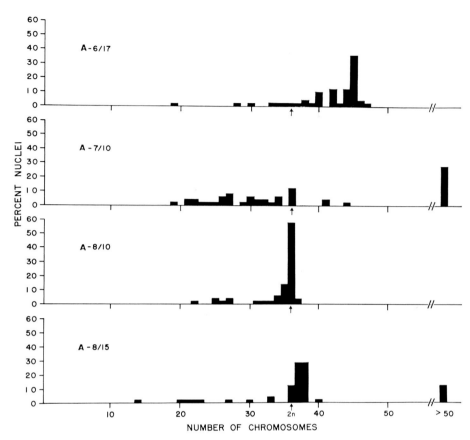

Fig. 13. Chromosome counts of Lines A-6 (*Xenopus* kidney), A-7 (*Xenopus* kidney), and A-8 (*Xenopus* liver). Although from a similar source, Lines 6 and 7 were of different epithelioid types (Figs. 6 and 7). Line 7, which was slow growing, showed a high degree of chromosomal instability. However, the most vigorous line yet encountered, Line 8, also showed some instability, as well as a double mode.

Karyotypes of Diploid Cell Lines

Line A-1 remained diploid for 90 cell generations in culture, after which it was accidentally lost. Since Hayflick (17) has proposed that the euploid longevity of cultured cells is limited by life expectancy of the donor, and since human fibroblasts survive for about 50–70 cell generations *in vitro,* the lines become of especial interest because of the relatively brief longevity of the frog. For this reason, a detailed karyotype analysis of Line A-1 was completed, and compared with a similar analysis of chromosomes from embryonic lines (18) and from adult marrow of the donor species. For this study, karyograms of 25 nuclei of the 79th subculture, and of 25 nuclei from marrow of an adult female were prepared and measured. Chromosome images were cut from photographs and arranged as pairs in order of descending length.

Figs. 14 and 15 illustrate typical preparations made from Line A-1 nuclei and from marrow nuclei, respectively. Fig. 16 represents a preparation of human chromosomes from peripheral blood. The comparison permits an appreciation of the differ-

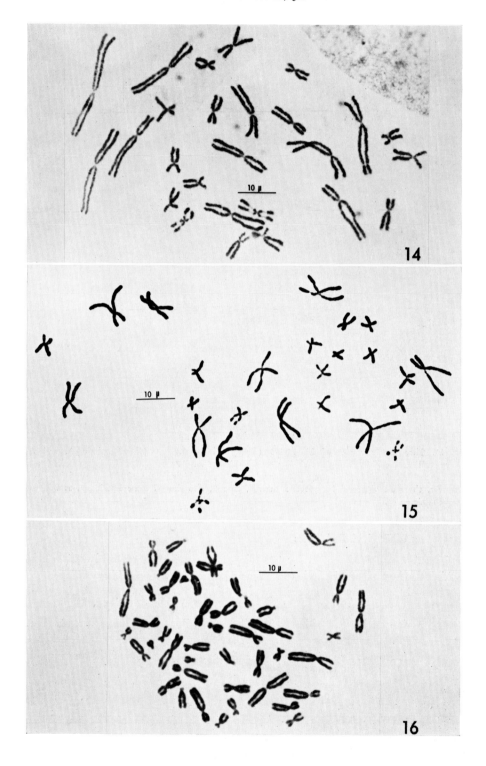

TABLE 2

COMPARATIVE ANALYSIS OF CHROMOSOMES FROM RANA SYLVATICA MARROW AND
TISSUE CULTURE CELL LINE A-1

Chromosome pair number	Mean arm ratio and range *		Mean rel. length (%) and range	
	Bone marrow	Tissue culture	Bone marrow	Tissue culture
1	1.0 (1.2) 1.4	1.0 (1.2) 1.3	14.1 (15.6) 18.0	14.3 (15.7) 16.4
2	1.6 (1.9) 2.1	1.6 (1.9) 3.0	11.2 (12.5) 13.8	11.9 (12.9) 14.0
3	1.2 (1.4) 1.6	1.2 (1.4) 1.8	11.3 (12.2) 13.3	10.7 (11.6) 13.3
4	1.6 (2.0) 2.2	1.7 (2.0) 2.4	10.4 (11.4) 12.4	10.5 (11.4) 12.8
5	1.0 (1.4) 1.6	1.2 (1.4) 1.6	9.0 (10.0) 10.6	9.1 (10.0) 10.7
6	1.0 (1.2) 1.8	1.2 (1.4) 1.8	5.2 (6.3) 6.7	5.6 (6.6) 7.3
7	1.0 (1.1) 1.4	1.0 (1.2) 1.5	4.3 (5.3) 6.2	4.2 (5.7) 6.4
8	1.1 (1.4) 1.7	1.1 (1.4) 1.7	4.8 (5.2) 6.0	4.8 (5.4) 5.9
9	1.1 (1.4) 1.8	1.0 (1.6) 1.8	4.1 (5.1) 6.1	4.5 (5.0) 5.6
10	1.8 (2.1) 2.7	1.6 (2.0) 3.2	4.4 (4.9) 5.5	4.2 (4.6) 5.0
11	1.0 (1.5) 1.9	1.1 (1.5) 1.8	3.4 (4.2) 5.0	3.5 (4.3) 4.7
12	1.6 (1.8) 2.7	1.6 (1.9) 2.3	3.4 (3.9) 4.5	3.4 (3.9) 4.3
13	1.1 (1.5) 1.9	1.3 (1.6) 1.9	2.9 (3.6) 4.4	3.1 (3.6) 4.2

* Arm ratios calculated as length of long arm ÷ length of short arm.

ences in length between anuran and mammalian chromosomes. Figs. 17 and 18 depict karyograms made from duplicates of Figs. 14 and 15, respectively.

All measurements were made from the karyograms, using a Keuffel and Esser map measuring device. Means and ranges of the measurements are given in Table 2. It is evident that the relative measurements are essentially identical within the limits of expected error. In the comparison of mean relative lengths between culture and marrow chromosomes the greatest difference—5.3% vs. 5.7% of the total length of chromosomal material—is seen in pair 7. However, this pair is characterized by quite prominent secondary constrictions in each arm (Figs. 17 and 18), and their length varied greatly in the pairs from both sources. Measurements of the constricted segments revealed that they were comparatively more extended in culture cells, amounting to 0.91% of the total length of all chromosomes, vs. 0.75% in the marrow chro-

Fig. 14. Metaphase chromosomes of Line A-1 (*R. sylvatica*), 79th subculture. Photographic composite reconstructed from three negatives. Pairs are matched and arranged in order of descending length in Fig. 17.

Fig. 15. Metaphase chromosomes from bone marrow of an adult female *R. sylvatica*. Composite reconstructed from two negatives. Pairs are matched and arranged in order of descending length in Fig. 18.

Fig. 16. Metaphase chromosomes from human peripheral blood, included to permit a comparison of size with amphibian chromosomes.

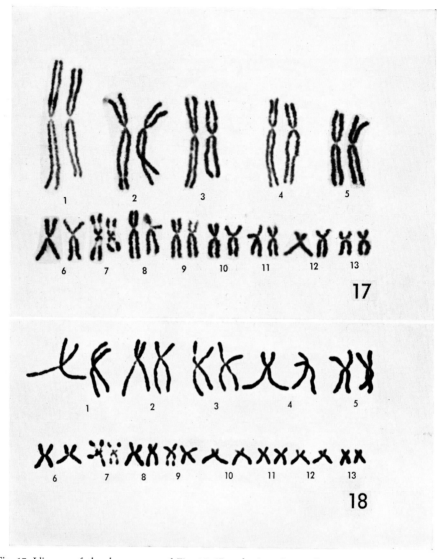

Fig. 17. Idiogram of the chromosomes of Fig. 14 (*R. sylvatica*: tissue culture strain A-1).

Fig. 18. Idiogram of the chromosomes of Fig. 15 (*R. sylvatica*: adult marrow). The marrow chromosome preparations were slightly more contracted (see text). In addition to the large secondary constrictions of pair 7, a small but relatively constant constriction is seen in the long arms of pair 9, but seldom seen in the corresponding pair of tissue culture chromosomes. The constriction or lesion in the short arms of one member of pair 3 may be regular but is so small that it is not often clearly present.

mosomes. Since the constricted segments are thought to be the nucleolar organizers it is perhaps not surprising that this segment might be relatively extended in rapidly growing culture cells.

All other pairs differ by less than 5% in mean relative length, except for the 6.1% difference in pair 10. However, the ranges within each group vary by about

20%, so any real differences between groups would require very large measurement series for detection.

Arm ratio comparisons were very close, although variations within groups were surprisingly high, amounting to as much as 40%.

Differences in total chromosome length were evident, however. Marrow chromosome preparations from the adult *R. sylvatica* averaged 181.1 μ for diploid sets, while the cultured chromosomes from larval kidney cells were 80% longer, averaging 325.1 μ. These differences do not appear to be due entirely to progressive shrinkage in metaphase arrest, since the frog used for marrow chromosome preparation was exposed to colchicine for 4.25 hours, while the cultures were exposed for 4 hours to colcemid. Di Berardino has suggested (8) that chromosomes of early developmental stages may be longer than those from later ones, a finding of potential interest in this case because of the fact that the culture chromosomes were derived from larval kidney.

In order to examine further the discrepancy between the constriction chromosome (No. 7) in culture vs. marrow cells, the pairs from 27 randomly chosen nuclei of Line A-1 were cut from photographs and grouped together (Fig. 19). In homologues of about equal length (7 cases) a single constriction is seen in each arm, as in the case of embryonic liver chromosomes (18) and marrow chromosomes. In the 19 pairs in which homologues were markedly unequal in length, however, an additional constriction was observed in the longer member but was seldom encountered in marrow chromosomes. This third constriction consists essentially of a long constricted segment divided into two by an intervening heterochromatin knob. Inspection of such chromosomes suggests that the third constriction is formed at the expense of a portion of the heterochromatin segment located next to the centromere in the long arm, since that segment appears shorter when the third segment is present. Thus, the distal constriction of the long arm is probably the one regularly seen, the proximal one being newly formed. If so, the figure suggests that constricted segments represent quite short chromosome lengths when compacted by coiling into heterochromatin. In any case, the third constriction cannot be regarded as a duplication, since they are occasionally seen in marrow cells as well. Hence the detailed analysis of Line A-1 chromosomes provides no evidence of pseudodiploidy, and the line is therefore regarded as euploid at the 79th cell generation in culture.

Recently, two more lines from embryonic *R. sylvatica* have been established which proved to be predominantly diploid in early subculture; these are Lines A-22 and A-23 (Table 1). These are being followed to determine whether they also are euploid and will persist as such.

Line Derived from *R. Clamitans*

Table 3 gives the results of length measurements made from photographic prints of 18 nuclei of Line A-5, 6th subculture. Chromosomes of one other nucleus photographed for analysis were omitted because of an apparent deletion. The table indicates a karyotype of satisfactory constancy and supports the view that each pair member of the karyotype can be distinguished on the basis of arm ratio, relative length, and other characteristics. The similarity between culture and marrow chromosomes is perhaps the more remarkable because the former tended to be more highly

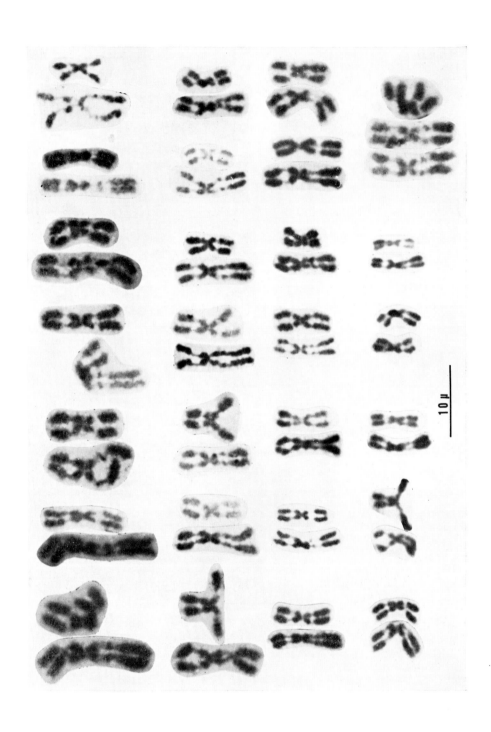

10 μ

TABLE 3

A Comparative Analysis of Chromosomes from Rana clamitans Bone Marrow and Tissue Culture Cell Line

Chromo-some pair number	Mean arm ratio and range						Mean rel. length (%) and range					
	Bone marrow			Tissue culture			Bone marrow			Tissue culture		
1	1.1	(1.2)	1.4	1.0	(1.1)	1.4	13.2	(15.6)	17.1	14.3	(15.3)	16.9
2	1.6	(1.9)	2.4	1.6	(1.8)	2.0	10.2	(12.3)	13.6	10.8	(12.4)	13.6
3	1.0	(1.3)	1.4	1.1	(1.3)	1.7	9.3	(11.4)	13.2	10.3	(11.3)	12.0
4	1.8	(2.1)	2.6	1.6	(2.1)	2.4	9.7	(10.8)	11.9	10.1	(11.0)	11.8
5	1.3	(1.4)	1.7	1.1	(1.4)	1.6	9.0	(9.8)	10.9	8.9	(9.9)	10.9
6	1.0	(1.1)	1.5	1.0	(1.2)	1.4	5.9	(6.5)	7.3	5.7	(6.4)	7.5
7	1.3	(1.6)	2.0	1.4	(1.7)	2.6	5.0	(5.6)	5.9	4.9	(5.5)	5.9
8	1.6	(2.2)	3.5	1.9	(2.4)	3.3	4.8	(5.3)	5.9	4.8	(5.5)	6.2
9	1.1	(1.5)	2.3	1.0	(1.4)	1.9	4.0	(5.0)	5.9	4.1	(4.9)	5.5
10	1.5	(2.0)	2.7	1.6	(2.0)	2.8	4.2	(4.8)	5.2	3.9	(4.9)	5.3
11	1.0	(1.4)	1.7	1.0	(1.2)	1.5	3.6	(4.7)	5.5	4.1	(4.6)	5.0
12	1.1	(1.6)	2.2	1.3	(1.9)	2.6	3.6	(4.3)	4.8	3.9	(4.3)	4.9
13	1.0	(1.2)	1.5	1.0	(1.2)	1.6	3.0	(3.9)	4.4	3.7	(4.2)	4.6

elongated, while the available preparations of marrow chromosomes were quite con-tracted. Hence, the diploid chromosome sets of the cultured cells averaged 242.7 μ in length, while those from marrow were only 63% as long (152.4 μ). In the former case, cultures were treated for 3 hours with colcemid; in the latter, adult frogs were exposed to colchicine for 5½ hours, so that the more prolonged period of metaphase arrest may account for the differential contraction observed.

In terms of group differences in mean relative length, the smallest pair (#13) differed by 7.7% in culture vs. marrow chromosomes; the next greatest group differ-ence, seen in pair 8, was 3.8%. As in the case of R. sylvatica culture and marrow chromosomes, however, range extremes within groups were much greater, and so group differences in mean relative length are best explained on the basis of intrinsic variability and random variation as a result of the preparative method. Again, ranges were, if anything, less extreme in the culture chromosomes in spite of the fact that they were less contracted.

Mean arm ratios also seem satisfactorily close between culture and marrow chro-

Fig. 19. The constricted chromosomes (pair 7) from 27 randomly encountered nuclei of Line A-1, 79th subculture (R. sylvatica). In 19 cases, one member shows triple constrictions, with the two constrictions of the long arm separated by a small heterochromatin knob. The triply constricted member is always longer than its homologue, but often even longer than can be accounted for by the newly elongated segment. Of the 8 pairs in which a third constriction is not seen, one member is usually distinctly longer than the other. The remaining case (at the lower right of the figure) is a trisomic in which two members show triple constrictions.

mosomes. Pair 10 differs by 0.3 unit; two pairs differ by 0.2 unit; five differ by 0.1 unit; and no difference was seen in the mean arm ratios for five pairs. Equally extreme range variations were observed in both groups, and again were much larger than group differences. Hence the measurements do not reveal differences between culture and marrow chromosomes. If any real differences do exist, they could be shown only by a much larger series of measurements.

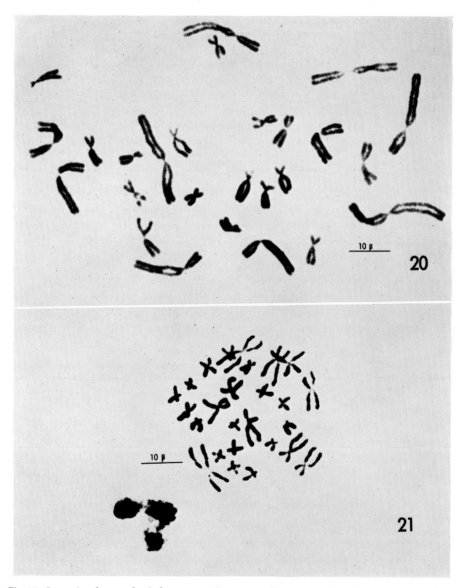

Fig. 20. Composite photograph of chromosomes from a metaphase preparation of strain A-5 (*R. clamitans*). Shown arranged in order of descending length in Fig. 22.

Fig. 21. Photograph of metaphase chromosomes from marrow of an adult *R. clamitans*. Idiogram in Fig. 23.

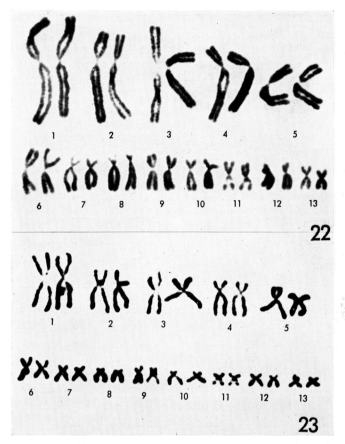

Fig. 22. Idiogram of the chromosomes of Fig. 20. (*R. clamitans:* tissue culture strain A-5.) Note satellites in pair 8 and secondary constrictions in the long arm of pair 11.

Fig. 23. Idiogram of the chromosomes of Fig. 21. (*R. clamitans:* adult marrow.) The marrow chromosome preparations were somewhat more contracted than were the culture chromosomes.

The Karyotype of *Rana Clamitans*

Since the karyotype of *Rana clamitans* has not previously been reported, it will be described in more detail. Figs. 20 and 21 represent metaphase spreads of tissue culture (6th subculture) and bone marrow origin. For analysis, chromosomes were arranged in order of descending length (Figs. 22 and 23). They thus fall naturally into two groups, as in the case of other *Rana* (8, 16, 18), on the basis of a pronounced size differential between the 5th and 6th pairs. The first group contains 3 submetacentric and two subtelocentric pairs, in alternate order. In most instances, all five pairs are distinguishable with no difficulty, although in individual nuclei, pair #4 may be longer than pair #3 and perhaps confused with pair #2. However, it is somewhat more telocentric than is pair #3 (Table 3). No secondary constrictions or other distinguishing features are seen in the chromosomes of the first group.

The second group consists of the remaining eight pairs, with adjacent members being of rather similar size; however, in most spreads, all members can be distinguished with some confidence. Pairs six, eleven, and thirteen are metacentric, but the first and last are the largest and smallest of the group, respectively, and #11 has a prominent secondary constriction in its long arm. Pair #7 is a relatively long telocentric, distinguished from #8 by the fact that the latter is more telocentric and is satellited. Pairs #9 and #12 are submetacentric but sufficiently different in length so that they are probably seldom confused. Pair #10 is more telocentric than pair #7 and usually distinguishable from pair #8 because it lacks satellites.

Discussion

Comparative Behavior of Amphibian and Mammalian Cells in Culture

Almost all cell culture is of mammalian or avian provenance. Because of difficulties in the study of avian chromosomes, karyotype analysis of cultured cells has been confined largely to those derived from mammals, notably the hamster, mouse and human. Unfortunately, morphological studies of dissociated cells have favored the use of chicken tissues because of presently inexplicable difficulties in the clonal analysis of mammalian cell types. During the last few years it has been shown that at least five types of avian embryo cells—skeletal muscle and fibroblasts (19), cardiac muscle (4), retinal pigment (5), and cartilage (7) can be grown as clonally purified culture strains with careful attention to medium composition and technique. Such cells can be positively identified either by means of distinctive differentiated morphology, a characteristic cell product, or both. But to date, only deep tissue cells of homoiotherms (with the possible exception of retinal pigment cells) have yielded to manipulation to the extent of being made reproducibly available for study in the normal chromosomal state. Amphibian cells which are epithelioid in morphology may represent epithelia themselves and hence organ parenchymal cells. The inference is strong that this is indeed the case, since, as previously noted, experience indicates that amphibian cultures usually come to be dominated by cells of epithelioid morphology except when they are begun from tissues lacking epithelium. Since amphibian chromosomes are unusually favorable for study, improvements in methodology could result in a source of normal organ parenchymal cells for *in vitro* analysis. Current general experience (11) indicates that although primary epithelioid cultures may be derived from mammalian tissues such as amnion or kidney, these either give rise to predominantly fibroblastic cell lines after a few subcultures or else (rarely) yield chromosomally abnormal lines of epithelioid cells. Human fibroblastic lines from whatever tissue seldom transform chromosomally but become senescent and die within 50–70 cell generations; fibroblastic lines of murine origin usually do transform and give rise to permanent cell lines (17).

The limited experience with amphibian cell lines suggests that there are some species-related differences within the class, as well as features common to the class. Tissues of *Rana* species often yield cultures which become predominantly epithelioid upon serial subculture; these may resemble mammalian cultures in being chromosomally abnormal (Line A-2) or may differ by remaining apparently euploid, as in the case of Lines A-1, A-5, A-22, and A-23R. Although fibroblastic lines do not often arise from mixed primary cultures of amphibian cells, two of the known cases (27), from *R. catesbeiana,* and Line A-5, from *R. clamitans,* were aneuploid, as in the first case, or else not shown to be diploid beyond the 6th subculture in the second case, since that line was lost before chromosome studies of older cultures could be made. Two other fibroblastic lines (A-19 and A-20) grow very slowly but are aneuploid. Freed *et al.* (14) have produced fibroblastic lines which appear to be diploid or near-diploid, but it is not clear how many cell generations these lines have passed through in culture. Whether fibroblastic lines of amphibian cells can remain diploid for extended periods in culture is therefore not known.

Experience with the four lines of cells derived from *X. laevis* suggests differences from both mammalian and *Rana* cells; all were judged to be epithelioid, but were chromosomally abnormal. Similar tissues from mammalian sources would be expected to give rise to fibroblastic cultures after repeated subcultivation, as already mentioned. Although chromosomally normal lines of *Xenopus* cells have not yet been observed, experience is too limited for conclusions regarding the probability of developing diploid cultures from this source.

Longevity of the Donor Species

The *in vitro* lifetime of amphibian diploid cells is of particular interest because of Hayflick's finding that the culture lifetime of diploid fibroblasts from human fetal lung is limited to 100 cell generations or less (17). As a result of this finding and those of others working with cells of human and murine origin, Hayflick has proposed that cells which do not become aneuploid are limited in the number of possible *in vitro* cell generations by intrinsic factors related to the longevity of the donor. Since the frog cell Line A-1 survived in diploid form for more than 90 generations, and in euploid form for at least 79 generations before being accidentally lost, without apparent decline in vigor, the question of donor longevity is of interest.

Although reliable records of amphibian longevities are few, enough are available to allow some conclusions dealing with certain genera. The data of Table 4 are based upon zoo records or upon first-hand accounts which were regarded as reliable by Flower (12). For the 13 represented species of *Rana*, the range of longevities is 6 to 16 years, with a mean of 8.9 years. Six years is the maximum recorded for *R. pipiens*, the donor species for Line A-2, which was lost accidentally after 3.5 years *in vitro* (47 subcultures). This line, however, developed a modal number one less than the diploid number. Although no record has been reported for *R. sylvatica*, it is more closely related to the short-lived than to the longer-lived species. The closest American relatives for which data are reported (*"halecina,"* probably *palustris*, and *R. pipiens*) have records of 7 and 6 years. At any rate, *R. sylvatica* is the donor species for Line A-1, which survived for 90 subcultures and at least that many cell generations *in vitro*, over a span of 3.4 years.

Xenopus laevis and species of *Hyla* appear to have somewhat longer lifetimes, in the vicinity of 15 years. Although a record of 31 years is said to have been observed in a zoo specimen of *X. fraseri*.[1] Three cell lines were derived from *X. laevis*; but since all became heteroploid rather early, they provide no information bearing upon Hayflick's proposal. Similarly, the *Hyla* strain appears to be established as a hypodiploid line. Thus, in a single case, a diploid amphibian cell line appears to have survived in

---

[1] Michael Balls, personal communication.

TABLE 4

Maximum Recorded Longevities of Some
Anuran Amphibians

Scientific name	Maximum Recorded longevity (years)
Rana adspersa	11 [1]
R. bibroni	7 [1]
R. catesbeiana	16 [2]
R. clamitans	10 [2]
R. esculenta	10+ [1]
R. guentheri	6 [1]
R. halecina	7 [2]
(*R. palustris?*)	
R. livida	6 [1]
R. oxyrhynchus	9 [1]
R. pipiens	6 [2]
R. ribibunda	9 [1]
R. temporaria	Approx. 12 [1]
R. tigerina	7 [2]
Hyla arborea	14 [2]
H. cerulea	16 [2]
Xenopus laevis	15 [2]

[1] International Zoo Yearbook, 6:492–493, 1966.

[2] Flower, S. S.: Further notes on the duration of life in animals. II Amphibians. Proc. Zool. Soc. Lon., pp. 369–394, 1936.

culture for more cell generations than would have been predicted on the basis of donor longevity.

Problems in Interpretation

Several factors make for caution in drawing conclusions concerning a relationship between longevity potential *in vitro* and *in vivo*. The first is that any rearrangement, deletion, or duplication of chromatin means that the cells are no longer euploid and must be regarded as potentially permanent aneuploid cell lines. It follows that small changes in the amount or distribution of chromatin may have occurred without having been large enough to be detectable by the method of analysis that was used for Line A-1. An additional factor is that the karyotype of the donor has not been studied in great detail in large numbers of individuals and thus is not so well known as some other karyotypes, notably the human. Second, doubt remains whether the longevity potential (as distinguished from observed record lifetimes of captured animals) has been established in the case of *Rana* species. Aside from the paucity of reliable reports, Comfort (6) has pointed out that the conditions of both field and captivity may not be favorable for long life, or that the accumulating risk of death from factors other than aging becomes a large element when small numbers of animals are kept for long periods. This may be especially true in the case of *Rana* species which require live food and are generally considered troublesome to keep. Some animals thought to have short lifetimes have, in fact, been shown to live for surprisingly long periods; the chaffinch, as an example, has a longevity potential of at least 29 years (6). Among amphibia, although the greatest age reliably recorded for any anuran is 16 years, ages in excess of 50 years have been recorded for urodeles (12), many of which eat prepared food and are generally more likely to be maintained for long periods in aquaria or as pets. The conclusion that species of *Rana* have relatively short lifetimes is therefore not established beyond doubt.

Amphibian Cells and Aging

The long-term survival of a diploid line of amphibian cells raises a question whether cells of epithelioid morphology are subject to the same limitation that seems to apply to fibroblastic cells. It is worth noting that it has not been possible to test epithelioid mammalian cells for senescence in culture because when they have proved vigorous, they have always proved to be aneuploid after a few subcultivations. Hence, it may be desirable to restrict the theory of cellular senescence to cell types of fibroblastic morphology. If so, the behavior of amphibian Line A-1 obviously suggests that epithelioid, and possibly therefore, organ parenchymal, cells do not undergo senescence. Indeed, the studies of Leblond and his co-workers (20) present difficulties in understanding how epithelial cells can be limited to 100 divisions in man, since all cells of the basal stratum of the (rat) esophagus incorporate large amounts of tritiated thymidine within 6 days of exposure and thus presumably undergo at least 60 divisions a year. This interpretation is complicated by a number of factors, including the important consideration that the size of the stem cell population is not known beyond all doubt; for example, the basal cell population could be supplemented by migration of cells from deeper layers. In any case, the data from isotope studies suggest that populations of stem cells in intestinal and cutaneous epithelia are in continuous rapid division throughout life and may have a much higher limit on the number of cell divisions than appears to be the case for fibroblastic cells.

Summary

Experience to date indicates that cultured amphibian cells are capable of aneuploid rearrangement and development into permanent, vigorous cell lines, but that diploid cultures have generally slower growth rates and are more difficult to maintain. In at least these respects, amphibian and mammalian cells behave similarly. Although experience with amphibian cell culture is quite limited, both class and species differences apparently occur. Whereas mammalian tissues have not been observed to give long-term diploid cultures which are epithelioid in morphology, an epithelioid line from embryonic kidney of *Rana sylvatica* produced at least 79 cell doublings in culture without detectable deviation from the normal karyotype. Other *Rana* cell lines, of both epithelioid and fibroblastic morphology, have transformed chromosomally. Three cell lines derived from *Xenopus laevis* were predominantly epithelioid and also aneuploid. Although senescence of diploid amphibian cells has not been observed as yet, experience is too limited to allow the conclusion that it does not occur.

Appendix

Nutrient Medium (1 liter). NCTC-109: 550 ml; fetal bovine serum (heated to 65°C for one hour): 100 ml; SS (Supplementary saline) A: 120 ml; SS-B: 120 ml; SS-C: 60 ml; amino acid solution (Eagle's 50X): 24 ml; glutamine to 2 mM total. Titrate to pH 6.8 with 1.0 N NaOH and sterilize by membrane filtration. Other commercially available complex media may be substituted for NCTC-109 (see text).

Supplementary saline A (SS-A). For each 120 ml distilled water, dissolve: $CaSO_4 \cdot 2H_2O$: 0.035 gm; $MgSO_4$: 0.053 gm.

SS-B. For each 120 ml distilled water, dissolve: Na_2HPO_4: 0.07 gm; KH_2PO_4: 0.02 gm; glucose: 0.14 gm.

SS-C. For each 60 ml distilled water, dissolve: $NaHCO_3$: 0.10 gm.

Wash Medium (1 liter). In approximately 800 ml, dissolve NaCl: 3.80 gm; KCl: 0.37 gm; Na_2HPO_4: 1.065 gm; glucose: 0.40 gm. Add phenol red (0.5% solution): 10 ml, and bring to 1 liter by addition of distilled water. Filter sterilize.

Versene Solution (1 liter). Dissolve in approximately 900 ml distilled water; Na-EDTA: 0.020 gm; NaCl: 4,500 gm; KCl: 0.300 gm; Na_2HPO_4: 1.065 gm; Glucose: 0.400 gm. Add phenol red (0.5% solution): 5.0 ml, and bring to 1 liter by addition of distilled water. Filter sterilize.

Trypsin Solution (Difco #0153-61). Contents of an ampule are dissolved in 10 ml. sterile distilled water and stored frozen. Immediately before use, the thawed solution is added to wash medium to 4% and the remainder re-frozen. In the case of cell lines which are difficult to remove from the surface (i.e., Line 6), the trypsin solution is used at 2–4% in versene solution. Thawed ampules may be refrozen several times without undue loss of activity.

Pronase Solution (B Grade, Calbiochem. #53702). Contents of a 1.0 gm bottle are dissolved in 200 ml distilled water and sterilized by membrane filtration (Millipore HA), collecting the filtrate in an iced flask. Aliquots are distributed in ampules and stored frozen. The thawed solution is used at 2–4% (100 μgm/ml) in wash medium or versene. Thawed ampules may be re-frozen several times without undue loss of activity.

References

1. Auclair, W.: Cultivation of monolayer cultures of frog renal cells. Nature *192*:467–468, 1961.
2. Balls, M., and L. N. Ruben: Cultivation *in vitro* of normal and neoplastic cells of *Xenopus laevis*. Exptl. Cell Res. *43*:694–695, 1966.
3. Bouroncle, B.: Preservation of living cells at 79°C with dimethyl sulfoxide. Proc. Soc. Exptl. Biol. & Med. *119*:958–961, 1965.

4. CAHN, R.: Maintenance of beating and dissociation of biochemical and functional differentiation in clones of chick embryo heart cells. J. Cell Biol. 23:17A, 1964.

5. CAHN, R. and M. CAHN: Heritability of cellular differentiation: clonal growth and expression of differentiation in retinal pigment cells *in vitro*. Proc. Nat'l. Acad. Sci. U.S. 55:106–114, 1966.

6. COMFORT, A.: The life span of animals. Sci. Amer. 205:108–119, 1961.

7. COON, H.: Clonal stability and phenotypic expression of chick cartilage cells *in vitro*. Proc. Nat'l. Acad. Sci. U.S. 55:66–73, 1966.

8. DiBERARDINO, M.: The karyotype of *Rana pipiens* and investigation of its stability during embryonic differentiation. Devel. Biol. 5:101–126, 1962.

9. DiBERARDINO, M. and T. KING: Karyotype of a serially transplanted frog renal adenocarcinoma. Am. Zool. 2:95, 1962.

10. DiBERARDINO, M., T. KING and R. McKINNELL: Chromosome studies of a frog renal adenocarcinoma line carried by intraocular transplantation. J. Nat'l. Cancer Inst. 31:769–790, 1963.

11. EAGLE, H.: Metabolic controls in cultured mammalian cells. Science 148:42–51, 1965.

12. FLOWER, S.: Further notes on the duration of life in animals. II Amphibians. Proc. Zool. Soc. Lon. 1936:369–394, 1936.

13. FREED, J. J. and S. ROSENFELD: Frog renal adenocarcinoma: cytological studies *in situ* and *in vitro*. Ann. N.Y. Acad. Sci. 126:99–114, 1965.

14. FREED, J. J., L. MEZGER-FREED and S. A. SCHATZ: Characteristics of cell lines from haploid and diploid *Rana pipiens* embryos. *In* Biology of Amphibian Tumors (M. Mizell, ed.), Springer-Verlag New York Inc., 1969, pp. 101–111.

15. GARTLER, S. M.: Genetic markers as tracers in cell culture. *In* Second Decennial Review Conference on Cell, Tissue and Organ Culture (B. B. Westfall, ed.), NCI Monograph #26, pp. 167–181, 1967.

16. GUILLEMIN, C.: Caryotypes de *Rana temporaria* (L) et de *Rana dalmatina* (Bonaparte). Chromosoma 21:189–197, 1967.

17. HAYFLICK, L.: The limited *in vitro* lifetime of human diploid cell strains. Exptl. Cell Res. 37:614–636, 1965.

18. HENNEN, S.: The karyotype of *Rana sylvatica*. J. Heredity 55:124–128, 1964.

19. KONIGSBERG, I.: Clonal analysis of myogenesis. Science 140:1273–1284, 1963.

20. LEBLOND, C.: Classification of cell populations on the basis of their proliferative behavior. *In* Internat. Symp. on the Control of Cell Division and the Induction of Cancer. Nat'l. Cancer Inst. Monograph 14:119–150, 1964.

21. MAKINO, S.: An atlas of the chromosome numbers in animals. The Iowa State College Press, Ames, Iowa, 1951.

22. MATSUDA, K.: Culture techniques with some amphibian tissues and a chromosome study of the tree frog, *Hyla arborea japonica*. Zool. Mag. 72:105–109, 1963.

23. MOORHEAD, P. and P. NOWELL: Chromosome cytology. *In* Methods in Medical Research, Vol. 10 (H. N. Eisen, ed.), Year Book Medical Publishers, Inc., Chicago, pp. 310–322, 1964.

24. REGAN, J. D., J. S. COOK, and W. H. LEE: Photoreactivation of amphibian cells in culture. J. Cell Physiol. 71:173–176, 1968.

25. SCHMID, W.: Autoradiography of human chromosomes. *In* Human Chromosome Methodology (J. J. Unis, ed.), Academic Press Inc., New York, pp. 91–110, 1965.

26. SETO, T.: Cultivation of tissues from cold-blooded amphibians with special reference to the culture methods in amphibia. Japanese J. Genet. 39:268–275, 1964.

27. WOLFE, K. and M. QUIMBY: Amphibian cell culture. Permanent cell line from the bullfrog (*Rana catesbeiana*). Science 144:1578–1580, 1964.

Dependence of Tumor Formation in Frogs on Abnormal Nucleolar Function

WILLIAM R. DURYEE [1]

Department of Pathology
The George Washington University School of Medicine
Washington, D.C.

During the past three years, in contrast with earlier tumor-filtrate and infective DNA initiations of growth (2), experiments with heavy metals such as lead, chromium, and cobalt were begun. Heavy metals were found capable of stimulating nucleolar organizers and initiating adenocarcinomas in the kidney, with comparable pathology of the lung, liver, and occasionally spleen. Thus, in effect, it was found possible to induce in the frog kidney a so-called virus tumor by an *inorganic* reagent. A related cytological study of DNA and RNA inhibitory effects on nucleoli and ribosomes by several Actinomycins and Puromycin was also begun. These preliminary experiments in frogs are reported for the first time in this paper.

As a background for my conclusions and for the current experimental design, the reader is referred to the Transcript of the First Frog Kidney Adenocarcinoma Conference (3) which I organized in 1961. From many conversations with Dr. Balduin Lucké, beginning in 1935 soon after he published his first paper on this tumor, I became interested in its cellular and possibly viral oncogenesis. From my earliest experiments with tumor filtrates I agreed with its probable causation by a virus. Without benefit of the techniques of electron microscopy, now so well developed, it was not possible to decide then between the virus theory and a simpler hypothesis I designated by the term: *infective* or *infectious DNA*. This was based on large numbers of observations of DNA nuclear extrusions that were capable of being engulfed by neighboring cells (8, 9).

With the continued and convincing finding that so-called spontaneous renal tumors in frogs are nearly always associated with parasite-induced granulomas, the virus theory became less attractive. Following the announcement in 1962 by Boyland *et al.* (1) and Van Esch *et al.* (16) that high percentages of renal tumors in rats could be produced by feeding lead acetate, it was then decided to try similar experiments in frogs. Van Esch pointed out that viruses were not involved in his animals, but that enlarged nuclei and eosinophilic inclusion bodies could be demonstrated after four weeks. Since nucleolar changes preceded all others in cells transforming toward malignancy, our experimental plan included feeding other lead salts and other heavy metals, such as cobalt and chromium, to provide wider understanding of cation effects.

[1] This work was supported by grant DRG 848 from the Damon Runyon Memorial Fund, by NCI grant award 5-KO-3-CA225, and by the William H. Donner Foundation.

82

TABLE 1

HUMAN TUMORS SHOWING NUCLEAR EXTRUSIONS OF DNA AND RNA
(FEULGEN STAIN)

Carcinoma:		Adenocarcinoma:		Sarcoma:	
Ear	1	Tonsil	1	Chest	1
Mouth	1	Lung	4	Elbow	1
Parotid gland	1	Breast	1	Vagina	1
Nose	1	Stomach	2	Vulva	1
Tonsil	1	Cecum	1		
Esophagus	3	Colon	4	Cystosarcoma:	
Neck	1	Kidney	5	Breast	1
Larynx	2	Endocervix	2	Carcino-sarcoma:	
Thyroid	1	Uterus	4	Ovary	1
Breast	18	Ovary	11	Uterus	1
Lung	5	Fallopian tube	1		
Hand	1			Lymphoma:	
Testis	1	Melanoma:		Hodgkin's disease	3
Cervix	12	Neck	2	Lymphoblastic	
Ovary	4	Vulva	1	thymoma	1
Vulva	1	Leg	2	Cervical and	
				inguinal node	1
Choriocarcinoma:		Mesothelioma:			
Uterus	1	Spermatic cord	1	Para-ganglioma:	
				Mediastinum	1
Rhabdomyosarcoma:		Leiomyosarcoma:			
Arm	1	Uterus	1		
Chest	1	Pelvis	1		
Astrocytoma:					
Astrocyte tumor	1			TOTAL STUDIED	115

Thanks are due to Dr. William P. McKelway and Dr. Frank S. Jannotta and to other colleagues in the Departments of Pathology and Surgery for supplying tissue specimens used in this study.

Attention is directed to the very recent review of organic carcinogen effects on nucleoli presented by Svoboda and Higginson (15). Directly comparable nucleolar changes have now been observed in human cancers by this laboratory and by other investigators. The range of human tissue examples in our series is shown in Table 1. Multiple extrusions were found in every case.

Carcinogenesis and the Control of Growth

Oncologists must continue to ask two searching questions: (1) What confers on a normal cell the *competitive advantage* to outgrow its sister cells? and (2) What allows a transforming neoplastic cell to leave its normal position and to become *invasive?* Preliminary answers to these questions focus attention on the overlooked fact that cancer is indeed a combined nuclear and cell surface disease. It is never an all-or-none phenomenon. Consequently, oncologists need not always seek a single inciting agent, such as a virus, because the list of inciting or triggering agents is a very long one. We can now answer the first question by identifying nucleolar organizer DNA as the controlling genetic locus for growth. And we can answer the second question by time-lapse films of surface secreted mucopolysaccharides which lessen intercellular adhesiveness.

In the present paper a revised hypothesis for carcinogenesis is put forward as follows: Depending on the *amount* of nucleolar organizer DNA, "bursts" of colloidal messenger RNA are released intermittently from the nucleolus, through the nuclear envelope, into the cytoplasm every five to thirty minutes. Rates of synthesis and bursting also depend on temperature (cf. Diagram 1 and Figs. 7, 8, 9 of Plate 3). This extruded RNA or RNP, being exceptionally hydrophilic (cf. Fig. 10) disperses rapidly in the cytoplasm.[1] There it catalyzes many syntheses, presumably aided by ribosomal action, leading to increase in cell mass, i.e., increase of the cytoarchitecture proteins.

Increase in cell size, or *growth*, can be followed, roughly quantized, and evaluated by time-lapse cinephotography. On a per cell basis we designate this process as *positive growth*. Similarly, loss of cell mass or shrinkage in cell size is designated as *negative growth*.

Attention must be confined in this instance not to all varieties of proteins but to the major one or ones concerned in growth. Because the nucleolus is the principal source and by far the largest center for manufacture of the essential growth catalysts, cytogeneticists generally agree that nucleolar DNA, that is to say the *nucleolar organizer*, represents the primary catalyst or template for extruded RNP. It should be noted that all larger cells, such as giant cells in tumors, ovarian eggs, Purkinje cells of the cerebellum, and many other types, have large hyperactive nucleoli. Indeed this relationship is well-known, and may be verified wherever there is a heavy protein demand on the cell.

There is ample evidence both in frog kidney cells and in the general cell physiology literature that protein is quantitatively synthesized on the secondary RNA templates. Parenthetically, it may be observed that the term "template" was first introduced into cytogenetics in my 1941 paper.

Careful study of primary DNA templates of the nucleolar organizers (there may be more than two per cell) yields increasing evidence that replication of these genetic loci correlate excellently with situations of increased growth. It must be emphasized again that nucleolar organizers are genetic loci by the most exact definition, i.e., DNA centers on a chromosome engaged in a specific biochemical function. Normally one would expect two such loci in every normal diploid cell—one deriving from the father, the other from the mother. As recently pointed out by Gall (12) and earlier observed in this laboratory, in amphibian oocytes with enormous germinal vesicles,

---

[1] Some authors, notably Reynolds, Montgomery and Hughes (13), have described structures observed in nucleoli as "Nucleolar Caps." Not only do we believe that they have misinterpreted transient vacuoles as permanent structures, but also that they have not understood the continuing physiological control mechanisms which nucleoli dominate during growth.

there may be over 2000 nucleoli, each with its attached nucleolar organizer fragment. In all types of malignant cells, human and animal, marked replication of the organizers can be observed. Most anaplastic Feulgen-stained tumors show DNA fragments of the organizers escaping into the cytoplasm and occasionally outside the cell membranes. It is hardly necessary to point out that for two decades clinical pathology has used the term *perinucleolar chromatin* (=DNA) as one of the criteria for malignancy. Emphasis must henceforth be put on the nucleolar organizer as targets for carcinogens and hormones and as the "Pacemaker" for growth (5).

Materials and Methods

Leopard frogs (*Rana pipiens*) used in these series were obtained from dealers in Alburg, Vermont. One small shipment originated in Wisconsin. Ninety-six percent had mature Trematode lung parasites—*Haematoloechus*, syn. *Pneumoneces*. (?). Approximately 80 percent also contained lung Nematodes. A much smaller percentage (58 percent) had histological evidence of larval parasitic invasion of their kidneys. All frogs were maintained at 16°C and were fed once a week with beef liver. Parasites and insect diets conceivably could introduce many types of viruses. This possibility cannot be ruled out.

Autopsied animals were examined grossly under a dissecting scope immediately thereafter, both lungs and both kidneys were fixed in Telly's solution [1] for 24 hours, and then transferred to 70 percent alcohol for storage before imbedding. This procedure avoided loss of RNA from both nuclei and cytoplasm, which commonly results from utilization of other fixatives. Our standard techniques were also found ideal for human biopsy material.

Since complete semi-serial sections of both kidneys and both lungs were *indispensable* to identify early cancers, entire ribbons from each organ were made. Acceptable sampling for identification of micro-adenocarcinomas (less than 200 micrometers) was achieved by dividing each ribbon into segments of five sections, each mounted separately. Slides were then assembled in lots of three, the first of each was stained with Feulgen reagent for DNA, the second treated with standard Periodic Acid Schiff reagents (PAS) for mucopolysaccharides, and the third with routine Hematoxylin and Eosin for pathologists. Thus, virtually every micronodule could be examined and interpreted in the light of three histochemical criteria. Occasionally other stains employed were: Alcian Blue, Luxol Fast Blue, Biebrich Scarlet, and Crystal Violet.

For establishing tissue cultures, sterily obtained organs, nodules, or tumors were washed with sterile media, immediately transsected, and the major portion carefully removed for immediate use in the culture room. The minor portion of each organ was fixed as described for further histological and cytological study.

Tissue cultures were prepared in the shortest possible time: explants again washed three times in an excess of media and mounted in hanging drops, using the flying coverslip method over an optically flat Romicron slide. To prevent drying, 1 cm squares of Earle's perforated cellophane, presoaked in media, were used to cover ex-

---

[1] Tellyesniczky's Acetic Alcohol Formalin (Fekete's modification): 70 percent Ethyl Alcohol—20 parts; Glacial Acetic Acid—1 part; Neutralized Formalin—2 parts.

plants and to promote adhesion of cells to the cover glass. Frequently minute pieces of male rudimentary oviduct were added to provide vigorous stirring by everted ciliated cells. During the past year, however, Dr. E. R. Burns, an NCI post-doctoral Fellow in this laboratory, found that cellophane could be dispensed with, provided extreme caution and speed were used in setting up and sealing the cultures. Optical conditions for phase-contrast microscopy of nucleolar details were thus greatly enhanced.

Previous media, such as NCTC 109 (modified), as recommended by others, were occasionally found unsatisfactory for frog and newt cells. Fortunately we were able to secure the generous help of Dr. Raymond C. Parker and G. M. Healy of the Connaught Medical Research Laboratories in Toronto. Parker's latest mammalian cell medium #1490 (greatly superior to his earlier medium #199 developed during polio research) was further modified by Healy for amphibian cells. Long-term cultures and high mitotic rates resulted from this improved formula (CMRL 1490-6).[1] It was routinely supplemented with frozen millipore-filtered Chick Embryo Extract at the level of 10 percent and with 10 percent bovine calf serum. All cultures were routinely fed twice a week and maintained at 16°C. Since nucleolar RNA output is increased immediately after feeding as well as by heat, mitotic studies henceforth need to be correlated with the feeding cycle and with accurate temperature control.

In the course of our experiments a number of other new techniques have been developed. These included direct unilateral injection of tumor-filtrates into kidneys to compare with effects of combined tumor and normal cells in tissue cultures, and improved culture methods for long-term (6–12 months) optical phase-contrast analysis. Special techniques were developed for single cell records of growth and temperature-change effects on cultured cells using time-lapse cinephotography. As noted above, for direct histochemical comparisons of each tissue, not only was it necessary to make complete semi-serial sections of both kidneys and lungs from every experimental frog for varied staining of groups of slides, but also each tissue culture was routinely fixed and Feulgen-stained. Thus, interlocking information was obtained for each donor animal, for its induced transforming cells, and for every sub-culture.

Time-lapse motion picture records have become standard in many laboratories. For precision, long-term, vibration-free, phase-contrast photography, the Arriflex camera without shutter but with revolving prisms was adopted. Cultures were illuminated only at the moment of photography by a precise intervalometer.

At appropriate times accurately controlled temperature rises of 2.5°C were provided by a nichrome wire heater mounted above the sub-stage condenser directly under the culture. Temperature was monitored by a thermocouple applied directly to the coverslip. A Galileo microscope fitted with Zeiss Neofluar optics, except for the long-working distance condenser, proved indispensable. Its built-in focusing telescope for phase centering saved many hours. During the past five years, over 23,000 feet of ciné records were made, largely on intranuclear and intranucleolar physiology. Reference is made to a film on nucleolar reconstruction in frog cells following mitosis recently presented at the XXIVth International Physiological Congress (10). It is believed that this constitutes the first motion picture record of a living genetic locus catalyzing the synthesis of RNA.

---

[1] The new medium CMRL 1490-6 is commercially available from the Connaught Medical Research Laboratories, Media Division, University of Toronto, Toronto 5, Ontario, Canada.

Inhibition of nucleolar activity was achieved by addition of micro amounts of Actinomycin D,[1] Actinomycin C_1 and C_2. A small number of comparisons were made with Daunomycin. In three experiments cytoplasmic RNA synthesis of protein was blocked by addition of Puromycin. Antimetabolite dosages ranged from 0.001 of a milligram to .01 mg per culture.

Experimental tumors in frogs were physiologically induced by weekly oral intubation of 0.5 ml solutions of lead acetate or lead nitrate (0.03–0.05M). Chronic plumbism was very difficult to achieve in these animals. Preliminary experiments led us to avoid intraperitoneal injection techniques. Since animals had to be maintained from two to ten months under optimal conditions, feeding cycles had to be scheduled accurately. Acetate treated animals were maintained at room temperature (21–23°C) and nitrate treated ones at 16°C. Controls were similarly intubated with 0.03M $NaNO_3$ or NaCl and kept at the lower temperature. Untreated stock animals also served for base line comparisons. The majority of animals were sacrificed; approximately 30% died.

A small preliminary series of animals were likewise intubated with comparable solutions of cobalt, chromium, and cadmium salts. Results from these series are not reported here in detail.

Experimental Results

Experimental results are presented in three sections: first information from Feulgen and PAS-stained slides, next information from living tissue cultures, and finally results brought out by time-lapse cinephotography.

Following repeated oral intubation of diluted lead acetate, frog kidneys showed early lesions of tubules in three to five weeks. However, on the average, invasive cells did not appear in numbers until after three months. It was then decided to change from use of lead acetate to lead nitrate, because of our earlier experience with oocytes which showed nitrate had more hydrating effects on nucleoli than did the other anion. For convenience all experiments were combined and summarized in Table 2.

While interpretations may vary, the table brings out clearly that after a latent period the degree of abnormality increased with time and duration of exposure. This was also true of tubule hyperplasia. Lymphocytic infiltration was difficult to estimate quantitatively and was not as closely related to the process of carcinogenesis. Lymphocytes do congregate in areas of hyperplasia and pre-cancer, so they may be considered as a supplementary physiological index. Nephrosis was expected as a result of heavy metal toxicity, but does not appear as a major variable, although mortality reached 29 percent. A surprising result was the relatively large proportion of lung cancers and their neoplastic involvement with pulmonary fibrosis and melanosis.

Data in Table 2 are derived from a detailed study of several hundred thousand tubule cross sections. However, more important information comes from much fewer random longitudinal sections in which progressive malignant transformations were observed along the axis of a renal tubule.

---

[1] Actinomycin D and other DNA antimetabolites were kindly supplied through courtesy of Dr. Alfred R. Stanley of the Cancer Chemotherapy National Service Center, NIH.

TABLE 2

SUMMARY OF RENAL AND LUNG PATHOLOGICAL CHANGES IN FROGS RESULTING
FROM ORAL INTUBATION OF LEAD ACETATE AND LEAD NITRATE

No.	Days	Nephrosis	Lymphocyte infiltration	Tubule hyperplasia	Emboli	Type of abnormality
1-A	4	—	—	—	—	—
2-A	13	—	+	—	—	—
3	13	—	—	—	+	—
4-A	14	+	+	—	—	— ?
5	21	+	+	+	—	—
6	23	+	+	+	—	*in situ* Transformations
7	23	—	++	++	—	Early ACa & Lymphosarcoma?
8-A	25	+	+	+	—	— ?
9-A	25	—	+	—	—	—
10	30	—	+	++	—	Early ACa & Fibrosis
11	30	+	+++	++	+++	Lymphosarcoma? Lung ACa++
12	33	+	++	++	++	Lung ACa++, Renal *in situ*
13	35	++	++	++	+++	Lung ACa+++
14	40	+	+	+++	+	Bilateral renal ACa +
15	41	+	+	+	++	Adrenal tumor, Lung ACa +
16	41	—	+	—	—	— ?
17	51	—	+	+	—	Early bilateral ACa +
18	70	++	+	++	+	Lung ACa +, met. to kidney
19	90	+	+	+	—	*in situ* Transformations
20	96	+	++	+++	++	Early renal ACa +
21	103	—	—	—	++	Lung ACa +, met. to kidney
22	105	—	+	+	++++	Lung ACa +, Melanosarcoma ++
23-A	107	+	+	++	—	Bilateral renal ACa ++
24	116	++	+	++	+++	Hepatoma +, Melanosis in lung

Early adenocarcinoma (ACa) may rarely be accompanied by fibrosis (cf. Animal 10) in the kidney, as contrasted with extensive and more frequent fibrogenesis in lungs (Animals 11, 22, 28, 39, 40). Melanosis (3 cases) and melanosarcoma (2 cases) of lung tissue were also observed. Kidneys from these cases showed numerous melanocytes trapped in glomeruli, as well as circulating in the blood.

Bilateral multiple adenocarcinomas (Nos. 14, 23, 29, and 44) were considered especially conclusive of the carcinogenic action of lead on renal parenchyma. However, numerous primary lung cancers, such as Nos. 12, 13, 21, 22, 32, 38, 39, were unexpected. Possibly lead solutions were regurgitated into lungs through an open glottis, as well as circulating in the blood. Fibrosis, fibrosarcoma, and lymphosarcoma of the lung were likewise encountered. Each needs to be studied in detail to be fully appreciated and cannot be adequately described in writing.

All tumors in these series exhibited marked hypersecretion of mucus from the outer columnar cells oriented perpendicularly to each nodular surface. This important observation would have been missed with only routine H&E staining, where secretion

TABLE 2 (cont.)

No.	Days	Nephrosis	Lymphocyte infiltration	Tubule hyperplasia	Emboli	Type of abnormality
25-A	120	+	++	++	+	Unilateral renal ACa +
26-A	120	+	++	+	—	Melanosis in lung
27-A	120	+	++	+++	+++	Early unilateral ACa +
28	120	+	++	++	++	Early Melanosarcoma in lung
29	130	+	+	++	—	Bilateral renal ACa ++
30	135	+	+	+	—	— ?
31	145	+	++	++	+	Early lung ACa +, Melanosis
32	145	+	++	++	+	Lung ACa +
33	150	+	+++	++	—	*in situ* Transformations
34	165	—	+	+	—	— ?
35	165	—	+	+	—	*in situ* Transformations
36	170	—	++	++++	+	Unilateral renal ACa ++++
37	175	—	+	+		*in situ* lung ACa
38	180	+	+++	+++	+	Lung ACa +
39	185	++	++	++	+	Lung ACa +, Fibrosis
40	185	++	+++	+++	+	Lung fibrosarcoma +
41	185	+	+++	+++	+	Lung lymphosarcoma ?
42	185	+	++	+++	+++	Lung ACa ++
43	185	++	++	++	+++	Early renal ACa +
44	185	+	+++	+++	+	Bilateral renal ACa ++
45	210	++	+++	++	+	Lung ACa ++

+ denotes slight, localized changes; ++ denotes marked changes in numerous areas; +++ denotes advanced changes in a large number of areas; ++++ denotes highly anaplastic changes throughout; -A denotes intubation with lead acetate, others with lead nitrate; ACa denotes Adenocarcinoma.

droplets were almost invisible. However, alternate slides, PAS-stained, invariably showed such droplets stained a brilliant pink-red. The arrangement, illustrated in Fig. 12, would have been without meaning were such cells not studied with time-lapse cinephotography, where the repetitive, rhythmical pumping was striking. It should not be overlooked that mucoid hypersecretion has deep significance for loosening of intercellular adhesiveness and the promotion of invasiveness.

A pertinent and impressive review of mucin histochemistry in adenocarcinomas had recently been published by Esterly and Spicer (11).

It should be emphasized that in six control animals intubated with 0.03M sodium nitrate, no cancers, either in kidneys or in lungs, were found in an eight-month period. Also, none were found in four other controls intubated for a three-month period. No cancers were found in three frogs intubated with dilute NaCl for four months. Over a period of years from normal animals kept in our cold boxes only two out of 59 have developed malignancies in less than five months.

Since voluminous data and individual protocols on each frog cannot be presented

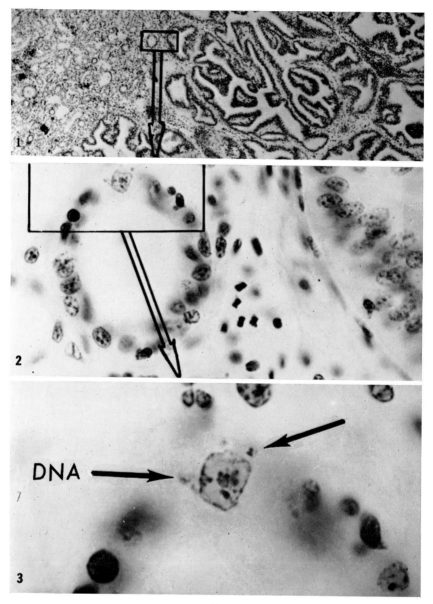

PLATE 1

Fig. 1. Low-power photomicrograph of filtrate-induced adenocarcinoma of frog kidney. Transformation zone of normal tubules into cancer. Inset shows area enlarged in Fig. 2. (Stained with Feulgen-Fast green FCF. Approx. ✕56.)

Fig. 2. Enlarged view of transforming frog renal tubule. Note hyperplasia evidenced by increased number of cells in cross section. Portion of malignant area visible at right. Note changing nucleolar patterns in tubule wall. Approx. ✕730.

Fig. 3. Greatly enlarged view of renal cell nucleus from inset of Fig. 2. Arrows point to extruded DNA and RNA from the hyperactive nucleolar organizer. Approx. ✕1800.

in a brief paper, attention is directed to the mechanisms of tubule transformation as illustrated in Figs. 1–6 (Plates 1, 2, and 3). The essential problem of carcinogenesis is visualized first. In Fig. 1 of Plate 1 the zone of junction between a filtrate-induced tumor and the normal frog kidney is shown. Fig. 2 is an enlarged view of the transforming tubule marked by the inset. Feulgen-positive DNA in the transforming nephron is noticeably greater than in completely normal tubules. It also has a significantly different intranuclear distribution, visible only under 100x oil-immersion. The nucleus in Fig. 3 is already malignant, and more transformed than its sister nuclei in the same tubule. Three fragments of nucleolar organizer material may be seen in the cytoplasm, having escaped with nucleolar-core messenger RNA colloid. There is no escape from the fact that each tubule adjacent to the tumor shown in Fig. 1 would ultimately transform into adenocarcinoma if left in the living animal. As will be shown later in this paper, such a mechanism is "infective DNA" particles entering new host cells and locking in on their homologous genetic loci.

A closely related experimental situation is next shown in Figs. 4, 5, and 6. The early adenocarcinoma was induced by lead acetate treatment for 120 days (Animal 25, Table 2). Fig. 5 illustrates the slightly different mechanism of tubule hyperplasia and early transformation. In Fig. 6 the lead effect on nucleoli is clear. Infiltrating lymphocytes and transforming cells are also visible. Here lead replaces infective DNA as the triggering agent.

New cytological information supplemented that obtained in earlier studies (2, 7) and that found in human cancers (4, 8) listed in Table 1. Degrees of nucleolar DNA extrusion from their "organizers" correlated well with anaplasia, agressive growth, and metastasis.

Turning to studies on tissue cultures, we found rates of nucleolar RNA extrusion ("halo" formation) could be speeded from average times of 20–25 minutes per burst to 4 or 5 minutes by increasing heat 2.5 degrees. Cooling slowed nucleolar function dramatically. Heating experiments are typified in Diagram 1.

Living nucleolar phenomena are illustrated in Figs. 7, 8, and 9. Between Figs. 7 and 8 is an interval of 45 minutes. One small colloidal coacervate droplet has burst. The nucleolus has changed shape and size. Of interest is the same nucleolus, four days later, shown in Fig. 9. Note four intranucleolar droplets (sometimes mis-identified as nucleolini) and a subsequent burst. Messenger RNA proceeds from the central nucleolar area between the chromosomes and nucleogel and into the cytoplasm. As earlier shown (9), it there disperses as a subtemplate and all-important catalyst for protein synthesis and "positive" growth.

In the past numerous experiments were devised to test the validity of our infective DNA theory for cell transformation. Some of these centered on the method of combining normal and malignant frog renal tissue on the same cover-slip of a culture. After several days growth it was often difficult to distinguish normal from malignant cells in the zone of junction. A solution presented itself through use of triploid cells as normal markers. Results are presented here for the first time in Figs. 10 and 11 (Plates 4 and 5). Through courtesy of Dr. Robert G. McKinnell of Tulane University, who presented us with a triploid *Rana kandiyohi*, cultures of triploid kidney cells were established. When monolayers of normal explants had grown out, pieces of

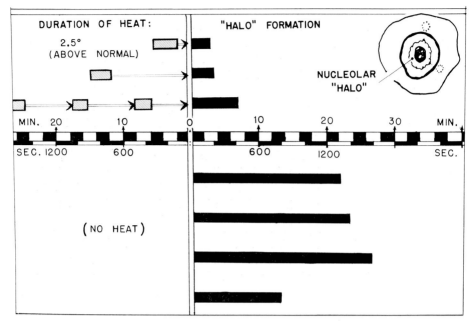

Diagram 1. Effects of pre-heating on nucleolar secretion activity and "halo" formation in cultured frog kidney cells.

typical high-malignancy renal tumors were added to the same cover-slips and the cultures continued.

A non-exposed typical triploid cell is shown in Fig. 10. Feulgen staining brought out the DNA arrangements of the two double and one single sets of nucleolar organizers. Also the figure beautifully illustrates three RNA nucleolar extrusions in sequential degrees of cytoplasmic hydration. Fig. 11 at slightly higher magnification, also Feulgen stained, shows the new DNA derived from nearby cancer cells during a 4-day exposure. Arrows indicate infective DNA masses replicating on host genetic templates. Unfortunately no biological test was available to test whether the exposed cells were capable of malignant growth. It can, however, be pointed out that human laryngeal carcinoma cells of the Hep-2 line, when similarly stained, present identical DNA patterns on their nucleolar surfaces.

Experiments designed to test the theory of nucleolar growth control were set up using various Actinomycins. Actinomycin D, even at widely different concentrations, uniformly produced its characteristic binding and blocking DNA template activity. In eleven experiments recorded by time-lapse motion pictures, the nucleoli could be seen to empty in approximately 40–60 minutes at room temperatures. Small nucleoli always emptied first, followed by the larger in complete synchrony. Inspection of a cell monolayer, one hour after Actinomycin treatment, showed all cells alive and in vigorous motion, but without nucleolar cores. Attempts to reverse inhibition by washing away excess Actinomycin was successful in only two instances. Actinomycin C_2 and C_3 appeared to be less efficient DNA-inhibitors in two experiments.

The result of Actinomycin D blockage of nucleolar organizer DNA activity was

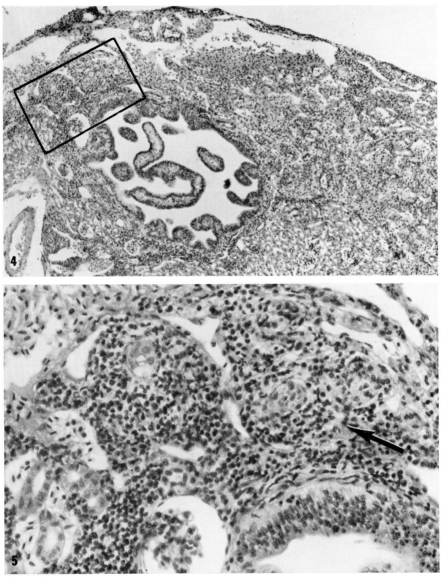

PLATE 2

Fig. 4. Early renal adenocarcinoma induced by oral administration of lead acetate (120 days). Edge of tumor with transforming tubules and granuloma area shown in inset, and enlarged in Fig. 5. (Feulgen stain.) Approx. ×56.

Fig. 5. Medium-power view of transforming tubules from inset in Fig. 4. Note malignant tissue at lower right and transforming tubules with early invasion areas, and numerous lymphocytes. Approx. ×220.

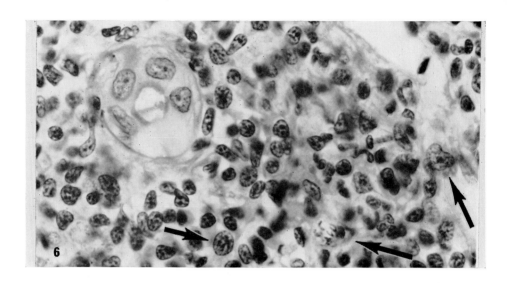

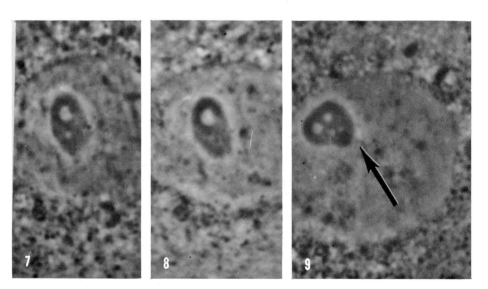

PLATE 3

Fig. 6. Enlarged view of lead acetate induced transforming tubule shown in Fig. 5. Early nucleolar organizer changes visible. Arrows indicate three invasive cancer cells—one undergoing mitosis, surrounded by lymphocytes. (Feulgen stain.) Approx. ×700.

Figs. 7, 8, 9. Sequential views of the same living nucleolus from a transforming normal kidney cell in culture. Fig. 7 shows a bursting nucleolus with two RNA colloidal droplets. Fig. 8, taken 45 minutes later, shows one remaining droplet with dispersing "halo." Fig. 9, taken four days later, illustrates nucleolus now with four RNA coacervate droplets. Arrow indicates an emerging one with beginning halo formation. RNA material also visible outside nuclear membrane. Approx. ×1900.

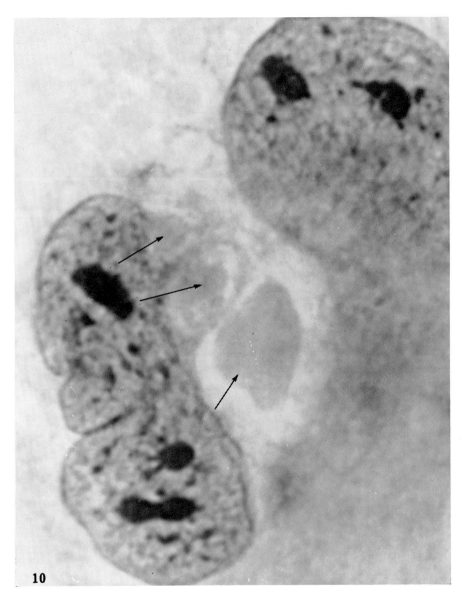

PLATE 4

Fig. 10. Central area of cultured kidney cell from a triploid frog (*R. Kandiyohi,* courtesy of Dr. R. G. McKinnell). Upper nucleus with two nucleoli, lower with three nucleoli. Arrows indicate three RNA nucleolar extrusions in sequential degrees of cytoplasmic hydration. (Photographed through 100× oil imm. planapochromat objective, Telly's fixation, Feulgen-Fast green FCF.) Approx. ×4700.

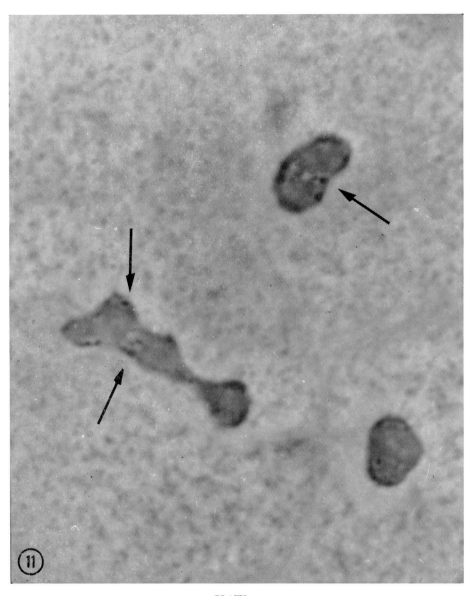

PLATE 5

Fig. 11. Central nuclear area of one cell from another explant of the same kidney of R. *Kandiyohi* frog as in Fig. 10, at slightly higher magnification, but grown on a coverslip with adjacent R. *pipiens* adenocarcinoma explant 1 mm distant for four days. Arrows indicate "infective DNA" masses on triploid nucleolar organizers of the host cell nucleoli. (Feulgen stain.) Approx. $\times$4900.

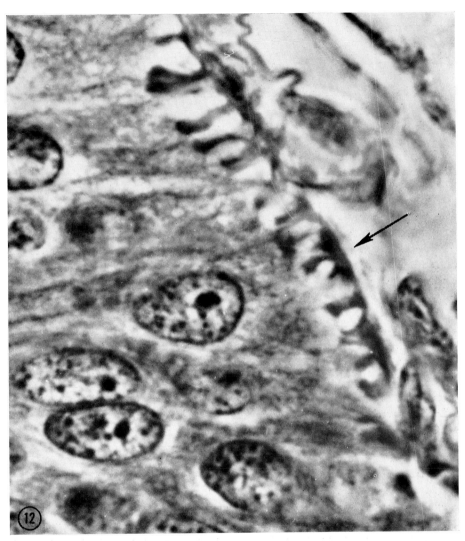

PLATE 6

Fig. 12. High magnification of edge of lead nitrate induced adenocarcinoma showing massive production of mucopolysaccharide on the *outer* border of the nodule. Arrow indicates heavily PAS-positive secretion droplets, typical of all lead-induced cancers. During life these droplet vacuoles pulsate rhythmically. Approx. ✕2400.

invariably followed by cell shrinkage. Motion pictures strikingly demonstrated thinning and retraction of pseudopodia, and as much as 50 percent diminution in cell size. This finding clearly justifies the term *negative growth*. It fully supports our earlier use of the term "Pacemaker" for all growth applied to the nucleolar organizers (5).

Cells were also filmed following Puromycin blockage of cytoplasmic protein synthesis. All shrank, converting thick pseudopodia into filamentous, active strands, and many were reduced to cannibalism. Experimental negative growth was thus again induced, but by a different metabolic mechanism.

Discussion

Intensive study of amphibian adenocarinomas has yielded other unexpected results. For example, there is not just one disease in frogs—the Lucké Adenocarcinoma. There is a whole spectrum of cancers, grading from adenomas of the kidney and lung to lymphosarcomas, melanoma, mesothelioma, and presumably benign tumors of bone, skin, adrenals, and fat. It is no longer unusual for pathologists to inquire whether there are common denominators in amphibian neoplasms, as well as in human multiple primary cancers, "mixed" tumors, recurrent tumors following long intervals, tumors in contra-lateral organs, and in rapidly spreading malignant disease as in the colon. There is clear implication of a common factor. This factor is designated "infective DNA."

In early cancer, the acquired ability of genetically transformed cells to invade and to metastasize is of paramount importance. However, mechanisms of the invasive process are until now poorly explained. Our data show that DNA genetic changes in the nucleolar organizer invariably *precede* and then accompany cytoplasmic phenomena which transform renal tubules into adenocarcinoma. In long-term tissue cultures, as well as *in vivo*, it has been observed that secreted mucopolysaccharide distribution, covering the cell surface, is profoundly altered.

Our observations have clearly shown by direct cinephotography and in PAS-stained sections that lysosomal secretion of mucopolysaccharide in tumor cells increased. We also demonstrated that because of lower viscosity and hence greater solubility, the stainable material dispersed more rapidly into parenchymal spaces.

Our motion picture studies have yielded hundreds of examples of to-and-fro oscillations of the nuclear membrane involving deep indentations by mucin-secretory vacuoles. Transfer of material from the nucleus to the vacuole has repeatedly shown on our films. While the biochemical nature of this process is imperfectly understood, the essential sequence of facts is indeed clear: cell motion, creeping, and cell surface events are directly dependent on nuclear metabolism. In other words, to a certain degree, surface activity is directly under genetic control. Without question, the rhythmical "pumping" of mucopolysaccharide aids cells in breaking away from a contiguous sheet and thus offers a definitive understanding for the mechanism of early metastasis. It is regrettable that numerous color photomicrographs and film records cannot be published here to supplement important relationships barely indicated in Plate 6.

It is hoped that bringing together a study of inorganic carcinogens with tumor filtrate experiments and at the same time relating changes in cell surface mucin secretion to nuclear behavior will be an advance in the area of oncogenesis. As pointed out by Sabin (14) in a recent symposium, the search for a direct viral etiology of human cancer is still "faced with repeated frustrations."

Summary

Studies based on the oral administration of lead salts showed that it was possible to produce in leopard frogs (*Rana pipiens*) a wide variety of malignancies. While these consisted primarily of renal adenocarcinomas and lung adenocarcinomas arising in a period of three to six months, other types were noted. Examples were fibrosarcoma, hepatoma, and melanosarcoma, and possibly lymphosarcoma. In all cases the primary target in the cell appeared to be the nucleolar organizer.

Progressive tubule transformations were essentially similar to those described earlier following injections of tumor filtrates.

A new finding based on PAS staining was that mucopolysaccharides are secreted more actively on transforming tubule surfaces than on normals. By means of correlated time lapse photography it was shown that renal cells secrete mucins from rhythmically bursting surface vacuoles. This phenomenon can be related to increased invasiveness of the cells. Likewise DNA-controlled nucleolar output of RNA could be filmed, inhibited by Actinomycin D, and accelerated by two degrees C of heat.

Experiments have led us to conclude that the nucleolar organizers are the genetic pacemakers for cell growth, and warrant introduction of the terms: *positive growth* and *negative growth* to describe the resulting cell behavior.

Acknowledgments

I wish to thank Mr. J. Russell Gilbert, Mrs. Joan L. Chadbourn, Miss Laura L. Chang, and Mr. J. Richard Thistlethwaite, Jr., for their expert and helpful technical assistance.

References

1. BOYLAND, E., DUKES, C. E., GROVER, P. L., and MITCHLEY, B. C. V.: The induction of renal tumors by feeding lead acetate to rats. Brit. J. Cancer *16*:283–288, 1962.

2. DURYEE, W. R.: Precancer cells in amphibian adenocarcinoma. Ann. N.Y. Acad. Sci. *63*: 1280–1302, 1956.

3. DURYEE, W. R.: Morphology and pathogenesis of frog kidney adenocarcinoma. *In* Transcript of Proceedings: First Frog Kidney Adenocarcinoma Conference (W. R. Duryee and L. Warner, eds.). N.I.H. Bethesda, Md., 1961, pp. 19–34.

4. DURYEE, W. R. and McKELWAY, W. P.: Nuclear control of cell growth. (Demonstration: 76th Meeting Am. Assoc. Anat.), Anat. Rec. *145*:361, 1963.

5. DURYEE, W. R.: Rate and volume of nucleolar extrusion as the pacemaker for cell growth. (Abstr.) XIth Internat. Congress of Cell Biology. Series *77*:17–18, Excerpta Medica, 1964.

6. DURYEE, W. R.: Nucleolar extrusion in living cells: effect of temperature on normal and malignant cultures of amphibian kidneys. *Film* presented at: XIth Internat. Congress of Cell Biol., Providence, R.I., 1964.

7. DURYEE, W. R.: On the frog kidney tumor review by Dr. Rafferty. Cancer Res. *24*:518–519, 1964.

8. DURYEE, W. R.: Nucleolar physiology in human tumors of divergent types. (Abstr.) Proc. Am. Assoc. Cancer Res. 5:15, 1964.

9. DURYEE, W. R.: Factors influencing development of tumors in frogs. Ann. N.Y. Acad. Sci. 126, I:59–84, 1965.

10. DURYEE, W. R.: Nucleolar reconstruction of lung and kidney cells following mitosis. *Film* presented at: XXIVth Internat. Congress of Physiol. Sci., Washington, D.C., Proc. I.U.P.S., VII:484, 1968.

11. ESTERLY, J. R. and SPICER, S. S.: Mucin histochemistry of human gallbladder: Changes in adenocarcinoma, cystic fibrosis, and cholecystitis. J. Nat. Cancer Inst. 40:1–11, 1968.

12. GALL, J. G.: Differential synthesis of the genes for ribosomal RNA during amphibian oogenesis. Proc. Nat. Acad. Sci. 60:553–560, 1968.

13. REYNOLDS, R. D., MONTGOMERY, P. O'B. and HUGHES, B.: Nucleolar "caps" produced by Actinomycin C. Cancer Res. 24:1269–1278, 1964.

14. SABIN, A. B.: Viral carcinogenesis: phenomena of special significance in the search for a viral etiology in human cancer. Cancer Res. 28:1849–1858, 1968.

15. SVOBODA, D. and HIGGINSON, J.: A comparison of ultrastructural changes in rat liver due to chemical carcinogens. Cancer Res. 28:1703–1733, 1968.

16. VAN ESCH, G. J., VAN GENDEREN, H., and VINK, H. H.: The induction of renal tumors by feeding of basic lead acetate to rats. Brit. J. Cancer 16:289–297, 1962.

Characteristics of Cell Lines from Haploid and Diploid Anuran Embryos[1]

Jerome J. Freed,[2] Liselotte Mezger-Freed and Susan A. Schatz

The Institute for Cancer Research
Fox Chase, Philadelphia, Pennsylvania

Haploid anuran embryos can readily be obtained by the classical methods of experimental embryology and provide a source of tissue for the initiation of haploid cell cultures. In order to exploit the obvious advantages for genetic experimentation of cell populations with a single chromosome set, we have for some time been studying cell lines initiated from haploid as well as diploid frog embryos (1). Since our initial publication in 1962, we have evaluated a number of growth media; the most useful appears to be that of Leibovitz (2) as modified for amphibian cells by Balls and Ruben (3), which we have employed since 1966. Using this medium, 35 lines have been initiated by passaging primary cultures. Of these, 23 have successfully been maintained in serial culture, i.e., carried through 10 or more passages. Clonal isolates have been obtained from some of these lines and passaged separately. Thus, 36 distinct lines are at present maintained in frozen storage or continuous culture. Our purpose in this paper is to describe how such lines are initiated, the morphological changes which the cells undergo, their chromosome constitution, and their properties as experimental material. We will consider in detail features of four lines of particular interest because of their origin or behavior.

Materials and Methods

Parent Animals. *Rana pipiens* (Schreber) were obtained from J. M. Hazen Co., Alburg, Vermont, and maintained in artificial hibernation until required for breeding (4). Ovulation was induced by injection of frog pituitary and mammalian progesterone (5). *Bufo americanus* (Holbrook) were collected April 25, 1968 near Sellersville, Pennsylvania, and bred naturally in an aquarium in the laboratory. These embryos were furnished to us by Dr. G. L. Slemmer, The Institute for Cancer Research.

[1] Research supported by USPHS grants CA-05959, CA-06927 and FR-05539 from the National Cancer Institute, and by contract AT(30-1)2356 with the U.S. Atomic Energy Commission (Report NYO-2356-32). Additional support was received from grant IN-49 from the American Cancer Society and an appropriation from the Commonwealth of Pennsylvania.

[2] Recipient of Research Career Development Award 5-K3-CA3401 from the National Cancer Institute.

Embryos. Normal diploid embryos of R. *pipiens* were obtained by fertilization *in vitro* using precautions to minimize bacterial contamination. Androgenetic haploids were produced by removal of the maternal nucleus (6), gynogenetic haploids by fertilization with photodynamically-inactivated sperm (7). Embryos were reared in 0.25 percent sodium sulfadiazine in sterilized artificial spring water; before use for culture, the embryos were freed of all jelly or adhering membranes, treated for 15 minutes in merthiolate (100 μg/ml), and washed in sterile artificial spring water.

Primary Cultures. The epidermis was removed from a batch of embryos (stage 17-18) by treatment with versene and pipetting (1). The carcasses of 5 embryos were transferred to a drop of balanced salt solution in a plastic petri dish (Falcon, cat. no. 3001) and minced with needles. The dish was then flooded with 2.5 ml growth medium (3) and incubated at 25 °C. In the case of line RPH 67.194, pooled somite tissue from several embryos was isolated by manual dissection and handled further as above.

Subculture Procedure. Primary cultures with a sufficient outgrowth of monolayer cells were treated with trypsin to produce a cell suspension for further passage as monolayer cultures in plastic flasks (Falcon, cat. no. 3012). After removal of growth medium, the monolayer was washed with a salt solution free of divalent cations and supplemented with bovine serum albumin (8). The cells were detached with trypsin 1:250 (0.5 percent in the salt solution mentioned above), suspended in fresh growth medium, and distributed to new culture vessels. This procedure was repeated as soon as the cultures became confluent. The frequency of subcultivation (7–10 days) and the degree of dilution (1:2 to 1:5) into the new cultures are adjusted according to the multiplication rate and growth characteristics of the individual cell lines.

Clonal Isolation. Plastic petri dishes (Falcon, cat. no. 3002) containing 5.0 ml growth medium were seeded with 10^5 x-irradiated cells of a frog line (exposed to 5,000 rad 250 kV x-rays, unfiltered). After incubating the dishes for 48 hours to promote medium conditioning, 300 viable cells were added. After further incubation for 20 days, individual clonal colonies were harvested using stainless steel rings (9) and transferred to new dishes containing feeder layers. After mass cultures were established, further subcultures were made by the procedure described above.

A more complete description of the methods used in culturing frog cell lines is to appear elsewhere (10).

Results

Primary Outgrowth. Within 24 hours, sheets of attached cells laden with yolk platelets are found in association with many tissue fragments: other flattened cells occur free or in small groups on the plastic growth surface. Two predominant types can be recognized: epithelial-like (Fig. 1) and fibroblast-like cells (Fig. 2). On further incubation sheets of yolk-free cells appear which resemble mammalian monolayer cultured cells in their structure.

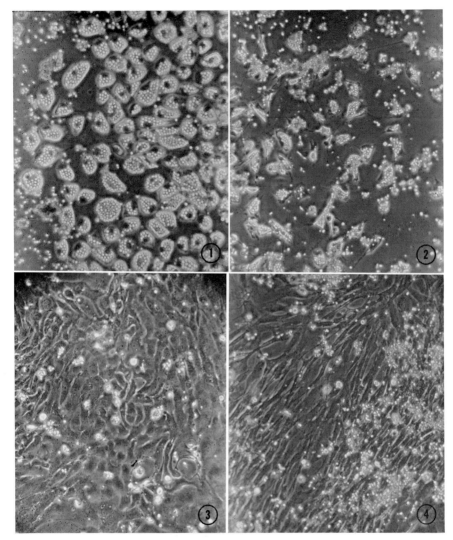

Fig. 1. Yolk-filled, epithelioid cells in primary culture at 48 hrs. Diploid *R. pipiens,* phase contrast, ✕78.

Fig. 2. Yolk-filled, fibroblastic cells in primary culture at 48 hrs. Diploid *R. pipiens,* phase contrast, ✕78.

Fig. 3. Epithelioid cells in first subculture. Some free yolk platelets are visible, but most cells are free of yolk. Diploid *R. pipiens* (line RPD 67.7), phase contrast, ✕78.

Fig. 4. Fibroblastic cells in first subculture, showing parallel orientation. Free yolk platelets overlie part of the cell sheet. Diploid *R. pipiens* (line RPD 67.7), phase contrast, ✕78.

Morphologically differentiated cell types also occur in the primary outgrowth. These include neural cells, myoblast-like spindle cells, myotubes, beating heart muscle and pigment cells.

Subcultures. When primary outgrowths are trypsinized and subcultured, only a minority of the cells reattach. The critical population density for multiplication at this stage is not known, but it has been our experience that successful initiation of a line is likely if the attached cells are separated from each other by only a few cell diameters.

As growth of the first subculture continues, some areas expand by cell multiplication. Morphologically differentiated cells become even rarer than in primary cultures. The following two cell types (11), now free of yolk platelets, continue to dominate the culture:

(a) Epithelial-like (Fig. 3): cells tend to be isodiametric in the plane of the growth surface and remain in contact with one another over extended common borders even in sparsely seeded cultures.

(b) Fibroblast-like (Fig. 4): cells tend to be highly anisodiametric, forming only limited contacts in sparse cultures. In dense culture they tend to become oriented in parallel arrays as shown in Fig. 4.

In some areas of the cultures both cell types occur as localized populations within the cell sheet.

The above observations are based on studies of both haploid and diploid cultures from *R. pipiens* and on diploids from *B. americanus*. As a general rule, if diploid embryos have given successful cultures, haploids from the same clutch of eggs have also grown well. Our observations suggest that haploids require a higher population density for optimal growth than their diploid counterparts but that above this critical density the multiplication rate is equal to that of the diploids.

Serially Cultured Lines. Of the 36 lines now in culture in our laboratory, four are described below to illustrate the diversity of characteristics in cells cultured from anuran embryos.

(1) RPD 67.7. This was established in February 1967 from normal diploid *R. pipiens* embryos as described above. The mode of growth of the cells is fibroblastic, leading to formation of parallel arrays as shown in Fig. 5. The population doubling time in moderately dense culture is about 60 hours. A typical metaphase from the 40th passage is shown in Fig. 14. While many characteristic chromosomes of *R. pipiens* (12) may be recognized, the stem-line is hypotetraploid and not uniform from cell to cell. This line was put in liquid nitrogen storage at passages 19 and 39. A series of clonal isolates has been obtained, carried through 18 passages and also stored in liquid nitrogen.

(2) RPH 67.134. Established in April 1967 from gynogenetic haploid *R. pipiens* embryos, it accumulated a substantial fraction of diploid variants with continued passage. An initially rapid rate of multiplication was observed, but at the present time the population doubling time lies near 50 hours. The cell morphology is moderately fibroblastic, parallel arrays forming in dense cultures. The cells are marked by prominent formation of stress lines, as shown in Fig. 6. The present karyotype is near-

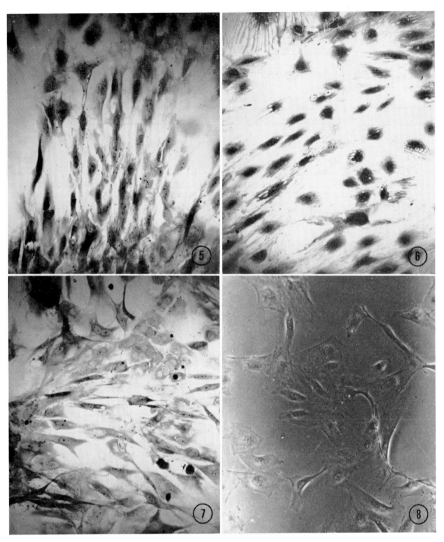

Fig. 5. Cells of line RPD 67.7, passage 30, showing tendency to parallel alignment in a dense culture. Coverslip preparation, fixed in glutaraldehyde and stained in Giemsa, ×120.

Fig. 6. Cells of line RPH 67.134, passage 49. These cells show parallel alignment in dense culture. Formation of prominent stress lines is characteristic of this line. Coverslip preparation, glutaraldehyde-Giemsa, ×120.

Fig. 7. Cells of line RPH 67.194, passage 13. In dense culture, these cells tend to form pavement-like sheets, although elongated, bipolar cells are present, as shown here. Coverslip preparation, glutaraldehyde-Giemsa, ×120.

Fig. 8. Cells of line BA 68.1, passage 25. Cells are large, and tend to form epithelioid areas, with extended lines of contact at cell borders. Phase contrast, ×78.

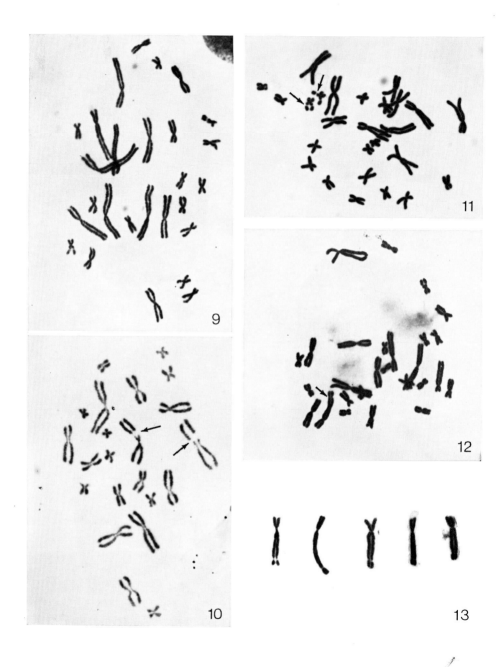

diploid, with most chromosome counts falling in the range 25–28. As shown in Fig. 9, the standard diploid chromosome set is found, with aneuploidy usually confined to the smaller chromosomes.

At the 11th passage, a series of 6 clonal sublines was isolated, designated RPH 67.134c1, c2, etc. These all proved to be diploid (e.g., Fig. 11); no haploid clones were recovered. Population doubling times of these clones ranged from 30 hours to 70 hours. The pattern of growth within a clone was stable on serial passage. An epithelial-like clone (c2) is shown in Fig. 15, a fibroblast-like example (c3) in Fig. 16.

(3) RPH 67.194. This line was established in May 1967 from somite tissue of gynogenetic haploid R. pipiens in an attempt to initiate a line of known tissue origin. Although bipolar, myoblast-like cells were noted in early passages, it has since grown as a mixed cell population; both epithelioid cells and elongated cells occur (Fig. 7).

The chromosomes of this cell line exhibit an unusual marker. The karyotype is near-diploid, with minor aneuploidy (Fig. 12). Both normal secondary constrictions on chromosome 10 are present, but in addition a third secondary constriction regularly occurs near the terminal end of a large acrocentric. Several examples of this chromosome are shown in Fig. 13.

(4) BA 68.1. This line was established from tissue of B. americanus, to be used for future attempts at hybridization with cultures of R. pipiens, and to provide cells for use as feeder layers which could be distinguished from R. pipiens cells by chromosome analysis. The cells show an epithelioid mode of growth, becoming extensively flattened on the plastic surface (Fig. 8). Dividing cells tend to remain in extended contact, leading to formation of cell plaques which eventually coalesce to form a confluent sheet. The population doubling time is near 30 hours. Chromosome number is near the diploid number for Bufo (13), and the chromosomes may readily be distinguished from those of R. pipiens. Useful markers are the pair of large chromosomes bearing secondary constrictions (Fig. 10); these differ notably from the smaller submetacentrics which bear the secondary constrictions in R. pipiens (Fig. 11).

Morphological Diversity of Clonal Isolates. Although the serially cultured lines of frogs' cells are usually predominantly either epithelioid or fibroblastic, individual

Fig. 9. Characteristic metaphase from line RPH 67.134, passage 44, containing 27 chromosomes. ×875.

Fig. 10. Characteristic metaphase from line BA 68.1, passage 19. Note that secondary constrictions (arrows) occur on a pair of large submetacentrics, readily distinguishable from the smaller and more asymmetric chromosomes which bear the secondary constrictions in R. pipiens (compare with Fig. 11). ×875.

Fig. 11. Characteristic metaphase from cloned line RPH 67.134c1, passage 6. Isolated from the parent line at passage 11, while both haploid and diploid cells were present, this and other clones proved to have standard diploid karyotype as shown here. Arrows indicate the secondary constrictions on chromosome 10. ×875.

Fig. 12. Characteristic metaphase from line RPH 67.194, passage 7, showing 27 chromosomes. In addition to the secondary constrictions on chromosome 10, a constriction (arrow) near the end of the long arm of a large acrocentric is characteristic of this line. ×875.

Fig. 13. Examples of the large acrocentric with secondary constriction in line RPH 67.194. Each occurred singly in a separate metaphase. ×875.

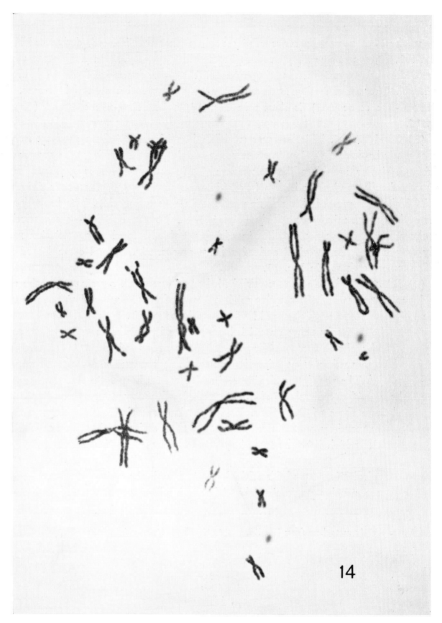

Fig. 14. Photo montage to show a hypotetraploid metaphase ($s = 45$) from line RPD 67.7, passage 40. $\times$1100.

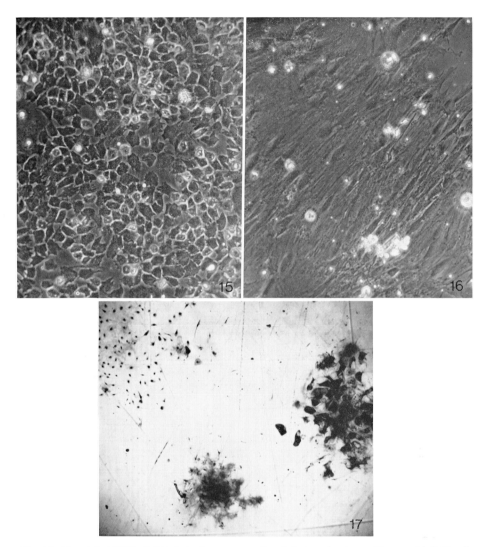

Fig. 15. Cloned line RPH 67.134c2, in first passage after isolation, showing uniform, epithelioid cell morphology. Phase contrast, ×84.

Fig. 16. Cloned line RPH 67.134c3, in first passage after isolation, showing parallel orientation, fibroblastic morphology. This clone was isolated in the same experiment, and from the same parental cell pool, as that shown in Fig. 15. Phase contrast, ×84.

Fig. 17. Clonal colonies shown *in situ* on the surface of a petri dish, from line RPH 67.133, passage 14. Three distinct morphological types are seen: at upper left, fibroblastic cells forming a loose colony; at right, large basophilic epithelioid cells; at bottom, stellate cells. Fixed and stained with Wright's stain 10 days after inoculation. ×12.6.

colonies arising from cells plated out at high dilution show pronounced morphological differences. Fig. 17 shows three adjacent colonies from RPH 67.133, a near-diploid line of haploid origin which is epithelioid when in mass culture. Each colony is a uniform population, but considerable differences from colony to colony are evident.

Discussion

The cultivation of anuran cells in our laboratory has resulted in lines of quite diverse properties. The retention of a near-euploid karyotype, perhaps with minor aneuploidy involving small chromosomes, is common. However, one line (RPD 67.7) is a hypotetraploid and thus repeats the pattern of evolution of altered cell lines found in some mammalian species (14, 15). Whether the unaltered lines become senescent, in the manner of human diploid lines (16), is not yet clear. Decreased growth rates and loss of lines have occurred in our laboratory but have usually been associated with contamination.

Other evidence, from work still in progress, suggests that most of our lines still have the properties of unaltered cells and differ from "established" mammalian lines. The cells of many lines show contact inhibition of movement, forming few overlaps. The cell population density reaches a characteristic stable value at confluence, suggesting a density-dependent inhibition of cell division. Further, when these cells are incubated in spinner flasks, using media with reduced concentrations of divalent cations, they remain suspended and morphologically intact, but fail to multiply.

The behavior of our haploid lines in culture is by no means predictable. Often the haploid cells are overgrown by diploid variants as was the case in our previous culture medium (1). However, two recently derived lines from androgenetic haploids appear to have retained the haploid karyotype. If these lines prove stable on continued passage, they will provide an optimal material for genetic work.

Experiments currently in progress, using these lines, include attempts to isolate drug-resistant and auxotrophic mutants. The nuclear transfer procedure is also being employed to test the capacity of cells from various strains to mediate embryonic development. As noted elsewhere in this symposium, line RPD 67.7 and clones of RPH 67.134 have been employed in other laboratories for virus propagation and support growth of the herpes-like virus of the Lucké tumor (8, 17).

Summary

Tissue from tailbud *Rana pipiens* embryos (haploids and diploids) and from normal diploid embryos of *Bufo americanus* has been used to establish a number of serially cultured lines, of which four are considered in this communication. Primary cultures yield an outgrowth of morphologically undifferentiated cells, which are presumed to act as precursors of the serially cultured populations. Both epithelioid and fibroblastic growth patterns are observed; clonal isolates are usually of a single cell type. The karyotype of haploid *R. pipiens* lines frequently becomes diploid, with development of minor aneuploidy on continued passage; one such line bears a potentially useful chromosome marker. An altered, hypotetraploid stem-line has arisen in one normal diploid *R. pipiens* line which is described. A line of epithelioid cells has been obtained from *B. americanus,* and can be distinguished from *R. pipiens* lines by chromosome analysis.

References

1. FREED, J. J.: Continuous cultivation of cells derived from haploid *Rana pipiens* embryos. Exp. Cell Res. *26:*327–333, 1962.
2. LEIBOVITZ, A.: The growth and maintenance of tissue cell cultures in free gas exchange with the atmosphere. Am. J. Hyg. *78:*173–180, 1963.
3. BALLS, M., and RUBEN, L. N.: Cultivation *in vitro* of normal and neoplastic cells of *Xenopus laevis.* Exp. Cell Res. *43:*694–695, 1966.
4. DiBERARDINO, M.: Frogs. *In* Methods in Developmental Biology (F. H. Wilt and N. K. Wessells, eds.). New York: Thomas Y. Crowell Co., 1966, pp. 53–74.
5. WRIGHT, P. A. and FLATHERS, A. R.: Facilitation of pituitary-induced frog ovulation by progesterone in early fall. Proc. Soc. Exp. Biol. Med. *106:*346–347, 1961.
6. PORTER, K. R.: Androgenetic development of the egg of *Rana pipiens.* Biol. Bull. *77:*233–257, 1939.
7. BRIGGS, R.: An analysis of the inactivation of the frog sperm nucleus by toluidine blue. J. Gen. Physiol. *35:*761–780, 1951–1952.
8. RAFFERTY, K. A.: Personal communication.
9. PUCK, T. T., MARCUS, P. I., and CIECIURA, S. J.: Clonal growth of mammalian cells *in vitro.* Growth characteristics of colonies from single HeLa cells with and without a "feeder" layer. J. Exp. Med. *103:*273–284, 1956.
10. FREED, J. J., and MEZGER-FREED, L.: Culture methods for anuran cells. *In* Methods in Cell Physiology, IV (D. M. Prescott, ed.). New York: Academic Press (in press).
11. Proposed Usage of Animal Tissue Culture Terms, Cancer Res. *27:*828–831, 1967.
12. DiBERARDINO, M.: The karyotype of *Rana pipiens* and investigation of its stability during embryonic differentiation. Devel. Biol. *5:*101–126, 1962.
13. WITSCHI, E.: Chromosomes in the spermatocyte divisions of five North American species of toads. Cytologia *4:*174–181, 1933.
14. HSU, T. C.: Chromosomal evolution in cell populations. Intern. Rev. Cytol. *12:*69–161, 1961.
15. HARRIS, M.: Cell Culture and Somatic Variation. New York: Holt, Rinehart and Winston, 1964.
16. HAYFLICK, L.: The limited *in vitro* lifetime of human diploid cell strains. Exp. Cell Res. *37:*614–636, 1965.
17. GRANOFF, A., GRAVELL, M., and DARLINGTON, R. W.: Studies on the viral etiology of the renal adenocarcinoma of *Rana pipiens* (Lucké tumor). *In* Biology of Amphibian Tumors (M. Mizell, ed.). Springer-Verlag New York Inc., 1969, pp. 279–295.

Species Identification of Poikilothermic
Tissue Culture Cells[1]

Arthur E. Greene, Lewis L. Coriell and Jesse Charney

Institute for Medical Research
Camden, New Jersey

For a number of years this laboratory has been one of those engaged in a program to develop a Central Cell Line Bank and Registry for the characterization and preservation of valuable cell cultures (1).

At the outset of this project it became clear that some cell lines were contaminated with cells of a different species, so that one of our first problems was the development of methods for the identification of the species of origin of tissue culture cell lines.

The rapidly increasing interest in the use of cell cultures of poikilothermic species as necessary tools for research on viral diseases and oncology of cold-blooded vertebrates has further increased the need for constant surveillance and characterization of these cultures in the laboratory in order to assure freedom of contamination with cells of other species.

Several techniques have proved useful in species identification of mammalian cell cultures including: chromosomal analysis, virus susceptibility, immunologic identification and, more recently, the use of isoenzyme analysis. For the purpose of identifying the species of mammalian cell lines characterized for the Cell Culture Collection, immunological techniques were the most practical, rapid and inexpensive. Such techniques as indirect hemagglutination (2), mixed agglutination (3), immunofluorescence (4), immunodiffusion (5) and cytotoxicity (6) have been used and are all reliable and accurate.

In our laboratory we have used the cytotoxic antibody dye exclusion test for species identification because of the rapidity with which the test may be carried out and its freedom from requirement for expensive equipment or experienced personnel. An alternate method which we have also used with success has been the agar gel microimmunodiffusion test. This paper reports the application of the cytotoxic antibody test, the agar gel immunodiffusion test, and isoenzyme analysis for species identification of poikilothermic cell cultures.

Materials and Methods

Tissue Culture

FT— Bullfrog tongue (*Rana catesbeiana*) fibroblasts were obtained from Dr. Kenneth Wolf (7). The cells were grown in Eagle's minimal essential medium (8)

[1] This investigation was supported by Public Health Service Research Grant C-4953 from the National Cancer Institute and Damon Runyon Memorial Fund Grant DRG 924A.

112

in Earle's balanced salt solution (EMEM) and 10% fetal calf serum diluted 4:1 with distilled water to adjust the osmolarity for amphibian tissues.

RTG-2— The line of rainbow trout (*Salmo gairdneri*) epithelial cells, was obtained from Dr. Kenneth Wolf (9). The cells were grown in EMEM and 10% fetal calf serum.

FHM— A continuous cell line of fathead minnow (*Pimephales promelas*) developed by Gravell and Malsberger (10); the cells were grown in Eagle's minimum essential medium in Hanks' balanced salt solution (HMEM) and 10% calf serum.

Grunt Fin— A continuous cell line from the fin tissue of the adult salt-water blue-stripped grunt (*Haemulon sciurus*) developed by Clem *et al.* (11). The cells were grown in HMEM containing 0.196M NaCl and 10% calf and 10% human serum.

Car— An established goldfish (*Carassius auratus*) fin cell line obtained from Dr. L. Moewus-Kobb (12) and grown in HMEM and 15% fetal calf serum.

BF-2— A continuous line of bluegill fry (*Lepomis macrochirus*) cells obtained from Dr. Kenneth Wolf (13). The cells were grown in EMEM and 10% fetal calf serum.

TH-1— A terrapene heart (*Terrapene carolina*) cell line established by Dr. H. F. Clark (14) and grown in HMEM and 10% fetal calf serum.

IgH-2— An established Iguana heart (*Iguana iguana*) cell line established by Dr. H. F. Clark and grown in BME and 10% fetal calf serum.

A6— A continuous cell line obtained from the kidney of a South African clawed toad (*Xenopus laevis*) from Dr. K. Rafferty, Jr., and grown in NCTC 109, 15% distilled water and 10% fetal calf serum.

Human— HeLa cells were grown in HMEM and 10% calf serum.

Chick Embryo— These were secondary chick cells grown from RIF free embryos obtained from Kimber farms. The cells were cultivated in Medium 199 and 6% calf serum according to procedures described by Rubin (15).

Bovine— These were secondary bovine kidney cells grown in Medium 199 and 10% calf serum.

Mouse— The mouse cell lines tested were the 70IP line obtained from Dr. Irene Koprowska (16) and the MMT (mouse mammary tumor line) obtained from Dr. John Sykes (17). The 70IP line was cultivated in HMEM and 10% inactivated calf serum and the MMT line in HMEM and 10% uninactivated calf serum.

Chinese Hamster— A continuous fibroblast-like cell line known as the B14-150 cell line obtained from Dr. T. C. Hsu (18). The cells were grown in McCoy's 5a medium and 10% fetal calf serum (19).

Preparation of Antisera

Antisera were prepared in rabbits by the intraperitoneal injection of human (HeLa), mouse, bovine, chinese hamster, chick, bullfrog tongue, fathead minnow and rainbow trout cells or tissues as detailed previously in publications from this laboratory (6, 20). Antisera to blue-stripped grunt, CAR (goldfish), terrapene heart and South African clawed toad were prepared by the same method except that 6 intramuscular injections of 1 ml of cell suspension or homogenate antigen at 3 day intervals were used instead of the earlier intraperitoneal injections.

The animals were bled 7 days after the last injection and the antisera tested for specific cytotoxic activity against the homologous antigens. The preimmunization sera were found to be negative. All test sera were inactivated at $56°$ for 30 minutes and stored at $-20°$C.

Absorption of Antisera

Absorption of antisera was sometimes required to remove cross-reactivity between antisera of several different species. This was accomplished by absorbing antisera 3 times at $37°$C with an equal volume of packed cell suspensions of the homogenates of heterologous muscle tissue.

The cytotoxic antibody test has been previously described in detail (6) and consists of mixing 100,000 viable tissue culture cells with antisera and fresh guinea pig serum complement. The death of 50% or more of the cells, as shown by trypan blue uptake, is considered evidence of antiserum cytotoxicity. Controls consist of cell suspensions, normal rabbit or calf serum and complement. The results are recorded as percent of viable cells.

Agar Microimmunodiffusion Test Method

The method used was that of Crowle (21) with modifications by Charney and Coriell (22). Extracts of cell cultures were placed in the central well and antisera against different animal species were placed in peripheral wells. The cell extracts were prepared by freezing and thawing centrifuged cell pellets three times.

Isoenzyme Techniques

Isoenzyme patterns of cells were studied by electrophoresis on polyacrylamide gel in a vertical gel apparatus described by Raymond (23). Poikilothermic cell lines were cultured in 250 ml plastic flasks until the cell sheets were confluent at which time the medium was removed and cell sheets washed 3 times with physiological saline. The excess fluid was drained from the cells and 0.5 ml of saline containing a drop of octyl alcohol was added to each flask. Octyl alcohol was used to gently release enzymes from the cells instead of repeated freezing and thawing, to prevent damage to the enzymes. The flasks were stored overnight at $4°$C, then scraped with a rubber policeman and the cells and supernate were centrifuged at 1500 RPM for 15 minutes. The supernate was clarified at 12,000 RPM for 2 hours.

Isoenzyme extracts were also prepared by the above technique from cells taken from ampules containing approximately 1 to 2 million cells/ml after recovery from the frozen state. When the extracts were ready to be added to the acrylamide gel an equal amount of 50% sucrose containing phenol red was mixed with the extract to insure layering of the samples.

Development was carried out by overlaying the polyacrylamide slab with a glass plate coated with agar gel containing the substrate. The substrate preparation for glucose-6-phosphate dehydrogenase (G6PD) consisted of 50 mg of glucose-6-phosphate, 10 mg of MTT (2,5-Diphenyl-3-4 N4, 5-dimethylthiazolyl-2) tetrazolium bromide, 1 mg of PMS (methyl phenazonium methosulfate) and 10 mg NADP in 5 ml of Tris (hydroxymethyl aminomethane) buffer pH 7.4; 5 ml of Tris buffer pH 7.4, 0.1M in $MgSO_4$ containing 1.6% ionagar at $50°$C were added and the solution spread on the glass plate to gel.

The lactate dehydrogenase (LDH) developer gel was prepared as above using 10 mg NAD, 10 mg MTT and 1 mg PMS in 5 ml of 0.3M lactate in Tris buffer pH 7.4. The malate dehydrogenase developer was identical with the lactate developer except that 0.15M malate replaced the lactate.

Results

The data presented in Table 1 demonstrate that it was easy to differentiate the species of a frog and two fish cell lines from each other and from mammalian and chick cells by means of the cytotoxic antibody test.

The homologous antiserum was strongly cytotoxic to the frog tongue cell line. However, cytotoxicity in lesser degree was observed with the heterologous antisera to fathead minnow and to a lesser extent by anti-human, anti-mouse and anti-Chinese hamster sera.

This slight cross-reactivity between bullfrog tongue cells and several non-homologous antisera was eliminated by a 1:4 dilution of the antisera. As shown in Table 2 the frog tongue cells were killed by their homologous sera but not by the heterologous sera when diluted 1:4. Table 1 also shows that whereas the rainbow trout antiserum killed rainbow trout cells better than fathead minnow cells, the fathead minnow antiserum killed the cells of both species. Following cross absorption of these two antisera, both were species specific as shown in Table 3.

The data obtained using the cytotoxic antibody test to distinguish goldfish cells from grunt fin cells is presented in Table 4.

The agar gel immunodiffusion method is an effective test for species identification. Figs. 1 and 2 are examples of this technique. In Fig. 1, terrapene or box turtle

TABLE 1

POIKILOTHERMIC CELL CULTURE SPECIES IDENTIFICATION
WITH THE CYTOTOXICITY TEST

Specific animal antisera [3]	Cells lines tested							
	Bullfrog tongue	Fathead minnow	Rainbow trout	Human (HeLa)	Chick	Mouse	Bovine	Chinese hamster
Bullfrog tongue	10 [1]	93	80	92	80	95	91	93
Fathead minnow	43	7	3	85	95	91	91	96
Rainbow trout	79	86	0	91	83	92	93	96
Human	56	92	76	8	95	88	88	87
Chick	74	94	74	91	3	98	95	95
Mouse	65	94	77	81	94	6	95	90
Bovine	84	90	76	92	90	92	2	89
Chinese hamster	68	89	71	91	81	90	88	1
Control [2]	81	93	77	93	86	91	89	93

[1] Percentage of viable cells after one hour incubation at 37°C.

[2] Preimmunization normal rabbit or normal calf serum.

[3] Specific animal antisera were unabsorbed.

TABLE 2

EFFECT OF SERUM DILUTION ON THE IDENTIFICATION
OF BULLFROG TONGUE (FT) CELLS

Antisera dilution [tested]	Specific animal antisera tested against bullfrog tongue cells								
	Bullfrog	Fathead minnow	Rainbow trout	Human (HeLa)	Chick	Mouse	Bovine	Chinese hamster	Control [2]
Undiluted	10 [1]	43	79	56	74	65	84	68	77
1:4	6	84	90	91	89	91	84	92	90

[1] Percentage of viable cells after one hour incubation at 37°C.

[2] Preimmunization normal rabbit or normal cell serum.

heart cell extract is in the center well, surrounded by antisera prepared against fathead minnow, grunt fin, terrapene and bullfrog cells. The terrapene heart cells formed precipitin lines with the homologous anti-terrapene serum but not with the antisera prepared to minnow, grunt fin or frog.

In Fig. 2, South African clawed toad cell extract is in the center well and in the surrounding wells are antisera prepared against fathead minnow, rainbow trout, CAR (goldfish) and clawed toad. The clawed toad cell extract formed a precipitin line with anti-serum prepared against toad tissue but not the other 3 species.

A recent and interesting development has been the use of isoenzyme analysis for identifying cell populations which have arisen from different species of animals or different individuals within the species. Fig. 3 shows the isoenzyme patterns for glucose-6-phosphate dehydrogenase, lactate dehydrogenase and malate dehydrogenase of grunt fin, bluegill fry, goldfish and fathead minnow cell cultures. These extracts were prepared from cells taken from ampules containing from 1 to 2 million cells after recovery from the frozen state. It is apparent that each species differs in the

TABLE 3

ELIMINATION OF CROSS-REACTIVITY BY ABSORPTION

Antisera	Cell lines	
	Fathead minnow	Rainbow trout
Fathead minnow (unabs.)	9 [1]	9
Fathead minnow (abs.) [2]	5	71
Rainbow trout (unabs.)	83	1
Rainbow trout (abs.) [2]	94	0
Normal rabbit or calf serum (control)	93	71

[1] Percentage of viable cells after one hour incubation at 37°C.

[2] Sera absorbed 3 times with equal volume of fresh heterologous tissue.

TABLE 4

POIKILOTHERMIC CELL CULTURE SPECIES IDENTIFICATION
WITH THE CYTOTOXIC ANTIBODY TEST

	Species antisera tested									
Cell lines tested	Grunt [3] fin	Car [2] (goldfish)	Fat-head [2,3] minnow	Rain-bow [2,3] trout	Human	Mouse	Syrian hamster	Chinese hamster	Bovine	Control [1]
Grunt fin	0	90	89	91	89	90	89	83	88	91
Car	89	5	92	82	90	94	89	95	93	94

[1] Control consisted of preimmunization normal rabbit serum and complement.

[2] Anti-sera to fathead minnow, car (goldfish) and rainbow trout were absorbed with grunt fin tissue.

[3] Anti-sera to fathead minnow, rainbow trout and grunt fin were absorbed with car (goldfish).

Car (*Carassius auratus*) = goldfish.

Fig. 1 (left). Center well: extract of terrapene (box turtle) heart cells: (1) Rabbit anti-fathead minnow; (2) Rabbit anti-grunt fin; (3) Rabbit anti-terrapene (box turtle); (4) Rabbit anti-bullfrog tongue. Precipitin lines are bright as visualized by indirect illumination.

Fig. 2 (right). Center well: extract of South African Clawed Toad: (1) Rabbit anti-fathead minnow; (2) Rabbit anti-rainbow trout; (3) Rabbit anti-CAR (goldfish); (4) Rabbit anti-clawed toad. Stained precipitin line is dark as visualized by direct illumination.

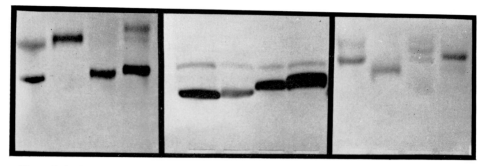

Fig. 3. *Left:* isoenzyme patterns for glucose-6-phosphate dehydrogenase (G6PD); *center:* lactate dehydrogenase (LHD); *right:* malate dehydrogenase (MDH). Cell lines from left to right: grunt fin, bluegill fry, CAR (goldfish) and fathead minnow.

number and mobility of its isoenzymes. This demonstrates how different isoenzymes can assist in identifying the species of a cell line.

Discussion

The development in the 1950's of many permanent cell lines from cells of homeothermic animals resulted in the isolation, identification and study of a multitude of new human and animal viruses of importance to the understanding of human and animal diseases. A similar development is occurring in the field of cold-blooded vertebrate animal research with the establishment of many new poikilothermic tissue culture cell lines and the subsequent isolation and identification of new viruses in these cell lines.

The contamination of mammalian cell lines with cells of different species has been described by a number of investigators and many techniques have been advocated to prevent contamination. The addition of new poikilothermic cell lines in the tissue culture laboratory calls for an extension of cell identification techniques to monitor these new cell cultures.

This study shows that a cytotoxic antibody dye exclusion test which is rapid, inexpensive and easy to perform can distinguish between homeothermic and poikilothermic cells and accurately identify species within the poikilothermic cell cultures. An alternate method which we have also used with success has been the agar gel microimmunodiffusion test in which cell extracts or supernates have been used to type the species of the cells. The use of both cytotoxic antibody and immunodiffusion has enabled us to verify the species of 5 fish, 2 amphibian and a reptilian cell culture. These have been accepted by the Cell Culture Collection Committee for inclusion in the Cell Bank.

A new approach to species identification of cell cultures is the utilization of electrophoretic methods for isoenzyme analysis. Gartler (24) observed that most human heteroploid cell lines contain an abnormal variant form of the isoenzyme glucose-6-phosphate dehydrogenase which suggested that many of the heteroploid human cell lines developed by investigators in the 1950's were derived from HeLa cells through contamination. This was suggested because 100% of the human permanent cell cultures he examined contained the type A+ variant of G6PD which is found in less than 30% of the Negro population and is absent in Caucasians. Gartler's findings have been confirmed in a cooperative study by three of the participating laboratories in the Cell Bank program (1). This study has focused the attention of cell culturists on the utility of isoenzyme techniques for the identification of interspecific and intraspecific cell variants. Preliminary data presented in this paper using glucose-6-phosphate dehydrogenase, lactate dehydrogenase and malate dehydrogenase demonstrate that isoenzyme analysis is a valuable test for species of poikilothermic as well as mammalian cell cultures.

Summary

One of the problems associated with use of tissue cultures has been the contamination of cell lines with cells of different species. This has been a problem with homeothermic cultures and is now of similar importance to investigators using poikilothermic cell lines for biochemical, virus and oncologic investigations. A number of techniques for identifying the species of origin of cell lines have been developed. Two of these methods, the cytotoxic antibody dye exclusion test and agar gel microimmunodiffusion test, were reported here to distinguish between homeothermic and poikilothermic cells and between species within poikilothermic cell cultures. Isoenzyme techniques were also used for interspecies identification of a number of piscine, amphibian and reptilian cell cultures and may eventually be useful for intraspecies identification.

References

1. STULBERG, C. S., CORIELL, L. L., KNIAZEFF, A. J. and SHANNON, J. E.: The animal cell culture collection. In Vitro, in press.
2. BRAND, K. G. and SYVERTON, J. T.: Immunology of cultivated mammalian cells. 1. Species specificity determined by hemagglutination. J. Nat. Cancer Inst. 24:1007–1019, 1960.
3. COOMBS, R. R. A., DANIEL, M. R., GURNER, B. W., and KELUS, A.: Recognition of the species of origin of cells in cultures by mixed agglutination. Use of antisera to red cells. Immunology 4:55–66, 1961.
4. STULBERG, C. S., SIMPSON, W. F., and BERMAN, L.: Species-related antigens of mammalian cell strains as determined by immunofluorescence. Proc. Soc. Exp. Biol. Med. 108: 434–439, 1961.
5. FURMINGER, I. G. S.: Analysis of intracellular antigen to determine the species of origin of cells. J. Path. and Bact. 89:337–342, 1965.
6. GREENE, A. E., CORIELL, L. L., and CHARNEY, J.: A rapid cytotoxic antibody test to determine species of cell cultures. J. Nat. Cancer Inst. 32:779–786, 1964.
7. WOLF, K. and QUIMBY, M. C.: Amphibian cell culture: permanent cell line from the bullfrog (Rana catesbeiana). Science 144:1578–1580, 1964.
8. EAGLE, H.: Amino acid metabolism in mammalian cell cultures. Science 130:432–437, 1959.
9. WOLF, K. and QUIMBY, M. C.: Established eurythermic line of fish cells in vitro. Science 135:1065–1066, 1962.
10. GRAVELL, M. and MALSBERGER, R. G.: A permanent cell line from the Fathead Minnow (Pimephales promelas). Ann. N.Y. Acad. Sci. 126:555–565, 1965.
11. CLEM, L. W., MOEWUS, L. and SIGEL, M. M.: Studies with cells from marine fish in tissue culture. Proc. Soc. Exp. Biol. Med. 108:762–765, 1961.

12. CLEM, L. W., SIGEL, M. M. and FRIIS, R. R.: An orphan virus isolated in marine fish cell tissue culture. Ann. N.Y. Acad. Sci. *126*:343–361, 1965.

13. WOLF, K., GRAVELL, M. and MALSBERGER, R. G.: Lymphocystis virus: isolation and propagation in Centrarchid fish cell lines. Science *151*:1004–1005, 1966.

14. CLARK, H. F. and KARZON, D. T.: Terrapene heart (TH-1), a continuous cell line from the heart of the box turtle *Terrapene carolina*. Exp. Cell Res. *48*:263–268, 1967.

15. RUBIN, H.: An analysis of the assay of Rous Sarcoma cells in vitro by the infective center technique. Virology *10*:29–49, 1960.

16. FERNANDES, M. R. A., and KOPROWSKA, I.: The usefulness of tissue culture cell lines in the development of ascites tumors from a transplantable squamous cell carcinoma. Cancer Res. *25*:444–450, 1965.

17. DMOCHOWSKI, L., GREY, C. E., LANGFORD, P. L., WILLIAMS, W. C., SYKES, J. A., YOUNG, E. L. and MIGLIORI, P. L.: Viral factors in mammary tumorigenesis. Carcinogenesis: a broad critique, 211–256, M. D. Anderson Tumor Institute, Twentieth Annual Symposium, 1966.

18. HUMPHREY, R. M., and HSU, T. C.: Further studies on biological properties of mammalian cell lines resistant to 5-Bromo-deoxyuridine. Texas Reports on Biol. & Med. Supplement 1 to volume *23*:321–336, 1965.

19. HSU, T. C., and KELLOGG, D. S.: Primary cultivation and continuous propagation in vitro of tissues from small biopsy specimen. J. Nat. Cancer Inst. *25*:221–235, 1960.

20. GREENE, A. E., GOLDNER, H., and CORIELL, L. L.: The species identification of poikilothermic tissue culture cells by the cytotoxic antibody test. Growth *30*:305–313, 1966.

21. CROWLE, A. J.: A simplified micro double-diffusion agar precipitin technique. J. Lab. Clin. Med. *52*:784–787, 1958.

22. CHARNEY, J. and CORIELL, L. L.: Demonstration, purification, and partial characterization of abnormal (HSL) antigens in stable human cell lines. J. Nat. Cancer Inst. *33*:285–301, 1964.

23. RAYMOND, S.: Acrylamide gel electrophoresis. Ann. N.Y. Acad. Sci. *121*:350–365, 1964.

24. GARTLER, S.: Genetic markers as tracers in cell cultures. Nat. Cancer Inst. Monogr. *26*:167–178, 1967.

Amino Acid and Nucleoside Incorporation in
Frog Kidney Cells: An Autoradiographic Study

Daniel Malamud [1] and John Tinker

Fels Research Institute, Temple University School of Medicine
Philadelphia, Pennsylvania, and Peter Bent Brigham Hospital

The adult frog (*Rana pipiens*) kidney is of particular interest due to the existence of a spontaneous renal adenocarcinoma (1). Although protein and RNA syntheses have been studied extensively in mammals with autoradiographic methods (for reviews see 2, 3), there is little information regarding macromolecular synthesis in adult amphibian cells. The present study provides an autoradiographic investigation of precursor incorporation into RNA and protein of frog kidney cells cultivated *in vitro* as compared with their *in vivo* counterparts. In addition to the relevance of frog kidney for tumor formation, the preparation of primary cell cultures leads to a stimulation of DNA synthesis and cell proliferation (4, 5). This then provides a model in which to study alterations taking place when a non-dividing cell population is stimulated to enter into DNA synthesis.

Materials and Methods

Radioactive precursors were purchased from Schwarz BioResearch at the following specific activities (C/mmole): ^{3}H-uridine, 2.0; ^{3}H-cytidine, 2.0; ^{3}H-leucine, 1.8; ^{3}H-proline, 1.15; ^{3}H-aspartic acid, 0.3; and ^{3}H-glycine, 1.0. The technique for preparing cell cultures has been described in detail (5, 6). Briefly, kidneys were digested in 0.025 percent Pronase and plated in Eagle's Minimum Essential Medium, diluted with water and supplemented with 20 percent calf serum, 10 percent whole egg ultrafiltrate, and 1 percent non-essential amino acids. Cells were grown on glass coverslips in Falcon culture dishes at 25°C in the presence of 5 percent CO_2.

For pulse labeling, cultures were exposed to radioactively labeled precursor for the times indicated. For "chase" studies, cultures were washed with Ringer's solution containing a one thousand fold excess of unlabeled precursor and the cells then grown in fresh medium. Cells in culture, or tissue slices, were fixed in glacial acetic acid-absolute ethanol (1:3) and extracted with 5 percent cold trichloroacetic acid.

Autoradiograms were prepared by dipping coverslips, mounted on glass microscope slides, into Kodak NTB-2 emulsion, diluted 1:1 with water. Slides were exposed at 4°C for about 2 weeks. After developing, slides were stained through the emulsion with methyl green-pyronin (7). Nuclease extractions were carried out as described previously (5).

---

[1] Present address: Massachusetts General Hospital, Boston, Massachusetts.

For *in vivo* studies, only grain counts over proximal tubule cells were assessed. Tubules were selected under low magnification ($10\times$), with only those tubules presenting a clean cross section being studied. For each determination, at least 10 tubules comprising about 100 cells were counted. Autoradiograms from *in vivo* material were virtually free of background grains. For *in vitro* studies, random cells were selected using low magnification and counted with high magnification ($43\times$). Background in these studies varied and it was necessary to establish a background count for each set of autoradiograms. The data presented in the graphs represent number of grains above background.

Results

Amino Acid Incorporation

Following intraperitoneal injection of ³H-amino acids (1 μ C per gram of body weight), both nuclear and cytoplasmic grains increased to a maximum within 1–3 hours (Fig. 1). Incorporation of ³H-proline was considerably higher than that of the other amino acids studied. Leukopoietic nodules, previously shown to be more active in DNA synthesis (8), showed more intense labeling after injection of ³H-amino acids than adjacent tubule cells. The number of silver grains was not reduced by treatment

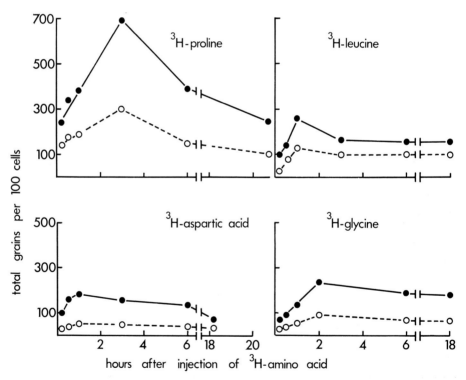

Fig. 1. Incorporation of ³H-amino acids into protein of frog kidney *in vivo*. Frogs were injected with 1 μC per gram body weight of the indicated ³H-amino acid. Grain counts presented for cytoplasmic (●) and nuclear (○) grains located over proximal tubule cells.

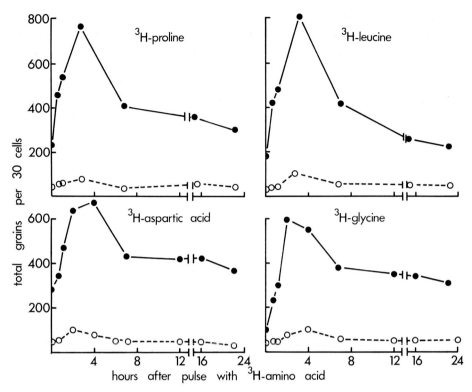

Fig. 2. Incorporation of ³H-amino acids into protein of frog kidney cells *in vitro*. Monolayer cultures were 5–7 days old at start of experiment. Cultures were pulsed with ³H-amino acids (1 μC per ml) for 15 minutes, washed with excess unlabeled amino acid, and chased for the times indicated. Grain counts represent cytoplasmic (●) and nuclear (○) grains.

with 5 percent cold trichloroacetic acid, suggesting that precursor was incorporated into protein. Some of the grains, however, could be due to radioactive aminoacyl-transfer RNA (9).

Cells in culture for 5–7 days were pulse labeled with ³H-amino acids (1 μ C per ml) for 15 minutes, washed with Ringer's solution containing a one thousand fold excess of unlabeled amino acid, and chased with fresh medium for various times. As shown in Fig. 2, the patterns of incorporation for the 4 amino acids investigated were similar. The number of grains over both cytoplasm and nuclei increased for 2–4 hours, cytoplasmic labeling being 6–8 times higher than nuclear labeling. Grain counts decreased from the maximum value, at first rapidly for about 3 hours, and then gradually for at least 40 hours. The decline in grain counts from the maximum value suggested the existence of two classes of proteins, which could be resolved by plotting the grain count semi-logarithmically against time (10). Assuming that there are only two components, the activity may be expressed by the following equation:

$$A = x_1 e^{-k_1 t} + x_2 e^{-k_2 t}$$

where A is the total activity, x_1 and x_2 the activity of each component, and k_1 and k_2 the respective turnover constants. Using data obtained for ^{3}H-proline *in vitro*, it was determined that the protein fraction with a rapid turnover had a half-life of 5.4 hours, while the other fraction had a half-life of 52 hours.

Since increased ^{3}H-proline incorporation characteristic of proximal tubules *in vivo* was not seen in monolayer cultures, it became of interest to follow the early changes which take place when cells are put in culture. Cells were plated (zero time) and pulse labeled with ^{3}H-amino acids (5μ C per ml) for 15 minutes at various times after initiation of cell cultures. As shown in Fig. 3, there was an initial decrease in the number of grains during the first 2 hours in culture. ^{3}H-leucine and ^{3}H-aspartic acid incorporation then increased to above the zero time level. ^{3}H-proline incorporation also decreased, but did not return to the level observed at zero time.

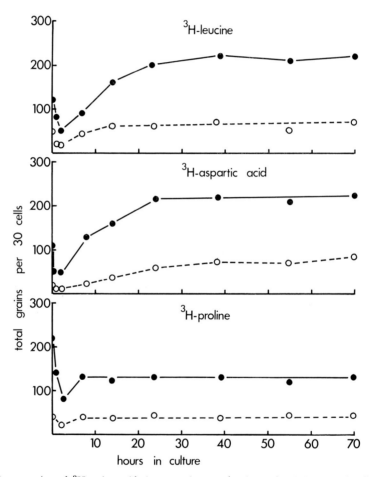

Fig. 3. Incorporation of ^{3}H-amino acids into protein at early times after initiation of cell cultures. Frog kidney cells in suspension (zero time) and at various times after preparation of cell cultures were pulsed with ^{3}H-amino acids (5μC per ml) for 15 minutes and then fixed. Grain counts represent cytoplasmic ($\bullet$) and nuclear ($\bigcirc$) grains.

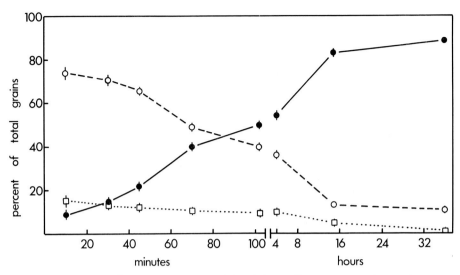

Fig. 4. Incorporation of ^{3}H-uridine into RNA of frog kidney cells *in vitro*. Monolayer cultures were 12 days old at start of experiment. Cultures were pulsed with ^{3}H-uridine (1 μC per ml) for 5 minutes, washed with excess unlabeled nucleoside, and chased for various times. Data presented as percent of total grains over cytoplasm (●), nucleus (○), and nucleolus (□). The total number of grains for each point was 705, 970, 1355, 1950, 767, 768, 543, and 755 respectively. Bars indicate standard error.

Nucleoside Incorporation into RNA

In vivo nucleoside incorporation was studied following intraperitoneal injection of ^{3}H-uridine (1 μ C per gram of body weight). Leukopoietic nodules and glomeruli were labeled 15 minutes after injection of nucleoside. Labeled proximal tubule cells were first seen at 60 minutes after injection of ^{3}H-uridine. At this time, grains were predominantly nuclear. The number of grains was increased 4 hours after injection of ^{3}H-uridine, with leukopoietic nodules still being more heavily labeled than tubule cells. By 12 hours after injection, grains were equally distributed between cytoplasm and nucleus.

For nucleoside incorporation in monolayer cultures, cells were pulse labeled with ^{3}H-uridine or ^{3}H-cytidine (1 μ C per ml) for 5 minutes and washed and chased as described above. Fig. 4 shows that at early times after a pulse with ^{3}H-uridine nuclear grains were predominant, while cytoplasmic labeling became predominant after about 1½ hours. Grains over nucleoli represented only about 10 percent of the total grains. Similar results were obtained with cells in culture from 9–12 days. Using ^{3}H-cytidine as precursor (Fig. 5A), the results were similar, except that nucleolar grains represented about 20 percent of the total grains. Since ^{3}H-cytidine is also incorporated into DNA, it was desirable to use slides incubated in DNase and RNase. These control slides indicated that, over the time interval studied, about 40 percent of the nuclear grains were due to nucleoside incorporation into DNA. Grain counts corrected for incorporation into DNA (Fig. 5B) show that a maximum of 30 percent of the total grains were located over nucleoli.

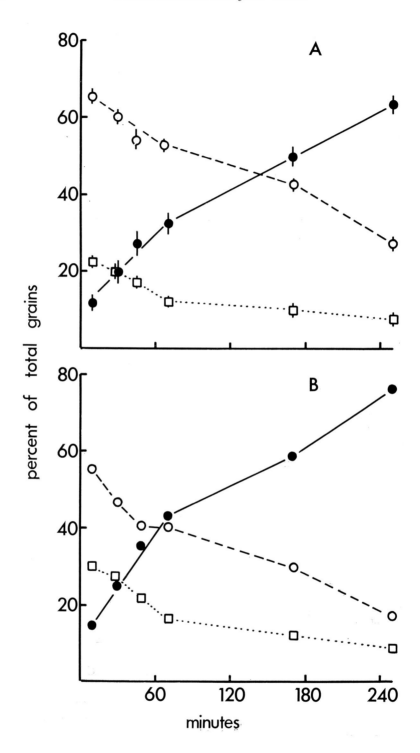

Discussion

The results provide qualitative information regarding incorporation of precursors into protein and RNA of frog kidney cells. No attempt has been made to evaluate the autoradiographic efficiencies of the various cell organelles. Due to self-absorption, grain yield will be lowest in nucleoli, intermediate in nuclei, and greatest from radio-activity present in cytoplasm (11). Thus the observation that 30 percent of the total grains were found over nucleoli after a pulse with ^{3}H-cytidine is an underestimate of the actual radioactivity present in this organelle. Similarly, without precise data on the amino acid pool, it is not possible to equate ^{3}H-amino acid incorporation with protein synthesis. The high proline incorporation observed *in vivo*, for example, may be the result of a small proline pool in the animal. It is clear, however, that there is an alteration in amino acid incorporation when frog kidney cells are placed in culture. The initial decrease in amino acid incorporation may result from the injury inflicted on the cells. It has been shown that there is a leakage of protein and enzymes from Ehrlich ascites cells incubated in isotonic buffer (12, 13). This could result in a decreased incorporation of amino acids into protein. Primary cultures prepared from mammalian kidney cortex, however, showed an immediate increase in amino acid incorporation (4).

In the present study we observed that the striking differences in amino acid incorporation occurring *in vivo* with the four amino acids studied disappear when cells are placed in culture (Figs. 1, 2). There are several possible explanations for these changes: (a) varying incorporation *in vivo* may reflect differences in pool sizes in the animal which are not present *in vitro*; (b) there may be an alteration in the type or amount of protein synthesized *in vitro*; or (c) the observed changes may reflect a change in the cell population. The *in vivo* studies were concerned only with proximal tubule cells. It is not known which types of cells are proliferating *in vitro*, and it is thus possible that cell cultures represent a sub-population of kidney cells. It has been shown, by prelabeling *in vivo* with ^{3}H-thymidine, that leukopoietic cells do not proliferate in culture (unpublished results).

The half-life of proteins determined for frog kidney cells in culture is comparable to results from mouse skeletal tissues in which the rapidly turning over component has a half-life of 2.5–7 hours while the slowly turning over fraction has a half-life of 1.6–5.2 days (14). It appears that the half-life of proteins in frog kidney cells is the same in the animal and in primary cultures (Figs. 1, 2).

The patterns of ^{3}H-uridine and ^{3}H-cytidine incorporation in frog kidney cells are similar to those reported for other cell types (15, 16, 17) with radioactivity being detected first in the nucleus and at later times in the cytoplasm. As reported by Sisken and Kinosita (15), even after a wash with excess unlabeled nucleoside, there is a

---

Fig. 5A. Incorporation of ^{3}H-cytidine into nucleic acids of frog kidney cells *in vitro*. Monolayer cultures were 11 days old at start of experiment. Cultures were pulsed with ^{3}H-cytidine (1 µC per ml) for 5 minutes, washed with excess unlabeled nucleoside, and chased for the times indicated. Percent of total grains over cytoplasm (●), nucleus (○), and nucleoli (□). The total number of grains for each point was 1019, 805, 1092, 1088, 1358, and 1309 respectively.

Fig. 5B. Same as above corrected for ^{3}H-cytidine incorporation into DNA.

continued incorporation of ³H-nucleoside into RNA. The net effect of this phenomenon is to delay the decrease in nuclear radioactivity due to continued incorporation.

Summary

An autoradiographic study of amino acid and nucleoside incorporation into frog kidney cells has been carried out. *In vivo* results indicated considerable differences with the various amino acids used, ³H-proline giving the highest incorporation. These differences disappeared shortly after initiation of primary cultures. In monolayer cultures, results were similar for all of the amino acids studied. By analyzing the decrease in grain count with time it was possible to estimate the turnover of labeled proteins. The patterns of nucleoside incorporation into RNA were similar to those reported for mammalian cells with grains initially located over nuclei, and at later times over cytoplasm.

Acknowledgments

We thank Dr. W. Auclair for his role in the formulation of this study, Dr. T. Sasaki for the calculation of protein half-life, and Drs. R. Baserga, F. Wiebel and R. Hanson for critical reading of the manuscript. This research was supported by American Cancer Society Institutional Grant IN-79.

References

1. Lucké, B.: A neoplastic disease of the kidney of the frog, *Rana pipiens*. Am. J. Cancer 20:352–379, 1934.

2. Leblond, C. P. and Warren, K. B. (eds.): The use of radioautography in investigating protein synthesis. Academic Press, New York, 1965.

3. Baserga, R. and Malamud, D.: Autoradiography: techniques and applications. Paul Hoeber (in press).

4. Lieberman, I., Abrams, R., Hunt, N. and Ove, P.: Levels of enzyme activity and deoxyribonucleic acid synthesis in mammalian cells cultured from the animal. J. Biol. Chem. 238:3955–3965, 1963.

5. Malamud, D.: DNA synthesis and the mitotic cycle in frog kidney cells cultivated *in vitro*. Exp. Cell Res. 45:277–280, 1967.

6. Malamud, D.: Preparation of monolayer cultures from adult frog kidney. Am. Zool. 6:246, 1966.

7. Long, M. E. and Taylor, H. C., Jr.: Nucleolar variability in human neoplastic cells. Ann. N.Y. Acad. Sci. 63:1095–1106, 1956.

8. Malamud, D. and Auclair, W.: Leukopoiesis in the adult frog kidney. Am. Zool. 5:252, 1965.

9. Studzinski, G. P., Jackson, L. G. and Perry, R. P.: Contribution of aminoacyl-transfer ribonucleic acid to protein label in autoradiographic experiments. J. Histochem. Cytochem. 15:702–703, 1967.

10. Droz, B.: Fate of newly synthesized proteins in neurons. *In* The use of radioautography in investigating protein synthesis (C. P. Leblond and K. B. Warren, eds.). Academic Press, New York, pp. 159–174, 1965.

11. Maurer, W. and Primbsch, E.: Grosse der β-selbstabsorption bei der ³H-autoradiographis. Exp. Cell Res. 33:8–18, 1964.

12. Wu, R.: Leakage of enzymes from ascites tumor cells. Cancer Res. *19*:1217–1222, 1959.

13. Holmberg, B.: On the *in vitro* release of cytoplasmic enzymes from ascites tumor cells as compared with strain L cells. Cancer Res. *21*:1386–1393, 1961.

14. Tonna, E. A.,: Protein synthesis and cells of the skeletal system. *In* The use of radio-autography in investigating protein synthesis (C. P. Leblond and K. B. Warren, eds.). Academic Press, New York, 1965.

15. Sisken, J. E. and Kinosita, R.: Intranuclear incorporation of tritiated cytidine. Exp. Cell Res. *24*:168–170, 1961.

16. Rho, J. H. and Bonner, J.: The site of ribonucleic acid synthesis in the isolated nucleus. Proc. Nat. Acad. Sci. *47*:1611–1619, 1961.

17. Feinendegen, L. E., Bond, V. P., Shreeve, W. W. and Painter, R. B.: RNA and DNA metabolism in human tissue culture cells studied with tritiated cytidine. Exp. Cell Res. *19*:443–459, 1960.

Immunity and Tolerance in Amphibia*

EDWIN L. COOPER

Department of Anatomy
School of Medicine
University of California
Los Angeles, California

This section of the symposium will treat immunity and tolerance in Amphibia presenting adult information in all three orders and in larvae where available. The data will be presented as a review of immunity to transplantation antigens, as information pertaining to antibody and immunoglobulin synthesis, and as lymphomyeloid organ control of immunity. This paper is not intended to be an exhaustive account of the subject which would list every known reference, but where feasible pertinent comprehensive reviews are presented. Lastly the information will be considered in light of cancerogenesis.

All aspects of immunity have been investigated in the anurans (Fig. 1) while only one known paper has dealt with urodele humoral immunity (1). A review of transplantation immunity in urodeles can be found in this symposium in the pioneer work of Cohen (2) and will not be dealt with here. In addition, his work treats the maturation of immunity emphasizing thymic control of graft rejection. The Apoda have apparently been largely neglected experimentally; most studies have been confined to taxonomic descriptions. Thus, only one report dealing with transplantation immunity in a caecilian is presented (3). The Urodela and Apoda remain, therefore, uninvestigated groups with respect to immunoglobulin structure and lymphomyeloid organ control of immune responses.

Tolerance and Transplantation Immunity

Some of the earliest transplantations in amphibians were performed by experimental embryologists in eggs, embryos and larvae. Dramatic experiments like those of Spemann and Mangold (4) who transplanted the dorsal lip of the blastopore remain classic in developmental biology and ever remind us of induction, a concept central to cellular differentiation. Tolerance to these transplants of ectoderm (prospective neural plate and epidermis) did not develop during early gastrula; these cells are more plastic with greater differentiating potentials than older cells. Tolerance develops when the capacity to distinguish self from not-self is differentiated in older stages. These early experiments were direct forerunners of the exciting studies of Volpe (5) on parabiotic induced tolerance in *Rana pipiens* larvae to be reported in this symposium.

---

* This work was supported mainly by research grants E-492 from the American Cancer Society and GB 7607 from the National Science Foundation.

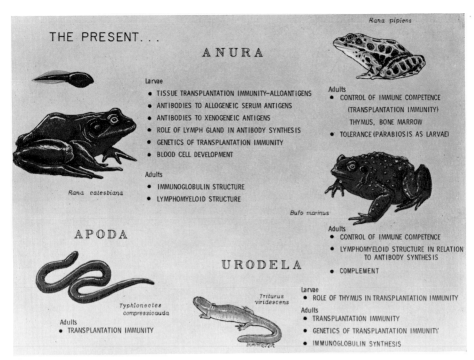

THE PRESENT...

ANURA

Rana pipiens

Rana catesbiana

Larvae
- TISSUE TRANSPLANTATION IMMUNITY–ALLOANTIGENS
- ANTIBODIES TO ALLOGENEIC SERUM ANTIGENS
- ANTIBODIES TO XENOGENEIC ANTIGENS
- ROLE OF LYMPH GLAND IN ANTIBODY SYNTHESIS
- GENETICS OF TRANSPLANTATION IMMUNITY
- BLOOD CELL DEVELOPMENT

Adults
- IMMUNOGLOBULIN STRUCTURE
- LYMPHOMYELOID STRUCTURE

Adults
- CONTROL OF IMMUNE COMPETENCE
  (TRANSPLANTATION IMMUNITY)
  THYMUS, BONE MARROW
- TOLERANCE (PARABIOSIS AS LARVAE)

Bufo marinus

Adults
- CONTROL OF IMMUNE COMPETENCE
- LYMPHOMYELOID STRUCTURE IN RELATION
  TO ANTIBODY SYNTHESIS
- COMPLEMENT

APODA

URODELA

Typhlonectes compressicauda

Triturus viridescens

Adults
- TRANSPLANTATION IMMUNITY

Larvae
- ROLE OF THYMUS IN TRANSPLANTATION IMMUNITY

Adults
- TRANSPLANTATION IMMUNITY
- GENETICS OF TRANSPLANTATION IMMUNITY
- IMMUNOGLOBULIN SYNTHESIS

Fig. 1. This figure summarizes current areas of emphasis in amphibian immunology. Note that the three orders Anura, Urodela, and Apoda have been investigated. The bullfrog has been central in all aspects of immunology.

Loeb (6) reviewed the status of transplantation in Amphibia and cited instances of graft incompatibility in adults and even larvae in his treatise on individuality. It was not until the pioneer work of Hildemann and Haas (7) on transplantation immunity in bullfrog larvae that the incompatibilities cited by Loeb were firmly recognized as immune phenomena. Their work was extremely important since it showed for the first time that a larval animal was capable of mounting an immune response. Going one detailed step further Hildemann and Haas (8) studied the genetic basis of allograft immunity in bullfrog tadpoles by describing the degree of antigenic sharing in several populations.

No doubt the observations of older workers were accurate but certain crucial questions asked during the period when embryonic transplantations were common were different from those of today. Organismic differentials are now considered to be genes (histocompatibility loci) which control acceptance or rejection of tissue grafts (9).

Lymphomyeloid Organ Control of Anuran Transplantation Immunity

The amphibian lymphomyeloid system includes the thymus, spleen, bone marrow and the various lymph nodules found, at least for now, in most anurans throughout the life cycle (10). One of the earliest accounts of lymphomyeloid organ control of immunity in anurans was published by Vogel (11) who showed that splenectomy failed to protect skin allografts from destruction in adult *Rana pipiens*. With regard to transplantation immunogenesis, its control is apparently influenced by the thymus. Bullfrog larvae that have been thymectomized early do not reject transplants as rapidly as animals that have been sham thymectomized (12). Studies on adult control of immunity by lymphomyeloid organs have been investigated by Mandell and Cooper (13). The thymus of adult *Rana pipiens* may assist in renewing immune competence in those animals rendered incompetent by irradiation but protected by autogeneic bone marrow. Frogs without viable autogeneic thymic transplants, after immuno-suppressing doses of irradiation (CO^{60}) and marrow therapy, accepted skin allografts for a longer period than did frogs without transplants. This suggests that the thymus, although exerting its greatest effect on frogs during early life, can be recalled to function, as in young stages, during adult life.

Lymphomyeloid Organ Control of Anuran Humoral Immunity

One of the important contributions to understanding the role of LM organs in antibody synthesis have come from the studies of Evans *et al.* (14). Their work has shown that *Bufo marinus* possesses much cervical lymphoid tissue with pyronino-philic cells which, appear by immunofluorescent methods to synthesize antibodies to BSA (bovine serum albumin). Antibody-forming cells were consistently found in the lymph nodes, kidneys, and spleens in both primary and tertiary responses. Primary follicles were found in the spleen and antibody-forming cells were most numerous at the periphery of the follicles (15). They (15) reported that primary, secondary and tertiary immunization of *Bufo* with STH (*Salmonella typhosa* H antigen) over a period of several months produced persistent 19S response without detectable con-version to 7S antibody. Further contributions from Evans' laboratory on the role of complement in immunity and immunoglobulin synthesis in their amphibian system will be reported by Legler in this symposium (16).

Larval anurans, notably bullfrog tadpoles, have been the subject of investigations of lymphomyeloid organ control of antibody synthesis. Bullfrog tadpoles can synthe-size antibodies to diverse antigens (17) but without the thymus they cannot syn-thesize serum antibodies to certain antigens. Recently it was shown that bullfrog larvae with their lymph glands removed failed to synthesize serum antibodies to BSA (18). Whether control of serum antibody synthesis and tissue graft rejection reside solely in the thymus and lymph gland, independently, is being carried out in our laboratory (19). We strongly suggest that factors such as age and temperature at the time of organ removal affect the results; the lymph gland may be the primary center for antibody synthesis during larval development but the thymus is involved in trans-plantation immunity. What the delicate balance is between lymph gland and thymus control remains to be determined.

Immunoglobulin Structure in Anurans

The work of Legler *et al.* in this symposium (16) will treat the immunoglobulins of *Bufo*. Of much interest in this connection are the studies of Marchalonis and Edelman (20) on immunoglobulins in adult *Rana catesbeiana*. They found that in response to a single injection of bacteriophage, bullfrogs produced two classes of antibodies that resembled γM and γG-immunoglobulins of higher forms. The order of appearance of phage-neutralizing activity in the frog immunoglobulin classes was (a) γM and then γG antibodies. They have suggested that the genes for heavy chains of γG-type (γ-chains) arose at or prior to the phylogenetic level of anuran amphibians.

Relationships Between Immunoglobulin Classes and Lymphoid Structure in Anurans

Of much interest is the apparent conflict between two laboratories involved in studies of immunoglobulins in *Bufo marinus*. Evans (15) and his group have observed cervical lymph nodules in *Bufo*, as well as follicular structure in the spleen. Studying anamnesis using several types of antigen they found: 1) no higher antibody level following second injections of *Salmonella* H antigen nor did they find a conversion from 7S to 19S by means of gel filtration; 2) a doubled mean titer for the secondary response when T_2 coliphage was used as antigen, indicating memory; 3) a reduction in the latent phase after secondary immunization with BSA, additional evidence for the existence of memory.

Diener and Nossal (21) by contrast, believe that the jugular bodies of Amphibia are functionally analogous to lymph nodes of mammals, in that they trap antigen (*Salmonella*) selectively and respond to antigenic stimulation with antibody production. They found no anamnestic response which paralleled the absence of antigen localization in defined areas such as primary and secondary lymphoid follicles. Indeed, Evans *et al.* (14) also found no anamnestic response with *Salmonella* type antigen but anamnesis was demonstrated to T_2 coliphage and BSA. In larval and adult bullfrogs we have observed no follicular structure in LM organs (22, 23, 24) yet Marchalonis and Edelman (20) found an anamnestic response in adult bullfrogs after immunization with bacteriophage T_2. I submit, therefore, that antibody synthesis is solely dependent upon lymphoid and/or plasma cells and macrophages. Anamnestic responses with both types of immunoglobulin are dependent upon kinds of antigens and immunization routes but not the precise arrangement of lymphoid cells into follicles with a large area containing central pyroninophilic cells and peripheral small lymphocytes. If anamnesis were dependent upon strict follicular structure then this could well develop after repeated antigenic stimulation.

Alternatively, escaping vigorous concomitant histologic analysis, the cells could be dispersed singly or only in small groups throughout the parenchyma of a lymphoid organ. Otherwise mammalian type follicular lymphoid structure is not *sine qua non* for memory in amphibians. Obviously, these relationships require more rigorous and precise investigation and remain crucial when dealing with the phylogenesis of immunoglobulin structure. The situation in birds and other vertebrates reported in this symposium by Pollara *et al.* (25) may be different and apparently dependent upon strict follicular structure.

Relationship Between Amphibian Immunity and Neoplasia

The development of cancer in homothermic vertebrates is dependent theoretically upon an immune response, the graft-versus-host reaction (26, 27). According to this theory carcinogenesis begins by the inactivation or loss of histocompatibility genes of normal cells by either irradiation, virus or chemical carcinogen; cell surfaces are correspondingly changed resulting in the proliferation of a now foreign cell in a normal environment like cells do in a graft-versus-host reaction (28). Precise experimental evidence of histocompatibility genes is available in axolotl populations (29) adult leopard frogs (30) and larval bullfrogs (8) and in *Xenopus* clones produced by nuclear transplantation (31). Undoubtedly the central raw materials necessary for this theory, namely genes, are present in the Amphibia.

A plausible analogy between a tissue graft and a neoplasm is suggested; both are foreign inasmuch as they are not normal constituents of the organism. Theories which attempt to explain how an animal handles experimental tissue transplants and spontaneous or transplanted tumors are dependent upon immune responses. The response of an immunologically competent animal to a tissue graft is usually rejection, but enhancement, which is the opposite reaction and dependent on antibody, has been observed (32). Presumably neoplasms are handled in like manner but when enhancement occurs a tumor grows because it escapes, paradoxically, control by the immune system and may operate autonomously. Although we have no information on the presence of antibodies to normal and/or tumor antigens in amphibians second-set normal skin grafts in urodeles and apodans are accelerated and prolonged.

One widely held view about the evolution of immune mechanisms is that the immune system acts to rid an organism of cells which have undergone mutation leading to the production of "not self" cells (33). Whatever may have occurred in the evolution of immune responses as future investigations will continue to reveal (Fig. 2) the Amphibia are at a crucial point in phylogeny because of the first appearance of well defined diverse types of lymphoid accumulations. Thus amphibians, particularly

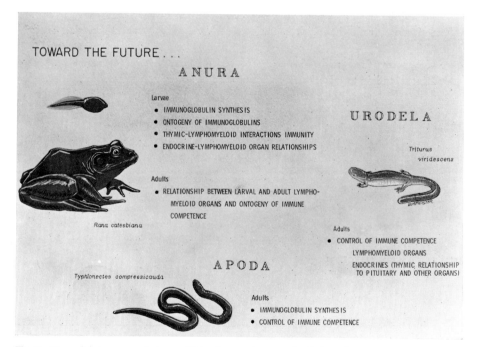

Fig. 2. Areas of future research in amphibian immunology are detailed in this figure which represents a summary of directions that these investigations should go relative to the findings in Fig. 1.

the apodans and urodeles, which may be devoid of these extra lymphoid appendages are even more provocative since their immune control mechanisms may well be correspondingly less complex. Neoplasia would be easier studied where fewer sources of "overseers" or immunologically competent cells are present.

Summary

This paper reviewed evidence for tolerance and immunity in amphibians. Transplantation immunology was emphasized in all three groups with the greater amount of information derived from the Anura and Urodela. Only one work has been cited relative to graft rejection in the Apoda. Tolerance was treated from a historical viewpoint and in relation to current experiments on tolerance to transplantation alloantigens after embryonic parabiosis. The important area of lymphomyeloid structure in relation to immunoglobulin synthesis exclusively in Anura was reviewed. Lastly, the contribution that immunology might make to understanding cancer was also presented.

References

1. CHING-CHUAN-YI, and R. J. WEDGWOOD: Immunologic responses in the axolotl, *Siredon mexicanum*. J. Immunol. 99:191–200, 1967.
2. COHEN, N.: Immunogenetic and developmental aspects of tissue transplantation immunity in urodele amphibians. *In* Biology of Amphibian Tumors (M. Mizell, ed.), Springer-Verlag New York Inc., 1969, pp. 153–168.
3. COOPER, E. L., and F. GARCIA-HERRERA: Chronic skin allograft rejection in the apodan *Typhlonectes compressicauda*. Copeia 2:224–229, 1968.
4. SPEMANN, H. und H. MANGOLD: Über induktion von embryonalanlagen durch implantation artfremder organisatoren. Wilhelm Roux' Arch. Entwicklungsmech. Organ. 100:599–638, 1924.
5. VOLPE, E. P., B. M. GEBHARDT, S. CURTIS and E. M. EARLEY: Immunologic tolerance and blood cell chimerism in experimentally produced parabiotic frogs. *In* Biology of Amphibian Tumors (M. Mizell, ed.), Springer-Verlag New York Inc., 1969, pp. 137–152.
6. LOEB, LEO: The Biological Basis of Individuality. Charles C. Thomas, Publisher, Springfield, Ill. 711 pp., 1945.
7. HILDEMANN, W. H., and R. HAAS: Homotransplantation immunity and tolerance in the bullfrog. J. Immunol. 83:478–485, 1959.
8. HILDEMANN, W. H., and R. HAAS: Histocompatibility genetics of bullfrog populations. Evolution 15:267–271, 1961.
9. SNELL, G. D.: The immunology of tissue transplantation "Conceptual Advances in immunology and Oncology." Hoeber Medical Div. Harper & Row, N.Y., 557 pp., 1963.
10. COOPER, E. L.: Some aspects of the histogenesis of the amphibian lymphomyeloid system and its role in immunity. *In* Ontogeny of Immunity (R. T. Smith, R. A. Good and P. A. Miescher, eds.), University of Florida Press, Gainesville, pp. 87–102, 1967.
11. VOGEL, H. H., JR.: Autoplastic and homoplastic transplantation of skin in adult *Rana pipiens* Schreber. J. Exp. Zool. 85:437–474, 1940.
12. COOPER, E. L., and W. H. HILDEMANN: Allograft reactions in bullfrog larvae in relation to thymectomy. Transplantation 3:446–448, 1965.
13. MANDELL, M. L., and E. L. COOPER: Transplantation immunity in anuran amphibians; bone marrow-thymic interactions. (In preparation.)

14. EVANS, E. E., S. P. KENT, R. E. BRYANT, and M. MEYER: Antibody formation and immunological memory in the marine toad. *In* Phylogeny of Immunity (R. T. Smith, R. A. Good and P. A. Miescher, eds.), University of Florida Press, Gainesville, pp. 218–226, 1966.

15. EVANS, E. E., S. P. KENT, M. H. ATTLEBERGER, C. SEIBERT, R. E. BRYANT, and B. BOOTH: Antibody synthesis in poikilothermic vertebrates. Ann. N.Y. Acad. Sci. *126*:629–646, 1965.

16. LEGLER, D. W., E. E. EVANS, M. H. ATTLEBERGER, and R. T. ACTON: Immunoglobulin and complement systems of amphibian serum. *In* Biology of Amphibian Tumors (M. Mizell, ed.), Springer-Verlag New York Inc., 1969, pp. 169–176.

17. COOPER, E. L., and W. H. HILDEMANN: The immune response of larval bullfrogs. (*Rana catesbeiana*) to diverse antigens. Ann. N.Y. Acad. Sci. *126*:647–661, 1965.

18. COOPER, E. L.: Lymphomyeloid organs of Amphibia III. Antibody synthesis in larval bullfrogs. J. Exptl. Zool. (in press), 1968.

19. BACULI, B. S., and E. L. COOPER: Lymphomyeloid organs of Amphibia V. Antibody synthesis in relation to organ structure. (In preparation.)

20. MARCHALONIS, J. and G. M. EDELMAN: Phylogenetic origins of antibody structure II. Immunoglobulins in the primary immune response of the bullfrog, *Rana catesbeiana*. J. Exp. Med. *124*:901–913, 1966.

21. DIENER, E., and G. J. V. NOSSAL: Phylogenetic studies on the immune response. I. Localization of antigens and immune response in the toad, *Bufo marinus*. Immunology *10*:535–542, 1966.

22. COOPER, E. L.: Lymphomyeloid organs of Amphibia I. Appearance during larval and adult stages of *Rana catesbeiana*. J. Morph. *122*:391–393, 1967.

23. BACULI, B. S., and E. L. COOPER: Lymphomyeloid organs of Amphibia II. Vasculature in larval and adult *Rana catesbeiana*. J. Morph. *123*:473–480, 1967.

24. BACULI, B. S., and E. L. COOPER: Lymphomyeloid organs of Amphibia IV. Normal histology in larval and adult *Rana catesbeiana*. J. Morph. *126*:463–476, 1968.

25. POLLARA, B., W. A. CAIN, J. FINSTAD and R. A. GOOD: The amphibian as a key step in the evolution of lymphoid tissue and diverse immunoglobuin classes. *In* Biology of Amphibian Tumors (M. Mizell, ed.), Springer-Verlag New York Inc., 1969, pp. 177–183.

26. TYLER, A.: Clues to the etiology, pathology and therapy of cancer provided by analogies with transplantation disease. J. Nat. Can. Inst. *25*:1197–1229, 1960.

27. SCHWARTZ, R., J. A. SCHWARTZ, M. Y. K. ARMSTRONG, and L. BELDOTTI: Neoplastic sequelae of allogeneic disease. I. Theoretical considerations and experimental design. Ann. N.Y. Acad. Sci. *129*:804–821, 1966.

28. SIMONSEN, M.: Graft-Versus-Host Reactions. Their natural history and applicability as tools of research. *In* Progress in Allergy (Paul Kallos and Byron H. Waksman, eds.), *6*:349–467, 1962.

29. DELANNEY, L. E., and M. K. BLACKLER: Acceptance and regression of a strain specific lymphosarcoma in Mexican axolotls. *In* Biology of Amphibian Tumors (M. Mizell, ed.), Springer-Verlag New York Inc., 1969, pp. 399–408.

30. NACE, G. W., and C. RICHARDS: Development of biologically defined strains of Amphibia. *In* Biology of Amphibian Tumors (M. Mizell, ed.), Springer-Verlag New York Inc., 1969, pp. 409–418.

31. SIMNETT, J. D.: Histocompatibility in the platanna, *Xenopus laevis laevis* (Daudin) following nuclear transplantation. Exptl. Cell Res. *33*:232–239, 1964.

32. KALISS, N.: Immunological enhancement: Conditions for its expression and its relevance for grafts of normal tissues. Ann. N.Y. Acad. Sci. *129*:155–163, 1966.

33. BURNET, F. M.: Evolution of the immune process in vertebrates. Nature *218*:426–430, 1968.

Immunologic Tolerance and Blood Cell Chimerism in Experimentally Produced Parabiotic Frogs[1]

E. Peter Volpe, Bryan M. Gebhardt,[2] Sherill Curtis [3]
and Elizabeth M. Earley

Department of Biology, Tulane University
New Orleans, Louisiana

Introduction

In 1951, Anderson, Billingham, Lampkin, and Medawar (1) confidently expected that the interchange of skin grafts between members of pairs of cattle twins would serve to distinguish between twins of monozygotic and those of dizygotic origin. It was not unreasonable to presuppose that tissue reciprocally transplanted between two-egg twins would be victimized by the same host immune response that regularly destroys allografts between siblings of separate births. On the other hand, grafts exchanged between one-egg twins should behave as autografts and survive indefinitely. It came therefore as a curious surprise when these investigators found that dizygotic cattle twins freely accept skin grafts from each other, even when the twin pairs are of unlike sex.

The failure of two-egg twins to reject one another's grafts was inevitably linked to Owen's dramatic discovery two decades ago (2) that the blood cell population of each twin is a mosaic of cells of two different genetic constitutions. Each member of a pair possesses not only its own antigenically distinct kind of erythrocyte, but also the antigenic type of its twin. Primordial blood cells are reciprocally exchanged between the twins through vascular anastomoses in embryonic life, and the translocated red cell precursors became established and perpetuate themselves in the hematopoietic tissues of the respective hosts. The chimeric twin calves are incapable of reacting against each other's blood antigens and, as attested by the mutual acceptance of skin grafts, the state of unresponsiveness extends as well to antigens of the skin cells. Skin grafts transplanted to the twins from other calves are destroyed in the expected fashion. From these intriguing findings emerged the thesis that immunological reactivity is suppressed when the animal is exposed to antigenic stimuli before its faculty of immunological response has developed. This is the phenomenon of "acquired immunologic tolerance," as initially set forth by Billingham, Brent and Medawar (3).

The concept of acquired immunologic tolerance was given a definite status by the experimental work of Billingham, Brent, and Medawar (4, 5). Tolerance was experimentally induced in a CBA-strain mouse by injecting the fetus *in utero* with

[1] This investigation was supported by grant GM-11782 from the United States Public Health Service.

[2] *Present address:* Department of Pathology, University of Florida, Gainesville, Florida.

[3] *Present address:* Department of Biology, University of Denver, Denver, Colorado.

137

a suspension of living lymphoid cells from an adult A-line mouse. When the CBA recipient after birth was grafted with A-line skin, it readily accepted the A-line graft as if it were its own. Strict specificity of the induced tolerance was revealed when a skin transplant from an unrelated AU-strain mouse was rejected by the CBA mouse tolerant of A-strain cells. In another laboratory and at about the same time, Hašek (6, 7) simulated experimentally the natural twinning in cattle by fusing the chorio-allantoic membranes of two chick embryos. The artificially paired chicks separated upon hatching, and, in postembryonic life, were incapable of forming antibodies against each other's erythrocytes or of eliciting an immune response against one another's skin. In essence, then, tolerance has been shown to be antigenically specific and systemic. A similar, if not identical, type of specific unresponsiveness can be induced in adult individuals by massive injections of foreign antigen (8–11).

Tolerance conferred in twin cattle may be viewed as a providential natural experiment. The establishment of blood cell chimerism, accompanied by tolerance, depends upon the fortuitous anastomosis of fetal vessels. In approaching the phenomenon of tolerance from an experimental standpoint, it is desirable to use organisms which can be joined in parabiosis at such an early period of development as to ensure the free interchange of blood cells. This desideratum is satisfied by the use of the avian embryo and equally well, if not better, by the amphibian embryo. Indeed, the amphibian embryo holds pride of place in the field of experimental embryology because of the incredible variety of ways that the embryo can be surgically manipulated without seriously impairing its chances of survival. The parabiotic union of frog embryos can be effected at a very early stage of development, before there is any differentiation of blood cells whatever. The present paper embodies results obtained from an extensive series of experiments on embryonal parabiosis in the leopard frog, *Rana pipiens*. Brief reports of some of the experimental findings have already been published (12–14).

Results

A large number of parabiotic pairs of frogs have been experimentally produced, beginning with a small series in September 1964, and continuing until the present. The initial experiments were pilot trials, and the approaches and methodology have become refined as the work has progressed. The data are presented in more or less summary form, and only the more meaningful aspects of the work are copiously considered.

Common Circulation Between Parabionts

The parabiotic union of amphibian embryos is a classical experimental procedure, dating back to the dawn of experimental embryology (15). Whereas early workers tended to join two embryos in the flank region, we proceeded to unite them side-to-side in the area of the gill primordium to ensure vascular communication. As revealed in Fig. 1 (a and b), the embryos were united together at the tail bud stage of development (stage 17, defined in Shumway, 16), approximately 60 hours after fertilization (at 20°C). The operation is performed under a dissecting microscope. The ectoderm covering the gill arch is removed, with a fine glass needle, from the adjacent sides of

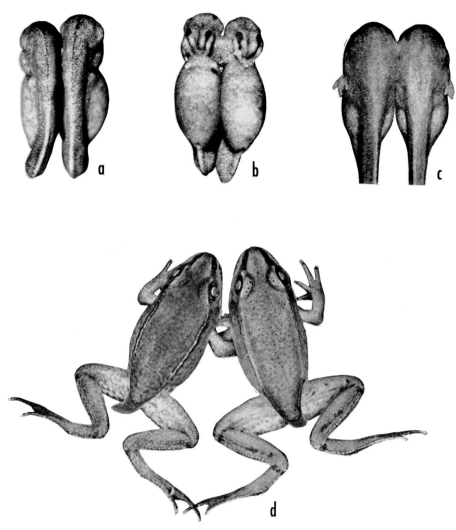

Fig. 1. Postoperative dorsal (a) and ventral (b) views of two embryos in tail bud development (68 hours after fertilization at 20°C) joined in parabiosis in the region of the gill primordium. External gills appear at the free lateral surfaces of the paired members during late embryonic development, 124 hours after fertilization (c). The connection between the parabionts becomes severed during the closing stages of metamorphosis, 82 days after fertilization (d). (In this particular case, the paired members are nonspotted or *burnsi* frogs, well known pattern mutants of the common spotted leopard frog.)

two embryos. The pair, with their cut surfaces closely apposed, are placed in a shallow depression in an agar-bottomed stender dish and are held tightly together by glass bridges. The wounds heal and a connection is established within three to five hours. Fig. 1c shows the period when circulation is established, approximately two days after the operation. In later development, a striking feature of the paired larvae is the failure of the left-hand member to develop an operculum, a fold of skin that normally encloses the gill, or branchial, chamber. As a consequence, the gill chamber of the left-

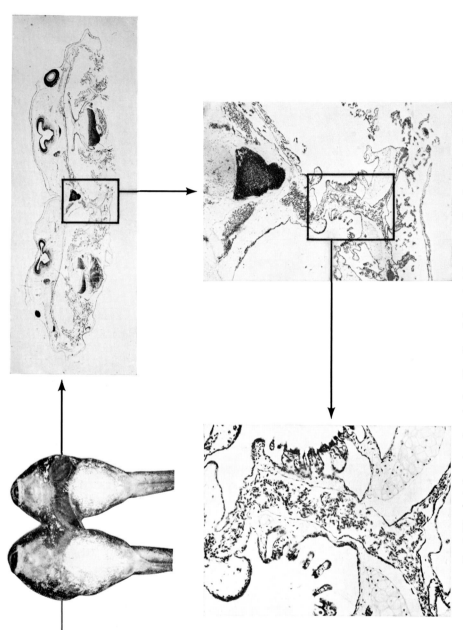

Fig. 2. Histological section through the gill region of the paired larvae revealing the union of circulatory channels of the parabionts. The lateral branchial vessels are fused into a single large median vessel supplying the internal gills of each parabiont.

hand partner remains open to the exterior throughout larval development. This odd condition does not adversely affect the development of either parabiont. That there is actually an intimate association of the circulatory channels is revealed in histological section through the gill region (Fig. 2). Specifically, the lateral branchial vessels leading from the dorsal aortae in the apposed gill regions are coalesced into a single large median vessel supplying the internal gills of each parabiont. There is obviously a complete intermingling of blood.

The co-parabionts typically become disunited during their metamorphosis into juvenile frogs (Fig. 1d). The common skin joining them shrivels and becomes necrotic after the resorption of the internal gills. If, however, tissue areas other than the gill primordium (such as the pronephric swelling) are included in the initial fusion of the embryos, the parabionts remain permanently together. Both types of parabiotic pairs—disjoined and conjoined—offer certain unique advantages for experimental work. We will consider first the experimentation on the conjoined pairs, and then turn to studies on the disjoined or disunited parabiotic frogs.

Skin Grafting Between Conjoined Pairs

As might have been expected, conjoined parabiotic frogs are highly tolerant of one another's skin grafts. As revealed in Fig. 3, the square pieces of exchanged dorsal skins have blended in so perfectly with the host skin that the borders of the skin are scarcely perceptible. These allografts behave like autografts, i.e., they behave like grafts transplanted from one site to another in the same individual. The tolerance is long-enduring; the grafts have persisted in parabiotic frogs for up to a year without any outward sign of deterioration. A few remarks on the technique of free skin grafting employed may be instructive. No special dressings are required. The frogs are anesthetized in pond water containing tricaine methanesulfonate (100 mg/L) and placed side-by-side on cotton, soaked in pond water, in a petri dish. Under a stereoscopic microscope, a piece of dorsal skin, approximately 2 mm square, is cut from each frog with finely sharpened iridectomy scissors. The excised skin is transferred from one frog to the other with watchmaker's forceps. Each graft bed is cleared of excess plasma exudate and the implanted piece of skin is maintained in place, under adequate pressure, with a small strip of moistened lens paper. The grafts typically become affixed within a few hours.

The state of tolerance is specific, for a given parabiont accepts allografts from no donor other than its partner. The fact that the tolerant pair reacts normally to the tissue antigens of a third unrelated party can be used to demonstrate, in its simplest form, the familiar principle of adoptively acquired immunity. That is to say, it can be shown that the sensitivity of one parabiont to an allograft from an unrelated donor is readily transferred to its conjoined partner. The experimental design is shown in Fig. 4. One member only of the parabiotic pair was grafted with skin from an unrelated donor. This transplant was destroyed in typical primary fashion. When the partner was then exposed for the first time to a skin allograft from the same donor frog, he responded by rejecting the graft in an accelerated and violent manner. The heightened reactivity, or secondary response, to the graft may be taken as a vivid demonstration that the faculty of "immunologic memory" had been conferred upon

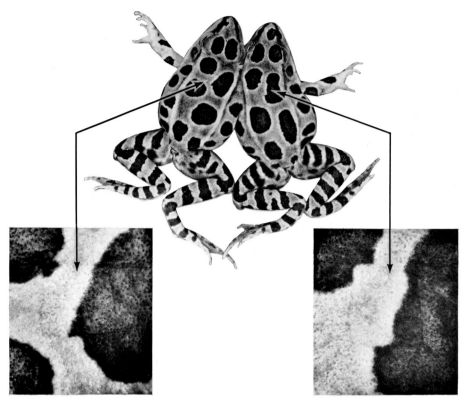

Fig. 3. Successful reciprocal exchanges of square pieces of dorsal skin between the conjoined partners. The enlarged views of the skin allografts reveal the perfectly healthy condition of each graft.

the partner. Nevertheless, the results of this experiment are subject to another interpretation. The alternative, perhaps simpler, explanation is reserved for later discussion.

Skin Grafting Between Disunited Pairs

As with conjoined twins, disunited or separated partners are tolerant of grafts from each other and are intolerant of grafts from unrelated frogs. The viable tolerated grafts are not at all affected by the degeneration of skin allografts from third parties.

One of the distinctive findings emerged when the two members of an ex-parabiotic pair each received skin transplants from an unrelated individual. Ordinarily, skin allografts between genetically diverse frogs are rejected within 18 days at 21°C (17, 18). First-set skin allografts heal in well. The grafted skin vascularizes and thrives for 5 or 6 days, but then progressively deteriorates as manifested by hemostasis, hemorrhaging, and pigment cell destruction. During the period of rejection, the graft bed becomes heavily infiltrated with mononuclear cells, principally lymphocytes (17). The end point of survival of the graft is considered as that day in which there is no or scarcely any trace of viable graft xanthophores (yellow chromatophores).

When pieces of skin from the same donor frog are transplanted to each member of an ex-parabiotic pair, the allografts are rejected but they tend to survive longer than allografts between frogs of ordinary genetic diversity (Fig. 5). At 21°C, skin

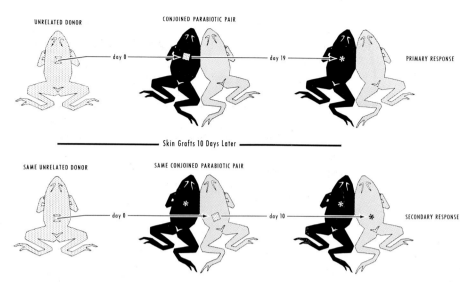

Fig. 4. Demonstration of transfer of allograft immunity. When one member only of a conjoined parabiotic pair is grafted with skin from an unrelated donor, the skin transplant is destroyed in typical primary, or first-set, fashion. Subsequently, the previously unchallenged partner responds anamnestically to a skin allograft from the same donor frog.

grafts transplanted to parabionts may survive for 26–37 days, and as long as 48 days. Apparently, then, each parabiont has a broader spectrum of antigens than does a single frog. This phenomenon does not occur in all cases; the data in Table 1 show that the survival time of allografts from unrelated frogs may either be prolonged ($\geqq$26 days) or fall within the usual limits (14–21 days).

The mutual specific tolerance exhibited by ex-parabiotic frogs and the extended survival of skin allografts from unrelated donors provided strong presumptive evidence that blood cells were interchanged when the ex-parabionts shared a common circulation in embryonic life. The experimental demonstration of chimerism constituted the next phase of the investigation.

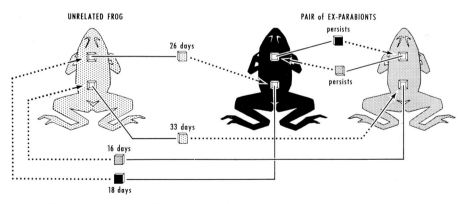

Fig. 5. Skin allografts from a third party to each member of an ex-parabiotic pair of frogs survive longer (26 and 33 days, respectively) than allografts from the ex-parabionts to the same third party (16 and 18 days, respectively).

TABLE 1

Transplantation of Skin Grafts from a Third Party to Each Member of an Ex-Parabiotic Pair, and Reciprocal Transplantations to the Third Party *

Pair		Survival time (in days) of allografts	
		FROM unrelated party	TO unrelated party
1	A	26	16
	B	33	18
2	A	16	17
	B	19	17
3	A	17	14
	B	16	16
4	A	28	15
	B	34	17
5	A	48	19
	B	37	17
6	A	35	18
	B	30	19
7	A	18	17
	B	20	16
8	A	17	18
	B	19	21

* Ex-parabiotic members of a pair are designated "A" and "B."

Blood Cell Chimerism

Owen (2) employed the immunologists' standard technique of differential hemolysis to test for blood cell chimerism in dizygotic twin cattle. Such a procedure is inapplicable to the leopard frog since the necessary lytic reagents or specific antisera are currently unavailable. The problem of testing for blood cell chimerism was approached by bringing into play and combining two experimental procedures that are ideally suited to the leopard frog, namely, the induction of triploidy and the *in vitro* cultivation of leucocytes. Triploidy was induced by pressure treatment, after the method of Dasgupta (19). The second maturation division spindle of the ovulated egg is highly sensitive to hydrostatic pressure. The formation of the second polar body is suppressed when the ovulated egg, 5 minutes after insemination, is subjected to hydrostatic pressure of 5,000 lb/in² for 6 minutes. The resulting embryo is triploid in constitution. One set of chromosomes is paternal (the contribution of the sperm pronucleus) and two sets are maternal (the normal maternal haploid contribution to the zygote and the complement that would normally enter the second polar body).

Triploid embryos obtained by pressure shock were joined to diploid embryos. When the diploid-triploid parabionts became disunited during their metamorphosis into juvenile frogs, blood was taken from the femoral artery of the thigh of each separated member. Two to three drops of whole blood into 4 ml of medium were used to initiate the leucocyte cell cultures (20). Eagle's minimum essential medium for Spinner cultures (Grand Island Biological Co., New York) diluted to isotonicity for amphibian cells was supplemented with 0.5% lactalbumin hydrolysate, 0.03 ml/ml phytohemagglutinin M, 0.4% whole egg ultrafiltrate, 10% fetal bovine serum, and penicillin and streptomycin at final concentrations of 100 units and 100 mcg/ml, respectively. After 3–4 days growth at 25 °C, 3.7 gamma of Colcemid per ml of culture medium was added for 8–12 hours. The cultures were harvested according to the method of Moorhead et al. (21) and the ignition-drying modification of Saksela and Moorhead (22). The preparations were stained in Giemsa.

The chromosome preparations of the cultured leucocytes of each ex-parabiont invariably contained both diploid ($2n = 26$) and triploid ($3n = 39$) metaphase plates (Fig. 6). The foreign, or donor, cells are distinctly in the minority in each postmetamorphic parabiont. As seen in Fig. 7, the incidence of donor cells is low, 15 percent or less, and approximately equal in both parabiotic partners.

The above data indicated only that two genetically distinct kinds of leucocytes were circulating in the bloodstream of each ex-parabiont. The next consideration was to provide evidence that the donor-type stem cells, or hematocytoblasts, had actually homed in the hematopoietic tissues of the host. Cytological preparations of marrow cells from the femur and tibiofibula of the ex-parabiotic frogs revealed the presence of both diploid and triploid metaphase plates. The technique for preparing the marrow cells for cytological study is treated in detail in Volpe and Gebhardt (13). As in peripheral blood, the proportion of donor cells is low, 15 percent or less. It is thus evident that the peripheral blood cell chimerism previously encountered is a permanent condition.

The Larval Blood Cell Populations

In light of the opportunities for a free, if not wholesale, interchange of blood cells between the parabionts in embryonic life, we were unprepared to find the exceedingly low-grade chimerism in the postmetamorphic ex-parabiotic frogs. The finding that donor-type cells are regularly in the minority in the transformed chimeric frog is in contrast to the usual situation in chimeric twin calves, where if one of the two cell types is in the majority in one twin, the same cell type is commonly also in the majority in the other twin (23–25). In other words, in cattle twins, there seems to be no selective advantage to the host's own cell type, and, as a rule, similar equilibria are established in both twins.

In our most recent studies, we have proceeded to take samples of blood from the two members of the parabiotic pair during the larval period. The data indicate that the frequencies of the two cell types in the paired larvae differ considerably from those of the transformed frogs. In two cases (pairs "2" and "4" in Table 2), the

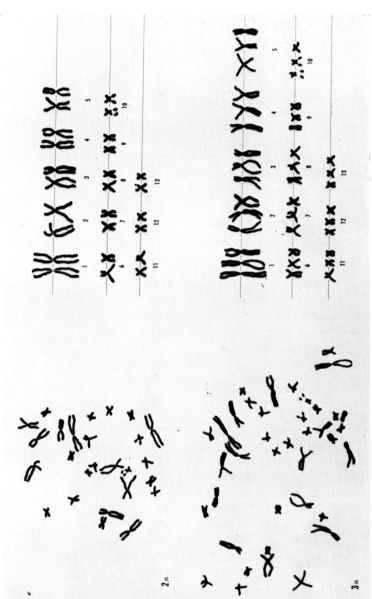

Fig. 6. Metaphase chromosomes from a short-term culture of peripheral leucocytes of an ex-parabiotic frog, accompanied by karyotypes, to reveal the chimeric composition of the leucocyte population ($2n = 26$ chromosomes; $3n = 39$). The chromosomes of the leopard frog, Rana pipiens, comprise a graded size series, divisible into two groups: five large (1–5) and eight relatively small (6–13). The No. 10 chromosome is characterized by a prominent secondary constriction in the long arms.

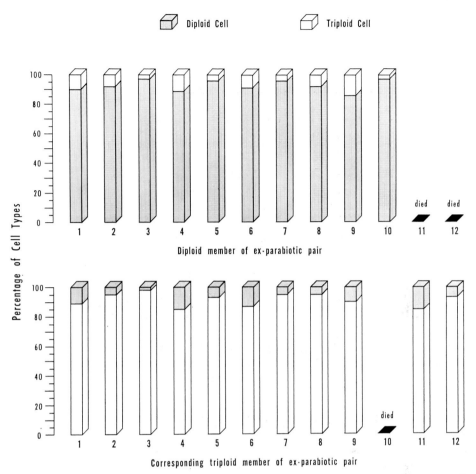

Fig. 7. Ex-parabiotic pairs of frogs in postmetamorphic life contain both diploid ($2n = 26$) and triploid ($3n = 39$) leucocytes. The incidence of donor, or foreign, blood cells in each member is 15 percent or less.

parabiotic larvae contained approximately equal amounts (50%) of each cell type. In three other pairs, the diploid cell type predominated, irrespective of whether the larvae were diploid or triploid (Table 2). Diploid cells may constitute from two-thirds to three-quarters of the total blood cell population of the diploid or triploid larva. Thus, one parabiont may actually possess more of its co-partner's cell type than of its own. A systematic study is now in progress to ascertain the quantitative changes throughout the course of development.

The dividing cells in culture have been identified as either diploid or triploid. Karyotypic analyses of selected metaphase plates have shown that the cells are faithfully diploid or triploid (Fig. 6). No unequivocal case of a third cell type, or "hybrid" cell, has been found.

Finally, we have posed the question as to whether the migration of cells across the vascular bridge is limited to blood cells. In other words, does the chimerism extend to tissues other than blood? Experiments designed to test for germ cell chimerism have

TABLE 2

Cytological Analysis of Peripheral Leucocytes of Conjoined Parabionts
During Mid-larval Development *

Pair		Metaphases Counted	Number of		Percentage of	
			2n cells	3n cells	2n cells	3n cells
1	A	302	197	105	65%	35%
	B	394	263	131	67%	33%
2	A	123	59	64	48%	52%
	B	35	17	18	49%	51%
3	A	257	187	70	73%	27%
	B	187	133	54	71%	29%
4	A	188	91	97	49%	51%
	B	227	122	105	54%	46%
5	A	307	230	77	75%	25%
	B	339	267	72	79%	21%

* The "A" member of a given pair is the triploid individual; the "B" member is the diploid partner.

been negative (14). Whether primitive embryonic cells of other tissues or organs migrate, and are able to establish themselves in the co-partner, awaits additional experimentation.

Discussion and Conclusions

We have seen that two genetically dissimilar frogs that had been joined in parabiotic union in embryonic life are each chimeric with respect to their blood cells. The interchange of primordial blood cells through the enforced common embryonic circulation results in the establishment, in each parabiont, of a genetically foreign cell line which persists into postmetamorphic or adult life. The detection of foreign, or donor-type cells, in parabiotic hosts was made possible by combining diploid ($2n = 26$) and triploid ($3n = 39$) embryos. The co-parabionts, whether conjoined or disunited in postmetamorphic life, freely accept allografts of one another's skin. Ex-parabiotic frogs have been reared apart for periods up to one year, and they have remained highly tolerant of skin grafts from their former partners.

In postmetamorphic ex-parabiotic frogs, we have not witnessed any abatement of the specific mutual tolerance nor any spontaneous disappearance of blood cell chimerism. Stone et al., (26) unexpectedly found that more than 50 percent of the cattle twins, despite their erythrocyte chimerism, lost their capacity to accept one another's grafts. Hašek (27) reported that ex-parabiotic chicks were not capable of forming antibodies against the partner's erythrocytes in later life, even when the chimerism had disappeared.

The tolerant ex-parabiotic frogs are intolerant of skin grafts from unrelated third parties. In several cases, however, skin grafts transplanted from an unrelated frog to both members of a parabiotic pair survived beyond the usual limits (Fig. 5). The prolongation of survival may be attributed to the circumstance that the co-partners, being tolerant of one another's tissue antigens, are in effect tolerant to a broader spectrum of antigens. In other words, the probability of substantial matching of the antigens of donor and host is increased by the wider array of antigens in the host parabionts.

Co-partners that remain permanently attached after metamorphosis permit a novel kind of experiment. When one member only of a conjoined parabiotic pair is grafted with skin from an unrelated frog, it destroys the skin transplant in typical primary fashion. Subsequently, the previously unchallenged partner responds anamnestically to a skin allograft from the same donor frog (Fig. 4). This would seem to be, at first glance, a dramatized demonstration of the classic principle of adoptively acquired immunity, i.e., the stimulated member of the pair transfers its immune state to its previously unconditioned partner. Sensitized cells migrate across the vascular bridge, and the unconditioned partner behaves as if it itself had been immunized with the skin graft placed on the other member. However, it may very well be that sensitized cells were produced in *both* parabionts after one of them had received a skin graft. Since the animals were conjoined, both may have participated in the primary (first-set) response to the single graft placed only on one member. The subsequent heightened responsiveness of the "unchallenged" partner would thus be the consequence of this partner having had previously acquired its immunity actively rather than adoptively.

These deliberations should not obscure an important point: the experiment does show that the agents which participate in an immune response in one partner are present in or can reach the other partner. It is of interest to speculate on the kind of cell that mediates the immune response. The only detectable cells which traverse the vascular connection are blood cells. We may state with assurance that small lymphocytes are among the blood elements that pass across the vascular bridge. We are reasonably certain of this because our means of detecting blood cell chimerism is the *in vitro* cultivation of leucocytes, and small lymphocytes have been implicated as the cells which are stimulated to divide in culture (28). We may even say that the small lymphocytes are provoked by antigenic stimuli to enlarge, divide, and form a large population in much the same manner that they are triggered by phytohemagglutinin to divide in culture. It may be, then, that the small lymphocytes not only are involved in the initiation of transplantation reactions, but are also the vectors or carriers of immunologic memory.

The proportion of the two antigenic types of blood cells apparently changes from the time the parabionts are joined in larval development to the time when the parabionts separate in postmetamorphic life. The percentage of foreign, or donor-type, leucocytes is small in the transformed ex-parabiotic frogs in comparison to the conjoined larvae, where the donor-type leucocytes may be equal to, or even exceed, the percentage of host leucocytes. Perhaps during larval development the donor-type blood cells are able to compete successfully with the resident blood cells in the host, but with the transition to juvenile (transformed) life, the donor-type blood cells become at a selective disadvantage. It is known that profound changes take place in the biochemical characteristics of blood cells and in the hematopoietic sites of the frog during the transition from larval to adult existence. The active sites of hematopoiesis shift from the kidneys in the larva to the spleen and long bones in the transformed frog (29–31). As the larva undergoes metamorphosis, there occurs a change in the type of hemoglobin as well as changes in the nonheme proteins of red blood cells (32–34). The disappearance of larval-type hemoglobin apparently is accompanied by the disappearance of larval-type erythrocytes. Recent studies by Hollyfield (35) indicate that the entire red cell population of the larva is replaced by new erythrocytes at the close of metamorphosis.

These dramatic changes during metamorphosis may place a selective premium on the donor-type blood cells. In other words, selection against the donor-type cells manifests itself or becomes rigorous during and after transformation. There may be a gradual selective overgrowth of the host-type cells at the expense of the donor-type cells. Nevertheless, the shifts in relative proportions of donor and resident cells do not affect the viability of skin allografts exchanged between the partners. As we have seen, skin transplants between the partners during larval development persist unharmed when the larvae transform into juvenile frogs. Evidently, the size or proliferative activity of the donor cell population does not fall below a level as to endanger the state of tolerance.

It would be amiss of us not to mention that the greatest mortality among the parabionts occurs during or shortly after metamorphosis. The causes of death during this period are largely unknown, but it is not inconceivable that the competition between the populations of donor and host cells may frequently have deleterious consequences on the lymphoid tissues and on the animals themselves. In their discussion of parabiotic disease in mice, Nakić, Teplitz, and Ohno (36) have expressed the idea that lymphoid atrophy and eventual death ensues when the rate of destruction of lymphoid tissue resulting from competitive interaction of donor and host cells far exceeds the rate of production of lymphoid cells. Surviving or healthy parabionts are apparently those in which the resident cells are able to largely replace the donor cells without being destroyed themselves in the process.

If the dramatic metamorphic changes upset the earlier stable equilibrium between the two antigenically dissimilar types of cells, then these same altered environmental conditions might furnish the proper setting for somatic cell mating of the two different blood stem cells. Stone, Friedman, and Fregin in 1964 (37) found one case in twin cattle indicative of somatic cell mating *in vitro*. We have yet to uncover evidences of somatic hybridization or segregation in our artificial frog chimeras.

Summary

Genetically dissimilar frogs that had been joined in parabiotic union in embryonic life are each chimeric with respect to their blood cells. The interchange of primordial blood cells through the enforced common embryonic circulation results in the establishment, in each parabiont, of a genetically foreign cell line which persists into postmetamorphic or adult life. The co-parabionts, which become separated from each other during their metamorphosis into juvenile frogs, freely accept allografts of one another's skin. The detection of foreign, or donor-type, cells in parabiotic hosts was made possible by combining diploid ($2n = 26$) and triploid ($3n = 39$) embryos. The proportion of the two antigenic types of blood cells changes from the time the parabionts are joined in larval development to the time when the parabionts separate in postmetamorphic life. The percentage of donor-type leucocytes is small (15 percent or less) in the transformed ex-parabiotic frogs in comparison to the conjoined larvae, where the donor-type leucocytes may be equal to, or even exceed, the percentage of host leucocytes. Apparently, donor-type blood cells during larval development are able to compete successfully with the resident blood cells in the host, but after the transition to juvenile (transformed) life, the donor-type blood cells are at a selective disadvantage.

References

1. ANDERSON, D., BILLINGHAM, R. E., LAMPKIN, G. H., and MEDAWAR, P. B.: The use of skin grafting to distinguish between monozygotic and dizygotic twins in cattle. Heredity 5:379–398, 1951.

2. OWEN, R. D.: Immunogenetic consequences of vascular anastomoses between bovine twins. Science 102:400–401, 1945.

3. BILLINGHAM, R. E., BRENT, L., and MEDAWAR, P. B.: Quantitative studies on tissue transplantation immunity. III. Actively acquired tolerance. Phil. Trans. Roy. Soc. London 239B:357–414, 1956.

4. BILLINGHAM, R. E., BRENT, L., and MEDAWAR, P. B.: "Actively acquired tolerance" of foreign cells. Nature 172:603–606, 1953.

5. BILLINGHAM, R. E., BRENT, L., and MEDAWAR, P. B.: Acquired tolerance of skin homografts. Ann. New York Acad. Sci. 59:409–416, 1955.

6. HAŠEK, M.: Parabiosis in birds during embryonic development. Čsl. Biol. 2:29–31, 1953.

7. HAŠEK, M.: Vegetative hybridization of animals by means of junction of blood circulation during embryonic development. Čsl. Biol. 2:267–282, 1953.

8. BRENT, L., and GOWLAND, G.: Cellular dose and age of host in the induction of tolerance. Nature 192:1265–1267, 1961.

9. GUTTMAN, R. D., and AUST, J. B.: Acquired tolerance to homografts produced by homologous spleen cell injection in adult mice. Nature 192:564–565, 1961.

10. SHAPIRO, F., MARTINEZ, C., SMITH, J. M., and GOOD, R. A.: Tolerance of skin homografts induced in adult mice by multiple injections of homologous spleen cells. Proc. Soc. Exp. Biol. Med. 106:472–475, 1961.

11. BILLINGHAM, R. E., and SILVERS, W. K.: Some factors that determine the ability of cellular inocula to induce tolerance of tissue homografts. J. Cell. and Comp. Physiol. 60 (suppl.):183–200, 1962.

12. VOLPE, E. P., and GEBHARDT, B. M.: Evidence from cultured leucocytes of blood cell chimerism in ex-parabiotic frogs. Science 154:1197–1198, 1966.

13. VOLPE, E. P., and GEBHARDT, B. M.: Chimerism of bone marrow cells in ex-parabiotic frogs. Exp. Cell. Res. 49:194–229, 1968.

14. VOLPE, E. P., and CURTIS, S.: Germ cell chimerism: absence in parabiotic frogs. Science 160:328–329, 1968.

15. BORN, G.: Über verwachsungsversuche mit amphibienlarven. Arch. Entwicklungsmech Organ 4:349–465, 517–623, 1897.

16. SHUMWAY, W.: Stages in the normal development of Rana pipiens. I. External form. Anat. Record 78:139–144, 1940.

17. Volpe, E. P.: Fate of neural crest homotransplants in pattern mutants of the leopard frog. J. Exp. Zool. *157*:179–196, 1964.

18. Volpe, E. P., and Gebhardt, B. M.: Effect of dosage on the survival of embryonic homotransplants in the leopard frog, *Rana pipiens*. J. Exp. Zool. *160*:11–28, 1965.

19. Dasgupta, S.: Induction of triploidy by hydrostatic pressure. J. Exp. Zool. *151*:105–116, 1962.

20. Tips, R. L., Smith, G., Meyer, D. L., and Ushijima, R. N.: Karyotype analysis of leucocytes as a practical laboratory procedure. Texas Rept. Biol. Med. *21*:581–586, 1963.

21. Moorhead, P. S., Nowell, P. C., Mellman, W. J., Batipps, D. M., and Hungerford, D. A.: Chromosome preparations of leucocytes cultured from peripheral blood. Exptl. Cell. Res. *20*:613–616, 1960.

22. Saksela, E., and Moorhead, P. S.: Enhancement of secondary constrictions and the heterochromatic X in human cells. Cytogenetics *1*:225–244, 1962.

23. Owen, R. D., Davis, H. P., and Morgan, R. F.: Quintuplet calves and erythrocyte mosaicism. J. Hered. *37*:291–297, 1947.

24. Mange, A. P., and Stone, W. H.: A spectrophotometric technique for measuring erythrocyte chimerism in cattle. Proc. Soc. Exp. Biol. Med. *102*:107–110, 1959.

25. Stone, W. H., Berman, D. T., Tyler, W. J., and Irwin, M. R.: Blood types of the progeny of a pair of cattle twins showing erythrocyte mosaicism. J. Hered. *51*:136–140, 1960.

26. Stone, W. H., Cragle, R. G., Swanson, E. W., and Brown, D. G.: Skin grafts: delayed rejection between pairs of cattle twins showing erythrocyte chimerism. Science *148*:1335–1336, 1965.

27. Hašek, M.: Abolition of tolerance of skin heterografts by means of serum antibodies. Folia Biol. (Prague) *8*:57, 1962.

28. Edwards, J. H.: Chromosome analysis from capillary blood. Cytogenetics *1*:90–96, 1962.

29. Jordan, H. E., and Speidel, C. C.: Studies on lymphocytes. 1. Effect of splenectomy, experimental hemorrhage and a hemolytic toxin in the frog. Am. J. Anat. *32*:155–188, 1923.

30. Jordan, H. E., and Speidel, C. C.: Blood cell formation and distribution in relation to the mechanism of thyroid-accelerated metamorphosis in the larval frog. J. Exp. Med. *28*:529–542, 1923.

31. Foxon, G. E. H.: Blood and respiration. *In* Physiology of the Amphibia (J. A. Moore, ed.), Academic Press, New York, 151–209, 1964.

32. Frieden, E.: Biochemical adaptation and anuran metamorphosis. Am. Zoologist *1*:115–149, 1961.

33. Baglioni, C., and Sparks, C. E.: A study of hemoglobin differentiation in *Rana catesbeiana*. Develop. Biol. *8*:272–285, 1963.

34. Moss, R., and Ingram, V. M.: The repression and induction by thyroxin of hemoglobin synthesis. Proc. Natl. Acad. Sci. (U.S.) *54*:967–974, 1965.

35. Hollyfield, J. G.: Erythrocyte replacement at metamorphosis in the frog, *Rana pipiens*. J. Morph. *119*:1–6, 1966.

36. Nakić, B., Teplitz, R. L., and Ohno, S.: Cytological analysis of parabiotic disease in mice. Transplantation *4*:22–31, 1966.

37. Stone, W. H., Friedman, J., and Fregin, A.: Possible somatic cell mating in twin cattle with erythrocyte mosaicism. Proc. Natl. Acad. Sci. (U.S.) *51*:1036–1044, 1964.

Immunogenetic and Developmental Aspects of Tissue Transplantation Immunity in Urodele Amphibians[1]

NICHOLAS COHEN

Department of Microbiology
University of Rochester School of Medicine and Dentistry
Rochester, New York

For the past 50 years, transplantation of tissues, organs, and their primordia in embryonic, larval, and adult urodele amphibians has been an essential tool in the continuing study of development (1), regeneration (2), and oncogenesis (3). It is only recently that systematic studies of the immunologic consequences and parameters of transplantation in these ectothermic vertebrates have been undertaken (4–9). This paper will review much of our current knowledge of transplantation immunity in this vertebrate order from the perspectives of comparative and developmental immunology and immunogenetics.

First-set Urodele Allografts

In our laboratory, the transplantation immune response to skin allografts of six genera of randomly breeding salamanders from four different families (Proteidae, Ambystomatidae, Plethodontidae, and Salamandridae) has been systematically evaluated (7). Additional species from the above families have been studied by others (10). The rejection response of all species examined can be divided into a latent phase followed by a rejection phase. The latent phase encompasses that period of full viability when skin allografts heal in, establish vascular connections with host vessels, and remain identical to autografts. In salamanders, this phase lasts approximately two to three weeks (4). The rejection phase is indicated by several externally observable events which are not manifested in autografts. In chronological order these events are secondary vasodilation, hemostasis, hemorrhaging, and melanophore destruction. Histologically, all those gross morphological changes that distinguish allografts from autografts are paralleled first by an increasing infiltration of lymphocytes and second by a gradual destruction of donor tissue. The rejection phase or the interval between its onset (vasodilation and hemostasis) and its completion (melanophore death) lasts between two and four weeks (5). At 25 °C, zero end points of the hundreds of grafts in the different species studied were noted between 8 and 155 days post transplantation. Many instances of indefinite allograft survival (>300 days) have also been observed (5, 7). Typical median survival times (MST's) from a variety of first-set allograft experiments in several species were between 32 and 50 days (Table 1; 7). This long

[1] Supported by grant 553-4-770 from the American Cancer Society and G. R. S. G. grant FRO 5403 to the University of Rochester.

term graft survival, which is usually but not always followed by gradual destruction, is known as chronic rejection. It is in direct contrast to the more typical acute allograft rejection response of other outbreeding vertebrates including fishes (11), frogs (12), and mammals (13). This chronic alloimmune response is not restricted to skin transplants. Although many developmental studies involving diverse allogeneic tissue and organ implants in urodeles have not presented detailed data on the timing and histology of graft rejection, prolonged and indefinite survival were invariably reported (2, 14–22).

First-set Urodele-to-Urodele Xenografts

Orthotopically transplanted mammalian and avian skin xenografts between different species, genera, and orders commonly elicit a more rapid rejection response than allografts (23, 24). Such a statement, however, cannot be broadened to include the Urodela since reciprocal first-set xenografts between four genera (*Diemictylus, Ambystoma, Taricha, Cynops*) of adult urodeles resulted in chronic rejection in six combinations (MST: 32–50 days) and subacute rejection in two combinations (MST: 19 and 24 days). Like urodele allografts, several interfamilial xenografts survived indefinitely (Table 2). Several generalizations which have been dealt with in detail elsewhere

TABLE 1

Median Survival Times (at 25°C) of First- and Second-set Skin
Allografts in Six Genera of Salamanders from Four Families

Species	Total number of allografts scored *		MST values (days)		Range of individual graft survivals (days)	
	1st-set	2nd-set	1st-set	2nd-set	1st-set	2nd-set
Taricha						
torosa	20	19	43.5	23.7	17–72	10–41
Cynops						
pyrrhogaster	15	10	33.0	15.0	28–44	8–33
Diemictylus						
viridescens	30	28	39.5	20.2	21–>200	10–29
Ambystoma						
tigrinum	27	7	39.0	39.0	21–72	36–>100
Desmognathus						
fuscus	25	15	31.5	18.5	22–>100	12–27
Necturus †						
maculosus						
(I)	10	9	46.0	34.0	38–67	25–74
(II)	4	1	116.0	74.0	113–120	—
(III)	4	0	>200		>200	

* Each host received a single first-set and a single second-set transplant.
† A clearly trimodal response was observed (8).

TABLE 2

MEDIAN SURVIVAL TIMES (AT 25°C) OF FIRST- AND SECOND-SET
INTERGENERIC XENOGRAFTS

Donor species	Host species	Total number of xenografts scored *		MST values (days)		Range of individual graft survivals (days)	
		1st-set	2nd-set	1st-set	2nd-set	1st-set	2nd-set
Diemictylus	Cynops	45	16	18.5	7.7	7–27	5–12
Cynops	Diemictylus	19	15	32.5	15.5	29–>500	9–28
Taricha	Cynops	14	14	23.9	9.3	16–32	6–16
Cynops	Taricha	14	12	41.9	18.3	34–52	15–26
Diemictylus	Taricha	19	14	32.0	12.1	20–55	8–21
Taricha	Diemictylus	17	11	50.0	23.5	27–97	11–59
Ambystoma	Diemictylus	53	36	41.2	7.1	17–>200	6–28
Diemictylus	Ambystoma	17	13	32.0	6.6	11–41	3–13

* Each host received a single first-set and a single second-set graft.

(8) are as follows: (1) In each of the four reciprocal xenograft combinations studied, rejection was significantly more rapid in one direction (Fig. 1); (2) Based on MST's, all xenografts on *Diemictylus* recipients survived longer than the control *Diemictylus* allografts used (MST = 22 days) in this particular experimental series. All other hosts rejected xenografts either at the same time as or somewhat more rapidly than allografts (Fig. 1); (3) Not all xenografts were chronically rejected. MST's of both *Taricha* (24 days) and *Diemictylus* (19 days) grafts on *Cynops* recipients were relatively rapid. Although such survival values are still long by mammalian standards, these two rejection reactions differed qualitatively as well as quantitatively from the other six xenograft combinations studied. Significant differences were occasional graft slough- ing, rapid graft lysis, and ischemia throughout the life of most *Diemictylus* grafts on *Cynops* hosts.

Other studies have indicated that in the urodele-to-urodele xenograft system, tissues and organs other than skin also exhibit chronic rejection (25–27).

Allogeneically implanted whole *Diemictylus* embryos develop into teratoma-like growths of extreme histological complexity and diversity (28). When intact swim- ming but not yet feeding larvae from five different species were implanted subcutane- ously or intraperitoneally into adult *Diemictylus,* these grafts also continued to differ- entiate, grow, and metamorphose without obvious immunologic interference in a high percentage of cases (Figs. 2, 3). Even in this xenogeneic system involving older tissues, histological examination of the resulting growths many months or years after implan- tation revealed viable muscle, cartilage, nerves, brain, spinal cord, notochord, meso- nephros, heart, skin, and intestine (29).

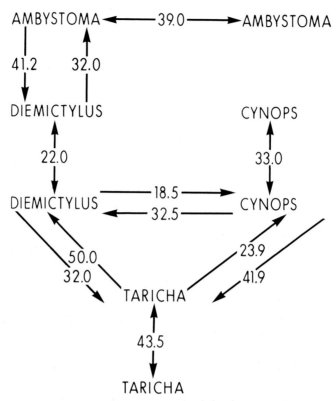

AMBYSTOMA ◄——— 39.0 ———► AMBYSTOMA

41.2   32.0

DIEMICTYLUS   CYNOPS

22.0   33.0

DIEMICTYLUS ——— 18.5 ———► CYNOPS
            ◄——— 32.5 ———

50.0   23.9
32.0   41.9

        TARICHA

         43.5

        TARICHA

Fig. 1. Comparison of the MST (in days) of first-set allografts and xenografts within four genera of salamanders. All *Diemictylus* donors and hosts were from a single population of newts that gave this comparatively rapid allograft rejection time of 22 days (9).

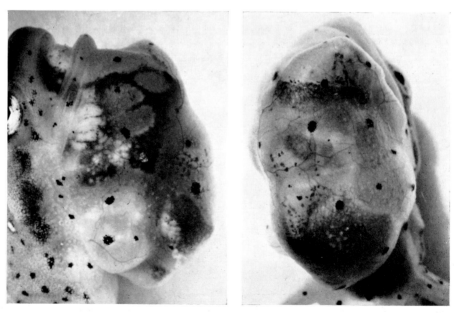

Fig. 2. Implant of *Ambystoma maculatum* larva (stage 40) into *Diemictylus viridescens* throat. Note the extensive growth 537 days post implantation.

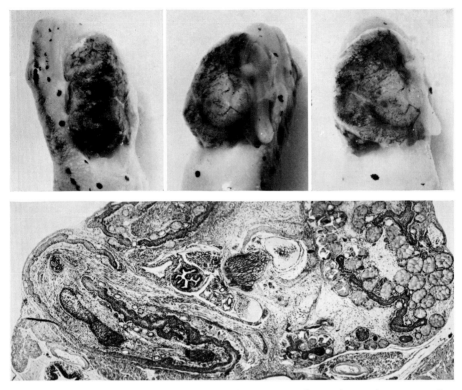

Fig. 3. *Pleurodeles waltlii* larva (stage 53) *implanted* into *Diemictylus viridescens* throat at 500 days. Host skin has been removed. Histological section through one level of the implant reveals skin glands, epidermis, muscle, cartilage, spinal cord, notochord, gut, and mesonephros.

First-set Frog to Salamander Xenografts

When *Rana pipiens* embryos (Shumway stages 18–25) were subcutaneously implanted into the throats of adult *Diemictylus,* extremely rapid implant cytolysis (within 1–2 days) rather than differentiation and growth occurred (29). Cartilage was the only tissue that occasionally differentiated and persisted (Fig. 4). Because of the rapidity of this rejection, cellular immune phenomenon did not appear to be involved. In an extensive series of experiments involving over 100 transplants of adult *Rana pipiens* skin xenografts on *Diemictylus* hosts, two apparently quite different rejection mechanisms were revealed. Between approximately 75% and 100% (depending on the experimental series) of all the ventral and dorsal frog xenografts examined were progressively destroyed between five and fifteen days post transplantation. These grafts constituted a distinct group (group 1) which for reasons to be discussed shortly appeared to be nonimmunologically rejected. A second much smaller group of grafts (group 2) passed through a definite latent period before they were slowly destroyed between 15 and 30 days post transplantation. Rejection of these grafts was accompanied by specific immunological features. The rejection reaction for the group 1 transplants was in part characterized by the early and continual detachment of graft epidermal layers which histologically seemed to be caused by host epidermal ingrowth

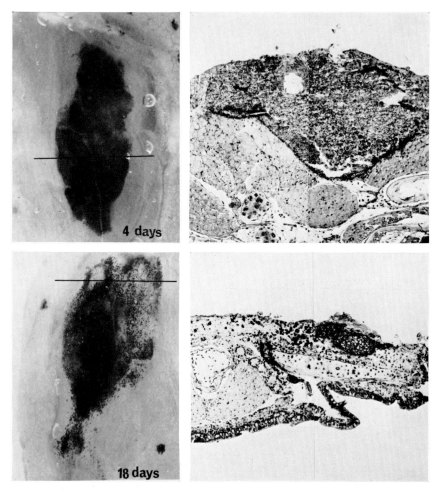

Fig. 4. *Rana pipiens* embryos (stage 18) implanted in the throat of *Diemictylus viridescens*. Host skin has been removed to reveal extensive necrosis at four days. By 18 days all that has differentiated are two nodules of cartilage.

rather than by cell death. Concurrent with epidermal loss was extreme and rapid depigmentation and glandular destruction so that by 12 to 15 days post transplantation only a donor collagen pad covered by host epidermis remained (Fig. 5). This rejection reaction was characterized histologically by donor cell pycnosis and by the influx of host macrophages and polymorphonuclear leukocytes which became engorged with cell debris. However, frequent and periodic histological examinations during these first two post-operative weeks failed to reveal any significant numbers of lymphocytes in either the viable, degenerating, or dead frog tissues. This is in direct contrast to the histopathological picture of urodele allograft and urodele-to-urodele xenograft rejections as well as rejection reactions in other vertebrate orders. Since lymphocytes invading a transplant are known to be the cellular effectors of rejection, and the destruction of group 1 grafts occurred without lymphocytic infiltration, it was

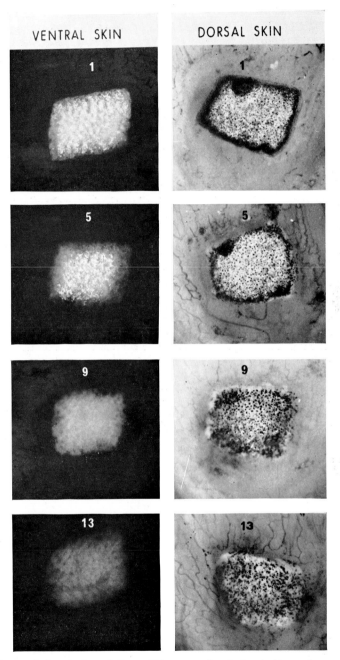

Fig. 5. Nonimmunologic rejection of *Rana pipiens* ventral and dorsal skin grafts transplanted to *Diemictylus* and photographed at 1, 5, 9, and 13 days post transplantation. Note the peripheral melanophore breakup at 9 days and total death by 13 days for the dorsal graft. Xanthophore destruction on the ventral graft is peripheral by 5 days and total at 9 days. Note that only collagen remains at 13 days and that no vascularization has occurred.

hypothesized that this xenograft rejection is not immunologically mediated. Results from three additional critical experiments supported this hypothesis.

1. Following or preceding rejection of first-set frog xenografts, *Diemictylus* recipients received repeat grafts from their original donors. Unlike results in allogeneic combinations, these second-set grafts were not rejected in an accelerated fashion. Therefore, in the absence of demonstrable immunological memory it is doubtful that the first-set rejection response was itself immune.

2. Five hundred to 3000r of whole body x-irradiation administered to newt allograft recipients prevented lymphocyte infiltration and blocked allograft rejection for at least 30 days (7). However, the same dosages of x-irradiation to newt hosts followed by their transplantation with frog skin failed to cause a different pattern of rejection from that of the controls. Since comparable dosages of x-irradiation in mammals suppress not only cellular immunity but the humoral antibody response as well, these data argue quite strongly for a nonimmunologic rejection mechanism.

3. Maintaining allografted newts at 10–15 °C prevents graft destruction and lymphocyte infiltration for over 100 days (7). The MST of allografts on newt hosts kept at 30 °C did not differ significantly from MST's recorded at 23.5 °C. On the other hand, frog skin xenografts on *Diemictylus* maintained at 10–15 °C were totally destroyed (without lymphocyte infiltration) although the rate of destruction was considerably slower than that at 23.5 °C. Frog skin xenografts also underwent accelerated destruction at 30 °C relative to 23.5 °C. In other words, depressed or elevated temperatures in alloimmune transplantation systems appears to exert its effect at the level of the immunocompetent cell (7) while in the frog to salamander xenogeneic system, temperature only seems to influence the kinetics of tissue destruction and removal of debris. The literature reporting the relatively rapid necrosis of xenogeneic implants of frog ganglia (14), kidney (20, 30), and liver (20) into newts also supports the validity of a nonimmunologic rejection mechanism. This type of group 1 graft rejection may well be the result of some as yet unknown physiologically-based incompatibility such as the absence of specific transplant-requiring metabolites or the liberation of some host produced factors toxic for frog tissue. To further test this hypothesis of physiologic incompatibility, studies on the fate of frog skin xenografts on larvally thymectomized immunologically incompetent urodeles are planned. Ruben and others have postulated that the higher success rate of supernumerary limb formation following xenogeneic frog to salamander implants compared with newt allogeneic implants is initially due to the increased immunologic activity and stress set up by the greater immunogenetic disparity between donor and host (3, 31). In the absence of any demonstrable cellular or humoral immune response in the majority of *Rana* to *Diemictylus* transplants we may have to look elsewhere for an explanation of the initial inductive stimulus in such systems of differentiation (31).

Although this nonimmunologic rejection mechanism is responsible for death of the majority of frog xenografts, I have observed some extremely provocative although puzzling instances where frog skin grafts on newt hosts underwent a more chronic loss of epidermis, xanthophores, melanophores, and skin glands between 15 and 30 days post transplantation. Of greatest import is that the cellular infiltrate noted during the course of this more chronic rejection was primarily lymphoid. This suggests that unlike the rejection of group 1 grafts, these group 2 transplants are rejected immunologically. The donor or host factors that determine which type of rejection will occur are unknown. For example, the slow lymphocyte-involved or the rapid nonimmune rejection of a first-set transplant does not dictate the mechanism by which a repeat graft will be rejected.

Regardless of the rapidity with which frog skin grafts are rejected, they remain ischemic throughout their life on salamander hosts. This has been determined by stereomicroscopic observation, by intracardiac injections of hosts with India ink, and by histological analysis. The inability of salamander and frog tissues to establish vascular connections is not restricted to adult systems. When whole tail buds from Shumway stage 17 *Rana pipiens* embryos were transplanted to the ventral flanks of Harrison stages 25–31 *Ambystoma punctatum* embryos, they continued to differentiate and elongate. However, no blood flow occurred in the differentiated frog vessels since donor and host blood vessels failed to establish connections. Although the importance of this phenomenon in the rejection reaction is unknown, its occurrence certainly suggests a basic but nonimmunologic lack of affinity between frog and salamander tissues.

Immunogenetic Basis of Chronic Allograft and Xenograft Rejection

Acute and subacute rejection of the lytic type has characterized the fate of intrapopulation allografts on *Diemictylus v. viridescens* collected from a single geographically isolated population (9). Therefore, it is clear that the more typical chronic urodele graft rejection does not result from an impaired or deficient immune response capacity. Since the rapid rejection of these intrapopulation grafts (MST = 22 days) was quite different from the chronic MST (41 days) of intrapopulation grafts on newts from another isolated pond, the opportunity to study the immunogenetic basis of chronic allograft rejection was presented. Two possibilities were considered and verified by interpopulation transplantation and by second-set and third-party test grafting. First, chronic rejection appears to be due to the interaction of "weak" histocompatibility antigens only. In other words, urodeles, unlike mice (32), rats (33), chickens (34), and man (35), do not have a detectable major or "strong" histocompatibility locus. Second, chronic rejection is also attributed to extensive sharing of transplantation antigens by donor and host (9). In view of this apparent lack of a major histocompatibility locus, instances of acute and subacute rejection have been tentatively explained by the cumulative interactions of several weaker alloantigenic specificites. This synergistic action in urodeles, however, is only a logical extrapolation from experiments with congenic strains of mice (36). In the absence of appropriate mating studies with amphibians, no firm deductions concerning the number of histocompatibility loci, the number of alleles per locus, or allele frequencies within populations can be made.

Since chronic xenograft rejection also seems to result from the interaction of "weak" histocompatibility antigens, these "weak" transplantation alloantigens also function as "weak" antigens in xenogeneic hosts (8). Whether significant transplantation, species-specific, and tissue-specific antigens are common to different genera and families of urodeles—and as such are partly responsible for chronic rejection or indefinite survival—is a most important phylogenetic and immunogenetic question whose definitive answer awaits additional experimentation.

In the past two years well over 75 allografts of the subspecies *Diemictylus viridescens dorsalis* collected from many sites in North Carolina and Florida have been studied. In all experiments, MST's were rather unique for outbreeding urodeles from *diverse* locations in that they were consistently subacute (between 19 and 24 days). Individual graft rejection was lytic, a response that had hitherto been seen routinely only in allografts within one geographically isolated population of *viridescens* and in *Diemictylus* to *Cynops* xenografts. The immunogenetic basis of this more rapid urodele response is currently being investigated by studying the fate of reciprocal *dorsalis-viridescens* transplants and third-party test grafts. Whether speciation of *Diemictylus* involved any major alteration in the histocompatibility gene system will be explored.

The possibility of a sexually dimorphic *dorsalis* or *viridescens* allograft response has been raised but not verified by several authors (5, 37). However, we cannot at this time categorically rule out the possible existence of sex-linked transplantation antigens in urodeles since we are not dealing with inbred strains. In all mammalian species where such antigens have been detected, they have been found to be quite "weak"; hence, their effective presence would not be manifest in outbred salamanders.

The Second-set Response in Allografts and Xenografts

Accelerated second-set rejection has generally been accepted as "proof" of the immunological nature of transplant rejection (38). In view of recent data from my laboratory with urodeles, from Cooper's laboratory with iguanas (39), earthworms (40), and apodans (41), and from Hildeman's laboratory with Syrian hamsters (42), this generalization must now be reevaluated from a phylogenetic and immunogenetic perspective. These data demonstrate that even though original donor second-set MST's for urodele allografts and xenografts are more accelerated than first-set MST's, the overall values do not always reflect the relative survival of individual first- and second-set grafts on the same host. In other words, second-set grafts can survive as long as or longer than first-set grafts as well as being rejected more rapidly (8, 9). This prolonged second-set survival does not appear to be causally related to the interval between first-set rejection and second-set transplantation, since immunological memory in the newt does not wane for at least three months post first-set destruction. Prolonged repeat graft survival may simply be an indication that although different weak alloantigenic combinations are responsible for the same first-set survival times of two different urodele transplants, the state of immunity they confer can differ.

The second-set response of two species, *Taricha* and *Cynops*, has been evaluated with respect to the relative duration of first- and second-set latent and rejection phases (8). The curtailed second-set survival of 50% of the *Taricha* and 60% of the *Cynops* grafts was referable only to a comparatively shorter latent phase. In these hosts, the times required to actually destroy repeat and initial grafts were quite similar. For an almost equal number of repeat grafts in these two species, the second-set rejection phase as well as the latent phase was accelerated. It is only this latter type of overall accelerated rejection that is typically associated with the classic second-set response in mammals differing at "strong" histocompatibility loci (38). This type of secondary response involving only the accelerated latent phase may not be unique to the Urodela. From data on the second-set response of the Syrian hamster (42) it may turn out to be the result of the immunity engendered across "weak" histocompatibility barriers regardless of species.

Ontogeny of Transplantation Immunity

In order to determine at what chronological age the ability to reject allografts in the adult fashion develops, larvae were challenged with tail tip grafts at 20 days and with skin allografts at 30, 40, 50, 60, and 80 days post hatching (43). Grafts which were from nonsiblings of the same chronological age as the recipient, were scored for 100 days post transplantation. By this time either the grafts had remained fully viable, had been totally destroyed, or had undergone partial but not complete rejection. Transplants in this last class either remained at some percentage of full viability or else recovered and appeared fully viable by 100 days. In Table 3 and Fig. 6, the following data are based on the percent of fully viable or totally rejected grafts at various post transplantation intervals. All old adult control allografts exhibited a progressive loss of melanophores; all but one were totally destroyed by 100 days (MST = 39 days). By contrast, all the tail tip grafts remained fully viable by 100 days suggesting complete immunologic immaturity and tolerance induction at 20 days post hatching. Likewise, less than 10% of the grafts placed on 30–50 day old animals were totally destroyed, while 45–61% retained full viability. The remainder of the grafts underwent a 5% to 50% loss of viability. Rejection reactions of the 60 day post hatching animals were indicated in 80% of the grafts by 55 days. However, as the probable result of graft regeneration and incomplete immunologic maturation, many of these grafts returned to an apparent state of full viability by 100 days. Since only 12% of the grafts on 60 day old animals were totally destroyed, this age appears to be transitional in the maturation of immunologic competence.

TABLE 3

The Maturation of Transplantation Immunity in Ambystoma Tigrinum at 25°C

Days post hatching when grafted	Number of grafts scored	Percent scored as zero by 100 days post transplantation	Percent scored as fully viable by 100 days post transplantation
20 days	21 *	0	100
30 days	12	8	50
40 days	20	5	45
50 days	13	8	61
60 days	16	12	20
80 days	40	48	12
Adults †	35	95	0

* In this experiment tail tip grafts were made; in all others skin grafts were used.

† Adults were several years old.

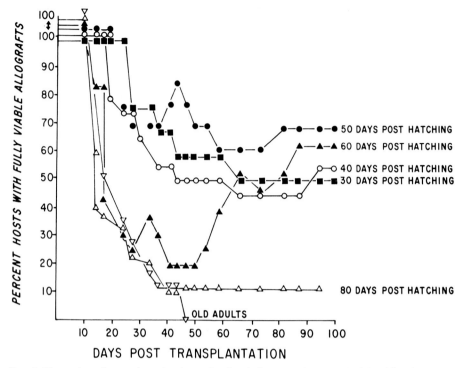

Fig. 6. Maturation of transplantation immunity in *Ambystoma tigrinum* (25°C). The decrease in percent of fully viable skin allografts in each group is plotted against the increasing chronologic age of the hosts.

The fate of transplants on 80 day post hatching animals was more similar to that of adult grafts since 88% of the transplants showed some loss of viability without full recovery. However, even at this age, full immunologic maturity was not reached since only 48% of the 40 grafts examined were totally rejected. These data, then, indicate that the development of immunologic competence to transplantation antigens in *Ambystoma* is quite gradual and does not reach the full level of adult reactivity until at least three months post hatching.

To determine whether this late development of immunologic maturity is under thymic control, tiger salamander larvae were completely thymectomized at 30, 40, 50, and 60 days post transplantation. At 80 days post hatching both intact and previously thymectomized animals received skin allografts from 80 day old donors. The ability to initiate rejection and to carry it to its completion were once again scored in each group over a 100 day period. Fig. 7 presents the percent of fully viable skin allografts at various times following transplantation. Grafts on the intact 80 day old animals studied in the previous experiment served as controls. By 60 days post transplantation the lowest percentage of grafts scored as "less than fully viable" was seen in all groups. It is clear that the younger the recipient at the time of thymectomy the greater the number of fully viable grafts observed at this time. Thymectomy of 30 and 40 day old animals resulted in their treating 80 day old grafts in an identical fashion to that of the 30–40 day old intact animals (Fig. 7) even though they were transplanted at 80 days of age. Hence, the thymus is of critical importance at this time. By 60 days post transplantation, thymectomy of 50 and 60 day old animals was seen to have moderate to no influence, respectively, on the numbers of grafts showing any indication of rejection. However, between 60 and 100 days post transplantation many of these partly rejected grafts in all but the control group recovered in that they were unrecognizable from autografts. It is provocative that the percent of recovery to the fully viable stage was directly related to the age of the animal at thymectomy, i.e., the earlier the ablation, the greater the recovery. Even some of the grafts on animals thymectomized at 60 days fully recovered indicating that the thymus played some role as late as two months post hatching.

Since the maturation of transplantation immunity in this species was assayed with skin allografts of the same chronological age as the recipients, we questioned whether a lack of "maturity" of transplantation antigens themselves might be contributing to or be totally responsible for the apparently slow development of the immune response capacity. Therefore, the fate of skin allografts from 20, 30, 40, 50, 60, and 80 day post hatching *Ambystoma* transplanted to adult *Diemictylus* was compared with the survival of adult *Ambystoma* to adult *Diemictylus* transplants. Both adult and 80 day old *Ambystoma* skin grafts underwent the same typical chronic rejection reaction with MST's between 39 and 45 days. However, the rejection of 20–60 day old skin allografts was much more chronic and many more of the younger grafts exhibited indefinite survival when compared with the older transplants. In view of these data, the relatively slow maturation of transplantation immunity in *Ambystoma* is at least in part a reflection of the "gradual maturing" of the transplantation

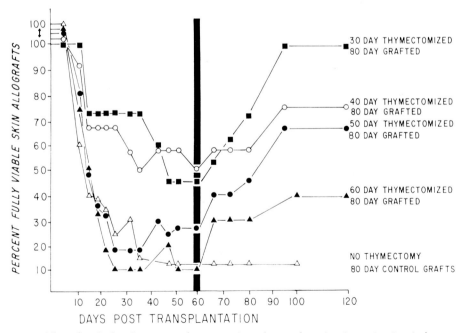

Fig. 7. The role of the thymus on the maturation of transplantation immunity in *Ambystoma tigrinum*.

antigens themselves. However, when salamanders thymectomized during the first month of larval life were challenged at 80 days post hatching with antigenically mature 80 day old skin, they rejected the grafts like an intact one month old larva rather than a three month old adult. Therefore, there must be a relatively slow development of the immune response capacity itself. In summary, the age of the transplant, the age of the recipient, and the presence of the thymus gland are three interacting variables which together with the interplay of weak histocompatibility antigens make the analysis of the ontogeny of immunity a very complex task.

The importance of these studies is, I believe, three-fold. First, a thorough understanding of immunologic responsiveness in this order is significant in the context of comparative and developmental immunology. Second, certain results have proved to be significant in a more broadly based immunogenetic perspective. Since recent evidence reveals chronic rejection phenomena in outbreeding hagfish (44), earthworms (40), apodans (41), iguanas (39), turtles (45), as well as urodeles, we may now have to deal with the evolution of histocompatibility genes and their products themselves. Finally, a better understanding of the immunological aspects of tissue transplantation in the urodeles makes the transplantation technique itself an even more valuable tool in the ongoing studies of development and oncogenesis.

Summary

Skin allografts and urodele-to-urodele xenografts are typically rejected in a chronic fashion. Since newts are capable of a prompt and vigorous rejection when confronted with potent immunogens, chronic rejection does not result from an impaired immune response capacity. Rather, it appears due to a lack of a major histocompatibility locus and to a high degree of antigen sharing.

Most *Rana* skin xenografts to newts undergo a rapid rejection which appears to result from physiologic rather than immunologic incompatibility. A minority of such frog transplants, however, are more chronically destroyed in a lymphocyte-involved reaction.

Unlike endothermic vertebrates, the alloimmune response of at least one urodele species develops quite gradually during the first two months of larval life. This developmental sequence is dependent upon the thymus and upon the maturation of transplantation antigens themselves.

References

1. HAMBURGER, V.: A Manual of Experimental Embryology. The University of Chicago Press, Chicago, Illinois, 1950.
2. BODEMER, C. W.: Observations on the mechanism of induction of supernumerary limbs in adult *Triturus viridescens*. J. Exp. Zool. *140*:79–99, 1959.
3. BALLS, M., and RUBEN, L. N.: Lymphoid tumors in amphibia: a review. Progr. Exp. Tumor Res. *10*:238–260, 1968.
4. COHEN, N.: Tissue transplantation immunity in the adult newt, *Diemictylus viridescens*. I. The latent phase: healing, restoration of circulation, and pigment cell changes in autografts and allografts. J. Exp. Zool. *163*:157–172, 1966a.

5. COHEN, N.: Tissue transplantation immunity in the adult newt, *Diemictylus viridescens*. II. The rejection phase: first and second-set allograft reactions and lack of sexual dimorphism. J. Exp. Zool. *163*:173–190, 1966b.

6. COHEN, N.: Tissue transplantation immunity in the adult newt, *Diemictylus viridescens*. III. The effects of x-irradiation and temperature on the allograft reaction. J. Exp. Zool. *163*:231–240, 1966c.

7. COHEN, N.: 1968 Chronic skin graft rejection in the Urodela. I. A comparative study of first- and second-set allograft reactions. J. Exp. Zool. *167*:37–48, 1968.

8. COHEN, N.: Chronic skin graft rejection in the Urodela. II. A comparative study of xenograft rejection. Transplantation *7*:332–346, 1969.

9. COHEN, N., and HILDEMANN, W. H.: Population studies of allograft rejection in the newt, *Diemictylus viridescens*. Transplantation *6*:208–217, 1968.

10. DELANNEY, E. L.: Homografting of sexually mature Mexican axolotls. Am. Zool. *1*:349, 1961.

11. HILDEMANN, W. H., and HAAS, R.: Comparative studies of homotransplantation in fishes. J. Cell. and Comp. Physiol. *55*:227–234, 1960.

12. HILDEMANN, W. H., and COOPER, E. L.: Immunogenesis of homograft reactions in fishes and amphibians. Fed. Proc. *22*:1145–1151, 1964.

13. RUSSELL, P. S., and MONACO, A. P.: The Biology of Tissue Transplantation. Little, Brown and Company, Boston, Mass., 1965.

14. KAMRIN, A. A., and SINGER, M.: The growth influence of spinal ganglia implanted into the denervated forelimb regenerate of the newt, *Triturus*. J. Morphol. *104*:415–440, 1959.

15. GOSS, R. J.: The relation of bone to the histogenesis of cartilage in regenerating forelimbs and tails of adult *Triturus viridescens*. J. Morphol. *98*:89–123, 1956.

16. HOROWITZ, N. H.: Tissue reactions to the transplantation of muscle in the urodele *Triturus viridescens viridescens*. J. Exp. Zool. *76*:105–113, 1937.

17. STONE, L. S.: The role of retinal pigment cells in regenerating neural retinae of adult salamander eyes. Anat. Rec. *106*:89–110, 1950.

18. STONE, L. S.: Experiments testing the capacity of iris to regenerate neural retina in eyes of adult newts. J. Exp. Zool. *142*:285–308, 1959.

19. STONE, L. S., and ZAUR, I. S.: Reimplantation and transplantation of adult eyes in the Salamander (*Titurus viridescens*) with return of vision. J. Exp. Zool. *85*:243–269, 1940.

20. RUBEN, L. N., and STEVENS, J.: Post-embryonic induction in urodele limbs. J. Morphol. *112*:279–302, 1963.

21. NEWSOME, T. W., and OLCOTT, C.: Transplantation of liver and spleen tissues in *Triturus viridescens*. Senior Thesis Biology Dept., Princeton University, 1963.

22. ADAMS, A. E.: Sexual conditions in *Triturus viridescens*. Artificial hermaphroditism. J. Exp. Zool. *78*:233–269, 1938.

23. PERPER, R. J., and NAJARIAN, J. S.: Experimental renal heterotransplantation. II. Closely related species. Transplantation *4*:700–712, 1966.

24. EGDAHL, R. H., VARCO, R. L., and GOOD, R. A.: Local reactions and lymph node response to skin heterografts between rabbits and rats. Int. Arch. Allergy *13*:129–144, 1958.

25. STONE, L. S.: Vision in eyes of several species of adult newts transplanted to adult *Triturus v. viridescens*. J. Exp. Zool. *153*:57–68, 1963.

26. STONE, L. S., and ELLISON, F. S.: Return of vision in eyes exchanged between adult salamanders of different species. J. Exp. Zool. *100*:217–227, 1945.

27. AMBROSIUS, H.: Heteroplastische gonadentransplantationen bei urodelen. Wissenschaft zeit Karl-Marx Universität *1*:57–100, 1962.

28. FANKHAUSER, G., and STONESIFER, G. L., Jr.: The fate of newt embryos implanted with or without jelly under the skin of adults. J. Exp. Zool. *132*:85–104, 1956.

29. COHEN, N.: The fate of xenogeneic whole larval implants in the newt, *Diemictylus viridescens*. Am. Zool. *4:664*, 1965.

30. CARLSON, B. M.: Studies on the mechanism of implant-induced supernumerary limb formation in urodeles. I. The histology of supernumerary limb formation in the adult newt, *Triturus viridescens*. J. Exp. Zool. *164:227–241*, 1967.

31. RUBEN, L. N.: An immunobiological model of implant-induced urodele supernumerary limb formation. Amer. Nat. *94:427–434*, 1960.

32. SNELL, G. D., and STIMPFLING, J. H.: Genetics of tissue transplantation. *In* Biology of the Laboratory Mouse, 2nd ed., McGraw-Hill, New York, 457–491, 1966.

33. ELKINS, W. L., and PALM, J.: Identification of a single strong histocompatibility locus in the rat by normal spleen cell transfer. Ann. N.Y. Acad. Sci. *129:573–580*, 1966.

34. SCHIERMAN, L. W., and NORDSKOG, A. W.: Immunogenetic studies with fowl: relationship of blood groups to transplantation immunity and tolerance. Ann. N.Y. Acad. Sci. *120:348–355*, 1964.

35. DAUSSET, J., IVANYI, P., and FEINGOLD, N.: Tissue alloantigens present in human leukocytes. Ann. N.Y. Acad. Sci. *129:386–407*, 1966.

36. GRAFF, R. J., SILVERS, W. K., BILLINGHAM, R. E., HILDEMANN, W. H. and SNELL, G. D.: The cumulative effects of histocompatibility antigens. Transplantation *4:605–617*, 1966.

37. ERICKSON, R. P.: Reactions to homografts in *Triturus viridescens*. Transpl. Bull. *30:137–140*, 1962.

38. MEDAWAR, P. B.: A second study of the behavior and fate of skin homografts in rabbits. J. Anat. *79:157–176*, 1945.

39. COOPER, E. L., and APONTE, A.: Chronic allograft rejection in the iguana, *Ctenosaura pectinata*. Proc. Soc. Exp. Biol. Med. *128:150–154*, 1968.

40. COOPER, E. L.: Transplantation immunity in annelids. I. Rejection of xenografts exchanged between *Lumbricus terrestris* and *Eisenia foetida*. Transplantation 6:322–337, 1968.

41. COOPER, E. L., and GARCIA-HERRERA, F.: Chronic skin allograft rejection in the apodan, *Typhlonectes compressicauda* Copeia, No. 2, 224–229, 1968.

42. HILDEMANN, W. H., and WALFORD, R. L.: Chronic skin homograft rejection in the Syrian hamster. Ann. N.Y. Acad. Sci. *87:56–77*, 1960.

43. COHEN, N.: The maturation of transplantation immunity in the salamander, *Ambystoma tigrinum*. Amer. Zool. *7:763*, 1967.

44. HILDEMANN, W. H.: Personal communications, 1968.

45. BORYSENKO, M.: Studies on the immune response of the snapping turtle, *Chelydra serpentina*, to allogeneic and xenogeneic transplants. Doctoral Dissertation S.U.N.Y. Upstate Medical Center, Syracuse, N.Y., 1968.

Immunoglobulin and Complement Systems
of Amphibian Serum*

Donald W. Legler, E. Edward Evans, Peter F. Weinheimer,
Ronald T. Acton and Marie H. Attleberger

Department of Microbiology
University of Alabama Medical Center
Birmingham, Alabama

Current advances in knowledge of mammalian immunoglobulin structure have spurred investigative efforts directed toward the development of more primitive study models. Historical observations of Metchnikoff (1) and Widal and Sicard (2) described the capacity for antibody production and its temperature dependence in amphibians. These early observations provided the basis for recent renewed emphasis on research in this field.

Progress with mammalian systems, primarily utilizing guinea pig serum as a source, has shown that serum complement is a complex reaction sequence consisting of at least nine serum components (3). Considerable interest has developed recently in the role of complement in graft rejection phenomena and certain auto-immune diseases (4). In addition to the reaction of whole complement with specific antibody which effects cellular lysis, certain complement components are intimately involved with the chemotaxis of leukocytes, increases in vascular permeability, and other aspects of inflammation, (5).

The phylogenetic development of immunity has been under investigation in our laboratory for several years (6–10). Although the origins of immune competence have been shown to develop at a more primitive phylogenetic level (11), our interest has continued to be focused on the *Amphibia*. An anuran amphibian, *Bufo marinus*, has been our experimental model for immunoglobulin research. For our studies concerning the phylogeny of serum complement systems several species of amphibians have been utilized.

Materials and Methods

Adult specimens of *Bufo marinus*, the marine toad, were imported from South America by commercial sources. Antigens used were the H antigen of *Salmonella typhosa* (STH), T_2 coliphage, and bovine serum albumin (BSA). Details of environmental conditions, antigen preparation, immunization procedures and antibody measurement have been described (9). Gel filtration and chromatographic procedures were based on standard methods (12, 13).

* Supported by Public Health Service Research Grants AI-02693 and AI-08068; Training Grants DE-7 and AI-00293.

Specimens of *Bufo marinus*, *Necturus maculosus*, and *Rana pipiens*, were obtained commercially and maintained in a 25°C controlled temperature environment for complement studies. Quantitative studies followed standard procedures (14) with the exception that samples were incubated at 30°C for two hours. Other procedures related to complement are as previously described (15).

Immunoglobulins

Synthesis

In a consideration of the biological aspects of the immune response in amphibians, a primary question involves the capacity for specific antibody production in this animal class. Many amphibians respond to antigenic stimulation with antibody titers comparable to those observed in mammals. *Bufo marinus* responds to a primary injection of 2×10^9 STH antigen with geometric mean agglutinin titers ranging from 320–800 at the optimal temperature of 25°C (7). Maximum titers of 2560 have been recorded in individual animals. Peak titers in the primary response were reached in 7–28 days, with considerable variation between individual animals.

Substantial antibody responses have been observed in other anuran species (16, 17), larval and adult forms of the urodele amphibian *Ambystoma mexicanum* (formerly *Siredon mexicanum*) (18) and in bullfrog larvae (*Rana catesbeiana*) (19, 20). Findings in the latter group were of special interest since a thymus dependent immune capacity in larvae was demonstrated against both xenogeneic and allogeneic serum proteins.

Although not a new finding, the effect of temperature on the rate of the immune response in amphibians is one of the more unique phenomena observed. In a group of ten *Bufo marinus* immunized with STH as above and maintained at 15°C, only one animal exhibited a detectable agglutinin titer at 28 days post immunization (7). Other investigators have reported similar results with even longer periods of observation. The South African toad, *Xenopus laevis*, failed to produce antibodies at 8°C over a 95 day period following immunization with a similar antigen (16). Circulating antigen was found in the serum of the urodele amphibian, *Ambystoma mexicanum*, for a 10–12 month period following injection with ϕX 174 phage at 8°C. Antibody became detectable within 12–14 months post immunization, however, suggesting an inducible capability with extended periods of immunization at low temperature.

Other studies dealing with the effect of temperature on immune responses of amphibians are reviewed in previous articles (6, 7, 9).

The anamnestic response in amphibians is of interest as a parameter of immune competence. As observed in *Bufo marinus* the presence of an anamnestic response is related among other variables, to the species, type of antigen, and immunization schedule. A secondary injection of STH antigen given 90 days following primary injection of 2×10^9 STH, resulted in little or no increase in titer or reduction in latent period. There was no prolongation of the duration of response (7). Clearly the criteria for specific anamnesis were not fulfilled in the response to this particulate antigen. These findings are consistent with the results of Diener and Nossal obtained by using a bacterial flagellar antigen as the immunogen in *Bufo marinus* (21).

The secondary response of *Bufo marinus* to T_2 phage does suggest an anamnestic response. There was a reduced latent period, rapid elevation in antibody titer, and a lengthened peak response. Similar findings were also noted in the responses of *Bufo marinus* following primary, secondary, and tertiary injections of BSA (7, 9).

Structure

Five classes of immunoglobulins have been demonstrated in human sera. The two major classes of present comparative interest are IgG and IgM. The IgG molecule has a molecular weight of approximately 160,000 and is dissociable by appropriate chemical means into four polypeptide subunits consisting of two L (light) chains and two H (heavy) chains (22). The IgM molecule has a molecular weight of approximately 1,000,000 and represents a pentamer of 7S units (23). The chemical compositions, antigenic specificities, electrophoretic mobilities, and molecular weights of the H chains differ in these classes of mammalian immunoglobulins and impart the characteristics of each immunoglobulin class. The molecular weights and amino acid compositions of the L chains in both classes, however, are indicative of a greater degree of structural similarity.

IgG represents 85–90% of the total human serum immunoglobulin population and has a sedimentation coefficient of approximately 7S. IgM is a 19S macroglobulin and comprises 5–10% of the total immunoglobulins. Current data suggest that these two classes of immunoglobulins are found in mammals (22), birds (24), and reptiles (25).

The characteristics of the immunoglobulins produced are of obvious interest in relation to the biological aspects previously noted. An investigation was initiated in our laboratory to determine the classes of immunoglobulins possessed by *Bufo marinus* and their ranges of immunological activity.

The immunoglobulins of *Bufo marinus* injected with STH antigen were separated from other serum proteins by passage through a DEAE-Sephadex anion exchange column. The STH agglutinin activity was confined to the first fraction eluted. When this fraction was pooled, concentrated, and subjected to gel filtration on a Sephadex G-200 column, two components were resolved in the 19S and 7S regions as determined by standard markers. STH agglutinin activity was associated only with the 19S fraction. Over a 241 day period of observation there was no indication of 7S antibody formation even after secondary and tertiary injections.

This is in contrast to our results following immunization of *Bufo marinus* with T_2 phage. T_2 neutralizing activity was found to be evenly distributed between the 19S and 7S components of immune serum separated by gel filtration. This distribution remained constant as observed from 21 days post-primary injection until 14 days after the secondary immunization (9).

Our findings in *Bufo marinus* are consistent with the results of Marchalonis and Edelman with the bullfrog *Rana catesbeiana* (26). Following a single injection of f2 phage these workers found two classes of antibodies which physicochemically correspond to the IgM and IgG immunoglobulins of mammals. The phage neutralizing activity was found to be associated with the macroglobulin, or 19S antibody, in the early stages of immunization. There was a gradual increase of activity in the 7S fraction in time with over 90% of the neutralizing activity present in this fraction at 90 days. The 19S macroglobulin of the bullfrog represented 40% of the total immunoglobulin population which is in contrast to the lower proportion of IgM found in mammals.

Further observations were made by Marchalonis and Edelman (26) on the physicochemical properties of bullfrog immunoglobulins. Sub-unit chain structures were found to be similar to their counterparts in higher animal species. Light chains of both immunoglobulins had molecular weights of 20,000. Heavy chains of the IgM class had molecular weights of 72,100 while those of the IgG class had molecular weights of 53,600. These values were in close agreement with those reported in mammalian species (22, 27). Carbohydrate content, amino acid composition, and immunoelectrophoretic analyses also suggested a close similarity between bullfrog immunoglobulins and the corresponding IgM and IgG immunoglobulin classes in mammals.

From existing data it appears that IgM is found in all vertebrates; however, the stage of phylogenetic development in which the IgG class emerges has not been clearly defined. Only the IgM class is found in elasmobranchs (28) and cyclostomes (29). The teleosts (30) may synthesize antibodies only of the macroglobulin class, although more data will have to be collected from various species before the presence of 7S antibody in this class can be ruled out. From an evolutionary standpoint, present evidence suggests that the amphibians may be the most primitive class of animals to exhibit IgG immunoglobulins. As pointed out by Archer (31) the amphibians are intermediate between the bony fishes and mammals as far as anatomical structures and the primary structure of the neurophypophyseal hormones are concerned. If the genes which code for the heavy chain of the IgG molecule did actually emerge with the amphibians, then these animals would well serve as models in which the genetic processes of immunoglobulin evolution could be more clearly understood.

Complement

Evidence suggests that complement (C') exists in many species of fish and elasmobranchs (8, 32, 33), although no evidence exists for the presence of complement in more primitive species. The lamprey has been found to possess a non-complement lysin in low titer (34). Certain species of shark appear to possess relatively highly developed hemolytic complement systems (32) and the component structure in one species has been described in some detail (33). Cushing studied complement and its component interaction in the bullfrog. *Rana catesbeiana,* and found close similarities to guinea pig complement (35, 36).

We first investigated the natural lytic activity of sera from *Rana pipiens, Necturus maculosus,* and *Bufo marinus* as directed against standardized erythrocyte suspensions from a number of heterologous species (15). Sheep, rabbit, dog, chicken, duck, turtle, goldfish, and human group A cells were used. Lysis of these suspensions by amphibian sera was selective depending upon the species of erythrocyte in the hemolytic system which suggested lytic systems composed of specific antibody plus complement, rather than a non-specific uniformly directed lysin.

Specific antibodies were produced for use in a hemolytic system with amphibian test sera by injecting rabbits, catfish, and turtles with sheep erythrocytes. Rabbit antibody reacted well with *Bufo marinus* and *Rana pipiens* complement; less well with that from *Necturus maculosus*. The *Necturus maculosus* system was the only one of the three which reacted with turtle antibody, however. There was no reaction between any amphibian system and fish antibody. This ability of *Bufo marinus* and *Rana pipiens* complement to be activated by rabbit antibody was confirmed by complement fixation experiments utilizing rabbit antibody to egg albumin. Such reaction with mammalian antibody was not observed in our experiments with complement from more primitive poikilotherms (8, 30).

Gel filtration of *Rana pipiens* serum on Sephadex G-200 was done to correlate the hemolytic activity with molecular dimensions as determined from the eluant peaks. Concentrates were made of eluates from the 19S peak and the 7S peak. Neither concentrate contained hemolytic activity to a standard sheep erythrocyte suspension. When the 19S peak concentrate was combined with the 7S peak concentrate, however, lysis occurred. This indicated at least a two component system with components distributed in the 7S and 19S peak. This is consistent also with data derived from guinea pig complement fractionation.

Quantitative estimates of the complement titers for the amphibian group were derived in terms of their C'H50 titer (14). Mean titers were recorded of 44.0 C'H50 units for *Rana pipiens*, 20.8 C'H50 units for *Necturus maculosus*, and 12.8 C'H50 units for *Bufo marinus* (15). These figures compare with values which we obtained in the same system of 36 C'H50 units for human serum and 264 C'H50 units for guinea pig serum.

Complement could also be measured by a bactericidal assay using a gram-negative bacillus, *Salmonella typhosa*, as the test organism. The antibody necessary in this system could be obtained by immunizing animals with S. *typhosa* vaccine or from normal antibody present in low concentration in some non-immunized animals. Heat labile complement, reactive in this system, was found in *Bufo marinus* and *Rana catesbeiana*.

EDTA (ethylenediamine tetra-acetic acid) inactivated the hemolytic activity of each of the amphibian sera, suggesting the inhibition of the C'1 and C'2 steps of the complement reaction which are dependent on calcium and magnesium ions. Addition of these ions to the EDTA-inactivated sera restored activity. Hydrazine, which inactivates C'4 and C'3, and heat, which inactivates C'1 and C'2, were effective in abolishing lytic activity in test sera. Hydrazine treated sera, which possessed intact C'1 and C', when added to heat inactivated sera lacking these components, restored hemolytic ability (15). Dose response curves and kinetic analyses of *Bufo marinus* complement in a standard rabbit antibody-sheep erythrocyte system showed a close similarity to the data obtained with the classical guinea pig complement system.

Amphibian complement seems closely related to that of mammals. The relatively low titers, as compared to guinea pig complement, and extreme lability of specific activity in these species makes further progress difficult. We are continuing our efforts to identify and separate individual components and their activities.

The demonstration of intact hemolytic and bactericidal complement systems in these species of amphibians suggests that a capacity for cellular lysis resides in amphibian serum. The possibility suggests itself that rejection of certain tumor cell implants, reported to involve cellular lysis (37), may be mediated in part by the action of complement.

Summary

Anuran amphibians, as represented by *Bufo marinus*, respond to antigenic stimulation with substantial antibody production which is temperature dependent. Specific anamnestic responses were produced after secondary injections with T_2 phage and BSA. This was not observed after secondary injections of STH antigen. T_2 phage neutralizing activity was found in both 19S and 7S fractions, whereas STH agglutinin antibody was demonstrable only in the 19S fraction.

Serum complement systems have been found in three amphibian genera (*Rana*, *Bufo* and *Necturus*). Potentiation by heterologous antibody and responses to specific inactivating agents such as heat, EDTA, and hydrazine suggested complement components similar to those of mammalian sera. Complement in the anuran amphibians was activated by rabbit antibody. Complement titers were measured by both hemolytic and bactericidal assays. Dose response studies and kinetic analyses of *Bufo marinus* complement showed a close similarity to the data obtained with the classical guinea pig complement system.

References

1. METCHNIKOFF, E.: Lectures on Comparative Pathology of Inflammation. London, K. Paul, Trench, Trubner Co., Ltd. 1893, p. 51.
2. WIDAL and SICARD: Influence de l'organisme sur les proprietes acquises par les humeurs du fait de l'infection. Compt. Rend. Soc. Biol. *49*:1047–1050, 1897.
3. MULLER-EBERHARD, H. J.: Chemistry and reaction mechanisms of complement. Adv. in Immunol. *8*:2–80, 1968.
4. GEWURZ, H.: The immunologic role of complement. Hospital Practice, Sept., 45–56, 1967.
5. NELSON, R. A., JR.: The role of complement in immune phenomena. *In* The Inflammatory Process. Academic Press, New York and London, 1965.
6. EVANS, E. E.: Antibody response in Amphibia and Reptilia. Fed. Proc. *22*:1132–1137, 1963.
7. EVANS, E. E., KENT, S. P., ATTLEBERGER, M. H., SEIBERT, C., BRYANT, R. E., and BOOTH, B.: Antibody synthesis in poikilothermic vertebrates. Ann. N.Y. Acad. Sci. *126*:629–646, 1965.
8. LEGLER, D. W., EVANS, E. E., and DUPREE, H. K.: Comparative immunology: serum complement of freshwater fishes. Trans. Amer. Fish. Soc. *96*:237–242, 1967.
9. EVANS, E. E., KENT, S. P., BRYANT, R. E., and MOYER, M.: Antibody formation and immunological memory in the marine toad. *In* Phylogeny of Immunity. Univ. of Florida Press, Gainesville, 1966, pp. 218–226.
10. EVANS, E. E., LEGLER, D. W., PAINTER, B., ACTON, R. T., and ATTLEBERGER, M.: Complement-dependent systems and the phylogeny of immunity. In Vitro III:146–153, 1968.
11. PAPERMASTER, B. W., CONDIE, R. M., FINSTAD, J., and GOOD, R. A.: Evolution of the immune response. I. The phylogenetic development of adaptive immunologic responsiveness in vertebrates. J. Exp. Med. *119*:105–130, 1964.

12. GELOTTE, B., FLODIN, P., and KILLANDER, J.: Fractionation of human plasma proteins by gel filtration and zone electrophoresis or ion-exchange chromatography. Arch. Biochem. Suppl. *1*:319–326, 1962.

13. FAHEY, J. L., McCOY, P. F., and GOULIAN, M.: Chromatography of serum proteins in normal and pathological sera: the distribution of protein-bound carbohydrate and cholesterol, siderophilin, thyroxin-binding protein, B_{12}-binding protein, alkaline and acid phosphatases, radio-iodinated albumin and myeloma proteins. J. Clin. Invest. *37*:272–284, 1958.

14. KABAT, E. A., and MAYER, M. M.: Experimental Immunichemistry. 2nd ed. Springfield, C. C. Thomas, 1961, pp. 149–152.

15. LEGLER, D. W., and EVANS, E. E.: Hemolytic complement in Amphibia. Proc. Soc. Exp. Biol. Med. *121*:1158–1162, 1966.

16. ELEK, S. D., REES, T. A. and GOWING, N. F. C.: Studies on the immune response in a poikilothermic species (*Xenopus laevis Daudin*). Comp. Biochem. Physiol. *7*:255–267, 1962.

17. ALCOCK, D. M.: Antibody production in the common frog, *Rana temporaria*. J. Path. Bact. *90*:31–43, 1965.

18. CHING, Y., and WEDGEWOOD, R.: Immunologic responses in the axolotl, *Siredon mexicanum*. J. Immunol. *99*:191–199, 1967.

19. COOPER, E. L., PINKERTON, W., and HILDEMANN, W. H.: Serum antibody synthesis in larvae of the bullfrog *Rana catesbeiana*. Biol. Bull. *127*:232–238, 1964.

20. COOPER, E. L., and HILDEMANN, W. H.: The immune response of larval bullfrogs (*Rana catesbeiana*) to diverse antigens. Ann. N.Y. Acad. Sci. *126*:647–661, 1965.

21. DIENER, E., and NOSSAL, G. J. V.: Phylogenetic Studies on the immune response. I. Localization of antigens and immune response in the toad, *Bufo marinus*. Immunology *10*:535–542, 1966.

22. COHEN, C., and PORTER, R. R.: Structure and biologic activity of immunoglobulins. Adv. in Immunol. *4*:287–343, 1964.

23. MILLER, F., and METZGER, H.: Characterization of a human macroglobulin I. The molecular weight of its subunit. J. Biol. Chem. *240*:(8), 3325–3333, 1965.

24. ROSENQUIST, G. L., and GILDEN, R. V.: Chicken antibodies to bovine serum albumin. Molecular size and sensitivity to 2-mercaptoethanol. Biochim. Biophys. Acta *78*:543–545, 1963.

25. GREY, H. M.: Phylogeny of the immune response. Studies on some physical, chemical, and serologic characteristics of antibody produced in the turtle. J. Immunol. *91*:819–826, 1963.

26. MARCHALONIS, J. J., and EDELMAN, G. M.: Phylogenetic origins of antibody structure II. Immunoglobulins in the primary immune response of the bullfrog, *Rana catesbeiana*. J. Exp. Med. *124*:901–913, 1966.

27. LAMM, M. E., and SMALL, P. A., JR.: Polypeptide chain structure of rabbit immunoglobulins. II. γM immunoglobulin. Biochemistry *5*:267–276, 1966.

28. CLEM, L. W., and SMALL, P. A., JR.: Phylogeny of immunoglobulin structure and function I. Immunoglobulins of the lemon shark. J. Exp. Med. *125*:893–920, 1967.

29. MARCHALONIS, J. J., and EDELMAN, G. M.: Phylogenetic origins of antibody structure III. Antibodies in the primary immune response of the sea lamprey, *Petromyzon marinus*. J. Exp. Med. *127*:891–914, 1968.

30. HODGINS, H. O., WEISER, R. S., and RIDGWAY, G. J.: The nature of antibodies and the immune response in rainbow trout *Salmo gairdneri*. J. Immunol. *99*:534–544, 1967.

31. ARCHER, R.: Evolutionary aspects of the structure of proteins. Angewandte Chemie *5*:798–806, 1966.

32. Legler, D. W., and Evans, E. E.: Comparative immunology: hemolytic complement in elasmobranchs. Proc. Soc. Exp. Biol. Med. *124*:3034, 1967.

33. Jensen, J. A., Sigel, M. M., and Ross, G. D.: Natural antibody (A_N) and complement (C'_N) of the nurse shark. Fed. Proc. (Abstract) *27*:491, 1968.

34. Gewurz, H., Finstad, J., Muschel, L. H., and Good, R. A.: Phylogenetic inquiry into the origins of the complement system. *In* Phylogeny of Immunity. Univ. of Florida Press, Gainesville, 1966, pp. 105–117.

35. Cushing, J. W., Jr.: A comparative study of complement. I. The specific inactivation of the components. J. Immunol. *50*:61–75, 1945.

36. Cushing, J. W., Jr.: A comparative study of complement. II. The interaction of components of different species. J. Immunol. *50*:75–89, 1945.

37. Ruben, L. J.: Possible immunological factors in amphibian lymphoma development. *In* Biology of Amphibian Tumors (M. Mizell, ed.), Springer-Verlag New York Inc., 1969, pp. 368–384.

The Amphibian as a Key Step in the Evolution of Lymphoid Tissue and Diverse Immunoglobulin Classes*

B. Pollara, W. A. Cain, J. Finstad and R. A. Good

Pediatric Research Laboratories of the Variety Club Heart Hospital
University of Minnesota, Minneapolis, Minnesota

Numerous studies have revealed that the lymphoid tissue of the chicken comprises two distinct peripheral components with basically separate functions. If newly hatched chicks are subjected to complete extirpation of the bursa of Fabricius plus near lethal total body irradiation, these chickens grow up as immunological cripples unable to produce demonstrable amounts of circulating antibodies (1, 2). Such chickens lack both of the known immunoglobulins, IgM and IgG. Nevertheless, even though grossly defective in ability to synthesize antibody and gamma globulin, such chickens have normal or essentially normal ability to develop and express cell-mediated immunity. In contrast, chickens subjected to total body irradiation and complete thymic extirpation grow up as immunological cripples unable to execute the cell-mediated immunities; i.e., delayed allergy, homograft immunity, and capacity to execute the graft-versus-host reactions. This division of immunological functions on the basis of influence of two separate central lymphoid organs is reflected in specialization of structure in the peripheral lymphoid organs; e.g., spleen, lymph nodes, skin, and intestinal lymphoid aggregates. Chickens irradiated and bursectomized in the newly hatched period completely lack plasma cells and germinal centers, but possess normal numbers of circulating small lymphocytes and normal aggregates of lymphocytes in the spleen, lymph nodes and other lymphoid cell organs and tissues. The thymus-dependent lymphocyte population is responsible for the cell-mediated immune reaction while the bursa-dependent germinal centers and plasma cells are responsible for the synthesis of immunoglobulin and antibody.

Studies of genetically-determined immunological deficiencies show convincingly that in man, as well as in chickens, the lymphoid apparatus is organized into thymus-dependent and thymus-independent components (3–5). Similarly, in mice and rabbits abundant evidence reveals as well that the lymphoid tissue has separate peripheral components with essentially distinct functions (6–8). The small lymphocyte population in circulating blood and deep cortical regions of lymph nodes and the small lymphocyte population in the white pulp of the spleen are directly dependent on the thymus for development. Plasma cells and germinal centers, on the other hand, are

* Aided by grants from The National Foundation, The American Heart Association, The American Cancer Society and the United States Public Health Service (AI-08372, AI-08677, AI-00292, NB-02042 and 5FO2 AI-35728).

independent of the thymus (7) and presumably dependent for development upon a central lymphoid organ equivalent to the bursa.

Attempts to study the phylogenetic origins of these two types of lymphoid activities are complicated by the diversity and extraordinary variability of the invertebrates and lower vertebrates. The most primitive of cold-blooded vertebrates, the cyclostomes, exhibit immunological responses. Immunoglobulin, antibody, delayed allergy, humoral immunity, and immunological memory have been demonstrated in the lamprey, *Petromyzon marinus* (9). Germinal centers and plasma cells, on the other hand, have not been unequivocally identified in the lamprey (10). Thus if we compare the elements of "thymic-dependent" immunity and "bursa-dependent" immunity in the lamprey, it would seem that the bursa-dependent systems have not been completely separated at the evolutionary stage reflected in this modern representative. In the lamprey, bursa-dependent immunity apparently comprises but one class of immunoglobulin and immunoglobulin-producing cells (10–12). In birds, at least two classes of immunoglobulins are present and a new lymphoid component, the germinal center, has evolved (13, 14). In man, at least four classes of immunoglobulins have been defined (15). Further studies of the avian model in our laboratory have revealed that the ontogeny of bursa functions may recapitulate certain key steps in the phylogenetic transition (16).

In critical experiments based on extirpation of the bursa *in ovo*, Good *et al.* (17) found that bursal function could be interrupted at different stages in chick embryos. Animals whose bursa had been removed on or prior to the 17th day of a 21-day embryonic period were regularly found to lack both 19S and 7S immunoglobulins as well as lack both germinal centers and plasma cells in their peripheral lymphoid tissues. By contrast, animals bursectomized at the 19th embryonic day were found regularly to lack 7S IgG-type immunoglobulins and germinal centers. Chickens bursectomized later, at or near the time of hatching, possessed both classes of immunoglobulins, germinal centers, and plasma cells, but had a sluggish, slowly developing antibody response. Cell-mediated immunity seemed intact irrespective of the developmental stage at which bursal extirpation was executed.

In the phylogenetic experiments a striking parallelism of immunological development to that observed in ontogenetic perspective has been elucidated. The lamprey, a representative cyclostome, shows ability to execute vigorous homograft immunity and readily develops delayed allergy (9). By contrast, these animals produce peculiar immunoglobulins of intermediate size (11, 12). Although these animals exhibit clear evidence of immunological memory, they do not demonstrate mammalian-type secondary responses. The lymphoid tissue of the lamprey is comprised of a primitive lymphoepithelial thymus, a system of lymphocytes in blood and hematopoietic tissues, and cells suggestive of plasmablasts of higher forms (10). Lymphoid cell aggregates are present in a primitive spleen, but there is no suggestion of true germinal centers or Marschalko-type plasma cells.

In representative elasmobranchii and chondrosteans the lymphoid system and immunological functions have achieved a higher order of development. In modern representatives of both of these evolutionary lines one finds the thymus developed as a discrete organ (10). The spleen is also developed as an organ in representatives of both lines. The spleen shows a sharp division into red pulp and lymphoid white pulp.

Plasma cells are present in the red pulp of the spleen and hematopoietic foci. However, structures which could be considered germinal centers are completely lacking. Immunologically, the representative elasmobranchii and chondrosteans exhibit homograft rejections with vigorous second set responses (18) and antibody synthesis with immunologic memory (19). These animals respond with appreciable vigor to most antigens. They do not, however, exhibit true mammalian-type secondary responses. Morphological study of their lymphoid tissue, although showing clusters of plasma cells (10, 20) and immunoglobulin producing cells (21, 22), does not reveal structures morphologically comparable to the germinal centers of birds and mammals. These stages in phylogenetic development are also characterized by the presence of 19S IgM-type immunoglobulins (12, 23–25). Although they possess a lower molecular weight immunoglobulin with a sedimentation constant of approximately 7S which, after prolonged immunization, can contain antibodies in some species, the small immunoglobulin molecules have H-chains immunologically identical to that of the larger molecular weight immunoglobulin. Thus, in both the chick manipulated during embryonic life by bursal extirpation preventing development of 7S IgG-type antibody and in phylogenetic stages prior to development of true 7S IgG-type immunoglobulin, we witness a lymphoid system possessing plasma cells and a small lymphocyte population but entirely lacking the germinal center component of the peripheral lymphoid system.

Marchalonis *et al.* (26) have shown recently that ability to synthesize more than one class of immunoglobulins evolved prior to birds. The amphibian bullfrog (*Rana catesbiana*) possesses high and low molecular weight antibodies which have antigenically distinct H-chains. It was of interest, therefore, to ascertain whether germinal centers were present in these amphibians.

Following the lead provided by Marchalonis and Edelman (26) who showed the presence of IgM and IgG-type immunoglobulins in *Rana catesbiana*, we proceeded to examine these amphibians for the presence of germinal center structure before and after antigenic stimulation. Examination of the spleen showed no germinal centers but only collections of reticular cells and lymphocytes in a white pulp lacking plasma cells or pyroninophilic cells. Following stimulation, this pattern was not appreciably changed except for an apparent increase in number of reticular cells and accumulation of few plasma cells (Fig. 1). This failure to demonstrate germinal center structure in *Rana*, despite the proven presence of two immunoglobulins, led us to examine the lymphoid tissue of *Bufo marinus* in search of such structures. Collections of lymphoid cells exhibiting pyroninophilia are seen in sections of *Bufo marinus* spleen before and after antigenic stimulation (Fig. 2). These collections of cells do not possess the characteristics of true mammalian germinal centers. Although lymphocytes and plasma cells may be present, especially at the periphery of these accumulations, a true collar of small lymphocytes is lacking in the mantle zone. These structures were found only in the poorly formed germinal centers in the spleen and not seen in the propericardial and procorocordial bodies. Using immunofluorescent techniques combined with electron microscopy, Cowden *et al.* (27) identified cells with features characteristic of mammalian plasma cells in long-term stimulated *Bufo marinus*. Thus, in this toad, lymphoid organs are encountered which may be considered as primitive germinal centers. Certainly the correlation of immunoglobulin classes with the presence of

Fig. 1. Section of *Rana catesbeiana* spleen following multiple stimulations with killed Brucella cells. Note organization into red and white pulp. White pulp contains accumulations of lymphocytes and reticular cells, but certainly no germinal centers such as are found in mammalian spleen after repeated immunizations. Hematoxylin-eosin. Low power.

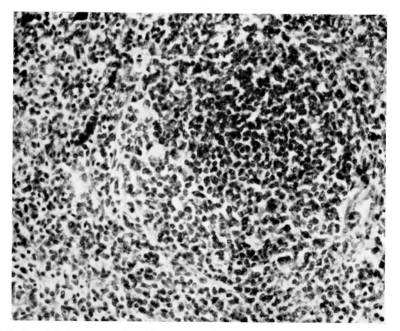

Fig. 2. Section of *Bufo marinus* spleen following stimulation with killed Brucella cells. Lymphoid cells which are pyroninophilic are present in follicular arrangement. Certain hallmarks of true germinal centers are absent. Hematoxylin-eosin. High power.

germinal centers in this developmental perspective, as well as mammals and birds, offers further evidence on the sequential development of the lymphoid system responsible for humoral immunity.

An exhaustive analysis of larval forms has failed to reveal an organ in amphibians equivalent to the bursa. Recent studies of Sidky and Auerbach (28), confirmed by Perey and LaPointe (29), have revealed a posterior gut organ in the young snapping turtle which resembles the bursa of the bird. This organ initially is a simple epithelial sac which later develops into a follicular lymphoid organ; in later life, the lymphoid tissue regresses. There are several indications that the turtle possesses a bursa of Fabricius. However, the bursal function in immunological development of the organ in turtles remains to be defined. Similarly, we are impelled to continue the search for the bursal equivalent in the amphibian.

Cooper (30) has postulated that the bursa offers an environment for a stepwise differentiation of stem cells into precursor cells, which in turn differentiate, perhaps in the periphery, into IgM producing cells. Longer residence in the microenvironment of the bursa may lead to the differentiation of a second precursor cell population, from which cells migrate to the periphery and develop as germinal centers. Finally, expansion of this population at the germinal center site may result in the differentiation of a population of cells that elaborates 7S IgG-type immunoglobulins and specific 7S IgG antibody. If this hypothesis is correct, germinal centers would be the requisite for production of diverse immunoglobulin classes. Our phylogenetic studies and extirpative manipulations in the chicken tend to support this viewpoint. Diversity of immunoglobulin classes has not been demonstrated in representative forms below amphibians.

References

1. COOPER, M. D., PETERSON, R. D. A., GOOD, R. A.: Delineation of the thymic and bursal lymphoid systems in the chicken. Nature 205:143 (1965).
2. COOPER, M. D., PETERSON, R. D. A., SOUTH, M. A., GOOD, R. A.: The functions of the thymus system and the bursa system in the chickens. J. Expt. Med. 123:75 (1966).
3. GOOD, R. A.: Agammaglobulinemia: an experimental study. Amer. J. Dis. Child. 88:625 (1954).
4. CRAIG, J. M., GITLIN, D., JEWETT, T. C.: The response of lymph nodes of normal and congenitally agammaglobulinemic children to antigenic stimulation. Amer. J. Dis. Child. 88:626 (1954).
5. NEZELOF, C., JAMMET, M. L., LORTHOLARY, P., LABRANE, B., LAMY, M. L.: L'hypoplasie hereditaire du thymus. Arch. Fr. Pediat. 21:897 (1964).
6. COOPER, M. D., PEREY, D. Y. E., McKNEALLY, M., GABRIELSON, A. E., SUTHERLAND, D. E. R., GOOD, R. A.: A mammalian equivalent to the bursa of Fabricius. Lancet 1:1388 (1966).
7. PARROTT, D. M. V., DeSOUSA, M. A. B., EAST, J.: Thymus depleted areas in the lymphoid organs of neonatally thymectomized mice. J. Expt. Med. 123:191 (1966).
8. McKNEALLY, M. F., KELLUM, M. J., SUTHERLAND, D. E. R.: Functional studies in thymectomized and appendectomized rabbits. Fed. Proc. 25:613 (1966).
9. FINSTAD, J., GOOD, R. A.: The evolution of the immune response. III. Immunologic responses in the lamprey. J. Expt. Med. 120:1151 (1964).

10. FINSTAD, J., PAPERMASTER, B. W., GOOD, R. A.: Evolution of the immune response. II. Morphologic studies on the origin of the thymus and organized lymphoid tissue. Lab. Invest. *13*:490 (1964).

11. MARCHALONIS, J. J., EDELMAN, G. M.: Phylogenetic origins of antibody structure. III. Antibodies in the primary immune response of the sea lamprey, *Petromyzon marinus*. J. Expt. Med. *127*:891 (1968).

12. POLLARA, B., FINSTAD, J., GOOD, R. A.: The phylogenetic development of immunoglobulins. *In* Phylogeny of Immunity (R. T. Smith, P. A. Miescher and R. A. Good, eds.), Gainesville, University of Florida Press, p. 88, 1966.

13. DREESMAN, G., LARSON, C., PINCHARD, R. N., GROYON, R. M., BENEDICT, A. A.: Antibody activity in different chicken globulins. Proc. Soc. Exp. Biol. Med. *118*:292 (1965).

14. THORBECKE, G. J., GORDON, H. A., WOSTMAN, B., WAGNER, M., REYNIERS, J. A.: Lymphoid tissue and serum gammaglobulin in young germ-free chickens. J. Infect. Dis. *101*:237 (1957).

15. COHEN, S., MILSTEIN, C.: Structure and properties of immunoglobulins. Adv. Immunol. *7*:1 (1967).

16. CAIN, W. A., COOPER, M. D., VAN ALTEN, P. J., GOOD, R. A.: Development and function of the immunoglobulin-producing system. II. Role of the bursa in development of humoral immunological competence. J. Immunol. *102*:671 (1969).

17. GOOD, R. A., PEREY, D. Y. E., CAIN, W., COOPER, M. D.: Relationship of germinal center development to development of capacity for immunoglobulin synthesis. *In* Proceedings of the 2nd Conference on Germinal Centers of Lymphatic Tissue, Padova, Italy, 1969 (in press).*

18. PEREY, D. Y. E., FINSTAD, J., POLLARA, B., GOOD, R. A.: Evolution of the immune response. VI. First and Second set skin homograft rejection in primitive fishes. Lab. Invest. *19*:591 (1968).

19. FINSTAD, J., GOOD, R. A.: Phylogenetic studies of adaptive immune responses in the lower vertebrates. *In* Phylogeny of Immunity (R. T. Smith, P. A. Miescher and R. A. Good, eds.), Gainesville, University of Florida Press, p. 173, 1966.

20. GOOD, R. A., FINSTAD, J., POLLARA, B., GABRIELSEN, A. E.: Morphologic studies on the evolution of the lymphoid tissues among the lower vertebrates. *In* Phylogeny of Immunity (R. T. Smith, P. A. Miescher and R. A. Good, eds.), Gainesville, University of Florida Press, p. 149, 1966.

21. POLLARA, B., FINSTAD, J., GOOD, R. A.: Specific immunoglobulin synthesis in lower vertebrates lacking germinal centers. *In* Proceedings of the 2nd Conference on Germinal Centers of Lymphatic Tissue, Padova, Italy, 1969 (in press).*

22. POLLARA, B., FINSTAD, J., GOOD, R. A.: Unpublished observations on immunoglobulin producing cells of the paddlefish.

23. MARCHALONIS, J. J., EDELMAN, G. M.: Phylogenetic origins of antibody structure. I. Multichain structure of Immunoglobulins in the smooth dogfish (*Mustelus canis*). J. Expt. Med. *122*:601 (1965).

24. CLEM, L. W., SMALL, P. A.: Phylogeny of immunoglobulin structure and function. I. Immunoglobulins of the lemon shark. J. Expt. Med. *125*:893 (1967).

25. FISH, L. A., POLLARA, B., GOOD, R. A.: Characterization of an immunoglobulin from the paddlefish (*Polyodon spathula*). *In* Phylogeny of Immunity (R. T. Smith, P. A. Miescher, and R. A. Good, eds.), Gainesville, University of Florida Press, p. 99, 1966.

26. MARCHALONIS, J. J., EDELMAN, G. M.: Phylogenetic origins of antibody structure. II. Immunoglobulins in the primary immune response of the bullfrog, *Rana catesbeiana*. J. Expt. Med. *124*:901 (1966).

27. COWDEN, R. R., DYER, R. F., GEBHARDT, B. M., VOLPE, E. P.: Amphibian plasma cells. J. Immunol. *100*:1293 (1968).

28. SIDKY, Y. A., AUERBACH, R.: Tissue culture analysis of immunological capacity of snapping turtles. J. Expt. Zool. *167*:189 (1968).

29. PEREY, D. Y., LaPOINTE, N.: Personal communication.

30. COOPER, M. D., WELLER, E. H.: Development suppression of germinal center and IgG production by prednisolone and 6-mercaptopurine. *In* Proceedings of the 2nd Conference on Germinal Centers of Lymphatic Tissue, Padova, Italy, 1969 (in press).*

---

* To be published *In* Lymphatic Tissue and Germinal Centers in Immune Response. Plenum Publ. Corp., New York.

Some Morphological and Biological Characteristics of a Tumor of the Newt, *Triturus cristatus* Laur.

VINCENZO G. LEONE and TERESA ZAVANELLA

Laboratory of Embryology and Experimental Morphology
University of Milan, Italy

We are presenting the results of research work done in our laboratory on a malignant tumor induced in the crested newt *Triturus cristatus* Laur. by a single methylcholanthrene (MC) treatment, consisting of the introduction of a small amount of MC crystals into the subcutis. In our experience tumors developed in about 30% of the cases after more than five months.

These tumors are transplantable to animals of the same species (homoplastic transplants) and of different genus and even order (*Pleurodeles waltlii* Michah., *Xenopus laevis* Daudin., xenoplastic transplants) without conditioning of the recipient animals. They metastasize all over the viscera, nervous system and the body walls (1, 2). In a series of experiments (3) it has been found that the take is about 80% both for homo- and xenotransplants when the graft is located in the anterior chamber of the eye; it drops to 64% for homografts, and to 54% for xenografts when the tumor is grafted into the subcutaneous tissues. We should mention, however, that in several other groups of experiments the homografts in the subcutis took in about 100% of the cases.

The transplant grows slowly in the winter and fast in the summer; in this latter season metastases spread extensively and the host can die within 15–20 days after the operation.

Recently *spontaneous* tumors have been found which present the same morphological aspect of MC induced and grafted tumors.

The induced and spontaneous tumors are initially located in the dermis, at the dermoepidermal junction; they then invade subcutaneous and muscular tissues (Figs. 1 and 2).

The primary tumors and metastases consist of cells of epithelioid aspect, round or oval, with relatively abundant cytoplasm which stains lightly and may contain a variable amount of melanin granules. The nucleus is round, but sometimes reniform, with a delicate chromatin network. The neoplastic cells are sparse or grouped in nests of various dimensions which generally lack vessels and stroma. Mitoses are rare and can be atypical (Figs. 1–9).

In the site of the graft, ulceration of the skin is a frequent event; in neighboring areas the epidermis may be hyperplastic, with numerous mitoses, and proliferate toward the neoplastic tissues underneath. The epidermal cells display, in fact, a tendency to disjoin from each other, with rupture of intercellular bridges, and move down into

184

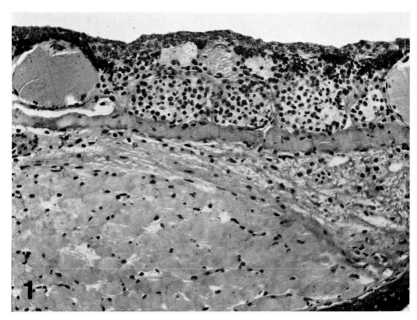

Fig. 1. Nests of malignant cells in the derma of the newt 1718, two months after the subcutaneous grafting of a tumor at 9th passage. Hematoxylin and eosin, ×110.

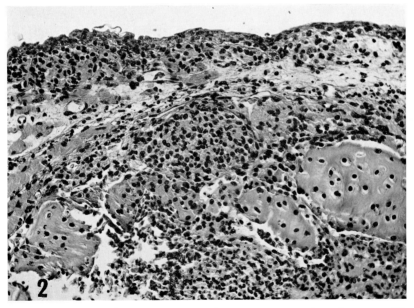

Fig. 2. Newt 1933, one month after receiving a subcutaneous tumor graft (9th passage). The epidermis appears thinner and superficial and deep nests of neoplastic cells are evident in the region of the graft. Partial destruction of the sternal cartilage is also evident at the site. Hematoxylin and eosin, ×110.

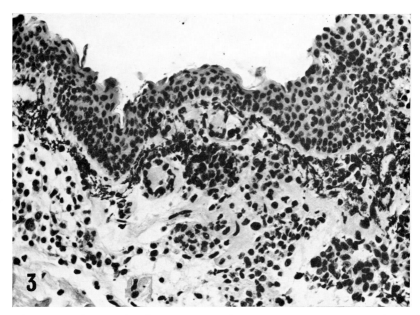

Fig. 3. Newt 2152, four months after receiving a subcutaneous injection of cell-free filtrate from an 8th passage tumor. This tumor developed at a distance from the site of injection. Note that the cells in superficial neoplastic nests are heavily pigmented whereas the deeper nests lack melanin. Hematoxylin and eosin, ×160.

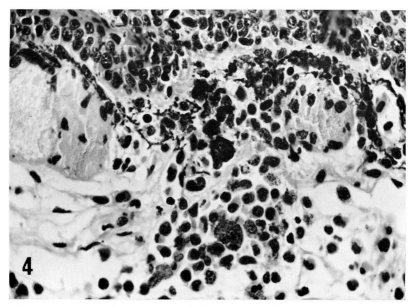

Fig. 4. Same case as Fig. 3. The melanocytes which migrate inwardly become round and clear. Hematoxylin and eosin, ×250.

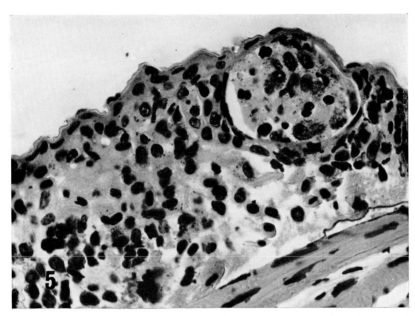

Fig. 5. Same case as Fig. 3. An epithelial nest of neoplastic cells. Note that the epidermis on the left appears thin, with no definite separation from the underlying tumor. Hematoxylin and eosin, ×320.

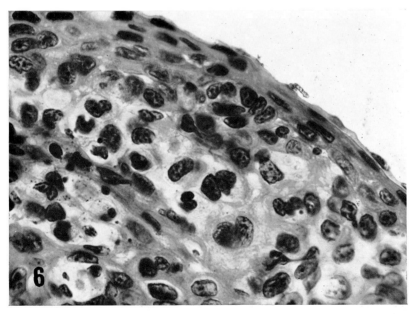

Fig. 6. Junctional alteration of the epidermis at the site of the graft in newt 3287. A 15th passage tumor was grafted subcutaneously two months before. Note neoplastic cell cytoplasm characteristically clearer than the surrounding malpighian cells. Hematoxylin and eosin, ×500.

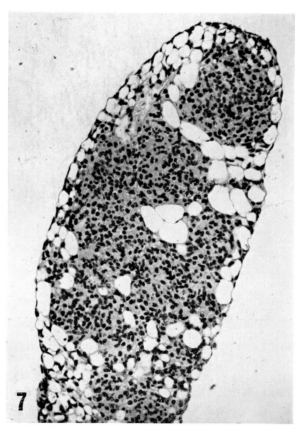

Fig. 7. Metastases in the fat bodies adjoining the gonads in newt 2706. This animal received a subcutaneous graft of a 9th passage tumor three months before. Hematoxylin and eosin, ×81.

the underlying tumor. In some cases this phenomenon results in an extreme reduction of the thickness of the epidermis, which may be reduced to a single layer of cells. Sometimes one can find in the epidermal layers "theques" or niches, containing nests of neoplastic cells which appear characteristically clearer than the surrounding epithelial cells, and sometimes lack pigment granules (Fig. 5). Another prominent feature of the epidermis overlying the tumor is the presence, at various levels, of single or clustered malignant cells.

The basal membrane is sometimes destroyed and several of the dendritic melanocytes under the membrane seem to disappear; actually they change shape, becoming roundish (Fig. 4) and the nucleus, normally masked, becomes visible because of a decrease in the amount of melanin pigment. Most of these cells migrate towards deeper sites. It has been noted that in the more superficial layers the tumor cells may appear pigmented, but in the nests situated deeply (Fig. 3) and in the metastases in the organs (Figs. 7–9) the majority of cells contain little or no pigment.

In histological preparations a weak tyrosinase activity has been detected in the transplanted tumors and in the metastases, when DOPA is used as substrate; such activity is not shown when tyrosine is used as substrate.

Studying these neoplastic cells with the electron microscope, Ceresa Castellani and Zavanella (4) have found in the cytoplasm membrane-limited bodies, round, oval or rod-shaped, with homogeneous or finely granular matrix of varying density (Figs. 10 and 11). In some cases a series of parallel or concentric membranes is visible within these dark bodies, a configuration similar to the lamellar structure described by various authors as being typical for normal and neoplastic melanocytes of mammals; cigar-shaped bodies with an internal lamellar structure have been found especially in the dendritic process occasionally observed in the neoplastic cells (Fig. 12). All these categories of bodies can be interpreted as melanin granules at different stages of maturation (premelanosomes, melanosomes).

In order to ascertain the nature of these bodies, electron microscopic preparations of metastatic nodules from the spleen and from fat bodies were incubated with DOPA after ordinary glutaraldehyde fixation and sectioned with the Sorvall TC-2 (tissue cutter) apparatus. The results showed that most of the granules exhibit tyrosinase activity. It has also been seen that the reaction is generally incomplete (5) (Figs. 13 and 14).

Because of the morphological characteristics observed, we maintain that the tumor

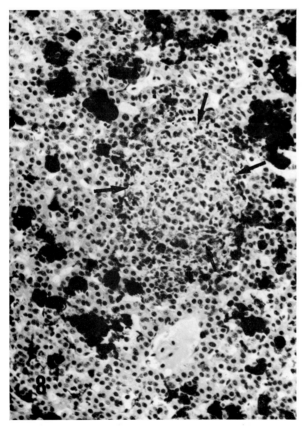

Fig. 8. Metastatic nodule (arrows) in the liver of newt 2982 four months after subcutaneous injection of nucleic acid extracted from normal newt tissues. Hematoxylin and eosin, $\times 96$.

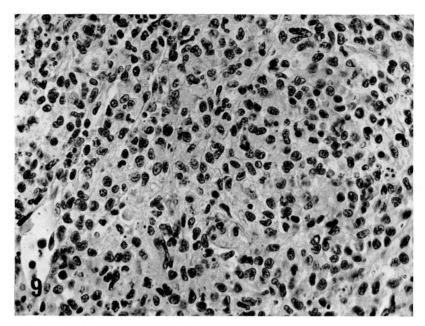

Fig. 9. The spleen of the newt 1412 completely occupied by neoplastic cells four months after the grafting of a tumor, at 5th passage, in the subcutis. Hematoxylin and eosin, ×220.

with which we are dealing should be classified as a malignant melanoma, characterized by the predominance of amelanotic cells and by junctional alterations. It is quite difficult to decide whether the tumor originates from dendritic melanocytes (melanophores) adjacent to the basal membrane of the epidermis or from the particularly pale cells found in the epidermis and interpreted as intraepidermal melanocytes by Pillai (6). This latter hypothesis finds strong support in the increased number of clear intraepidermal cells noticed in some newts treated with MC.

During the last few years our research has been aimed principally toward detecting oncogenic viruses ultimately responsible for, or associated with, the appearance of a tumor and perhaps unmasked by MC treatment.

In a previous experiment a cell-free filtrate prepared from a melanomna at the fifth passage was injected subcutaneously into 15 newts, 9 of which developed tumors of the same histological type after 1–4 months (Membranfilter Göttingen No. 8) (7). In other series of experiments using 182 recipient newts, 25 cell-free filtrates out of 32 were completely inactive. The remaining 7 filtrates gave rise to tumors in 19 of the 61 injected animals (unpublished data) (Fig. 3).

Tumors have been induced also in a high percentage of animals treated with homogenates of tumors kept at 0 °C and at −25 °C in 50% glycerol or 8% sucrose solution. The induced tumors show the same morphological characteristics as the donor tumor (8).

It is hard to believe that living cells, responsible for the initiation of tumors in all the responding animals, were present in the homogenates; the hypotheses that a viral agent is implicated in this carcinogenic process is very suggestive, but as yet we do not have conclusive evidence. Viral particles have never been found in these tumors.

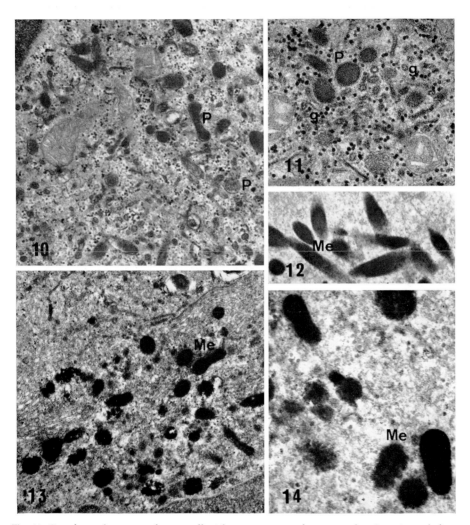

Fig. 10. Cytoplasm of a newt melanoma cell with numerous premelanosomes of various size and shape. P = premelanosome; ×24,000.

Fig. 11. Premelanosome ultrastructure: the membrane surrounding the premelanosome in a newt melanoma cell is evident. P = premelanosome; g = glycogen; ×35,000.

Fig. 12. Cigar-shaped melanosomes present in a dendritic process of a malignant cell: an internal lamellar structure is recognizable. Me = melanosomes; ×21,000.

Fig. 13. Numerous melanosomes are evident in a malignant cell of the newt melanoma after DOPA incubation. Me = melanosome; ×30,000.

Fig. 14. Higher magnification of Fig. 13. Me = melanosome; ×48,000.

Electron micrographs courtesy of Dr. L. Ceresa Castellani.

Since some virus-induced tumors of mammals are transmissible by nucleic acids, the possibility that nucleic acids (NA) extracted from neoplastic and corresponding normal tissues of the newt might demonstrate oncogenic activity was explored. Experiments were carried out in cooperation with the Institute of Zoology of Milan (9, 10) and with the "Istituto Nazionale dei Tumori" of Milan (11, 12, 15). Nucleic acids were prepared by three different methods of extraction, two based on phenol (cold and hot phenol) extraction; and the other on employment of cold phenol and sodium-p-amino salicylate (13). Almost 400 animals were treated with NA extracted by use of the first two methods; melanomas were found, with similar incidence, both in animals injected with neoplastic NA and in those treated with NA extracted from tissues of normal newts (Fig. 8). When the third method was employed, a higher incidence of tumors was induced with NA from tumor tissues than with NA from normal ones (4.8%); however, statistical analyses of the latter results have not yet been carried out (12).

After subcutaneous injection of NA extracted from tumors, serious alterations of the cartilage situated beneath the site of treatment were observed in some animals (9). In one newt treated with NA from normal tissues a new cartilage trabecula was found adjacent to the scapular cartilage near the site of the injection; the controlateral scapula was unaffected (11).

In another group of 78 animals used as controls, the activity of heterologous NA and of phosphate buffer solutions was tested. To our astonishment tumors of the same histological type were found in 28.2% of cases, independent of the type of treatment. Because it is improbable that a phosphate solution could induce the appearance of tumors, it must be inferred that a high incidence of spontaneous melanoma exists in the newts (11, 14, 15).

Camerini and Zavanella (15) noticed that the incidence of tumors in different groups seems less dependent on the type of treatment than on the season when treatment was performed. For instance, in our register we found that melanomas were detected in 12 out of 15 newts inoculated in September–October 1965 (80% of the cases); in a second group of 18 animals treated in January–February 1966, nine developed tumors (50%); but in a third group of 45 newts treated in June–July 1966 only 2.2% of the subjects developed melanomas.

It is striking that the incidence is so strictly dependent on seasonal factors; and the importance of seasonal factors is reported also by Seilern-Aspang *et al.* (16) with regard to the susceptibility of newts to benzopyrene.

Another point to consider with regard to the incidence of spontaneous tumors in the newt is the existence of geographical factors which may be linked to the genetical background of different newt populations. The records on our material indicate that there is a difference in spontaneous tumor incidences between northern and southern newt populations, that is, more tumors were found in *Triturus* collected in the fields around Pavia than in those collected in the surroundings of Naples (15). Statistical and genetical data are, however, completely lacking.

On the other hand one could also consider the hypothesis that the higher incidence found in the northern region could depend on specific environmental factors such as the pollution of the streams caused by industrial discharges.

To conclude, the high incidence of melanomas found in some groups of *Triturus* that we have studied could have been influenced by a variety of factors (seasonal, environmental, climatic, genetic or viral) working independently of each other, or in cooperation. It is interesting to note the similarity between newt melanoma and frog adenocarcinoma behavior (17), based probably on the biological cycle similarities in these two amphibians.

We are dealing with a many faceted and very complex problem. In the quest for a solution a series of investigations with different approaches is planned; one of these will involve a search for the presence of virus in winter and summer tumors.

Summary

Malignant tumors can be induced in newts (*Triturus cristatus*) by methylcholanthrene treatment in the subcutaneous tissues. These tumors can be successfully transplanted by cell-graft into other newts of the same species, and of a different genus (*Pleurodeles waltlii*), and into anurans (*Xenopus laevis*), with an 80–100 percent take. The tumors can be transmitted by cell-free extracts, and some experimental data suggest that nucleic acids extracted from them can show oncogenic properties; these properties have been observed only with some methods of extraction, not with other methods. Transplanted tumors grow quite slowly in winter time, while in the summer the animals can die within 15–20 days, with metastases in all organs. These methylcholanthrene-induced tumors can be classified as malignant melanomas; their morphology remains unchanged throughout passage in animals of the same species. Recently, spontaneous-occurring melanomas have been observed, with high incidence, in newts of some populations in the northern regions of Italy.

References

1. LEONE, V. G.: Ricerche e considerazioni sulla cancerizzazione negli Anfibi. Tumori 39:420–442, 1953.

2. LEONE, V. G.: Tumori da metilcolantrene in tritoni. Ist. Lomb. Sci. e Lett. Rend. Cl. Sci. 92:220–240, 1957.

3. LEONE, V. G., and ZAVANELLA, T.: Trapianti omo ed eteroplastici di tumori sperimentali in Anfibi. Tumori 50:39–63, 1964.

4. CERESA CASTELLANI, L., and ZAVANELLA, T.: Ultrastructural features of a methylcholanthrene-induced tumor in the newt. Atti V Congr. Ital. Micr. Elettr. 62–65, Bologna 5–7 ottobre 1965.

5. ZAVANELLA, T., and CERESA CASTELLANI, L.: Osservazioni ultrastrutturali e istochimiche sui melanociti normali e tumorali in *Triturus cristatus* Laur. XXXVII Convegno dell' Unione Zool. Ital., Siena 11–16 ottobre 1968 (in press).

6. PILLAI, A. P.: Electron microscopic studies on the epidermis of the newt with an enquiry into the problem of induced neoplasia. Protoplasma 55:10–62, 1962.

7. ZAVANELLA, T.: Trasmissione dei tumori da metilcolantrene negli anfibi mediante filtrati acellulari. Tumori 50:485–498, 1964.

8. ZAVANELLA, T.: Trasmissibilità dei tumori da metilcolantrene degli anfibi mediante materiale glicerinato. Atti Soc. Ital. Cancer V:416, 1964.

9. ZAVANELLA, T.: Acidi nucleici infettanti da tumori indotti con metilcolantrene. Atti Soc. Ital. Patol. IX Congr.: 875–879, Torino-Saint Vincent 10–12 giugno 1965.

10. Zavanella, T., and Protti Necchi, M.: Proprietà oncogene degli acidi nucleici estratti da un melanoma indotto chimicamente. Il Cancro *20*:171–191, 1967.

11. Zavanella, T., and Camerini, E.: Cancerogenesi da acidi nucleici negli anfibi urodeli. Boll. Soc. Ital. Patol. *9*:210–213, 1965/66.

12. Zavanella, T., Camerini, E., and Leone, V. G.: Attività biologiche degli acidi nucleici in anfibi urodeli. Folia Hered. et Patol. *16*:195–202, 1967.

13. Hays, E. F., and Carr, J. A.: Oncogenic properties of deoxyribonucleic acid isolated from parotid gland tumors. Cancer Res. *22*:1319–1322, 1962.

14. Zavanella, T., and Leone, V. G.: Caratteristiche del melanoma del tritone. Atti Accad. Med. Lomb. Simposio sulla biologia normale e patologica dei melanociti. Milano 8–9 ottobre 1967.

15. Camerini, E., and Zavanella, T.: Attività degli acidi nucleici eterologhi in anfibi urodeli. Il Cancro *21*:379–394, 1968.

16. Seilern-Aspang, F., and Kratochwil, K.: Die spontanheilung eines infiltrierenden und metastasierenden, epithelialen tumors von *Triturus cristatus* in abhängigkeit von seinem entstehungsort und vom jahreszeitlichen cyclus. Arch. f. Geschwultforsch. *21*:293–300, 1963.

17. Rafferty, K. A.: Kidney tumors of the leopard frog: a review. Cancer Res. *24*:160–185, 1964.

Skin Carcinogenesis, Mammals Versus Amphibia

BEPPINO C. GIOVANELLA

McArdle Laboratory for Cancer Research
University of Wisconsin, Madison, Wisconsin

The successful induction of cancer on the skin by means of topical applications of appropriate chemicals has been known to depend largely on the species employed and on the method of application. Carcinogenesis results in a high percentage of mice when their skins are treated with solutions of polycyclic aromatic hydrocarbons, but much less frequently in rats and rarely in guinea pigs. Only recently have studies been undertaken to try to elucidate the reasons for these profound differences in susceptibility. It was suspected for a long time that the pilosebaceous apparatus was the site of origin of the chemically induced cutaneous cancers. In 1945 Lacassagne and Latarjet (1) found that areas of skin depilated by ultraviolet light irradiation or hairless surgical scars were refractory to carcinogenesis by 3-methylcholanthrene. In 1947 Suntzeff, Carruthers and Cowdry (2) demonstrated that the epidermis of newborn mice, before the appearance of hair follicles, was refractory to a single dose of 3-methylcholanthrene. In 1949 Liang (3) studied the site of origin of cutaneous tumors after application of the same carcinogen by means of an ingenious method of epidermal whole mounting, and localized this site at the junction between the hair follicles and the basal epidermal layer. In 1951 Billingham, Orr and Woodhouse (4) found by epidermal transplantation that interfollicular epithelium treated with carcinogens and transplanted to another site without its hair follicles did not give rise to any tumors, whereas epithelial tumors developed from the area of origin, grafted with untreated epidermis, where the only epithelial structures exposed to the carcinogen were the hair follicles. The results of this experiment were somewhat misinterpreted, but recently Steinmuller (5) with an elegant experiment has definitely demonstrated that these tumors originated from the hair follicles by repeating the above experiment using F_1 hybrid mice as the carcinogen-treated hosts and parent strain of mice as donors of untreated epidermal grafts. All the carcinomas which arose on the graft site grew in F_1 hybrids, and none grew in the parental strain, which demonstrates that they arose from treated epithelial cells of the F_1 hybrid. Unfortunately, this issue has been somewhat clouded by the appearance of numerous papers describing the induction of epithelial tumors in the skin of hairless strains of mice following application of polycyclic aromatic hydrocarbons (cf. 6). In considering these apparently contradictory results our attention was drawn to the fact that hairs are present in hairless mice during their first weeks of life and undergo abortive hair growth subsequently (7). Sometimes a few hairs are present even in adult hairless mice.

We chose to re-examine this problem in a strain of mice inbred except for the hair locus. When a hairy female is mated with a hairless brother, the progeny is roughly

50% hairy and 50% hairless. We carefully chose adult hairless mice of both sexes that did not have any hair left. As controls we used their hairy isogenic litter-mates. All the animals were given one application of 100 μg of 9,10-Dimethyl-1,2-benzanthracene (DMBA) followed two weeks later by bi-weekly applications of 2 drops of 0.5% croton oil in acetone, which were continued for 30 weeks or more. One papilloma was obtained in 20 female mice treated for 40 weeks and 3 papillomas (one on the top of the head and two at the origin of two whiskers) in 14 male mice treated for 30 weeks. In the hairy controls 69 papillomas and 2 epitheliomas were obtained in 15 mice (8). The obvious possibility of a lack of penetration of the hydrocarbon into the skin was ruled out by measuring with radioactive DMBA the amount of binding to the macromolecules of the skin. The binding of DMBA to the DNA, RNA and proteins of skin epithelium was identical in hairless and Swiss hairy mice (9); when the latter were used in an experiment identical to the one mentioned above, 68 papillomas and 6 epitheliomas were induced in 26 females after 40 weeks. It is therefore probable that in mouse skin the only cells capable of becoming malignant belong to the pilosebaceous apparatus. Here a comparison can be drawn with the amphibian skin where the majority of tumors induced have been of glandular origin and were obtained not by painting but by sub-epithelial injection of carcinogens; see Balls (10). This situation is similar to what has been found for some mucosa in mammals and the amphibian skin, especially the one of urodela is anatomically a structure sharing some of the characteristics of the skin and mucosa of the mammals. It is evidently too early to generalize, but it would seem that interfollicular epithelia are not as easily cancerized, as the epithelium of the annexa.

Now I would like to examine another difference between chemical carcinogenesis in amphibia and in mammals, which until recently was more apparent than real. In our definition of malignant tumors we are implying the concept of an irreversible, progressive growth. Accordingly, many epithelial overgrowths in amphibia, which histologically were similar to epithelial malignancies, were looked upon with skepticism, because many of them had a tendency to regress. However, in 1954 when Rous (11) transplanted tumors obtained from embryonic skin into adult mice, he observed that histologically malignant epitheliomas regressed. In 1964 Kleinsmith and Pierce (12) demonstrated that from single *in vivo* clones of a teratocarcinoma of the mouse they could obtain up to 14 different normal tissues plus neoplastic cells. In the same year Foley and Drolet (13) observed that tissue culture cells from sarcoma 180 after many passages in tissue culture lost malignancy, as demonstrated by the progressively larger inocula necessary to induce tumors both in mice and in the cheek pouch of hamsters. The following year Foley *et al.* (14) confirmed this observation with another tumor. Goldstein (15) in 1964 found that malignant neuroblasts cultured for a long time *in vitro* tended to differentiate and to lose their reproductive ability, a fact described *in vivo* as early as 1927 (16). We were able to obtain similar results simultaneously *in vivo* and *in vitro* (using suboptimal conditions) (17). Malignant epidermal tumors were induced in the skin of *Swiss* albino and C$_3$H mice (Swiss mice are not inbred and have a high rate of tumor production under these experimental conditions; C$_3$H mice are inbred but have a low rate of tumor production) by bi-weekly topical applications of DMBA (25 μg) or by a single application of DMBA (100 μg) followed by bi-weekly applications of croton oil. The primary tumors were then transplanted as single cell suspensions or into newborn (in the case of Swiss tumors we always used a first passage in the newborn) and adult mice and into the cheek pouch of hamsters by trocar. Cells obtained from the primary tumor or from successive early passages *in vivo* were cultured *in vitro* indefinitely. It was found that the majority of the tumors obtained grew in transplants as an agglomeration of epidermal cysts, associated sometimes with a solid tumor mass. The cavity of the cysts was filled with cells demonstrating various degrees of keratinization and degeneration, none of them being viable as shown in Figs. 1 and 2. In successive transplants the tumors obtained were also cystic; especially if thin walls of cysts were used for transplantation. When the solid tumor masses associated with the cysts were transplanted serially by trocar it was possible to obtain after some passages, tumor lines which were mostly solid. This cystic form of growth is characteristic of these neoplastic cells and is not the result of a host reaction, since they were obtained from transplants performed both in non-inbred and inbred mice and in the cheek pouch of cortisonized hamsters. Cells injected into the animals after one passage *in vitro* were more malignant than the primary tumor. In the course of further passages *in vitro* their ability to form tumors decreased and finally disappeared altogether, although the cells continued to grow vigorously *in vitro*.

Tables 1 to 5 summarize part of the natural history of tumor T5. The original material was an axillary metastasis of a highly malignant epidermoid carcinoma obtained in a female Swiss mouse by bi-weekly painting of 25 μg of DMBA for three months. Tumors that developed late after transplantation or that were transplanted

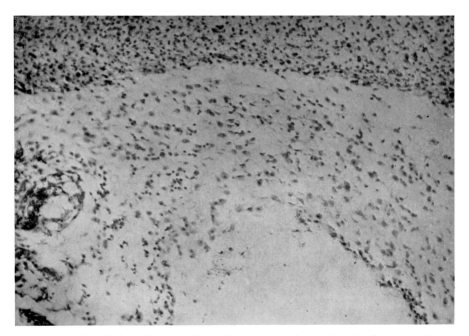

Fig. 1. Section through the wall of an early cystic tumor, second transplantation by trocar of tumor T10, a highly malignant epidermoid carcinoma obtained in a female C_3H mouse by biweekly painting of 25 μg of DMBA. The recipient was an adult female C_3H mouse.

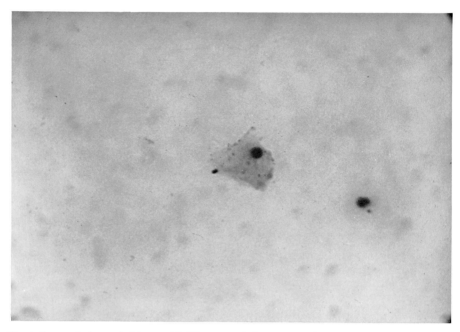

Fig. 2. Smear of the semisolid material filling one of the cysts of the tumor of Fig. 1. A cell in advanced state of keratinization is visible.

TABLE 1

T5 (Epidermoid carcinoma DMBA induced)
    Trypsinized and 500 cells injected Sc
    in 14 48 hrs. old mice.

100 days later	1/11 solid ⊕ 1 cm.
180 days ,,	2/5 ♀ 0/3 ♂ both cystic— one large 5 × 4 cm—put in culture.
225 days ,,	1/3 ♀ 1/3 ♂ both large and cystic. 38 ml fluid from one, 10 ml from the other.
280 days ,,	1/2 ♀ 0/2 ♂ cystic.

Total 6/11

TABLE 2

T5 After 16 days in culture $5 \cdot 10^5$ cells are injected Sc in 4 ♀ and 4 ♂ (adults)

28 days later 4/4 ♀ 2/4 ♂

All solid, one of the ♀ regresses, the others grow progressively until very large; last of the tumor carrying animals dies 80 days after inoculation.

TABLE 3

T5 After 56 days in culture and 5 passages

$1 \cdot 10^5$ cells Sc in	6	♀	adults		
$1 \cdot 10^4$ ”	” in	6	”	”	
$1 \cdot 10^3$ ”	” in	5	”	”	
$1 \cdot 10^2$ ”	” in	10	”	”	

Tumors

	43 days after inoculation	340 days after inoculation
$1 \cdot 10^5$	0/6	1/6
$1 \cdot 10^4$	1/3	0/2
$1 \cdot 10^3$	0/5	0/2
$1 \cdot 10^2$	0/10	0/10

TABLE 4

T5 After 56 days and 5 passages in tissue culture

$1 \cdot 10^2$ cells are injected Sc in	12	24 hrs.	old mice			
” ” ” ”	” ”	11	48 hrs.	”	”	
” ” ” ”	” ”	9	72 hrs.	”	”	
$1 \cdot 10^3$ ” ” ”	” ”	13	48 hrs.	”	”	

Tumors

		50 days		290 days		335 days	
$1 \cdot 10^2$	24 hrs.	0/4 ♀	1/2 ♂	0/4 ♀	0/1 ♂	0/4 ♀	0/1 ♂
”	48 hrs.	0/5	0/6	0/5	0/5	1/4	0/5
”	72 hrs.	0/8	0/1	3/7	0/1	0/4	0/1
$1 \cdot 10^3$	48 hrs.	1/5	1/2	0/2	0/1	1/2	0/1

TABLE 5

T5 After 13 passages in tissue culture six clones are
isolated and after 4 more passages $1 \cdot 10^4$ and
$1 \cdot 10^5$ cells from each are injected into 10
♀ adults.

1/120 with tumor at 110 days, all the others
negative after 200 days.

many times developed into enormous multiple cysts, twice and thrice the size of the
animal as shown in Figs. 3, 4, and 5. These large cysts were filled with a clear, serum-
like fluid instead of the semi-solid material of the early ones. It seems that the keratinization process in the wall of these cysts is much less active than in the early cysts.
The malignancy (infiltrative growth, metastases) of these tumors was found to be
rather low, although they were transmissible by means of very small inocula (100–500
cells).

In view of the above-mentioned results it is clear that our past definitions of malignant tumors ought to be revised. Malignancy can be lost and malignant cells can
differentiate into non-malignant cells. The reasons for these phenomena are not understood, and probably the answers will come only when we understand differentiation,
for which the Amphibia have always been the best material of study.

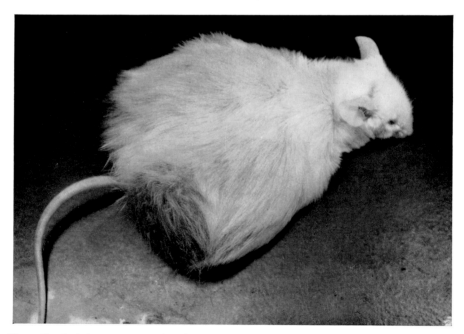

Fig. 3. Female Swiss mouse injected with 500 cells from the primary tumor T5, 48 hrs after birth.
The picture was taken seven months later.

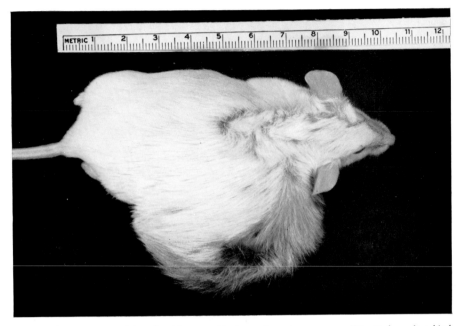

Fig. 4. Male Swiss mouse injected with 500 cells from the primary tumor T5, 48 hrs after birth. The picture was taken seven months later.

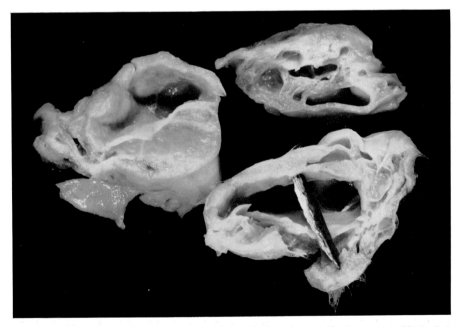

Fig. 5. Cross sections of cystic tumors obtained by injection of 500 cells from tumor T5 in Swiss mice 48 hrs after birth.

Summary

Carcinogenesis of the skin follows different patterns in amphibia and in mammals. Some of these divergences are traceable to structural and functional differences between the two classes. Carcinogenesis by painting the skin with polycyclic aromatic hydrocarbons has been largely unsuccessful in amphibia compared to what has been found in mammals. Recent experiments, however, have demonstrated that in a high tumor incidence strain of mice, lack of hair has made the animals completely refractory to cutaneous carcinogenesis. If, as these experiments suggest, the hair follicle cells are responsible for the production of cutaneous epithelial malignancies, the lack of hair follicles in the amphibia would be sufficient explanation for the refractoriness of these animals to carcinogenesis by painting. Conversely, some intriguing phenomena originally observed in amphibia have also been recently observed in mammals.

In our definition of malignant tumors we are implying the concept of an irreversible, progressive, inarrestable growth. Accordingly many epithelial overgrowths in amphibia which histologically were extremely similar to epithelial malignancies were looked upon with skepticism because many of them had a tendency to regress, especially during regenerative processes. Now it is a common observation that in long term tissue cultures of highly malignant tumors frequently a lessening and even a total loss of malignancy can occur. The same phenomenon has been observed by us *in vivo;* subcutaneous transplants of highly malignant epitheliomas of mice give rise in some cases to progressively less malignant growths, most of them cystic.

The causes of these phenomena are at present very imperfectly understood and in order to clarify them comparative studies offer the best approach.

References

1. LaCASSAGNE, A. and LATARJET, R.: Action of methylcholanthrene on certain scars of the skin in mice. Cancer Res. 6:183–188, 1946.
2. SUNTZEFF, V., CARRUTHERS, C. and COWDRY, E. V.: The role of sebaceous glands and hair follicles in epidermal carcinogenesis. Cancer Res. 7:439–443, 1947.
3. LIANG, HSU-MU: Localized change in methylcholanthrene-treated epidermis. Cancer Res. 8:211–220, 1948.
4. BILLINGHAM, R. E., ORR, J. W. and WOODHOUSE, D. L.: Transplantation of skin components during chemical carcinogenesis with 20-methylcholanthrene. Brit. J. Cancer 5:416–432, 1951.
5. STEINMULLER, D.: Epidermal transplantation during chemical carcinogenesis: a reinvestigation. Proc. Am. Ass. Cancer Res. 9:66, 1968.
6. IVERSEN, O. H. and IVERSEN, U.: A study of epidermal tumorigenesis in the hairless mouse with single and with repeated applications of 3-methylcholanthrene at different dosages. Acta Path. Microbiol. Scand. 62:305–314, 1964.
7. IVERSEN, U. and IVERSEN, O. H.: Cycles of hair growth in hairless mice. Acta Path. Microbiol. Scand. 59:50–62, 1967.
8. GIOVANELLA, B. C. and HEIDELBERGER, C.: Studies on the role of the hair follicle in epidermal carcinogenesis. Proc. Am. Ass. Cancer Res. 8:21, 1967.
9. GOSHMAN, L. M. and HEIDELBERGER, C.: Binding of tritium-labeled polycyclic hydrocarbons to DNA of mouse skin. Cancer Res. 27:1678–1688, 1967.

10. BALLS, M. and RUBEN, L. N.: A review of the chemical induction of neoplasms in amphibia. Experientia 20:241–247, 1964.

11. ROUS, P. and SMITH, W. E.: The neoplastic potentialities of mouse embryo tissues. I. The findings with skin of C. strain embryo transplanted to adult animals. J. Exp. Med. 81:598–619, 1945.

12. KLEINSMITH, L. J. and PIERCE, G. B.: Multipotentiality of single embryonal carcinoma cells. Cancer Res. 24:1544–1552, 1964.

13. FOLEY, G. E. and DROLET, B. P.: Loss of neoplastic properties in vitro. I. Observations with S 180 cell lines. Cancer Res. 24:1461–1467, 1964.

14. FOLEY, G. E., HANDLER, A. H., LYNCH, P. M., WOOLMAN, S. R., STULBERG, C. S. and EAGLE, H.: Loss of neoplastic properties in vitro. II. Observations on K. B. sublines. Cancer Res. 25:1254–1261, 1964.

15. GOLDSTEIN, M. N., BURDMAN, J. A. and JOURNEY, L. J.: Long-term tissue culture of neuroblastomas. II. Morphological evidence for differentiation and maturation. J. Nat. Cancer Inst. 32:165–199, 1964.

16. CUSHING, H. and WOLBACH, S. B.: The transformation of a malignant paravertebral sympathicoblastoma into a benign ganglioneuroma. Am. J. Path. 3:203–216, 1927.

17. GIOVANELLA, B. C., RÖLLER, M. R. and CHRISTENSON, R. H.: Biological characteristics of cells from primary hydrocarbon—induced skin carcinomas. Ninth Int. Cancer Congress, 36:1966.

Plasmacytoma in a *Rana pipiens*

Sydney S. Schochet, Jr., and Peter W. Lampert

Neuropathology Branch, Armed Forces Institute of Pathology, and
the Veterans Administration Special Reference Laboratory for
Pathology at the AFIP, Washington, D.C.

Though the occurrence of tumors among amphibians has been recognized for many years, these lesions have been considered quite rare. Lucké and Schlumberger (1) reviewed the problem of neoplasia in cold-blooded vertebrates and concluded that amphibians are no less susceptible to neoplasms than other vertebrates. Recent studies have vastly expanded our knowledge of some of these tumors, especially renal cell carcinoma in the frog (2–6) and lymphosarcoma in the toad (7–9). The transmissibility of these lesions has been demonstrated, and viral pathogenesis has been suggested.

The present study reports the first example of a plasmacytoma in a frog (*Rana pipiens*) and describes the intracytoplasmic inclusions found in this lesion.

Material and Methods

The "Principles of Laboratory Animal Care" as promulgated by the National Society for Medical Research were observed during this study.

Two and one-half months after implanting a fragment of a typical Lucké renal cell carcinoma into the anterior chamber of the eye of an adult female *Rana pipiens,* a soft tissue tumor was noted in the thigh. The tumor grew rapidly, approximately doubling its volume during the subsequent month before the animal was killed. Grossly, the lesion was a fleshy grayish-white tumor that infiltrated the thigh muscles. The overlying skin and underlying femur were not involved.

Attempts to propagate the tumor in the anterior chamber of the eye of other *Rana pipiens* were unsuccessful.

For light microscopy, tumor tissue was fixed in Bouin's solution and embedded in paraffin. The sections were stained by hematoxylin-eosin, periodic acid-Schiff, Masson's trichrome, Wilder's reticulum, Holmes' silver, alcian blue, Giemsa, and methyl green-pyronin techniques.

For electron microscopy, the tumor tissue was immersed in phosphate-buffered 3% glutaraldehyde, postfixed in osmic acid, dehydrated, and embedded in Maraglas. Sections two microns thick were stained with toluidine blue for screening. Suitable blocks were selected, and the thin sections were stained with uranyl acetate and lead citrate prior to examination in a Siemens IA electron microscope.

Results

By light microscopy, the tumor was highly cellular, and infiltrated among degenerating skeletal muscle fibers (Fig. 1). The neoplastic cells appear to be plasma cells

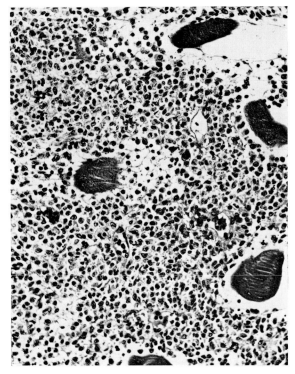

Fig. 1. A plasmacytoma from the thigh of a frog showing neoplastic cells infiltrating among degenerating skeletal muscle fibers. Hematoxylin and eosin. ×130. AFIP Neg. 68-6239.

of varying degrees of maturity (Fig. 2). Some of the cells were mature plasmacytes characterized by amphophilic cytoplasm, perinuclear clear zones, and large eccentric nuclei that had peripherally situated chromatin. Most of the cells were atypical or immature plasmacytes containing abundant finely granular amphophilic cytoplasm and large nuclei that had prominent nucleoli. Many mitotic figures were encountered. Scattered throughout the neoplasm were infrequent but highly characteristic cells containing either multiple small intracytoplasmic inclusions (the so-called "Mott cells") or a few large inclusions (Russell bodies) that displaced and deformed the nucleus. The Russell bodies were eosinophilic but not PAS positive. Other cells contained multiple fine granules of PAS-positive material, but they were not recognizable when the hematoxylin and eosin stain was used.

By electron microscopy, the majority of the neoplastic cells were readily recognized as plasma cells displaying varying degrees of protein storage (Fig. 3). The nuclei had an oval or indented configuration, and the chromatin was clumped against the nuclear membrane. The cytoplasm contained an abundant network of granular endoplasmic reticulum and numerous mitochondria. The Golgi network was not as prominent nor as completely localized to the juxtanuclear region as in normal mammalian plasma cells. The cisterns of the rough endoplasmic reticulum often were markedly dilated by finely granular material (Fig. 4). Occasionally the stored material

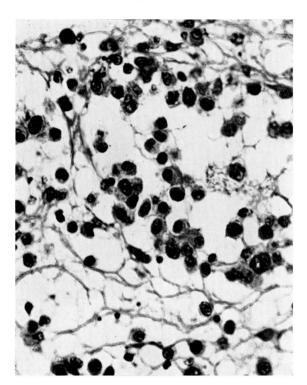

Fig. 2. A plasmacytoma from the thigh of a frog showing the characteristic morphologic features of the neoplastic cells. Hematoxylin and eosin. ×400. AFIP Neg. 68-6237.

was further condensed into multiple small osmophilic masses corresponding to the Mott cell (Fig. 5). Rarely, further aggregation was observed to be giving rise to Russell bodies (Fig. 6). Regardless of the degrees of condensation, the stored protein was always clearly within dilated cisterns of rough endoplasmic reticulum (Fig. 7).

The most striking ultrastructural feature of this neoplasm was the presence of multiple tubular intracytoplasmic inclusions (Fig. 8). The involved cells displayed abundant cytoplasm and a large eccentric, often indented nucleus. The inclusions were closely aggregated and usually occupied only a portion of the cytoplasm. Within these distinct but unbounded areas, the other cellular organelles were reduced in number. The tubules were frequently oriented parallel to one another, forming interwoven fascicles (Fig. 9). At higher magnification it was evident that the tubules possessed a double wall formed by two concentric osmophilic shells (Fig. 10). The diameter of the outer shell was approximately 400 Å; the diameter of the inner shell was approximately 200 Å, while the length was indeterminable. In longitudinal section, continuity between the outer walls and dilated cisterns of the rough endoplasmic reticulum could be demonstrated frequently (Fig. 11). In cross section, the association was less obvious. The central core of tubules was generally lucent, although an occasional punctate density was seen. The space between the two concentric shells was also lucent.

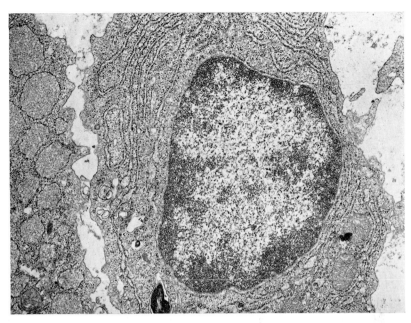

Fig. 3. Electron micrograph of the predominant neoplastic cell type showing the abundant rough endoplasmic reticulum characteristic of plasma cells. Uranyl acetate and lead citrate. $\times 12,750$. AFIP Neg. 68-6427-1.

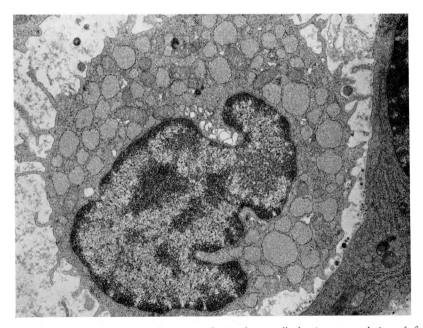

Fig. 4. Electron micrograph of an "active" neoplastic plasma cell showing accumulation of finely granular proteinaceous material within the cisterns of the rough endoplasmic reticulum. Uranyl acetate and lead citrate. $\times 8,500$. AFIP Neg. 68-6427-2.

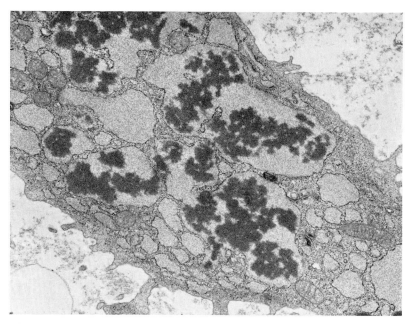

Fig. 5. Electron micrograph of a neoplastic plasma cell that shows increased osmophilia of the accumulated proteinaceous material within the cisterns of the rough endoplasmic reticulum. Uranyl acetate and lead citrate. ✕12,750. AFIP Neg. 68-6427-3.

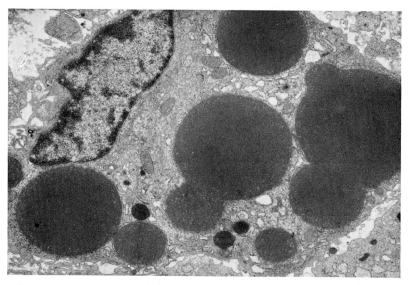

Fig. 6. Electron micrograph of a neoplastic plasma cell containing Russell bodies. Uranyl acetate and lead citrate. ✕6,800. AFIP Neg. 68-6427-4.

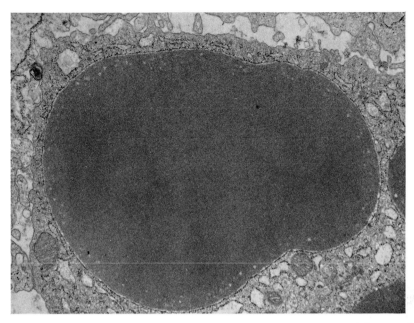

Fig. 7. Electron micrograph of a neoplastic plasma cell showing the intracisternal location of the Russell body. Uranyl acetate and lead citrate. ×30,000. AFIP Neg. 68-6427-5.

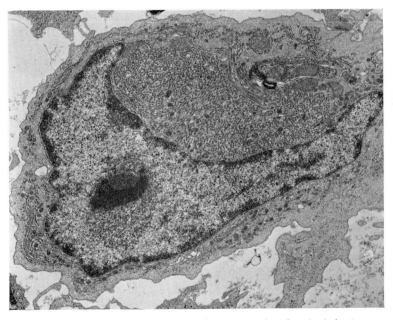

Fig. 8. Electron micrograph of a neoplastic plasma cell containing fascicles of tubular intracytoplasmic inclusions. Uranyl acetate and lead citrate. ×8,500. AFIP Neg. 68-6427-6.

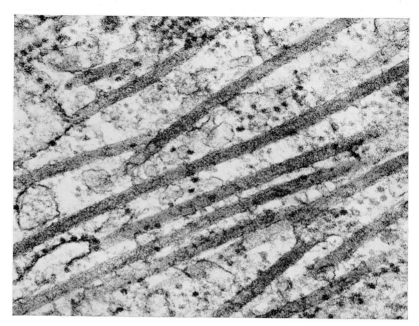

Fig. 9. Electron micrograph of a neoplastic plasma cell showing the interwoven fascicles of tubular intracytoplasmic inclusions. Uranyl acetate and lead citrate. ×85,000. AFIP Neg. 68-6427-7.

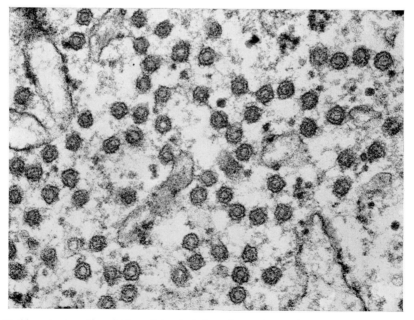

Fig. 10. Transverse sections of the tubular inclusions demonstrating the two concentric osmophilic shells and the lucent core. Uranyl acetate and lead citrate. ×130,000. AFIP Neg. 668-6427-8.

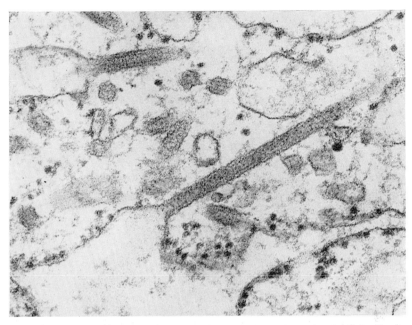

Fig. 11. Longitudinal sections of the tubular inclusions demonstrating the continuity between the outer shell and the rough endoplasmic reticulum. Uranyl acetate and lead citrate. $\times$100,000. AFIP Neg. 68-6427-9.

In other areas, the cytoplasm of the inclusion-bearing cells contained abundant collapsed or moderately dilated cisterns of rough endoplasmic reticulum. No intra-nuclear inclusions were recognized.

Discussion

Two and one-half months after transplantation of a Lucké renal cell carcinoma into the anterior chamber of the eye, a rapidly growing tumor was noticed in the thigh of a female *Rana pipiens*. Microscopically, this infiltrative tumor was composed of mature and immature plasma cells (plasmablasts) along with occasional Mott cells and Russell bodies. Mitotic figures were frequent. By electron microscopy, the neo-plastic cells displayed the abundant rough endoplasmic reticulum with manifestations of protein production and storage observed in plasma cell dyscrasias (10–12). Unfortu-nately, no blood serum was available to study the immunoglobulins being produced by this neoplasm.

The nature of the tubular intracytoplasmic inclusions constitutes the most in-triguing ultrastructural aspect of this tumor. Consideration must be given to the possibility that the inclusions represent a modification of one of the normal cyto-plasmic organelles. Microtubules form the mitotic spindle, make up the 9 + 2 array of filaments in cilia and sperm tails, and are particularly abundant in neuronal proc-esses. Microtubules, however, have a smaller diameter (150–200 Å) and lack the double-walled structure of these inclusions (13).

Another possibility is that these tubules represent stored or accumulated proteinaceous material. Bessis (10) reported that protein produced by plasma cells within the cisterns of the endoplasmic reticulum may occasionally condense into crystals with a periodicity of 100–140 Å. In hyperplastic nodules in mouse liver, Essner (14) has described dilated cisterns containing filaments measuring 330 Å in diameter. In both of these situations, the stored material was within the cisterns of the endoplasmic reticulum, whereas the tubules we have described in the frog plasmacytoma are attached to the endoplasmic reticulum, but they extend out into the surrounding cytoplasm.

Highly ordered pseudocrystalline aggregates of undulating tubules associated with the endoplasmic reticulum in tissue cultures were described by Chandra (15). These, however, displayed a more precise spatial orientation, were sharply curved, and had a smaller diameter (240 Å) than the tubules from our plasmacytoma.

Ikuta and Zimmerman (16–17) and Popoff *et al.* (18) described the development of double-walled tubules in brain and muscle following the implantation of certain carcinogens. These inclusions were observed in the cytoplasm of reactive cells adjacent to the particles of carcinogen, prior to the actual development of neoplasms. While the appearance of these inclusions is quite similar to the double-walled tubules we found in the tumor in a *Rana pipiens*, the diameters of the shells are almost twice as large. The authors compare the rod-shaped particles to viruses, but they suggest that the particles are the result of an interaction between carcinogen and certain cytoplasmic components.

Elongated or tubular viral forms were described in studies of a number of oncogenic viruses, including the Moloney agent (19), the Shope papilloma virus (20), the polyoma virus (21), and the human wart virus (22). They were also described in the Lucké renal cell carcinoma (2, 23) and in cultures of the Burkitt lymphoma (24). The tubular structures have been variously regarded as a stage in viral development or as an aberrant form of virus. In both spontaneous and experimentally induced murine plasmacytoma, virus-like particles have been described (25). These are spherical intracytoplasmic and intracisternal type-A particles, however. Furthermore, recent studies (26) have shown that the intracytoplasmic particles are due to the mammary tumor agent (MTA) harbored in the host animal. Based on the results of transmission studies, a viral pathogenesis has been proposed for the toad lymphosarcoma (7–9), but ultrastructural studies have not yet been reported.

By analogy it seems appropriate to regard the double-walled inclusions in the plasmacytoma of a frog as virus-like particles. Whether or not these are indeed complete viruses, responsible for the induction of the neoplasm, remains to be established.

Summary

A plasmacytoma in the thigh of a frog, *Rana pipiens*, is reported. The neoplastic plasma cells displayed varying stages of maturation and evidence of protein accumulation. Many of the tumor cells contained double-walled tubular virus-like particles in their cytoplasm.

References

1. LUCKÉ, B., and SCHLUMBERGER, H. G.: Neoplasia in cold-blooded vertebrates. Physiol. Rev. *29*:91–126, 1949.

2. FAWCETT, D. W.: Electron microscope observations on intracellular virus-like particles associated with the cells of the Lucké renal adenocarcinoma. J. Biophys. Biochem. Cytol. *2*:725–742, 1956.

3. LUNGER, P. D.: The isolation and morphology of the Lucké frog kidney tumor virus. Virology *24*:138–145, 1964.

4. MIZELL, M., and ZAMBERNARD, J.: Viral particles of the frog renal adenocarcinoma: causative agent or passenger virus? II. A promising model system for the demonstration of a "lysogenic" state in a metazoan tumor. Ann. N.Y. Acad. Sci. *126*:146–169, 1965.

5. TWEEDELL, K. S.: Induced oncogenesis in developing frog kidney cells. Cancer Res. *27*:2042–2052, 1967.

6. MIZELL, M., STACKPOLE, C. W., and HALPERN, S.: Herpes-type virus recovery from "virus-free" frog kidney tumors. Proc. Soc. Exp. Biol. Med. *127*:808–814, 1968.

7. BALLS, M.: Lymphosarcoma in the South African clawed toad, *Xenopus laevis*: a virus tumor. Ann. N.Y. Acad. Sci. *126*:256–273, 1965.

8. RUBEN, L. N., and BALLS, M.: Further studies of a transmissible amphibian lymphosarcoma. Cancer Res. *27*:293–296, 1967.

9. BALLS, M., and RUBEN, L. N.: The transmission of lymphosarcoma in *Xenopus laevis*, the South African clawed toad. Cancer Res. *27*:654–659, 1967.

10. BESSIS, M.: Ultrastructure of lymphoid and plasma cells in relation to globulin and antibody formation. Lab. Invest. *10*:1040–1067, 1961.

11. WELSH, R. A.: Light and electron microscopic correlates of the periodic acid-Schiff reaction in the human plasma cell. Amer. J. Path. *40*:285–296, 1962.

12. MALDONADO, J. E., BROWN, A. L., JR., BAYARD, E. D., and PEASE, G. L.: Ultrastructure of the myeloma cell. Cancer *19*:1613–1627, 1966.

13. PORTER, K. R.: Cytoplasmic microtubules and their functions. *In* Ciba Foundation Symposium Principles of Biomolecular Organization (G. E. W. Wolstenholme and M. O'Connor, eds.), Boston, Little, Brown and Co., 1966, p. 308.

14. ESSNER, E.: Ultrastructure of spontaneous hyperplastic nodules in mouse liver. Cancer Res. *27*:2137–2152, 1967.

15. CHANDRA, S.: Undulating tubules associated with endoplasmic reticulum in pathologic tissues. Lab. Invest. *18*:422–428, 1968.

16. IKUTA, F., and ZIMMERMAN, H. M.: Intramuscular precancerous lesions induced by carcinogenic hydrocarbons. Arch. Path. *78*:377–389, 1964.

17. IKUTA, F., and ZIMMERMAN, H. M.: Virus particles in reactive cells induced by intracerebral implantation of dibenzanthracene. J. Neuropath. Exp. Neurol. *24*:225–243, 1965.

18. POPOFF, N., SUTTON, C. H., and ZIMMERMAN, H. M.: Virus-like particles in reactive cells associated with crystals of implanted carcinogen. Acta Neuropath. *10*:308–323, 1968.

19. DALTON, A. J., HAGUENAU, F., and MOLONEY, J. B.: Further electron microscopic studies on the morphology of the Moloney agent. J. Nat. Cancer Inst. *33*:255–275, 1964.

20. WILLIAMS, R. C., KASS, S. J., and KNIGHT, C. A.: Structure of the Shope papilloma virus particles. Virology *12*:48–58, 1960.

21. HOWATSON, A. F., and ALMEIDA, J. D.: Observations on the fine structure of polyoma virus. J. Biophys. Biochem. Cytol. *8*:828–834, 1960.

22. NOYES, W. F.: Structure of the human wart virus. Virology *23*:65–72, 1964.

23. ZAMBERNARD, J., VATTER, A. E., and McKINNELL, R. G.: The fine structure of nuclear and cytoplasmic inclusions in primary renal tumors of mutant leopard frogs. Cancer Res. 26:1688–1700, 1966.

24. EPSTEIN, M. A., BARR, Y. M., and ACHONG, B. G.: Avian tumor virus behavior as a guide in the investigation of a human neoplast. *In* Avian Tumor Virus, National Cancer Institute Monograph No. 17 (J. W. Beard, ed.), Washington, D.C., U.S. Government Printing Office, 1964, pp. 637–650.

25. DALTON, A. J., POTTER, M., and MERWIN, R. M.: Some ultrastructural characteristics of a series of primary and transplanted plasma cell tumors of the mouse. J. Nat. Cancer Inst. 26:1221–1267, 1961.

26. DALTON, A. J., and POTTER, M.: Electron microscopic study of the mammary tumor gut in plasma cell tumors. J. Nat. Cancer Inst. 40:1375–1385, 1968.

Structures of Spontaneous and Transplanted Tumors in the Axolotl (*Siredon mexicanum*)

VICTOR V. BRUNST

Roswell Park Memorial Institute
Buffalo, New York

Spontaneous and transplanted melanoma and olfactory neuroepithelioma and spontaneous teratoma have been observed in the axolotl, *Siredon mexicanum* (also known as *Ambystoma mexicanum*). Spontaneous and transplanted melanoma, identical in structure, consisted of melanophores, black pigment cells. The spontaneous teratoma consisted of tissues derived from all three embryonic layers. Its most significant cells were epithelial, partly organized in gland-like structures. Mitosis was observed only in these cells. A second predominant tissue probably resulted from differentiation and degeneration of epithelial tissue. The tissues of the tumor resembled none of the tissues of normal adult axolotls. Spontaneous and transplanted melanoma (1), transplanted olfactory neuroepithelioma (2, 3), and spontaneous teratoma (4) in the axolotl have been or will be reported in detail elsewhere, and hence the present paper is concerned chiefly with spontaneous olfactory neuroepithelioma.

Normal olfactory chambers in axolotls are comparatively long. They contain small cavities that are generally very long and narrow, characteristically tubiform. The walls of the chambers are mostly very thick, especially on one side. In adult axolotls, the interior surfaces of the chambers are covered with a specialized type of sensitive epithelium, namely the olfactory epithelium. This type of epithelium is stratified, columnar, and ciliated. The cells of the most proximal (basal) layers have round nuclei, those of the less proximal layers have an intermediate type of nuclei, those of several more distal layers have nuclei that are comparatively large and elongated, and those of the most distal portion are almost without nuclei. The surface facing the interior of a normal olfactory chamber is concave and is covered with cilia.

A completely different picture was created by the presence of the tumor. The olfactory chambers were modified by the tumor so much that it is even difficult to compare them with normal olfactory chambers (Fig. 1). The cavities inside were greatly enlarged and were atypical in form. The walls of the olfactory chambers were abnormally thin in some places, but were thick in others, with extensive irregularities, atypical folds, and deep cracks.

The most severe changes, however, occurred in the structure of the epithelium lining the walls of the internal cavities. Only in one place, in the central part of the anterior wall of the chamber, was it possible to observe epithelium somewhat similar to normal (Fig. 3). All other epithelium lining the walls was transformed into tumor tissue that had the structure typical of neuroepithelioma. In many places, this tumor tissue had an obviously tubular structure, with a central cavity or lumen (Fig. 2).

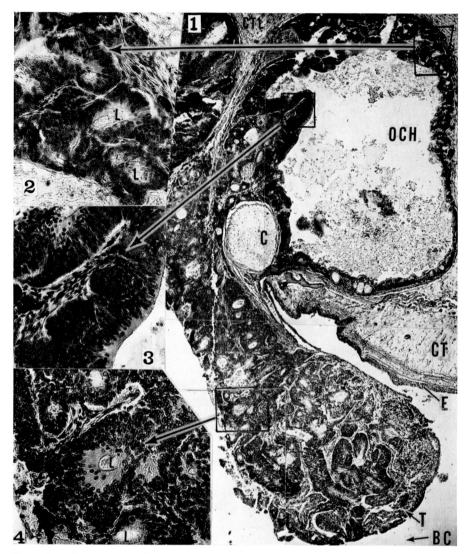

Fig. 1. Sagittal sections through modified olfactory chamber (OCH) and surrounding tissues, including tumor. (Compound photomicrograph consisting of several separate photomicrographs under low magnification.) BC, buccal cavity; C, cartilage; CT, loose connective tissue; E, surface epithelium of buccal cavity; T, tumor (neuroepithelioma). ×32.

Fig. 2. Upper right posterior portion of epithelium of olfactory chamber, transformed into tumor tissue (medium magnification). L, lumen or central cavity of tumor lobe. ×136.

Fig. 3. Central anterior portion of epithelium of olfactory chamber, preserving structure somewhat similar to that of normal olfactory epithelium (medium magnification). ×136.

Fig. 4. Portion of tumor tissue (medium magnification). L, lumen or central cavity of tumor lobe. ×136.

Large masses of tumor surrounded a region of epithelium with a relatively normal structure (Figs. 1 and 3). The abnormal size of the olfactory chamber was evidently a result of the destructive activity of the tumor tissue. In some areas, portions of the tumor were separated by layers of connective tissue (Fig. 1). The largest tumor masses were concentrated in the lower portion of the anterior corner of the olfactory chamber (Fig. 1), and the tumor grew through the roof of the mouth into the buccal cavity, where it developed more in the posterior direction (Fig. 1). The structure of the tumor was remarkably similar in the wall of the olfactory chamber (Fig. 2) and in the buccal cavity (Fig. 4).

It is evident that this spontaneous neuroepithelioma had an appreciable capacity for invasion and destruction. The tumor did not intrude into tissues posterior to the olfactory chamber (Fig. 1), but it did invade all of the anterior portion of the lower jaw up to the end. All tissues in its path, including the skin epithelium, disappeared and were replaced with tumor tissue. Obviously the anlagen of the teeth of the lower jaw disappeared in the process. In the dorsal direction, the tumor was limited by the wall of the olfactory chamber. Above the tumor were a layer of normal loose connective tissue and the skin epithelium. The distal portion of the upper jaw was completely normal, with skin epithelium, loose connective tissue, cartilaginous skeletal elements, and tooth anlagen, in striking contrast to the tumorous distal portion of the lower jaw.

The spontaneous and transplanted tumors showed appreciable differences in behavior and structure. The spontaneous tumor gave a definite impression of greater aggressiveness and invasiveness. For one thing, it exhibited some sort of special antagonism toward skin epithelium. The transplanted tumor was so tolerant of skin epithelium as to be always covered with it, but the spontaneous tumor destroyed skin epithelium. Furthermore, a lack of surface epithelium was characteristic of the spontaneous tumor (Figs. 1 and 6–8). The neuroepitheliomal tubes were bare at the surface of the tumor in some places (Fig. 1), although generally isolated by a layer of connective tissue, thin in most places but very dense in structure elsewhere (Fig. 6). The amount of connective tissue was considerable in a few areas. Certain lobes of the tumor were separated by thick layers of connective tissue (Fig. 1). Some sort of interstitial membrane, possibly collagen, covered the surface of the tumor in certain areas, clearly visible in some places, especially under high magnification (Fig. 7), but almost invisible in others (Fig. 8). In a few areas, this membrane was obviously separate from the underlying connective tissue.

The spontaneous tumor was characterized by a very rich blood supply provided by great numbers of blood vessels ranging from occasional extremely large ones (Fig. 5) through medium-sized ones (Fig. 9) to small ones (Figs. 8 and 11) and capillaries. In contrast, the blood supply to the neuroepithelioma transplants was provided mostly by small capillaries (2).

In both types of tumor, spontaneous and transplanted, certain parts of the neuroepitheliomal tubes were very similar to the olfactory epithelium and exhibited the types of layers of cells that are characteristic of the olfactory epithelium. Even so, cilia, which were observed in the transplanted tumor only in very rare cases, if at all, were often very clearly observable in the spontaneous tumor (Fig. 10).

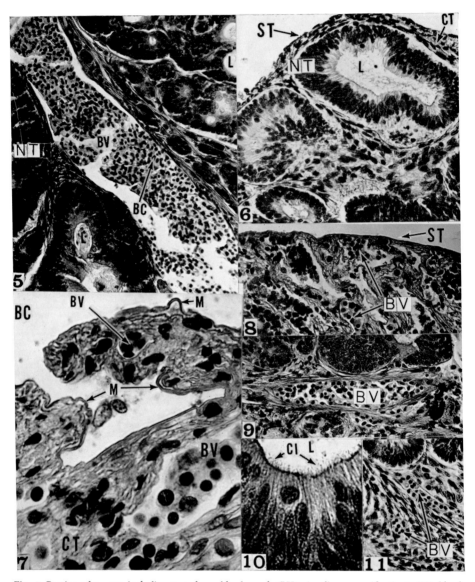

Fig. 5. Portion of tumor, including very large blood vessel (BV) (medium magnification). BC, blood cells; L, lumen or central cavity of tumor lobe; NT, neuroepitheliomal tubes or lobes. ×136.

Fig. 6. Surface portion of tumor (medium magnification). CT, connective tissue; L, lumen or central cavity of tumor lobe; NT, neuroepitheliomal tubes or lobes; ST, surface of tumor. ×136.

Fig. 7. Surface portion of tumor (high magnification). BC, buccal cavity; BV, blood vessel; CT, connective tissue; M, surface interstitial membrane. ×456.

Fig. 8. Surface portion of tumor (medium magnification). BV, blood vessel; ST, surface of tumor. ×136.

Fig. 9. Portion of tumor, including large blood vessel (BV) (medium magnification). ×136.

Fig. 10. Central portion of neuroepitheliomal tube (NT) (high magnification). CI, cilia; L, lumen or central cavity of tumor. ×456.

Fig. 11. Portion of tumor, including small blood vessels (BV) (medium magnification). ×136.

Conclusions

Histological study of a spontaneous neuroepithelioma occurring in a Mexican axolotl (*Siredon mexicanum*) showed that the tumor originated in the olfactory epithelium of the nasal cavities. This tumor destroyed almost all of the olfactory epithelium as well as all other tissues in the anterior portion of the lower jaw. The spontaneous tumor differed from a transplanted tumor derived from it in that the spontaneous tumor had a much richer blood supply, was much more invasive, and exhibited some sort of special antagonism toward skin epithelium.

References

1. SHEREMETIEVA-BRUNST, E. A., and BRUNST, V. V.: Origin and transplantation of a melanotic tumor in the axolotl. Special Publ. N.Y. Acad. Sci. *4*:269–287, 1948.
2. BRUNST, V. V., and ROQUE, A. L.: Tumors in amphibians. I. Histology of a neuroepithelioma in *Siredon mexicanum*. J. Nat. Cancer Inst. *38*:193–204, 1967.
3. BRUNST, V. V.: Cytological study of transplanted neuroepithelioma in *Siredon mexicanum*. Exper. Cell Res. *53*:401–409, 1968.
4. BRUNST, V. V., and ROQUE, A. L.: Spontaneous teratoma in an axolotl (*Siredon mexicanum*). Cancer Res. *29*:223–229, 1969.

Tumors of the Testis in the Mexican Axolotl
(*Ambystoma,* or *Siredon, mexicanum*) *

R. R. Humphrey

Department of Zoology, Indiana University
Bloomington, Indiana

Although neoplasms in the Amphibia occur with considerable frequency, ones originating in the testis seem to be very rarely encountered. In an extensive review published in 1962 Balls (1) was able to include only a single case, that of a carcinoma in *Megalobatrachus maximus* reported by Pick and Poll (2). In view of this apparent scarcity of neoplasms in the amphibian testis, it is rather remarkable that 16 have been found in Mexican axolotls of the writer's colony. The first of these was discovered in 1941 in a white male about 6 years of age which had been obtained in 1935 from Dr. Cranford Hutchinson, then at the Morris Biological Farm of the Wistar Institute. Fundamentally similar tumors have since been found in 15 additional animals, most of them of the same white strain. The last of the series was found in 1968; the tumors have thus been appearing at intervals over a period of 27 years. Five of them were found while the axolotl colony was at the University of Buffalo, and the remaining 11 since its transfer to Indiana University in 1957.

In 10 of the axolotl males the tumors were of large size and had caused such a reduction of the non-tumorous parts of both testes as to make them almost unrecognizable. Such tumors are classed as definitive. In 6 animals the tumors constitute relatively small parts of testes which usually are otherwise of normal structure. These can be identified with certainty only by microscopic examination and are classed as incipient.

Definitive Tumors

Although of large size, these were all of benign type. None had caused the death of the animal carrying it. Often they were attached to a testis by a rather slender vascular stalk (Fig. 2), but a few had a broader attachment (Fig. 3). One tumor appeared to constitute the cephalic third of the testis to which it was related, and another had seemingly replaced the entire right testis (Fig. 4). In shape and size they ranged from a sphere of about 8 mm diameter to an oval mass about 45 mm in its longest dimension. Some were subdivided by deep fissures into a number of lobes

---

* Contribution No. 817 from the Department of Zoology, Indiana University. This study was supported in part by research grant RO1 GM 05850 from the Research Grants Division, National Institutes of Health, United States Public Health Service. The author wishes to acknowledge the assistance of Dr. Robert Briggs and Mrs. Carolyn Huffman in the preparation of the illustrations.

(Figs. 1 and 21). Much or all of the surface of any tumor showed a pebbled appearance under low magnification. Usually they were of fairly compact structure; some, however, were of a spongy character or contained cysts of various sizes (Fig. 5).

Stained sections show the tumors to be composed of tubules which are much elongated and branched, unlike the normal tubules of the axolotl testis, which are short unbranched conical or pyramidal structures (Figs. 15–17). Larger and presumably older stems or trunks in the interior branch repeatedly (Fig. 7). Their terminal branches near the tumor surface are usually arranged perpendicular to the covering peritoneum (Figs. 8 and 10); here their bulging ends give the tumor surface its characteristic pebbled appearance.

Although the tumors vary somewhat in their finer structure, and differences may occur even in different parts of a single tubule, one type of lining epithelium is present in much or all of every tumor and appears to be essential to tumor development. This "tumor epithelium" consists of spermatogonia with relatively large spherical nuclei, surrounded and separated by smaller irregular cells (Figs. 8 and 9); the latter have a scanty cytoplasm and a hyperchromatic nucleus of variable shape. In regions in which the spermatogonia are widely spaced or lacking the smaller cells assume the form of a simple columnar epithelium (Fig. 10), or if the tubule becomes much distended, an epithelium of squamous type. They are frequently seen in mitosis, especially in those parts of the tubules nearest the tumor surface. Mitotic figures in the spermatogonia also tend to be more frequent in this region. Degenerating spermatogonia, on the other hand, are usually more numerous in the more internal (presumably older) parts of the tubules.

Two striking modifications of the characteristic tumor epithelium have been encountered. In much of one lobe of the tumor shown in Fig. 1 all spermatogonia had disappeared. The associated small cells remaining constitute a simple epithelium with fairly tall columnar cells (Fig. 10). The other modification of the tumor epithelium, found in the *A. mexicanum-opacum* hybrid whose tumor is shown in Fig. 4, consists in its marked thickening or stratification apparently following a considerable dilatation of the tubules at some earlier time (Fig. 11). Relative numbers of the spermatogonia and smaller cells had been maintained as the thickening occurred, and none of the spermatogonia had transformed into spermatocytes. These two modifications of the tumor epithelium were found in the two oldest males with tumors—animals of 6 years or over.

The tubules of the tumors are surrounded by a rather scanty loose connective tissue, continuous with that of the covering peritoneum (Figs. 9 and 10). This becomes more conspicuous in regions in which many tubules have undergone degeneration. It contains no interstitial cells.

Incipient Tumors

In contrast with the bulky definitive tumors, one classed as incipient is, as a rule, merely a small pathological part of an otherwise normal testis (Fig. 6). It is actually a tumor in an early stage of development (Fig. 14).

Incipient tumors have been found in 6 males, one of which had 2 in the same testis. Usually they appear to be modifications of one of the small subdivisions or lobes of the normal testis, such as appear in Fig. 6. They consist of elongated tubules instead of the normal conical or pyramidal ones. These tend to radiate outward from the interior of the mass to end beneath its covering peritoneum. They are not as extensively branched as in the definitive tumors. They have become highly atypical, however, in their pattern of spermatogenesis. In the normal tubule there is an approximate synchrony of development of all the germ cells. After a series of mitotic divisions, all the spermatogonia of a normal young tubule, except a few at its junction with its duct (the residual spermatogonia; see Fig. 15) transform into growing primary spermatocytes (Fig. 16). Meiotic divisions eventually follow, and the resulting spermatids transform simultaneously throughout the tubule (Fig. 17). The tubules of the incipient tumors lack this synchrony in development of their germ cells. Instead, each tubule has a seriation of stages along its length (Fig. 12). The more advanced stages (spermatozoa or spermatids) occupy its central end in the interior of the mass, with meiotic divisions, growing primary spermatocytes, and spermatogonia in sequence toward its peripheral end. Directly beneath the peritoneum the spermatogonia are distributed singly in an epithelial layer structurally similar to the tumor epithelium of the definitive tumors (Fig. 9). Such an epithelial layer is a characteristic feature of an early developmental stage of the normal tubule (Fig. 15); there, of course, it disappears as its spermatogonia, by a series of mitoses, produce groups of isogenic cells which soon become growing spermatocytes. In the tubules of the incipient tumors, however, this epithelial layer persists and through its continued unregulated growth produces the bulky definitive tumors.

Although the definitive tumors agree in attaining a large size and in having as an essential constituent the tumor epithelium found originating in the incipient tumors, they do fall into two rather distinct categories with regard to their structural pattern. The first type is essentially an incipient tumor grown to large size. It is represented by only 2 of the 10 definitive tumors. In these, the spermatogonia crowded away from the end of the tubule continue, perhaps indefinitely, to become primary spermatocytes which progress to meiosis and later stages. Thus an abortive spermatogenesis continues in the interior of the tumor, the germ cells produced there degenerating as spermatozoa if not in some earlier phase. The tubules degenerate and disappear progressively from their inner ends outward; this leaves a central core of connective tissue (Fig. 21) external to which is a zone in which an abortive spermatogenesis continues, and external to this, at the tumor surface, a narrow zone in which the slender tubules have the usual tumor epithelium of spermatogonia and indifferent cells. The tumor epithelium thus constitutes a relatively small part of the total bulk of the tumor. The second type of structure is found in 8 of the 10 definitive tumors. In these an abortive spermatogenesis is either completely lacking or remains only in scattered tubules. It would appear that the tumor epithelium established in the early development of the tumor had soon ceased to give origin to spermatocytes, and that it had then extended inward as a lining for the tubules, surrounding the spermatocytes, spermatozoa or other germ cells contained therein, which would finally disappear completely through degeneration (Fig. 13). The deep ends of the tubules, now lined by tumor epithelium, become the larger trunks or stems of the branching tubules. Stages in this type of transformation in the tubules occur in some of the small incipient tumors as well as occasionally in some of the older ones.

In what are probably the oldest tumors no germ cells remain except the spermatogonia of the tumor epithelium, which here constitutes the bulk of the tumor substance (Figs. 8, 9, and 11).

Physiological Action of Tumors

In all males with definitive tumors the non-tumorous parts of both testes showed an extreme reduction in size (Figs. 2, 3, and 4). Normally in the axolotl the tubules from which spermatozoa have been discharged undergo degeneration, becoming reduced finally to a few large spermatogonia and their associated indifferent cells at the junction of the tubule with its duct. These residual spermatogonia, characterized by large lobulated lightly staining nuclei, had remained quiescent during the months in which the tubule had produced and discharged its crop of spermatozoa (Figs. 15–17). Shortly following the degeneration of the emptied tubule they begin to increase by mitosis, and together with the associated indifferent cells soon produce a small new tubule (Fig. 15). In males in which a tumor has attained a large size this regeneration of normal tubules is inhibited. Mitoses occur, but the resulting new spermatogonia then degenerate. Finally the entire non-tumorous portions of both testes become reduced to narrow flattened structures, mere rudiments in which only ducts and small numbers of spermatogonia remain (Figs. 2, 4, and 18). The tumor of Fig. 3 is apparently of fairly recent origin and the testes are less reduced in size; those tubules which had developed beyond spermatogonial stages before the tumor had attained a large size had been able to continue development. Quite different is the testis shown in Figs. 4 and 18. Subjected to the influence of a large tumor for perhaps 3 years, this testis lacks spermatogonia in much of its extent.

Whether the inhibition of the testes by definitive tumors is brought about by androgens or by other substances from the tumor carried by the blood remains uncertain. It is evident, however, that in males with definitive tumors and vestigial testes, sufficient androgens are being produced to maintain an active state in the glands of the cloaca (Fig. 19) and the epithelium of the ductus deferens (Fig. 20). These are not reduced to the condition seen in castrated males. A vestigial testis such as that of Figs. 4 and 18 would seem unlikely to be the source of the androgens maintaining the duct epithelium of Fig. 20. The bulky tumor in this male, consisting as it does of testicular components, might be expected to produce androgens as does the normal testis, although not necessarily in the same quantity.

Incidence and Etiology of Tumors

Since the tumors have not been found in males under two years of age, only males of about that age and over have been taken into account in computing their rate of occurrence. Of 497 such males 16 had tumors, an incidence of 3.2 percent. Fourteen of these 16 tumorous males were closely related, one of them being among the white animals obtained from the Wistar Institute in 1935, and the other 13 being descended from the one female which produced offspring, an animal probably a sib of the male with the tumor. The possible role of heredity in the etiology of the tumors is strongly suggested by one family group in which a male with a tumor had a brother, a son, two grandsons, a great-grandson, and a great-great-grandson with tumors. Although the fact that a tumorous male may have no immediate ancestor or descendant with a tumor would suggest a recessive type of inheritance if heredity is involved, this type of genetic basis is contraindicated by the occurrence of a tumor in a hybrid male whose father was a marbled salamander (*Ambystoma opacum*) rather than an axolotl. The axolotl mother, closely related to several tumorous males, might here seem to have transmitted a dominant gene. Of the two unrelated dark axolotls with tumors, one is known to have had a remote white ancestor, and the other may have had. In any event, all of the tumorous males may have a common ancestry, since all are descended from animals obtained from European sources. It is, of course, quite probable that the tumors do not result from the action of a single specific gene, but develop in response to non-genetic influences acting upon a pattern of testis structure common to all axolotl males, and that in the absence of influences which might trigger abnormal development of tubules, no tumor arises. In this connection it may be noted that the multilobed form of the testis characteristic of axolotl males after their first breeding season (Fig. 6) is not found in any other urodele with which the writer is acquainted, and tumors of the testes were never found in several hundred males of 12 other urodele species which have been autopsied.

Study of the incipient tumors suggests as a possible factor in their development the loss of the usual connection of testis tubules to ducts. The atypical elongated tubules of the incipient tumors usually appear to lack such connections. That the related duct may exert an influence upon the tubule is suggested by the fact that a few spermatogonia adjacent to the duct cease division and remain quiescent while those of the remainder of the tubule continue dividing and then after a time transform into spermatocytes (Figs. 15 and 16). Whether the relation of duct to tubule, or some other factor, regulates or limits the division of spermatogonia as the tubule develops, this regulation has been lost in the tubules of the incipient tumors, permitting spermatogonia to persist and multiply indefinitely in the tumor epithelium at their subperitoneal ends.

The possible role of a virus in the formation of these testicular tumors cannot be excluded. The action of either a virus or a chemical product of the tumors is suggested by a finding in a few of the males with definitive tumors: although inhibiting tubule regeneration in the opposite testis and in more distal parts of the testis in which it developed, the tumor appears to stimulate or promote development of tubules in the region contiguous with it and induce their differentiation into tumor tubules. These young tubules become elongated and branched, with their spermatogonia continuing to divide as in the tumor epithelium instead of transforming into spermatocytes. Such tubules apparently become incorporated into the edge of the tumor.

The addition of new tubules through a change in young tubules or tubule anlagen in adjacent parts of the atrophic testis may explain the condition shown in Fig. 4, in which the tumor in an old male appears to have replaced the entire right testis. The cephalic part of this tumor is apparently the oldest: its tubules have the peculiar stratification of the tumor epithelium shown in Fig. 11. The caudal part has tubules of the character found in tumors known to be of recent origin, such as those of Fig. 9. It may be surmised that this part of the tumor had arisen by formation of new tumor tubules in what had earlier been atrophic testis caudal to the original tumor site.

Two of the 16 males with tumors of the testis also had tumors in the roof of the mouth. These were comparable in structure to the tumor described by Brunst and Roque (3) and believed by them to be a neuroepithelioma originating from the olfactory epithelium of the adjacent nasal chamber. These oral tumors probably preceded in development the tumors of the testes. If they were of viral origin the same virus might well have been a factor in the later formation of a tumor at another site. In 14 of the axolotl males, however, no tumors were found except those of testicular origin.

The case records of the 16 affected males offer little suggestion as to other possible etiological factors. Advanced age, hormonal imbalance, trauma, and malnutrition may be dismissed, since none could have affected more than one or two animals at most. Almost all of the males were probably under three years of age and in good condition when their tumors first began development.

Summary

Tumors of the axolotl testis arise from the proliferation of a "tumor epithelium" consisting of the spermatogonia and associated indifferent cells at the peripheral (subperitoneal) ends of a group of tubules, usually those of a testicular lobe in which tubules are regenerating after emptying. These tumors may attain a bulk several times that of a normal testis; a tubular structure is maintained, with the tubules becoming much branched and elongated. Ultimately they may contain no germ cells other than spermatogonia. They inhibit regeneration of the normal tubules in the non-tumorous portions of both testes, thus reducing these to mere rudiments. In view of this condition of the testes, the maintenance of secretory activity in the accessory reproductive glands and in the ductus deferens of tumorous males must be interpreted as the result of androgen output by the tumors. The etiology of the tumors is uncertain. Although possibly resulting from a disturbed relationship between growing parts (ducts and tubules) in a lobe of the testis, they may perhaps be produced by a reaction to the presence of a virus.

References

1. BALLS, M.: Spontaneous neoplasms in amphibia: a review and descriptions of six new cases. Cancer Res. 22:1142–1154, 1962.
2. PICK, L., and POLL, H.: Uber einige bemerkenswerthe Tumorbildungen aus der Thierpathologie, inbesondere uber gutartige und Krebsige Neubildungen bei Kaltblutern. Berlin Klin. Wchnschr. 40:572–574, 1903.
3. BRUNST, V. V., and ROQUE, A. L.: Tumors in amphibians. I. Histology of a neuroepithelioma in Siredon mexicanum. J. Nat. Cancer Inst. 38:193–204, 1967.

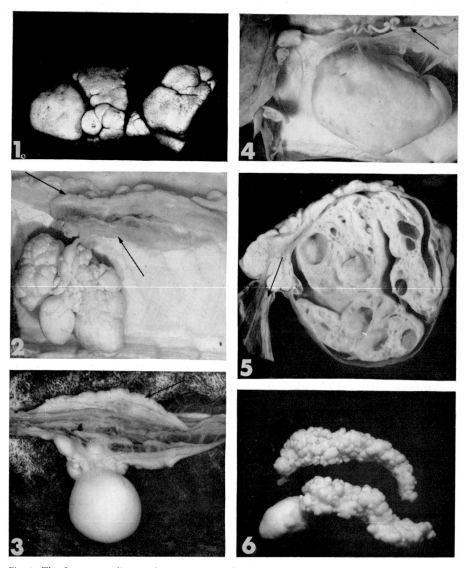

Fig. 1. The first tumor discovered, in a 6 year male. ✕1.6.

Figs. 2–4. Definitive tumors *in situ,* with other viscera removed or displaced. Left side upmost. Arrows indicate the atrophic testes. ✕1.6, ✕2.4, ✕1.4.

Fig. 5. Definitive tumor cut open to show cysts. ✕1.6. This tumor was attached to the cephalic end of the right testis, indicated by arrow.

Fig. 6. Testes of male of 4 years, 3 months. The left testis (below) has an incipient tumor at its cephalic end. ✕1.6.

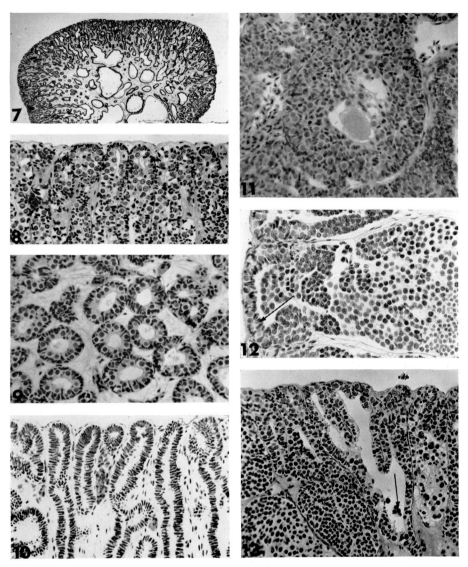

Fig. 7. Section of one lobe of the tumor of Fig. 1. ×10.

Fig. 8. Peripheral (subperitoneal) ends of tubules, from tumor of Fig. 1, showing tumor epithelium. ×80.

Fig. 9. Tumor tubules cut transversely. ×96.

Fig. 10. Tubules with tumor epithelium lacking spermatogonia. ×80.

Fig. 11. Tubule with much thickened tumor epithelium; compare with Fig. 9. ×96.

Fig. 12. Tubule from incipient tumor; peripheral end (at left) shows tumor epithelium (arrow). To right are spermatogonia, spermatocytes, spermatids. ×96.

Fig. 13. Incipient tumor. Growth of tumor epithelium has produced a branching tubule; arrow indicates degenerating germ cells. ×80.

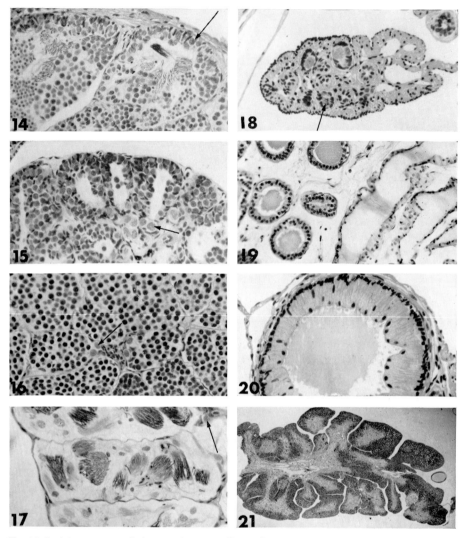

Fig. 14. Incipient tumor; tubules contain germ cells in all stages from spermatogonia to spermatozoa (filamentous). Tumor epithelium at arrow. ✕92.

Figs. 15–17. Normal testes illustrating synchronous development of all germ cells in any tubule: 15, spermatogonia; 16, spermatocytes; 17, spermatozoa. Residual spermatogonia at arrows. ✕92.

Fig. 18. Cross section of atrophic testis of *mexicanum-opacum* hybrid of 6 years (see Fig. 4). Few spermatogonia remain. One in mitosis at arrow. ✕92.

Fig. 19. Actively secreting cloacal glands of two types from male whose tumor is shown in Fig. 1. ✕154.

Fig. 20. Ductus deferens from male whose testis is shown in Fig. 18. Note tall epithelial cells and secretion in lumen. ✕92.

Fig. 21. Tumor of type showing degeneration of central ends of tubules after abortive spermatogenesis; connective tissue occupies interior of lobes. ✕3.5.

Simulated Transmission of Renal Tumors in Oocytes and Embryos of *Rana pipiens**

Kenyon S. Tweedell

Department of Biology, University of Notre Dame
Notre Dame, Indiana

Introduction

The susceptibility of the frog embryo to infective transmission of the renal adenocarcinoma was shown following inoculation of R. *pipiens* embryos with subcellular fractions and filtrates from inclusion body tumors (1). The cytoplasmic fractions injected were rich in the herpes-like virus also seen in the source tumor. Induction of renal carcinomas, identical to spontaneous actively growing primary adenocarcinomas occurred in 66% to over 90% of the hosts. Tumors were found in both pronephric and mesonephric kidneys and were palpable prior to or during metamorphosis. While the success of the injections depended upon the embryonic stage, all recipients from the blastula through hatching stage were inducible. Subsequently, Mulcare (2, 3) has found that similar fractions will transmit renal tumors through the embryos of a closely related species *Rana palustris*.

These experiments helped to affirm the suspected viral nature of the tumor and presented evidence that transmission in natural populations could have been through the embryo or larva, a route suggested by Rafferty (4). If so, passage might be horizontal from one animal to another. Infection of the young could either take place at fertilization actively aided by entrance of the sperm, or when the larvae are free of the fertilization and jelly membranes. Attempts were made to simulate transmission of the tumor into the fertilized egg or via the larvae, as if from a natural source of infection such as a tumor bearing adult. Alternatively, if developing eggs already harbor the tumor inducing virus, a latent infection of either the sperm or egg could take place during gametogenesis as proposed by Mizell and Zambernard (5). Exposure of the gamete, presumably from a tumor bearing adult host, could also occur later during transportation of the gametes through the urogenital system (♂) or within the pleuroperitoneal cavity during ovulation (♀). Experiments were designed to simulate tumor transmission through both routes—horizontal and vertical. The embryo injection experiments cited earlier could support both hypotheses.

Materials and Methods

Animals. Adult *Rana pipiens* were obtained from Vermont (C. H. Mumley, Alburg, Vt.) and Wisconsin (E. G. Steinhilber, Oshkosh, Wis.). Frog eggs, embryos and larvae

---
* This research was supported by Grant CA-07849 from the National Cancer Institute, NIH, Bethesda, Md.

were produced by induced ovulation in *R. pipiens* adults. After fertilization, embryos were raised at 18°C until hatching when they were moved to 23°C and maintained as described earlier (1).

Tumor Source and Analysis. All tumors used were spontaneous renal adenocarcinomas from either Vermont or Wisconsin *R. pipiens*. Each tumor was stored at 9°C for 3 or more months to induce inclusion bodies (6), a visible sign of viral infection. Nuclear inclusion bodies were verified by frozen section prior to fractionation.

All experimental and control animals were autopsied and their organs examined grossly for abnormalities. Tumors and suspect tissues were examined histologically after fixation in Carnoy's and staining in Jenner Giemsa.

Tumor Fraction Inoculum. The preparations of the active cytoplasmic tumor fractions used were mitochondrial (P_2) and microsomal (P_3) components isolated after the method of Tweedell (1). Some tumors were sonicated in a Willems Polytron at a pulse frequency of 9400 cps (22,000 rpm) for 90 sec just after separation of the crude nuclear-cytoplasmic fractions but before further fractionation. Tumor fractions were used undiluted or in dilutions of 10^{-1} or 10^{-2} made in phosphate buffer (0.02 M, pH 7.6). E. M. checks of the P_2 pellet were made for the presence of the herpes-like virus.

Perivitelline Inoculation of Eggs. Eggs from a *R. pipiens* Vt. animal (subsequently shown to be free of any neoplasia) were obtained and fertilized with sperm from a tumor free male. After membrane elevation and egg rotation, 5μ filtrates of the P_2 or P_3 tumor fractions undiluted or diluted up to 10^{-2} were injected (0.1 μl/egg) through the jelly layers beneath the fertilization membrane prior to the first cleavage. Controls received similar amounts of phosphate buffer as a blank.

Inoculation Into Embryos. An aliquot of the undiluted P_2 fraction previously used for inoculation of the eggs was stored in ice for 6 days. Tailbud embryos (S18) were demembranated and injected with 0.2 to 0.4 μl of 10^{-2} dilutions of the P_2 filtrates into the nephrogenic ridge or into the rhombocoel of the hindbrain as described elsewhere (1). Uninoculated controls were also maintained.

Exposure of Embryos. Newly hatched embryos from Shumway (7) stage 19 to stage 21 were reared in 500 ml of water and 0.25 ml of the tumor fractions were introduced into the water periodically. In the first experiment the embryos were exposed to the P_2 and then to the P_3 fractions of two inclusion body tumors derived from both Wisconsin and Vermont animals. Twelve inoculations (0.25 ml/dish) were given over a period of 32 days for a total of 3 ml of tumor inoculum. In a second experiment both fractions from three different inclusion body tumors were administered alternately 9 times over a period of 36 days. Subsequently, the animals were raised at 19–21°C through metamorphosis. Phosphate buffer dilutions of 10^{-1} through 10^{-3} were also tested and blank controls were run simultaneously. During the exposure period, the animals were gradually reduced from 25/culture dish to 8–9/dish at the time of the last injection. The same inoculum ratio was maintained. Culture dishes were changed and food added the day following inoculation so that tumor fractions containing the virus were present approximately 24 hours. Each inoculation was repeated every 3rd to 4th day.

Incubation of Spermatozoa. Testes from non-tumor bearing animals were removed and crushed in 20 ml of spring water. Aliquots of either the P_2 or the P_3 tumor fraction were added to the sperm suspension (0.5 ml tumor fraction/20 ml sperm suspension). The sperm were incubated at 23 °C for $\frac{1}{2}$ hour prior to their use in fertilization. Another aliquot of the original sperm suspension without tumor incubation was used to fertilize control eggs.

Exposure of Oocytes. Adult female *R. pipiens* (later determined to be non-tumor bearing) were injected with pituitaries to induce ovulation. Initial follicular rupture occurs from 18 to 22 hours after injection (8). Twelve hours after the pituitary injections, two females were injected intraperitoneally with either 0.1 or 0.2 ml of the undiluted P_2 tumor fractions. Since follicular rupture and egg emergence lasts for 10 to 12 hours at 22 to 25 °C, the adults were placed at 9 °C for 12 hours after the first injection to prolong exposure of the oocytes to the virus in the P_2 fraction. The hosts were then returned to 23 °C and inoculation of the tumor fraction was resumed. Each animal was given a total of 5 injections over a period of 20 hours, totaling from 0.5 ml to 1.0 ml of P_2 tumor fraction. Another adult was treated with injections of the filtrates from presonicated P_2 fractions 6 hours after the pituitary injection and lasting over a period of 11 hours at 23 °C. At the end of 48 hours the eggs were shed and fertilized by sperm from males later determined to be free of tumor loci. After fertilization the embryos were reared at 23 °C except one group that was kept at 9 °C for a period of $3\frac{1}{2}$ months.

Results: Simulated Horizontal Transmission

Perivitelline Injection of Tumor Cell Fractions

In a latent infection of the egg, entry of the infective tumor virus could have taken place at the time of fertilization, during amplexus from contaminated spawning waters. Filtrates of the P_2 and P_3 cytoplasmic fractions from an established oncogenic renal tumor (RT 165) that possessed herpes-type viruses were used to mimic this condition. The injected tumor fractions showed a lethal effect on early embryos. From 40 to 54% of the inoculated embryos died in the first 7 days (Table 1) but this level subsided by the time the embryos reached hatching (S19). Of these survivors, 50 to 85% reached metamorphosis with a direct relationship demonstrated between the percentage of survivors and the dilutions of the tumor fractions. At the end of 6 months none of the surviving young adults in any of the inoculated groups, or controls, had developed tumors.

Direct Inoculation of Tailbud Embryos. In order to substantiate the potency of the donor tumor in the above experiment, part of the undiluted P_2 fraction was retained for direct injection into embryos raised from the same clutch. After an initial attrition from the operations, most of the surviving injected animals reached metamorphosis

TABLE 1

Effect of Injecting Renal Tumor Cell Fractions Beneath the Membranes
of Fertilized Eggs or into Tailbud Embryos of Vermont R. pipiens

Inoculum renal tumor 156 Vt.	Site	Number inoculated	Number of survivors (hatching)	Number of adults (6 mo.)	Number of tumors (6 mo.)
P₂ Undiluted	Membrane	117	74	22	0
10⁻¹		114	71	25	0
10⁻²		85	39	22	0
P₃ 10⁻¹		106	56	14	0
10⁻²		93	58	22	0
Controls		48	45	22	0
				(3 mo.)	
P₂ 10⁻²	Nephric ridge	18	17	10	4
10⁻²	Brain	24	22	10	2
Controls		18	17	9	0

and between 60 to 65% completed the transition (Table 1). Renal tumors began to appear in recently metamorphosed adults at 3 to 4 months after the injections. Adeno-carcinomas affecting both the pronephric and mesonephric kidneys were discovered in animals inoculated into the nephrogenic ridge. Additional tumors were produced in the brain injected animals but these were not detected until after autopsy. In one of these metamorphosed animals a 2 mm tumor mass was found attached to the dorsal side of the medulla oblongata at the junction with the spinal cord. The tumor was encapsulated and continuous with periodic septa that projected inward, occasionally accompanied by blood vessels. The septa were bordered with large cuboidal cells having large round nuclei and 1 to 2 nucleoli (Fig. 1). Numerous pockets of erythrocytes and necrotic cells were found throughout the tumor that resembled an adenoma. The induction of tumors by both inoculation routes established the potency of the tumor fraction used in the previous experiment even though the fractions had been stored for 6 days (in ice) after extraction. No tumors were found in the uninoculated controls.

Continuous Exposure of Late Embryos and Larvae to Tumor Cell Fractions

Combinations of mitochondrial and microsomal fractions of three different inclusion body renal tumors (RT 140, Wis., RT 141 and 148 Vt.) were placed in the culture water of recently hatched Wis. R. *pipiens* embryos for a period of 32 to 36 days.

In the first experiment 3 groups of 25 animals were exposed to undiluted, 10⁻¹ and 10⁻² dilutions of the P₂ and P₃ fractions from two renal tumors, RT 140 and 141. Equal numbers of controls were maintained. The second experiment consisted of 3 more groups of 25 that were treated with fractions from all three tumors and a control group. At the termination of the inoculation period the larvae had a median length of 38 mm (range 25–80 mm).

There was no apparent effect upon the larvae from exposure to the tumor cell fractions nor upon the survival rate when compared to the controls. Of the 150 experimental animals, from 48% to 52% of all groups completed metamorphosis. None of the experimental or control animals developed any signs of neoplasia before, during or after metamorphosis. At least 2 dozen animals from each experiment were kept under observation for 1½ years with no subsequent appearance of tumors in any group.

Results: Simulated Vertical Transmission

Exposure of Spermatozoa to Tumor Cell Fractions

Sections of normal frog kidneys often showed that spermatozoa penetrated the ureter back into the kidney tubules. Presumably then mixing of the sperm and renal tumor viruses could have taken place easily in the cloaca of a tumor bearing adult. The spermatozoa could act as a carrier and transmission of the tumor virus would be aided by sperm penetrance.

Eggs from a non-tumor bearing Wis. R. *pipiens* were fertilized with sperm exposed to the cytoplasmic fractions of a Vt. R. *pipiens* tumor. The exposure of the sperm to either tumor fraction had a strong lethal effect and resulted in only 10% fertility among the progeny. The untreated sperm produced 80% fertility in the controls. The subsequent mortality of the treated group was extremely high; after 1 week only 15 of the 570 P_2 treated and 86 of the 350 P_3 treated embryos remained alive. After metamorphosis 10 of the P_2 survivors and 17 of the P_3 exposed survivors remained alive. The metamorphosed animals were kept for one year after fertilization. The 27 animals were autopsied and their kidneys examined for neoplasia. There were no cases of neoplasia in either the experimentally treated or control animals. Spermatozoa exposed in this manner seemed incapable of transmitting the tumor causing agent, although later experiments showed that the tumor used, RT 150, was oncogenically active.

Exposure of Oocytes to Tumor Cell Fractions

If the tumor causative virus is present in oocytes at the time of fertilization, this infection could have taken place during development in the ovary. The oocytes may also be vulnerable to infection during ovulation and these experiments attempted to simulate the latter condition.

Untreated P_2 Fractions. After exposure of the oocytes *in vivo* to i. p. injections of the tumor cell fractions the eggs were fertilized and treated routinely. Development of the treated embryos was normal but there was 18 to 22% mortality in the first 3 months leaving 363 and 199 survivors from frog A and B respectively. At this time 70 late larvae from donor animal A were randomly selected before initiating metamorphosis and transferred to 9 °C in the dark to determine the possible effect of cold treatment on tumor induction. The remaining embryos from both donor frogs were left at 23 °C when 57% and 67% respectively of the surviving larvae from

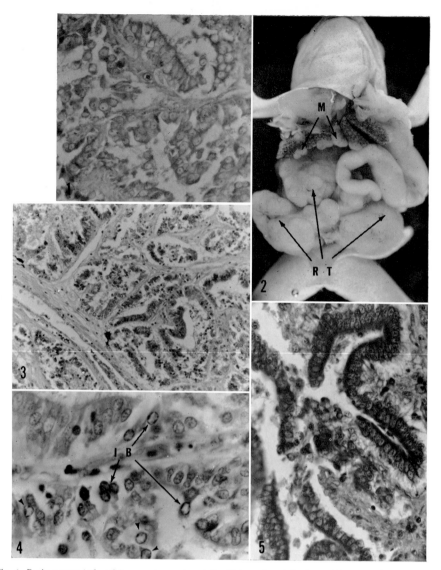

Fig. 1. Brain tumor induced in a metamorphosed *R. pipiens* after injection with a mitochondrial (P_2) renal tumor fraction into the hindbrain of a tailbud (S 17) embryo. $\times$311.

Fig. 2. Induced renal adenocarcinoma in a *R. pipiens* adult yearling (37 mm head-body length) after exposure of the oocytes to the P_2 fraction of an inclusion body tumor (RT 150). The renal tumor (RT) was a bilateral mesonephric tumor with multiple metastases (M) to the lung, liver and ovaries. $\times$1.5.

Fig. 3. A renal adenocarcinoma induced in a young adult *R. pipiens* that had been exposed as an oocyte to injections of the P_2 fractions from a renal carcinoma, RT 150. The unilateral tumor nodule was an atypical adenocarcinoma with heavy stroma and intranuclear inclusion bodies. $\times$112.

Fig. 4. A nuclear inclusion body renal carcinoma induced in a *R. pipiens* yearling (39 mm snout body length) after oocyte exposure to the P_2 fraction of RT 150A-4. The carcinoma was a non-palpable renal tumor node adjacent to a large hemorrhagic area in the kidney. $\times$450.

Fig. 5. A carcinoma of the pyloric stomach from a young metamorphosed *R. pipiens* (6 mo.) with inclusion bodies in some areas. The adjacent mesonephroi were a continuous anaplastic carcinoma. Induced after exposure of the oocyte to P_2 fractions of RT 150A. $\times$311.

234

donors A and B entered metamorphosis. During this period the cold treated animals continued to grow to an exceptionally large size. After $3\frac{1}{2}$ months the cold treated animals were returned to the room environment ($23°C$) but almost all of the survivors remained in permanent prometamorphosis (well developed adult hind limbs). Only 10% metamorphosed after being returned to room temperature. This compared to 33% and 40% of the progeny from donor frogs A and B that had completed their transformation into adults on schedule at room temperature.

Renal Tumor Development. None of the treated animals had developed detectable tumors at the time of metamorphosis. This varied from earlier results (1) following injection of the tumor cell fractions since the majority of these were detectable at metamorphosis. Renal tumors did appear later in the young adults derived from each of the donor frogs (Table 2). All tumors developed from the mesophric kidneys which suggested they had arisen after disappearance of the pronephros. The carcinomas were bilateral and found in both sexes. The first tumor palpated (Fig. 2) was detected in a young adult from donor B at 8 months after fertilization. The rest of the palpable tumors appeared between 9 months and a year after fertilization. Their gross pathology resembled spontaneous renal adenocarcinomas of mature adults (Fig. 3). The first tumor, 150B-1, possessed multiple necrotic areas with intranuclear inclusion bodies (Fig. 4), a characteristic that differed from those tumors induced by injection of cell free filtrates into embryos. Another feature seen previously only in advanced, highly malignant tumors of the mature adult was the presence of multiple metastases to the liver, lung, intestines and ovary (Fig. 2). There were 3 palpable tumors and 5 animals with tumor loci detected upon autopsy in both males and females. The earliest tumor loci were found 6 months after fertilization. While all animals were autopsied, only

TABLE 2

EXPOSURE OF R. PIPIENS OOCYTES DURING THE OVULATORY PERIOD TO P_2 FRACTIONS OF RENAL TUMOR CELLS

Donor	Total tumor inoculum RT 150 Vt.	Number completed	Metamorphosis hemorrhagic lesions	Tumors	Young adults	
					Number	Tumors
Frog A (Wis.)	0.5 ml	118	1 *	0	44	3
Frog B (Wis.)	1.0 ml	76	9	0	46	8
Frog A (Wis.) (Cold treated)	0.5 ml	6 †	9 *	0	4	0
	RT 162 Vt. (Sonicated)					
Frog C (Vt.)	1.0 ml	26	0	0	26	5

* One each with anaplasia.

† Forty-one remained in permanent prometamorphosis.

suspects were checked histologically which possibly allowed some tumor loci to go undetected.

The first tumor that appeared in the progeny from donor animal A was found 10 months after exposure of the oocytes. The adjacent pyloric region of the stomach was enlarged; histologically it appeared to be an adenocarcinoma of the pyloric region (Fig. 5). The remaining tumors were detected 13 months after exposure and consisted of multiple tumor nodules with necrotic centers that were often associated with massive hemorrhagic areas as described below. Other animals in this group showed pretumor anaplasia of the kidneys.

The metamorphosed survivors from both adults were kept under observation for 1¾ years. No further tumors appeared in the second year among 36 adult yearlings. It is perhaps significant that none of the *cold* treated larvae from Donor A developed renal tumors during the entire period of observation, although relatively few of this group ever became adults.

Sonicated P_2 Fractions. Previous sonication of the cytoplasmic fraction used to derive the P_2 fraction of RT 162 caused a greater disintegration of the fragmented mitochondria, endoplasmic reticulum, etc., and virus clumps. There was little observable effect upon the tumor inducing capacity and presumably the herpes-like virus. Renal tumors of the mesonephroi were again delayed and appeared between 5 to 6 months after exposure to the tumor fraction (Table 2). In general they were actively growing tumors although some nuclear inclusion bodies were present.

Hemorrhagic Lesions. Larvae and metamorphosing animals from donors A and B often developed subdermal hemorrhagic areas (Table 2). The cold treated larvae were particularly affected. The affected areas developed on the ventral side over the entire pleuroperitoneal regions and extended up to the gills or posteriorly toward the anal opening and extending onto the bases of the hind limbs. Internal hemorrhagic areas were also often found on the fat bodies, liver and intestine. The largest proportion of the animals with this syndrome were in the cold treated progeny from donor A while only one of the non-cold treated animals from the same adult became hemorrhagic. While hemorrhagic areas also formed in the progeny from donor B these cases represented only 4% of the original survivors. The latter cases did not form in the same animals developing tumors.

Discussion

Horizontal Transmission. The prospects of establishing a latent infection of the embryo by transmission at fertilization appeared quite promising. Rafferty (10, 11) had shown that the urine of tumor bearing frogs does contain large amounts of virus. The spawning waters containing the virus would allow virus entrance at the time of fertilization and in this way establish a latent infection. Both prior incubation of the sperm with the tumor fractions and injection of the tumor cell-virus fraction beneath the egg membranes at the time of fertilization failed to substantiate this possibility. Continuous exposure of the post hatched embryos and larvae also seemed a likely time for virus entrance from spawning waters. The present experiments also failed to support this hypothesis. Failure to induce tumors via this route parallels attempts by Rafferty to transmit tumors with the purified FV-4 virus (tumor urine virus) by exposure to larvae in the water (10, 11). Similar attempts to transmit tumors after exposure of older R. *pipiens* larvae to FV-4 failed to demonstrate tumors in the post metamorphosed adults (12). Further challenges to larvae with the cytoplasmic viruses FV-1 and FV-2 (derived from normal kidney) had an acute lethal effect upon the tadpoles when added to the water (13). Thus far, attempts to induce tumors horizontally in embryos, or larvae with either viral tumor cell fractions or cultivated viruses have been negative.

The early experiments of Lucké (14) had suggested that natural transmission of the tumor agent might be from adult to adult. Later evidence has been contradictory since Rafferty (15) and Roberts (16) found that the incidence of tumors in untreated isolated laboratory animals varied little from that in crowded laboratory frogs. Recently, DiBerardino and King (17) reported that tumor incidence in adults did increase significantly in crowded laboratory animals when compared to those kept isolated. Apparently some other unknown factor is involved here. A possible explanation is activation of a latent virus acquired as an embryo such as the present experiments demonstrate.

Hemorrhagic Lesions. The appearance of subdermal and internal hemorrhagic areas was possibly related to viral activity. These conditions resembled that seen when frog larvae were infected with frog virus FV-3 (9) and that reported by Mulcare (2, 3) in R. *palustris*. It is possibly significant that this syndrome was more prevalent in animals without induced renal tumors. In this regard the lesions were proportionately higher in the cold treated progeny from the exposed oocytes that failed to form tumors yet practically absent in the siblings reared at room temperature that did develope tumors. If this phenomenon is viral related it suggests either a dual action of the same virus or more probably (due to its resemblance to the reaction of FV-3 in embryos and larvae) an expression of the cytoplasmic virus (3).

Vertical Transmission. Only the freshly emerged oocytes proved susceptible to tumor transmission when they were exposed to the cytoplasmic-virus fractions of the tumor during ovulation. Their vulnerability may be due in part to the non-elevated vitelline membrane and the absence of jelly membranes added in the oviduct. The breakdown of the germinal vesicle and the 1st maturation division also takes place while the exposed eggs are transported toward the oviduct. Another reason for receptivity of the oocyte to viral infection may be the absence of antiviral lysozymes L-1 and L-2 that are present in normal kidney but absent in frog eggs and tumor cells (18). The L-3 form of the lysozyme found in eggs does not inhibit the FV-3 virus in tissue culture. Under natural conditions, a tumor bearing gravid female emerging from hibernation could serve as a direct focus of infection for the oocyte. Assuming the presence of the tumor virus in the blood and lymphatic system at this time, passage into the oocyte could take place in the ovary or possibly penetration into the pleuroperitoneal cavity from the ventral lymph sacs would cause direct exposure of the ovulated oocytes.

Aside from the mode and relative incidence of tumor induction, the most striking difference in the tumors induced by exposure of the oocytes resided in their charac-teristics. All of the tumors found in these experiments were malignancies of the mesonephros; those resulting from injection of embryos often involved the pronephros, strictly a phenomenon of the embryonic state. For the first time metastatic tumors were encountered in the oocyte related tumors; only non-metastatic actively growing tumors were found in those induced through injection of the embryo. Tumors with inclusion bodies were frequently derived by induction through the oocyte. These inclu-sions occurred in animals raised at 19–20°C with no low temperature induction. However, they were rarely seen in dozens of tumors induced from injections of tumor fractions. Finally, the delay in tumor formation until the young adult and yearling in the present experiments departed from the usual formation of tumors prior to or during metamorphosis in those animals injected as embryos.

The above facts may form the basis for a hypothesis of natural tumor transmission, assuming that most embryos possess a latent tumor causing agent. First, renal tumors are never encountered in laboratory produced embryos and larvae nor have they been discovered in natural tadpoles. Juvenile frogs are seldom found with tumors (4). A recent field collection of 2000 frogs by McKinnell and McKinnell (19, 20) showed the mean head-body length of tumor bearing frogs was 67 mm to 91 mm, a size exceeding many two year old adults. However, a tumor bearing juvenile female (57 mm) was recovered recently (20).

The amount of virus injected into the embryos is probably many times that present in natural embryos and the presumed natural titer was exceeded to a lesser degree by the experimentally exposed oocytes. If the natural level of the viral titer is accelerated by cold temperature periods as shown (6), only to subside during the spring and summer months, each succeeding hibernation period might tend to increase the viral titer until a sufficient threshold is reached resulting in tumor induction.

Summary

Previous experiments had demonstrated induction of renal tumors after the in-jection of virus-containing tumor cell fractions and filtrates into frog embryos.

Subcellular cytoplasmic fractions of spontaneous renal tumors containing a herpes-like virus were used to test if the embryonic and larval period of the frog is the natural infective period and secondly whether transmission is horizontal from an external source of infection or vertical through the embryo. Simulated sperm borne infection at fertilization was tried by injection of the tumor fractions beneath the membranes of fertilized eggs. No tumors were produced although the same fractions were oncogenic when injected into tailbud embryos. Post hatched embryos and larvae were continuously exposed to the tumor fractions placed in the culture medium but no tumors had formed in young adults after 1½ years. Spermatozoa incubated with the tumor virus fraction and used to fertilize normal eggs caused heavy mortality but no tumors formed in the survivors. Oocytes were exposed to tumor-virus fractions *in vivo* during ovulation. Latent renal tumor developed in the young adults 5–12 months after exposure. These tumors were often metastasized and sometimes formed intranuclear inclusion bodies, a sign of high viral activity.

References

1. TWEEDELL, K. S.: Induced oncogenesis in developing frog kidney cells. Cancer Res. 27:2042–2052, 1967.

2. MULCARE, D. J. and TWEEDELL, K. S.: Renal tumors induced in *Rana palustris* by tumor implants or subcellular fractions from *Rana pipiens*. Amer. Zool. 7:176, 1967.

3. MULCARE, D. J.: Non-specific transmission of the Lucké tumor. *In* Biology of Amphibian Tumors (M. Mizell, ed.), Springer-Verlag New York Inc., 1969, pp. 240–253.

4. RAFFERTY, K. A., JR.: Kidney tumors of the leopard frog: a review. Cancer Res. 24:169–185, 1964.

5. MIZELL, M. and ZAMBERNARD, J.: Viral particles of the leopard frog renal adenocarcinoma: Causative agent or passenger virus? II. A promising model system for the demonstration of a "lysogenic" state in a metazoan tumor. Ann. N.Y. Acad. Sci. 126:146–169, 1965.

6. MIZELL, M., STACKPOLE, W. and HALPERN S.: Herpes-type virus recovery from "virus-free frog kidney tumors. Proc. Soc. Exp. Biol. Med. 127:808–814, 1968.

7. SHUMWAY, W.: Stages in the normal development of *Rana pipiens*. Anat. Rec. 78:139–148, 1940.

8. RUGH, R.: Ovulation in the frog. II. Follicular rupture to fertilization. J. Exper. Zool. 71:163–193, 1935.

9. TWEEDELL, K. and GRANOFF, A.: Viruses and renal carcinoma of *Rana pipiens*. V. Effect of frog virus 3 on developing frog embryos and larvae. J. Nat. Cancer Instit. 40:407–410, 1968.

10. RAFFERTY, K. A., JR.: The biology of spontaneous renal carcinoma of the frog. *In* Renal Neoplasia (J. King, ed.), Little, Brown and Co., Boston, Mass., 1967.

11. RAFFERTY, K. A., JR.: The cultivation of inclusion associated viruses from Lucké tumor frogs. Ann. N.Y. Acad. Sci. 126:3–21, 1965.

12. GRANOFF, A. and TWEEDELL, K. S.: Unpublished observations.

13. GRANOFF, A., CAME, P. E., and RAFFERTY, K. A., JR.: The isolation and properties of viruses from *Rana pipiens*: their possible relationship to the renal adenocarcinoma of the leopard frog. Ann. N.Y. Acad. Sci. 126:237–255, 1965.

14. LUCKÉ, B.: Kidney carcinoma of the leopard frog: a virus tumor. Ann. N.Y. Acad. Sci. 54:1093–1109, 1952.

15. RAFFERTY, K. A., JR.: Spontaneous kidney tumors in the frog: rate of occurrence in isolated adults. Science 141:720–721, 1963.

16. ROBERTS, M. E.: Studies on the transmissibility and cytology of the renal carcinoma of *Rana pipiens*. Cancer Res. 23:1709–1714, 1963.

17. DiBERARDINO, M. A., and KING, T. J.: Renal adenocarcinomas induced by crowded conditions in laboratory frogs. Cancer Res. 25:1910–1912, 1965.

18. RUBIN, M. L., AR, D. B., and NACE, G. W.: The virus inhibiting action of a lysozyme present in normal frogs but lacking in tumor frogs and eggs. Amer. Zool. 6:510, 1966.

19. McKINNELL, R. G., and McKINNELL, B. K.: Seasonal fluctuation of frog renal adenocarcinoma prevalence in natural populations. Cancer Res. 28:440–444, 1968.

20. McKINNELL, R. G., and ZAMBERNARD, J.: Virus particles in renal tumors obtained from spring *Rana pipiens* of known geographic origin. Cancer Res. 28:684–688, 1968.

Non-specific Transmission of the Lucké Tumor[1,2]

DONALD J. MULCARE [3]

Amphibian Facility, Department of Zoology
University of Michigan, Ann Arbor, Michigan

Introduction

Living fragments of Lucké tumors were successfully grown in the anterior eye-chambers of adults from an assortment of vertebrate species (1); however, anterior eyechamber implants induced adenocarcinomas only in hosts from the same *R. pipiens* population as the tumor donor (1, 2, 3). Tumors were induced in hosts of a heterologous population and species when the oncogenic agent was adapted to the new host (2, 3, 4), but this only emphasized the existence of the barriers to tumor induction that lay in the path of the unadapted oncogenic agent.

Although the unadapted tumor agent did not induce tumors in adults of heterologous *R. pipiens* populations, it did induce tumors when inoculated into heterologous embryos (5) and young larvae (4). This revealed that the host interaction with the tumor agent depended on the stage at which the host was inoculated.

This report is concerned with the interaction between the host and the unadapted Lucké tumor inducing agent and how this interaction participates in the specificity of tumor transmission. The hosts were *R. pipiens*, *R. palustris*, their interspecific hybrids and *R. clamitans*. This provided tumor susceptible hosts, tumor resistant hosts, and intermediate host types. The tumor agent was presented to embryos before the immune system was functional (6), to larvae before the immune system was completely mature (7, 8) and to adults by way of the dorsal lymph space, allowing doses many times larger than the anterior eyechamber could accommodate. Other adults were implanted intraocularly as many times as was necessary to produce a take.

A determination of the conditions under which heterologous host resistance could be circumvented or overcome would explain much about the natural defenses of the host. This information could be useful in explaining why purified frog virus could not

[1] Part of a dissertation submitted to the Graduate School of the University of Notre Dame in partial fulfillment of the requirements for the degree of Doctor of Philosophy.

[2] This investigation was supported in part by Grant IN 84A from the American Cancer Society, Grant CA-07849 from the National Cancer Institute made to Kenyon S. Tweedell, N.I.H. 5T 01 GM 00989 and NSF GB 4677 and a Damon Runyon Memorial Foundation Grant DRG-980 made to George W. Nace, and N.I.H. 1-F2-CA-23-476 made to Donald J. Mulcare.

[3] Present address: Department of Biology, Southeastern Massachusetts University, North Dartmouth, Massachusetts.

induce tumors (9, 10, 11), whereas Feulgen positive filtrates (12, 13), virus rich subcellular fractions of inclusion tumors (5, 14) and desiccated and glycerinated tumor tissue did induce tumors (15, 16, 17).

Nace *et al.* (18) suggested that a lysozyme found in the kidneys of *R. pipiens* adults may have an antiviral potency. Another aim of this report is to describe the effects of a lysozyme preparation on a virus-rich oncogenic inoculum.

Materials and Methods

Experimental Animals. Adult *pipiens* were obtained commercially from Clarence Mumley, Alburg, Vermont and the E. G. Steinhilber Company, Oshkosh, Wisconsin. *Rana palustris* adults were obtained from the Connecticut Valley Biological Supply Company, Southampton, Massachusetts and Glenn Gentry of Donelson, Tennessee, or were caught in Cass County, Michigan. Adult *Rana clamitans* were collected in Wisconsin by Steinhilber and in West Virginia by William Frye.

Ovulation was induced by injection of pituitaries (19). The eggs of *R. pipiens* (Vermont and Wisconsin) and *R. palustris* (Tennessee) were fertilized with spermatozoa from males of their own species or of the other species to produce *R. pipiens*, *R. palustris* and reciprocal interspecific hybrid embryos. *R. clamitans* (Wisconsin) were ovulated and the eggs fertilized with *R. clamitans* (West Virginia) spermatozoa.

Procurement of Renal Tumors. Kidney tumors were either spontaneously or experimentally induced in *R. pipiens* from both Vermont and Wisconsin. The tumor bearing animals were kept at 9°C in order to induce formation of viral inclusion bodies (14). These animals were anesthetized in a small cage containing 1 g of tricaine methane-sulfonate (MS-222, Sandoz) and 250 g of crushed ice. The tumors were removed and teased clean of non-tumorous tissue. After several washings in amphibian Ringers #1 (20), the tumors were cut into pieces varying from 0.2 mm^3 to 5.0 mm^3. All of the tumor fragments were stored in 100 ml of sterile Ringers containing 100 to 200 mg of sulfadiazine and chloramphenicol 1:1 and stored at 4°C. Representative pieces of each tumor were placed in Carnoy's fixative and were subsequently used to classify the tumor.

Intraocular Implants into Adults. *R. pipiens* and *R. palustris* adults of both sexes were anesthetized with MS-222 and ice. The left cornea was punctured with an iris knife and one or more tumor fragments with a total volume of 2 mm^3 to 3 mm^3 were inoculated. The incisions were then powered with sulfadiazine and chloramphenicol.

Implantation of the Dorsal Lymph Space of Adults. A transverse incision was made through the loose dorsal skin just anterior to the urostyle and 5 mm^3 to 7.5 mm^3 of tumor tissue was implanted through this incision. The growth of the implant was estimated by periodically measuring the bulge that it caused in the skin.

Inoculation of Embryos and Larvae. Tumors containing high percents of nuclear viral inclusion bodies were homogenized in 0.02M Gomori sodium phosphate buffer (pH 7.2 to 7.35) [1] and then centrifuged at 800 $\times$ g. The mitochondrial fraction was extracted from the first supernatant by centrifugation at 5090 $\times$ g. The second precipitate was suspended in 0.1 ml of buffer (14). This stock solution was inoculated at full strength or diluted in the same buffer. Mitochondrial fractions (5090 $\times$ g) were extracted from R. *pipiens* (Wisconsin) kidney and injected into R. *pipiens*, R. *palustris* and hybrid embryos as a control of the effect of kidney proteins and as a possible source of virus (9).

Testing for Antiviral Activity of Lysozyme Containing Material. Nace first suggested that tumor-free R. *pipiens* kidneys, especially those of adults from the Wisconsin population, may contain an antiviral lysozyme (18). The 800 $\times$ g supernatants of lysozyme containing kidneys were incubated with 800 $\times$ g supernatants of virus containing tumors for 22 minutes at 22°C. From the combined 800 $\times$ g supernatants of the two homogenates, a common 5090 $\times$ g precipitate was extracted and inoculated into embryos in the same manner as was the tumor precipitate in order to test the effect of the lysozyme on the tumor fraction.

The basic proteins were isolated from R. *pipiens* (Wisconsin) kidneys. Kidneys were washed in tris-tris phosphate buffer (20 mM, pH 7.4). They were then homogenized with 100 ml of this buffer and the homogenate centrifuged for 45 minutes at 0°C and 32,800 $\times$ g. The supernatant was dialysed against three changes of the tris buffer for 9 hours.

A 35 $\times$ 2.5 cm column was packed with carboxy-methyl cellulose (Na form) using tris buffer. The tissue supernatant was slowly introduced into the column. The basic proteins were held by the column while the acid and neutral proteins were washed out with the tris buffer. The basic proteins were washed out with a NaCl gradient (0 to 0.5M in 1500 ml, the low molarity point was tris buffer alone).

The fractions of basic protein were tested for lytic activity against *Micrococcus lysodeicticus* substrate in agar. Samples of each successive basic protein eluent fraction were put into 4.5 mm diameter wells in the agar and incubated for 10 hours at 37°C. The diameter of lysis was measured with calipers. The basic proteins with the greatest lytic activity were contained in the fraction collected at 300 ml after the beginning of the NaCl gradient wash.

The crude lytic material was lyophilized. The lysozyme containing preparation was diluted in tris buffer to produce 15 mg/ml, 1.5 mg/ml, and 0.15 mg/ml solutions. These were mixed 1:1 with separate aliquots of a 5090 $\times$ g fraction of inclusion body containing tumors. A fourth aliquot of the tumor fraction was diluted 1:1 in plain tris buffer. These four preparations were incubated at 14.5°C for 2 hours or 10°C for 2.5 hours before use.

Inoculation of Embryos and Larvae. Demembranated R. *pipiens*, R. *palustris*, their hybrids, and R. *clamitans* embryos were injected with the mitochondrial fraction of either an inclusion body tumor, a tumor-free kidney from adult R. *pipiens* or a precipitate derived from a mixture of kidney and tumor supernatants or one of the tumor plus lysozyme preparations. A volume of 0.2 to 0.6 μl of either full strength or a

---

[1] With 0.24M sucrose.

diluted preparation was administered beneath the left pronephros of Ranid embryos of Shumway stages 17 through 19 (22) by means of a 10 μl syringe (Hamilton syringe model 701 fitted with a 31 gauge needle with a Kel F nylon hub, Model KF 731). The embryos injected with Wisconsin tumor received a full strength or a 10-fold diluted preparation. The other embryos received a 1:1 dilution of the tumor fraction.

Larvae of Taylor-Kollros stage I to III (17 to 22 mm) (23) were anesthetized in 1:3000 MS 222 and injected intracoelomically with 0.5 to 0.7 μl of the mitochondrial fraction of inclusion body containing tumor.

The Scoring of Tumors. Hosts implanted as adults were not included in the experimental data unless they survived at least 3 months after inoculation. Hosts injected as embryos that did not survive until detection of the first tumor of the experiment were eliminated from the calculations. The remaining hosts in each treatment group were compared as to the percent of tumors induced. Tumors were determined on the basis of the presence of kidney growths. Samples of about half of the growths were observed histologically to confirm their tumor nature.

Histology. Samples of the tumor used as an implant, tumors fractionated or tumors resulting from the inoculations were fixed in Carnoy's 6:3:1 (20) fluid and imbedded in 56° or 61° Paraplast (Fisher) and sectioned at 7 or 8 μ. Sections were stained in Jenner-Geimsa, a modified May-Grundwald stain prepared from Harleco Giemsa Blood Stain solution (NGe-18) and Harleco Jenner Stain (Methylene Blue Eosinate, LJr-r) according to the formula of Humason (21). Harris hematoxylin and eosin were also used.

Results

Specific Tumor Induction in Adults. R. *pipiens* and R. *palustris* adults received anterior eyechamber implants. The majority of the first implants were takes, otherwise inoculations were repeated until an implant grew or was vascularized or the host died. Tumors were induced in R. *pipiens* adults but none were produced in 77 adult R. *palustris* implanted intraocularly with R. *pipiens* tumor (Table 1), although implants into R. *palustris* anterior eyechamber had a high percentage of takes. This result was also observed by Rose (24) and Tweedell (4).

Non-specific Tumor Induction in Adults. R. *pipiens* and R. *palustris* adults received 0.5 to 0.75 cc dorsal lymph space heterologous implants. These were 2 to 4 times larger than the eyechamber implants. The percentage of dorsal lymph space takes in R. *pipiens* was low in comparison with eyechamber implants of homologous tissue (Table 1). Three adult R. *palustris* were implanted with Wisconsin inclusion body renal tumor. In each case the dorsal lymph space implant had increased in size after 50 days. One R. *palustris* developed a huge, bilateral, multilobed renal tumor. It had the color and appearance of liver tissue but was not attached to the liver. Its pathology (Fig. 1) showed a series of epithelial folds and acini. The lumina were larger and longer than those in the R. *pipiens* renal tumor. The adult R. *palustris* tumor had larger spaces basal to the epithelial layers (Fig. 1). The space contained a netlike

TABLE 1

THE FREQUENCY OF TUMOR INDUCTION IN ADULT RANID HOSTS
IMPLANTED WITH LUCKÉ TUMOR TISSUE

Host species	R. pipiens tumor implant source population	Implantation site	Animals	Implants accepted No.	Implants accepted %	Tumors induced No.	Tumors induced %
R. pipiens (Wis.)	Wisconsin	AEC [1]	26	11	42	3	12
R. pipiens (Vt.)	Wisconsin	AEC	30	7	23	6	20
	Vermont	AEC	15	3	20	5	33
R. palustris	Vt. & Wis.	AEC	77	49	64	0	0
R. pipiens (Vt.)	Wisconsin	DLS [2]	7	1	14	0	0
R. pipiens (Wis.)	Vermont	DLS	7	1	14	1	14
R. palustris (Mich.)	Wisconsin [3]	DLS	3	3	100	1	33
R. pipiens (Vt.)	Control	Control	20	0	0	3	15
R. pipiens (Wis.)	Control	Control	26	0	0	1	4
R. palustris	Control	Control	53	0	0	0	0

[1] AEC-Anterior Eyechamber.
[2] DLS-Dorsal Lymph Space.
[3] Had many inclusion bodies.

eosinophilic stroma with erythrocytes and fibroblasts. In contrast, opposed layers of epithelium in R. *pipiens* tumors compressed the basal space and stroma between them so that there was only a band of eosinophilic stroma, and little if any space.

Non-specific Tumor Induction Through Inoculation of Larvae and Embryos. Very few of the larvae injected with $5090 \times g$ fraction of Vermont viral inclusion tumor developed adenocarcinomas but tumors were induced in both R. *pipiens*, R. *palustris*, and the R. *pipiens* × R. *palustris* hybrids (Table 2). Embryos inoculated with this $5090 \times g$ fraction of Vermont viral inclusion tumors have shown a high percentage of tumor induction during later life (Table 2). Tumors were induced in R. *clamitans*, R. *pipiens*, and R. *palustris* and the interspecific hybrids that were injected as embryos.

The relative susceptibility of the three species and two hybrids have not been determined because of the variable inductive power of each tumor (14, 27) and the resulting inability to pool data since there was variation in the number of individuals from each species or hybrid group that was injected with each of the four Vermont tumors. The R. *palustris* × R. *pipiens* hybrids consistently had a higher percentage of tumors than any other host type but this must yet be established by injection of more hosts with many more tumors.

Lysozyme preparations. The supernatant of tumor-free kidneys incubated and later centrifuged at $5090 \times g$ with the supernatant of an inclusion tumor gave no signifi-

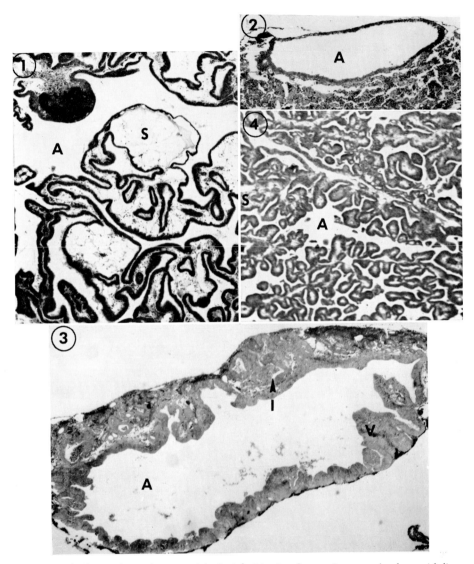

Fig. 1. Renal adenocarcinoma from an adult R. *palustris*. A = lumen; S = space basal to epithelium. Jenner-Giemsa. ×22.

Fig. 2. Kidney vesicle induced in R. *palustris* after inoculation as an embryo. Simple columnar epithelium, not invasive of kidney. Jenner-Giemsa. ×22.

Fig. 3. Tumor vesicle induced in R. *pipiens* after inoculation as an embryo. Columnar epithelium folded into villi (V). Invasive of kidney (I). Jenner-Giemsa. ×22.

Fig. 4. Renal adenocarcinoma induced in R. *clamitans* after inoculation as an embryo. Harris hematoxylin and eosin. ×22.

TABLE 2

Induction of Tumors in a Variety of Ranid Hosts by the 5090 × g. Fraction
of R. pipiens (Vermont) Inclusion Tumor

	Injected as embryos		Injected as larvae		Uninoculated	
	animals	tumors	animals	tumors	animals	tumors
Hosts	No.	No. %	No.	No. %	No.	No. %
R. pipiens	67	26 38	14	2 14	79	0 0
R. pipiens × R. palustris	44	10 23	44	1 2	72	0 0
R. palustris × R. pipiens	70	37 53	4	0 0	70	0 0
R. palustris	61	16 26	11	1 9	99	0 0
R. clamitans	11	3 27	0	0 0	8	0 0

cant information on the potential antiviral activity of the lysozyme that was found
in tumor-free kidneys (Table 3). Incubation of tumor inducing fractions with lytic
basic proteins extracted from R. *pipiens* tumor-free kidneys has shown that the rate
of tumor induction was not reduced by incubation, but that it may have been increased (Table 4).

The total of tumors induced among all hosts injected with the 5090 × g tumor
fraction plus buffer was compared by X^2 analysis to the total of tumors in all hosts
injected with the 5090 × g tumor fraction plus the (0.15, 1.5 and 15 mg/ml)
lysozyme preparation (Table 4).

$$X^2 = \left\{ \frac{[\text{Tumors induced by tumor fraction} + \text{lysozyme} - \text{tumors induced by tumor fraction} + \text{buffer}]^2}{\text{Tumors induced by tumor fraction} + \text{lysozyme}} + \frac{[\text{Tumor-free animals injected with tumor} + \text{lysozyme} - \text{tumor-free animals injected with tumor} + \text{buffer}]^2}{\text{Tumor-free animals injected with tumor} + \text{lysozyme}} \right.$$

$$X^2 = \frac{[T1 - Tb]^2}{T1} + \frac{[NT1 - NTb]^2}{NT1} = \frac{[110 - 45]^2}{110} + \frac{[103 - 73]^2}{103} = 47.15$$

(one degree of freedom). The probability that $X^2 \geqq 47.15$ might arise by chance
is less than 0.001. The results are significantly different.

Tumor-Free Fraction. Subsequent to injection with the 5090 × g fraction of
tumor-free kidney no tumors were detected in the R. *pipiens* hosts (Table 3). This was
observed by Tweedell (5, 14). No tumors were found in the hybrids but renal tumors
were found in R. *palustris* that were injected similarly (Table 3).

Characteristics of Induced Tumors. There are several generalizations that can be
offered regarding all of the tumors induced by the treated or untreated Vermont tumor
fraction injected into embryos. Tumors were observed at necropsy in hosts of Taylor-

TABLE 3

THE EFFECT OF KIDNEY EXTRACT ON TUMOR INDUCTION BY THE 5090 × g. FRACTION OF R. PIPIENS (VERMONT) INCLUSION BODY TUMOR

Hosts	Tumor fraction animals No.	tumors No.	%	Tumor and Wis. kidney fraction animals No.	tumors No.	%	Kidney fraction (Wisconsin) animals No.	tumors No.	%	Uninoculated animals No.	tumors No.	%
R. pipiens	29	9	31	13	3	23	12	0	0	33	0	0
R. pipiens × R. palustris	6	3	50	—	—	—	2	0	0	19	0	0
R. palustris × R. pipiens	51	27	53	12	3	25	4	0	0	19	0	0
R. palustris	38	5	13	33	8	24	23	9	40	87	0	0

DONALD J. MULCARE

TABLE 4

THE EFFECT OF A LYSOZYME PREPARATION ON TUMOR INDUCTION BY THE 5090 × g. FRACTION OF R. PIPIENS (VERMONT) INCLUSION CONTAINING TUMOR

| | One part of tumor fraction mixed with one part of lysozyme preparation | | | | | | | | | | | | Buffer | | | Uninoculated | | |
| | 15 mg/ml | | 1.5 mg/ml | | | 0.15 mg/ml | | | total | | | | | | | | | |
Hosts	anim. No.	tumors No. %	anim. No.	tumors No. %		anim. No.	tumors No. %		anim. No.	tumors No. %			anim. No.	tumors No. %		anim. No.	tumors No. %	
R. pip.	18	13 72	51	28	55	25	13	52	94	54	57		38	17	45	46	0	0
R. pip. × R. pal.	19	10 52	49	16	33	2	0	0	70	26	37		38	7	18	53	0	0
R. pal. × R. pip.	34	26 76	11	1	9	—	—	—	45	27	60		19	10	52	51	0	0
R. pal.	1	0 0	3	3	100	—	—	—	4	3	75		23	11	48	12	0	0

Kollros stage 5 to 25 (23) in postmetamorphic or juveniles as early as 80 days after injection. The bulk of the tumors were found between 110 and 160 days after inoculation. Some tumors were still found 200 days after injection. Tumors were usually located near the site of injection. They were predominantly unilateral, left and mesonephric. Some were pronephric and larger tumors extended from the pronephric into the mesonephric region. Two tumors were found on the nephric duct between the mesonephric and pronephric regions.

The adenocarcinomas induced by the various preparations injected into embryos took two forms, the solid tumor and also vesicular growths. Fluid filled *kidney vesicles* (25) were composed of a single layer of basophilic columnar cells, with numerous mitoses and covered by a connective tissue sheath. This resembled the epithelium of the Lucké tumor (Fig. 2). The epithelium had a sparse basal border of connective tissue similar to that seen on the basal side of tumor epithelium. Kidney vesicles were encapsulated and did not invade normal tissue.

The epithelium of *tumor vesicles* (25) was also a layer of basophilic columnar cells but it was elaborated into folds and villi that resembled those found in the Lucké tumor and it invaded normal kidney tissue (Fig. 3). Neither of the vesicular formations were found in uninoculated controls.

The tumors induced in some *R. palustris*, the hybrids and in *R. clamitans* (Fig. 4) resembled the adenocarcinomas of larvae and adult *R. pipiens*. Some *R. palustris* solid tumors induced in young animals did closely resemble the tumor found in a *R. palustris* adult. The majority (65%) of *R. palustris* tumors were vesicular. *R. pipiens* tumors were vesicular on only 7% of the cases observed, whereas 30% of the tumors in the hybrids were vesicular. Each host seems to affect the morphology of the tumor induced by the same tumor agent.

Results of Injection with Wisconsin Tumor Fraction. Embryos injected with the 5090 × g fraction of *R. pipiens* (Wisconsin) inclusion body tumor induced adenocarcinomas in *R. pipiens* (Wisconsin) and the hybrids but not in *R. palustris* (Table 3). The *R. palustris* had been devastated as larvae with subcutaneous hemorraghic lesions (26).

Between 30 and 80 days after hatching, when the larvae varied from 18 to 45 mm (median 25 mm) and Taylor-Kollros stages V to XIV (23), a subcutaneous hemorrhagia appeared in some of all of the following sites: posterior to the ventral lip, randomly distributed about the abdominal epidermis, in blotches along the dorsal epidermis and on either side of the tail. This was sometimes accompanied by blood in the coelom but was always followed by the death of the afflicted larvae. Histologically, the subcutaneous lesions appeared as an accumulation of blood between the muscles and the dermal connective tissue.

Hemorrhagic lesions apeared in *R. pipiens* (Wisconsin and Vermont), *R. palustris* (Tennessee) and their reciprocal interspecific hybrids (Table 5). They have not as yet been observed to follow the inoculation of embryos with *R. pipiens* (Vermont) inclusion tumor, Wisconsin kidney of both.

R. palustris had the highest percentage of lesions; *R. pipiens* had very few even after concentrated doses. The frequency of lesions in the hybrids was intermediate between the rates in *R. pipiens* and *R. palustris* (Table 5).

TABLE 5

The Incidence of Pathologies Resulting from Inoculation of Embryos with the Mitochondrial Fraction of R. pipiens (Wisconsin) Inclusion Body Renal Tumor

Host Egg × Sperm	Inoculum	Sur-vivors[1]	Lesions No.	Lesions %	Sur-vivors[2]	Tumors No.	Tumors %
R. pipiens × R. pipiens	1/1	57	11	17	5	0	0
(Wisconsin) (Wisconsin)	1/10	44	3	7	21	6	29
	Total	101	14	14	26	6	23
	Control	78	0	0	39	0	0
R. pipiens × R. palustris	1/1	45	21	47	6	1	16.6
	1/10	57	6	11	9	2	22
	Total	102	27	27	15	3	20
	Control	55	3	5	14	0	0
R. palustris × R. pipiens	1/1	62	29	45	16	1	6.3
	1/10	45	8	18	11	0	0
	Total	107	37	35	27	1	3.7
	Control	58	1	2	14	0	0
R. palustris × R. palustris	1/1	51	27	53	9	0	0
	1/10	65	18	28	14	0	0
	Total	116	45	39	23	0	0
	Control	130	2	1.5	41	0	0

[1] Based on the number of animals that survived to grow to at least 18 mm.

[2] Based on the number of animals that survived until late larval development.

Discussion

Lucké tumors were thought to induce renal adenocarcinomas only in hosts of the homologous R. pipiens population (1). Subsequently tumors were induced in disparate populations and species. Renal tumors were induced in individuals of the Wisconsin and Vermont populations of R. pipiens that were injected as embryos with the mitochondrial fraction, microsomal fraction or the filtrate of the viral inclusion-rich tumor from either population (5, 14). R. clamitans, R. palustris, and interspecific hybrids between R. palustris and R. pipiens have also developed renal adenocarcinomas when injected as embryos with the mitochondrial fraction of R. pipiens viral inclusion tumor (25, 26, 27).

The barriers to transpopulation tumor induction were overcome by tumor tissue implants into the dorsal tail mesenchyme of 18 mm larvae (4). However, eyechamber implants into postmetamorphic hosts induced tumors only in the homologous population (4). This demonstrated that a selective barrier to tumor induction had developed in the older disparate hosts. The barrier discriminated against the same tumor agent on the basis of its source population. A difference between the 18 mm larvae and the postmetamorphic hosts responsible for this result may have been the more effective immune system in the older hosts.

An adult R. *palustris* has formed a tumor subsequent to its implantation with a large viral-rich fragment of a R. *pipiens* (Wisconsin) tumor, yet numerous adult R. *palustris* were resistant to tumor induction by smaller eyechamber implants of similar R. *pipiens* tumor (3, 23). The barriers to tumor induction were apparently overcome by the high dosage of the tumor agent contained in the large, virus-rich implant.

These results suggest that the barrier to the tumor agent's inductive power was not an inability to transform heterologous cells, but rather was due to the ability of the host to defend itself. This defense was present in adult and late larval hosts, but not present in embryonic hosts.

In the interaction between the host and the tumor inducing agent, the host immune system may be responsible for the specific barrier to tumor induction by its action on the Herpes-like virus associated with the Lucké tumor oncogenesis (5, 14). The Herpes-like virus would be antigenic by virtue of the plasma membrane envelope it acquires from the cell in which it originates (28, 29). The hosts immune system would discriminate against a Herpes particle on the basis of the antigens of the envelope.

The immune system of an adult R. *pipiens* may not recognize and attack a Herpes-like virus enveloped in compatible antigens, such as those from the plasma membrane of a homologous tumor cell. Were the same Herpes-like virus enveloped in antigens from a nonhomologous tumor or tissue culture cell, it may be attacked by the same host. A R. *pipiens*, R. *palustris*, hybrid, or R. *clamitans* embryo which lacks the active immune system of the adult or larval frog (6, 7, 8) could not attack a virus regardless of its antigenic envelope. As a result there would be no host specific barriers to tumor induction. This hypothesis may explain the host specificity of the Lucké adenocarcinoma. The hemorrhagic lesions resulting from injection with the $5090 \times$ g fraction of Wisconsin inclusion tumor may have been due to the hexagonal-cytoplasmic virus often found in R. *pipiens*. Tweedell and Granoff (11) have reported dermal hemorrhages resulting from injection of embryos and young larvae with Frog Virus-3, a hexagonal-cytoplasmic virus. Lunger (30) reported in this symposium that the hexagonal-cytoplasmic virus was found only in connective tissue. The hemorrhagic lesions were found between muscle and dermal connective tissue.

Basic proteins with lysozyme activity may increase the tumor inductive ability of the viral-rich fractions of tumors by protecting the host from bacteria since lysozymes are used as anti-bacterial agents (31), or perhaps by eliminating competition to the herpes-like virus by killing the hexagonal-cytoplasmic viruses which were susceptible to lysozyme *in vitro* (32).

Summary

Solid and vesicular renal adenocarcinomas, hemorrhagic lesions and other pathologies were induced in *Rana pipiens*, R. *palustris* and reciprocal hybrids that were injected as embryos with a mitochondrial fraction of inclusion tumors. Solid tumors were induced in *R. clamitans* similarly injected. An adult *R. palustris* implanted subcutaneously with a large *R. pipiens* inclusion tumor developed a renal adenocarcinoma. Intraocular implants into *R. palustris* induced no tumors. These and previous results reported by Tweedell (3, 5, 14) indicated that the resistance to tumor induction developed after embryonic life and parallels the development of the immune system. A hypothesis of host specificity was based on the reaction between the antigenic envelope of a Herpes-like virus and the immune systems of the various hosts throughout their life cycle. The effect of lysozyme on tumor induction is discussed.

Acknowledgments

The author wishes to thank Prof. Kenyon S. Tweedell of the University of Notre Dame for suggesting and directing this research and Prof. George W. Nace of the University of Michigan for the use of the Amphibian Facility and for providing viral-rich Lucké tumors when they were otherwise unavailable. The "lysozyme" preparation was provided by Mr. John Snyder and Mr. David Ostrovski. The *R. clamitans* embryos were prepared by Mr. Dennis Pence. The statistical advisor was Dr. William Hirschfeld. Photographs were taken by Mr. Louis Martonyi. Special thanks to Prof. Tweedell, Prof. Nace, Dr. Martin Blumenfeld, and Mrs. Nancy Ann Mulcare who aided in the preparation of this text.

References

1. LUCKÉ, B. and SCHLUMBERGER, H.: Heterotransplantation of frog carcinoma: character of growth in the eyes of an alien species. J. Exp. Med. *72*:311–320, 1940.

2. ROSE, S. M. and ROSE, F. C.: Tumor agent transformation in amphibia. Cancer Research *12*:1–12, 1952.

3. TWEEDELL, KENYON S.: Adaption of an amphibian renal carcinoma in kindred races. Cancer Research *15*:410–418, 1955.

4. TWEEDELL, KENYON S.: Modification of an amphibian renal tumor by intraocular transplantation and subculture in kindred races. Transplan. Bull. *1*:26–27, 1953.

5. TWEEDELL, KENYON S.: Renal tumor transmission in frog embryos by subcellular fractions. Am. Zool. *5*:711, 1965.

6. VOLPE, E. PETER and GEBHARDT, BRYAN M.: Effect of dosage on the survival of embryonic homotransplantations in the leopard frog, *Rana pipiens*. J. Exp. Zool. *160*:11–28, 1965.

7. COOPER, E. L., PINKERTON, W. and HILDEMANN, W. H.: Serum antibody synthesis in larvae of the bullfrog, *Rana catesbeiana*. Biol. Bull. *127*:232–238, 1964.

8. COOPER, E. L. and HILDEMANN, W. H.: The immune response of larval bullfrogs (*Rana catesbeiana*) to diverse antigens. Ann. N.Y. Acad. Sci. *126*:647–661, 1965.

9. GRANOFF, ALLAN, CAME, PAUL E. and RAFFERTY, KEEN A.: The isolation and properties of viruses from *Rana pipiens*: their possible relationship to the renal adenocarcinoma of the leopard frog. Ann. N.Y. Acad. Sci. *126*:237–255, 1965.

10. RAFFERTY, KEEN A., JR.: The cultivation of inclusion-associated viruses from Lucké tumor frogs. Ann. N. Y. Acad. Sci. *126*:3–21, 1965.

11. TWEEDELL, KENYON S. and GRANOFF, ALLAN: Viruses and renal carcinoma of *Rana pipiens* V. Effect of frog virus 3 on developing frog embryos and larvae. J. Natl. Cancer Inst. *40*:407–410, 1968.

12. DURYEE, WILLIAM R.: Precancer cells in amphibian adenocarcinoma. Ann. N.Y. Acad. Sci. 63:1280–1302, 1956.

13. DURYEE, WILLIAM R.: Factors influencing development of tumors in frogs. Ann. N.Y. Acad. Sci. 126:59–84, 1965.

14. TWEEDELL, KENYON S.: Induced oncogenesis in developing frog kidney cells. Cancer Research 27:2042–2052, 1967.

15. LUCKE, BALDWIN: A neoplastic disease of the kidney of the frog Rana pipiens. Am. J. Cancer 20:352–379, 1934.

16. LUCKE, BALDWIN: Carcinoma in the leopard frog: its probable causation by a virus. J. Exp. Med. 68:457–468, 1938.

17. LUCKÉ, BALDWIN: Kidney carcinoma in the leopard frog: a virus tumor. Ann. N.Y. Acad. Sci. 54:1093–1109, 1952.

18. NACE, GEORGE W., SUYAMA, TADAKAZU and IWATA, TAKUZO: The relationship between a lysozyme-like enzyme and frog adenocarcinoma. Ann. N.Y. Acad. Sci. 126:204–221, 1965.

19. RUGH, ROBERTS: Ovulation in the frog. I. Pituitary relations in induced ovulation. J. Exp. Zool. 71:149–162, 1935.

20. CAVANAUGH, GAIL M.: Formulae and Methods IV of the Marine Biological Laboratory Chemical Room, 1956.

21. HUMASON, GRETCHEN L.: Animal tissue techniques. W. H. Freeman and Company, San Francisco, 468 pp., 1962.

22. SHUMWAY, WALDO: Stages in the normal development of Rana pipiens. Anat. Record 78:139–147, 1940.

23. TAYLOR, A. CECIL and KOLLROS, JERRY J.: Stages in the normal development of Rana pipiens larvae. Anat. Record 94:7–13, 1946.

24. ROSE, S. M.: Interaction of tumor agents and normal cellular components in amphibia. Ann. N.Y. Acad. Sci. 54:1110–1119, 1952.

25. MULCARE, DONALD J. and TWEEDELL, KENYON S.: Renal tumors induced in Rana palustris by tumor implants or sub-cellular fractions from R. pipiens. Am. Zool. 7:748, 1967.

26. MULCARE, DONALD J.: Induction of tumors in hybrids between Rana pipiens and R. palustris. Am. Zool. 6:212, 1966.

27. MULCARE, DONALD J.: The host specificity of the Rana pipiens renal adenocarcinoma inducing agent. A dissertation submitted to the University of Notre Dame, Notre Dame, Indiana, 93 pp., 1968.

28. FAWCETT, D. W.: Electron microscopic observations of intercellular virus-like particles associated with the cells of the Lucké renal adenocarcinoma. J. Biophys. Biochem. Cytol. 2:725–742, 1956.

29. LUNGER, P. D., DARLINGTON, R. W. and GRANOFF, A.: Cell-virus relationships in the Lucké renal adenocarcinoma: an ultra structural study. Ann. N.Y. Acad. Sci. 126:289–314, 1965.

30. LUNGER, PHILIP D.: Fine structure studies of cytoplasmic viruses associated with frog tumors. In Biology of Amphibian Tumors (M. Mizell, ed.), Springer-Verlag New York Inc., 1969, pp. 296–309.

31. Atti Del 2⁰ Symposium Internazuenale Sul Di Fleming Vol. II Museo Della Scienza E Della Techina, Milano, 1961.

32. RUBIN, MONA L., AR, DIANE B. and NACE, GEORGE W.: The virus inhibiting action of a lysozyme present in normal frogs but lacking in tumor frogs and eggs. Am. Zool. 6:510, 1966.

Lucké Renal Adenocarcinoma:
Epidemiological Aspects[1]

Robert Gilmore McKinnell [2]

Department of Biology
Newcomb College of Tulane University
New Orleans, Louisiana

Although the renal tumor of the common leopard frog, *Rana pipiens*, has been studied for over 34 years, exceedingly little has been known concerning its natural history until the past few years. Several localities in northern Vermont and adjacent Canada were identified as the sites of tumor-bearing frog populations in 1961 (1). Prior to this date, no precise geographic locality was known to contain frogs with tumors. Montana frogs had been examined but were reported to be tumor-free (2). Tumors were generally available from commercial dealers but the origin of tumor frogs was at best conjectural. An extensive collecting trip from South Dakota to the eastern United States identified several localities with tumor susceptible populations (3). The only continuing epidemiological studies, however, have been made by our laboratory.

Our research has concerned Minnesota frogs primarily but some studies have been made of North Dakota, South Dakota, and Louisiana frogs. Our interest has focused on Minnesota because of its abundance of leopard frogs, the several genetic variants of the leopard frog, and the diversity of ecological conditions within the state.

The abundance of leopard frogs in Minnesota makes it feasible to collect large numbers of frogs from each locality that is studied. Frogs can be taken from a variety of habitats associated with different phases of their annual behavioral cycle. Frogs prepare to leave lakes in the spring as the ice recedes from the shores. They may be netted in the cold lake water at that time. Breeding ponds, with water warmed by spring sunshine, are located adjacent to overwintering lakes. Pairs, triplets, or groups up to six or more may be taken in amplexes from the breeding ponds. Northern *R. pipiens* move to marshes, meadows, and cultivated fields where they forage during the summer. Roadside ditches in the vicinity of a lake offer a copious supply of frogs for the collector who does not desire to trespass. The frogs move closer to the large overwintering lakes as colder weather approaches in the fall. They mass in great numbers on the shores just prior to entering the lakes for hibernation. They remain submerged

[1] This study was supported by American Cancer Society, Inc. Research Grant E-369-B.

[2] The author acknowledges the valuable assistance of Mrs. Beverly Anderson Deggins, Mrs. Deidre Dumas Labat, and Mr. Louis A. Reed. The author would like to express his appreciation to Mr. Leo M. Kirsch, Wildlife Research Biologist, Woodworth, North Dakota, for his cooperation that made the study of frogs from Stutsman County, North Dakota, possible.

while the lake is covered with ice during the winter. Thus, frogs can be taken from a variety of habitats in each locality at different seasons. The effect of water temperature and other ecological factors can be correlated with tumor biology.

The non-spotted mutant, burnsi, and the mottled mutant, kandiyohi, range primarily in Minnesota (4, 5). Tumors from these pigment pattern variants are potentially of value in nuclear transplantation studies and accordingly, we desired to know whether or not they are equally susceptible to tumor formation as the wild-type leopard frog.

Northeast Minnesota originally was covered by evergreen forests. Now much of the formerly coniferous forest area is cut-over land covered mostly by aspen and birch. Prairie characterizes southwestern Minnesota. A belt of deciduous forest separates the original northern coniferous forest from the tall grass prairie region. Additionally, Minnesota includes flat plains of the Red River Valley, hills and lakes of much of central Minnesota, rolling plains of southwestern Minnesota, and a profusion of lakes adjacent to the eastern half of the border with Canada. Thus, it is apparent that Minnesota has a diversified ecology.

If there is a non-random distribution of tumor-susceptible frogs and if the non-randomness is associated with environmental factors, it would seem that Minnesota affords an excellent opportunity to correlate environment to tumor development.

What value is there in epidemiological studies? We believe that the following are some of the ways epidemiological studies may be useful.

Identification of tumor-prone and tumor-resistant or tumor-free populations permits experiments designed to appraise the relative roles of genetic and environmental factors involved in tumor progression. Suggested methods of natural transmission of the proposed etiological agent can be evaluated in the field if adequate information is available concerning the natural history of tumor-bearing frogs. Commercial dealers in leopard frogs are now obtaining their merchandise from three nations; the United States, Canada, and Mexico. Since the tumor seems not to be equally prevalent in all populations in its distribution, the buyer of commercial frogs can be alerted to request from the dealer those leopard frogs most appropriate for his planned experimentation.

The following is an account of an examination of over four thousand frogs collected from known localities during the years 1965 through 1968.

Seasonal Fluctuation of Renal Tumor Prevalence in Natural Populations in Leopard Frogs

An examination of 1,088 frogs by autopsy in November, 1963, revealed that frogs originating from the north central United States are particularly prone to the renal adenocarcinoma (6). Prevalence [1] rates of 6 to 9% among adult leopard frogs stimulated us to survey the distribution of leopard frogs in Minnesota.

---

[1] Epidemiology is the science that relates disease to environment. Students of the science use terms concerning frequency of occurrence differently than students of other sciences. Thus, "prevalence" refers to the number of individuals with a disease at a particular time. It is not synonymous to "incidence," which refers to the number of new cases per unit time. These and other epidemiological terms are defined elsewhere (7, 8).

The initial field study was disappointing because, although 1,081 leopard frogs were collected in a number of different localities throughout Minnesota during the summer of 1965, no tumors were detected. Purchase of tumor-bearing frogs during the following winter led us to postulate a seasonal fluctuation in tumor prevalence (9). Data suporting the hypothesis was obtained in spring collections in the following years, i.e., renal tumors were found to be abundant in frogs obtained in April as ice recedes from the shores of lakes (10, 11). It would seem unlikely that tumors appear while amphibians are hibernating in water near its freezing point. Accordingly, tumors were looked for, and found, among frogs just prior to hibernation (12). Data from 3,367 autopsies performed on frogs collected from known localities during four years is summarized in Table 1. An examination of Table 1 reveals that samples of summer frog populations indeed differ from spring and fall populations. Summer tumor prevalence is low (0.14%) in contrast to the higher tumor prevalence of both spring (5% and autumn (4.4%).

The increasing prevalence rates in the springs of three years from 2.8% to 12.5% (Table 1) reflect, in our judgment, not an increase in morbidity, but an increased awareness of *where* tumor-bearing frogs can be collected. The increase in summer rates, from 0.0% to 0.36% (Table 1), is believed to have a similar explanation. We deliberately collected in previously unstudied localities in fall, 1968. Several of the collections were tumor negative but were included in the data. The reduced prevalence rate, from 6.0% to 3.9% (Table 1) among fall frogs, reflects data from several county collections that were tumor-free.

Where are summer frogs with tumors? Among several proposed possibilities, we favor the hypothesis of selective predation. It seems reasonable to suggest that tumor-bearing frogs cannot escape potential predation with the same proficiency as their more healthy compatriots. Accordingly, fewer surviving frogs during the summer foraging months would be expected, and fewer are found. Death from the effects of the tumor itself or spontaneous regression cannot be eliminated as factors reducing the prevalence of tumors in summer frogs.

TABLE 1

SEASONAL VARIATION IN TUMOR PREVALENCE AMONG MINNESOTA LEOPARD FROGS

Spring	No. frogs	No. tumors	%	Summer	No. frogs	No. tumors	%	Fall	No. frogs	No. tumors	%
1966	212	6	2.8	1965	1,081	0	0.0	1967	150	9	6.0
1967	279	12	4.3	1966	473	1	0.21	1968	534	21	3.9
1968	88	11	12.5	1967	550	2	0.36				
TOTALS	579	29	5.0		2,104	3	0.14		684	30	4.4

The results of 3,367 autopsies of frogs collected in Minnesota are summarized above. Prevalence of tumors among spring and fall frogs (5% and 4.4% respectively) exceeds tumor prevalence in summer frogs (0.14%).

Seasonal Fluctuation of Virus Particles in Tumors
Obtained from Natural Populations of Frogs

Once methods were developed that permitted obtaining tumor-bearing frogs from their natural habitat, it was possible to study tumors that were unaffected by storage in either a dealer's or laboratory facility. We considered an examination of spontaneous tumors fixed in the field necessary because of the changes that occur in tumor fine structure with storage (13). Earlier fine structure studies reported a pleomorphism with respect to the presence or absence of virus particles (14, 15). We asked the question: are tumors obtained from frogs of similar environmental origin as variable in fine structure as tumors from commercially obtained frogs? Our studies suggest a negative answer to this question.

Leopard frogs were collected prior to their emergence from hibernation. The frogs were autopsied shortly after capture, tumor fragments were fixed in the field, and examined by electron microscopy in the laboratory. The fine structure of eleven tumors was studied and herpes-type virus particles were observed in all (16).

Frogs caught immediately prior to hibernation in October, 1967, were examined in a similar manner. Eleven renal tumors were detected, and fixed in the field. Careful examination of electron micrographs of these autumn renal tumors failed to disclose the presence of virus particles (12).

Thus, our studies indicate that the presence or absence of a herpes-type virus is *not* random in a population examined at different times of the year, but the presence of electron-microscope detectable virus particles seems to be climatologically determined. These findings are in harmony with laboratory studies of the relationship of cold temperature to the induction of the virus particles in "virus-free" renal tumors (17, 18).

Geographic Distribution of Tumor Susceptible Populations

Localities known to have populations of tumor-prone frogs have been published previously (11, 12, 16). These sites, together with more recent findings, are summarized in Table 2. We have detected renal adenocarcinomas in leopard frog populations in nine Minnesota counties thus far.

Although the county distribution record is still fragmentary, it may be noted that tumor-bearing frogs have been taken from a county that was primitively covered with conifer forests (Aitkin County), from areas of deciduous forests (Kandiyohi County, Otter Tail County, etc.), and from a prairie region (Cottonwood County).

Two of the counties with tumor-bearing frogs, Sherburne County and Aitkin County, were discovered by autopsy of museum specimens. Frogs preserved in formaldehyde were dissected and suspicious-appearing kidneys were removed and prepared for light microscope examination. The museum frogs were collected in September 1958, by Professor David J. Merrell of the University of Minnesota in a study of the distribution of the burnsi and kandiyohi variants (4). The autopsies were performed by Mr. Charles F. Rodell of the University of Minnesota, and the study is still in progress. The discovery of tumors in specimens fixed for several years suggests the possibility of detecting tumors in even older museum material. The study of old fixed

TABLE 2

GEOGRAPHIC DISTRIBUTION OF TUMOR-BEARING FROGS IN MINNESOTA

County	Sum of spring and fall collections	Tumors	Prevalence
Kandiyohi	482	31	6.4%
Otter Tail	124	13	10.5%
Todd	85	1	1.8%
Douglas	7	1	14 %
Scott	183	11	6 %
Le Sueur	107	1	0.9%
Cottonwood	41	1	2.4%
Sherburne	(46)*	1	2.2%
Aitkin	(85)*	1	1.2%
Becker	28	—	—
Wright	61	—	—
Isanti	10	—	—
Anoka	43	—	—
Itasca Park	46	—	—
Hubbard	15	—	—

* Based on museum specimens.

Tumors have been found in frogs from nine Minnesota counties. No tumors were detected in frogs from six other counties. All collections were made at seasons of high tumor prevalence.

animals, a beginning of paleopathology, would afford a means of detecting tumors in chronologically earlier populations of frogs and would comment cogently whether or not there has been a spread of the kidney neoplasm to new ranges in the recent past. We now know that the frog renal tumor has been present in Minnesota since 1958 despite the fact that it was first reported in 1965 (6).

Nine counties in Minnesota have been shown to have tumor susceptible frog populations. In addition, frogs from six counties have been examined at a season of the year when a high tumor prevalence would be expected, but no tumors have been found. Additional collections from these areas may or may not reveal the presence of renal tumors.

Are There Tumor-Free Populations of Leopard Frogs in Other Localities?

We have examined to date 618 leopard frogs collected at Woodworth Station, Northern Prairie Wildlife Research Center, Stutsman County, North Dakota. The collections were made during April, September, and October, 1968. The April and October collections were bracketed in time by tumor positive collections in Minnesota; i.e., tumors were detected in Minnesota leopard frogs both before and after the North Dakota tumor-free collections were made. The tumor positive collections made elsewhere are important because of the seasonal fluctuation of tumor prevalence (11). No renal adenocarcinoma was found in the Stutsman County, North Dakota, frogs.

One hundred and ten leopard frogs collected 21 April 1968 near Whitman Dam, 70 miles west of Grand Forks, North Dakota, by Dr. John O. Oberpriller and Mr. Mark Carlson of the University of North Dakota, were autopsied. No renal adenocarcinoma was detected.

We believe that the size of the collections from Stutsman County and Whitman Dam, North Dakota, argues convincingly that either the frogs are completely tumor-free, or that there is an exceedingly low tumor prevalence in these areas.

We desired to know if the infrequency of tumors among North Dakota leopard frogs is attributable to a high natural immunity, or if it is due to environmental factors that protect the animal from the effects of infection. Leopard frogs from susceptible populations develop a high rate of renal tumors when held at room temperatures in the laboratory for eight months (19, 20).

We have been maintaining a sample of Stutsman County frogs under crowded conditions at room temperature since April, 1968. A few of the frogs have died during this time. A histologically confirmed renal adenocarcinoma has been found in one of the frogs that died. Although our study of tumor susceptibility is still in progress, the finding of a renal tumor among these frogs suggests that the frogs may be as susceptible to tumor formation as other more eastern populations, but are protected by one or more environmental factors.

Because we know of no report of tumor prevalence among southern leopard frogs, we are beginning a study of the southern leopard frog, R. pipiens sphenocephala. Frogs were collected in Morehouse Parish in northern Louisiana during September, 1968, by Mr. Dennis Duplantier of Tulane University. Two hundred forty-seven frogs have been autopsied. Although all suspicious appearing areas were fixed for microscopic examination and studied, no renal adenocarcinomas have been detected thus far.

Summary

A seasonal fluctuation of prevalence has been described for renal tumors obtained from Minnesota leopard frogs. High prevalence rates are reported for spring and autumn populations contrasted with low tumor prevalence during summer.

Tumor fine structure seems to be climatologically determined. Tumors from prehibernating leopard frogs appear to be "virus-free." Virus particles were detected in all tumors of frogs emerging from hibernation.

Nine Minnesota counties are cited as containing populations of leopard frogs afflicted with renal tumors. Frogs from six other counties were examined, but no tumors were detected.

Autopsies of North Dakota and Louisiana frogs shortly after capture failed to reveal renal tumors. One renal tumor was found in a North Dakota leopard frog maintained under tumor promoting conditions for six months.

References

1. AUCLAIR, W.: Monolayer culture of Rana pipiens kidney and ecological factors. In Proceedings of Frog Kidney Adenocarcinoma Conference (W. R. Duryee and L. Warner, eds.), Bethesda, Maryland, National Institutes of Health, 1961, pp. 107–113.

2. MATEYKO, G.: Studies on renal neoplasms in western frogs. Anat. Record *128*:587, 1957.

3. RAFFERTY, K. A.: The biology of spontaneous renal carcinoma of the frog. *In* Renal Neoplasia (J. S. King, ed.), Boston, Massachusetts: Little, Brown, and Company, 1967, pp. 301–315.

4. MERRELL, D. J.: The distribution of the dominant burnsi gene in the leopard frog, *Rana pipiens*. Evolution *19*:69–85, 1965.

5. McKINNELL, R. G. and McKINNELL, B. K.: An extension of the ranges of the burnsi and kandiyohi variants of *Rana pipiens*. J. Minnesota Acad. Sci. *34*:176, 1967.

6. McKINNELL, R. G.: Incidence and histology of renal tumors of leopard frogs from the north central states. Ann. N.Y. Acad. Sci. *126*:85–98, 1965.

7. LILIENFELD, A., PEDERSEN, E., and DOWD, J. E.: Cancer Epidemiology: Methods of Study. Baltimore, Maryland: The Johns Hopkins Press, 1967.

8. SHIMKIN, M. B.: Epidemiology in cancer research. *In* Methods in Cancer Research (H. Busch, ed.). Vol. 1. New York, N.Y.: Academic Press, 1967, pp. 289–305.

9. McKINNELL, R. G.: Evidence for seasonal variation in incidence of renal adenocarcinoma in *Rana pipiens*. J. Minnesota Acad. Sci. *34*:173–175, 1967.

10. McKINNELL, R. G.: Renal tumors obtained from pre-breeding Minnesota lake frogs. Am. Zoologist *6*:558, 1966.

11. McKINNELL, R. G., and McKINNELL, B. K. Seasonal fluctuation of frog renal adeno-carcinoma prevalence in natural populations. Cancer Res. *26*:440–444, 1968.

12. ZAMBERNARD, J., and McKINNELL, R. G.: "Virus-free" renal tumors obtained from prehibernating leopard frogs of known geographic origin. Cancer Res. *29*:653–657, 1969.

13. ZAMBERNARD, J., and VATTER, A. E.: The effect of temperature change upon inclusion-containing renal tumor cells of leopard frogs. Cancer Res. *26*:2148–2153, 1966.

14. FAWCETT, D. W.: Electron microscope observations on intra-cellular virus-like particles associated with the cells of the Lucké renal adenocarcinoma. J. Biophys. Biochem. Cytol. *2*:725–742, 1956.

15. LUNGER, P. D., DARLINGTON, R. W., and GRANOFF, A.: Cell-virus relationships in the Lucké renal adenocarcinoma: an ultrastructure study. Ann. N.Y. Acad. Sci. *126*:289–314, 1965.

16. McKINNELL, R. G., and ZAMBERNARD, J.: Virus particles in renal tumors obtained from spring *Rana pipiens* of known geographic origin. Cancer Res. *28*:684–688, 1968.

17. TWEEDELL, K. S.: Induced oncogenesis in developing frog kidney cells. Cancer Res. *27*: 2042–2052, 1967.

18. MIZELL, M., STACKPOLE, C. W., and HALPERN, S.: Herpes-type virus recovery from "virus-free" frog kidney tumors. Proc. Soc. Exptl. Biol. and Med. *127*:96–98, 1968.

19. RAFFERTY, K. A., JR., and RAFFERTY, N. S.: High incidence of transmissible kidney tumors in uninoculated frogs maintained in a laboratory. Science *133*:702–703, 1961.

20. DIBERARDINO, M. A., and KING, T. J.: Renal carcinoma promoted by crowded conditions in laboratory frogs. Cancer Res. *25*:1910–1912, 1965.

Chromosome Studies of Primary Renal Carcinoma from Vermont *Rana pipiens*[1]

Marie A. DiBerardino and Nancy Hoffner [2]

Department of Anatomy
Woman's Medical College of Pennsylvania
Philadelphia, Pennsylvania

The kidney carcinoma of *Rana pipiens* first described by Lucké (1) has been the subject of numerous investigations relating to problems of carcinogenesis and development (2–5). Although this tumor has long been suspected to be of viral origin (6), only recently has induced oncogenesis been demonstrated significantly by injecting sub-cellular fractions of inclusion-bearing tumors into developing frog embryos and larvae (7).

Studies on the frog renal adenocarcinoma have now extended over three decades; however, little information is available concerning the ploidy and karyotypic constitution of this primary neoplasm. Previously, a limited number of karyotype analyses, made on 3 diploid primary neoplasms, revealed chromosomal alterations in 2 tumors (8), but no changes were observed in the third carcinoma (9). Earlier reports of a general nature, regarding chromosome number of primary carcinoma in cell culture, indicated the tumors were diploid (10–12). In order to determine the chromosome status of this tumor, we have carried out detailed studies on the chromosomes of 9 primary kidney carcinomas. The results of these studies are reported below.

Materials and Methods

Source of Primary Tumors

The chromosome studies reported in this paper were made on 9 primary renal carcinomas that arose in adult male *Rana pipiens*, originally derived from the Lake Champlain region of Vermont. Two of the tumors (Table 1: RA 43, RA 40) were detected by palpating frogs that were shipped by the dealer to our laboratory during the autumn and spring. The remaining 7 neoplasms arose in frogs that had received tumor implants in the anterior eye chamber; 6 of the hosts were recipients of primary renal carcinoma and 1 (host of RA 29) received a piece of lung tumor. With the

[1] This study was initiated at the Institute for Cancer Research, Philadelphia, Pa., and aided by research grant CA-05755 from the National Cancer Institute; subsequently, at Woman's Medical College this work was aided by research grant GB-7702 from the National Science Foundation.

[2] The authors acknowledge the valuable assistance of Miss L. Bohl during the initial stages of this study.

261

exception of 2 intraocular tumors (hosts of RA 39, RA 31), the other transplanted tumors regressed.

All of the frogs bearing intraocular implants were maintained in the laboratory (22 ± 2°C) for 11–33 months and were palpated monthly for the presence of renal tumors. At first, they were maintained separately in glass aquaria, but when regression of the intraocular tumors occurred, the animals were housed in groups of 6 to 8 in rectangular aquaria tanks. Details relating to the care of adult frogs maintained in the laboratory have been summarized previously (4).

Animals were sacrificed from 4 days to 3 months following detection of the tumors (Table 1). At this time, the body length of the frog was determined by measuring the dorsum from the tip of the snout to the anus. After the neoplastic kidneys were removed and placed into Steinberg's salt solution (13), the entire thoracic and abdominal cavities were examined for the presence of additional tumors (i.e., metastases of the original primary renal adenocarcinoma or new neoplasms).

A healthy portion of the tumor including some adjacent kidney was fixed in Zenker's acetic acid fluid for 1 hour and then processed for histological study. Sections were cut at 7μ, stained with basic fuchsin according to the Feulgen procedure and counterstained with fast green.

Chromosome Preparations

Tumor Cells

The following procedure used for preparing metaphase chromosomes by the air drying method consists of modifications of the techniques reported previously by Rothfels and Siminovitch (14) and Ford and Woollam (15). All the operations including fixation were performed at 18°C.

After the initial rinse in Steinberg's salt solution, healthy portions of the tumor were transferred to fresh salt solution and cut into small pieces (2–3 mm). These pieces were transferred to a small amount of salt solution (~3 ml) and further minced with fine scissors and forceps. Finally, the tumorous fragments were sucked in and out of a fine bore pipette (0.5–1 mm diameter) for 5 minutes in order to obtain small clumps of cells and some free cells.

The concentrated suspension of tumor cells was transferred to a 6.5 ml centrifuge tube and centrifuged for 10 minutes in an International Clinical Centrifuge at 450 rpm (all subsequent centrifugations were carried out at this speed). The pellet was resuspended in 25% Steinberg solution, added to the 5 ml level, and the preparation was intermittently agitated with a pipette for a 15 minute interval. Exposure of normal and tumorous frog cells to hypotonic salt solutions prior to fixation has previously been found to produce adequate spreading of metaphase chromosomes, so that reliable chromosome studies can be made (9, 16). Subsequent to the hypotonic treatment, the cell suspension was centrifuged for 5 minutes, then fresh fixative (glacial acetic acid:absolute ethyl alcohol, 1:3) was added to the pellet until a volume of 2 ml was reached, and the cell suspension was left undisturbed for 10 minutes. Next, the fixed cells were recentrifuged for 5 minutes, then 45% acetic acid was

TABLE 1

Case Histories of Primary Renal Carcinoma Arising in Male Vt. Rana pipiens

	Host			Tumor				
Tumor number	Laboratory age (month) [a]	Body length (mm) [b]	Source of host [c]	Unilateral, bilateral	Volume (mm³)	Age (month) [d]	Other tumors	Percent normal karyotype
RA 41	33	78	AEC regressed	U	180	1	Fat body, urinary bladder	100
RA 29	12	80	AEC (lung) regressed	B	3960	2	Stomach	91
RA 43	(4 days)	71	Shipment	B	7326	?	Small intestine	90
RA 38	24	78	AEC regressed	U	360	1	Lung	89
RA 35	19	83	AEC regressed	B	7920	3	—	80
RA 39	11	68	AEC	B	720	1	—	73
RA 40	2	78	Shipment	U	720	?	—	25
RA 31	13	74	AEC	U	504	1	—	—
RA 42	27	74	AEC regressed	U	210	1	—	Not done

Note: Data obtained at autopsy.

[a] Interval that frogs were maintained in the laboratory at 22 ± 2°C.

[b] From snout to anus.

[c] AEC refers to frogs that received primary renal carcinoma implants into the anterior eye chamber; in the case of RA 29 a piece of lung tumor was implanted.

[d] Estimated age: interval from time of detection by palpation to time of sacrifice; palpations performed monthly.

added to the pellet until a volume of 2 ml was attained and the tumor cells were left undisturbed for 10 minutes. The cells were then subjected to a final centrifugation for 10 minutes, and the pellet was resuspended in 45% acetic acid up to the ½ ml level in order to obtain a concentration of free cells. The use of 45% acetic acid in the final steps of this procedure softens the cells and permits better spreading of the chromosomes on the microscopic slides.

The final cell suspension was gently agitated with a pipette (0.5–1 ml diameter) and 3 to 5 drops of cell suspension were placed on a microscope slide previously heated on a histological slide warmer (49–50°C). After a 10 minute drying period, the slides were removed from the warmer and stained for 30 minutes in filtered orcein (1% Gurr's natural orcein in 60% acetic acid). Subsequently, the slides were washed in 3 changes of 45% acetic acid (½ minute each), air dried at room temperature and mounted in Technicon. In some cases, slides were stored up to 3 weeks prior to staining.

Normal Cells

Chromosomal analyses of testes from adult and recently metamorphosed frogs constitute the control series since normal kidney cells rarely undergo mitosis. Some of the adult testes were processed according to the procedure described above for obtaining spread cells by the air-drying method. Other adult testes and all of the testes from juvenile frogs were pretreated with hypotonic salt solution, stained in acetic-orcein and then squash preparations were made as previously described (9, 16).

Results

Normal Cells

Metaphases of spermatogonial cells from 3 adult and 4 juvenile testes were studied. A diploid number of 26 chromosomes was present, and this number is in agreement with previous reports for this species (9, 16–17). Occasionally, polyploid metaphases ranging from 4N to 8N were present in the adult testes; presumably, these metaphases are derived from Sertoli cells.

A total of 10 metaphases derived from the 7 individuals was subjected to karyotype analysis; these metaphases conformed to previous karyotype analyses of embryonic and larval cells (16) and adult bone marrow cells (9) in which no detectable pair of heteromorphic (sex) chromosomes was observed. A representative karyotype from spermatogonial cells is illustrated in Fig. 1.

Tumor Cells

The 9 primary renal tumors whose chromosome constitution will be described below were examined microscopically and all conformed to the histopathology of a frog renal carcinoma (1).

Chromosome Counts

Table 2 summarizes the chromosome number of metaphases from 9 renal carcinomas. In every tumor the chromosome counts are predominantly diploid. Five

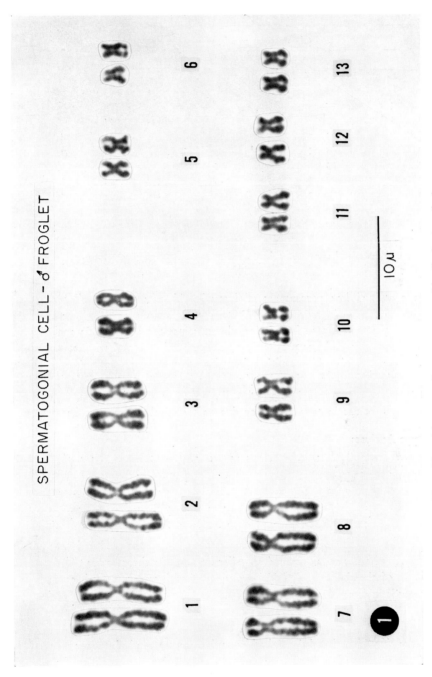

Fig. 1. Normal karyotype from a spermatogonial cell of a juvenile frog.

TABLE 2

Primary Renal Carcinoma (Vt. Rana pipiens)

Tumor	Chromosome number									Percent			Diploid karyotypes		
	23	24	25	26	27	30	31	50	Total counts	<2N	2N	>2N	Total	Abnormal	Percent normal
RA 41	1	2	2	25					30	17	83	—	4	—	100
RA 29	1	2	3	17					23	26	74	—	11	1	91
RA 43 *	4	2		23					29	21	79	—	10	1	90
RA 38		1	1	25	1				28	7	89	4	9	1	89
RA 35	2			23					25	8	92	—	5	1	80
RA 39	9	5	9	85	3	3	1		115	20	74	6	11	3	73
RA 40		1	3	24	2				30	13	80	7	4	3	25
RA 31	2	2	3	30				1	38	18	79	3	12	12	—
RA 42			2	18	1				21	9	86	5	—	—	—

* One cell contained approximately 48 chromosomes.

tumors contained low percentages of hyperdiploid cells, whereas all tumors possessed some hypodiploid cells. Some of this hypodiploidy is due to chromosome loss, inherent in the techniques of preparing chromosomes for microscopic analysis. More extensive studies carried out previously on normal cells revealed that, approximately, 10–15% were hypodiploids, resulting from broken metaphase plates (9, 16). In the present study, 5 tumors had a slightly higher incidence of hypodiploidy (2–11% higher) than that present in normal cells. Whether this is a true expression of numerical deviations in tumor cells or due to technical loss cannot be ascertained.

Karyotype Analyses

Karotype analyses performed on diploid cells from 8 tumors revealed that there was no uniformity of chromosome constitution among the renal carcinoma. One tumor, RA 41 (Table 2) displayed no karyotypic alterations in the metaphases analyzed; 5 tumors possessed non-specific chromosomal abnormalities in a minority of cells; 1 tumor contained variable aberrations in the majority of cells; and finally, 1 tumor (RA 31) had deviations from the normal karyotype in all the cells analyzed; furthermore, many of these cells possessed a similar acrocentric chromosome.

Details of the abnormal diploid karyotypes of each tumor, as well as analyses on some hypodiploids are described below.

RA 29

Eleven diploid and 2 hypodiploid metaphases were studied. Among the diploid cells, 10 were normal in karyotype (Fig. 2) and 1 was abnormal. In the abnormal diploid, one of the no. 1 chromosomes was absent and an apparent normal chromosome similar to the pair of no. 8 chromosomes was present. Since the length and arm

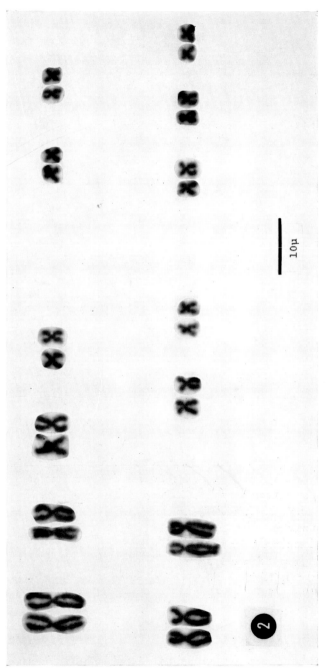

Fig. 2. Normal karyotype from primary renal carcinoma, RA 29.

ratio of this extra element was similar to the homologous no. 8 chromosomes, this metaphase was interpreted as consisting of a trisomic no. 8 and a monosomic no. 1.

One hypodiploid cell consisted of 24 chromosomes and lacked a pair of no. 4 chromosomes. The other hypodiploid (Fig. 3) contained 25 chromosomes: one no. 8 and one no. 12 chromosome were absent and a deviate chromosome with a median centromere was present.

RA 43

One of the 10 diploid metaphases examined was abnormal. This metaphase lacked one homologue of no. 8 and contained an extra small sub-metacentric chromosome whose length ranked it between nos. 12 and 13 chromosomes; since its long arm was equal in length to the short arm of the no. 8 present in the cell, this new sub-metacentric element may be derived from a portion of the missing no. 8.

RA 38

Among the 9 diploid metaphases analyzed, 1 karyotype was found to be abnormal. The abnormalities comprised no. 1 monosomy and no. 13 trisomy.

RA 35

One of the 5 diploid cells examined displayed abnormalities; these consisted of no. 2 monosomy and no. 3 trisomy.

RA 39

Eleven diploid and 1 hypodiploid metaphases were studied. Among the diploid cells 8 exhibited no deviations from the standard karyotype (Fig. 4), but 3 were abnormal.

One diploid cell displayed no. 1 monosomy and no. 12 trisomy (Fig. 5).

The second abnormal diploid metaphase showed evidence of structural change in the karyotype (Fig. 6). One homologue of no. 7 was absent and an extra meta-centric chromosome was present; its length ranked it between chromosomes 2 and 3. In addition, an extraordinary constriction was present on both chromatids of one homologue of no. 1. One possible interpretation of the origin of these aberrations is as follows: the new metacentric chromosome could be derived from a no. 7 chromo-some that has lost the terminal portion of its long arm; the length of the short arm of the new chromosome is equal to the length of the short arm of the one no. 7 that is present in the cell. Other complex changes, however, could have occurred involving the one homologue of no. 1 that displays an extraordinary constriction in both chromatids of the longer arm.

The third abnormal diploid cell displayed such extensive deviations from the standard karyotype that speculation regarding the origin of these aberrations is impossible: one homologue of no. 1 and no. 13 and both homologues of no. 6 were absent; four new chromosomes not conforming to the standard karyotype were present, namely, 3 medium-sized chromosomes with median centromeres and 1 large submetacentric chromosome.

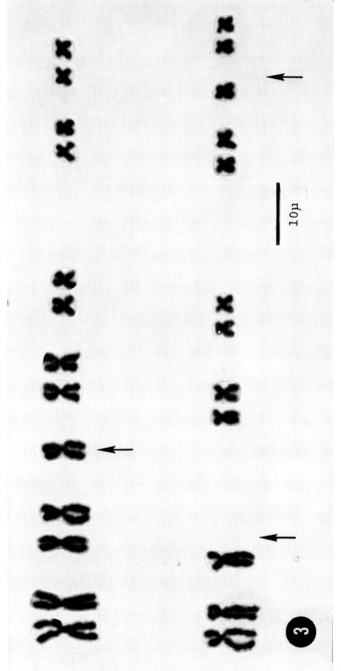

Fig. 3. Abnormal hypodiploid karyotype (25 chromosomes) from primary renal carcinoma, RA 29. One homologue each of no. 8 and no. 12 is absent and a deviate metacentric chromosome is present.

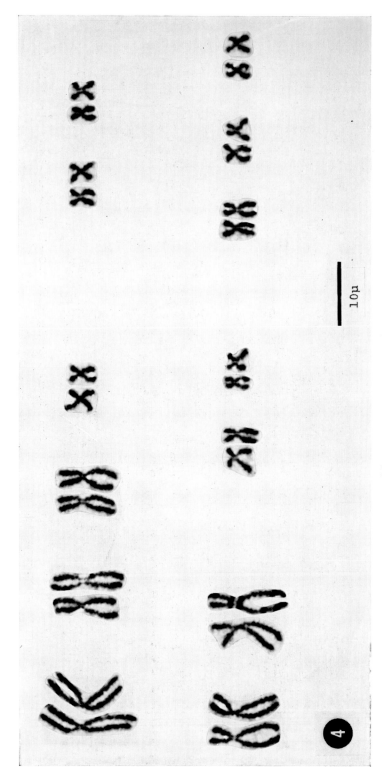

Fig. 4. Normal karyotype from primary renal carcinoma, RA 39.

10μ

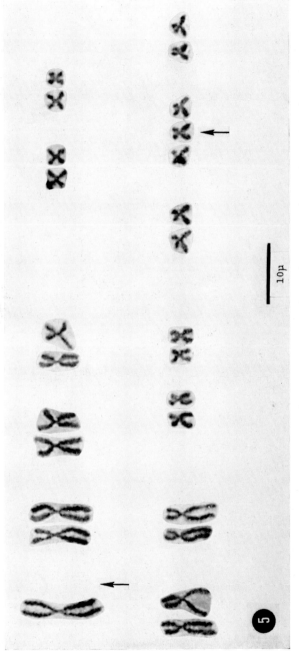

Fig. 5. Abnormal karyotype from primary renal carcinoma, RA 39. Abnormalities consist of monosomic no. 1 and trisomic no. 12.

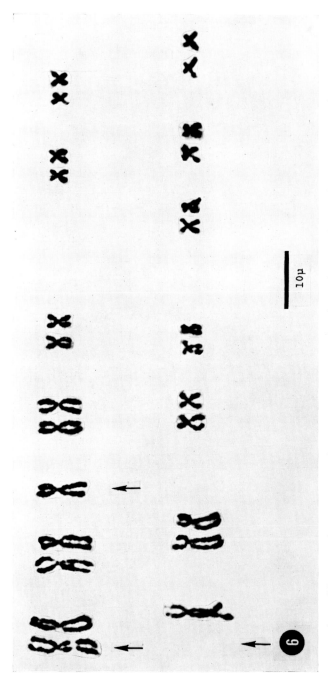

Fig. 6. Abnormal karyotype from primary renal carcinoma, RA 39. One homologue of no. 7 is absent, a deviate metacentric chromosome is present, and an unusual constriction is located on both chromatids of one homologue of no. 1.

Finally, the 1 hypodiploid analyzed contained 23 chromosomes. This aneuploid cell lacked one homologue each of no. 3, no. 9 and no. 10 chromosomes. No apparent structural abnormalities were detected in the chromosomes.

RA 40

Among the 4 diploid metaphases analyzed, 3 were abnormal. In all cases, monosomy and trisomy were involved: cell 1 (monosomy no. 1, trisomy no. 11); cell 2 (monosomy no. 2, trisomy no. 4); cell 3 (monosomy no. 2, trisomy no. 3).

RA 31

Although this tumor was relatively small compared to some of the others (Table 1), karyotype analysis of 12 diploid cells revealed extensive alterations in all the cells analyzed.

Six cells possessed an acrocentric chromosome, lacked one homologue of no. 1 and contained an extra large sub-metacentric chromosome (Fig. 7). Other abnormalities were present among these 6 cells involving the loss of either no. 3, 4, 5, 6, 9 or 10. The simplest interpretation for the derivation of the acrocentric is that it is derived from the centromere and short arm of the missing no. 1 chromosome.

Five cells lacked one homologue of no. 2 and contained an extra large sub-metacentric chromosome (Fig. 8). In addition, there are not two homologous no. 8 chromosomes. An interchange between the missing no. 2 and one of the no. 8 chromosomes may account for the origin of the extra large sub-metacentric element.

Finally, 1 diploid cell lacked a no. 1 homologue and contained one extra large sub-metacentric chromosome.

Two hypodiploid metaphases were analyzed, each containing 23 chromosomes. In both cases, only one no. 13 was present. In addition, one cell was monosomic for no. 2 and no. 11, while the other lacked one homologue of no. 5 and no. 8.

Karyotypic Constitution and Tumor Characteristics

The results of the karyotypic studies reported in the previous section demonstrate that these primary renal carcinomas differ in the percentage of cells that exhibit karyotypic alterations. Since the case histories of the hosts and the tumors were variable for a number of factors (Table 1), we examined the data to determine whether a relationship exists between the percentage of abnormal diploid metaphases found in the sample analysis and the following factors: unilateral vs. bilateral tumors, volume of tumor, estimated age of tumor and presence of metastases. No correlation was found; in fact, the characteristics that are considered common to advanced malignancy (bilateral involvement, large growth and metastases) were present in frogs who tumors exhibited few or no karyotypic changes.

Discussion

Chromosome studies of primary renal carcinoma in *Rana pipiens* have shown that this malignancy is not characterized by significant deviations from the diploid number. In addition to the 9 primary tumors reported in this paper, detailed studies

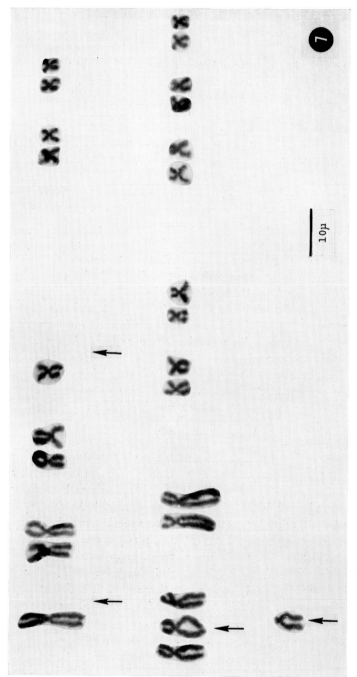

Fig. 7. Abnormal karyotype from primary renal carcinoma, RA 31. Aberrations consist of monosomic no. 1 and no. 4, one additional large submetacentric chromosome and one acrocentric chromosome.

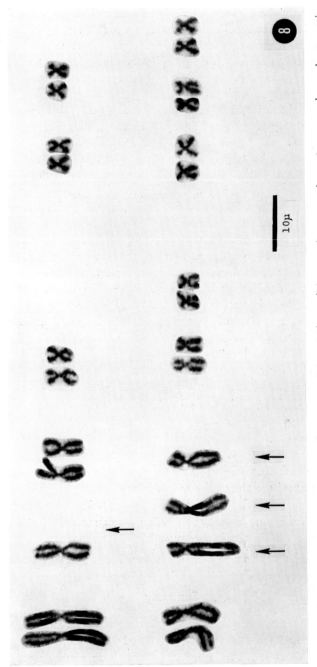

Fig. 8. Abnormal karyotype from primary renal carcinoma, RA 31. Abnormalities comprise monosomic no. 2, an extra large submetacentric chromosome and non-homologous no. 8 chromosomes.

on 4 other primary tumors and 3 intraocular tumors (8–9) as well as 1 cell culture strain (18) have demonstrated that these tumors are mainly diploid. Furthermore, the diploid state has persisted for at least 2.7 years in one intraocular tumor line (9) and for at least 25 subcultures in a tumor cell strain (18).

In contrast to the relatively stable diploid condition of these tumors, their karyotypic state is variable. All together 11 primary tumors have been subjected to karyotypic analysis [8 in the present study and 3 in previous studies (8–9)]. In these sample studies, 2 tumors displayed no deviations from the standard karyotype, 5 tumors contained aberrations in a minority of cells (9–27%), 1 tumor had abnormalities in the majority of cells, and finally, 3 tumors exhibited chromosome changes in all cells analyzed.

The origin of these karyotypic abnormalities appears to be twofold. Some may arise through non-disjunction during anaphase and the abnormalities are then displayed in metaphases as monosomy and trisomy. Others presumably originate from chromosome breaks followed by chromosomal interchange, resulting in the formation of new types of chromosomes not present in the standard karyotype. Among the 7 tumors displaying aberrations in this present study, 3 tumors exhibited evidence of non-disjunction in some cells, 2 tumors displayed structural alterations in a few cells, and finally, 2 tumors contained both types of abnormalities.

In assessing the significance of these results, at least three points should be considered. First, the relative stability of diploidy makes this tumor useful for analyzing developmental problems; however, since the karyological state is variable, it is essential to know the karyotype of each tumor, so that meaningful evaluations can be made. Second, the renal carcinomas examined for karyotypic constitution have been derived from male *Rana pipiens* obtained from the Lake Champlain region of Vermont. Whether similar or different chromosome complements exist in renal tumors derived from females of this locality is not known. Neither is the chromosome status known for spontaneous renal carcinoma arising in wild type (19–22) and mutant (19–21) *Rana pipiens* from the North Central States, nor is it known for renal carcinoma, induced in larval *Rana pipiens* (7) and larval and adult *Rana palustris* (23). Third, chromosomal changes do not appear to be primarily involved in the development of the tumor, for extensive malignancy does not necessarily involve significant changes in karyotype (Tables 1 and 2). What appears most probable is that the observed non-specific chromosome changes are secondary effects of the malignant state, and that the initial cause of malignancy is a genetic alteration arising through the interaction of a virus and the genome of the kidney cell.

Summary

Counts of metaphase chromosomes, made on 9 primary renal carcinomas derived from Vermont male *Rana pipiens,* demonstrated that these neoplastic cells are predominantly diploid; a small percentage of hyperdiploidy was observed in 5 of the tumors (range = 3 to 7 percent). Karyotype analyses of a sample of diploid cells from 8 carcinomas revealed that their chromosomal constitution was variable: 1 tumor displayed no deviations from the normal karyotype; 5 tumors possessed karyotypic alterations in a minority of cells; 1 tumor displayed abnormalities in the majority of metaphases; and 1 tumor had deviations from the normal karyotype in all the cells analyzed; in addition, many of these cells possessed an acrocentric chromosome. Some of the abnormalities comprised monosomy and trisomy and arose presumably through non-disjunction; the other deviations consisted of aberrant forms of chromosomes and originated through structural changes. These chromosomal changes do not appear to be primarily involved in the development of the tumor, because extensive malignancy did not necessarily involve significant changes in karyotype.

References

1. LUCKÉ, B.: A neoplastic disease of the kidney of the frog, *Rana pipiens*. Amer. J. Cancer 20:352–379, 1934.

2. RAFFERTY, K. A., JR.: Kidney tumors of the leopard frog: a review. Cancer Res. 24:169–185, 1964.

3. LUNGER, P. D.: Amphibia-related viruses. *In* Advances in Virus Research 12:1–33. K. M. Smith and M. A. Lauffer, eds. Academic Press, New York, 1966.

4. DiBERARDINO, M. A.: Frogs. *In* Methods in Developmental Biology, pp. 53–74. F. H. Wilt and N. K. Wessells, eds. T. Y. Crowell Co., New York, 1967.

5. RAFFERTY, K. A., JR.: The biology of spontaneous renal carcinoma of the frog. *In* Renal Neoplasia, pp. 301–315. J. S. King, ed. Little, Brown and Co., Inc., Boston, 1967.

6. LUCKÉ, B.: Kidney carcinoma in the leopard frog: a virus tumor. Ann N.Y. Acad. Sci. 54:1093–1109, 1952.

7. TWEEDELL, K. S.: Induced oncogenesis in developing frog kidney cells. Cancer Res. 27: 2042–2052, 1967.

8. DiBERARDINO, M. A., and KING, T. J.: Transplantation of nuclei from the frog renal adenocarcinoma. II. Chromosomal and histologic analysis of tumor nuclear-transplant embryos. Develop. Biol. 11:217–242, 1965.

9. DiBERARDINO, M. A., KING, T. J., and McKINNELL, R. G.: Chromosome studies of a frog renal adenocarcinoma line carried by serial intraocular transplantation. J. Nat. Cancer Inst. 31:769–789, 1963.

10. LUCKÉ, B.: Characteristics of frog carcinoma in tissue culture. J. Exp. Med. 70:269–276, 1939.

11. DURYEE, W. R., and DOHERTY, J. K.: Nuclear and cytoplasmic organoids in the living cell. Ann N.Y. Acad. Sci. 58:1210–1231, 1954.

12. FREED, J. J., and COLE, S. J.: Chromosome studies on haploid and diploid cell cultures from *Rana pipiens*. Amer. Soc. Cell Biol. 1:62, 1961 (Abstract).

13. STEINBERG, M.: Carnegie Inst. Washington Year Book 56:347 (report by J. D. Ebert), 1957.

14. ROTHFELS, K. H., and SIMINOVITCH, L.: An air-drying technique for flattening chromosomes in mammalian cells grown *in vitro*. Stain Technol. 33:73–77, 1958.

15. FORD, E. H. R., and WOOLLAM, D. H. M.: A colchicine, hypotonic citrate, air drying sequence for foetal mammalian chromosomes. Stain Technol. 38:271–274, 1963.

16. DiBERARDINO, M. A.: The karyotype of *Rana pipiens* and investigation of its stability during embryonic differentiation. Develop. Biol. 5:101–126, 1962.

17. PARMENTER, C. L.: The chromosomes of parthenogenetic frogs. J. Gen. Physiol. 2:205–206, 1920.

18. RAFFERTY, K. A., JR.: The cultivation of inclusion-associated viruses from Lucké tumor frogs. Ann N.Y. Acad. Sci. 126:3–21, 1965.

19. McKinnell, R. G.: Incidence and histology of renal tumors of leopard frogs from north central states. Ann N.Y. Acad. Sci. *126*:85–98, 1965.

20. Tweedell, K. S.: Renal tumors in a western population of *Rana pipiens*. Amer. Midland Naturalist *73*:285–292, 1965.

21. McKinnell, R. G.: Evidence for seasonal variation in incidence of renal adenocarcinoma in *Rana pipiens*. J. Minnesota Acad. Sci. *34*:173–175, 1967.

22. McKinnell, R. G., and McKinnell, B. K.: Seasonal fluctuation of frog renal adenocarcinoma prevalence in natural populations. Cancer Res. *28*:440–444, 1968.

23. Mulcare, D. J., and Tweedell, K. S.: Renal tumors induced in *Rana palustris* by tumor implants or sub-cellular fractions from *Rana pipiens*. Amer. Zool. *7*:748, 1967 (Abstract).

Studies on the Viral Etiology of the Renal Adenocarcinoma of *Rana pipiens* (Lucké Tumor) [1]

ALLAN GRANOFF, MANETH GRAVELL, and R. W. DARLINGTON

Laboratory of Virology
St. Jude Children's Research Hospital, and
University of Tennessee Medical Units
Memphis, Tennessee

Introduction

The presence of intranuclear acidophilic inclusion bodies and an increased incidence of tumors in frogs receiving cell-free tumor extracts led Lucké (1, 2) to postulate a viral etiology of the renal adenocarcinoma of *Rana pipiens* (Lucké tumor). Although this conclusion was reached over thirty years ago, propagation of a virus from *R. pipiens* capable of inducing renal tumors has not been achieved.

The electron microscope studies of Fawcett (3) demonstrated the presence of a herpes-like virus in inclusion-bearing tumors. The physical separation of the virus from tumor extracts (4) and characterization of its ultrastructure by negative staining firmly placed the virus in the herpesvirus group. Thus, a likely candidate as the causative agent of the Lucké tumor appeared to be a herpesvirus; but its candidacy was based primarily on guilt by association.

About six years ago we became interested in the Lucké tumor and its potential usefulness as an experimental model for studying virus-induced oncogenicity. Obvious from the outset was the need to firmly establish the virus etiology of this tumor. Toward this end, experiments were initiated for the purpose of isolating, propagating, and characterizing viruses from *R. pipiens*, particularly from tumor tissue, and for assessing their role in tumor formation. Our experience in these efforts is reviewed in this report.

Polyhedral Cytoplasmic Virus

The first virus isolated from *R. pipiens* originated from plaques appearing spontaneously in monolayers of frog kidney cells overlaid with agar (5). It was subsequently found that fathead minnow cells (FHM) (6) were susceptible to infection with the virus and using these cells a number of additional isolations of virus were made (5, 7). The source of virus included normal cultured frog kidney cells, homogenates of normal frog liver, and homogenates of Lucké tumors. Homogenates of 30 pairs of normal kidneys, each pair tested separately, did not yield

[1] Supported by Public Health Service Research Grant 5 RO1 CA 07055 and Training Grant 5 TO1 CA 05176 from the National Cancer Institute, and American Lebanese Syrian Associated Charities (ALSAC).

279

virus. Recently we have also isolated virus from livers of tumor bearing frogs. In some instances virus was isolated from the tumor of the same animal, in others it was not. Virus could also be isolated from tumor homogenates of an animal but not from the liver of the same animal. To date 16 separate isolations of virus have been made in our laboratory with the incidence of virus in normal (liver) and malignant tissue about 10% and 30%, respectively. The virus has been designated frog virus (FV) with a number given sequentially as isolates were obtained.

Following the initial isolation of virus, of prime importance was to determine whether the virus was the same as the herpes-type seen in inclusion-bearing Lucké tumors. Feulgen staining of virus-infected cells of each of the viruses isolated showed them all to induce Feulgen-positive cytoplasmic inclusions (7) (Fig. 1). Electron microscopy (8) clearly showed the virus to be morphologically distinct from the herpes-type virus and confirmed that the site of virus synthesis was the cytoplasm. Fig. 2 is an electronmicrograph of a FV 1-infected FHM cell showing the topography and several other aspects of virus replication. The sequential development of this virus in cultured cells has been detailed elsewhere (8). The virus is hexagonal in thin sections of infected cells and measures approximately 120×130 mμ. Regions of virus synthesis (Fig. 2, S) are seen in infected cells and contain virus particles in all stages of development from partial capsids to complete capsids with nucleoids. The virus acquires an envelope as it buds from the cytoplasmic membrane into either the medium or into cytoplasmic vacuoles.

The virus synthesizing sites contain viral DNA which has a G + C content of

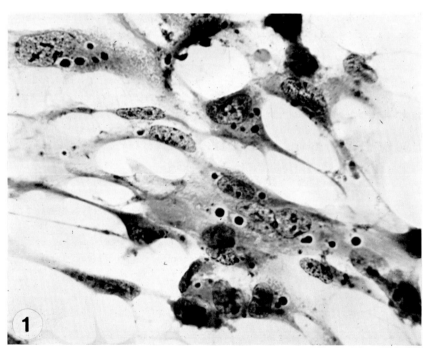

Fig. 1. Feulgen-stained polyhedral cytoplasmic virus (FV 3)-infected BHK 21/13 cells illustrating Feulgen-positive cytoplasmic inclusion bodies. Approximately $\times 375$.

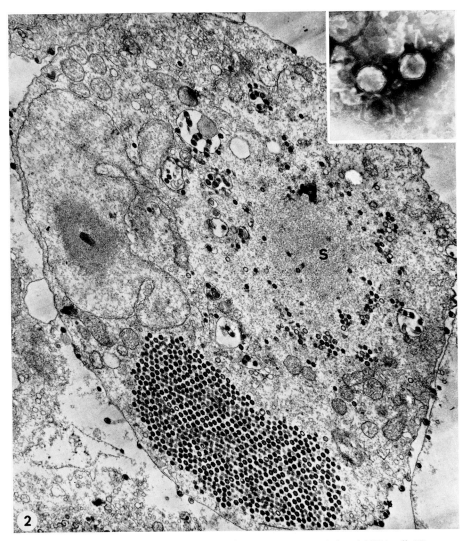

Fig. 2. Electron micrograph of a polyhedral cytoplasmic virus (FV 1)-infected FHM cell. Virus synthesis site (S), crystalline array of virus, and virus particles budding from the cytoplasmic membrane or into cytoplasmic vacuoles are shown. ×12,000. The insert shows 2 negatively stained virions. ×72,000.

53% (9) corresponding to a similar G + C content of DNA isolated from virions (10). Viral protein, as determined by immunofluorescence, is also found in distinct cytoplasmic sites.

Two unenveloped virions negatively stained with phosphotungstic acid are shown in Fig. 2 (insert). Viral ultrastructure (capsomeres) is not revealed. The nucleoid of the virus is surrounded by what appears to be a capsid morphologically similar to a unit membrane and which we have found susceptible to lipid solvent degradation. More concerted efforts are being made to elucidate the ultrastructure of this virus.

Comparative studies of two of the isolates, one from uninoculated kidney tissue culture (FV 1) and the other from a frog tumor (FV 3) have revealed no differences thus far between these isolates and most of our studies have been carried out with FV 3. This virus multiplies in piscine, reptilian, avian, amphibian, and mammalian (including human) cells (8, 11). It multiplies at temperatures ranging from 12°C to 30°C in fish (FHM), chick embryo (CE), and baby hamster kidney cells (BHK 21/13) (12). Fig. 3 illustrates growth curves of FV 3 in these cells at 12°C and 24°C. At 12°C (Fig. 3A) the viral latent period is much shorter (12 to 24

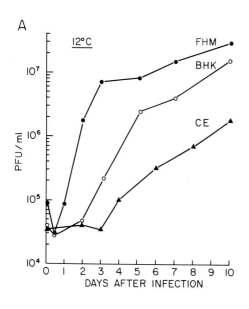

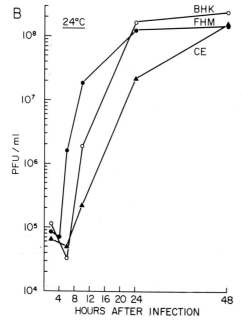

Fig. 3. Growth curves of polyhedral cytoplasmic virus (FV 3) in FHM, BHK 21/13, and CE cells at 12°C (A) and 24°C (B). Plaque titers are based on total virus yield (cell-associated plus released virus).

hours) in cells of poikilothermic origin (FHM) than in those of homeothermic origin, BHK 21/13 (2 to 3 days) and CE (3 to 4 days). As temperature is raised (Fig. 3B), the latent period decreases and the rate of FV 3 multiplication increases in all cells. At 30°C the latent period is shortest (4 hours) and the rate of virus production greatest. Although replication of infectious virus cannot be demonstrated at 33°C, both viral DNA (Feulgen-positive inclusions) and protein(s) (immunofluorescent inclusions) are made at this temperature but not at 37°C (13).

Of great importance was the test for *in vivo* activity of the cytoplasmic virus. Adult *R. pipiens* injected with 10^8 plaque-forming units (PFU) of FV 3 did not develop tumors after 8 months at 25°C nor has any pathology been observed. Indeed, we have failed to demonstrate significant virus replication in tissues of frogs over a period of 35 days after inoculation with FV 3.

Tweedell (14) has demonstrated that *R. pipiens* embryos and larvae receiving injections of cytoplasmic fractions of inclusion-containing Lucké tumors developed typical renal carcinomas as they reached metamorphosis. Using the same method, FV 3 was tested for tumorigenic activity (15) with the following results. Tailbud and hatching stage embryos were rapidly killed by as few as 900 PFU. Larvae (17–26 mm) were killed by $2.7 - 4.5 \times 10^6$ PFU, but survived 10^5 PFU. Animals dying from virus infection were edematous and had dermal hemorrhages. Depigmentation, lordosis and epithelial sloughing were also present. None of the larvae reaching metamorphosis which had received 10^5 PFU developed macroscopic tumors, nor was there any observable alteration in their development.

Studies on the pathology of FV 3 infection have been extended to Fowler's toads (*Bufo woodhousei fowleri*). These amphibia have been shown by Wolf *et al.* (16) to be susceptible to infection by tadpole edema virus (TEV), a virus similar to FV 3. Thus far, uninoculated toads have been found free of polyhedral cytoplasmic virus. Inoculation with 10^8 PFU of FV 3 killed 100% of toads within 9 days and 10^6 PFU 50% within 21 days. All animals survived lower concentrations of virus. Virus multiplication occurred in various tissues as indicated by high PFU titers found in kidney, liver, lung, skeletal muscle, and fat body. Virus infection was transmissible to other toads by pooled homogenates of liver and kidney. Toads dead or moribund from FV 3 infection were edematous and hemorrhagic. Microscopically the histopathology was compatible with a generalized virus infection with multiple focal or confluent necrosis and hemorrhage in the tissue examined. Fig. 4 is a section of a kidney from a moribund FV 3-infected toad. The glomeruli show considerable alteration; there is a loss of Bowman's space with fusion of glomerular tufts and capsular epithelium. The capillary pattern is destroyed in many areas of each glomerulus and varying numbers of erythrocytes are present in the glomeruli. The higher power magnification of a glomerulus shown in the insert of Fig. 4 illustrates the cellular necrosis that accompanies FV 3 infection. Many of the affected cells contain cytoplasmic inclusions identical to those seen in FV 3-infected cells *in vitro* (Fig. 1). Both the gross pathology and histopathology of FV 3 infection are similar to, but apparently less severe than, the pathology induced in the same host by TEV (16).

Polyhedral cytoplasmic DNA viruses antigenically related to our isolates have been isolated by others (11, 16, 17) and are reviewed in detail elsewhere in this symposium (18, 19).

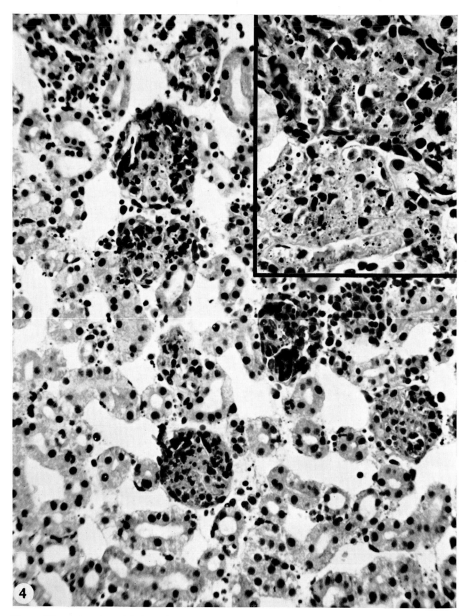

Fig. 4. FV 3-infected toad kidney showing glomerular alterations (×253). Insert shows many degenerating cells which appear to contain cytoplasmic inclusion bodies. ×753.

Although none of the cytoplasmic viruses has been shown to be causally related to the Lucké tumor, the frequency with which they have been isolated from, or observed in, (20) tumors requires that they remain suspect. The etiology of the Lucké tumor, if viral, may prove to involve a defective virus and the FV 3 type may play a role as a helper virus. Polyhedral cytoplasmic frog virus is also of additional interest as a model system for studying cell-virus interaction. Although this virus and poxvirus are DNA viruses multiplying in the cell cytoplasm, several differences exist in their mode of replication (21). It is now possible, therefore, to compare the requirements of one cytoplasmic DNA virus with those of another and to determine what is basic for replication of viral DNA in the cytoplasm.

Herpes-Type Virus

Several years ago Rafferty (22) isolated a virus from the urine of a tumor bearing frog. The virus, FV 4, multiplied only in a *R. sylvatica* embryo cell line developed by Rafferty in contrast to the polyhedral cytoplasmic virus which has a broad host range in cultured cells. Hematoxylin and eosin staining of infected cells revealed small, lightly eosinophilic, nuclear inclusions, and Feulgen and acridine orange staining indicated that the inclusions contained DNA. Additional work on this virus was hindered by loss of the embryo cell line supporting its replication.

During the past year we have tested a variety of cell cultures for susceptibility to FV 4 and have found that *R. pipiens* embryo cell lines initiated by Dr. Jerome Freed (Institute for Cancer Research, Philadelphia) and described fully elsewhere in this symposium (23) support replication of FV 4 (24). One cell line was established from minced tissue (epidermis removed) of pooled, stage 18 *R. pipiens* normal embryos and has been designated ICR-RPD 67.7 by Dr. Freed and redesignated RPE 67.7 by us. The second cell line was established from gynogenetic haploid embryos of *R. pipiens* produced *via* toluidine blue inactivation of sperm. They were cultured from whole minced tailbud embryos and carried through 11 serial passages before cloning. The cells were received by us after over 30 passages and had the diploid number at this time. The cells, designated ICR-RPH 134c2 by Dr. Freed have been redesignated RPE 134c2 by us. The reader should refer to a recent publication (25) for methods of culturing these cells and for other experimental procedures. All experiments were carried out at 25 °C.

FV 4 produces a cytopathic effect (CPE) 10 to 21 days after infection of RPE cells characterized first by spindling and contraction of cells followed by rounding, vacuolation, enlargement of nuclei, and polykaryon formation. Intranuclear inclusions form which, by acridine orange staining, contain DNA. An example of intranuclear inclusions and vacuolation in RPE 134c2 cells is shown in Fig. 5. On the basis of this CPE a quantitative plaque assay similar to that used for FV 3 (26) has been developed. Plaque formation requires 14 to 15 days. The number of plaques is directly proportional to the concentration of virus inoculated, indicating that a single particle is capable of initiating a plaque. Virus titers of disrupted (sonic vibration) infected cells in the infected culture medium have ranged from 1×10^5 PFU/ml to 2×10^6 PFU/ml. On the average 1 to 10 PFU are detected per cell. Virus infectivity is lost at pH 3.0 or by exposure to ethyl ether.

Fig. 6 shows a FV 4 growth cycle at 25 °C in RPE 67.7 cells initiated with a multiplicity of about 0.05 PFU/cell. Although it is not a single step growth curve it does reveal several important features. Cell-associated virus (CAV) is not measurable until 4 to 5 days after infection; release of virus (RV) follows between 6 and 7 days. The CAV and RV titers are equivalent by day 14. Although high multiplicities of infection would likely shorten the latent period, the data from the virus growth curve

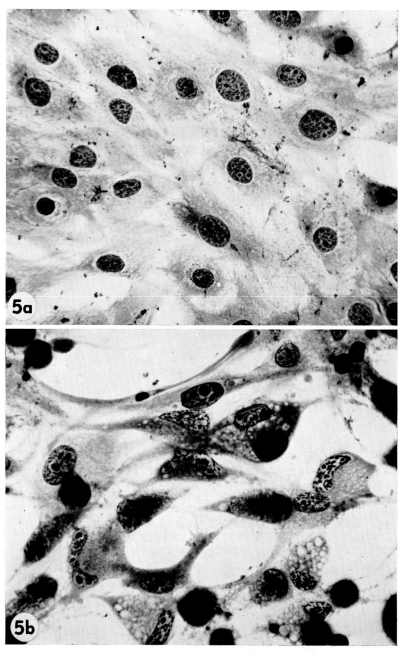

Fig. 5. RPE 134c2 cells infected with herpes-type virus (FV 4) illustrating cytoplasmic vacuolation and intranuclear inclusions: (a) uninfected, (b) FV 4-infected. (May-Gruenwald-Giemsa.) ×356.

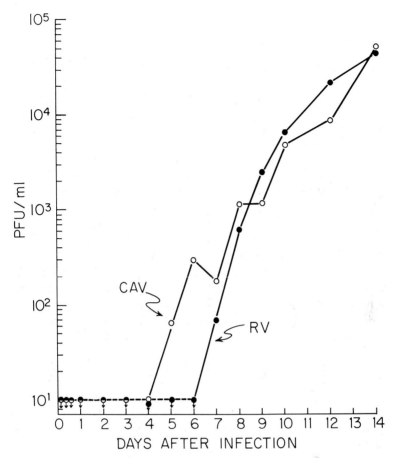

Fig. 6. Growth curve at 25°C of herpes-type virus (FV 4) in RPE 67.7 cells. CAV, cell-associated virus; RV, released virus.

together with the length of time required for development of CPE suggest that the virus has a relatively long growth cycle.

The next critical experiment was to determine by electron microscopy the site of synthesis and morphology of FV 4 for comparison with the herpes-type virus seen in inclusion bearing Lucké tumor cells. RPE 67.7 cells, infected at about 0.04 PFU/cell, were examined by electron microscopy at selected times after infection. Uninfected cultures were also examined. Four days after infection virus particles were seen in the nucleus of an occasional cell. By 12 days after infection about 80% of the cells were observed to be infected. The time of first appearance of virus as observed by electron microscopy was approximately the time CAV was detected by bioassay (Fig. 6). Fig. 7 shows several infected cells. Virus particles are either scattered throughout the nucleus (Fig. 7, right-hand cell) or aggregated in crystalline arrays (Fig. 7, left-hand cell). The predominant form was a single membrane particle, 95 to 100 mμ in diameter. About 10% of the particles were double membraned forms consisting of an outer membrane 95 to 100 mμ in diameter with an inner ring 45 to 50 mμ in diameter

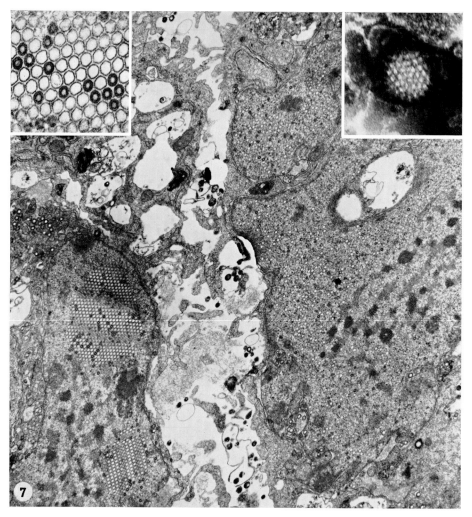

Fig. 7. Electron micrograph of two herpes-type virus (FV 4)-infected RPE cells. ×7,150. Upper left insert illustrates morphology of single and double membraned particles. ×33,800. Upper right insert shows a negatively stained unenveloped virion. ×130,000.

(Fig. 7, upper left insert). Although enveloped particles in large numbers were frequently seen extracellularly, particles were not seen budding from the nuclear membrane. Extracellular virions had an overall diameter of about 170 mμ; the viral capsid measuring 95 to 100 mμ in diameter. Few of the enveloped particles contained cores. Uninfected cells contained no demonstrable virus particles.

A negative stain of particles sedimented from fluid of infected cultures revealed cubic symmetry and hollow capsomeres (Fig. 7, upper right insert); the capsomere number was found to be 162. Thus, by morphological criteria, i.e., virion size, morphology and number of capsomeres, FV 4 is indistinguishable from virus seen in Lucké tumor cells (3, 4) and is identical to members of the herpesvirus group (27).

In collaboration with Dr. Kenyon Tweedell (University of Notre Dame) we have tested FV 4 for tumorigenic activity in developing R. *pipiens* embryos and larvae. Animals injected with and surviving about 400 PFU of FV 4 failed to develop tumors.

The availability now of cells which support the growth of herpesvirus make possible a critical assessment of the role of this virus in the Lucké tumor. Several obvious objectives have to be pursued, namely additional isolation of herpesviruses from tumors and tests for their presence in normal tissues of R. *pipiens* as well. A critical test for tumorigenic activity in Tweedell's embryo system will be dependent on obtaining higher titered virus preparations. Efforts in our laboratory continue towards these goals.

Another Virus from Lucké Tumors (?)

On the basis of the susceptibility of RPE cells to FV 4 infection, we have attempted to isolate herpes-type virus from several tumor homogenates. Two tumors chosen contained herpes-type virus as determined by the presence of intranuclear inclusions or of virus by electron microscopy; another was free of herpes-type virus. Each tumor had been tested for the presence of polyhedral cytoplasmic virus by isolation procedures (7) and were free of this agent.

RPE 67.7 cells were inoculated with 10% homogenates of each tumor and incubated at 23 °C to 25 °C. After about 3 to 4 weeks several changes in cell monolayers were observed. Some cell degeneration occurred but the most pronounced change was cell stranding and clumping. At this time the cells were removed into the medium and fresh RPE 67.7 cultures were inoculated with this cell suspension. Similar cell changes were observed to occur in the inoculated cells and at the 3rd passage the cells were suspended in the overlaying medium and disrupted by sonic vibration or by freezing and thawing. After low speed centrifugation to remove cellular debris the supernatant was used for subsequent passages. Cellular changes similar to those described above were seen about 2 weeks after inoculation with the cell free extract. An example of the change observed in RPE 67.7 cells is shown in Fig. 8.

RPE 134c2 cells infected with the 5th or 6th passage material from RPE 67.7 cells showed somewhat different alterations. Initial infection resulted in very little discernible cellular change. However, when the infected RPE 134c2 cells were subcultured a striking difference in their morphology, illustrated in Fig. 9, was observed. The cells had assumed a more fibroblastic nature and grew in whorls. These altered cells are presently in their 3rd passage. They multiply very slowly as compared with the original RPE 134c2 cells. In contrast, infected RPE 67.7 cells cannot be serially passaged.

The two inclusion tumors and the one free of inclusions each produced the same effect in RPE 67.7 cells. RPE 134c2 cells inoculated with cell free extracts of the infected RPE 67.7 cells responded as described above regardless of the tumor used initially for infection of RPE 67.7 cells. Tests for mycoplasma have been negative.

Electron microscopic examination by negative stain of both infected RPE 67.7 and RPE 134c2 culture material revealed the presence of particles 45 mμ in diameter. These are shown in Fig. 10. Although there is some evidence of viral capsomeres, we are unable to determine their number.

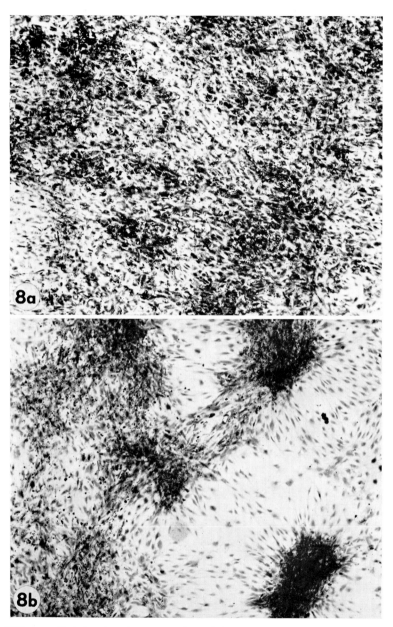

Fig. 8. RPE 67.7 cells infected with an agent obtained from Lucké tumors (both with and without inclusions) three weeks after infection at 25°C: (a) uninfected, (b) infected. (Crystal violet.) ×23.

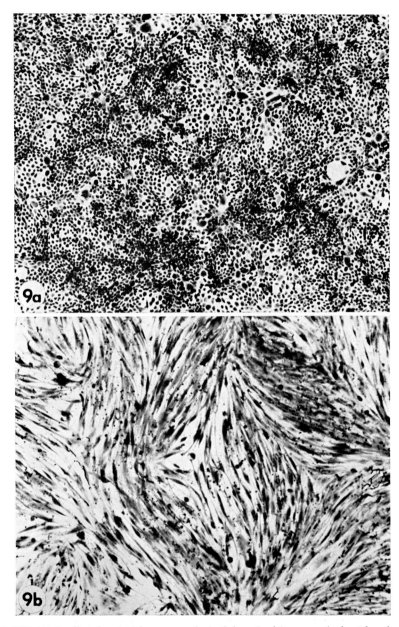

Fig. 9. RPE 134c2 cells infected with an agent obtained from Lucké tumors (both with and without inclusions) and twice serially passaged at 25 °C: (a) uninfected, (b) infected. (Crystal violet.) ×41.

Despite repeated attempts, no evidence of viral infection has been seen in inoculated RPE 67.7 or 134c2 cells on examination by thin section technique. Nevertheless, it appears certain that an infectious agent, a virus, is responsible for the effects observed in the two RPE cell lines. Significantly, the virus was isolated from both inclusion and non-inclusion tumors. We are currently directing our efforts to further characterizing this agent and to determining its relationship to the Lucké tumor.

The Lucké Tumor Revisited

Lunger *et al.* (28) called attention to the presence of 45 to 50 mμ particles in a Lucké tumor cell which also contained herpes-type virus. In a later publication (29) he favored the idea that these small particles were in some manner related to viral (herpes-type) synthesis. Less favored was the interpretation that they represented a passenger virus. More recently Stackpole and Mizell (30) reached similar conclusions.

We have also observed these particles in the nucleus and cytoplasm of inclusion-bearing Lucké tumor cells. Fig. 11 is an electron micrograph of the nucleus of a tumor cell containing both herpes-type and small particles. The small particles are double-ringed, many with a central electron dense area and are about 46 mμ in diameter. They may be related to the small particle, described in the previous section, or, they may indeed be related to the synthesis of the herpes-type virus as suggested by others (29, 30). The nature and importance of these particles in the Lucké tumor will be decided by further experimentation.

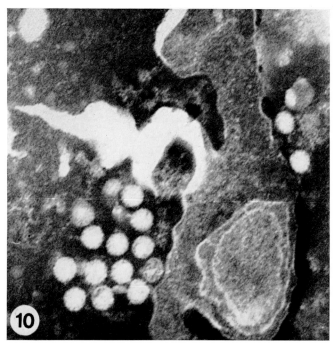

Fig. 10. Electron micrograph of negatively stained particles found in the growth medium of cells shown in Figs. 8b and 9b. ×180,000.

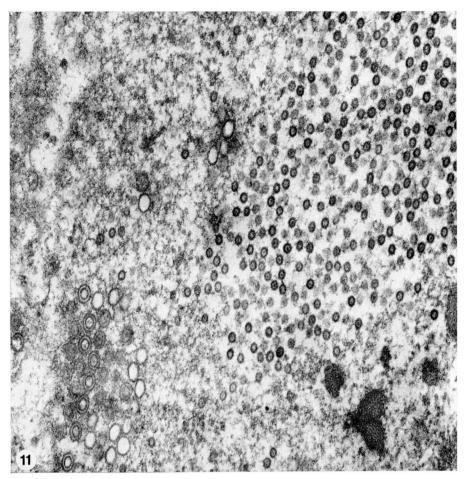

Fig. 11. Electron micrograph of a Lucké tumor cell showing small particles about 46 mμ in diameter in the nucleus. Herpes-type particles are also present. Similar small particles were also seen in the cytoplasm of cells. ×54,000.

A polyhedral cytoplasmic virus was isolated from a homogenate of the tumor shown in Fig. 11. Thus, if the small particle is a virus and not a component of herpes-virus replication, this particular tumor contained three distinct viruses.

Conclusions

With the development of tissue culture systems which support replication of viruses from R. *pipiens*, with knowledge of the nature of several frog viruses discussed in this and other papers in this symposium, and with application of Tweedell's elegant *in vivo* test for tumorigenicity, the role of a virus or viruses in the etiology of the Lucké tumor should be clarified in the near future. However, it does appear that the relation-ship of virus to tumor may not be a simple one and, indeed, may be complicated such as a defective plus helper virus-cell interaction. The fact that for years a herpes-type virus has been considered, but not proven to be, the causative agent of the Lucké tumor should not influence us emotionally in our search for what promises to be fascinating answers concerning the biology and natural history of this malignancy.

References

1. LUCKÉ, B.: A neoplastic disease of the kidney of the frog, *Rana pipiens*. Am. J. Cancer *20*:352–379, 1934.

2. LUCKÉ, B.: Carcinoma in the leopard frog: Its probable causation by a virus. J. Exptl. Med. *68*:457–468, 1938.

3. FAWCETT, D. W.: Electron microscope observations of intracellular virus-like particles associated with the cells of the Lucké renal adenocarcinoma. J. Biophys. Biochem. Cytol. *2*:725–742, 1956.

4. LUNGER, P. D.: The isolation and morphology of the Lucké frog kidney tumor virus. Virology *24*:138–145, 1964.

5. GRANOFF, A., CAME, P. E., and RAFFERTY, K. A.: The isolation and properties of viruses from *Rana pipiens*: Their possible relationship to the renal adenocarcinoma of the leopard frog. Ann. N.Y. Acad. Sci. *126*:237–255, 1965.

6. GRAVELL, M., and MALSBERGER, R. G.: A permanent cell line from the fathead minnow (*Pimephales promelas*). Ann. N.Y. Acad. Sci. *126*:555–565, 1965.

7. GRANOFF, A., CAME, P. E., and BREEZE, D. C.: Viruses and renal carcinoma of *Rana pipiens*. I. The isolation and properties of virus from normal and tumor tissue. Virology *29*:133–148, 1966.

8. DARLINGTON, R. W., GRANOFF, A., and BREEZE, D. C.: Viruses and renal carcinoma of *Rana pipiens*. II. Ultrastructural studies and sequential development of virus isolated from normal and tumor tissue. Virology *29*:149–156, 1966.

9. MAES, R., and GRANOFF, A.: Viruses and renal carcinoma of *Rana pipiens*. IV. Nucleic acid synthesis in frog virus 3-infected BHK 21/13 cells. Virology *33*:491–502, 1967.

10. GRAVELL, M.: Unpublished data.

11. CLARK, H. F., BRENNAN, J. C., ZEIGEL, R. F., and KARZON, D. T.: Isolation and characterization of viruses from the kidneys of *Rana pipiens* with renal adenocarcinoma before and after passage in the red eft (*Triturus viridescens*). J. Virol. *2*:629–640, 1968.

12. GRANOFF, A., and GRAVELL, M.: Influence of temperature and host cell on replication of frog virus 3 (FV 3). Bacteriol. Proc., p. 178, 1968.

13. GRANOFF, A.: Unpublished data.

14. TWEEDELL, K. S.: Induced oncogenesis in developing frog kidney cells. Cancer Res. *27*: 2042–2052, 1967.

15. TWEEDELL, K. S., and GRANOFF, A.: Viruses and renal carcinoma of *Rana pipiens*. V. Effect of frog virus 3 on developing frog embryos and larvae. J. Nat. Canc. Inst. *40*: 407–410, 1968.

16. WOLF, K., BULLOCK, G. L., DUNBAR, C. E., and QUIMBY, M. C.: Tadpole edema virus: A viscerotropic pathogen for anuran amphibians. J. Inf. Dis. *118*:253–262, 1968.

17. LEHANE, D. E., JR., CLARK, H. F., and KARZON, D. T.: Antigenic relationships among frog viruses demonstrated by the plaque reduction and neutralization kinetics tests. Virology *34*:590–595, 1968.

18. CLARK, H. F., GRAY, C., FABIAN, F., ZEIGEL, R. F., and KARZON, D. T.: Comparative studies of amphibian cytoplasmic virus strains isolated from the leopard frog, bullfrog, and newt. *In* Biology of Amphibian Tumors (M. Mizell, ed.), Springer-Verlag New York Inc., 1969, pp. 310–326.

19. WOLF, K. E., BULLOCK, G. L., and DUNBAR, C. E.: Tadpole edema virus: Pathogenesis and growth studies. *In* Biology of Amphibian Tumors (M. Mizell, ed.), Springer-Verlag New York Inc., 1969, pp. 327–336.

20. LUNGER, P. D.: Fine structure studies of cytoplasmic viruses associated with frog tumors. *In* Biology of Amphibian Tumors (M. Mizell, ed.), Springer-Verlag New York Inc., 1969, pp. 296–309.

21. KUCERA, L. S., and GRANOFF, A.: Viruses and renal carcinoma of *Rana pipiens*. VI. Interrelationships of macromolecular synthesis and infectious virus production in frog virus 3-infected BHK 21/13 cells. Virology *34*:240–249, 1968.

22. RAFFERTY, K. A., JR.: The cultivation of inclusion-associated viruses from Lucké tumor frogs. Ann. N.Y. Acad. Sci. *126*:3–21, 1965.

23. FREED, J. J., MEZGER-FREED, L., and SCHATZ, S. A.: Characteristics of cell lines from haploid and diploid *Rana pipiens* embryos. *In* Biology of Amphibian Tumors (M. Mizell, ed.), Springer-Verlag New York Inc., 1969, pp. 101–111.

24. GRAVELL, M., GRANOFF, A., and DARLINGTON, R. W.: Propagation of a nuclear frog virus: The Lucké tumor agent? Bacteriol. Proc., p. 178, 1968.

25. GRAVELL, M., GRANOFF, A., and DARLINGTON, R. W.: Viruses and renal carcinoma of *Rana pipiens*. VII. Propagation of a herpes-type frog virus. Virology, *36*:467–475, 1968.

26. MAES, R., GRANOFF, A., and SMITH, W.: Viruses and renal carcinoma of *Rana pipiens*. III. The relationship between input multiplicity of infection and inclusion body formation in frog virus 3-infected cells. Virology *33*:137–144, 1967.

27. WILDY, P., RUSSELL, W. C., and HORNE, R. W.: The morphology of herpesvirus. Virology *12*:204–222, 1960.

28. LUNGER, P. D., DARLINGTON, R. W., and GRANOFF, A.: Cell-virus relationships in the Lucké renal adenocarcinoma: An ultrastructure study. Ann. N.Y. Acad. Sci. *126*:289–314, 1965.

29. LUNGER, P. D.: A new intranuclear inclusion body in the frog renal adenocarcinoma. J. Morph. *118*:581–588, 1966.

30. STACKPOLE, C. W., and MIZELL, M.: Electron microscopic observations on herpes-type virus-related structures in the frog renal adenocarcinoma. Virology *36*:63–72, 1968.

Fine Structure Studies of Cytoplasmic Viruses
Associated with Frog Tumors

Philip D. Lunger

Department of Biological Sciences
University of Delaware
Newark, Delaware

A relatively short period of time has elapsed since the discovery of cytoplasmic, polyhedral frog viruses, first in both uninoculated "normal" and malignant kidney cultures (1), and then *in vivo* (2). Since that time particular emphasis has been placed on biochemical aspects of viral maturation events (3, 4, 5) and the relationship between input multiplicity of infection and inclusion body formation in tissue culture (6). Studies concerning the effect of these viruses on immature frogs (7), newts (8) and toads have also been conducted. From the viewpoint of morphology, particles observed *in vitro* (9) appear to be identical to those seen in certain cells of renal adenocarcinomas. Since this group or class of viruses appears in many respects to be unique, they have rapidly gained the attention of investigators interested in possible model virus systems.

The present report represents an extension and expansion of a previous study (2), and will be concerned with fine structural aspects *in vivo* of virus location (host cell type), general morphology, associated organelles, and maturation events.

Materials and Methods

Frogs bearing spontaneous renal adenocarcinomas utilized in this study were obtained from C. H. Mumley, Alburg, Vermont. Tissue preparation techniques for electron microscopy have been detailed previously (10), and, thus, need not be repeated here.

Observations

Polyhedral, cytoplasmic frog viruses, morphologically displaying close resemblance to those initially obtained from both malignant and allegedly normal kidney tissue cultures (1), have to date been observed by thin-section electron microscopy in 4 out of 38 (10.5%) virus-containing renal adenocarcinomas. These viruses measure approximately 135 mμ in diameter, and, at least visibly, have been found to be associated only with stromal tissue, presumed to represent interstitial cells (2), of the kidney. The precise characterization of these cells is not certain because many of them and their associated organelles appear to be in a high state of degeneration, a condition not uncommon in invasive adenocarcinomas of this type.

296

Fig. 1 is a low magnification electron micrograph illustrating the presence of a moderate number of viruses randomly scattered throughout the cytoplasm of an infected stromal cell. An aggregation of collagen fibrils (C), displaying a typical 640 Å banding periodicity, is discernible at the left of this particular cell. Although many of the particles can be observed to contain a dense center, or nucleoid, the interior of some of them is empty, or only partially filled with electron-dense material. Several incomplete capsids, also lacking dense internal material, can be seen in this field. The term capsid, rather than shell, is applicable here and throughout this report because visible substructure of the virus surface has been demonstrated (11). This rather marked degree of structural incompleteness suggests that many of the viruses illustrated here are in the process of maturation. The developmental sequence of these particles will be considered in further detail below.

At higher magnification (Figs. 2–6) a more detailed analysis of the morphology of these viruses and related organelles can be undertaken. Fig. 2 illustrates a loosely-arranged cluster of nearly mature viruses embedded in a distinct, but finely-granular background matrix, generally referred to as a viroplasm. Although criteria for maturity are normally based on infective potential, in a fine-structure study of this kind the criteria by necessity must be founded on somewhat arbitrary morphological features. Viruses in this system are considered mature if they 1) display a high degree of capsid and associated nucleoid completeness, 2) a relative absence of background viroplasm, and 3) are encircled by an envelope. Most of the particles illustrated in Fig. 2 contain a dense, well-developed (i.e., spheroid) nucleoid measuring 75–95 mμ in diameter occupying much of the virus center. Capsids are complete in most instances, but a considerable amount of viroplasm still exists and the particles have not yet acquired envelopes. Peripheral to the nucleoid is a moderately electron-lucent zone 13 mμ in width, followed by the viral capsid measuring approximately 8.5 mμ in thickness. The capsid itself can be seen to consist of at least two distinct dense layers (Fig. 3; Fig. 4, arrows) separated from each other by an intermediate light zone. Fine, spine-like projections, 11 mμ in length, extend perpendicularly from the capsid surface, and are spaced at regular 20 Å intervals from each other (see Fig. 6, arrow). Close examination of these projections reveals their distal ends to be slightly more dense than the proximal and middle portions. These structures, as well as vacuoles of varying sizes, are commonly observed at this stage of the maturation process.

Nearly mature cytoplasmic frog viruses, again as judged by their high degree of capsid and nucleoid completeness, are not invariably randomly clustered as illustrated in Fig. 2, but in some instances are packed in a symmetrical pattern suggestive of a crystalline array (Figs. 5 and 6). For the most part these particles, like those seen in noncrystalline clusters, are situated in a characteristic, flocculent viroplasm. The latter, incidentally, is not the only structural entity associated with the process of viral maturation. Several additional types of cytoplasmic organelles are also involved. The most striking of these consists of electron-opaque fibrils arranged in closely adhering, semiparallel aggregations or bundles (Figs. 7–9). Such aggregations are invariably associated with developing viruses, and, therefore, are situated within the viroplasmic zone; they are not observed in more advanced stages of development. Fig. 7 is a low magnification electron micrograph illustrating the relative position of dense fibrillar masses to viruses. In the left-central portion of the micrograph is a dense, granular

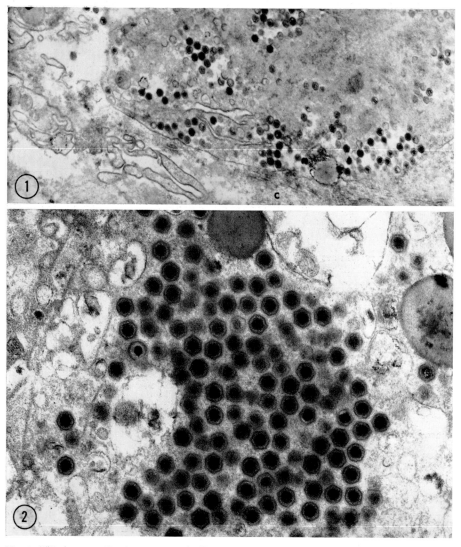

Fig. 1. This low-magnification micrograph illustrates a portion of a renal stromal cell containing a moderate number of cytoplasmic frog viruses in various stages of maturity. In most instances capsids are complete, but the amount and density of the viral nucleoid varies considerably. Collagen fibrils (C) and a lipid-like body are present at the lower right. ×11,000.

Fig. 2. A loosely-arranged cluster of nearly mature frog viruses embedded in a flocculent background viroplasm is illustrated in this figure. Capsids and nucleoids are generally complete, but the particles are still devoid of an envelope. ×34,500

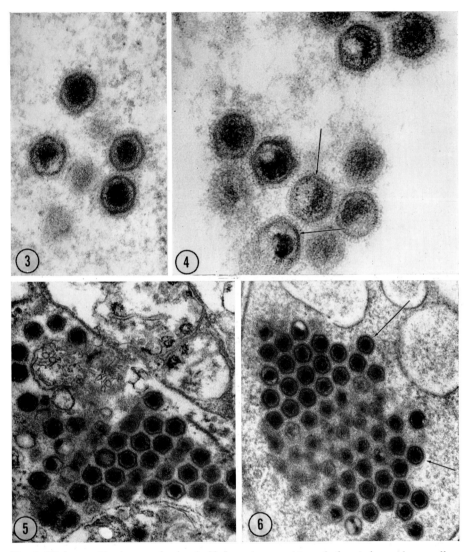

Fig. 3. High magnification reveals the double-layered composition of the viral capsid, as well as relative size and density of the nucleoid. ×72,450.

Fig. 4. At still higher magnification than Fig. 3 at least two distinct densities comprising the viral capsid can be discerned (arrows). ×96,600.

Fig. 5. A clearly-ordered array of nearly mature viruses is illustrated in this micrograph. Crystalline patterns are not often seen *in vivo*, suggesting that this transitory stage in development is rapid. A disorganized mitochondrion partially surrounded by particles can be seen in the upper portion of the figure. ×34,500.

Fig. 6. Like the preceding figure, this micrograph illustrates a cluster of nearly mature viruses arranged in a crystalline pattern. Regularly spaced "spines" are seen projecting from the surface of some particles (arrows). Several vacuoles containing flocculent material are evident above the virus cluster. ×34,500.

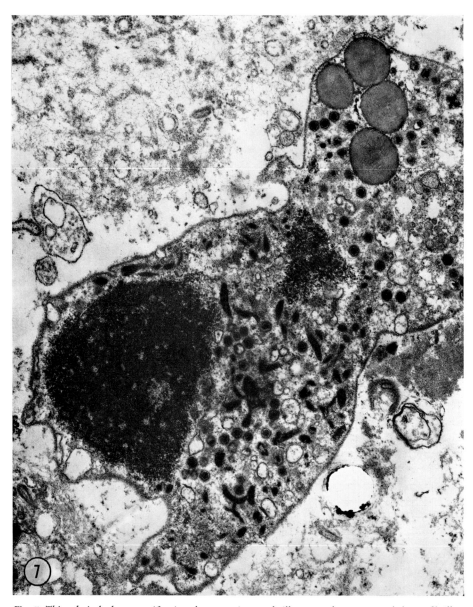

Fig. 7. This relatively low magnification electron micrograph illustrates the presence of dense, fibrillar masses scattered, apparently at random, among virus particles. At the left is a large, dense granular mass believed to represent a pyknotic nucleus whose envelope has disintegrated. A less compact mass, comprised of granules similar in size and density to certain of those in the nucleus, is seen in the upper-central portion of the figure. Situated above this mass are four osmophilic, lipid-like bodies. ×17,120.

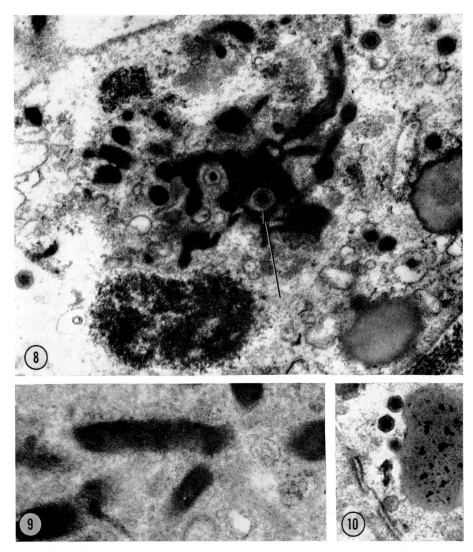

Fig. 8. The close relationship between dense fibrillar masses and viruses is demonstrated here. In one instance a particle is completely surrounded by this material (arrow); slightly above and to the left a particle is approximately ¾ surrounded. Note the close similarity in density between fibrillar material and the viral nucleoid. A dense granular mass is present at the periphery (lower-left) of the viroplasmic zone. ×34,500.

Fig. 9. This is a high-magnification micrograph of a dense fibrillar mass. The semiparallel arrangement of individual fibrils can be clearly discerned. ×72,450.

Fig. 10. Occasionally a close relationship between viruses and a lipid-like inclusion is apparent. The mottled appearance of the inclusion is believed to represent a staining artifact. ×34,500.

mass thought to represent a pyknotic nucleus whose envelope has completely degenerated. A mass of dense granules, similar to those comprising much of the interior of the nucleus, can be observed immediately above the fibrillar aggregations. Somewhat above these granules are four osmophilic, lipid-like bodies. At higher magnification (Fig. 8) dense, fibrillar material can in one instance be seen to completely encircle a virus particle (arrow); slightly to the left is a virus partially enclosed by this material. The electron density of the fibrillar mass appears to be similar, if not identical, to that of the viral nucleoid. This density is slightly greater than that of the viral capsid. Fig. 9 illustrates the fibrillar texture and semiparallel arrangement of the individual fibrils of several aggregations. Individual fibrils are estimated to measure approximately 25 Å in thickness.

Several other organelles, aside from viroplasm and fibrillar clusters, appear to be involved with the synthesis of these frog viruses. Dense, granular masses are often prominent usually at the periphery of the viroplasmic zone (Figs. 7 and 8). These granules, measuring 5–15 mμ in diameter, are similar in size and density to those observed in certain regions of rarely observed intact nuclei. Aggregations of this type have not been noted in more advanced stages of virus maturation (Figs. 5 and 6). Another organelle frequently seen in early stages of virus development is an osmophilic, lipid-like body (Figs. 2, 7 and 8). Like the dense granular aggregations these bodies tend to be situated on the periphery of the viroplasmic region. On rare occasions virus particles can be observed to be in close proximity to osmophilic bodies (Fig. 10).

The structural relationship in respect to development between viral capsid and nucleoid components is at best complex. A fundamental question that arises is, which of the two components is synthesized first? Or, on the other hand, are both elements formed concomitantly? Examples of partially and completely formed capsids, lacking definable internal material, are numerous (Fig. 11, A-arrows). Alternatively, an occasional nucleoid lacking any discernible surrounding capsid can be noted (Fig. 12, arrow). The most commonly observed relationship, however, appears to involve a simultaneous capsid-nucleoid assembly pattern (Fig. 11, B-arrows; Fig. 13). In Fig. 11, partially completed capsids can be seen enclosing nucleoid material of varying morphology. The latter is occasionally clumped or spheroid, but most frequently it is crescent shaped. When crescent shaped the material is usually closely adjacent to the inner surface of the forming capsid. Close inspection of this nucleoid material reveals that it may be composed of fine strands or filaments running in the plane of the crescent. At possibly a more advanced developmental stage (also Fig. 11) capsids can be seen to be complete, and the presumptive nucleoid often surrounds, in ring-like formation, the inner capsid border. In some instances nucleoid profiles within developing capsids appear as rod-shaped or spherical masses, rather than as crescent-shaped structures (Fig. 13).

Finally, as previously illustrated (9, 2), these cytoplasmic viruses egress from the cell by means of a budding process. Individual particles first come into close proximity to the plasma membrane. With gradual protrusion they are eventually surrounded by this membrane which fuses and buds off into the extracellular space. The particle, thereby, acquires a tight-fitting plasma membrane-derived envelope. The total diameter of such enveloped viruses approaches 160 mμ.

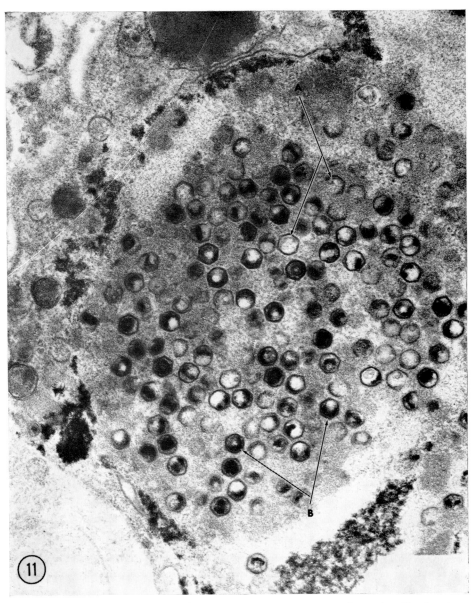

Fig. 11. This micrograph illustrates a cluster of viruses in various stages of maturity. The flocculent nature of the background viroplasm is particularly well defined. Note the frequent rod-like and crescent-shaped appearance of dense nucleoid material within capsids. A-arrows denote partially and completely formed capsids lacking nucleoids; B-arrows denote partially formed nucleoids within capsids. ×40,000.

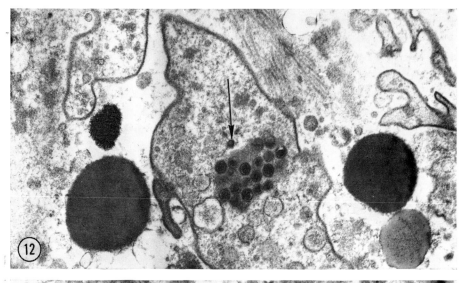

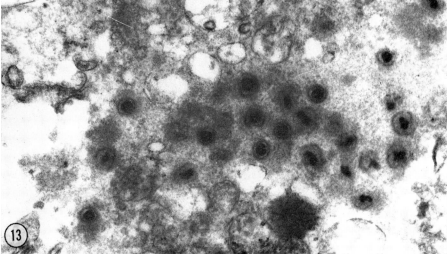

Fig. 12. A possible developing viral nucleoid devoid of surrounding capsid is seen on the periphery of the viroplasmic region (arrow). ×14,770.

Fig. 13. Viral nucleoids in various configurations surrounded by developing capsids are seen in this micrograph. Frequent observations of this kind indicate that both structures are assembled concomitantly in the same location. ×34,500.

Discussion

It is clear from this and a previous *in vivo* study (2) of cytoplasmic frog viruses that the particles described here are morphologically identical to those isolated from kidneys (as well as certain other organs) by tissue culture techniques (1, 9). A comparison of the *in vitro* and *in vivo* mode of replication of these particles reveals both similarities and differences, and these will be considered in detail below.

One perplexing, fundamental question that arises, among others, concerns the cell type harboring and propagating these viruses. Morphological evidence to date strongly suggests that the particles are restricted to renal stromal cells, possibly interstitial cells. (Other organs from which they have been isolated—liver and spleen—have not been examined by thin-section electron microscopy to confirm their presence or absence in a particular cell type.) Although these cells in no way resemble morphologically those comprising tubule epithelium, it is, of course, possible that through marked degeneration and/or virus-induced transformation they may be unrecognizable as epithelial cells. The relatively high frequency of virus isolation by tissue culture methods indeed suggests that the viruses may be more widespread than indicated by morphological studies; it has been reported (1) that cytoplasmic frog viruses may undergo an unmasking from a presumably latent state in nature by culturing infected cells *in vitro*. Nevertheless, a careful examination by thin-section electron microscopy of easily recognizable epithelial tubule cells in 38 virus-containing tumors failed to demonstrate the presence of cytoplasmic viruses in that cell type. It might be argued that the failure to detect such particles was a result of the limited scanning power of the electron microscope, but this seems unlikely considering the relatively large size of the sample examined.

In considering virus morphology per se, hexagonal profiles were frequently noted, especially when particles were sectioned through their maximum diameter; eccentrically-sectioned particles often displayed pentagonal profiles. These combined observations strongly indicate that these viruses may have icosahedral symmetry. Unpublished studies in our laboratory of purified, negatively stained FV 3 have, however, neither supported nor refuted this hypothesis, possibly because the intact viral envelope inhibited visualization of its inherent 5:3:2 symmetry. Triangular facets and associated protein subunits were not observed. Numerous fine, spine-like surface projections on capsids were resolved by the negative staining technique and are thought to be homologous to those illustrated here (Fig. 6). The distal ends of "spines" in PTA do not appear to be broader or club-shaped as they do in thin section. Apparent distal broadening, therefore, may reflect a staining artifact, whereby distal spine ends might somehow either collect more stain or prevent stain from entering proximal regions.

The general morphology of cytoplasmic frog viruses resembles in varying degrees that of certain other groups or classes of viruses. The iridescent virus group, in particular, displays a general morphology and developmental sequence similar in many respects to that of frog viruses. Both *Tipula* iridescent virus (TIV) and *Sericesthis* iridescent virus (SIV) are cytoplasmic icosahedra measuring approximately 130 mμ in diameter (12, 13). The former develops in association with aggregations of fibrous material believed to play a role in viral capsid formation (14). Also, capsid maturation occurs in a stepwise fashion like the sequence observed with frog viruses. In spite of the structural similarity of these insect viruses to those of frogs there is reason to believe that the two groups are not closely related to each other. Unlike insect viruses, frog viruses do not iridesce upon pelleting; they do not multiply in the mealworm (*Tenebrio*) whereas SIV does; frog viruses are susceptible to lipid solvents (1) whereas SIV is ether and chloroform resistant (15). In connection with this latter point, SIV *in vivo* has not been observed to acquire an envelope during egression from the cell.

Viruses, similar in many respects to frog viruses, have been isolated from edematous

Rana catesbeiana tadpoles (16). These "tadpole edema viruses" (ibid.) manifest poly-hedral symmetry and measure 120 by 130 mμ. *In vitro* they are associated with cyto-plasmic, Feulgen-positive inclusions. Sites of synthesis are often surrounded by mito-chondrial aggregates; typical virus maturation stages ranging from empty to full capsids were demonstrated. Upon maturity the virus acquires an envelope in the same manner as frog viruses.

Another cytoplasmic virus group that shows certain morphological features with frog viruses is African Swine Fever Virus (ASFV) described by Breese and De Boer (17). The mature ASFV typically displays a hexagonal profile in cross section consist-ing of an outer "membrane structure" (?capsid), an inner zone of lower density and a dense, central, DNA-containing nucleoid. The nucleocapsid measures 175–215 mμ in diameter, hence is considerably larger than frog viruses. Furthermore, the proposed maturation sequence of the porcine virus as studied in tissue culture (17) differs sig-nificantly from that of FV 3 and the viruses described in the present investigation. Finally, there are apparently no serological similarities between the two virus groups (18, 19).

A virus associated with lymphocystic disease of certain teleost fish species has been noted to resemble to some degree cytoplasmic frog viruses (13). These viruses are cyto-plasmic icosahedra and measure nearly 300 mμ in overall diameter as determined by thin-section electron microscopy (20, 21). Like FV 3, lymphocystis virus contains DNA and is ether sensitive. In certain species of fish mature viruses aggregate into crystalline arrays (22). No evidence was found of particles passing through the plasma membrane, thereby acquiring an envelope. Preliminary reciprocal neutralization studies utilizing FV 3 and lymphocystis virus antisera indicate no heterologous neutral-ization (18).

There are several limitations to be recognized when attempting to reconstruct events that occur during the *in vivo* development of these cytoplasmic frog viruses. Not only is there the constant problem of interpreting purely static images, but com-bined with this there is a lack of time-sequence control. However, the employment of a tissue culture system to study frog virus assembly and maturation has been under-taken (9) and provides at least certain guidelines, if not parallels, to permit a tentative interpretation of *in vivo* events. Morphological differences between the two systems are also to be expected since the *in vitro* analysis utilized foreign host cells. A number of well-defined structures are associated with early stages of viral maturation. The most prominent of these, a flocculent, background viroplasm, is characteristically present at this time. Its chemical composition is not precisely known, although there is strong indication that this material may be DNA; Feulgen-positive and immuno-fluorescent cytoplasmic inclusions, thought to correspond to sites of viral synthesis, have been observed in FV 3-infected culture cells of various types (5, 6). Combined studies utilizing Feulgen staining and labeling with tritiated thymidine demonstrated (5) that the label was incorporated in the inclusion zone, and presumably was indica-tive of DNA synthesis; a correlary experiment utilizing tritiated uridine resulted in the label accumulating *around*, rather than within, the inclusions. This observation implies, at least, that the dense granular masses frequently seen on the periphery of the viroplasmic regions may be composed of RNA. The size and density of individual granules conforms to that of ribosomes. Further, but less direct, support for the belief that the viroplasm may contain DNA comes from an analysis of SIV development [as reviewed by Bellett (13)]. Morphologically, SIV viroplasm is similar to that observed in infected frog cells, and the former has been shown to contain DNA as detected by Feulgen and acridine orange staining, and localization of tritiated thymidine within it.

The functional significance of the electron-dense fibrillar masses associated with virus assembly is obscure. Such structures have not been described in tissue culture infected cells. From a highly speculative standpoint, these fibrils may contain DNA since they are invariably found only within viroplasmic regions. It is evident that these fibrillar masses are present only during early stages of virus maturation, and from frequent observations of dense, finely-striated, crescent-shaped material on inner capsid profiles, it is conceivable that this material may be highly-organized (into fibrils) viroplasmic DNA required during the nucleoid-capsid assembly process.

Aside from the presence and absence of fibrillar masses in cells *in vivo* and *in vitro*, respectively, there are several other morphological differences between the two systems. Although both systems displayed evidence of extreme mitochondrial degeneration (swelling and highly-disorganized cristae), dense clusters of mitochondria surrounded sites of viral synthesis *in vitro*, whereas such clusters were not observed in the animal. Also, in the latter nuclei were infrequently observed in comparison to culture cells. This may imply that in the present study cells were in a more pyknotic state; plasma membranes were often noted to be incomplete indicating that nuclei may have egressed from the cells. Even in presumably healthier *in vitro* cells, nuclei were frequently observed to be displaced to the cell periphery. Tissue culture cell viroplasm was poorly defined (more so in FHM cells than in BHK21 cells) in comparison to that observed *in vivo*. Finally, bizarre, rod-shaped viral forms, indicative of incorrect capsid assembly were described (9) in tissue culture infected cells, but such forms were not observed in the present study.

Summary

In approximately 10 percent of virus-containing frog renal adenocarcinomas, thin-section electron microscopy has revealed the presence of cytoplasmic viruses in stromal, but not epithelial, cells. (The more frequently observed herpes-like, or Lucké, viruses are restricted to epithelial cells, and the nucleus is involved in their synthesis.) Cytoplasmic viruses, with no apparent nuclear involvement, display a frequently hexagonal morphology, suggesting icosahedral symmetry, and measure approximately 135 mμ in diameter. The first visible stage of maturation involves the formation of a spiney-surfaced "shell" within a flocculent viroplasm; as this shell becomes spheroid, internal material (the future nucleoid) assumes a high degree of electron density. The mature particle eventually acquires an envelope derived from the plasma membrane of the cell. In frogs the pathogenic potential, if any, of these viruses is unclear; however, certain frog-derived viruses of identical morphology produce lesions and rapid death in immature toads.

Acknowledgments

The author is indebted to Dr. Paul E. Came of the Schering Corporation for helpful suggestions concerning the manuscript, and to Mrs. B. L. Bojarski for technical assistance.

References

1. Granoff, A., Came, P. E., and Rafferty, K. A., Jr.: The isolation and properties of viruses from *Rana pipiens:* Their possible relationship to the renal adenocarcinoma of the leopard frog. Ann. N.Y. Acad. Sci. *126:*237–255, 1965.

2. Lunger, P. D., and Came, P. E.: Cytoplasmic viruses associated with Lucké tumor cells. Virology *30:*116–126, 1966.

3. Granoff, A., Came, P. E., and Breeze, D. C.: Viruses and renal carcinoma of *Rana pipiens.* I. The isolation and properties of virus from normal and tumor tissues. Virology *29:*133–148, 1966.

4. Kucera, L. S., and Granoff, A.: Requirement for DNA synthesis of frog virus 3 (FV 3). Bact. Proc., p. 158, 1967.

5. Maes, R., and Granoff, A.: Viruses and renal carcinoma of *Rana pipiens.* IV. Nucleic acid synthesis in frog virus 3-infected BHK 21/13 cells. Virology *33:*491–502, 1967.

6. Maes, R., Granoff, A., and Smith, W. R.: Viruses and renal carcinoma of *Rana pipiens.* III. The relationship between input multiplicity of infection and inclusion body formation in frog virus 3-infected cells. Virology *33:*137–144, 1967.

7. Tweedell, K., and Granoff, A.: Viruses and renal carcinoma of *Rana pipiens.* V. Effect of frog virus 3 on developing frog embryos and larvae. J. Nat. Cancer Instit. *40:*407–410, 1968.

8. Clark, H. F., Brennan, J. C., Zeigel, R. F., and Karzon, D. T.: Isolation and characterization of viruses of *Rana pipiens* with renal adenocarcinoma before and after passage in the red eft (*Triturus viridescens*). J. Virology *2:*629–640, 1968.

9. Darlington, R. W., Granoff, A., and Breeze, D. C.: Viruses and renal carcinoma of *Rana pipiens.* II. Ultrastructural studies and sequential development of virus isolated from normal and tumor tissue. Virology *29:*149–156, 1966.

10. Lunger, P. D., Darlington, R. W., and Granoff, A.: Cell-virus relationships in the Lucké renal adenocarcinoma: an ultrastructure study. Ann. N.Y. Acad. Sci. *126:*289–314, 1965.

11. Came, P. E., and Lunger, P. D.: Viruses isolated from frogs and their relationship to the Lucké tumor. Arch. f. ges. Virus-forschung *4:*464–468, 1967.

12. Smith, K. M.: A study of the early stages of infection with the *Tipula* iridescent virus. Parasitology *48:*459–462, 1958.

13. Bellett, A. J. D.: The iridescent virus group. Advances in Virus Research *13:*225–246, 1968.

14. Bird, F. T.: On the development of the *Tipula* iridescent virus particle. Can. J. Microbiol. *8:*533–534, 1962.

15. Day, M. F., and Mercer, E. H.: Properties of an iridescent virus from the beetle *Sericesthis pruinoso.* Australian J. Biol. Sci. *17:*892–902, 1964.

16. Wolf, K., Bullock, G. L., Dunbar, C. E., and Quimby, M. C.: Tadpole edema virus: A viscerotropic pathogen for anuran amphibians. J. Infectious Diseases *118:*253–262, 1968.

17. Breese, S. S., Jr., and DeBoer, C. J.: Electron microscope observations of African Swine Fever Virus in tissue culture cells. Virology *28:*420–428, 1966.

18. CAME, P. E., and DARDIRI, A. H.: Host specificity and serologic disparity of African Swine Fever Virus and amphibian polyhedral cytoplasmic viruses. Proc. Soc. Exp. Biol. Med. *130*:128–132, 1969.
19. CAME, P. E., GEERING, G., OLD, L. J., and BOYSE, E. A.: A serological study of polyhedral cytoplasmic viruses isolated from amphibia. Virology *36*:392–400, 1968.
20. WALKER, R.: Fine structure of lymphocystis virus of fish. Virology *18*:503–505, 1962.
21. ZWILLENBERG, L. O., and WOLF, K.: Ultrastructure of lymphocystis virus. J. Virology *2*:393–399, 1968.
22. WALKER, R., and WEISSENBERG, R.: Conformity of light and electron microscopic studies on virus particle distribution in lymphocystis tumor cells of fish. Ann. N.Y. Acad. Sci. *126*:375–395, 1965.

Comparative Studies of Amphibian Cytoplasmic Virus Strains Isolated from the Leopard Frog, Bullfrog, and Newt[1]

H. Fred Clark,[2] Claudia Gray, Frances Fabian, Robert Zeigel
and David T. Karzon [3, 4]

Department of Pediatrics, School of Medicine, State University of New York
at Buffalo, Buffalo, New York, and Roswell Park Memorial
Institute, Buffalo, New York

Alone among all the species of reptiles and amphibians, the leopard frog (*Rana pipiens*) has been the object of intensive virological investigations. The study of *Rana pipiens*, prompted by the frequent occurrence of inclusion-bearing kidney tumors in this species (1, 2), has already yielded at least two types of amphibian virus (3–6).

We originally attempted to "unmask" the "kidney tumor virus" by passage of tumor cells into the immature eft stage of the newt *Diemictylus viridiscens* (formerly *Triturus viridiscens*) (6), a method suggested by the "tumor agent transformation" studies of Rose and Rose (7). Eft tissues were subsequently subinoculated into cell cultures of the turtle cell line TH-1. Four cytopathic agents, designated LT1 to LT4, were recovered from efts inoculated with cells of 4 different frog tumors. Only one of the frog tumors yielded virus (L4) when inoculated directly into TH-1 cell culture. A fifth virus, L5, was isolated directly in TH-1 cell culture from a normal frog kidney.

These viruses grow readily at temperatures below 34°C in a wide variety of cultured vertebrate cells. Cytoplasmic inclusions and distinctive cytopathic effect are consistently produced. Electron microscopic studies reveal hexagonal particles lacking obvious capsomeric structure, approximately 150 mμ in diameter, and limited to the cytoplasm. Viruses LT1 to LT4, L4 and L5, and viruses FV1 to FV3 isolated from *Rana pipiens* by Granoff *et al.* (4), were found to be antigenically indistinguishable when compared by means of serum neutralization (8), complement fixation, and gel immunodiffusion (9) methods.

Each of the above-mentioned viruses replicates readily in efts and adult newts. However, individual newts may be refractory to infection, and occasionally virus has been recovered from uninoculated control newts. These observations prompted a search

[1] Supported in part by research grant AI2396 and training grant AI98, from the National Institute of Allergy and Infectious Diseases, and by research grant CA-08737, from the National Cancer Institute.

[2] Present address: Wistar Institute of Anatomy and Biology, Philadelphia, Pennsylvania.

[3] Recipient of Research Career Award AI-1136 from the National Institute of Allergy and Infectious Diseases.

[4] Present address: Department of Pediatrics, School of Medicine, Vanderbilt University, Nashville, Tennessee.

310

for virus in newts supplied by a number of different dealers. When viruses were isolated from newts, they were compared, using a number of parameters, with the previous isolates LT1–LT4, L4 and L5, with FV1–FV3, and with the similar isolate tadpole edema virus (TEV), recently isolated from bullfrogs (*Rana catesbeiana*) (10). These comparative studies are described in this report.

Materials and Methods

Amphibians

Adult newts were purchased from the following dealers: Illinois No. 1—General Biological Supply House, Chicago; Illinois No. 2—Coe-Palm Biological Supply House, Chicago; Illinois No. 3—National Biological Supply Co., Chicago; Minnesota No. 1—J. R. Schettle Biologicals, Stillwater; Wisconsin No. 1—The Lemberger Co., Oshkosh; Wisconsin No. 2—Nasco Inc., Fort Atkinson. All efts were purchased from dealer Illinois No. 1. Immature (<3.5 cm total length) Fowler's toads (*Bufo woodhousei fowleri*) were collected on the northern shore of Lake Erie, Ontario, Canada by Mr. E. R. Kaye, Jr.

Virus-inoculated newts and efts were given 0.05 ml intraperitoneally (IP) or subcutaneously (SC), administered at a midventral site with a 26 gauge needle. Toads were inoculated IP with doses of 0.05 ml.

Amphibians were sacrificed by MS 222 (Sandoz) anesthesia, or by freezing. Each harvested organ was triturated with mortar and pestle or Ten Broeck glass grinder in 1.0 ml of amphibian Ringer's solution and frozen at $-70\,^{\circ}$C. Organs were assayed for virus content by plaque assay (11) in *Terrapene* cell subline TH-1W (12).

Cell Culture

Terrapene heart (TH-1) cell sublines TH-1B$_2$ and TH-1W, established in this laboratory, were propagated by methods previously described (13). An additional subline of TH-1 cells was obtained from the American Type Culture Collection. Bluegill fry (BF) cells were kindly provided by Dr. Ken Wolf. BF cells were grown in Eagle's minimal essential medium containing 10% fetal calf serum. All cell cultures were grown at 23 $^{\circ}$C, except TH-1W which was grown at 30 $^{\circ}$C.

Virus

Viruses FV1 to FV3 were kindly supplied by Dr. Allan Granoff and Dr. Keen Rafferty. TEV and lymphocystis viruses were provided by Dr. Ken Wolf. Lymphosarcoma of *Xenopus laevis* was provided by Dr. Lauren Rubens. Amphibian cytoplasmic viruses were propagated in cell culture at 23 $^{\circ}$C or in chick embryos (chorioallantoic membrane—CAM) incubated at 30 $^{\circ}$C. Lymphocystis virus was propagated in BF cells at 23 $^{\circ}$C (14). *Xenopus laevis* lymphosarcoma was propagated by IP passage of tumor suspensions in newts (15).

Electron Microscopy

Viruses were grown in TH-1 or BF cell culture. When 25% to 50% of the cell sheet showed cytopathic effect, cells were scraped from the glass and sedimented at

200 g. Cell pellets were fixed in chrome-osmium fixative and stained with uranyl acetate prior to sectioning. Sections were observed and photographed by means of a Siemens Elmiskop I electron microscope.

Neutralization Tests

Antisera to LT1 propagated in RTG cell culture and in CAM and to *Tipula* iridescent virus (TIV) were prepared by Dr. Daniel E. Lehane, Jr. and Mrs. Suzanne Kaminski, by methods previously described (8, 9). Antisera to new amphibian isolates and to lymphocystis virus were prepared in rabbits by similar methods. Serum neutralization tests were performed by the plaque reduction method of Lehane *et al.* (8) in TH-1 cell culture, employing as endpoint 50% plaque reduction determined graphically.

Temperature Gradient Studies

The temperature gradient incubator employed will be described in detail elsewhere. It consists basically of an aluminum bar electrically heated at one end and thermoelectrically cooled at the other. Twenty positions for 30 ml plastic cell culture flasks are arranged in two rows along the bar. Actual temperature at each position is determined by thermocouples inserted in test flasks.

Results

Isolation of Viruses from Newts

Newts were purchased from different dealers at different seasons of the year and sacrificed immediately upon receipt. The animals were screened for virus infection by inoculation of liver suspensions into TH-1 cells.

The results of the newt virus screening are given in Table 1. Fifteen cytopathic agents, designated T6 through T20, were isolated from newts in 4 of 6 lots supplied by a single dealer, Illinois No. 1, over a span of $9\frac{1}{2}$ months. No cytopathic agents were recovered from 7 lots of newts supplied by 5 other dealers during the same period.

An additional isolate was subsequently recovered from a pool of fat body lymphosarcomas harvested from newts obtained from dealer Illinois No. 1 and inoculated with *Xenopus laevis* lymphosarcoma agent. Virus was again recovered from second generation tumors induced by this suspension in uninfected newts supplied by another dealer. This isolate was designated T21. No virus was recovered from the original lymphosarcoma inoculum nor from lymphosarcomas grown in this laboratory in newts obtained from other dealers.

The exact source of the virus infection commonly encountered in adult newts supplied by a single dealer was not determined. The dealer did not know the geographic origin of his animals, but insisted that they were kept well isolated from other amphibians on his premises. Indeed, virus was never recovered from immature eft stage newts supplied by the same dealer. Several of the newts yielding the more recent isolates (T16–T21) were identified as the subspecies *Triturus v. dorsalis*, native only to North and South Carolina (17). Unfortunately, the subspecies of animals sacrificed previously was not determined. Animals of the subspecies *Triturus v. dorsalis*,

TABLE 1

Recovery of Agents Cytopathic for TH1 Cells from Dealer-supplied
Adult Newts, Diemictylus viridescens

Source of newts[1]	Date shipment received	Condition of newts	Newts tested[2]		Cytopathic agents recovered
			Sacrificed	Dead	
Illinois #1	4/13/67	16 healthy; 8 dead		5	2 (T6, 7)
Wisconsin #1	5/3/67	100 healthy; 4 dead 4–5 days after receipt	5	4	0
Illinois #1	5/9/67	8 healthy	8		7 (T8–14)
Minnesota #1	6/12/67	23 healthy	11		0
Illinois #1	6/15/67	6 healthy	6		0
Wisconsin #1	6/22/67	21 healthy; 3 dead		2	0
Illinois #1	7/26/67	2 healthy; 11 dead	2	7	0
Illinois #2	7/26/67	14 healthy	14		0
Illinois #1	8/2/67	12 healthy	6		1 (T15)
Illinois #3	8/3/67	13 healthy	11		0
Wisconsin #2	9/7/67	12 healthy	12		0
Wisconsin #1	1/22/68	100 healthy	10		0
Illinois #1	1/25/68	13 healthy; 35 dead		6	5 (T16–20)

[1] Identity of dealer sources is listed in Materials and Methods.

[2] Animals were tested by inoculation of a 10% liver suspension into TH1 cells incubated at 23° and observed for 30 days.

as well as *Triturus v. viridescens*, were also identified in several shipments of non-infected newts supplied by other dealers.

Each of the newt isolates caused a destructive type of cytopathic effect (CPE) in TH-1 cell culture at 23 °C, characterized by early formation of numerous cytoplasmic inclusions. The CPE was indistinguishable from that caused by the other amphibian cytoplasmic viruses. CPE induced in TH-1 cells by newt isolates T6 and T21, by leopard frog-newt isolate LT1, and by bullfrog isolate TEV is illustrated in Fig. 1.

Electron Microscopy

Newt isolates were examined in TH-1 and BF cell culture and occasionally in the tissues of infected newts. For comparative purposes, LT1, FV1 and TEV strains were cultivated in TH-1 or BF cells and examined in parallel.

Virus was observed only in the cytoplasm of infected cells. The appearance of newt viruses T6 and T21, as well as LT1 and TEV, is shown in Fig. 2. Mature intracellular

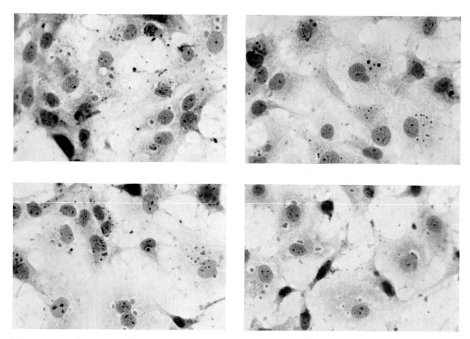

Fig. 1. Cytopathic effect, characterized by cytoplasmic inclusion formation, induced by several isolates in TH-1 cell culture at 23°. Upper left, virus T6; upper right, virus T21; lower left, virus LT1; lower right, virus TEV.

newt virus particles were composed of a hexagonal outer shell approximately 130 mμ in diameter containing a dense nucleoid 95 mμ in diameter. Virus particles formed in juxtanuclear viroplasmic regions which were composed of a uniform filamentous mesh-work. The filamentous material, presumably containing DNA, appeared to be accumu-lated inside the virions during virus synthesis. Completed virions acquired an envelope in the course of budding through the cell membrane.

This pattern of morphogenesis will be described in detail elsewhere (Zeigel and Clark, in preparation). No differences could be distinguished between several newt isolates studied and amphibian virus strains FV1, LT1 or TEV, either in the morphology of the mature virion, or in the pattern of morphogenesis *in vitro*.

Antigenic Studies

Representative cytoplasmic virus isolates from diverse sources were compared by means of the plaque reduction test (Table 2). Extensive cross reactions were demon-

Fig. 2. Fine structure of representative amphibian cytoplasmic viruses. All approx. $\times$34,000. (1) Virus FV1 in TH-1 cell culture—viroplasmic region; (2) LT1 virus in TH-1 cell culture—viroplasmic region; (3) and (4) virus TEV in TH-1 cell culture, virus particles in various stages of formation in a fibrillar matrix presumed to be DNA; (5) T6 virus in TH-1 cell culture viroplasmic region; (6) T6 virus in the bladder of an experimentally inoculated newt—two virions enclosed in a single membrane coat; (7) T8 virus in TH-1 cell culture—periphery of viroplasmic region, a particle acquiring a membrane-derived envelope can be observed at the cell surface; (8) T21 virus in TH-1 cell culture—viroplasmic region.

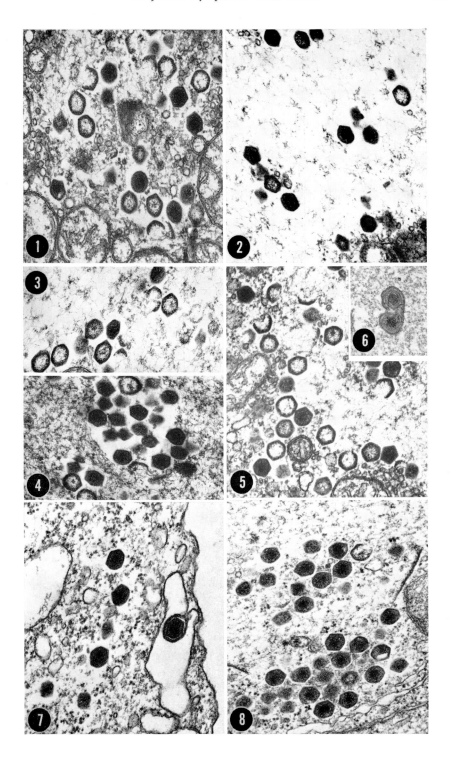

TABLE 2

CROSS-NEUTRALIZATION OF AMPHIBIAN CYTOPLASMIC VIRUSES [1]

Virus	LT1(RTG)[2]	LT1(CAM)	FV1(RTG)	TEV(TH1W)	T6(TH1W)	T8(TH1W)	T15(TH1W)
LT1	*484*	<4	22	24	84	62	38
FV1	268	—[3]	*56*	—	246	—	—
TEV	448	<4	35	*256*	56	—	172
T6	63	<4	24	24	*62*	174	192
T8	48	11	8	—	56	*168*	460
T15	>512	10	96	—	120	>512	—
T21	>512	—	—	64	36	—	—

[1] 50% plaque reduction serum dilution endpoints against virus propagated in TH1W cell culture. Homologous reactions are italicized.

[2] Immunizing antigen source: RTG = rainbow trout gonad cell line; CAM = chick chorioallantoic membrane; TH1W = *Terrapene* heart 1W cell line.

[3] — = not done.

TABLE 3

NEUTRALIZATION OF LT1 VIRUS BY ANTISERA TO THE VIRUS PROPAGATED
IN DIFFERENT HOST SYSTEMS [1]

| Virus | Source | Antisera | | | | |
		LT1-TH1W2	LT1-RTG	LT1-BF	LT1-CAM(1)	LTL-CAM(2)
LT1	TH1W	>256	484	62	15	<4
LT1	TH1B$_2$	192	50	10	<4	3
LT1	BF	256	118	30	<4	14
LT1	CAM	32	48	52	25	96

[1] 50% plaque reduction endpoint. Homologous reactions are italicized.

[2] TH1W, TH1B$_2$ = sublines of *Terrapene* heart cell line 1; RTG = rainbow trout gonad cell line; BF = bluegill fry cell line; CAM = chick embryo chorioallantoic membrane.

strated between all pairings tested of isolates from leopard frog, bullfrog or newt. No clear patterns distinguishing viruses or groups of viruses were observed.

The effect of the host cell system used for virus propagation on serum neutralization was investigated. LT1 virus propagated in several different systems was reacted with antisera to LT1 grown in a variety of systems. The virus was passaged two or more times in each host system before use. Antisera to LT1 grown in box turtle, rainbow trout and bluegill cell cultures, and in chick embryo CAM were reacted with virus propagated in box turtle and bluegill cell cultures and in the CAM. The results (Table 3) indicated that, in entirely virus-homologous tests, titers varied to an extent equal to that observed when diverse isolates were compared. There were suggestive indications that antisera to CAM-origin virus preferentially neutralized CAM-origin virus, but no similar patterns of preferential homologous neutralization by antisera to virus of cell culture origin were noted.

The plaque reduction test was also employed for an antigenic comparison of several amphibian isolates with the structually similar (16) *Tipula* iridescent virus (TIV). An antiserum to TIV [homologous complement fixation titer 1:256 (9)] tested at a dilution of 1:4 caused no plaque reduction when reacted with LT1, FV1, TEV, T6 and T8 viruses.

LT1 virus was further compared with the piscine DNA cytoplasmic virus "lymphocystis." An antiserum that neutralized 30 tissue culture infectious doses of lymphocystis virus at a dilution of 1:128 caused no LT1 plaque reduction at a dilution of 1:4.

Temperature Gradient Comparisons

The effect of temperature on the efficiency of plaquing (EOP) of representative amphibian cytoplasmic viruses was studied. Sets of 10 flasks containing TH-1 cell monolayers were inoculated with approximately 100 pfu each (determined at 23°C). Virus was adsorbed for one hour at 23°C after which starch overlay was applied. Cell

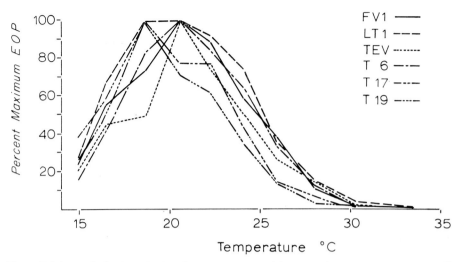

Fig. 3. Efficiency of plaquing (EOP) of representative amphibian cytoplasmic viruses in TH-1 cells incubated on a 15° to 35° temperature gradient.

cultures were incubated over a temperature gradient of approximately 15 °C to 34 °C. A staining overlay containing neutral red was added seven days after inoculation.

At and above optimum plaquing temperatures, maximum numbers of plaques were countable after 8 days incubation. At sub-optimal temperatures, plaque numbers continued to increase for several more days. Hence, the convention was adopted of counting plaques on the first day that plaques were clearly visible at the lowest temperature tested (15 °C), normally the tenth or eleventh day of incubation.

EOP curves obtained with six amphibian cytoplasmic viruses on the 15 °C to 34 °C gradient are shown in Fig. 3. Very similar curves were produced by each of the viruses tested. Peak plating efficiency was obtained at 18.7 °C and/or 20.6 °C. Observed differences between viruses with peak EOP at one or the other of these temperatures were not repeatable on retesting. Plaque numbers gradually increased with time at sub-optimal temperatures only and conceivably might eventually reach maximum levels. However, deterioration of warmer cell cultures prevented observation of experiments beyond 13 to 14 days after inoculation. No virus strain produced plaques at 33.6 °C, and all exhibited sharply reduced EOP at 30 °C and 28 °C.

Plaques reached the largest size, 0.5 to 1.2 mm diameter, at 9 days of incubation at temperatures from 20.6 °C to 28 °C. Plaque size was consistently reduced at temperatures below optimum and at 30 °C. It was apparent that the diverse isolates could not be distinguished on the basis of their plaquing behavior over a wide range of incubation temperatures.

Growth of Isolates in Amphibians

It was previously demonstrated that viruses LT1 through LT4, L4 and FV1 through FV3 could be recovered in high titer from the liver, spleen, and kidneys of IP-inoculated newts (6). A further study was made of the distribution of virus in six organs of newts inoculated with LT1 by several different routes and observed for 81 days. A small number of newts inoculated with T6 virus were also studied.

Recovery of virus from newts inoculated via the IP route is illustrated in Fig. 4. LT1 virus was rather evenly distributed through newt visceral organs for 21 days after inoculation, with peak titers observed on the 7th day. Newts sacrificed 35 and 49 days after inoculation were apparently clear of virus, but surprisingly, each of 2 newts sacrificed on the 81st day again yielded virus. It is interesting to note that one of these newts yielded virus in a titer of $10^{3.7}$ from testes, organs not routinely assayed. This was 50 to 100 times the titer recovered from liver, spleen or kidneys.

T6 virus similarly caused pan-visceral infection of newts. A limited number of samplings revealed higher titers than those obtained with LT1. Infection persisted at peak levels for 28 days.

Newts were not consistently infected by SC or oral inoculation of LT1. Only two of eight newts inoculated by each route yielded virus when sacrificed between 1 and 39 days after inoculation. Virus was recovered from only a few organs of such newts in titers not exceeding $10^{2.0}$.

In previous studies, newts refractory to IP inoculation of virus were occasionally observed. An experiment was designed to determine if the response of newts to inoculation with LT1 virus was affected by prior infection. Newts were challenged with LT1 virus 35 days after inoculation of a similar dose of LT1 virus or a control inoculation of TH1 cells only. The results are shown in Fig. 5. One of 2 virus vaccinated

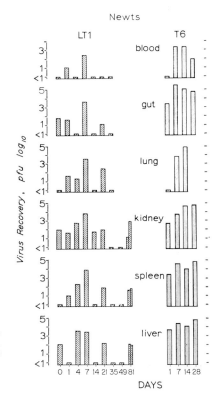

Fig. 4. Recovery of virus from the blood and visceral organs of adult newts inoculated via the IP route with LT1 or T6 virus. Inoculum doses: LT1 = 1.5 × 10⁵ pfu, T6 = 7.0 × 10⁵.

newts sacrificed at the time of challenge yielded virus. Three virus vaccinated and three cell control vaccinated newts all revealed similarly high titered visceral infections when sacrificed 7 days after challenge.

The effect of inoculation of efts by 3 different routes with LT1, and IP with T6 was studied. Results are shown in Fig. 6. Unlike adult newts, efts appeared to be equally susceptible to infection following administration of virus via IP, SC or oral routes. Virus was uniformly present in liver, spleen, and kidney, but not the gut. Assay of testes of a single newt, sacrificed 14 days after oral inoculation, revealed a titer of $10^{4.0}$ pfu, higher than that of any other organ tested. T6 appeared to reach higher titers than LT1.

Growth of several isolates inoculated in equivalent doses into efts was compared (Fig. 7). LT1 virus, frog isolates FV1 and TEV, and newt isolates T8 and T15 all caused widespread visceral infection. Relatively low titers of virus were recovered from FV1 inoculated efts, but differences in the level of infection of animals inoculated with the other four isolates were not marked.

Wolf *et al.* have reported that TEV replicates to high titer and causes severe disease in immature anurans (10). Hence, we studied the effect of IP inoculation of several amphibian viruses of diverse host origin into young Fowler's toads. Groups of 10 toads were inoculated with each of 6 different isolates. Six toads of each group were observed for study of gross pathology at time of death or at 30 days post-inoculation. Four toads from each group were sacrificed for study of viral growth.

The incidence of deaths and gross pathology induced by each virus is shown in

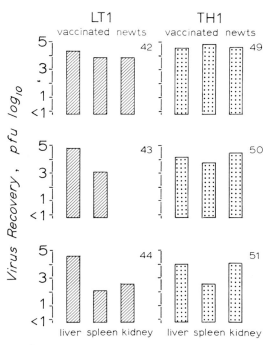

Fig. 5. Recovery of virus from LT1 "virus vaccinated" and TH-1 cell "control vaccinated" newts, 7 days after challenge with LT1 virus. "Vaccine" dose = 1.5×10^5 pfu, challenge dose = 5.0×10^5 pfu.

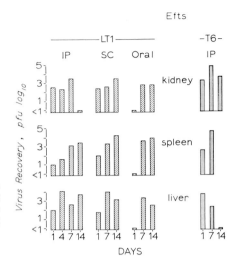

Fig. 6. Recovery of virus from efts inoculated with LT1 virus via the IP, SC or oral route or with T6 virus via the IP route. Inoculum doses: LT1 IP = 1.5×10^5 pfu, LT1 SC = 3.0×10^5 pfu, LT1 oral = 3.0×10^5 pfu, T6 IP = 7.0×10^5 pfu.

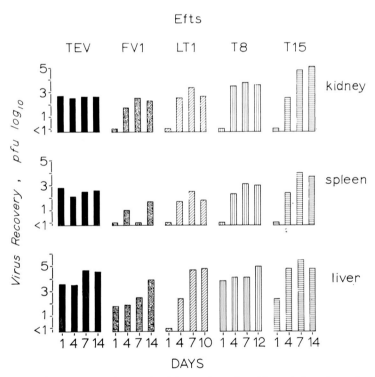

Fig. 7. The growth of virus in efts inoculated intraperitoneally with equivalent doses of several different amphibian isolates. Inoculum doses = approx. 1.0×10^5 pfu.

TABLE 4

Deaths and Gross Pathology Induced in Fowler's
Toads by Amphibian Virus Isolates

Virus	Inoculum (pfu)	Deaths[1]	Toads sacrificed 30 days post-inoculation	
			Visceral lesions	Normal
TEV	2.1×10^5	4	0	2
FV1	7.5×10^4	4	1	1
L5	6.5×10^4	0	0	6
LT1	5.0×10^4	3	0	3
LT2	5.0×10^5	2	2	2
T6	7.0×10^5	1	0	5
none	—	0	0	12

[1] All dead toads exhibited hemorrhagic lesions, except the single toad dead following T6 inoculation.

Table 4. Viruses TEV, FV1, LT1 and LT2, each caused a high incidence of deaths, usually occurring between 7 and 20 days after inoculation, and invariably accompanied by gross edema and/or visceral or skeletal muscle hemorrhages. Hemorrhagic lesions were also observed in LT2 and FV1 inoculated toads sacrificed 30 days after inoculation. T6, a newt isolate, and L5, a frog isolate, caused no deaths or gross pathology.

The distribution of virus in LT1 inoculated toads was studied in detail. Results of assay of virus in nine organs are given in Fig. 8. All visceral organs studied, the blood and skeletal muscle (gastrocnemius) were uniformly infected. Peak titers appeared in most organs in 4 to 7 days, declining by the 15th day after inoculation. However, virus continued to increase in the stomach through the 15th day, reaching the highest concentration observed in any organ.

Virus was assayed in the blood and livers only of toads inoculated with other isolates. Results are given in Fig. 9. The highest titers of virus infection and the most consistent viremia were noted in toads inoculated with TEV. However, no clear-cut correlation of levels of infection with virus pathogenicity was noted in toads infected with 5 other isolates. Livers usually yielded virus, but viremia was sporadic. Very low titers of virus were detected in toads inoculated with the non-pathogenic isolate L5, but also with the pathogenic strain FV1.

Maximum titers of virus detected in newts, efts, and toads in this study were lower than reported in previous studies with efts (6). This was probably explained by a change of technique. In the studies reported here, amphibian organs were triturated prior to storage at $-70°C$, instead of being frozen entire and triturated immediately prior to virus assay. Studies with infected newt organs divided and treated either way revealed that organs frozen entire yielded 50 to 100 times as much infectious virus as those triturated before freezing.

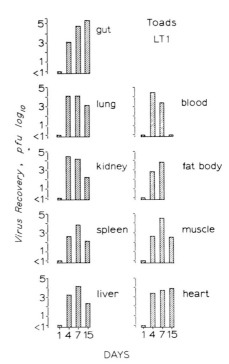

Fig. 8. Recovery of virus from the blood and visceral organs of immature toads inoculated via the IP route with LT1 virus. Inoculum dose = 5.0×10^4 pfu.

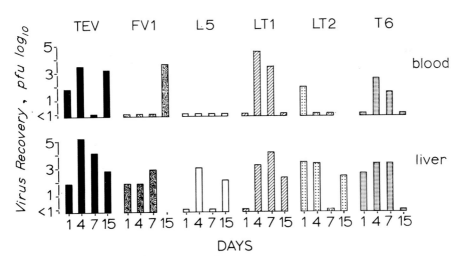

Fig. 9. The growth of representative amphibian virus isolates in IP inoculated baby toads. Inoculum doses: TEV = 2.1×10^5 pfu, FV1 = 7.5×10^4 pfu, L5 = 6.5×10^4 pfu, LT1 = 5.0×10^4 pfu, LT2 = 5.0×10^5 pfu, T6 = 7.0×10^5 pfu.

Discussion

A survey of adult newts supplied by several dealers has revealed frequent virus infection in animals supplied by one dealer only. Newt isolates resembled polyhedral cytoplasmic viruses isolated from leopard frogs and bullfrogs in inducing cytopathic effect characterized by cytoplasmic inclusions in cell cultures incubated at 23 °C, and in polyhedral morphology and cytoplasmic localization of the virions. However, there was no indication that infection of newts resulted from contact with frogs in captivity. While the exact geographic origin of infected newts was not determined, at least some were of a subspecies found only in North and South Carolina. It is remarkable that, in the present embryonic state of amphibian virology, polyhedral viruses have already been recovered from three amphibian species from widely diverse localities. One might predict that such viruses will be found in many other species as yet unstudied.

It was of particular interest to note that cytoplasmic newt viruses were recovered from lymphosarcomas induced in infected newts. This observation parallels the previous common isolation of similar viruses, presumably as "passenger agents," from kidney adenocarcinomas of leopard frogs.

Representative newt virus isolates were shown to cross-react extensively with other amphibian cytoplasmic viruses by means of the plaque neutralization test. Close antigenic relatedness of many of these isolates has also been demonstrated by means of agar gel immunodiffusion (9, 18) and complement fixation tests. By all criteria tested to date, all of the isolates must be considered a single antigenic type.

Comparison of amphibian virus isolates on the basis of the effect of temperature on EOP in TH-1 cell culture also revealed no differences. Each virus showed maximum EOP at 19 °C to 21 °C, with delayed plaque formation at lower temperatures and sharply depressed plaque numbers above 26 °C. Plaques that did appear at warmer temperatures up to 28 °C, were as large as those developing at optimal temperatures. The observation suggests that virions capable of initiating infection at slightly supraoptimal temperatures may then replicate at near-optimal rates. It has previously been reported (19) that LT1 virus replication in TH-1 cells is delayed at 30 °C, but titers near to those obtained at 23 °C are reached by 48 hours after infection. Total depression of FV1 replication at 34 °C has been described by Granoff et al. (5).

Detailed study of the growth of LT1 virus in adult newts revealed pantropic infection with peak virus levels obtained by 7 days after inoculation. However, no obvious pathology was induced. Virus infection persisted in some newts for at least 81 days after inoculation. The combination of low pathogenicity and long persistence of LT1 virus in newts would seem to provide an ideal system for maintaining the virus in nature. Immature eft stage newts were susceptible to LT1 virus inoculated via SC or oral routes, while adult newts were not. Selective susceptibility to amphibian cytoplasmic viruses of immature toads (10) and tadpoles (4) as compared with adult anurans has also been reported. The failure of amphibian cytoplasmic viruses to regularly replicate in large amphibians such as the bullfrog (6) and mudpuppy (Clark, H. F., unpublished) has made it difficult to perform complete pathogenesis studies including assessments of the role of humoral and cellular immune or non-specific responses.

Each of the viruses studied, of frog or newt origin, apparently replicated in efts and immature toads, consistently infecting all organs tested. Attempts to relate given isolates to their original host by comparing the infective titers attained in efts and toads met with limited success. The highest titered eft infections noted followed inoculation of newt isolates T8 and T15, but the level of these infections did not exceed that of LT1, FV1, or TEV infections consistently enough to provide a reliable tool for distinguishing strains.

Comparisons by several criteria of amphibian cytoplasmic viruses isolated from the leopard frog, bullfrog, and newt revealed remarkable uniformity in the different strains tested. A few strain differences, such as special plaquing characteristics of LT2 (11) and FV3 (5), and the lack of pathogenicity for baby toads of T6 and L5 may serve as usable strain markers. However, it is clear that each isolate described to date should be considered a representative of the same virus. The appropriate definitive name for this virus remains to be established.

Summary

Isolation of polyhedral cytoplasmic amphibian viruses has been described from tumor-bearing (FV3 and L4) and normal (FV1, FV2 and L5) leopard frogs and from bullfrogs (TEV). We have also described recovery of viruses from eft stage newts previously inoculated with leopard frog tumors (LT1–LT4).

This report describes a search for virus in uninoculated adult newts supplied by several dealers. Fifteen isolates, designated T6 to T20, were recovered from newts in 4 different lots supplied by one dealer. An additional isolate (T21) was recovered from a lymphosarcoma induced with the tumor agent of *Xenopus laevis* in a newt supplied by the same dealer. T isolates resembled the FV, LT and L isolates in fine structure and in the induction of cytopathic effect characterized by cytoplasmic inclusion body formation at an incubation temperature of 23°C. T isolates also cross-reacted extensively in neutralization tests with LT1, FV1 and TEV.

The effect of different temperatures on the efficiency of plaquing (EOP) of representative amphibian cytoplasmic viruses was tested on a temperature gradient incubator. Each virus exhibited maximum EOP at 19°C to 21°C with complete inhibition at 33.6°C.

Viruses of both newt and frog origin viruses infected efts and toads. Viruses LT1, LT2, FV1 and TEV caused disease in toads, while L5 and T6 did not. None of the isolates caused obvious disease in efts. It was concluded that the frog and newt cytoplasmic viruses described to date represent quite homogeneous strains of the same virus.

References

1. LUCKÉ, B.: A neoplastic disease of the kidney of the frog, *Rana pipiens*. Am. J. Cancer *20*:352–379, 1934.
2. RAFFERTY, K. A., JR.: Kidney tumors of the leopard frog: A review. Cancer Res. *24*:169–185, 1964.
3. RAFFERTY, K. A., JR.: The cultivation of inclusion-associated viruses from Lucké tumor frogs. Ann. N.Y. Acad. Sci. *126*:3–21, 1965.

4. Granoff, A., Came, P. E., and Rafferty, K. A., Jr.: The isolation and properties of viruses from *Rana pipiens:* Their possible relationship to the renal adenocarcinoma of the leopard frog. Ann. N.Y. Acad. Sci. *126:*237–255, 1965.

5. Granoff, A., Came, P. E., and Breeze, D. C.: Viruses and renal carcinoma of *Rana pipiens.* I. The isolation and properties of virus from normal and tumor tissue. Virology *29:*133–148, 1966.

6. Clark, H. F., Brennan, J. C., Zeigel, R. F., and Karzon, D. T.: Isolation and characterization of viruses from the kidneys of *Rana pipiens* with renal adenocarcinoma before and after passage in the red eft *Triturus viridescens.* J. Virol. *2:*629–640, 1968.

7. Rose, S. M., and Rose, F. C.: Tumor agent transformations in amphibia. Cancer Res. *12:*1–12, 1952.

8. Lehane, D. E., Jr., Clark, H. F., and Karzon, D. T.: Antigenic relationships among frog viruses demonstrated by the plaque reduction and neutralization kinetics tests. Virology *24:*590–595, 1968.

9. Kaminski, S.: Thesis, State University of New York at Buffalo, 1968.

10. Wolf, K., Bullock, G. L., Dunbar, C. E., and Quimby, M. C.: Tadpole edema virus: A viscerotropic pathogen for anuran amphibians. J. Infect. Dis. *118:*253–262, 1968.

11. Lehane, D. E., Jr., Clark, H. F., and Karzon, D. T.: A plaque method for titration of frog viruses using starch gel overlay. Proc. Soc. Exper. Biol. & Med. *125:*50–54, 1967.

12. Clark, H. F., and Karzon, D. T.: Acquired tolerance to elevated temperatures in a poikilothermic cell line (*Terrapene* heart, TH-1). Exper. Cell Res. *48:*269–275, 1967.

13. Clark, H. F., and Karzon, D. T.: *Terrapene* heart (TH-1), a continuous cell line from the heart of the box turtle, *Terrapene carolina.* Exper. Cell Res. *48:*263–268, 1967.

14. Wolf, K., Gravell, M., and Malsberger, R. G.: Lymphocystis virus: Isolation and propagation in Centrarchid fish cell lines. Science *151:*1004–1005, 1966.

15. Ruben, L. N., and Balls, M.: Further studies of a transmissible amphibian lymphosarcoma. Cancer Res. *27:*293–296, 1967.

16. Darlington, R. W., Granoff, A., and Breeze, D. C.: Viruses and renal carcinoma of *Rana pipiens.* II. Ultrastructure studies and sequential development of virus isolated from normal and tumor tissue. Virology *29:*149–156, 1966.

17. Bishop, S. C.: *Handbook of Salamanders,* Comstock, Ithaca, XIV +555, 1943.

18. Came, P. E., Geering, G., Old, L. J., and Boyse, E. A.: A serological study of polyhedral cytoplasmic viruses isolated from amphibia. Virology *36:*392–400, 1968.

19. Clark, H. F., and Karzon, D. T.: Temperature optima of mammalian and amphibian viruses in cell cultures of homeothermic and poikilothermic origin. Arch. ges. Virusforsch. *23:*270–279, 1968.

Tadpole Edema Virus: Pathogenesis and Growth Studies and Additional Sites of Virus Infected Bullfrog Tadpoles

Ken Wolf, G. L. Bullock, C. E. Dunbar and M. C. Quimby

Bureau of Sport Fisheries and Wildlife
Eastern Fish Disease Laboratory
Kearneysville, West Virginia

Introduction

Considering geographic origin, method of isolation, and the life stage, health and host species, the polyhedral cytoplasmic amphibian viruses thus far cultured belong to one of three categories. The first category consists of viruses obtained directly from adult *Rana pipiens*—with or without renal adenocarcinoma—either from northcentral United States or from New England and adjacent Canada (1, 2, 3, 4). The second category comprises viruses from larval or adult *Diemictylus viridescens* (formerly, *Triturus viridescens*) from New England or southeastern United States—efts previously inoculated with New England *R. pipiens* kidney tumor cells (4, 5) and more recently virus has been isolated directly from newts (6). The third category is a group of viruses isolated directly from normal adult or normal and diseased tadpoles of *Rana catesbeiana* from northcentral or southeastern United States (7).

While much of the information consists of negative results and circumstantial evidence, the accumulated evidence today overwhelmingly indicates that polyhedral cytoplasmic viruses are not causally related to the Lucké tumor. The known effects of these viruses in experimental hosts do not in themselves preclude tumorigenesis; they do, however, show clearly that polyhedral cytoplasmic viruses have a role in disease production that is both direct and immediate.

In 1965 we made a microbiological examination of 3 diseased larval bullfrogs (*Rana catesbeiana*) from the White Sulphur Springs National Fish Hatchery in West Virginia and found 2 pathogens; one a virus, and the other *Aeromonas liquefaciens*, a bacterium implicated in red leg disease of frogs. The bacterium and the virus were both present in numbers lower than we usually see in poikilotherms with clinical infectious disease. Experimentally, however, the virus rapidly caused death, usually with edema, in 3 species of toads and in some metamorphosing bullfrogs; therefore, we named it TEV for tadpole edema virus (7).

TEV is one of the polyhedral cytoplasmic frog viruses having the size, shape, and biophysical properties of FV-1 and LT type viruses. Subsequently, newer data show that regardless of their host or geographic origin, the polyhedral cytoplasmic viruses of amphibia are antigenically related. Using plaque reduction and neutralization kinetics, Lehane *et al.* (8) found that LT-1, LT-2 and FV-1 viruses belonged to a single serotype. Came *et al.* (9) used neutralization and immunodiffusion techniques, but could not distinguish between 9 representative isolates of amphibian agents including TEV. In addition, the 9 viruses all produced in toads acute fatal disease with gross pathology similar to that described for TEV. Clark *et al.* (6) have confirmed the antigenic relationship of representative viruses of this group but found differences in degree of pathogenicity for newts and toads.

The biology and epizootiology of TEV, and related viruses, are almost completely unknown, but existing facts appear to follow a pattern that has been reported for the known viruses of North American salmonid fishes (10). These particular fish viruses produce disease and death of the very young. However, some victims usually recover to grow to functional sexual maturity; many of them acquire a persistent carrier state but to all outward appearances are normal healthy fish. One year after the original isolation of TEV we revisited the West Virginia site and made additional isolations from normal appearing metamorphosing tadpoles and from mature adult bullfrogs. We could not obtain consistent disease production among experimentally inoculated bullfrog tadpoles of comparable development stage. This failure was attributed to effects of preexisting viral infection which was demonstrated among bullfrog tadpoles from a commercial source in Wisconsin and another in North Carolina.

Considering the foregoing, our purpose was threefold: (a) to determine reasons why bullfrog tadpoles were often refractory to TEV, (b) to search selected geographic areas for other sources of polyhedral cytoplasmic amphibian viruses, and (c) to resolve some aspects of the biology, pathology and epizootiology of TEV. This report covers our findings.

Materials and Methods

Search for Virus

Considering the geography of the known occurrences of frog virus, the mobility and habitat requirements of the hosts, and the continuity of stream environments, we looked for viruses among frogs from major watersheds of the continental United States. Friends and collaborators in our Bureau collected the specimens and sent them live to our laboratory.

Detection and Quantification of Virus in Animals

In our earlier work we had readily found virus by inoculating BF-2 cells with visceral homogenates; therefore, we used the same procedures in the present study. With the exception of very small animals such as *Hyla regilla* and tadpoles less than 50 mm long which were used whole, only the viscera (minus the gall bladder) were taken. The organs of 3 to 5 animals were pooled, weighed, homogenized by hand with mortar and pestle, diluted 10-fold with Hanks' balanced salt solution (BSS), centrifuged to separate gross solids and lipids, then filtered through a 0.45μ porosity membrane. Ten confluent tube cultures of either FHM or BF-2 cells were each inoculated with 0.1 ml filtrate, and additional 10-fold dilutions were made in BSS and inoculated into 5 or 10 cultures. After 10 days incubation at $23°$ to $30°C$ cultures were examined and scored.

Experimental Tadpoles

A mass of eggs, presumably *R. catesbeiana* but possibly *R. clamitans*, was obtained from a local pond during late July and hatched in a building away from experimental facilities. Most of the eggs hatched within 24 hours and the larvae were soon feeding on boiled lean beef, boiled leafy vegetables, yeast and commercial trout ration. A pool of 15 tadpoles was assayed for virus when they were 69 days old.

Susceptibility Trials with Tadpoles

Duplicate lots of 10 or more tadpoles were tested at 25 °C for susceptibility to TEV at 3, 18, 28, 35, 49 and 63 days of age. In all trials, infected animals were kept in one room and were tended by one of us while control lots which received heat killed virus were kept isolated in a separate room. Virus was added to the water, and food was provided to insure virus ingestion.

Trials with 18- and 49-day-old tadpoles were intended to yield data for mortality curves and so employed replications of 100 (10 mm) and 50 (17 mm) animals each. Duplicate aerated aquaria holding 700 ml water were slanted to provide depths of from 0 to 15 mm. Approximately 10^8 cell culture infective doses, 50 percent end point (ID_{50}) of 15th cell culture passage TEV were added to the infected pair of aquaria on the day each trial started. Control aquaria received an identical volume of virus which had been held at 60 °C for 1 hour. Each day animals were fed lightly, aquaria were cleaned, and afterward the water levels were returned to the starting volume.

Sequence of Pathology

The pathogenesis of TEV was studied in young tadpoles and in young Fowler's toads (*Bufo woodhousei fowleri*). Two-month-old tadpoles were held at 25 °C in water containing 15th cell culture passage TEV. Each day, several specimens were preserved in Bouin's solution. Mortality began on the 5th day, and the last living, but sick, specimens were preserved on the 8th day.

Small Fowler's toads (16 to 25 mm) were collected locally and inoculated intraperitoneally (I.P.) with 0.03 ml TEV in 15th cell culture passage; this was approximately 10^6 ID_{50} per gram of body weight. Each day a random sample of 4 toads was killed, examined grossly and fixed in 10 percent neutral formalin for paraffin embedding, hematoxylin and eosin staining and histological examination. Concurrently, a lot of bluegill sunfish (*Lepomis macrochirus*) and older toads (45 to 80 mm, 9 to 62 gms) were inoculated I.P. with TEV at the same dosage rate. All animals were held at 25 °C.

Cell Cultures

BF-2, a line of cells originating from bluegill fry and currently in development at this laboratory, and the permanent FHM line (11) were grown in Eagle's Minimal Essential Medium plus 10 percent fetal bovine serum, 100 units penicillin, 100 μg streptomycin, and 25 units nystatin per ml.

Virus Growth Curve

Replication of TEV in BF-2 cells grown at 25 °C was studied by inoculating confluent 2-ounce prescription bottle cultures containing approximately one million cells in 31st subculture with 10^8 ID_{50} TEV in 13th passage. After 60 minutes adsorption, cell sheets were washed 4 times with Hanks' BSS and incubated. At selected intervals, random duplicate cultures were examined and their supernatant fluids harvested and stored at $4°C$ until assayed for released virus. Culture fluid was diluted in serial 10-fold steps each of which was inoculated into 5 tube cultures. Titrations were read and scored after 7 days incubation at $25°C$.

Results

New Areas with Infected Frogs

Three species of frogs, a total of 158 animals from 9 locations across continental United States, were examined for virus. Bullfrog tadpoles from 2 locations were found to harbor agents which were filterable, transferable and produced in BF-2 cells a cytopathic effect which was indistinguishable from that caused by TEV (Table 1). All 4 lots of Alabama animals showed virus and titers ranged from $10^{1.1}$ to $10^{3.3}$ ID_{50} per ml. All lots of Arkansas tadpoles were also positive, but the titer was somewhat higher—$10^{2.8}$ to $10^{4.3}$ ID_{50} per ml.

Susceptibility of Bullfrog Tadpoles to TEV

Passage 15 TEV was highly pathogenic for bullfrog tadpoles from 3 days to 2 months of age, and when virus was simply added to the animals' aquarium water, mortality began at about 5 days and was rapidly complete. Eighteen-day-old tadpoles sustained total loss within 9 days; mortality began on the 5th day and peaked at 53 percent for the 8th day (Fig. 1). There was no mortality among control animals which had received heated virus. Forty-nine-day-old tadpoles showed the same 5 day incubation period, but peak rate of mortality was only 37 percent; it occurred on the 9th day and while the loss was complete, the last animals in each aquarium

TABLE 1

Occurrence of Virus Among Frogs Collected from 9 Locations in the United States

Major watershed	State	Species	Number examined	Results
Apalachicola	Alabama	R. catesbeiana	20	+
Colorado	Utah	R. pipiens	20	−
Colorado (of Texas)	Texas	R. catesbeiana	20	−
Columbia	Washington	Hyla regilla	16	−
Mississippi	Arkansas	R. catesbeiana	20	+
Missouri	South Dakota	R. pipiens	20	−
Sacramento	California	R. catesbeiana	7	−
Snake	Idaho	R. pipiens	15	−
Susquehanna	Pennsylvania	R. catesbeiana	20	−

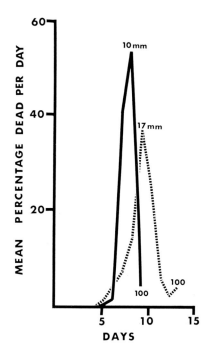

Fig. 1. Response of young (10 mm, 18 days old) and older bullfrog tadpoles (17 mm, 49 days old) held at 25°C to Tadpole Edema Virus.

survived for 13 days. Four control tadpoles which had received heated virus died from undetermined cause between the 3rd and 6th days, but there was no evidence of a contagious disease.

Assay for virus among 69-day-old tadpoles which had not been infected showed no virus.

Sequence of Pathology

We qualify our histopathological findings for bullfrog tadpoles. Reference material consisted solely of normal animals which were fixed on the day the experimental tadpoles were infected. We lacked prior experience with small tadpoles and found their size and the changes of organogenesis to be troublesome. We report only clear-cut pathology; accordingly, our findings might be the minimal effects of TEV.

The effects of TEV in tadpoles are characterized as severely degenerative with necrosis of liver, kidneys, and digestive tract and associated edema in those organs and in skeletal muscle. Beginning focal liquefactive necrosis was found in most livers 2 days post-infection. Thereafter, the severity of hepatic pathology was greater. Necrosis often appeared to originate in the area of the gall bladder and bile duct and from there it spread to other parts of the liver. By the 5th day, stomach, intestine or mesentery adjacent to areas of strong hepatic necrosis were similarly involved. Advanced liver necrosis was accompanied by edema, and the latter was a general finding through the 8th and last day that specimens survived. Beginning kidney tubule necrosis was found in one of 4 specimens 24 hours post-infection; that finding was more common thereafter, and by the 4th day it too was accompanied by edema. Glomeruli were not involved. Skeletal muscle showed beginning edema in one of 4 specimens on the 3rd day. On succeeding days this was strongly evident in all specimens.

Pathology in Fowler's toads was readily identified both macroscopically and microscopically. The very earliest change was microscopic, slight focal necrosis in the liver of one specimen 2 days after infection. Liquefactive necrosis of the liver with concomitant edema was the rule from the 3rd through the 6th day when the last specimens died. Multiple macroscopic focal hemorrhages were clearly evident in kidneys and skeletal muscle on day 4, and on day 5 hemorrhages appeared in stomach tissues also. Microscopically, kidney tubules showed focal necrosis on day 4 and was common thereafter.

Larger toads inoculated with TEV died from 6 to 8 days after injection, slightly later than the smaller and younger toads. Bluegills similarly injected survived and were apparently healthy 40 days later, and at that time an assay of filtered visceral homogenate showed no virus.

Growth of TEV in BF-2 Cells

During the first 5 hours post-inoculation, the level of TEV remained essentially unchanged, but soon thereafter virus increased and by the 8th hour the amount had doubled (Fig. 2). The finding of new virus coincided with the very earliest appearance of cytopathology. Exponential growth occurred during the period from about 10 to

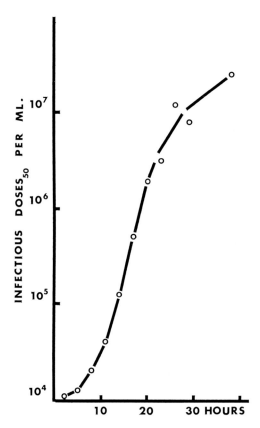

Fig. 2. One-step growth curve of released Tadpole Edema Virus in BF-2 cells grown at 25°C.

20 hours post-inoculation. By the 29th hour 100 percent of the cells appeared affected and by 38 hours about three-fourths had been lysed and were off the glass. A final level of about $10^{7.3}$ ID_{50} per ml—close to the usual maximum for this cell system—was reached at 38 hours. Following exposure to a multiplicity of infection of 1000 ID_{50}, a residual level of 0.05 ID_{50} per cell (10^4 ID_{50} per ml) was found. After 38 hours at 25°C, the yield was calculated to be about 1260 ID_{50} per cell.

Discussion

In this study TEV was again shown to lack pathogenicity for fish, and its virulence for toads was confirmed. More important, however, was the clear-cut evidence that young specific pathogen-free bullfrog tadpoles quickly succumbed to TEV infection and in so doing they showed progressive pathology which was comparable in time of occurrence and tissue tropism to that produced in toads (*Bufo*).

In young tadpoles the liver, kidneys, digestive tract and skeletal muscle were early targets for virus effects. Among young *Bufo*, these organs were also affected although skeletal muscle showed hemorrhage instead of edema. In our earlier work with older *Bufo*, we did not find pathology in livers. The discrepancy might be resolved by virological assay. The liver pathology does agree with occurrence of virus in livers of *R. pipiens* (3).

Rana pipiens and its sub-species are found throughout much of the United States, but polyhedral cytoplasmic virus has been found thus far only in the northcentral and northeast portions of the country. *R. catesbeiana* has been widely introduced, but we found no virus in frogs from the western half of the United States. This may simply be a matter of sample size, but it could reflect an absence of ecological requirements for virus transmission or even the absence of a needed vector.

Our own experience and that of others attests to the prevalence of polyhedral cytoplasmic virus among amphibians from commercial sources. If such animals do not have natural infections when captured it seems likely that transmission could occur in the dealers' facilities.

The acute disease course, an incubation time of 5 days at 25°C in all animals, worked against development of more involved pathology, but this very acute course is apparently characteristic for polyhedral cytoplasmic amphibian viruses.

TEV replication in BF-2 cells at 25°C resembles growth of FV-1 in FHM cells at 24°C (3). The latent period is approximately the same though the peak of released FV-1 occurred at about 48 hours, somewhat later than that of TEV. It should be noted that FHM cells were not the most efficient host system for either agent. The short growth cycle is consistent with the acute disease course of this DNA virus at 25°C. Lymphocystis, a much larger polyhedral cytoplasmic DNA virus which is pathogenic for fish, produces chronic disease and has a growth curve of at least 12 days at 25°C.

In 18- and 49-day-old specific pathogen-free bullfrog tadpoles TEV produced acute disease and death following a short incubation. Among the older animals, however, the peak rate of mortality was lower and survival was extended; this was interpreted as evidence that some resistance was acquired with age. The clear-cut production of mortality vindicated an earlier hypothesis (7) that TEV would prove virulent for young tadpoles, and the differential response supports the idea that the biology of this polyhedral cytoplasmic virus is like that of the known viruses of North American salmonids. TEV bears similarities to infectious pancreatic necrosis (IPN) virus, for both viruses are widespread and produce acute serious degenerative disease in the very young, both viruses also encounter resistance with increasing host age. TEV and IPN virus are similarly found in the carrier state among normal appearing adults and vertical transmission probably occurs with both agents. As noted by Clark *et al.* (4), Kaminski found precipitating antibody against LT virus, a polyhedral cytoplasmic agent, in adult bullfrogs. Though less specific, IPN virus and TEV both are water-borne and undoubtedly have adaptations for survival and transmission in the aquatic environment. Considering the viruses, the host animals, and the nature of their environments, spread is easily assured especially in lotic habitats.

The isolations of polyhedral cytoplasmic amphibian viruses can be considered from a hydrographic point of view because of the broad influence geography has on the distribution of the host and ecologically on the transmission and hence the long-term survival of the virus as a biological entity.

The first polyhedral cytoplasmic frog viruses were isolated from animals obtained in northcentral United States. Depending on the actual source, the animals were from the Great Lakes basin or the Mississippi River drainage. Assuming greater probability of the latter, the isolation of TEV in West Virginia—actually in the Ohio River drainage—was a second site for frog virus occurrence in the Mississippi watershed. By the same token, the Arkansas isolation of the present work documents a third site

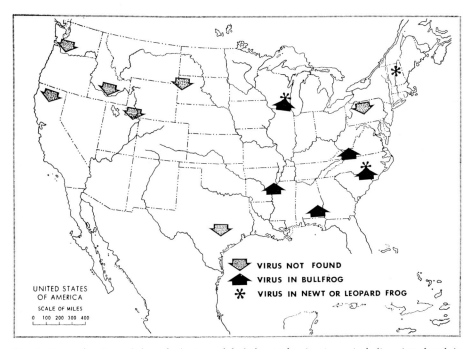

Fig. 3. Known locations of frogs harboring polyhedral cytoplasmic viruses including sites found in this study.

of infected animals (Fig. 3). The Alabama site is new; it is on the Chatahoochee river, part of the Apalachicola River system which empties into the Gulf of Mexico. The Alabama site therefore is comparable in its hydrographic isolation to the North Carolina site which is in the Cape Fear river drainage.

The occurrence of polyhedral cytoplasmic amphibian viruses is of course inseparably related to the host animals themselves. The work reported here adds 2 occurrences—making 5 in all—in which hosts have been infected bullfrog tadpoles. All occurrences of amphibian virus are in the eastern half of the United States (Fig. 3). Although all the amphibia indigenous to each area have not been virologically examined—and this certainly would be a worthwhile study—the Alabama, Arkansas and West Virginia sites are thus far known only for infected bullfrogs. North Carolina and Wisconsin have infected bullfrogs and either infected leopard frogs or infected newts. The New England area has had infected leopard frogs, but we cannot help but wonder what would be found among the bullfrogs.

We realize that epizootiological data are meager, but they do suggest that the principal host for polyhedral cytoplasmic amphibian virus might be the bullfrog and secondarily other members of the class.

Summary

Tadpole edema virus (TEV), a polyhedral cytoplasmic agent from West Virginia bullfrogs (*Rana catesbeiana*) always produced acute degenerative disease in toads but inconsistent disease production in bullfrog tadpoles. Erratic results in the latter were attributed to virus already present in commercial tadpoles used in the trials. The present study sought to resolve the problem of bullfrog susceptibility, to determine the sequence of pathology, to learn some aspects of virus biology, and to gain some idea of the national distribution of frog virus.

In the present study, specific pathogen-free bullfrog tadpoles proved consistently susceptible to TEV. A 5-day incubation was followed by acute disease and death, but older tadpoles showed signs of increased resistance. Sequential pathology in similar young tadpoles and in toads (*Bufo*) conformed to that reported earlier. Additional frog viruses were sought from 9 widely separated locations in the United States, and isolations were made from bullfrog tadpoles from Alabama and Arkansas. The biology of the bullfrog tadpole virus is similar to that of infectious pancreatic necrosis virus of salmonid fishes. Both viruses are widespread; they are virulent for the very young, and their transmission includes carrier adults.

Acknowledgments

We gratefully acknowledge the cooperation of the following people who provided live specimens for this study: James L. Billi, Coleman NFH (National Fish Hatchery), Anderson, California; Harry Bishop, BSFW (Bureau of Sport Fisheries and Wildlife), Austin, Texas; Dr. N. Fijan and T. L. Wellborn, Jr., Auburn University, Alabama; Ronald W. Goede, Utah State University, Logan; Harlan E. Johnson, Little White Salmon NFH, Cook, Washington; Edward Larsen, BSFW, Hagerman, Idaho; Dr. Fred P. Meyer and Jordan A. Robinson, BSFW, Stuttgart, Arkansas; Lyle L.

Pettijohn, Leetown NFH, Kearneysville, West Virginia, and Charles L. Sowards, McNenny NFH, Spearfish, South Dakota.

References

1. GRANOFF, A., CAME, P. E., and RAFFERTY, K. A., JR.: The isolation and properties of viruses from *Rana pipiens*: Their possible relationship to the renal adenocarcinoma of the leopard frog. Ann. N.Y. Acad. Sci. *126*:237–255, 1965.

2. RAFFERTY, K. A., JR.: The cultivation of inclusion-associated viruses from Lucké tumor frogs. Ann. N.Y. Acad. Sci. *126*:3–21, 1965.

3. GRANOFF, A., CAME, P. E., and BREEZE, C. D.: Viruses and renal carcinoma of *Rana pipiens*. I. The isolation and properties of virus from normal and tumor tissue. Virology *29*:133–148, 1966.

4. CLARK, H. F., BRENNAN, J. C., ZEIGEL, R. F., and KARZON, D. T.: Isolation and characterization of viruses from the kidneys of *Rana pipiens* with renal adenocarcinoma before and after passage in the red eft (*Triturus viridescens*). Jour. Virology *2*:629–640, 1968.

5. CLARK, H. F., and KARZON, D. T.: Temperature dependence of growth in cell culture of herpes simplex, vaccinia, and two viruses isolated from amphibia. Fed. Proc. *24*:319, 1965.

6. CLARK, H. F., GRAY, C., FABIAN, F., ZEIGEL, R. F., and KARZON, D. T.: Comparative studies of amphibian cytoplasmic virus strains isolated from the leopard frog, bullfrog and newt. *In* Biology of Amphibian Tumors (M. Mizell, ed.), Springer-Verlag New York Inc., 1969, pp. 310–326.

7. WOLF, K., BULLOCK, G. L., DUNBAR, C. E., and QUIMBY, M. C.: Tadpole edema virus: A viscerotropic pathogen for anuran amphibians. J. Inf. Dis. *118*:253–262, 1968.

8. LEHANE, D. E., JR., CLARK, H. F., and KARZON, D. T.: Antigenic relationships among frog viruses demonstrated by the plaque reduction and neutralization kinetics tests. Virology *34*:590–595, 1968.

9. CAME, P. E., GEERING, G., OLD, L. J., and BOYSE, E. A.: A serological study of polyhedral cytoplasmic viruses isolated from amphibia. Virology *36*:392–400, 1968.

10. WOLF, K.: The fish viruses. *In* Adv. Virus Res. *12*:35–101, 1966.

11. GRAVELL, M., and MALSBERGER, R. G.: A permanent cell line from the fathead minnow (*Pimephales promelas*). Ann. N.Y. Acad. Sci. *126*:555–565, 1965.

Herpestype Virus Latency in the Lucké Tumor[1]

MERLE MIZELL, CHRISTOPHER W. STACKPOLE [2] and J. JOYCE ISAACS

Department of Biology [3]
Tulane University
New Orleans, Louisiana

Although the presence of a herpestype virus (HTV) in Lucké renal adenocarcinoma cells was confirmed by electron microscopy over a decade ago (2), a definite etiological link between HTV and the Lucké tumor was not established until recently. Tweedell's recent experiments elegantly demonstrated the oncogenicity of cell-free fractions of "winter" tumor and the *lack* of oncogenicity in similarly prepared fractions of "summer" tumors (16). In our recent studies we further purified Tweedell's "winter" tumor mitochondrial fraction, so that a zonal centrifuge purified fraction rich in HTV was obtained. This zonal fraction retained the ability to induce tumors in developing tadpoles whereas other, adjacent fractions did not (9, 11).

Since previous studies have indicated that "summer" and "winter" renal carcinomas are merely temperature-mediated states of the same tumor (10, 12, 14), the study of the transition from "virus-free" ("summer") to virus-containing ("winter") state should yield insight into the phenomenon of viral latency. The present study represents an attempt to gain further understanding of the emergence of virus in the Lucké tumor.

Although low temperature treatment of *in situ* "virus-free" kidney tumors has proved to be an efficient means of obtaining virus,* primary tumors cannot be used to follow the time course of virus induction during low temperature treatment. A major factor which makes primary tumors unsatisfactory is the inherent sampling errors attributable to the multicentric origin of many Lucké tumors (Figs. 1, 2 and 3). This obviously limits the usefulness of employing *in situ* primary tumors for repeated bioassay. The culture of small portions of tumor tissue in the frog anterior eyechamber (Figs. 4 and 5) is an *in vivo* method which overcomes most of the disadvantages of repeated bioassay and also has many intrinsic advantages. A more de-

---

[1] Aided by grant #E-494 from the American Cancer Society.

[2] Present address: Division of Immunology, Sloan-Kettering Institute for Cancer Research, New York, New York.

[3] The Chapman H. Hyams III Laboratory of Tumor Cell Biology.

* By subjecting frogs with "summer" tumors to low temperature ($7.5 \pm 0.5°C$) for several months we have been able to recover high concentrations of the frog HTV (average = 5×10^{11} virus particles per gram of tumor); purification procedures were devised to separate and concentrate the virus from these cold-treated tumors (17). Virus prepared in this manner provided antigen for immunological comparison of the frog HTV with other known herpestype viruses (3, 4, 5).

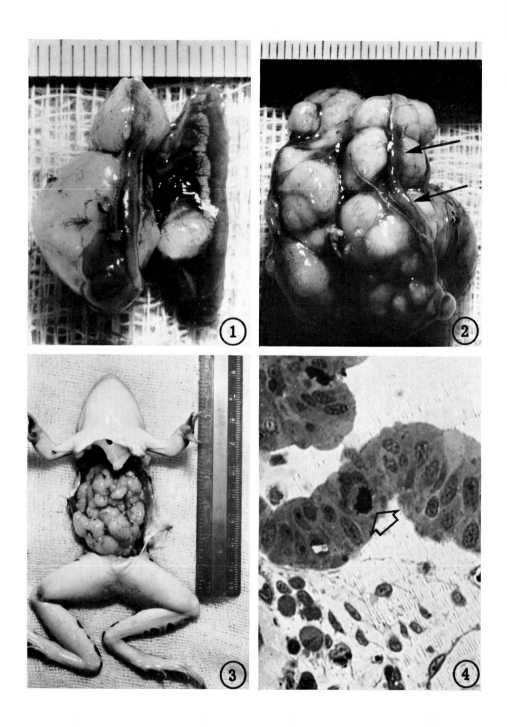

tailed discussion of the advantages of employing eyechamber transplants rather than *in situ* primary tumors has previously been presented (12).

Virus Induction in the Anterior Chamber of the Eye

The following procedures have been used to study the time course of virus production:

(a) A frog containing a primary tumor was sacrificed; the tumor was removed and placed in chilled saline and a single tumor nodule was dissected free from the main tumor mass.

(b) At the outset of these experiments, both light and electron microscopy were utilized to confirm the absence of virus in the nodule used for transplants.*

(c) The nodule was cut into small pieces (1–2mm^3) and a single piece was placed into the right anterior eyechamber of several dozen animals.

(d) Soon after transplantation the hosts were placed in the low temperature environment. (All virus-induction experiments were carried out at 7.5 ± 0.5°C).

(e) Periodically, an animal was sacrificed and its implant examined by light and electron microscopy for the presence of virus.

In light microscopy examination, the criteria used as an indication of the presence of virus were: (a) enlarged nucleus, (b) margination of the chromatin, and (c) Cowdry Type A intranuclear inclusions (Fig. 6)—characteristics known to be associated with herpesvirus infection. If two or more of these characteristics were noted, the transplant was scored as *indicating* viral presence. Visualization of virus with the electron microscope was used to confirm HTV presence (Fig. 7).

Homologous Host Eyechambers

Our earlier study of virus induction in *Rana pipiens* eyechambers had shown that virus was present in 1 to 6% of the tumor cells in the transplants as early as 11

---

* It should be noted that all "summer" tumors used in these experiments were "virus-free" tumors which developed in frogs housed in our laboratory at 20–26°C.

PLATE 1

Fig. 1. Ventral aspect of *Rana pipiens* kidneys with bilateral, multicentric Lucké tumors. Two large nodules can be recognized on the right kidney, and a single nodule is present on the left. Scale in millimeters.

Fig. 2. Another primary renal tumor in which the kidneys are almost entirely replaced by tumor nodules. Only a small strip of normal kidney tissue remains (arrows). Scale in millimeters.

Fig. 3. Another tumor demonstrating multicentric origin, shown *in situ*. All viscera removed to show the extent of tumor growth.

Fig. 4. Histological section of eyechamber growth (pulse-labeled with tritiated thymidine). Silver grains over a heavily labeled nucleus (arrow) are evident in this autoradiograph. ×480.

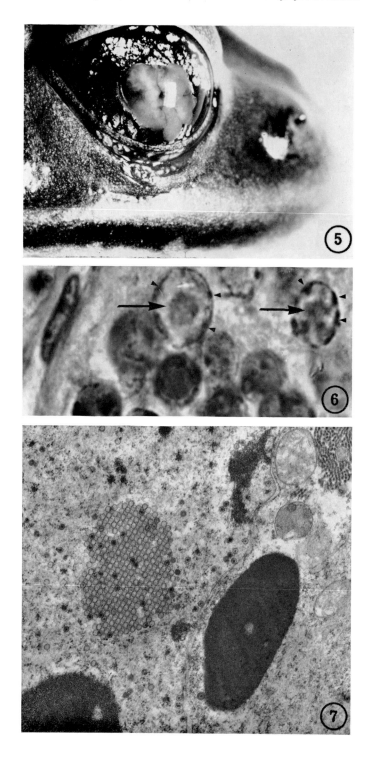

weeks after low temperature treatment was begun (10). In the present study a larger number of animals was employed and tumor implants were examined at more frequent intervals. In this study we were unable to detect virus in any transplant examined during the first 8 weeks. In one series of 44 *Rana pipiens* hosts, the first appearance of virus occurred at $9\frac{1}{2}$ weeks. In another series of 90 *Rana pipiens*, the presence of HTV was first observed at 10 weeks. This experiment was continued for 32 weeks; the number of virus-containing cells increased with time until a plateau was reached at about 20% infection after 14–16 weeks. This level was then maintained and no significant change in the number of virus-containing cells could be noted during the subsequent course of these experiments. The ultrastructural details of virus particle development under these conditions will be published elsewhere (Stackpole, in preparation).

Although sampling errors are eliminated by the use of eyechamber transplants in these experiments, the use of *pipiens* eyechambers does not exclude another possible explanation for the appearance of virus in low temperature-treated tumor tissue. Since the Lucké tumor is endemic in *Rana pipiens*, it is quite possible that at elevated temperatures virus may reside in distant organs and tissues. Reduction in temperature may permit the HTV to demonstrate an affinity for tumor cells and thus trigger the migration of virus from other tissues. Therefore, although virus accumulation and replication is seen to take place within the tumor cells, virus may not have *originated* in the tumor cells. This possibility takes on added meaning since herpesviruses are notorious for their ability to reside in distant reservoir tissues until activated, whereupon they make their appearance in specific regions of circumscribed infection (1).

Heterologous Host Eyechambers

The following heterologous eyechamber experiments were performed to eliminate the possibility that the virus might arise from a distant site. Since the Lucké tumor is a tumor of *Rana pipiens*, a different species of frog, *Rana clamitans*, was chosen to serve as host; and in an additional series, the toad, *Bufo americanus*, representing a different amphibian family, was used. The same primary tumor that served as the source of tumor tissue for one series of *Rana pipiens* transplants was transplanted to 58 *Rana clamitans* and 29 *Bufo americanus* eyechambers (See Table 1). Again we were unable to detect virus in any transplant examined during the first 8 weeks of low temperature treatment. In *Rana clamitans* the first appearance of virus occurred in implants examined at 9 weeks (see Fig. 8); in *Bufo americanus* (Fig. 9) the pres-

---

PLATE 2: HOMOLOGOUS HOST IMPLANTS

Fig. 5. Macrophotograph of tumor growth in anterior eyechamber of *Rana pipiens*. Growth of the implant has progressed until it now obscures most of the pupil.

Fig. 6. Photomicrograph of virus-containing tumor showing enlarged nuclei with marginated chromatin (small arrows) and Cowdry Type A inclusions (large arrows). These light microscopy characteristics indicate the presence of virus. ✕2,000.

Fig. 7. Tumor in *Rana pipiens* eyechamber after 20 weeks of low temperature treatment. Various stages of virus development can be recognized. ✕9,700.

TABLE 1

LOW TEMPERATURE VIRUS INDUCTION IN EYECHAMBER TRANSPLANTS (7.5 ± 0.5°C)

Host species	Number of transplants‡	No. of transplants examined before 9 weeks		Indications of virus	Presence of virus	No. of transplants examined after 9–32 weeks		Indication of virus	Presence of virus
		Light micro.	Electron micro.	L/M	E/M	L/M	E/M	L/M	E/M
Rana pipiens	44*	5	10	0	0	4	3	4	3
Rana pipiens	90†	—	20	—	0	—	65	—	65
Rana clamitans	58*	8	2	0	0	19	12	17	11
Bufo americanus	29*	4	3	0	0	14	9	13	9

* Tumor VR 2-67A used for transplantation.
† Tumor VR 2-67C used for transplantation.
‡ In some cases a single transplant was large enough to be examined by both light and electron microscopy. On the other hand, some animals did not survive long enough to have their implants examined. Because of these facts the total number of transplants examined does not equal the number of animals which received transplants.

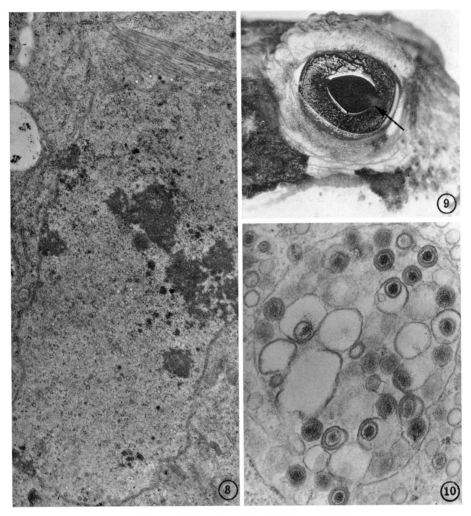

PLATE 3: HETEROLOGOUS HOST IMPLANTS

Fig. 8. Electron micrograph of *Rana clamitans* implant after 13 weeks low temperature treatment. Various stages of herpesvirus development can be seen within the nucleus. ×7,000.

Fig. 9. Macrophotograph of tumor implant in *Bufo americanus* eyechamber. The small tumor implant is indicated by the arrow.

Fig. 10. Electron micrograph of *Bufo americanus* implant after 16 weeks low temperature treatment. A nuclear sac of enveloped virus particles, surrounded by some empty capsids, can be seen. ×74,000.

ence of virus was first detected at 9½ weeks (see Fig. 10). As in the homologous eyechamber transplants, low temperature treatment was continued for 32 weeks and it was noted that virus production increased from the initial levels until a plateau was reached. Furthermore, the amount of virus, the various types and distribution of virus, and the morphology of this herpestype virus were essentially the same in all tumor cells, regardless of the host species (Figs. 7, 8 and 10).

"Virus-Free" State—Latency

Low temperature induction of virus in "summer" tumor implants maintained in foreign hosts suggests the *de novo* production of virus within the transplanted tumor cells and eliminates the possibility that virus originates in other host tissue and merely migrates into the tumor cells for replication. Furthermore, it is rather striking that, with little regard to the eyechamber in which the tumor implant resided (whether it be *pipiens*, *clamitans* or *Bufo*), virus first made its appearance at approximately the same time.

This evidence, that the herpesvirus which appears in low temperature-treated tumor originates from the tumor cells themselves, suggests that these cells contain a relatively complete viral genome in a masked or latent form. However, this assumption awaits definitive proof that the "virus-free" summer tumor state is truly virus-free. Although careful survey by light microscopy has shown that the obvious cytopathic effects of herpesvirus infection are lacking in "summer" tumors and virus is not seen with the electron microscope, a *small* number of virus particles would not exhibit overt signs and could easily escape detection by electron microscopy. Immunological reagents which will permit more effective screening for virus are just becoming available; antibody * against frog HTV harvested from sucrose gradient rate zonal purified, low temperature-treated primary tumors is now being employed to study the "virus-free" state. The results of these studies should make it possible to determine if "summer" tumors are virus-free in the sense that they lack virus particles and yet contain virus genetic information in an integrated or provirus state.

Regardless of the form in which herpesvirus information exists within summer tumor cells, low temperature treatment does activate the production of frog HTV. Although we do not yet understand the sequence of events which is triggered by low temperature and results in virus activation, the above experiments allow us to draw some tentative conclusions about the process.

Low Temperature Viral Activation—Exogenously Mediated?

In several instances, cold-blooded vertebrates have been shown to produce antibody primarily during the period of the year in which they are active. With the onset of cold weather, and a decrease in their activity, there is also a decrease in antibody production [see Legler *et al.*, this volume (8)]. Indeed, various studies have implied that during lowered temperature, several cold-blooded animals must subsist on previously produced antibody.

Could low temperature activation of virus production in summer tumor cells be explained by such a mechanism: at summer temperatures does antibody keep virus production in check; then after periods of low temperature does antibody titer fall to a level which allows virus production to occur? This type of phenomenon could account for the absence of virus in the "summer" tumor and would also explain the appearance and production of virus in winter primary tumors. However, such a scheme could not explain the results of our eyechamber transplant experiments. The

---

* Prepared by Dr. John Wallace, Department of Surgery, Tulane University.

delayed emergence of virus in both homologous and heterologous host eyechambers argues strongly against viral inhibition by host antibody.

Low Temperature Viral Activation—Endogenously Mediated

Since the available evidence indicates that low temperature viral activation is not exogenously mediated, it appears that low temperature acts directly upon an intrinsic cellular mechanism. What endogenous (intrinsic) mechanism might be operative at low temperature, but inoperative at elevated temperatures? Elevated temperature has been shown to selectively inhibit other herpes-virus DNA synthesis, e.g., infectious bovine rhinotracheitis (15). Although detailed knowledge of viral replication is currently lacking in the frog system, several possible pathways of inhibition can be envisioned. At elevated temperatures nuclease activity may degrade viral DNA synthesis. The initiation of viral DNA synthesis may be heat-sensitive; or the process of viral DNA synthesis may in itself be heat-sensitive; or a specific step in viral DNA synthesis, for example viral DNA polymerase, may be heat-sensitive. In any event, at normal or elevated temperature frog HTV synthesis is inapparent, whereas cellular DNA synthesis and tumor cell replication are accentuated (Fig. 4).

Low temperature activation of viral antigen synthesis has recently been attained in "virus-free" cultures of Shope papilloma virus infected cells (13). This example of temperature activation *in vitro* provides evidence from still another DNA virus-tumor system to support the concept of endogenously mediated expression of a previously masked viral genome. In all probability, low temperature acts directly on the tumor cell to activate a temperature-sensitive step in virus production. It is likely that the temperature-sensitive step affected is one involving enzymatic activity.

Until recently it was thought that cells transformed by DNA viruses were nonproductive because they retained only a fragment of the viral genome. A popular view emerged which represented neoplastic cells as containing merely a portion of the viral genes. In the SV40 system, limited recovery of complete virus by chemical or physical means was explained by recombinational events involving several partial ("defective") SV40 molecules or two SV40 mutant molecules within a single cell. This type of reasoning could explain the rescue of *small* numbers of complete viral particles. Recently it has been possible to recover *infectious* virus via co-cultivation of transformed cells with susceptible indicator cells (7). This fusion procedure produces heterokaryons, and rescue of infectious SV40 DNA from as many as 10% of the cells has been reported (6). Such *massive* recovery cannot be explained by recombinational events. Kit *et al.* suggest intact SV40 DNA integration within the malignant cell (6). These authors propose that the nuclear membrane or a linear insert in a chromosome, per se, may represent the site of integration.

Similar integration of intact HTV genome in "summer" renal carcinoma cells of the frog is suggested by the now routine recovery of large quantities of herpestype virus after low temperature treatment. This possibility is currently being tested.

Summary

Induction of virus in tumor cells which were previously "virus-free" suggests that these cells contain a relatively complete viral genome in a masked or latent state.

We have previously reported virus induction in "virus-free" ("summer") Lucké tumor cells which were transplanted to *Rana pipiens* eyechambers and maintained at low temperature. In our recent studies, amphibians in which the Lucké tumor does not occur (*Rana clamitans* and *Bufo americanus*) were chosen as hosts for eye chamber implants. Virus production was observed in these implants and the interval before appearance of virus in these tumor cells was similar to that observed in *R. pipiens* eyechamber transplants. The induction of virus in tumor implants maintained in foreign hosts suggests the *de novo* production of virus within the transplanted tumor cells and eliminates the possibility that virus originated in host tissue and merely migrated into tumor cells for replication. Evidence for the existence of a latent state of the herpestype virus within "summer" frog renal carcinoma cells is examined and discussed.

Acknowledgments

The authors wish to thank John Butler and Kenneth Fontenot for their splendid care of the animals. We also gratefully acknowledge Lorraine B. Mizell for her valuable assistance in preparation of the manuscript.

References

1. ANDREWS, C. H.: Latency and viral ecology. *In* Viruses of Laboratory Rodents (R. Holdenried, ed.), Monograph 20, Natl. Cancer Inst., Bethesda, 1966, pp. 1–11.
2. FAWCETT, D. W.: Electron microscope observations on intracellular virus-like particles associated with the cells of the Lucké renal adenocarcinoma. J. Biophys. Biochem. Cytol. *2:725–742, 1956.*
3. FINK, M. A., G. S. KING and M. MIZELL: Preliminary note: identity of a herpesvirus antigen from Burkitt lymphoma of man and the Lucké adenocarcinoma of frogs. J. Natl. Cancer Inst. *41:1477–1478, 1968.*
4. FINK, M. A., G. S. KING and M. MIZELL: Reactivity of serum from frogs and other species with a herpesvirus antigen extracted from a Burkitt lymphoma cultured cell line. *In* Biology of Amphibian Tumors (M. Mizell, ed.), Springer-Verlag New York Inc., 1969, pp. 358–364.
5. KIRKWOOD, J. M., G. GEERING, L. J. OLD, M. MIZELL and J. WALLACE: A preliminary report on the serology of Lucké and Burkitt herpes-type viruses: a shared antigen. *In* Biology of Amphibian Tumors (M. Mizell, ed.), Springer-Verlag New York Inc., 1969, pp. 365–367.
6. KIT, S., T. KURIMURA, M. L. SALVI and D. R. DUBBS: Activation of infectious SV40 DNA synthesis in transformed cells. Proc. Nat. Acad. Sci., USA. *60:1239–1246, 1968.*
7. KOPROWSKI, H., F. C. JENSEN and Z. STEPLEWSKI: Activation of production of infectious tumor virus SV40 in heterokaryon cultures. Proc. Nat. Acad. Sci., USA. *58:127–133, 1967.*
8. LEGLER, D. W., E. E. EVANS, P. F. WEINHEIMER, R. T. ACTON and M. H. ATTLEBERGER: Immunoglobulin and complement systems of amphibian serum. *In* Biology of Amphibian Tumors (M. Mizell, ed.), Springer-Verlag New York Inc., 1969, pp. 169–176.
9. MIZELL, M.: State of the art: Lucké renal adenocarcinoma. *In* Biology of Amphibian Tumors (M. Mizell, ed.), Springer-Verlag New York Inc., 1969, pp. 1–25.
10. MIZELL, M., C. W. STACKPOLE and S. HALPEREN: Herpes-type virus recovery from "virus-free" frog kidney tumors. Proc. Soc. Exp. Biol. and Med. *127:808–814, 1968.*

11. MIZELL, M., I. TOPLIN and J. J. ISAACS: Tumor induction in developing frog kidneys by a zonal centrifuge purified fraction of the frog herpes-type virus. Science *165*:1134–1137, 1969.

12. MIZELL, M. and J. ZAMBERNARD: Viral particles of the frog renal adenocarcinoma: causative agent or passenger virus? II. A promising model system for the demonstration of a "lysogenic" state in a metazoan tumor. Ann. N.Y. Acad. Sci. *126*:146–169, 1965.

13. OSATO, T. and Y. ITO: Immunofluorescence studies of Shope papilloma virus in cottontail rabbit kidney tissue cultures. Proc. Soc. Exp. Biol. and Med. *128*:1025–1029, 1968.

14. RAFFERTY, K. A.: Cultivation of an inclusion-associated virus from Lucké tumor frogs. Ann. N.Y. Acad. Sci. *126*:3–21, 1965.

15. STEVENS, J. G.: Selective inhibition of herpesvirus DNA synthesis at elevated temperature. Virology *29*:570–579, 1966.

16. TWEEDELL, K.: Induced oncogenesis in developing frog kidney cells. Cancer Res. *27*:2042–2052, 1967.

17. TOPLIN, I., P. BRANDT and P. SOTTONG: Density gradient centrifugation studies on the herpes-type virus of the Lucké tumor. *In* Biology of Amphibian Tumors (M. Mizell, ed.), Springer-Verlag New York Inc., 1969, pp. 348–357.

Density Gradient Centrifugation Studies on the Herpes-Type Virus of the Lucké Tumor

I. Toplin, P. Brandt and P. Sottong

The John L. Smith Memorial for Cancer Research
Chas. Pfizer & Co., Inc.
Maywood, New Jersey

The "virus-free" renal adenocarcinoma (Lucké tumor) of the frog has been shown by Mizell *et al.* (1) to develop herpes-type virus (HTV) when the tumor-bearing frogs are maintained at 7–8°C for several months. Tweedell (2) has shown that kidney tumors can be induced in frog embryos by HTV-positive tumor filtrates and subcellular fractions obtained by the differential centrifugation of tumor homogenates. We have fractionated several of these cold-treated tumors utilizing sucrose gradient zonal centrifugation followed by isopycnic banding of the virus zones for further purification. This report presents the results of these fractionation studies.

Materials and Methods

Tumor Preparation

Five tumors were supplied by M. Mizell of Tulane University and ranged in size from 1.4 to 9.0 grams. The histories of these frog tumors are given in Table 1. The first 3.4 grams of tumor (frogs A and B) were homogenized for 2 minutes in 10 volumes of 0.01M PBS [1] in a motor-driven Teflon-glass homogenizer (sample 1). The whole tumor homogenate served as the first zonal centrifuge sample.

The next three portions of tumor (samples 2, 3, and 4) weighed, respectively, 2.9 grams (frog C), 4.1 grams (frog C), and 6.9 grams (frogs D and E).

These samples were subjected to differential centrifugation prior to zonal centrifugation to effect preliminary fractionation of the tumors by procedures similar to those of Tweedell (2). The tumors were homogenized for 4 minutes in 10 volumes of 0.25M sucrose-TKM [1] (3) and centrifuged at 600 × g. for 15 minutes to deposit nuclei and intact cells. The supernatant (S1) was removed and the pellet (P1) was suspended in 10–20 ml 0.25M sucrose-TKM, rehomogenized 2 minutes and recentrifuged. The final washed P1 pellet, the "nuclear" fraction, was suspended in 20 ml 0.25M sucrose TKM (samples 2 and 3) or 40 ml hypotonic buffer [1] (sample 4). The combined S1 supernatants were centrifuged at 3000 × g. for 15 minutes to sediment mitochondria and subcellular debris. The P2 pellet, the "mitochondrial"

---

[1] The buffers used in this study were: PBS, 0.01M Na_2HPO_4, 0.14M NaCl, pH 7.0; TKM, 0.05M Tris, 0.025M KCl, 0.005M $MgCl_2$, pH 7.0 (See ref. 2); hypotonic buffer, 0.002M Tris, 0.002M EDTA, pH 7.0.

TABLE 1

Histories of Frog Tumors Used in Zonal Centrifuge Experiments [1]

Frog	Source	Sex	History	Tumor weight
A	Wisconsin	M	Natural "winter" tumor; frog received 12/67 and held 3 days at 7.5°C before sacrifice.	1.56 g.
B	Wisconsin	F	Natural "winter" tumor; frog received 12/67 and held 33 days at 7.5°C before death.	1.88 g.
C	Vermont	M	Normal frog received 2/67; tumor eye transplant 2/67; palpable kidney tumor [2] 6/67; held at 7.5°C from 9/67 until death on 2/68.	9.00 g.
D	Vermont	F	Normal frog received 2/67; tumor eye transplant 2/67; palpable kidney tumor [2] 12/67, held at 7.5°C from 2/68 until sacrificed on 5/68.	5.56 g.
E	Vermont	M	Normal frog received 2/67; tumor eye transplant 3/67; palpable kidney tumor [2] 11/67; held at 7.5°C from 2/68 until sacrificed on 5/68.	1.35 g.

[1] These histories were supplied by Dr. M. Mizell, Tulane University (supported by American Cancer Society Grant #E-494).

[2] After a tumor is palpated, the frog must be maintained at normal laboratory temperature for several months so that its tumor can grow to appreciable size before low temperature treatment is begun.

fraction, was suspended in 20 ml 0.25M sucrose-TKM (samples 2 and 3) or 40 ml hypotonic buffer (sample 4). The P2 supernatant was designated the "mitochondrial supernatant" fraction. For samples 2 and 3, the "mitochondrial" and "nuclear" suspensions were disrupted by 4 minutes sonication using the 60 watt MSE sonicator with the $\frac{3}{8}''$ probe. Sample 4 was freshly excised tumor which was treated rapidly at 0–4°C in an attempt to preserve potential infectivity. The "mitochondrial supernatant" and "mitochondrial" fractions were neither sonicated nor frozen, but were held at 0°C for 1 and 20 hours, respectively, before zonal centrifugation. All other samples were from frozen tumor and the fractions were stored at −70°C before zonal centrifugation.

Zonal Centrifugation

The B-XV rotor of the zonal centrifuge (4) with a total capacity of 1725 ml was used for the initial density gradient centrifugation of the various crude frog tumor fractions. One-liter sucrose gradients ranging from 10 to 60% (w/w) in 0.01M Tris, 0.002M, EDTA, pH 7, were employed. Samples were overlayed with 190 ml hypotonic buffer and the rotor contents were displaced at the end of the centrifugation period with either 60% sucrose or potassium citrate, density 1.35. The 50 ml fractions were collected through the flow cell of a recording spectrophotometer set at 265 mμ (Gilford Instruments, Oberlin, Ohio). The sucrose content of each fraction was determined by refractometry or pycnometry. The fractions of interest were diluted to 70 ml with hypotonic buffer and subjected to highspeed centrifugation at 66000 $\times$ g. for 90 minutes. The pellets from each fraction were suspended in 2–4 ml PBS by aspiration.

Isopycnic Banding

Selected viral concentrates from the rate-zonal separations in the B-XV rotor were banded isopycnically on preformed potassium tartrate or cesium chloride gradients using the Beckman SW 25.1 rotor. In these experiments, 2–3 ml of viral concentrate were layered on 25 ml of gradient, density 1.05 to 1.40 and centrifuged at 64000 $\times$ g. for 120–150 minutes. Sucrose gradients (10–60%) were also used in these studies although the centrifugation times were not sufficient to band the viruses isopycnically. After centrifugation, the tubes were bottom punctured and 1.5–2.5 ml fractions were collected. The density of each fraction was determined by refractometry. Fractions were diluted to 6 ml, overlayed with 6 ml mineral oil, and centrifuged at 93000 $\times$ g. for 60 minutes in the Beckman 40 rotor. In some cases, a drop of 6% gelatin was mixed with the diluted fractions before centrifugation to facilitate recognition of the virus pellet. The virus pellets were aspirated in 0.3–0.5 ml PBS and stored at $-70°$C until examined by electron microscopy.

Electron Microscopy

Virus suspensions were evaluated by a semi-quantitative negative staining method using 1:5 dilutions of sample in 2% potassium phosphotungstate, pH 4.5, containing 0.1% bovine serum albumin. The diluted sample was applied to 200-mesh carbon/Formvar-coated ionized copper grids and viewed in the Siemens Elmiscope 1A. Isopycnic banding fractions were also examined by a modification of the direct sedimentation virus quantitation method of Sharp and Beard (5), wherein known volumes of diluted samples were sedimented onto an agar plug. The virus layer was stripped off the agar on a film of parlodion and stained with potassium phosphotungstate (6).

Tumor tissue and pellets for sectioning were fixed in phosphate-buffered glutaraldehyde, postfixed in osmium and embedded in Epon. Thin sections were stained with lead citrate.

Protein Assays

Protein assays were carried out by the Lowry method (7) using crystalline bovine serum albumin as the assay standard.

Results and Discussion

All the frog tumor homogenates contained high concentrations of HTV with an estimated average of 5 $\times$ 10^{11} virus particles per gm of tumor. These tumors contained the range of morphological forms of the frog HTV previously observed in the cold-treated frog tumors (1). This included nucleated particles with and without outer envelopes, empty particles with and without outer envelopes, and a small percentage of particles having an amorphous outer coating on the capsid surface, presumably an antibody coating like that observed for the HTV from human lymphoma cells reacted with human HTV antisera (8). Empty uncoated particles without outer envelopes predominated. In addition, at least two of the tumors (frogs A and C) contained readily discernible structures in the tumor nuclei (Fig. 1) believed to be aberrant forms of viral protein (9). One of the frog tumors (frog D of sample 4) was distinguished by the large number of viral inclusions in the tumor nuclei; within the inclusion each virus was tightly enveloped by a closely bound membrane (Fig. 2). These tightly enveloped virus forms were observed to a lesser degree in frog C (Fig. 1b) and in the other frog tumors. Sample 1 also contained a high level of 55 mμ particles believed to be another frog HTV-related structure (9).

The rate-zonal centrifugation experiments on the various types of tumor preparations are summarized in Figs. 3–6. When sample 1, the whole tumor homogenate, was processed on the zonal centrifuge (Fig. 3), there was a wide spread of virus throughout the gradient. Some zones with elevated concentrations of certain morphological types of HTV were observed, as indicated in Fig. 3. The other zonal centrifuge experiments, where the "nuclear," "mitochondrial" and "mitochondrial supernatant" tumor fractions were processed individually, generally were more successful in separating the various forms of the frog HTV (Figs. 4, 5 and 6). Empty particles predominated in the lighter zones of the gradient, whereas nucleated particles concentrated in the denser zones of the gradients, above 40% sucrose, under the centrifugation conditions employed in these experiments.

Because of the observed oncogenicity of several fractions, the zonal centrifugation of the "mitochondrial" pellet from sample 4 is of particular interest (Fig. 5). Fractions 14 and 15, sucrose range 40.3 to 44.4% at ω^2t of 22.5 $\times$ 10^9 radians^2/sec, were highly enriched in the concentration of tightly enveloped particles (Fig. 7). The detailed results of the *in vivo* infectivity experiments with these and other fractions will be presented elsewhere (10).

In the isopycnic banding experiments, viral concentrates from the lighter, medium and denser zones of the sucrose rate-zonal runs were analyzed on preformed potassium tartrate, sucrose or cesium chloride gradients in the expectation of obtaining clean separation of the different morphological forms of the frog HTV. This is an application of the S-ρ principle of Anderson (4): sedimentation rate runs in the zonal centrifuge followed by isopycnic banding of the virus zones in small-tube rotors. To date, we have not been consistently successful in obtaining bands consisting exclusively of single morphological virus types. The zonal virus concentrates from the lighter end of the gradients generally yielded isopycnic tube fractions containing high (>90%) concentrations of empty virus particles. Similarly, isopycnic fractions high in nucleated particles (70–90%) were often but not always obtained from the zonal virus concentrates from the denser zones of the initial sucrose gradient centrifugation.

The isopycnic densities observed for the frog HTV can be compared to the isopycnic densities for infectious herpes simplex virions of 1.26–1.27 in cesium chloride (11). This was for fully nucleated enveloped herpes simplex virions. Most often the frog HTV empty naked particles banded at 1.17–1.21 in potassium tartrate and cesium chloride, whereas naked nucleated virus was observed at density 1.25–1.27 for potassium tartrate and 1.27–1.30 in cesium chloride. The so-called loosely enveloped frog HTV particles and the low numbers of coated particles observed after isopycnic band-

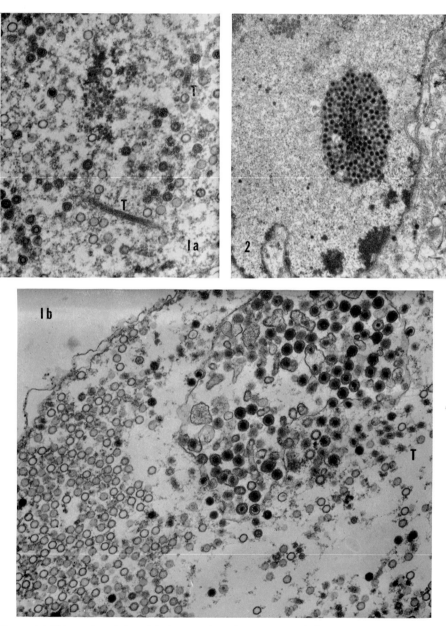

Fig. 1. (a) Thin-section of the original tumor from frog A. Note tubular structures (T). ×23,000. (b) Thin-section of "nuclear" pellet from frog C. Note tubular structures (T) and viral inclusion containing tightly enveloped viral forms. ×22,000.

Fig. 2. Thin-section of the original tumor from frog D. Note prominent viral inclusion within the nucleus containing tightly enveloped virus. ×9,000.

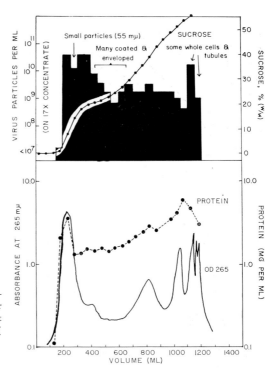

Fig. 3. Zonal centrifugation of whole tumor homogenate from 3.4 gms. of tumor (sample 1). The B-XV rotor was spun at 22,000 rpm for 20 minutes ($\omega^2 t$ of 6.8×10^9 radians^2/sec).

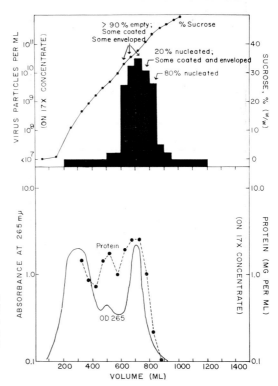

Fig. 4. Zonal centrifugation of the "mitochondrial supernatant" fraction of sample 4 from 7.0 gms. of tumor. The B-XV rotor was spun at 24,000 rpm for 60 minutes ($\omega^2 t$ of 22.9×10^9 radians^2/sec).

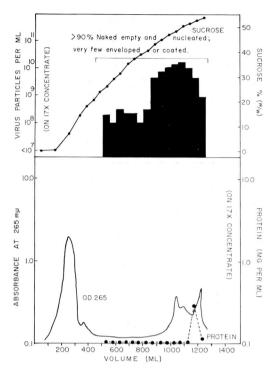

Fig. 5. Zonal centrifugation of the "nuclear" fraction of sample 2 from 2.9 gms. of tumor. The B-XV rotor was spun at 24,000 rpm for 120 minutes ($\omega^2 t$ of 46.1×10^9 radians^2/sec).

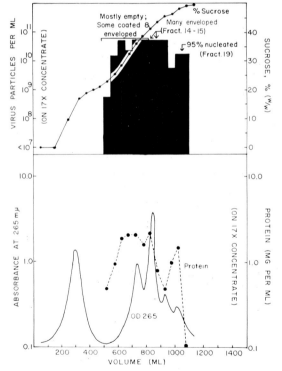

Fig. 6. Zonal centrifugation of the "mitochondrial" fraction of sample 4 from 7.0 gms. of tumor. The B-XV rotor was spun at 24,000 rpm for 60 minutes ($\omega^2 t$ of 22.5×10^9 radians^2/ sec).

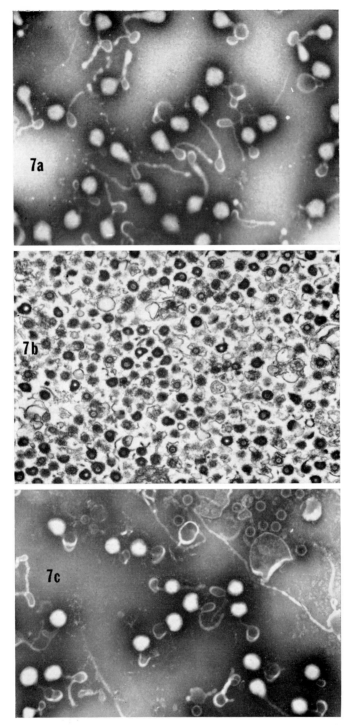

Fig. 7. Electron micrographs of viral concentrates from fractions 14 and 15 from zonal centrifugation of "mitochondrial" fraction of sample 4 (see Fig. 6). (a) Negative stain of fraction 14, concentrated 17-fold, ×26,500. (b) Thin section of pellet of fraction 14, ×17,500. (c) Negative stain of fraction 15, concentrated 17-fold, ×26,500.

ing were seen in a broad density range from 1.13–1.21 in potassium tartrate. Fraction 14 from the zonal centrifugation of the mitochondrial suspension of sample 4, rich in tightly enveloped frog HTV (Figs. 7a, b) banded sharply at density 1.20–1.21 in sucrose after three hours centrifugation at 25,000 rpm in the SW 25.1 rotor. The 55 mμ particles seen in sample 1 banded sharply at density 1.16 in potassium tartrate.

It should be mentioned that the amounts of virus placed on the 25 ml preformed gradients were in the range of 2–10 $\times$ 10^{10} particles, and often visible bands were not observable at certain isopycnic density levels in the tubes where significant concentrations of virus could be detected by electron microscopic examination. After concentration by high-speed centrifugation, these isopycnically banded virus fractions often contained greater than 10^{11} v.p./ml and less than 0.05 mg/ml total protein, an indication of their relatively high purity. But we are not at all satisfied with the results of our isopycnic banding work. Frequently, isopycnic fractions high in total virus concentration were observed to contain high percentages of both nucleated and empty particles. Assuming that our negative staining procedures are giving us the true picture of the virus types present in these tube bands, we are presently studying the possibilities that these anomalous results are caused by virus association or virus instability. The effects of such treatments as proteolytic enzyme digestion, fluorocarbon extraction, and formaldehyde stabilization are being investigated in the isopycnic work on the frog HTV in progress.

Summary

"Virus-free" kidney tumors of frogs which had been subjected to prolonged low temperature treatment to induce formation of herpes-type virus (HTV) were fractionated on sucrose gradients in the B-XV zonal centrifuge rotor under a variety of centrifugation conditions. The tumors consistently yielded fractions with high concentrations of HTV, covering the full range of herpesvirus morphology. This included nucleated and empty particles, enveloped particles, and a small percentage of virus coated presumably with antibody. Application of the S-ρ principle of Anderson (NCI Monograph 21, 1966), rate-zonal centrifugation in the B-XV rotor followed by isopycnic banding of the virus zones in small-tube rotors, resulted in highly purified virus concentrates enriched in single morphological types. Differential centrifugation as employed by Tweedell for this tumor (Cancer Research, 27:2042, 1967) was also used in the purification procedures. Virus fractions were used for *in vivo* infectivity experiments and fractions enriched in a tightly enveloped form of the virus have shown oncogenicity when injected into frog embryos.

Acknowledgments

We would like to acknowledge the guidance of Dr. J. Monroe for electron microscopy, and the technical assistance of K. Munch, V. Caferella, B. Stankaitis and C. Etelman.

This work was carried out under Contract PH 43-66-98 within the Special Virus Leukemia Program of the National Cancer Institute.

References

1. MIZELL, M., STACKPOLE, C. W., and HALPEREN, S.: Herpes-type virus recovery from "virus-free" frog kidney tumors. Proc. Soc. Exp. Biol. Med., *127*:808–814, 1968.

2. TWEEDELL, K. S.: Induced oncogenesis in developing frog kidney cells. Cancer Research, *27*:2042–2052, 1967.

3. BLOBEL, G., and POTTER, V. R.: Nuclei from rat liver: isolation method that combines purity with high yield. Science, *154*:1662–1665, 1966.

4. ANDERSON, N. G.: The development of zonal centrifuges and ancillary systems for tissue fractionation and analysis. National Cancer Institute Monograph 21, 1966.

5. SHARP, D. G., and BEARD, J.: Counts of virus particles by sedimentation on agar and electron micrography. Proc. Soc. Exp. Biol. Med., *81*:75–79, 1952.

6. SMITH, K. O., and BENYESH-MELNICK, M.: Particle counting of polyoma virus. Proc. Soc. Exp. Biol. Med., *107*:409–413, 1961.

7. LOWRY, O. H., ROSEBROUGH, N., FARR, A., and RANDALL, R.: Protein measurement with the Folin phenol reagent. J. Biol. Chem., *193*:265–275, 1951.

8. MAYYASI, S. A., SCHIDLOVSKY, G., BULFONE, L., and BUSCHECK, F.: The coating reaction of the herpes-type virus isolated from malignant tissue with an antibody present in sera. Cancer Research, *27*:2020–2024, 1967.

9. STACKPOLE, C. W., and MIZELL, M.: Electron microscopic observations on herpes-type virus-related structures in the frog renal adenocarcinoma. Virology, *36*:63–72, 1968.

10. MIZELL, M., TOPLIN, I., and ISAACS, J. J.: Tumor induction in developing frog kidneys by a zonal centrifuge purified fraction of the frog herpes-type virus. Science *165*:1134–1137, 1969.

11. ROIZMAN, B., and ROANE, P. R., JR.: A physical difference between two strains of herpes simplex virus apparent on sedimentation in cesium chloride. Virology, *15*:75–79, 1961.

Reactivity of Serum from Frogs and Other Species with a Herpesvirus Antigen Extracted from a Burkitt Lymphoma Cultured Cell Line

Mary A. Fink,[1] Gladys S. King,[2] and Merle Mizell [3]

Since 1964, when Epstein *et al.* (1) described the presence of herpesvirus in cultured cells of a biopsy of Burkitt lymphoma, many investigators from various parts of the world have confirmed and extended this observation. To date, cell lines have been successfully grown in culture from at least 125 individuals (2). Of those derived from malignant states, including leukemia and lymphoma, 44 of 105 tested or 42 percent contained a herpesvirus morphologically indistinguishable from that originally described by Epstein. Of those derived from normal persons or those with other diseases, 4 of 19 or 21 percent contained a similar herpesvirus. Despite intensive efforts in several laboratories, this virus has not been identified as a known herpesvirus. The term EBV—Epstein-Barr virus—has been suggested as a name for this unidentified herpesvirus strain.

Various serological methods have been used to test for antibody to antigens of EBV in the serums of man and animals. In a recent survey of methods (3), four were found to be positive only when virus was present and negative when virus was absent. These included complement fixation (4), indirect fixed-cell immunofluorescence (5), an antibody coating reaction (6), and immunodiffusion (7). One of these, immunodiffusion, is the reaction by which we have shown an antigen in common in EBV and a similar herpesvirus isolated from the Lucké adenocarcinoma of frogs (8).

The use of immunodiffusion in the human system was an outgrowth of work in murine leukemia (9, 10). While working on various serological procedures for the detection of antigen and antibody in this system, we adapted a highly sensitive immunodiffusion technique to the identification and the delineation of antigens of the nucleoid and of the outer coat of the virion of the murine leukemia virus. When a Rhesus monkey antiserum to the virus reacts with the virion, at least three bands of precipitation are characteristically seen. One of these represents antigen which has diffused little if at all; the two other precipitin lines represent much smaller antigenic components which obviously have diffused through the agar and reacted with antibody. What is the evidence that these are viral antigens? By treating the virus with tween and ether and isolating the antigen of the nucleoid in pure form on a sucrose

---

[1] Immunology Section, Viral Leukemia and Lymphoma Branch, National Cancer Institute, National Institutes of Health, Bethesda, Maryland.

[2] Department of Biology, Trinity College, Washington, D.C.

[3] Department of Biology, Tulane University, New Orleans, Louisiana, supported by American Cancer Society Grant #E-494.

gradient, we have identified which of the precipitin lines is attributable to "g," the group specific antigen of murine leukemia viruses (11). By using this isolated antigen in immunodiffusion on the same template as the intact virus, we can see clearly that one antigen which has diffused from whole virus is indeed identical to the isolated group antigen. This is unequivocal evidence that the virus undergoes degradation during its 48-hour incubation at room temperature, with consequent release of subviral components which diffuse through the agar.

In early work, using this technique with EBV antigen to test for antibody in human serums, one precipitin band was characteristically found (7). Regardless of the origin of the serums, only 50–60 percent reacted, with a somewhat higher percentage of adult serums reacting than those from children. When a stronger antigen, i.e., one containing much more virus, became available, over 90 percent of the serums tested reacted (Table 1). With the strong antigen, two precipitin lines, "a" and "b" indicative of reactivity with two antigens of EBV, were usually formed. Occasionally as many as four precipitin lines were present. Evidence that these reactions are due to viral antigens as opposed to cellular is as follows:

(1) When density gradient isolates of the extracted virus are tested, only isolates in which virus is detectable by electron microscopy are reactive. Bands above and below this point are negative.

(2) Even when the isolated band from virus containing material is tested, unless the virus is a high concentration—approximately 500 particles per grid square— negative results are consistently obtained. This material would be expected to contain all of the cellular debris characteristic of this density isolate, yet in the absence of sufficient virus it is not reactive.

TABLE 1

HUMAN SERUMS TESTED BY IMMUNODIFFUSION WITH
EBV ANTIGEN (P-3)

| | Reaction with | | | |
| | Low virus count antigen | | High virus count antigen | |
Diagnosis	No. +	% +	No. +	% +
Burkitt's lymphoma *	11/20	55	29/30 †	97
Control *	13/20	65		
Lymphoma	1/4	[25]	1/1 †	[100]
Leukemia	22/35	63	42/48 †	88
Other malignancy	8/16	50	7/7 †	100
Infectious mononucleosis			31/36	86
Other pathology			34/36 †	94
Normal	17/30	57	32/34 †	94

* Serums of African origin. All other are North American.

† The bulk of these serums were also tested with two non-virus containing cell lines, P-1 and N-37, with negative results.

(3) Antigens extracted from cell lines not known to contain the herpesvirus have been consistently negative in this reaction.

(4) In a double blind study using four antigens and 133 coded serums, positive reactions occurred only with extracts of the two cell lines containing virus, not with the two cell lines which lacked virus.

(5) Representative serums, absorbed with blood group substances and with cultured Hela, Chang liver, KB, Hep^2, and Wish cells, retained their reactivity with EBV, precluding the possibility that the reaction is specific for alloantigens.

The extent of reactivity of human serums shown by the immunodiffusion technique in our laboratory is in disagreement with that reported by Old et al. (12), who used an antigen extracted from similar cells. Not only do they find fewer serums reactive, but they also have been unable to demonstrate cross-reactivity between antigens of EBV isolated from different cell lines. We have shown reactions with virus isolated from five different cell lines. The discrepancy in results is explainable by the difference in sensitivity of the test as used in the two laboratories. At least three investigators have independently shown that the microimmunodiffusion test in which a template is used, and in which a cadmium developing buffer is used, increases the sensitivity to a remarkable degree.

Materials and Methods

Antigen

Antigens were prepared by Toplin from both the P-3 line of Burkitt lymphoma and from the adenocarcinoma of frogs supplied by Mizell. The methods used by Toplin have been described in this monograph. Four different preparations, each containing at least 0.5×10^{10} virus particles per ml., have given positive reactions. One preparation was negative.

Herpes simplex virus, obtained through the courtesy of Mr. George Yee, National Institute of Allergy and Infectious Diseases, was also used as an antigen.

Serums

Human serums from Burkitt lymphoma patients were obtained by the Resources Branch of the Special Virus-Cancer Program of the National Cancer Institute. Frog serums, including those from one, two, and three-year-old *Rana pipiens pipiens* from Vermont were supplied by Dr. Gladys King. She also supplied one serum from a North Carolina frog, *Rana pipiens sphenocephala*. Some of these frogs had been held in the laboratory under different storage treatments, as detailed later. Other serums tested included those from a variety of primates and domestic animals, largely supplied through the courtesy of Dr. Paul Gerber of the Division of Biologic Standards, National Institutes of Health.

Guinea pig anti-herpes simplex serum, obtained from National Institute of Allergy and Infectious Diseases, was also tested.

Technique

The immunodiffusion tests were performed as described previously using a plastic template which was impressed over agarose on a microscopic slide. After filling the reactant wells, the templates were incubated in a humidified chamber at room temperature for 48 hours, after which they were removed and the precipitin lines developed with a buffer containing cadmium.

Results

Results of the testing of frog serums with EBV are given in Table 2. Frogs in each age category reacted with the antigen. Only three frog serums, including one from a Vermont frog with a massive tumor, one from a three-year-old Vermont frog, and one from a frog of a species not known to be associated in any way with the Lucké adenocarcinoma, gave negative reactions. Because of the limited amount of antigen extracted from the frog tumor, only a few frog serums were tested with frog antigen. There was sufficient antigen, however, to demonstrate a reaction of complete identity between antigen "a" of EBV and the antigen of the herpesvirus of the Lucké tumor. This is represented in Fig. 1. Neither the EBV or the frog antigen reacted with the herpes simplex antibody, nor did positive frog serums react with herpes simplex antigen.

The results of testing serums from domestic animals and primates with EBV, and to a limited extent with the frog tumor antigen, are given in Table 3. At least one animal of each species of the domestic animals tested (including goat, cat, sheep, dog, horse, and cow) reacted strongly with the EBV antigen. The one goat serum tested and the one horse serum tested reacted strongly with the frog antigen, the two serums reacting in a line of identity. A cat serum reacted weakly with the frog antigen.

TABLE 2

REACTIONS OF FROG * SERUMS WITH EBV ANTIGEN

Years of age	Treatment	No. + "a" line	No. −
1	None	1	0
	5 mos. 25°	6	0
2	None	1	1 †
	1–2 mos. 25°	7	0
	5 mos. 25°	9	0
3	None	0	2 ‡
	5 mos. 25°	9 §	0
Total		33	3

  * *Rana pipiens pipiens* from Vermont with one exception.

  † *R. pipiens sephenocephala* from North Carolina.

  ‡ One bearing massive tumor with no residual kidney.

  § Including 1 serum with both "a" and "b" lines.

TABLE 3

REACTIONS OF VARIOUS ANIMAL SERUMS WITH ANTIGEN "a" OF EBV
AND LUCKÉ ADENOCARCINOMA

Species	No. +/Total (EBV antigen)		No. +/Total (Lucké antigen)	
	Strong reaction	Weak reaction	Strong reaction	Weak reaction
Goat	2/2		1/1	
Cat	1/2	1/2		1/1
Sheep	1/2	1/2 *		
Dog	2/2			
Horse	1/2	1/2	1/1	
Cow	2/2			
Rhesus	13/14	1/14	0/1	
Vervet	1/2	1/2		
Cynomologous	2/2			
Baboon	2/2			1/1

* This animal also reacted with "b" antigen of EBV.

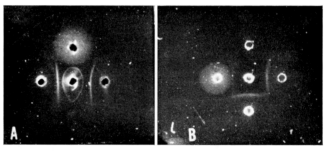

Fig. 1. Reaction of Burkitt lymphoma patient's serums and frog serums with virus isolated from Burkitt lymphoma and from Lucké frog tumor.

	9 o'clock	12 o'clock	3 o'clock	6 o'clock	Center well
A.	Burkitt Serum 48	Frog #3	Burkitt Serum 37	—	Burkitt herpesvirus
B.	Frog #1	—	Burkitt Serum 35	Burkitt Serum 35	Frog herpesvirus

Discussion

The studies described using the immunodiffusion test show clearly that a viral antigen, antigen "a" of the herpesvirus isolated from a Burkitt lymphoma cultured cell line, is identical to an antigen of a herpesvirus in the Lucké frog tumor. Antibodies to this antigen have been found in almost all human serums tested, regardless of the age, diagnosis or geographical origin of the donors. Antibodies to this "a" antigen have also been found in a high percentage of a limited number of serums from domestic animals, and from primates. This is in contrast to the report by Gerber (4) of a high incidence in primates, but an absence in the serum of domestic animals. This can be explained on the basis of the sensitivity of the reaction. The serum is used undiluted in immunodiffusion and at a 1:30 dilution in complement fixation. If technical problems in using complement fixation at a lower dilution could be worked out, it would be expected that the domestic animal serums would also be found to be positive in this test.

It has come to our attention that the coating reaction has been used in an attempt to show cross reactivity between the virus from the Lucké adenocarcinoma of the frog and EBV. No reaction was demonstrable when human Burkitt serums positive with the EBV were tested with virus of the frog tumor, although an antiserum prepared against the frog virus did react. This observation is in contrast to the results with immunodiffusion. If one considers the geographic site of antigens within the virion, however, the reason for this discrepancy becomes obvious. For example, if the antigen being tested is not on the surface of the virion, one would not expect the coating reaction to occur, even if antibody to an internal antigen were present. But one would expect, following viral degradation, that internal antigens of the virus would diffuse through the medium and that then a positive reaction would occur. Based on this negative coating reaction, the inference could be drawn that the antigen is not a surface antigen. When compared to antigens of a murine leukemia virus, in which the antigen of the nucleoid was shown to be the fastest diffusing antigen and outer coat antigens diffuse at a slower rate, the cross-reactive antigen in EBV and the Lucké tumor, not being the fastest diffusing antigen of EBV, could not be judged to be in the nucleoid. Thus, until definitive work is done, the hypothesis that this antigen is in the outer coat of the virion, but not at its surface, would appear to be tenable.

The observations reported indicate that there is broad reactivity throughout the animal kingdom to an antigen present in EBV and the virus associated with a frog tumor. That these observations are meritorious or of little consequence to oncology, depends upon the ultimate determination of the etiological significance of the herpesvirus described by Epstein *et al.* (1) to human lymphoma, and the significance of the herpesvirus first described by Fawcett (13) to the Lucké adenocarcinoma of frogs.

Summary

Since Epstein's isolation of a herpes virus from the tissues of a Burkitt lymphoma patient, several investigators have established similar cell cultures from Burkitt lymphoma and from the peripheral blood of leukemia cases and from individuals with no known pathology. These cultures often have yielded a herpes-type virus which is not identifiable as known herpesvirus. The technique of immunodiffusion has been used to test for antibodies in human serums to a viral concentrate prepared from selected virus-rich cell lines.

Similarly, the serums from frogs and other species were tested against the Burkitt herpes virus in immunodiffusion tests, to give positive results. An antigen extract rich in herpes virus from a renal adenocarcinoma of a frog was also used as an antigen in studies with both human and frog serums. The results of these tests are reported.

References

1. EPSTEIN, M. A., ACHONG, B. G., and BARR, Y. M.: Virus particles in cultured lymphoblasts from Burkitt's lymphoma. Lancet *1*:702–703, 1964.

2. RAUSCHER, F. J.: Virologic studies in human leukemia and lymphoma: the herpes-type virus. Cancer Res. *28*:1311–1318, 1968.

3. IMMUNOLOGY SUB-GROUP, Special Virus-Cancer Program: Results of a comparison of serological tests used to detect human antibodies to a herpesvirus (EBV) associated with Burkitt's lymphoma. J. Nat. Cancer Inst. *42*:623–631, 1969.

4. GERBER, P., and BURCH, S. M.: Complement-fixing antibodies in sera of human and non-human primates to viral antigens derived from Burkitt's lymphoma cells. Proc. Nat. Acad. Sci. *58*:478–484, 1967.

5. HENLE, G., and HENLE, W.: Immunofluorescence in cells derived from Burkitt's lymphoma. J. Bact. *91*:1248–1256, 1966.

6. MAYYASI, S. A., SCHIDLOVSKY, G., BULFONE, L. M., and BUSCHECK, F. T.: The coating reaction of the herpes-type virus isolated from malignant tissues with an antibody present in sera. Cancer Res. *27*:2020–2024, 1967.

7. FINK, M. A., and COWLES, C. A.: Use of immunological techniques in the study of human leukemia. In Proc. Intnl. Conference on Leukemia and Lymphoma (C. J. D. Zarafonetis, ed.), Philadelphia, Lea and Febiger: 155–162, 1968.

8. FINK, M. A., KING, G. S., and MIZELL, M.: Preliminary note: identity of a herpesvirus antigen from Burkitt lymphoma of man and the Lucké adenocarcinoma of frogs. J. Nat. Cancer Inst. *41*:1477–1478, 1968.

9. FINK, M. A., and COWLES, C. A.: Immunodiffusion: Detection of a murine leukemia virus (Rauscher). Science *150*:1723–1725, 1965.

10. FINK, M. A., COWLES, C. A., CHIRIGOS, M. A., and MESSORE, J.: A comparison by several techniques of the antibody prepared in various species against the Rauscher murine leukemia virus. NCI Monog. *22*:439–447, 1966.

11. FINK, M. A., SIBAL, L. R., WIVEL, N. A., COWLES, C. A., and O'CONNOR, T. E.: Some characteristics of an isolated group antigen common to most strains of murine leukemia virus. Virology *37*:605–614, 1969.

12. OLD, L. J., BOYSE, E. A., OETTGEN, H. F., DE HARVEN, E., GEERING, G., WILLIAMSON, B., and CLIFFORD, P.: Precipitating antibody in human serum to an antigen present in cultured Burkitt's lymphoma cells. Proc. Nat. Acad. Sci. *56*:1699–1704, 1966.

13. FAWCETT, D. W.: Electron microscopic observations on intracellular virus-like particles associated with the cells of the Lucké renal adenocarcinoma. J. Biophys. Biochem. Cytol. *2*:725–742, 1956.

A Preliminary Report on the Serology of Lucké and Burkitt Herpes-type Viruses: A Shared Antigen

John M. Kirkwood, Gayla Geering, Lloyd J. Old,[*]
Merle Mizell,[†] and John Wallace [‡]

Serological analysis of the Herpes-type virus (HTV) associated with cell lines derived from patients with Burkitt lymphoma has revealed two classes of antigens: a) soluble components detected by immunoprecipitation (12), and b) capsid antigens, most clearly demonstrated by coating reactions visualized by electron microscopy (4, 9). Immunoprecipitation, immunofluorescence, and complement-fixation tests indicate a high incidence of antibody to Burkitt HTV antigen in human populations (3, 5, 6, 7, 12). This antibody is found most frequently in patients with Burkitt lymphoma, lymphosarcoma, chronic lymphatic leukemia, and nasopharyngeal carcinoma (11). Naturally occurring antibodies to antigens related to this virus are not restricted to man, but are also found in the chimpanzee, and other subhuman primates (3, 11).

In Amphibia, two classes of virus have been associated with the Lucké renal adenocarcinoma: a) polyhedral cytoplasmic viruses, described in this volume by Drs. Granoff, Zeigel, and Lunger, and b) virus of Herpes type, first described by Fawcett (2).

Immunological studies of the polyhedral cytoplasmic viruses have not indicated any relation of these agents to the etiology of the Lucké tumor (1, 8). Recently, we have begun a serological study of the HTV associated with the Lucké tumor (10). Rabbits were immunized with Lucké HTV, purified by zonal centrifugation as described by Dr. I. Toplin in this volume. The preparations used for immunization consisted primarily of non-enveloped capsids. The resulting antisera (*Rabbit anti Lucké HTV*), after absorption with extracts of normal *Rana pipiens* kidney, gave a strong band of precipitation in micro-Ouchterlony immunoprecipitation tests (0.5% agar) with the Lucké HTV. This band appears to be complex, resolving under certain conditions into three distinct lines. Unrelated hyperimmune rabbit sera, including an antiserum to one of the polyhedral cytoplasmic frog viruses (*Rabbit anti FV3*) (1), did not precipitate Lucké HTV; nor did absorbed *Rabbit anti Lucké HTV* serum react with extracts of normal *R. pipiens* tissues—showing the reaction to be specific for Lucké HTV. Thus, serological reagents are now available for the study of both the polyhedral cytoplasmic viruses and HTV of amphibia.

---

[*] Division of Immunology, Sloan-Kettering Institute for Cancer Research, and Sloan-Kettering Division, Cornell University Graduate School of Medical Sciences, Cornell University Medical College, New York, New York. Supported by NCI grant CA 08748, and grants from the John A. Hartford Foundation, Inc. and the New York Cancer Research Institute, Inc.

[†] Department of Biology, Tulane University, New Orleans, Louisiana, supported by American Cancer Society Grant #E-494.

[‡] Departments of Microbiology and Surgery, Tulane University, New Orleans, Louisiana.

Investigation of the sera of a variety of amphibians, including *Pipa pipa*, *Bufo marinus*, *R. catesbeiana*, *R. clamitans*, *R. sphenocephala*, and *R. pipiens*, revealed the existence of natural antibody to HTV in 9 of 115 normal *R. pipiens* from Vermont, and 4 of 5 Wisconsin and Vermont *R. pipiens* with the Lucké tumor (E. G. Steinhilber & Co., Oshkosh, Wis. and Connecticut Valley Biological Co., Southampton, Mass.). Positive frog sera and *Rabbit anti Lucké HTV* gave reactions of identity in immunoprecipitation tests with Lucké HTV. This occurrence of natural antibody to the Lucké HTV in frogs invites comparison with the similar occurrence of natural antibody to the Burkitt HTV in man and subhuman primates (3, 11).

Purified Burkitt HTV (P3V) was kindly provided by Dr. E. M. Jensen, Chas. Pfizer & Co., Maywood, New Jersey. This preparation of P3V was strongly precipitated by *Rabbit anti Lucké HTV* serum. Fifteen unrelated hyperimmune rabbit sera did not react with Burkitt HTV. Absorption of the *Rabbit anti Lucké HTV* serum with Burkitt P3V eliminated precipitating activity against Lucké HTV, and against Burkitt HTV. The Burkitt and Lucké viruses thus share common antigens, presumably capsid components.

Fig. 1 illustrates the results obtained in immunoprecipitation tests with *Rabbit anti Lucké HTV (LV)* serum and *R. pipiens* serum. Both rabbit and frog sera precipitate the Lucké virus (LV), giving a reaction of identity. *Rabbit anti Lucké HTV* serum is shown also to precipitate the Burkitt P3V, giving reactions of identity with the Lucké virus; this is not well illustrated in Fig. 1, but was verified in other tests. *Rabbit anti FV3* serum reacts neither with Lucké HTV, nor with Burkitt HTV.

The antigenic similarity between Lucké HTV and Burkitt HTV was unexpected, considering their origin from such widely disparate species. This may indicate a com-

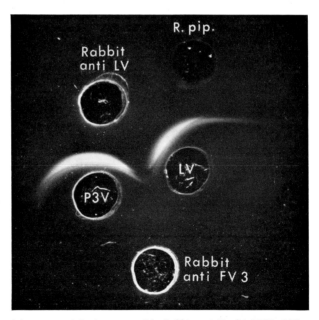

Fig. 1. Results of immunoprecipitation tests with *Rabbit anti Lucké HTV (LV)* serum and *Rana pipiens* serum.

mon group antigen of herpesviruses or, alternatively, an antigen shared by those HTV associated with neoplasia. In this regard, it will be rewarding to study the HTV associated with neurolymphomatosis of chickens (Marek's disease).

Addendum

Rabbit anti Lucké HTV has been found to precipitate nucleocapsid preparations of Herpes simplex virus (provided by Dr. B. Roizman, the University of Chicago, Chicago, Ill.) and cytomegalovirus strains C87 (human) and GR 2757 (simian) (provided by Dr. R. McCombs, Baylor University School of Medicine, Houston, Tex.). Ouchterlony analysis in conjunction with absorption tests indicate that *Rabbit anti Lucké HTV* detects a group antigen of the herpesviruses, presumably located on the virus nucleocapsid.

References

1. CAME, P. E., GEERING, G., OLD, L. J. and BOYSE, E. A.: A serological study of polyhedral cytoplasmic viruses. Virology 36:392–400 (1968).
2. FAWCETT, D. W.: Electron microscope observations of intracellular virus-like particles associated with the cells of the Lucké renal adenocarcinoma. J. Biophys. Biochem. Cytol. 2:725–742 (1956).
3. GERBER, P. and BIRCH, S. M.: Complement-fixing antibodies in sera of human and nonhuman primates to viral antigens derived from Burkitt's lymphoma cells. Proc. Natl. Acad. Sci. U.S. 58:478–484, 1967.
4. HENLE, W., HUMMLER, K. and HENLE, G.: Antibody coating and agglutination of virus particles separated from the EB3 line of Burkitt lymphoma cells. J. Bacteriol. 92:269–271, 1966.
5. HENLE, G. and HENLE, W.: Immunofluorescence in cells derived from Burkitt's lymphoma. J. Bacteriol. 91:1248–1256, 1966b.
6. HENLE, G. and HENLE, W.: Studies on cell lines derived from Burkitt's lymphoma. Trans. N.Y. Acad. Sci., Ser. 2 29:71–79, 1966a.
7. KLEIN, G., CLIFFORD, P., KLEIN, E. and STERNSWÄRD, J.: Search for tumor-specific immune reactions in Burkitt lymphoma patients by the membrane immunofluorescence reaction. Proc. Natl. Acad. Sci. U.S. 55:1628–1635, 1966.
8. LEHANE, D. E. JR., CLARK, H. F. and KARZON, D. T.: Antigenic relationships among frog viruses demonstrated by the plaque-reduction and neutralization kinetic tests. Virology 34:590–595, 1968.
9. MAYYASI, S. A., SCHIDLOVSKY, G. S., BULFONE, L. M. and BUSCHEK, F. T.: The coating reaction of the Herpes-type virus isolated from malignant tissues with antibody present in sera. Cancer Research 27:2020–2024, 1967.
10. MIZELL, M., STACKPOLE, C. W. and HALPEREN, S.: Herpes-type virus recovery from virus-free frog kidney tumors. Proc. Soc. Exp. Biol. Med. 127:808–814, 1968.
11. OLD, L. J., BOYSE, E. A., GEERING, G. and OETTGEN, H. F.: Serologic approaches to the study of cancer in animals and man. Cancer Research 28:1288–1299, 1968.
12. OLD, L. J., BOYSE, E. A., OETTGEN, H. F., DEHARVEN, E., GEERING, G., WILLIAMSON, B. and CLIFFORD, P.: Precipitating antibody in human serum to an antigen present in cultured Burkitt's lymphoma cells. Proc. Natl. Acad. Sci. U.S. 56:1699–1704, 1966.

Possible Immunological Factors in Amphibian Lymphosarcoma Development[1]

Laurens N. Ruben [2]

Department of Biology
Reed College
Portland, Oregon

Introduction

Spontaneous lymphoid cancers in *Xenopus laevis* (the South African clawed toad) were first described by Balls in 1962 (1). These growths are lethal, and appear primarily in the hematopoietic organs: the liver, spleen and kidneys. *Xenopus* is a primitive anuran and shares with the more primitive urodeles the use of the liver subcapsular epithelium as a granulocytic organ and with the more advanced anurans the kidney as an emergency source of lymphocytes (2, 3). The disease is not limited to these organs, however, and on occasions the cancer will develop in all other viscera and, less frequently, in the head, trunk and limb musculature.

When cellular implants of *Xenopus* lymphosarcoma were made into the abdominal cavities of *Triturus cristatus* (the European crested newt), lymphoid cancers developed in the visceral organs, particularly the liver, spleen and kidneys. Transfer of cellular fragments of these newt tumors back to *Xenopus* led to the development of toad lymphosarcomas. Since newt lymphoid cells are morphologically distinguishable from *Xenopus* cells, it could be shown that the tumors were always composed of host and not of donor cells (4). Lymphosarcoma implants from *X. laevis* also initiated the formation of similar tumors in other *Xenopus* species and subspecies, and in other anuran species, e.g., *Bufo bufo bufo* and *Rana esculenta* (5). All of these early heterogeneic implant experiments, along with allogeneic implant transfers into *Xenopus* forelimbs (6), suggested that the donor cancer material was destroyed and that a subcellular agent was thereby released to infect the host.

That particular allogeneic implant study called attention to several interesting characteristics of the phenomenon of transmission by viable lymphosarcoma which were recorded but not explicable at the time. For instance, it was noted that inflammatory responses to the implanted tumor tissue appeared to cycle. There was an initial

[1] The work upon which this report is based was partially supported by a grant (CAO-8268) of the National Cancer Institute, National Institutes of Health, Bethesda, Maryland, U.S.A.

[2] The author wishes to acknowledge the assistance of Jean M. Stevens and aid of Mr. Jeffrey Drucker and Mr. Martin Elliot for their contributions in studying the temperature effects described in the text, and is grateful to Dr. Michael Balls and Dr. Nicholas Cohen for critical reading of the manuscript.

phase which began by 17 days post-implantation and built dramatically during the following two weeks. By 41 days, however, the inflammation had subsided and the animals were free of grossly visible response in the implant site during the succeeding two weeks, only to be subjected to a renewal of inflammation. This second active period had all but disappeared by 61 days post-implantation and did not reappear before the end of the experiment at 72 days.

In addition to observing this cyclical activity, we pointed out that the intensity of the response to viable lymphosarcoma far exceeded any allograft response we had ever observed while using normal, non-lymphoid implants.

Finally, we noted that not only did implanted lymphosarcoma material undergo destruction during the third week following implantation, but metastases (or multi-focal sites) also broke down.

General experiences over the years with literally thousands of *Xenopus* used in tumor transmission experiments indicated that whether the tumor was observed to be healthy or necrotic depended on the time within the experimental period at which the animal was killed or died. These four observations set the stage for this report.

Further information concerning the transmission of this lymphosarcoma was obtained using *Xenopus, Diemictylus viridescens* (the common American newt, formerly *Triturus viridescens*) and *Rana pipiens* (the leopard frog). It was found, for instance, that freshly biopsied and frozen-killed lymphosarcoma implants from *Xenopus* donors could initiate lymphosarcoma in newt and frog and further that cell-free homogenates (10–15% w/v) made from *Xenopus, Diemictylus* and *Rana* lymphosarcoma could also be used to pass the cancer to any or all kinds of hosts utilized (7).

In characterizing the cancer-initiating agent biologically, we have found that it is resistant to freezing and thawing, freeze-drying, sonication, penicillin, streptomycin, and kanamycin, but is thermolabile and sensitive to ether and chloroform. It passes a 100 mμ but not a 10 mμ filter and while remaining in the supernatant fluid following one hour at 30,000 $\times$ g centrifugation, it is gradually lost from the supernatant fluid during centrifugation at 40,000 $\times$ g. Cultures of infective 30,000 $\times$ g supernatant fluid proved to be negative for bacteria or fungi and bacterial cultures, including those of acid-fast bacteria, made from tumor and normal tissue failed to pass the disease. Mycobacteria are ubiquitous in Amphibia and have been found as inconstant residents of more mature foci. Their presence seems more indicative of secondary invasion than of cancer causation. They are kanamycin sensitive and do not pass 220 mμ filtration (Ruben and Stevens, unpublished observations). The agent appears likely to be a small virus with a lipid component in the coat (8, 9). In sucrose density gradients (Ruben and Balls, unpublished) infectivity can be recovered from a number of fractions. This might be due to lipid variation in the coat, irregularity in agent shape, or to aggregation of the agent. Two important gaps in our knowledge at present are that the agent has not yet been visualized in the electron microscope and that we do not know its nucleic acid character.

The Intensity of Inflammation

In order to ascertain whether the extreme host response noted earlier to viable lymphosarcoma implants was peculiar to the tumor material or related to its lymphoid nature, 20 young, post-metamorphic *Xenopus laevis,* bred in the laboratory, were implanted with both allogeneic normal spleen and lymphosarcoma material. An implant of spleen (1 mm^3) was placed subcutaneously in a dorsal position on the radio-ulnar portion of the left forearm, while a comparably-sized piece of kidney-developed lymphosarcoma was implanted in a similar position in the right forearm. Three animals were chosen at random for sacrifice at five weekly intervals and histological preparations were made of each implant site and of the liver, spleen and kidney. In addition, macroscopic observations were recorded of the implant sites every four days post-implantation. These observations revealed a pattern of epidermal ulceration, local hemorrhage, hemostasis and implant enlargement in the tumor implant site beginning as early as six days post-implantation and continuing throughout the 35-day period. Some limbs bearing these implants showed proximo-distal foreshortening as early as the second week and one was essentially destroyed by the end of the third week. None of these gross activities could be observed in association with the normal spleen implants, which gradually lost their original reddish appearance, yellowed, and decreased in size. The histological preparations confirmed the gradual breakdown of the normal spleen implants and extraordinary growth of the tumor tissue during the first two weeks. By 14 days post-implantation, lymphosarcoma foci were common in the visceral organs. In two of the three limbs bearing the normal spleen implants a focus of lymphosarcoma had also appeared. All of the lymphosarcoma in the hosts, regardless of anatomical position, was at least partially necrotic by the end of the third week. The necrotic picture in the lymphosarcoma material continued to be found throughout the fourth week and not until the final animals died or were killed at 35 days was there some relatively healthy tumor present.

In summary, these results suggest that the intense "inflammatory" response we had previously reported for viable allogeneic lymphosarcoma implants was related to the tremendous volume of material which these implants are capable of generating before they finally degenerate. The intensity of the response does not appear to be related to their lymphoid nature since normal spleen did not elicit comparable degrees of activity. That the animals at the end of the experimental period had healthier tumors than those sacrificed a week earlier suggested that a renewal of cancer growth might be occurring of either host transformed cellular origin or of surviving cells of the donor tumor.

In order to shed light on the sequence of events suggested by these results, the following experiments were designed as detailed studies of the development of the lymphosarcoma following transmission by fresh and frozen-killed allogeneic and xenogeneic lymphosarcoma implants and by lymphosarcoma homogenates.

Viable Allogeneic Implant Transmission

Forty young, post-metamorphic *Xenopus laevis* bred in this laboratory were allogeneically implanted with a small, viable fragment (0.5 mm)^3 of spleen-developed lymphosarcoma in the right forelimb. Two host animals were sacrificed every other day from two through 40 days post-implantation. Their livers, spleens, kidneys and implant-bearing forelimbs were prepared for histological examination.

While the implanted lymphosarcoma appeared to take up to four days to recover fully from the operative shock, i.e., the cells were somewhat loosely massed in their subcutaneous site in the limb, by six days they seemed to be fully established. Within the next week they generated massive amounts of lymphosarcoma (Fig. 1) filling the skin lymph sac in which they were placed and additional foci appeared in a variety of internal positions within the implanted limb.

Meanwhile, within the viscera, as early as two days post-implantation, aggregations of small lymphocytes could be seen in the liver sinusoids (Fig. 2). These aggregations of small lymphocytes present in the sinusoids could not in themselves be distinguished from the plaques of similar cells which had been found in the liver and kidney following the injection of non-particulate antigen, e.g., fetal calf serum (Ruben and Bieber, unpublished observations) or after implantation of normal tissues (Ruben and Stevens, unpublished observations). It is only when the characteristic germinal center becomes established that one can distinguish the beginning of lymphosarcoma development from the initial cellular response to antigenic challenge. These centers were clearly discernible by four days post-implantation in both the subcapsular epithelium (Fig. 3) and the sinusoidal areas of the liver (Fig. 4). The foci had enlarged by eight days post-implantation and the halo of small lymphocytes which was commonly found surrounding the germinal centers in the early stages of lymphosarcoma development became less apparent (Fig. 5) and disappeared in more mature foci found in the viscera by 14 days (Fig. 6). Growth of the lymphosarcoma foci continued in the limb and viscera into the third week. Animals killed or dying from 16 days through 32 days post-implantation, however, all showed varying degrees of necrosis within the lymphosarcoma foci, regardless of their anatomical position. The necrotic activity appeared first in splenic foci but only one day separated the spleen from the liver and kidney in this regard. As a rule the necrosis began in the center of the larger foci, often near the vascular supply (Fig. 7), and progressed toward the periphery (Fig. 8). These foci became completely destroyed and consisted of granular eosiniphilic debris with scattered pycnotic nuclear remains (Fig. 9). Occasional healthy cells could be identified within the masses. The necrosis is non-caseating. It should be noted that the necrosis was not limited to large foci but affected smaller ones as well (Fig. 10). While the necrosis may have been initiated by mechanical phenomena, e.g., occlusion of the vascular supply causing anoxia, nutritional deficiency or waste product accumulation, the inclusion of smaller foci in this activity suggested that some systemic effect was being expressed.

Lymphosarcoma proliferated rapidly and developed in a variety of sites. The growth phase served to provide an extensive mass of cells which was subsequently destroyed. Because the destruction did not involve an extensive cellular response on the part of host small lymphocytes or plasma cells, one is led to suggest that humoral cytotoxic antibodies may be responsible. The timing of the necrosis fits the immunological expression of this species at $25^\circ C$ (10), the temperature used for this series. Because host death is most frequent during the necrotic period it is important to set the dead and dying animals apart from the randomly selected developmental series in order to avoid prejudicing the data. This was done for all series described in this report.

When animals were killed or died during the fifth week post-implantation they were found to bear healthy tumor foci (Fig. 11). Indeed, those killed or dead between 26 and 32 days post-implantation possessed partially necrotic foci which were clearly

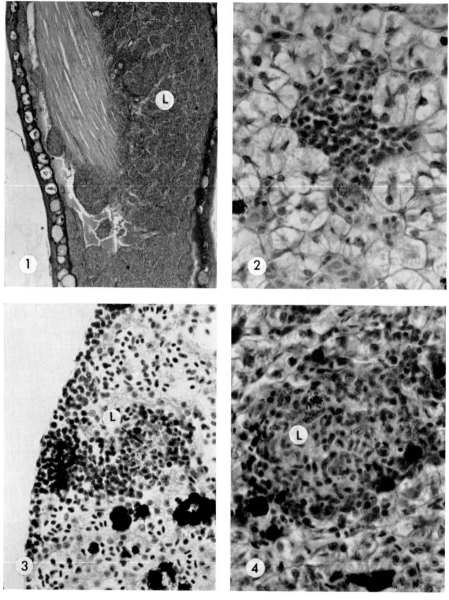

PLATE 1

Fig. 1. Lymphosarcoma (L) developed in limb of young post-metamorphic *Xenopus*, bearing 13-day old implant of viable allogeneic lymphosarcoma. H & E. $\times$12.

Fig. 2. Small aggregation of small lymphocytes in liver sinusoid, two days after implantation of viable allogeneic lymphosarcoma. H & E. $\times$325.

Fig. 3. Small tumor nodule (L) associated with the subcapsular epithelium of the liver showing characteristic germinal center of pleiomorphic lymphoid cells and histiocytes, six days after implantation of allogeneic tumor. H & E. $\times$200.

Fig. 4. Small tumor nodule (L) in sinusoidal area of liver eight days after implantation of viable allogeneic tumor. H & E. $\times$325.

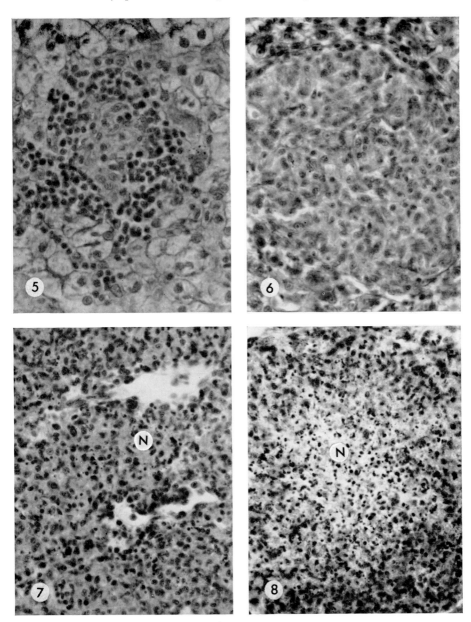

PLATE 2

Fig. 5. Early nodule showing halo of small lymphocytes surrounding germinal center at four days post-implantation. H & E. ×340.

Fig. 6. More mature focus showing absence of lymphocytic halo. H & E. ×207.

Fig. 7. Early stage of tumor necrosis (N) showing scattering of granular cellular debris in the center of a large nodule. H & E. ×207.

Fig. 8. Focal necrosis (N) has progressed peripherally, involving a large portion of this focus. H & E. ×166.

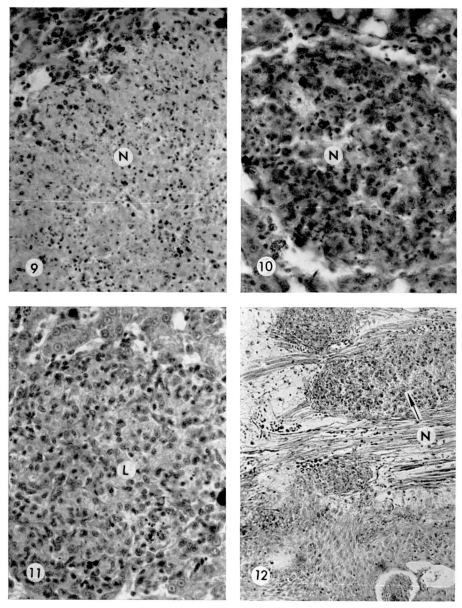

PLATE 3

Fig. 9. Destruction (N) of a tumor nodule, showing eosinophilic debris and pycnotic cellular remains. Note presence of scattered viable cells at periphery and through necrotic mass. H & E. ✕207.

Fig. 10. Necrosis (N) in small tumor nodule, suggesting the expression of some systemic effect (see text). H & E. ✕207.

Fig. 11. Healthy tumor (L) in liver, 38 days post-implantation. H & E. ✕207.

Fig. 12. Partially necrotic (N) tumor foci in limb of Xenopus, 26 days post-implantation. H & E. ✕85.

healthier than in earlier specimens of the series. Fig. 12 illustrates a 26-day limb with many partially necrotic foci. The removal of some of the necrotic material was achieved by the epidermis, which in amphibia can play an important clearance function. The destruction of so large a mass of lymphosarcoma must surely release a high titer of the agent. The renewal of growth may then represent lymphosarcoma formed of transformed host cells.

Transmission by Other Lymphosarcoma Implants

The results of the previous study with allogeneic lymphosarcoma were not un-expected. What proved surprising was that comparable studies utilizing methods which ensured the development of host-cell-originated lymphosarcoma led to the identical sequence of events, i.e., growth, necrosis and growth.

These descriptive studies were all carried out in the manner previously described for the viable allogeneic lymphosarcoma material. Implant transmission of lympho-sarcoma was followed using fragments of (a) twice frozen-thawed killed allogeneic lymphosarcoma developed in liver, (b) viable lymphosarcoma of *Diemictylus viri-descens* liver and (c) twice frozen-thawed killed *Diemictylus* lymphosarcoma. The freezing was accomplished in a Revco −70°C cabinet and thawing in a 37°C water bath. Histological examination of two-day implants in the limb site confirmed that no viable cellular structure remained (Fig. 13).

The sequence of events was comparable for all lymphosarcoma implant series. One additional feature of the phenomena described previously was the earlier activity on the part of the limb epidermis as it undercut, isolated and discharged implant debris to the environment. Perhaps the most interesting of these three series was the one utilizing viable xenogeneic lymphosarcoma fragments, since it offered an opportunity to take advantage of the difference between *Diemictylus* and *Xenopus* cell size and stainability to more accurately follow the steps involved. The freshly biopsied newt cancer implants degenerated quickly in the limb site. After six days only about a dozen viable *Diemictylus* cells could be identified and there was no evidence of proliferation or metastasis within or from the implant site. The donor cells were four times larger and took a heavier, more granular nuclear stain than the host *Xenopus* cells (Fig. 14). No donor cells were found after this date.

By nine days, host-cell lymphosarcoma was extensive in the limb site and some foci were observed in the viscera (Fig. 15). Lymphosarcoma growth was extremely rapid and by 16 days post-implantation the lymphosarcoma was of massive proportions in the limbs and multiple well-developed foci were present in the viscera. At 17 days necrosis was observed and it was found in all lymphosarcoma sites through 28 days when mixtures of foci were seen again and development was progressive.

While lymphosarcoma formation may have been slightly delayed in this series, perhaps until the implant had been sufficiently destroyed to provide an adequate agent titer, once it was established its growth was rapid enough to provide an enormous tumor mass by 16 days. That the frozen-killed allogeneic and xenogeneic fragment series did not show this delay suggests that the killed tissue could more readily yield sufficient agent titers for earlier tumor initiation.

In summary, then, even though the implanted lymphosarcoma material in these

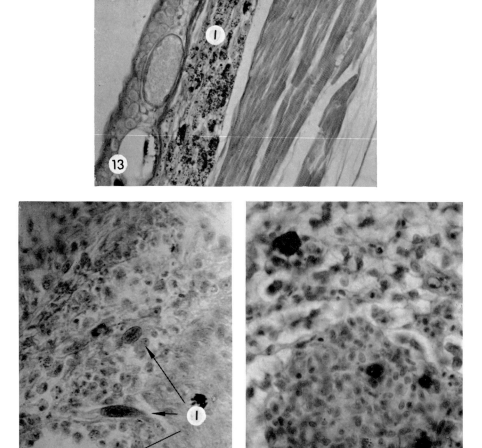

PLATE 4

Fig. 13. Two-day implant of frozen-thawed killed allogeneic lymphosarcoma. Note complete destruction of cellular structure of implant (I). H & E. ×166.

Fig. 14. Six-day implant of freshly biopsied newt cancer in *Xenopus* limb, showing a few viable implant cells (I). Donor newt cells can be distinguished from the *Xenopus* host cells by their larger size and more intense nuclear staining. H & E. ×200.

Fig. 15. Tumor nodule in *Xenopus* liver 12 days after implantation of viable newt lymphosarcoma in the limb. The tumor cells are clearly of host derivation, as distinguished by cell size and staining characteristics. H & E. ×207.

three groups initiated the development of host cell comprised lymphosarcoma, it was still destroyed or destroyed itself in the same manner and time period as that which had been observed for presumably allogeneically derived tumor. A renewal of growth followed this necrotic phase. The cycling of growth and necrosis could then account for the previously observed cycling of macroscopically observed "inflammatory" phenomena referred to in the introductory section of this report.

Agent Titer and the Growth-Necrosis Cycle

In the preparation of *Xenopus* cell-free lymphosarcoma homogenates there is a substantial reduction of agent titer as 10 or 15% w/v homogenates are prepared and are further diluted for standardization. I.P. injection of 0.05 ml of a 15% w/v homogenate diluted 100× with calcium-magnesium free amphibian Ringer's solution was used in a 72-day developmental study. The cycle was substantially slower. While aggregates of small lymphocytes were found in the liver as early as seven days postinjection, actual identifiable lymphosarcoma foci were not seen before 14 days. The growth of these foci did not show the burst of activity which followed implant initiation but instead remained about two weeks behind schedule. By 35 days large masses of lymphosarcoma were present and the first signs of necrosis were observed. Mixtures of necrotic and healthy foci were found in animals killed during the sixth and into the seventh week but from day 60 through 72 the foci were all healthy.

A more moderate slowing of the growth rate and delay in necrosis was achieved by using frozen-killed fragments of *Xenopus* liver which were histologically normal but were taken from a lymphosarcoma-bearing animal. The growth rate and necrosis were delayed by one week in this series. While we know that histologically normal tissue from a diseased animal is capable of transmitting the pathology (11, 12), it might be expected that the agent titer would be lower than in the actual lymphosarcoma cells.

In general, the total of the evidence suggests that the initiation time and growth rate of the lymphosarcoma varies with agent titer and that the point of necrosis onset depends on the production of a particular mass. This is most clearly seen in log dilution series of infective homogenates.

The Effect of Temperature Depression

One of the advantages in using poikilotherms to study phenomena of these kinds is that one can alter the rates of the biological processes involved by altering the environmental temperature. It is, for instance, well-known that one can suppress the immunological activity of Amphibia by depressing the temperature of their surroundings. Both humoral antibody (13, 14, 15, 16) and cell-mediated immunity (17) responses are temperature-sensitive. Three series of experiments have now been completed which were designed to investigate the existence of temperature-sensitive parameters in the lymphosarcoma growth-necrosis-growth cycle. Two were performed using two different concentrations of *Xenopus* lymphosarcoma cell-free homogenate and the third studied development following transmission by frozen-killed *Xenopus* lymphosarcoma implants made, as before, into the right forelimb. Also as before, the subjects for study were young but post-metamorphic *Xenopus* hosts. Since the results of all three series were in general agreement, I will discuss in detail only implant-induced lympho-sarcoma development which was the most recently completed and had a sequence of events and timing comparable to those implant groups described earlier in this report.

Eighty-five hosts were divided into five experimental groups. Groups IV (25 animals) and V (15 animals) were maintained at 25 °C and 15 °C respectively throughout the five weeks of the test period. Ordinarily all experiments are carried out at 25 °C, therefore a 10 °C temperature depression was used in these studies. These two groups were designed to provide information as to the effect of continuing temperature depression on the growth of the lymphosarcoma and on the time of onset of necrosis.

Groups I (17 animals), II (12 animals) and III (15 animals) were placed at 15 °C for one week only during the first, second, and third weeks post-implantation respectively. The animals were kept at 25 °C at all other times during the 35-day period. The odd numbers in the different groups result from counter controls established for recoveries of two animals every week from the 25 °C group (V) being matched by individuals from the various 15 °C temperature groups. The animal collection schedule was as follows: Two animals from groups I, IV, V on days 7, 14, 21 and 28, while collection of group II and III animals began on days 14 and 21, respectively. In this way only animals from groups which might contain new information were collected. All remaining animals were sacrificed on day 35. Gross observations on tumor development were recorded at the time of sacrifice and were correlated with slide material prepared from the liver, spleen and kidney of all hosts.

Our usual system of rough quantitative estimation of the amount of tumor per organ per animals was used, i.e., "+++" for an organ completely taken over by tumor; "+" for just visible lesions and "++" for all in-between states. While this is admittedly a crude system, it does avoid making subjective evaluations of the intermediate quantities. In order to determine the average amount of tumor per animal per group the total number of "+"'s was divided by the number of animals in that group. The data in Table 1 therefore reflect this quantitative method.

TABLE 1

THE EFFECT OF TEMPERATURE DEPRESSION ON TUMOR
GROWTH AND NECROSIS

Group	No.	Av. +'s spleen	Av. +'s liver	Av. +'s kidney	Av. total +'s	1st day of necrosis	Weeks at 15 °C
I	17	2.5 *	1.7	1.2	5.4	25	1st
II	12	2.8	1.4	1.4	5.6	none	2nd
III	15	2.8	1.4	1.9	6.1	21	3rd
IV	26	2.1	0.8	0.5	3.4	16	none
V	15	2.8	2.6	2.1	7.5	32	all 5

* The figures refer to estimates of the amount of lymphosarcoma in the spleens, livers, and kidneys expressed as the numbers of +'s (see text) divided by the number of animals in the group.

It was clear from these results that keeping the animals continuously at 15 °C (group V) greatly increased the average amount of lymphosarcoma developed per animal over the 25 °C controls (group IV). Further, the data reveal that even one week at 15 °C will initiate an increase in lymphosarcoma growth (groups I, II and III) over 25 °C controls, although the growth rate was less than that achieved by continuous 15 °C treatment. The import of these results on growth rate was that even though temperature depression would be expected to depress all biological processes, including cell division, in poikilotherms, lymphosarcoma growth was enhanced. It was interesting that even one week at the cooler temperature during the first week following implantation provided an increase in the amount of lymphosarcoma when the two 7-day specimens of groups I and IV were compared to the 7-day controls which had been at 25 °C. While immunological controls might play a role in lymphosarcoma growth, it is clear from the above that they are not the sole controlling factors, since the first 7 days post-implantation would probably be too early for them to become effective. Temperature depression must suppress a variety of other processes in the *Xenopus* and it may be that other systemic controls on lymphoid activity may also participate, e.g., cortisone production. That the increases in tumor development appear to be mainly in the liver and kidney and not the spleen is misleading in that the spleen was nearly totally involved in all groups in this experiment and therefore changes in liver and kidney content were more easily discernible. In other experiments the liver or the kidney may be more involved than the spleen. The preference in different experiments for extreme primary involvement of one organ or another may suggest the possibility of histiotropic specificity.

While weekly temperature depression failed to reveal any temperature sensitive period of growth control when implant initiation was studied, the use of homogenates proved to be illuminating in that when a 10^{-2} dilution of the infective homogenate was used, a drop in the environmental temperature during the second week post-injection *only* brought about the greatest increase in the amount of cancer generated through 50 days. Treatment in the second and third week periods proved to be about equally effective for enhancement of growth when a 10^{-3} dilution of the same infective homogenate was used. The failure to demonstrate a temperature sensitive period related to growth when implant initiation was used would seem to bear on the high titer of agent delivered by the implant which may have masked a temperature sensitive period. The results concerning necrosis of lymphosarcoma after implant initiation, however, are clear on this matter. At 25 °C (group IV), implant-initiated lymphosarcoma showed the first signs of necrosis at 16 days post-implantation. Continuous treatment at 15 °C delayed this until 32 days. The results from 15 °C treatment for specific weeks following implantation demonstrated that temperature depression during the second week (group II) post-implantation was at least as effective in delaying necrosis as continuous exposure to 15 °C. No animals showed necrotic tumor in group II. A 10 °C temperature depression during the first week following implantation was next most effective and delayed the necrotic phase until 25 days. Group III had the least significant delay and showed necrosis by day 21.

There are two points to make from these data. First, that these temperature-induced delays of necrosis agree well with the effects Simnett (17) achieved studying temperature and skin-graft rejection in the same species. It was his view that while antigenic information transfer may be somewhat affected by temperature depression, the lymphoid activation-antibody synthetic phase was most strongly suppressed. That the amnestic response was less affected by temperature depression than the primary response suggested that antibody release and antigen-antibody reaction were not so strongly involved. Our demonstration that cold treatment during the third week had little effect on necrosis could be considered to be in agreement with Simnett's experience. While the above data do not prove that necrosis is immunologically based, they are suggestive and at the very least show a clear differential effect of temperature depression. Delay in necrosis by temperature depression was something more than just the slowing of biological activity for the period of time that the animals were kept in the cold. If that had been the case necrosis should have begun around day 23 in all three groups put in the cold for only seven days.

The second point to make from these results is that while in experiments run at 25°C there appears to be a relationship between the amount of lymphosarcoma developed and the time of necrotic onset, temperature depression treatment clearly allows for greater tumor masses to be produced in conjunction with delayed necrosis. These data, coupled with the fact that there is a temperature sensitive period, support the view that the necrosis is imposed by the system, though it may be intrinsic in the lymphosarcoma cells themselves.

Resistance to the Disease

The following data should be considered as preliminary only. This study was done recently and it has not yet been repeated with sufficient numbers. I have included it nevertheless in this capacity as a preliminary report because of its interest and relationship to the ideas and data being considered here. Our routine method of standardizing infective homogenates made from lymphosarcoma has been to inject 0.05 to 0.1 ml of log dilutions of the homogenate i.p. into groups of *Xenopus* and to freeze and store the remaining homogenate at $-70°C$ until required for use. In this way we know what dilution will provide lymphosarcoma by 40 days, 60 days or whatever an experiment might require. In doing this, we have been concerned primarily with the individuals developing the tumor and not those remaining free of it. This report, however, concerns a test dilution series where our interest had passed to those free of the disease. Table 2 summarizes the data. Four test groups were used for the primary challenge with infective homogenate. Undiluted, 10^{-1}, 10^{-2}, and 10^{-3} dilutions of the homogenate with calcium-magnesium-free amphibian Ringer's solution were used. All animals receiving this particular undiluted homogenate (the supernatant fluid from a 30-minute $20,000 \times g$ centrifugation of 10% w/v homogenate) were dead with the disease by three months post-injection. Those receiving the 10^{-1} dilution were all dead with tumor by four months. Only three of those injected with 10^{-2} and one which received 10^{-3} dilution died of the disease within twelve months. It is interesting that while fewer animals get the disease in longer periods of time with dilution of infective solutions, the individuals dying from the disease have developed comparable amounts of lymphosarcoma. This observation supports the view provided by previously described experiments that mass and necrosis, the most frequent cause of death, are related unless special treatment is applied.

TABLE 2

RECHALLENGE OF SURVIVORS OF LOW TITER PRIMARY
CHALLENGE AFTER ONE YEAR

Group	No.	Homogenate dilution	No. +	Months
A1	8	None	8	3
A2	6	10^{-1}	6	4
A3	10	10^{-2}	3	12
A4	10	10^{-3}	1	12
RA3 *	5	10^{-1}	0	7
RA4	8	10^{-1}	3	7

* RA = rechallenge of some survivors of group A3
and A4 after one year.

Five of the survivors of the 10^{-2} dilution series and eight of those from the 10^{-3} dilution series were then rechallenged with 10^{-1} dilution. While a 10^{-1} dilution of the infective solution killed all animals by four months in the original group none of those which had been prechallenged with a 10^{-2} dilution one year before had developed lymphosarcoma when they were killed and examined histologically after seven months. Examination of those rechallenged from the 10^{-3} dilution group showed that three animals had developed small amounts of lymphosarcoma recognizable only on slides prepared from these specimens. These data suggest that animals vary in their resistance to low dosages of the agent and further that the resistant animals when rechallenged with a relatively infective homogenate remain resistant in accordance with the strength of their prechallenge titer. I should note that during that period of time the same homogenate was used effectively to initiate tumor in other groups, therefore we are not concerned with potency loss by the homogenate.

Liver and spleen fragments from one of the rechallenged (10^{-2} group) animals were implanted into the right forelimb of six post-metamorphic *Xenopus*. The donor animal showed no evidence of tumor either macroscopically or microscopically. Two of these implanted animals died early without the disease, but of the four survivors, three had developed moderate amounts of tumor by 70 days. It would appear then that after seven months the agent was still carried within the rechallenged animals, although its expression had been prevented in the resistant hosts. Transfer of the agent to animals not prechallenged with diseased tissue homogenate allowed for the tumor to develop within a 70-day experimental period.

Discussion: The Immunobiological Model

The presence of cycles of tumor growth and destruction raises certain questions and produces the need for certain assumptions to be made. Once the tumors composed of donor cells are destroyed, agent is released in titers sufficient to affect host lymphoid series cells and transform them into lymphosarcoma. Such a transformation would be likely to remove these cells from the host's immune system, allowing the cancer to develop unresisted. If tumors which develop during the initial two-week period or in the later growth period are subsequently destroyed as the data suggest, the host must have at its disposal a population of immunocompetent cells which has not been transformed. Such a population might become available if a low titer of agent existed during the growth phase of tumor development; this would prevent the transformation of the newly developed immunocompetent cells into tumor cells as they became available. A low titer of agent could be due to the persisting presence of an anti-agent antibody complex in the system, or to reduced agent production during the active growth period of the neoplastic cells. The latter suggestion is somewhat similar to one made by Rafferty (18) in regard to the development of the renal adenocarcinoma in *Rana pipiens*. The postulated life cycle in that case rested on the assumption that viral replication and tumor growth were mutually exclusive, the latter occurring at warm temperatures when the animals were immunologically competent, the former at cold temperatures when the immune capacity was impaired. Whether such a mutual exclusion of agent replication and tumor growth may apply to the *Xenopus* lymphosarcoma system kept at a constant 25°C temperature remains to be seen. One point clarified by this *Xenopus* data, however, is that the growth of this tumor is enhanced, not depressed, by cooler temperatures. Whatever the mechanism of their origin, the appearance of a new population of immunocompetent cells would have to arise if the necrosis of either donor or host cell lymphosarcoma were to be brought on by immunological events.

Each necrotic phase would cause the release of more agent; this new agent would in turn reinfect the next immunocompetent cell population produced and a new cycle of tumor growth would begin. The utilization of the immunocompetent cell population for growth renewal could explain why a second necrotic phase does not occur sooner since a primary rather than amnestic response would be involved.

It must be stated that it is not known whether secondary growth periods involve solely newly transformed cells, or mixtures of transformed cells with survivors of the necrotic phase. It is further not known whether the cells of the second growth are antigenically different from those of the primary growth when the primary growth is host-cell developed. It is possible too that the renewal of growth is encouraged by something akin to an immune paralysis in hosts brought on by the release of such an extraordinary quantity of material into the system during necrosis. A likely suggestion, for instance, as to why animals usually die during the necrotic phase would seem to be that the enormous quantity of material released to the system initiates anaphylactic shock. Whether animals die during the growth phase seems to depend on the amount of vital tissue occupied by the cancer.

The destruction of tumor composed of host cells requires that a further assumption be made: the host is capable of recognizing its own neoplastic cells as being antigenically non-self. Information concerning the unique antigenicity of tumors initiated by oncogenic chemicals (19, 20, 21, 22, 23) and by viruses (24, 25, 26, 27, 28) is readily available. It is further known that lymphoid diseases are particularly susceptible to humoral cytotoxic antibody (29, 30). Whether any of these features of mammalian cancer development apply to the present model of *Xenopus* lymphosarcoma development has not yet been determined. My view is that the data provided in this report are at least suggestive. The presence of an autochthonous growth-necrosis cycling of a lymphosarcoma would provide a unique opportunity to study immunological controls during oncogenesis.

Summary

Consistent features of lymphosarcoma development in *Xenopus laevis* are dramatic growth and spread, followed by equally dramatic necrosis of foci regardless of anatomical location. Following viable allogeneic lymphosarcoma implantation, growth appears to be donor cell proliferation. The timing and character of necrosis suggest humoral cytotoxic breakdown of foreign lymphosarcoma cells. However, allogeneic destruction cannot account for necrosis when transmission methods ensure lymphosarcoma development of host-cell composition.

Growth rate and necrosis timing relate to initiating agent titer. Cell-free lymphosarcoma homogenate injections stimulate slower growth and necrosis is delayed until the lymphosarcoma mass is comparable to that developed rapidly in response to implants.

When lymphosarcoma necrosis is complete, death usually results; if partial, in each focus *a second* growth-necrosis cycle develops bringing death in either phase.

Environmental temperature depression suppresses amphibian immunity, enhances lymphosarcoma development and inhibits necrosis.

Animals found resistant to low agent titers show resistance to rechallenge with higher titers in proportion to initial challenge strength. Tissues taken from an animal resistant to rechallenge after seven months initiated the disease in unprechallenged hosts by 70 days.

References

1. BALLS, M.: Spontaneous neoplasms in Amphibia: a review and descriptions of six new cases. Cancer Res. *22*:1142–1154, 1962.
2. FEY, F.: Hämatologische Untersuchungen an *Xenopus laevis* Daudin. Morph. Jahrbuch *103*:9–20, 1962.
3. HADJI-AZIMI, I. et FISCHBERG, M.: Hématopoïèse périhépatique chez le Batracien anoure *Xenopus laevis*. Comparaison entre les individus normaux et les porteurs de tumeurs lymphoides. Rev. Suisse Zool. *74*:641–645, 1967.
4. BALLS, M.: Cell transformation in xenoplastic transplantations of an amphibian lymphoid tumor. Rev. Suisse Zool. *71*:805–813, 1964.
5. BALLS, M.: Lymphoid tumor transfers from *Xenopus laevis laevis* to alien species and subspecies, including *Rana pipiens*. Cancer Res. *24*:1261–1267, 1964.
6. RUBEN, L. N. and BALLS, M.: The implantation of lymphosarcoma of *Xenopus laevis* into regenerating and non-regenerating forelimbs of that species. J. Morph. *115*:225–238, 1964.
7. RUBEN, L. N. and BALLS, M.: Further studies of a transmissible amphibian lymphosarcoma. Cancer Res. *27*:293–296, 1967.
8. BALLS, M. and RUBEN, L. N.: The transmission of lymphosarcoma in *Xenopus laevis*, the South African clawed toad. Cancer Res. *27*:654–659, 1967.
9. BALLS, M. and RUBEN, L. N.: Lymphoid tumors in Amphibia: a Review. Prog. Exptl. Tum. Res. *10*:238–260, 1968.

10. Simnett, J. D.: Histocompatibility in the Platanna, *Xenopus laevis* (Daudin) following nuclear transplantation. Exp. Cell Res. *33*:232–239, 1964.

11. Balls, M. and Ruben, L. N.: Variation in the response of *Xenopus laevis* to normal tissue homografts. Devel. Biol. *10*:92–104, 1964.

12. Balls, M. and Ruben, L. N.: The induction of lymphosarcoma in *Xenopus laevis* by cancerous and normal tissues of *Rana pipiens*. Ann. N.Y. Acad. Sci. *126*:274–288, 1965.

13. Allen, F. N. and McDaniel, E. C.: A study of the relation of temperature to antibody formation in cold-blooded animals. J. Immunol. *32*:143–152, 1937.

14. Bisset, K. A.: The effect of temperature upon antibody production in cold-blooded vertebrates. J. Pathol. Bacteriol. *60*:87–92, 1948.

15. Evans, E. E., Kent, S. P., Attleberger, M. H., Senbent, C., Bryant, R. E., and Booth, B.: Antibody synthesis in poikilothermic vertebrates. Ann. N.Y. Acad. Sci. *126*:629–646, 1965.

16. Elek, S. D., Rees, T. A. and Gowing, N. F. C.: Studies on the immune response in a poikilothermic species (*Xenopus laevis* Daudin) Comp. Biochem. Biophysiol. *7*:255, 1962.

17. Simnett, J. D.: Prolongation of homograft survival time in Platanna, *Xenopus laevis* (Daudin) by exposure to low environmental temperature. J. Cell Comp. Physiol. *65*:293–298, 1965.

18. Rafferty, K. A.: Kidney tumors in the leopard frog: a Review. Cancer Res. *24*:169–183, 1964.

19. Foley, E. J.: Antigenic properties of methylcholanthrene-induced tumors in mice of the strain of origin. Cancer Res. *13*:835–837, 1953.

20. Prehn, R. T. and Main, J. M.: Immunity to methylcholanthrene-induced sarcomas. J. Nat. Cancer Inst. *18*:769–778, 1967.

21. Prehn, R. T.: Tumor-specific immunity to transplanted dibenz (a, h) anthracene-induced sarcomas. Cancer Res. *20*:1614–1617, 1960.

22. Baldwin, R. W. and Barber, C. R.: Antigenic composition of transplanted rat hematomas originally induced by 4-dimethyl aminoazobenzene. Brit. J. Cancer *21*:338–345, 1967.

23. Prehn, R. T.: Tumor specific immunity to non-viral tumors. Can. Cancer Conf. *5*:387–395, 1963.

24. Habel, K.: Resistance of polyoma virus immune animals to transplanted polyoma tumors. Proc. Soc. Exptl. Biol. Med. *106*:722–725, 1961.

25. Sjögren, H. O., Hellstrom, I. and Klein, G.: Transplantation of polyoma virus induced tumors in mice. Cancer Res. *21*:329–337, 1961.

26. Klein, G.: Tumor Antigens. Ann. Rev. Microbiol. *20*:233–252, 1966.

27. Old, L. J., and Boyse, E. A.: Immunology of experimental tumors. Ann. Rev. Med. *15*:167–186, 1964.

28. Klein, G.: Tumor-specific transplantation antigens: G. H. A. Clowes Mem. Lect. Cancer Res. *28*:625–635, 1968.

29. Klein, E. and Klein, G.: Antigenic properties of lymphomas induced by the Moloney agent. J. Nat. Cancer Inst. *32*:547–568, 1964.

30. Slettenmark, B. and Klein, E.: Cytotoxic and neutralization tests with serum and lymph node cells of isologous mice with induced resistance against Gross lymphomas. Cancer Res. *22*:947–954, 1962.

Organ Cultures of Normal and
Neoplastic Amphibian Tissues[1,2]

MICHAEL BALLS, JOHN D. SIMNETT and ELIZABETH ARTHUR

School of Biological Sciences, University of East Anglia
Norwich, England, and Department of Pathology
Royal Victoria Infirmary, University of Newcastle-upon-Tyne, England

Although the organ culture technique has been widely used in studies on the growth and differentiation of mammalian tissues, there are few records of the use of the technique with the tissues of metamorphosed amphibians. We have recently shown that a variety of organs from recently metamorphosed, immature *Xenopus* may be maintained in culture for at least 6 days, with mitotic incidences comparable to or even higher than those *in vivo* (1).

This preliminary report concerns our continuing research on the culture of a variety of normal tissues from four amphibian species for longer periods than those used in our earlier experiments. We have also carried out experiments concerning the culture of *Xenopus* lymphoid tumor bearing organs and attempts at transforming *Xenopus*, *Triturus* and *Rana* cells *in vitro* by treating organ fragments with homogenates of tumor tissues containing the *Xenopus* lymphosarcoma agent (2). The lymphosarcoma was originally found in *Xenopus*, but can be transferred to adults of a number of amphibian species (including those used in the present experiments) by means of cellular implants or cell-free extracts [see review (3)].

Materials and Methods

Source of Animals

Adult *Xenopus laevis laevis*, *Rana pipiens*, *Triturus cristatus* and *Pleurodeles waltlii* (also known as *Pleurodeles waltl*) were obtained, respectively, from dealers in South Africa, Vermont (U.S.A.) and London (U.K.), and from J. C. Boucaud (University of Paris, France). Immature *Xenopus* were obtained from matings induced by injections of chorionic gonadotrophin (Organon Laboratories). Larvae were reared at 25 °C and fed on pea soup powder. Immature *Xenopus* were fed on *Tubifex* worms, adult *Xenopus*, *Triturus* and *Pleurodeles* on chopped beef liver, and *Rana* on flies or earthworms.

---

[1] This work is being supported by grants from the Medical Research Council of the United Kingdom (M.B. and E.A.) and the Northern Council of the British Empire Cancer Campaign (J.D.S.).

[2] We acknowledge the continuing benefit of discussions with Dr. L. N. Ruben and Dr. K. A. Rafferty, and thank Miss Mary Wade for her skilled technical assistance.

Measurement of Mitotic Incidence in vivo

Three adults of each of three species (*Xenopus, Rana, Triturus*) and three lymphoid tumor bearing *Xenopus* were given intra-abdominal injections of 0.02 ml of a 0.1% Colcemid (CIBA) solution per gram body weight to accumulate mitoses at metaphase. The animals were kept at 25°C for 4 hours, then killed in urethan, and portions of selected tissues were fixed in Worcester's fluid (1), dehydrated in cellosolve, embedded in paraffin wax and sectioned at 5 μ. The histological preparations were stained with Weigert's haematoxylin or Mayer's acid haemalum, and eosin.

Organ Culture Technique

Animals were killed and, using full aseptic technique, selected organs were transferred to culture medium and cut into 2–3 mm cubes. The fragments were then transferred to a dish containing a 26 mm grid of expanded titanium mesh on which rested two strips of ether cleansed lens paper. Using 7 ml medium per dish, the explants rested on the lens paper, moistened but not submerged in the medium. Each dish contained up to 10 explants, usually from different organ types. The dishes were placed in petri dishes and incubated at the required temperature. The fragments were thus in free gaseous exchange with the atmosphere.

Culture Medium

The culture medium used was a variant of that previously found suitable for the growth of normal and neoplastic cells in tissues culture (4, 5) and for maintaining immature and adult *Xenopus* tissues in organ culture [(1), R. A. Wallace, personal communication]. The medium originally suggested (4) contained 50% Leibovitz L-15 medium and 40% water, but we have since found that embryonic, larval and adult *Xenopus* cells also grow well in serial culture in media containing up to 90% L-15, though the growth rate falls off at concentrations above 70% L-15.[1] The media used in the present experiments consisted of 700–800 ml Leibovitz L-15

---

[1] Moser *et al.* (6) considered that the L-15 complete medium originally suggested was hypotonic for *Xenopus* cells and lethal for many cell types, having an osmolarity only 60% of that of mammalian culture media. We do not agree with this conclusion for the following reasons: (a) the original L-15 medium has been successfully used for the culture of a variety of cell types from various stages from a number of amphibian species [(1), (4), (5), our own unpublished observations]; (b) K. A. Rafferty (personal communication) has found the medium suitable for the culture of his *Xenopus*-derived cell lines A6 and A8, and for the establishment of new cell lines from other amphibian species; and (c) Rafferty has also provided the following osmometer readings:

L-15 complete amphibian medium	:	214 mOsm
NCTC-109 complete amphibian medium	:	204
Amphibian Hank's solution (i.e. 70%)	:	211
Brinster's mammalian organ culture medium	:	270
Fetal calf serum	:	301
Distilled water	:	000

These data suggest that the L-15 medium compares well with another amphibian culture medium and has an osmolarity much higher than 60% of that of mammalian culture media. We were unable to find in the literature a value for the osmolarity of amphibian serum.

(Grand Island Biological Co.), 0–160 ml triple distilled water, 80 ml fetal bovine serum and 40 ml calf serum (Flow Laboratories Ltd.) and 20 ml tryptose phosphate broth per litre, with 100 units/ml benzylpenicillin (Glaxo), 100 μgm/ml streptomycin sulphate (Glaxo) and 2 μgm/ml fungizone (Squibb).

Period of Culture

The organ fragments were maintained in culture for periods up to 18 days at 10°C, 18°C or 25°C, the medium being replaced by fresh medium every 3 days. At the end of the culture period, 0.28 ml of a 0.01% solution of Colcemid was added to the culture dish, to give a final concentration of 0.004 mgm Colcemid per ml of culture medium (7), and four hours later the explants were removed, fixed and processed in the same way as were the fresh tissues.

Quantitative Methods for Mitotic Counting

The mitotic incidence (MI) is the ratio of arrested metaphases to total cells. In tissues where mitoses were comparatively rare, the mitotic incidence was estimated in the following way [see (8)]. Using an eyepiece graticule, the area of the section was first estimated, and the numbers of nuclei were then measured in a number of small sample areas. From these two pieces of information, the total number of nuclei per section could be calculated and the number of arrested metaphases, obtained by scanning the whole section, was then recorded. At least 5 replicate samples were usually taken for each treatment, both *in vivo* and *in vitro,* which enabled a mean and a standard deviation to be calculated. For a series of such replicate samples the total number of nuclei was usually between 10^4 and 10^5 and the MI was accordingly expressed as the proportion of arrested metaphases per 10^5 nuclei. In a few tissues (e.g., lung, tumor spleen), the MI was so high that it could be estimated directly by counting the number of arrested metaphases in a sample of 1000 nuclei, but for the sake of consistency these figures were converted to the number per 10^5 nuclei. The MI thus represents the proportion of cells entering mitosis during the 4 hour period of Colcemid treatment.

Preparation of Homogenates

Normal or tumor-bearing *Xenopus* organs were ground up in 65% Hank's solution to give a 10% homogenate (w/v). The homogenate was then centrifuged at 10,000 × g for 1 hour (Sorval RC2B) and the supernatant fluid (I) was stored at −20°C or −190°C until used. The stored fluid was later centrifuged at 20,000 × g for 1 hour and the supernatant fluid (II) was used for treating fragments prior to organ culture or tested for infectivity by injection into recently metamorphosed *Xenopus* (0.1 ml per host). The organ fragments were incubated for 1 hour at 22°C in supernatant fluid II diluted 10 times with 65% Hank's solution. The fragments were then placed on the grids in dishes whose medium contained a 1:20 dilution of the homogenate. The medium was replaced with fresh medium without homogenate after 1 or 3 days.

Source of Tumor Animals

The animals used as sources of tumor-bearing organs had previously been given dorsal lymph sac implants of viable tumor tissues. After 69–87 days, the animals were either killed and the organs used for *in vitro* culture, or injected with Colcemid as a source of organs for *in vivo* MI estimation. When killed, all the animals bore advanced, grossly visible tumor nodules.

Treatment of Animals Prior to Organ Culture

The animals were kept in a weak potassium permanganate solution for 1–16 hours, then washed with 70% alcohol immediately prior to dissection. We have had problems with bacterial and fungal contamination, particularly with *Rana* liver and kidney cultures. In future experiments, we shall give the animals antibiotic injections a few days before their organs are required for culture.

Experiments and Results

Variety of Organs and Length of Culture Period

The range of organs cultured at 25 °C is summarized in Table 1, together with an estimate of the state of preservation of the tissue concerned. Necrosis was observed in most liver and kidney cultures, as was the case in our earlier studies (1), and similar results have been observed with mammalian liver and kidney (9). Similarly, ovary and testis did not culture well over long periods, so it is clear that such organs require rather more suitable conditions than those provided. Wallace (personal communication) notes that liver cultures are improved by the addition of amphibian serum, and Foote and Foote (10, 11) added hormones to improve their cultures of larval gonads. However, excellent, long term cultures were obtained of spleen, lung, oviduct, pancreas and intestine (Figs. 1–8, 11). In general, it appeared that organs from the urodeles (*Triturus* and *Pleurodeles*) cultured well more consistently than those from the anurans (*Xenopus* and *Rana*), but we do not have enough data to allow us to quantify this impression. Good preservation was observed in the fragments cultured at 10 °C and 18 °C.

Effect of Organ Culture on Mitotic Incidence (MI)

The changes of MI during spleen organ culture are summarized in Table 2. Although the information is incomplete as yet, it is clear that MI's significantly higher than those *in vivo* were obtained in cultures from *Rana*, *Triturus*, and immature and mature *Xenopus*. It is interesting to note that the highest MI in immature *Xenopus* spleen cultures was reached at day 1, whereas the peak in mature spleen cultures was at day 7. The highest MI in pancreas cultures was also reached at day 7 (MI = <10 *in vivo* and at days 1 and and 3, but 1533 ± 659 at day 7). The peak MI in stage 47–48 (12) *Xenopus* tadpole regenerating kidney is reached at 2 days in culture (Chopra and Simnett, unpublished), whereas the highest MI in immature *Xenopus* kidney cultures was reached at day 6 (1). Organs thus appear to reach their peak MI in culture progressively later if taken from larval, immature or mature *Xenopus*. It may be that the cells from mature animals take longer to become independent of the control mechanisms which were preventing their division *in vivo*. The immense increase in MI in pancreas cultures may prove to be important in this connection, since the *in vivo* MI in mature animals of <10 had increased to 1533 ±

TABLE 1

Variety of Organs Cultured and Maximum Length of Culture Period at 25°C

Species	Organ	Maximum culture period to date (days)	Comments on state of tissue[c]	
			0–7 days	8–18
Immature Xenopus[a]	spleen	18	g	g
	liver	7	f	—
	lung	7	g	—
	kidney	12	f	f
	skin	7	g	—
	ovary	7	g	—
	testis	7	g	—
Mature Xenopus	spleen	18	g	g
	liver	18	f	p
	lung	7	g	—
	kidney	12	f	p
	pancreas	10	g	g
	oviduct	12	g	g
	intestine	7	g	—
	ovary	10	g	f
	testis	12	g	p
Mature Rana	spleen	18	g	g
	liver	16	f	p
	lung	10	g	g
	ovary	10	g	f
	testis	10	f	p
Mature Triturus	spleen	17	g	g
	liver	17	g	g
Mature Pleurodeles[b]	spleen	7	g	—
	liver	7	g	—
	lung	7	g	—
	kidney	7	f	—

[a] Data from reference (1) and subsequent unpublished work.

[b] In collaboration with J. C. Boucaud.

[c] Preservation classed as follows: g = good, whole explant alive, normal histology preserved; f = fair, some areas of explant good, others poor; p = poor, widespread necrosis; — = no data available.

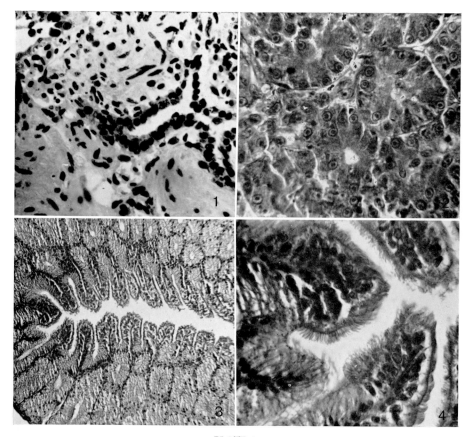

PLATE 1

Fig. 1. *Pleurodeles* lung after 7 days in culture. ✕200.

Fig. 2. Mature *Xenopus* pancreas after 7 days in culture at 25°C. Note the distinct nuclei containing a single, large nucleolus. ✕350.

Fig. 3. Mature *Xenopus* oviduct after 5 days in culture. ✕80.

Fig. 4. Detail of the oviduct shown in Fig. 3. ✕350.

659 after 7 days in culture, whereas mammalian pancreas rapidly autolyses in organ culture (13). A more extensive analysis will undoubtedly show further significant differences in the behaviour of amphibian and mammalian organs in culture.

Affect of Temperature on MI in Organ Culture

It is clear from Table 3 that the temperature at which the cultures are incubated must be carefully controlled, since the MI was significantly higher in both spleen and pancreas cultures at 25°C than at 18°C. We had earlier shown (1) that increasing the environmental temperature from 20°C to 25°C gave increases in immature *Xenopus in vivo* ranging from ✕1.52 (epidermis) to ✕7.67 (lung). The increases in organ culture were of the same order.

Mitotic Incidence in Tumor Tissues in Vivo and in Vitro (Table 4)

The *in vivo* MI's for tumor tissue were estimated from tumor-bearing spleens and livers taken from 3 immature *Xenopus* which had been given dorsal lymph sac tumor implants 69 days earlier. The MI of the tumor-bearing spleen and liver nodules was very much higher than in the normal spleen. Tumor tissue for culture was obtained from 25 animals which had received dorsal lymph sac tumor tissue implants 69–87 days earlier. While good cultures were obtained at 1 and 3 days (Fig. 9), organs in which the majority of the normal tissues had been replaced by lymphoid tumor did not preserve well in long-term culture, only 15% of the cells surviving. However, the surviving cells showed very high MI's at 7 days. Our data is again

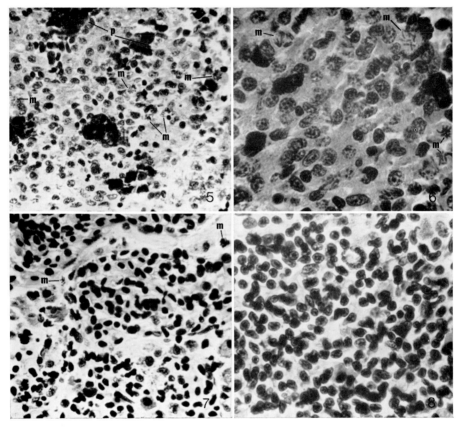

PLATE 2

Fig. 5. *Triturus* liver after 8 days in culture. Mitotic figures are arrowed (m). The organ is heavily pigmented *in vitro* as *in vivo* (p = pigment). This liver had been treated with tumor homogenate. ✕200.

Fig. 6. Detail of *Triturus* liver after 8 days in culture. It is clear that the cells were in good condition, and many were dividing (m). This liver had been treated with tumor homogenate. ✕375.

Fig. 7. *Triturus* spleen after 15 days in culture. Mitotic figures are indicated (m). ✕200.

Fig. 8. Detail of *Triturus* spleen after 8 days in culture. ✕300.

TABLE 2

Change in Mitotic Incidence (MI)[a] in Spleens in Organ Culture

Species	Xenopus immature[b]	Xenopus mature	Rana mature	Triturus mature
in vivo	198 ± 191.7	<10[c]	<10[c]	76 ± 37
Days in culture				
1	424 ± 380	25 ± 15		
2			21 ± 13	
3	203 ± 213			
4		103 ± 30	13 ± 4	
5				130 ± 56
6	94 ± 47			
7		429 ± 81		
8		122 ± 55	<10[c]	
12		138 ± 20		
15			37 ± 19	220 ± 25
18			77 ± 46	

[a] MI is the number of arrested metaphases per 10^5 cells after 4 hours of Colcemid treatment.

[b] These figures are taken from reference (1).

[c] No mitosis in a sample of 10^4 cells.

TABLE 3

Effect of Temperature on Mitotic Incidence [a] in Adult Xenopus Tissues in Organ Culture

Organ	Spleen		Pancreas	
Culture temperature	18°C	25°C	18°C	25°C
Days in culture				
1	350 ± 300	25 ± 15	<10[b]	<10[b]
4	91 ± 18	103 ± 30	<10[b]	<10[b]
7	131 ± 11	429 ± 81	185 ± 43	1533 ± 659
in vivo		<10[b]		<10[b]

[a] MI is the number of arrested metaphases per 10^5 cells after 4 hours of Colcemid treatment.

[b] No mitosis in a sample of 10^4 cells.

TABLE 4

MITOTIC INCIDENCE [a] IN NORMAL AND NEOPLASTIC XENOPUS LYMPHOID
TISSUES IN VIVO AND IN VITRO

	Normal spleen[b]	Spleen from tumor-bearing animal	Lymphoid tumor nodules
in vivo	198 ± 191	427 ± 28	2185 ± 64
in vitro			
day 1	424 ± 380		
3	203 ± 213	750 ± 295	
6	94 ± 47		
7		1176	8877

[a] MI is the number of arrested metaphases per 10^5 cells after 4 hours of Colcemid treatment.

[b] Data taken from reference (1).

incomplete, but it may be that the peak MI is reached later in tumor tissue than in normal spleen cultures from immature *Xenopus*. Poor preservation in culture is indicated by large necrotic areas, but there does seem to be a difference between the necrosis in normal and tumor tissues. Whereas in normal tissues the necrotic areas are uniform in that all cells in the area are dead or dying, in tumor tissue the necrotic areas contain a mixture of necrotic and dividing cells (Fig. 10). This suggests that the necrosis may be selective and with a different basis from the necrosis of, say, cultured normal liver. It is likely that the observed tumor necrosis was related to that seen in *Xenopus* lymphoid tumors *in vivo* and which has been discussed by Ruben (14), and the study of the growth-necrosis cycle in organ culture should be a rewarding one.

Effects of Lymphoid Tumor Homogenates on Xenopus, Rana and Triturus Tissues in Organ Culture

The effects of lymphoid tumor homogenates on tissues in organ culture could be estimated in at least four ways, namely: (a) change in mitotic incidence in the treated tissue as compared with that in similar tissues treated with homogenates made from normal tissues; (b) histological changes in the treated tissues; (c) an increase in lymphoid tumor inducing infectivity in the culture medium; and (d) an increasing ability of portions of the cultured fragments to induce tumors when implanted into immature *Xenopus*. To date, we only have evidence concerning the MI in treated tissues, and it appears that by day 8 there is a 50% increase in the MI in cultured *Xenopus* spleen previously treated with tumor homogenate. This conclusion is based on an analysis of only 28 spleen fragments and we do not consider this number sufficient to justify detailed presentation of the data here. Treated *Triturus* liver showed a very high MI by day 8, too (Figs. 5 and 6), but the control liver fragments were not sufficiently well preserved to permit a direct comparison to be made.

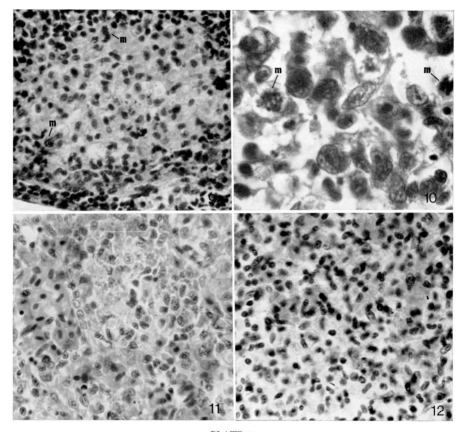

PLATE 3

Fig. 9. Tumor nodule in a *Xenopus* spleen after 3 days in culture. The nodule is typical of those observed *in vivo*, being surrounded by small lymphocytes. Mitotic figures = m. ✕300.

Fig. 10. Detail of *Xenopus* tumor tissue after 7 days in culture. Some cells are mitosing (m), although many other cells in the area were necrotic. ✕800.

Fig. 11. Mature *Rana* spleen after 18 days in culture. ✕300.

Fig. 12. Detail of *Xenopus* lymphosarcoma *in vivo*. These tumor cells are in the spleen of an animal previously given an implant of living tumor cells. ✕300.

Any comments on possibility (b) (histological changes in treated tissues) would need to be based on a detailed study of the behavior of the *normal* organ in culture. The change from normal to neoplastic in lymphoid tissue is not as clearly definable as is, say, the change from normal frog kidney tubule to *Rana* renal adenocarcinoma (15). For instance, although admittedly one organ is from *Rana* and the others from *Xenopus*, the 18 day normal *Rana* spleen fragment shown in Fig. 11 is similar to the *Xenopus* tumor *in vitro* (Fig. 9) and *in vivo* (Fig. 12). Clearly, then, morphological criteria alone are insufficient evidence of cell transformation.

Furthermore, since the immune response has been observed in *Xenopus* spleens *in vitro* (Auerbach and Ruben, personal communication), it is likely that lymphoid cells in cultured organs will respond to the serum proteins of the medium or other antigens in the homogenate by an increase in MI and/or some histologically visible change in cell morphology and/or change in the relative numbers of the different cell types present. Since implant-induced or homogenate-induced tumors appear rather more rapidly in *Triturus* than in *Xenopus* (3), and since *Triturus* tissues preserve so well in organ culture, we are continuing to use adult *Triturus* liver and spleen in our experiments, as well as *Xenopus* spleens.

Attempts at estimating an increase in infectivity in treated organ culture fragments or medium [possibilities (c) and (d)] are in progress, but success here may be dependent on the improvement of the small animal assay used at present (3).

Conclusions

We wish to emphasize that the MI provides an extremely sensitive parameter of changes in growth rate. Naturally occurring growth control factors may well be highly unstable and, in consequence, their duration of action is likely to be short in experimental systems, so that a consequential change in the mass of the tissue will not be detectable by measurement of gross size. Such changes of size can only be detected when the tissue exhibits a very high mitotic rate extending over a period of days—a condition which it is difficult to obtain in experimental situations.

The data presented in this and in a previous paper (1) have a bearing on a number of diverse problems, and we shall now comment on those observations which seem to us the most interesting.

Increase of MI in Culture

In a number of organs (kidney, liver, spleen, pancreas) the MI increased following explantation and culture. It could be argued that this was simply due to a presumed mitotic stimulating property of the biological additions in the culture medium. We do not consider this to be the correct explanation. The bronchial and prostatic epithelia of the mouse show a marked increase of MI in organ culture (16), even in a very simple, chemically defined medium, which contains no known mitotic stimulators. The increase in MI which occurs after the isolation of these mammalian tissues *in vitro* thus appears to be due to the absence of inhibiting factors present *in vivo*. It is likely that this explanation also holds for our results with amphibian tissues, and we put forward the following suggestion: that some organ systems show large increases in MI *in vitro* over the *in vivo* rate, while others do not, suggests that growth may be controlled differently in these two organ groups, by systemic and/or local factors.

Temperature Effects in Culture and in Vivo

Tissues from the animals used in our experiments were well preserved at 10°C, 18°C and 25°C. The temperature of culture must be carefully controlled, since the MI decreases as the temperature is lowered. However, the optimum temperature will surely vary with the species used, since, while 25°C is the temperature most commonly used for amphibian tissue culture, Stephenson has reported an optimum of 30°C for frog (*Limnodiastes*) organ culture (17). That the MI in amphibian cultures decreases at lower temperatures is a predictable result, but the degree to which the MI of lymphoid tissue is affected by temperature is worthy of comment. The extent to which the skin homograft reaction of *Xenopus* is depressed by low temperature is out of all proportion to the corresponding effect on other vital processes (18). In contrast, we find that the temperature depression of MI in *Xenopus* spleen is within the range exhibited by other organs. This suggests that depression of spleen MI cannot solely be responsible for the extreme sensibility of the immune response to low temperature.

Lymphoid Tumors in Organ Culture

The question of lymphoid tumor organ cultures is an intriguing one for various reasons. The *in vivo* enhancement of lymphoid tumor development at low temperatures and growth—necrosis cycling observed by Ruben (14) have already been mentioned. The apparently selective cell death we observed is no doubt a reflection of the cycling, but the great increase in MI may suggest that a mechanism exists *in vivo* which is partially successful in combatting the pathogenic effects of the tumor agent. Furthermore, since *Xenopus* have no lymphoid aggregations comparable to lymph nodes, it is not known whether lymphosarcoma in *Xenopus* is a systemic disease of multifocal origin or whether cell transformation occurs in one of the major centres of lymphoid cell activity (spleen, liver, kidney, gut). The organ culture situation provides the opportunity to study these organs in isolation, both with and without the addition of infective, sterile, cell-free tumor filtrates. Since tumor nodules composed of host cells appeared in the viscera *in vivo* only 4–9 days after *Triturus* lymphosarcoma fragments were implanted into the dorsal lymph sac of immature *Xenopus* (19), amphibian organs can certainly be cultured for sufficiently long periods for transformation to occur. As has already been suggested, the problem is one of devising sufficiently sensitive and reliable methods of quantitating any transformation that occurs. *Xenopus* spleen cultures treated with tumor homogenate showed a 50% increase in MI, but the small number of samples analysed so far does not permit this increase to be shown to be significant. If substantiated by further experiments, this increase might provide a useful advance indication of *in vitro* transformation. However, as discussed earlier, increases in MI or histological changes cannot alone serve as proof of transformation, since increased infectivity in the medium or the ability of the apparently transformed cells to induce tumors *in vivo* must also be involved.

Possible Advantages of Amphibian over Mammalian Organ Cultures

Skin. Mitotic control mechanisms have been subject to extensive study using short-term organ cultures of mouse skin (7). Unfortunately, mitotic activity in mammalian epidermis can only be maintained for the first few hours *in vitro*, which means that long-term experiments on growth control cannot be performed on this tissue. Amphibian material may prove useful in this respect, since *Xenopus* skin retains mitotic activity for at least 6 days in organ culture (1).

Liver and Kidney. These two organs are favorite subjects for experiments on causal mechanisms in compensatory hyperplasia (20). It is likely that the present state of conflicting hypotheses could be resolved by suitable experiments on liver and kidney explants isolated *in vitro*, but these two organs have proved difficult to maintain in mammalian organ culture systems. The frequently excellent preservation of cultured amphibian liver and kidney (particularly of adult urodeles) could provide a much needed alternative model, and our interest is sharpened by the recent observation (Chopra and Simnett, in preparation) that larval *Xenopus* kidney is sensitive to tissue-specific mitotic inhibitors.

Pancreas. Whereas mammalian pancreas rapidly autolyses in organ culture (13, 21), the pancreas of *Xenopus* can be maintained *in vitro*, where it exhibits a greatly increased MI. We do not envisage any difficulty in devising a method for quantitating enzyme production in the pancreas, and this tissue should provide an excellent model for studying the well-known antagonistic reaction between functional and mitotic activity in differentiated tissues (22).

Intestine. The kinetics of cell turnover in mammalian intestinal epithelium have been the subject of extensive investigations (23), but the causal mechanisms are poorly understood. We believe that the organ culture system could answer many of the relevant questions and point out that amphibian material has a distinct advantage over that of mammals, where the epithelium rapidly undergoes degenerative changes in culture.

Ovary. Immature *Xenopus* ovary showed excellent preservation in culture, with a very high MI in the follicle cells. This system could provide a method for studying the effect of exogenous factors on oogenesis under controlled conditions.

Further uses of amphibian organ cultures will inevitably become apparent as more work is carried out. Two additional possibilities come to mind. Firstly, the technique might prove useful in studies of the effects of frog viruses on the kidney tubules of embryonic, larval and adult *Rana pipiens*. Secondly, the extent to which the survival of amphibian tissues was prolonged in organ culture was surprising, and it may be that it will be possible to preserve organs such as skin for very long periods at low temperatures, with obvious benefits to immunological studies.

Summary

Organ fragments from mature adults of four amphibian species (*Xenopus laevis, Rana pipiens, Triturus cristatus* and *Pleurodeles waltlii*) have been maintained in organ culture for periods up to 18 days. Good preservation was observed in a number of organs, including spleen, lung, pancreas, oviducts and intestine, with mitotic incidences (MI) in some organs higher than those *in vivo*. The MI was significantly higher in spleen and pancreas cultures at 25 °C than at 18 °C. The MI was also higher in lymphoid tumor nodules *in vitro* than *in vivo*, and both these MI's were higher than those in normal *Xenopus* spleens *in vivo* or in culture. Preliminary attempts at studying neoplastic transformation in organ culture are discussed.

References

1. SIMNETT, J. D., and BALLS, M.: Cell proliferation in *Xenopus* tissues: a comparison of mitotic incidence *in vivo* and in organ culture. J. Morph. *127*:363–372, 1969.

2. BALLS, M.: Lymphosarcoma in the South African clawed toad, *Xenopus laevis:* a virus tumor. Ann. N.Y. Acad. Sci. *126:*256–273, 1965.

3. BALLS, M., and RUBEN, L. N.: Lymphoid tumors in amphibia: a review. Prog. Exptl. Tumor Res. *10:*238–260, 1968.

4. BALLS, M., and RUBEN, L. N.: Cultivation *in vitro* of normal and neoplastic cells of *Xenopus laevis.* Exptl. Cell Res. *43:*694–695, 1966.

5. FREED, J. J., MEZGER-FREED, L., and SCHATZ, S. A.: Characteristics of cell lines from haploid and diploid anuran embryos. *In* Biology of Amphibian Tumors (M. Mizell, ed.), Springer-Verlag New York Inc., 1969, pp. 101–111.

6. MOSER, H., HADJI-AZIMI, I., and SLATKINE, S.: Culture of cells and tissues derived from the South African frog *Xenopus laevis* (Daudin). Rev. Suisse Zool. *75:*619–630, 1968.

7. BULLOUGH, W. S., and LAURENCE, E. B.: The study of mammalian epidermal mitosis *in vitro:* a critical analysis of technique. Exptl. Cell Res. *24:*289–297, 1961.

8. SIMNETT, J. D., and HEPPLESTON, A. G.: Cell renewal in the mouse lung: the influence of sex, strain and age. Lab. Invest. *15:*1793–1801, 1966.

9. MACDOUGALL, J. D. B., and COUPLAND, R. E.: Organ culture under hyperbaric oxygen. Exptl. Cell Res. *45:*385–398, 1967.

10. FOOTE, C. L., and FOOTE, F. M.: *In vitro* cultivation of gonads of larval anurans. Anat. Rec. *130:*553–565, 1958.

11. FOOTE, C. L., and FOOTE, F. M.: The culture *in vitro* of urogenital organs of *Pleurodeles waltlii.* J. Embryol. Exptl. Morphol. *10:*465–470, 1962.

12. NIEUWKOOP, P., and FABER, J.: Normal Table of *Xenopus laevis* Daudin. Amsterdam: North Holland Publ. Co., 1956.

13. TROWELL, O. A.: The culture of mature organs in a synthetic medium. Exptl. Cell Res. *16:*118–147, 1959.

14. RUBEN, L. N.: Possible immunological factors in amphibian lymphosarcoma development. *In* Biology of Amphibian Tumors (M. Mizell, ed.), Springer-Verlag New York Inc., 1969, pp. 368–384.

15. RAFFERTY, K. A.: Kidney tumors of the Leopard frog: a review. Cancer Res. *24:*169–185, 1964.

16. SIMNETT, J. D., and MORLEY, A. R.: Factors controlling growth of prostatic epithelium. Exptl. Cell Res. *46:*29–36, 1967.

17. STEPHENSON, E. M.: Effects of temperature on tadpole hearts *in vitro.* J. Embryol. Exptl. Morphol. *17:*147–159, 1967.

18. SIMNETT, J. D.: The prolongation of homograft survival time in the Platanna, *Xenopus laevis laevis* (Daudin), by exposure to low environmental temperature. J. Cell and Comp. Physiol. *65:*293–298, 1965.

19. BALLS, M.: Cell transformation in xenoplastic transplantation of an amphibian lymphoid tumour. Rev. Suisse Zool. *71:*805–813, 1964.

20. GOSS, R. J.: Adaptive Growth. Logos Press, London, and Academic Press, New York, 1964.

21. JONES, R. O.: Factors affecting the survival of organ cultures of the mammalian pancreas. Exptl. Cell Res. *47:*403–407, 1967.

22. BULLOUGH, W. S.: Mitotic and functional homeostasis: a speculative review. Cancer Res. *25:*1683–1727, 1965.

23. CAIRNIE, A. B., LAMERTON, L. F., and STEEL, G. G.: Cell proliferation studies in the intestinal epithelium of the rat. Exptl. Cell Res. *39:*528–538, 539–553, 1965.

Acceptance and Regression of a Strain-specific Lymphosarcoma in Mexican Axolotls[1]

Louis E. DeLanney and Kate Blackler

Department of Biology
Ithaca College
Ithaca, New York [2]

A closed colony [3] of dark (DD) and white (dd) Mexican axolotls (*Ambystoma mexicanum*) was analyzed, by skin allografting, for acceptance or rejection. From this analysis three major histocompatibility factors were identified and designated A^h, B^h, and C^h (1, 2). These factors behave as codominants and segregate as would be expected (2), thus: $B^hB^h \times C^hC^h \rightarrow B^hC^h \times B^hC^h \rightarrow \frac{1}{4}B^hB^h : \frac{1}{2}B^hC^h : \frac{1}{4}C^hC^h$. Although the factors may turn out to be complex, they appear to be *relatively* rapid within the context of chronic rejection characteristic of urodeles. The onset of rejection occurs at 28 days ± 7 days. In addition to these factors, there are relatively "weak" factors that may produce chronic rejection initiated at about 90 days or later; no attempt has yet been made to analyze these in detail. Rapid chronic rejection has the characteristic manifestations (Plate I, upper left and right) described for several amphibia (4, 5, 6, 7): there is epidermal hyperplasia in the graft and replacement from the edges by the host's epidermis; if the graft is pigmented, the epidermal cells become punctate but if the graft is unpigmented on a pigmented host, the host's epidermal melanocytes move in with the replacing epidermis; there is marked vasodilation which is almost always followed by stasis and disintegration of the vascular bed.

The Lymphosarcoma: Its Origin. The lymphosarcoma (8) appeared as localized swellings in grafts reciprocally made between adult [4] $A^hC^h \times C^hC^h$ animals. The tumor was recognized and transplantable only after third set allografting. Attempts to pass the tumor were successful only in animals known to be either homozygous or heterozygous for C^h. Although the pathology of the solid tumor makes it appear

[1] Supported by Public Health research grant GM15363-02 from the Institute for General Medical Sciences.

[2] The assistance and involvement of Mr. Sven Warner in the execution of the experiments is gratefully acknowledged.

[3] The kind cooperation of Professor R. R. Humphrey of Indiana University is acknowledged with deep appreciation. He made possible the establishment of the axolotl colony, and has continually assisted in identifying genealogies of animals derived from his stock.

[4] The Mexican axolotl is neotenic. The term "adult" refers to an animal that has achieved most of its growth and is believed to be sexually mature; the term does not apply to a post-metamorphic condition in the context of this paper.

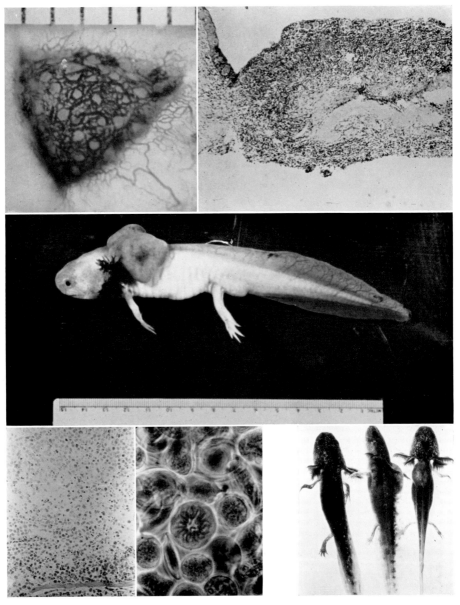

PLATE 1

Upper left: Vigorous rejection, with stasis, of a white graft on a white host (scale in mm). *Upper right:* Section of a graft in rejection. Host tissue on left. *Center:* White axolotl bearing a well-developed tumor passed as a small rod, ca. 2 mm $\times$ 0.5 mm, into the anterior base of the dorsal fin. *Lower left:* Segment of integument with tumor. The epidermis is at the upper left corner; the epimysial area is at the bottom. *Lower center:* Phase contrast photo of freshly drawn blood of a terminal lymphocytic leukemia stage. The lymphoid cells predominate over erythrocytes, one of which can be seen adjacent, lower left, to the cell in metaphase. *Lower right:* Three Netherlands darks that received small rods of tumor in the base of the dorsal fin at 28 days of age. Tumor flourished in all three, is present on the two on the right, has regressed on the one at the left at 58 days of age, and subsequently regressed on the other two.

to be a true lymphosarcoma, its terminal stages are often accompanied by a lympho-cytic leukemia and granulocytes are common in the blood (Plate I, lower left and right).

The Lymphosarcoma: Phenotypic Stability. The tumor (Plate I, center) is very stable, highly metastatic, shows no evidence of inducing host cell transformation, and appears to be passed intact to appropriate strains. This is confirmed by thymectomy of histoincompatible animals (3) which will then support tumor growth. Tumor grown in a histoincompatible thymectomized animal can be successfully passed back to the C^h strain, but can not be passed into thymus-intact siblings of the first thy-mectomized group.

The Lymphosarcoma: Karyotypic Analysis. Analysis of 169 axolotl cells shows that 69% of the cells believed to be tumorous bear an extra chromosome (n = 14) while only 6% of the cells from non-tumorous animals or tissues believed not to be tumorous possess 29 chromosomes. No specific trisomy is identified, but the extra chromosome appears in highest incidence to resemble chromosome 8 or chromosomes 12 and/or 13.

The Lymphosarcoma: Its Passage. The tumor can be passed by implants of solid tumor, enzyme dissociated tumor, whole blood, buffy coat, liver, spleen, testis, and coelomic fluid from tumorous animals. Cells in short term culture in modified Eagle's medium, cells kept for 21 days in Eagle's medium at 4°C, and short-term cultures of cells diluted 0.1^4 (statistically 80 cells/ml) also produced localized tumors when introduced intradermally.

Failure to Pass Tumor. The tumor has not been passed by cell-free means in any form. Heat treatment at 56° for 15 min. prevents its passage. However, three ani-mals of a group that received tumor subjected to a double freeze-thaw cycle did come in positive. Normally an animal that receives a tumor plant shows overt signs of a positive nature within 6–8 weeks after planting. The three animals cited above were not positive until 24 weeks after implantation. The possibility of survival of living cells from the freeze-thaw cycle is not definitely excluded.

Genealogical Background for Studies of Tumor Antigens and Tumor Immunity. The laboratory is stocked with axolotls from 4 sources: 1. A random sample of animals received from Humphrey included dark animals which tested as B^hB^h or B^hC^h, and light animals which tested as C^hC^h, A^hC^h or B^hC^h. Crosses were then made in order to select out homozygous B^h and C^h strains of both colors. The dark line in this laboratory originated from 4 of Humphrey's animals, three homozygous darks and a heterozygous dark (Fig. 1). Data show that the C^h-strain traces back to a stock of white animals Humphrey kept as a separate line since receiving them from the Wistar Institute in 1935; this subline of C^h is here designated *wis*. The other subline of C^h-strain traces to a remote dark ancestry. The significance of this differ-ence becomes apparent later. 2. Siblings imported from the Netherlands and having two "strong" histocompatibility factors which differ from A^h, B^h, and C^h. 3. Descend-

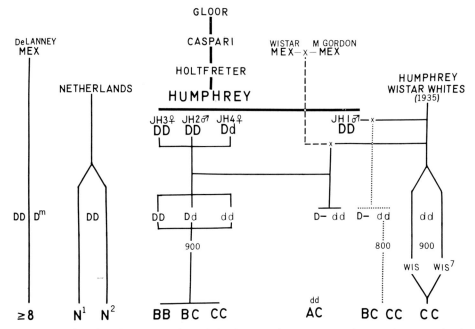

Fig. 1. Genealogical background of the axolotl colony. *Right:* White animals retained as an isolated strain, or as a true inbred strain presently for 9 generations, since 1935. *Center:* Four animals, JH1–JH4, received by Humphrey from Holtfreter and traced to animals randomly assembled by Gloor for shipment to Caspari. (No known descendants of imports from Mexico by the Wistar Institute or by M. Gordon remain in the colony.) *Left:* Thirty siblings received from Utrecht fall into two histocompatibility groups. Thirty randomly caught animals from near Mexico City could be classified for histocompatibility only upon minimal assignment of 8 alleles as a model. (Not shown are imports from England.) (Three-digit numbers refer to the number of spawnings to the nearest hundred at the time of the construction of the chart.)

ants of randomly caught axolotls from nature in Mexico and whose histocompatibility analysis shows a minimum of 8 factors. 4. White animals from Southampton (London stock) presumably not bred with darks. There are various crosses also in stock, e.g., Netherlands/C^h, Mexican/C^h, etc. derived from the sources named above.

Analysis of Strain-Specificity of the Tumor: the Role of Age. Two approaches to strain-specificity were undertaken. The first, the role of age in tumor development was based on the knowledge that the immunological competence of young animals is different from that of older animals and also that generally the young of many animals are more susceptible to viruses. Four hundred and ninety-five axolotls of ages ranging from 26 days to 107 days from spawning served as hosts. As Table 1 shows, no C^{wis} animals that become positive ever reject the tumor and it is always lethal. Young animals of the B^h strain allow tumor to develop but some of them, planted as young as 40 days of age, can later mount a rejection and cause an established tumor to regress completely. Conversely, in some others, tumor will develop when animals are planted at 100 days of age. In the B^h group, however, the tumor is rarely lethal; it will usually be regressed sooner or later by all individuals. Animals of

TABLE 1

AGE AND THE CAPACITY TO REJECT THE LYMPHOSARCOMA

Age in days	No. planted	No. +ve	No. −ve	Mean no. days to tumor onset	Mean no. days to death	Mean no. days to obvious regression	Host type
26	17	15	2	42	75		C
33	11	7	4	45	185		C
35	18	13	5	43			C^{wis}
43	19	19	0	47	97		C^{wis}
50	6	6	0	43	90		C^{wis}
55	13	12	1	56			C^{wis}
59	4	4	0	61	120		C^{wis}
63	4	3	1	19			C
64	8	8	0	23	68		C
70	9	6	3	50	98		C^{wis}
76	9	9	0	57	94		C^{wis}
83	4	4	0	19			C
85	10	10	0	31	94		C^{wis}
90	10	10	0	30	105		C
95	24	18	6	35	80		C
95	8	8	0	31	125		C
105	5	2	3	30			C
107	5	5	0	19			C^{wis}
34	18	0	18				B (dd)
40	18	13	5	43		72	B (dd)
45	14	13	1	43	98	72	B (dd)
51	15	15	0	38		59	B (dd)
29	3	3	0	12			B (DD)
30	25	22	3	35	90		B (DD)
88	15	15	0	25		46	B (DD)
90	15	12	3	33		50	B (DD)
100	6	4	2	36		58	B (DD)
99	9	9	0	32	73		BC
101	10	10	0	28	76		BC
35	23	8	15	34	125	65	Netherlands
43	11	2	9	50		80	Netherlands
51	15	0	15				Netherlands
54	15	8	7	25	58		Netherlands
58	10	1	9	42		61	Netherlands
64	23	16	7	28		56	Netherlands
78	5	2	3	28			Netherlands
83	4	1	3	38		58	Netherlands

TABLE 1 (cont.)

TABLE 1 (cont.)

Age in days	No. planted	No. +ve	No. −ve	Mean no. days to tumor onset	Mean no. days to death	Mean no. days to obvious regression	Host type
28	13	7	6	41	84	62	Mex (mm)
51	8	6	2	35			Mex
70	9	7	2	16		49	Mex (mm)
78	10	9	1	14		34	Mex (mm)
93	11	5	6	25		35	Mex (mm)
41	16	16	0	20			Mex/CxMex/C

dd = white.
DD = dark.
mm = melanoid.

the Netherlands and Mexican derivation reacted similarly, but show a lower percentage of individuals that allow an initial flourishing of tumor.

It should be noted that animals deriving from a B × C^{wis} spawning uniformly succumb to the tumor as juveniles and as adults. Animals deriving from a BC^{wis} × BC^{wis} spawning, however, succumb to the tumor in a 3:1 ratio (Table 2, spawning 67-33).

Strain-Specificity: Regression in Adult C^h-strain. The second study resulted from an unexpected observation that some adult animals of C^h-strain could proliferate large (2cm. diameter) tumors from small plants and then rapidly have the tumors regress. Siblings similarly planted would die with tumors but the regressed animals survived. Rarely did such survivors proliferate tumors from subsequent plantings either from the same or from a different donor. The preliminary review of the C^h-strains which regressed showed that they were closely related, and later studies showed that this line went back to the crossing of the white and dark animals. This observation made it obvious that genetic analysis for tumor regression was needed. Table 2 summarizes studies on 293 animals in 16 different spawnings. It is quite obvious that parents known to have either regressed tumor or to have failed to develop tumor when first planted, do not produce offspring who show competence to reject tumor in the first 4½ months. Regression is seen in only 2 of 217 animals younger than 137 days. On the other hand, in animals a year old or older, the ratio is 18/97. However, the data present contradictory information. Spawning 66-125 at 360 days produced 2 regressions out of 10 but in two plantings 80 days later and totalling 20 animals, none regressed. On the other hand, in spawning 66-10 only 1 of 20 regressed tumor when planted at 458 days of age but when another group of the same spawning was planted at age 717 days all but one regressed. The principal conclusion at this moment from these data (and other unpublished data) is that in animals of the C^h line the

TABLE 2

ANALYSIS OF REGRESSION OF LYMPHOSARCOMA

Spawning code	Age at planting in days	Parents ♀	Parents ♂	No. +ve	No. -ve	No. regressed	No. days to regression	No. days to +ve	No. days to death
				NO REGRESSIONS					
67-28	98 / 133 / 153	2066-9	1945-9	15/19	4/19				
67-33	100	1908-46BC	1908-7BC	16/20	4/20			58	118
67-42	105	2411-92wis	65-52-8 (B^h)	20/20				41	112
67-43	111	65-10-1	65-10-2	20/20				41	148
67-29	119	65-13-4	65-13-8	9/19	10/19			87	133
67-46	122	65-33-34	65-33-25	20/20				41	140
67-44	124	2068-38	2068-46	20/20				52	122
67-45	124	65-11-7	65-11-8	19/20	1/20			44	132
67-22	127	65-11-6	65-11-5	20/20				34	95
67-47	137	65-3-24	65-3-20	20/20				29	165
				REGRESSIONS					
67-26	94	65-33-19	65-33-28	18/19	1/19	2/19	95	49	117
66-135	200	65-16-42	64-36-7	7/7	0	0		81	129
	377			7/10	3/10	6/10	149		
66-125	360	65-23-7	65-13-2	10/10	0	2/10	136	51	187
	441			14/20	6/20	0			
				18/20	2/20	0			
66-10	458	64-16-42	64-16-40	20/20	0	1/20	201	62	211
	717			10/10	0	9/10	114	80	167

TABLE 3

C^{wis}		C^h non-wis	
(a) Two exposures to tumor before challenge	(b) One exposure to tumor before challenge	(a) Two exposures to tumor before challenge	(b) One exposure to tumor before challenge
2 +ve 3 −ve	4 +ve	4 −ve	1 +ve 8 −ve

capacity to mount a reaction against tumor appears usually to mature quite late. The data do not support a stable episome concept or give credence to a vertical transmission hypothesis.

Strain-Specificity: Immune Competence Compared Between C^{wis} and C^h. Because the evidence shows that C^{wis} always accept and succumb to the tumor, it was questioned whether the C^{wis} line possessed the ability to mount an immune reaction against tumor. Accordingly, the experimental design involved planting both C^{wis} and C^h non-wis with tumor into a limb. The limb could be amputated, thus hopefully removing the tumor completely after the putative tumor antigens had provided a challenge to the host. Twenty C^{wis} and 20 C^h non-wis strain animals were each planted with tumor to the rear right leg. After 55 days the leg was amputated on all animals. Each group of 20 animals was further subdivided into two groups of 10. Ten C^{wis} and 10 C^h non-wis, designated group (a) received tumor plants to the left rear leg; tumor developed on this leg and it was amputated 79 days later. Thirty-one days were allowed to elapse and then challenging tumor was planted to the dorsal fin of the pelvic region. The remaining 10 C^{wis} and 10 C^h non-wis, designated group (b), were challenged with tumor 50 days after the right rear leg was amputated. Thus, one set of animals included both C^{wis} and C^h non-wis, received two doses of tumor before the definitive challenge; the other set received only one dose. Table 3 shows the results. (This group composes the survivors of an *Oodinium* infestation in the colony.) The data confirm the existence of a tumor-specific transplantation antigen (TSTA). This TSTA provokes a stronger immune reaction in C^h non-wis than in C^{wis}.

Discussion

While the causative factors for the origin of the tumor can only be speculative, the present information does not show any evidence of viral involvement. On the other hand, the circumstances associated with its origin are not inconsistent with hypotheses proposed by Green (9), and Tyler (10), and they are similar to conditions reported in mice by Schwartz and Beldotti (11), namely, that the onset of the tumor may be associated with immune stress. This turned attention to possible tumor-specific immune mechanisms in the axolotl. The problem was approached from two points of view: the histoincompatible animals and the histocompatible animals within the 30 day range of allograft rejections.

The adult histoincompatible animals of the B^h, Netherlands and Mexican strains show no overt evidence of even transient flourishing of the transplanted tumor from C^h-strain donors. However, consistent with skin allograft studies in young animals of the same strains (12), the tumor flourishes transiently but is subsequently regressed. The tumor is never lethal to the adult and rarely lethal to the young host.

The C^h non-*wis* adults are histocompatible to skin allografts of C^{wis} strain within the 30 day period. (There is evidence of chronic rejection between C^h and C^{wis} that appears at the earliest at 90 days and often much later.) In C^{wis} animals the tumor is equally lethal to the young and to the adults. However, while the tumor can be lethal to both young and adult C^h non-*wis* animals, it is relatively rare for young animals to regress a flourishing tumor; this is not so rare in adults. This suggested that there was a differential capacity between the two C^h strains to mount a tumor immunity.

The evidence from a pilot study involving tumor planting and excision strongly suggests that when the host is not overwhelmed by proliferating lymphoma cells, it can indeed mount a tumor-specific immunity, but the evidence still stands that C^{wis} is less effective in accomplishing this. The axolotl, an atypical urodele, thus manifests a spectrum of immunological competences consistent with the evidence from the large body of literature dealing with other vertebrates. That is, it shows definable histocompatible strains, a capacity to develop tolerance (12), a competence to produce circulating antibodies (13), a stable non-transforming tumor bearing a tumor-specific transplantation antigen.

Summary

In a colony containing histocompatibility strains of Mexican axolotls (*Ambystoma mexicanum*), a lymphosarcoma is normally specific for the C^h strain. It is passed by several means, e.g., transplantation of skin, blood, liver, spleen, etc., which demonstrate the need for viable cells. No subcellular fractions have passed the tumor and there is no evidence clearly supporting host cell transformation. Adult histoincompatible hosts do not visibly proliferate tumor or pass it unless they were thymectomized at early larval ages or made tolerant to C^h strain prior to planting the tumor. Evidence accumulates that C^h strain possesses at least one substrain which allows the tumor to proliferate and then regress. Just as young animals mature in their capacity to reject skin allografts, histoincompatible strains also mature in ability to regress tumor. Also, the C^h strain animal that invariably dies from single plants of tumor can be made immune by a regimen of tumor planting and excision.

References

1. DeLanney, L. E.: Homografting of sexually mature Mexican axolotls. Amer. Zool. *1:* 349, 1961.
2. Meier, A. H. and Delanney, L. E.: Histocompatibility studies in the Mexican axolotl. Amer. Zool. 2:431, 1962.
3. DeLanney, L. E. and Prahlad, K. V.: unpublished.
4. Hildemann, W. H. and Haas, R.: Homotransplantation immunity and tolerance in the bullfrog. J. Immunol. *83:*478–485, 1959.

5. Erickson, R. P.: Reactions to homografts in *Triturus viridescens*. Transpl. Bull. *30*:137–140, 1962.

6. Bovbjerg, A. M.: Rejection of skin homografts in larvae of *Rana pipiens*. J. Exp. Zool. *162*:69–80, 1966.

7. Cohen, Nicholas: Tissue transplantation immunity in the adult newt, *Diemictylus viridescens*. I. The latent phase: healing, restoration of circulation, and pigment cell changes in autografts and allografts. J. Exp. Zool. *163*:157–172, 1965.

8. DeLanney, L. E., Prahlad, K. V. and Meier, A. H.: A malignant lymphoma in the Mexican axolotl. Amer. Zool. *4*:279, 1964.

9. Green, H. N.: Immunological aspects of cancer. *In* Ciba Foundation Symposium, Carcinogenesis: Mechanism of Action (G. E. W. Wolstenholme and M. O'Connor, eds.). London: J. A. Churchill Ltd., 131, 1959.

10. Tyler, A.: A developmental immunogenetic analysis of cancer. *In* Henry Ford Hospital International Symposium, Interactions in Normal and Neoplastic Growth. Boston: Little, Brown and Co. (Inc.), 533–571, 1962.

11. Schwartz, R. S. and Beldotti, L.: Malignant lymphomas following allogenic disease: transition from an immunological to a neoplastic disorder. Science, *149*:1511–1514, 1965.

12. DeLanney, L. E., Blackler, M. K. and Prahlad, K. V.: The relationship of age to allograft and tumor rejection in Mexican axolotls. Amer. Zool. *7*:763, 1967.

13. Ching, Y. and Wedgwood, R.: Immunologic responses in the axolotl, *Siredon mexicanum*. Jour. Immunol. *99*:191–200, 1967.

Development of Biologically Defined
Strains of Amphibians[1]

GEORGE W. NACE and CHRISTINA M. RICHARDS

Department of Zoology
and the Center for Human Growth and Development
The University of Michigan
Ann Arbor, Michigan

Throughout this Symposium (1) two threads of thought are implicit. The first is that the amphibian is a desirable organism on which to conduct tumor and virus research, but that living amphibian material, either in culture or as the whole animal, must be brought under more adequate biological control. Reference has repeatedly been made to the use of wild amphibians in a variety of experimental situations. In no case has reference been made to the nutritional or health status of the animals involved. The only attempts at genetic definition have been by reference to karyotyping, with the exception of work with some urodeles which have been maintained in laboratory colonies for significant periods. It is evident from the work of Moore (2) and McKinnell (3) that the biology of *Rana pipiens* from closely adjacent populations may differ markedly. Important genetic differences among animals from different commercial shipments must be expected. The second line of thought is that viruses are somehow associated with the development of the Lucké renal adenocarcinoma. Only the approach developed by Tweedell (4) and utilized by Mulcare (5) has routinely resulted in the induction of tumors by inoculation of a virus-containing fraction. Tumors have been induced in other cases (6) but the incidence has been below that desirable for routine analysis of the biology of this tumor. Granoff (7) has specifically indicated the failure to induce tumors in frogs with cultured agents isolated from tumor-bearing frogs.

It is common knowledge that the investigation of tumor biology in mammals made uncertain progress until inbred tumor-susceptible and -resistant strains became available. Amphibian tumor biology does not seem to be an exception.

At the last symposium which assembled investigators working with the Lucké renal adenocarcinoma, Nace *et al.* (8, 9) presented evidence for the absence of a normal kidney antigen from the tumor tissue. This antigen was found to be a bacteriolytic substance tentatively identified as a lysozyme. Crude assays of this material showed differences in concentration among frogs from different populations; one population seemed to be tumor-susceptible, the other tumor-resistant. Brief mention

[1] These investigations were supported by National Science Foundation grant GB 4677, by the U.S.-Japan Cooperative Science Program, National Science Foundation grant GF 242, by Damon Runyon Memorial Fund grant DRG-980, and by a grant from the Michigan Cancer Research Fund.

409

was also made to preliminary evidence which suggested that seasonal fluctuations occur in the level of lysozyme within the kidney of the frog. It was hypothesized that this enzyme might be related to the etiology of the tumor and initial tests of this hypothesis revealed that this enzyme inhibited plaque formation by FV-3 virus when tested on monolayer cultures of fathead minnow cells (10). Mulcare (5), however, has found some evidence for enhancement of tumor induction in tadpoles when his active fractions were incubated with lysozyme.

Subsequent efforts to test the hypothesis involved isolation of the enzyme now unequivocally identified as a lysozyme. This proved to be difficult when it was found that lysozyme in the frog exists in multiple-molecular forms—perhaps as many as 9— and that these forms are differentially distributed among the tissues. Indeed, it has been found that low levels of some of these lysozymes can even be found in the tumor tissue, although the selection of the molecular forms in the tumor seems to be different from that found in the normal kidney. Evidence is also developing which suggests individual variation with respect to the lysozyme composition of these animals. Quite clearly, it is impossible to test the hypothesis concerning the involvement of lysozyme in the etiology of the Lucké tumor without adequate biological and genetic control of the test organisms and without a strain of animals uniformly susceptible to a tumor-inducing agent. This need for defined strains of amphibians for the tumor studies and for other studies concerned with molecular aspects of embryonic development has forced the initiation of a program designed to produce them.

The description of such a program at the Amphibian Facility of The University of Michigan and of the equipment and procedures developed for the maintenance of large numbers of amphibians, particularly anurans, has recently appeared (11). This information will not be reiterated here. Briefly, the program has three objectives. First, research on defined strains of amphibians. Second, development of the strains themselves, and research on amphibian biology designed to answer questions as needed for the purpose of developing such defined strains. Third, production of animals from these strains in sufficient number to constitute a resource for the biological community.

The purpose of this presentation is to indicate a few of the observations which have emerged from the maintenance of large numbers of animals and to indicate some of the progress that has been made toward the objective of developing defined strains, including strains which would be useful in studies of the Lucké renal adenocarcinoma. This is not a definitive report inasmuch as the work is very much in progress and final results are not available. It is important to emphasize that while husbandry procedures have been fairly well established, many questions of the biology and pathology (12) of amphibians under laboratory conditions have arisen but have not yet been answered. In addition, many potential progenitors of important research strains have emerged, but the process of selecting strains for large scale propagation is still in progress.

Mode of Reproduction

The routine procedures for bisexual and diploid gynogenetic reproduction of R. *pipiens* in the Amphibian Facility has been described in detail (11). Diploid gynogenesis is a procedure which results in fertilization of the egg by its second polar body, thus reconstituting the diploid state without utilizing the haploid genome of the sperm. Our understanding of the mechanisms of meiosis and of gynogenesis suggests that this should result in the production of offspring homozygous at all loci except for those at which recombination has occurred. If true, a 50:50 ratio of simple Mendelian characters should appear from heterozygous females, and 100% production of traits should appear from homozygous females. Departures from the 50:50 ratio are a direct expression of recombination. It should be evident, then, that the basic outlines of a genetic map should be readily constructed within a few generations by combination of gynogenetic reproduction with selected bisexual matings.

As one result of gynogenesis, 100% females would be expected if the female is homogametic. If the female is heterogametic, however, 50% ZZ males to 50% WW females would be expected; this situation has not heretofore been reported for *Ranidae* although it does occur in other amphibians (13, 14). At the Amphibian Facility, heterosexual matings of *R. pipiens* have resulted in the expected 50:50 male-female ratio, but diploid gynogenetic eggs from the same females have produced 1:3 (34: 102) male-female ratios.[1] Such a ratio, plus the failure to identify sex chromosomes in the *Ranidae*, render difficult an understanding of normal sex control in these organisms until further studies have been completed. This is not the place to expand further on this question, but it must be emphasized that many observations on the biology or pathology of an organism must remain uninterpreted when such fundamental information as the normal mechanism of sex regulation within the species is not understood.

Other unusual observations have been made on the gynogenetic material. Distances from the kinetochore have been calculated (16) for three clearly recognizable color mutants: burnsi, a dominant color pattern in which there is a failure of spot development; kandiyohi, a dominant, which has a complicated patterning between the spots; and melanoid, a recessive, which will be described elsewhere[2] but which lacks both xanthophores and iridiophores [see color plate in Nace (11)]. Table 1 presents this data. Further analysis revealed that these mutants are not linked. The most interesting analysis resulted when the assumption was made that kinetochore division, i.e., equational division, occurs at meiosis I, rather than at meiosis II, the reverse of the situation recognized for most genetic systems. In this case, a 1:5 segregation ratio rather than a 50:50 ratio would be expected. The data show that the burnsi and melanoid segregation ratios do not differ significantly from 1:5, a figure which is in close agreement with the burnsi gynogenetic diploid segregation ratio observed by Volpe and Dasgupta (15) on a sample of 17 animals. This was not true, however, for the kandiyohi mutant. Two conclusions are possible from this analysis: either that two mutants, randomly selected for analysis, had, by chance, the same recombination frequency—a frequency which also is the same as the segregation frequency expected if kinetochore division occurs at meiosis I; or that kinetochore division can occur at meiosis I. Although further tests must be conducted, it now

---

[1] Volpe and Dasgupta (15) reported 6 males and 11 females among 17 gynogenetic diploid *R. pipiens*.

[2] See: Richards *et al.*, Copeia, in press.

TABLE 1

GYNOGENETIC PROGENY

Progeny \ Phenotype / Maternal	Burnsi Bb	Kandiyohi Kk	Wildtype Mm
B-, K-, mm	283	179	53
bb, kk, M-	53	126	220
Total progeny	336	305	273
% Heterozygotes	68.5	17.4	61.2
Distance from kinetochore in CMU *			
K = 0.20	41.4	8.9	35.6
K = 1.00	‡	10.1	‡
χ^2 for 1:5 ratio	.19	133.5 †	1.48

* Distance based on assumption of kinetochore segregation at meiosis II.

† $\chi_1^2 = 3.841$ at P = .05.

‡ Map distance undefined.

mm = Melanoid; CMU = Centi-Morgan Units (18); K = Coefficient of Coincidence (18).

seems quite possible that some chromosomes in R. *pipiens* may follow the classical pattern and undergo reduction at meiosis I, e.g., kandiyohi data, whereas others, e.g., burnsi and melanoid data, may undergo equational division at this meiotic step, a possibility also suggested by Lindsley *et al.* (17) in an analysis of three different markers in the Mexican axolotl.

These observations, plus those of Rafferty (19) on relative chromosome stability for amphibian cells in culture, suggest that some unusual processes may be associated with certain aspects of cell division in these amphibians, and further, suggest caution in the interpretation of all experiments which depend upon these two processes. In addition, these observations have significant implications with regard to the procedures required to develop isogenetic colonies of amphibians.

Reproductive Cycle

One circumstance which has arisen in the course of maintaining R. *pipiens* in the Amphibian Facility has been the dissociation of its life cycle from the seasonal cycles. It is now possible routinely to ovulate a mature female every three to five months, and animals produced in the laboratory may be ovulated for the first time within 12–13 months. However, isolation of the animals from the synchronizing influence of the seasonal cycles results in asynchrony of egg maturation. Whereas a female fresh from nature yields 2000–3000 eggs, a female which reaches the reproductive phase in the laboratory may produce only 200–300 mature eggs. Examination of the ovary reveals that many eggs have passed maturity and are at various stages of resorption, whereas other eggs are still in their growth stages.

By acrylamide electrophoresis Hejmadi, in my laboratory, has identified a minimum of two special components in serum during the period of egg growth in females obtained directly from nature. These proteins cannot be identified in the male or in the female after the eggs have reached maturity, i.e., during hibernation, or during the immediate post-ovulatory period prior to the initiation of major egg growth. At least one of these constituents may be similar to the lipophosphoprotein described by Wallace and Jared (20) and by Follett and Redshaw (21) for *Xenopus*. However, this situation does not prevail in most females raised or maintained for multiple ovulations in the laboratory; these females contain these proteins at all times. Observations on males and females injected with estradiol reveal that at least one of these proteins is under estrogen regulation. Preliminary evidence suggests that estrogen is responsible not only for the production of these proteins, but also for the growth of eggs, and for the resorption of over-ripe eggs. We are now testing this hypothesis, as well as the additional hypothesis that the final maturation of the egg and its retention without resorption involves FSH.

It is evident from these observations that full exploitation of *R. pipiens* as a laboratory animal will require control of this reproductive cycle. We hope that our current investigations of this physiology will result in such control.

Strain Selection and Skin Grafting

Several criteria enter into the selection of animals as progenitors of major strains to be developed in the laboratory. Of first importance is the detection and propagation of mutants which affect color and color pattern. This can be readily accomplished by the use of gynogenetic procedures. Though important for the analysis of questions of developmental genetics, the significance of these mutants in the context of developing tumor-susceptible and -resistant strains is the desirability of using color markers to simplify laboratory manipulations once the tumor strains are established, provided that the markers are closely linked to whatever factors may be involved in tumor resistance or susceptibility. In addition to the albino and blue frogs previously illustrated (11), and to the burnsi, kandiyohi, and melanoid mutants mentioned above, at least 10 color variants are now being tested for genetic stability. A number of biochemical variants have also been found, thus there is every reason to be optimistic concerning the possibility of developing biochemical strains linked to useful color markers.

A second objective in the selection of progenitors is to develop isogenetic strains in which tumors can be maintained by serial transplantation. To this end, skin grafting tests are routinely conducted on gynogenetic progeny. This will be reported in detail elsewhere, but it might be mentioned here that the mean survival time under our conditions for grafts between unrelated frogs is approximately 16 days, regardless of whether the animals have recently metamorphosed or are adults. Grafts between first generation gynogenetic siblings, however, show survival times which range from 11 to more than 216 days, whereas grafts between gynogenetic and normally fertilized siblings are rejected within approximately 16 days. There has not yet been sufficient time to collect data on graft survival time for second-generation gyno-genetic siblings, but long term or permanent survival is expected. The wide spread of rejection times between first generation gynognetic siblings reflects, of course, the independent segregation among the wild-type mother's eggs which causes some of these siblings to be as different from each other as are non-related wild-type animals, and causes others to have a high degree of genetic similarity. On the other hand, grafts from gynogenetic offspring to their mothers all survive permanently.

The results of our attempts to establish lines with unique color markings and lines within which grafts can be maintained has been most encouraging. Some hundreds of frogs in these categories are in the laboratory, and it is anticipated that animals from these lines will be available to other investigators after another generation of production.

Tumor Lines

The critical test of progress toward the objective of developing tumor-susceptible and -resistant lines of animals is the number of potential progenitors of such lines which have been processed through the laboratory. Emphasis is first being placed on the selection of tumor-susceptible animals. These must be available in order to develop procedures to test for possible resistance in other lines. Thus, if a test procedure does not result in the production of tumors in a susceptible line, it certainly cannot be used to evaluate the resistance of other lines.

Tumors are obtained through three routes: 1) by direct shipment from amphibian dealers alert to our needs; 2) by personal collection from a local population; and 3) by spontaneous appearance among animals maintained in the colony. Palpation is used to detect these tumors. Consequently, the tumors are usually far advanced and the gametes—especially ova—are of exceptionally poor quality, or the animals do not survive under the conditions required to bring them to sexual maturation. A technique for early diagnosis of the tumor would be most useful in producing progeny from tumor-bearing animals. It has been possible to circumvent this difficulty when progeny are obtained from animals which subsequently develop spontaneous tumors in the laboratory.

Table 2 shows a tabulation of tumor-bearing frogs and progeny of such frogs assembled from records coded in our Termatrex system (11). This system has only recently been activated in the Amphibian Facility and is not yet complete. Therefore, this tabulation is not a complete record but does indicate the sources of tumor-bearing animals in the colony and the kinds of material from which we expect to develop tumor-susceptible lines.

It is of particular interest to draw attention to the appearance of tumors in frogs collected at Milford, Michigan, by personnel from the Amphibian Facility. This is the first verified report of tumors from frog populations other than those in Vermont and Wisconsin-Minnesota. Their proximity to the Amphibian Facility should permit a study of a wild tumor population in close conjunction with laboratory studies.

It is evident from Table 2 that, although the numbers of possible tumor line progenitors are still minimal, procedures have been developed to identify animals for reproduction.

TABLE 2

PROGENITORS OF TUMOR LINES?

| Source | Sex | | | Totals |
	♂	♀	?	
Tumor-bearing				
Alburg, Vt.	12	20	2	34
Oshkosh, Wis.	3	4		7
Milford, Mich.	1	3	2	6
Lab. raised				4
F₁ Vt, tumor			1	
F₁ Vt			1	
F₂ Vt × Vt gyno.		2		
Progeny of tumor-bearing				
L × L	1	1		2
L × –	13	15	17	45
L gyno.				0

Dealer Information

In the establishment of the Amphibian Facility it has been necessary to maintain close liaison with amphibian dealers. Five major dealers are responsible for approximately 90% of the supply of R. pipiens to educational and research centers, either directly or through jobbers. They collect and ship approximately 5,000,000 frogs per year. These men have observed frogs in nature over many years and are privy to extensive practical knowledge of the biology and, particularly, the behavior of amphibians.

Mr. C. H. Mumley has made an observation which should be brought to the attention of amphibian tumor biologists. It was he who provided tumor-bearing frogs to Professor Lucké throughout his investigations of this tumor. The tumor-bearing frogs from Alburg, Vermont, have been collected primarily in the watersheds of Mud Creek and Pike River, both of which flow into the northern portion of Lake Champlain. Each stream has received the discharge from at least three cheese factories. Several years ago, a dairy farmer on the banks of Mud Creek brought suit against the Mud Creek cheese factories for contaminating the water source used by his cattle. The presence of tumor-bearing frogs in Mud Creek was one of the major points of evidence used in this successful litigation which resulted in the abandonment of cheese factories on Mud Creek. In the several years which have intervened, the number of tumor-bearing frogs collected on Mud Creek has drastically decreased, and none have been collected there in the past two years. Cheese factories still utilize Pike River, and apparently tumor-bearing frogs are still to be found in that watershed. However, in the past few years the access routes to Pike River, which is in Canada, have been acquired by private interests who no longer permit transit to frog collectors. As a consequence, very few tumor-bearing frogs are now coming to the amphibian dealers in Alburg, Vermont, and the major source of these animals would seem to be in serious jeopardy.

Perhaps more significant than the question of availability is the meaning of these observations in our attempts to understand the biology of this tumor. This observation of the association of tumor-bearing frogs with polluted water systems may have a direct bearing on the report by McKinnell (3) that tumor-prone and tumor-free populations of frogs exist within 150 miles of each other.

Amphibian Resources

It is important to take note here of a serious circumstance which confronts students of amphibian biology and pathology. The demand for frogs for educational and research purposes has risen markedly in recent years. Concurrently, the areas from which frogs may be collected have markedly diminished, and, more important, the major experienced amphibian dealers either have reached an age when they cannot long continue their activities or have encountered financial obstacles which make it unprofitable to remain in the business. Younger men are not appearing to fill the anticipated need for this service. It behooves those of us who are actively engaged in studies using amphibians to develop an active concern for this problem if these studies are to be continued.

The Amphibian Facility

Sufficient experience has now been gained in the operation of the Amphibian Facility to suggest that laboratory production of amphibians for research is possible and will expand, but that for the next few years it will be able to provide for only part of the need for animals used in critical studies. Those conducting preliminary investigations and routine procedures in which the character of the research animal is of little moment will be obliged to continue using animals collected from the wild.

The only way in which this restricted supply will be relieved is by a sustained interest in the laboratory maintenance and production of amphibians. In addition to the objectives noted above, the Amphibian Facility stands ready to serve as a resource to develop this interest. The Amphibian Facility can board valuable animals and accept visiting investigators who may wish to utilize the resource to conduct certain experiments. Arrangements can also be made to accept visitors who may wish to learn the techniques of amphibian husbandry and production.

Summary

Difficulties in proving the viral etiology of the Lucké renal adenocarcinoma and in testing hypotheses concerning the biology of this tumor can be directly traced to the absence of laboratory colonies of appropriate amphibians, particularly *Rana pipiens*. Such a colony has now been developed in the Amphibian Facility of The University of Michigan and progress has been made in developing genetically defined strains. It is expected that a tumor-susceptible strain will emerge. Offspring of tumor-bearing animals are now being tested for susceptibility to Tweedell's oncogenically active fraction. Gynogenetic offspring which permanently accept grafts from one another are available in limited numbers. This should permit serial transplantation of tumors. It is anticipated that a reliable source of tumors under laboratory control will soon be available. Hypotheses concerning the possible role of lysozyme in the etiology of this tumor are being tested. Procedures and current progress is described. In addition to the tumor and skin graft data, this includes presentation of genetic data on gyno-genetic diploid frogs relating to sex determination and three color mutants, and of data on the reproductive cycle of laboratory raised frogs. Contributions of amphibian dealers to problems of amphibian biology are also described.

References

1. Symposium: Biology of Amphibian Tumors, Royal Orleans Hotel, New Orleans, Louisiana, October 28–30, 1968.

2. MOORE, J. A.: Interrelations of the populations of the *Rana pipiens* complex. *In* Biology of Amphibian Tumors (M. Mizell, ed.), Springer-Verlag New York Inc., 1969, pp. 26–34.

3. MCKINNELL, R. G.: Lucké renal adenocarcinoma: epidemiological aspects. *In* Biology of Amphibian Tumors (M. Mizell, ed.), Springer-Verlag New York Inc., 1969, pp. 254–260.

4. TWEEDELL, K. S.: Lucké tumor transmission through the oocyte. *In* Biology of Amphibian Tumors (M. Mizell, ed.), Springer-Verlag New York Inc., 1969, pp. 229–239.

5. MULCARE, D. J.: Non-specific transmission of the Lucké tumor. *In* Biology of Amphibian Tumors (M. Mizell, ed.), Springer-Verlag New York Inc., 1969, pp. 240–253.

6. DURYEE, W. R.: Dependence of tumor formation in frogs on abnormal nucleolar function. *In* Biology of Amphibian Tumors (M. Mizell, ed.), Springer-Verlag New York Inc., 1969, pp. 82–100.

7. GRANOFF, A.: Studies on the viral etiology of the renal adenocarcinoma of *Rana pipiens* (Lucké tumor). *In* Biology of Amphibian Tumors (M. Mizell, ed.), Springer-Verlag New York Inc., 1969, pp. 279–295.

8. NACE, G. W., T. SUYAMA, and T. IWATA: The relationship between a lysozyme-like enzyme and frog adenocarcinoma. Ann. N.Y. Acad. Sci. *126*:204–221, 1965.

9. NACE, G. W. and T. SUYAMA: The loss of a bacteriolytic enzyme associated with the appearance of a frog kidney tumor. SABCO J. *1*:1–5, 1965 (In Japanese).

10. RUBIN, M. L., D. B. AR, and G. W. NACE: The virus inhibiting action of a lysozyme present in normal frogs but lacking in tumor frogs and eggs. Am. Zool. *6*(4):#29, 1966.

11. NACE, G. W.: The Amphibian Facility of The University of Michigan. BioScience *18*(8): 767–775, 1968.

12. ABRAMS, G. D.: Diseases in a frog colony. *In* Biology of Amphibian Tumors (M. Mizell, ed.), Springer-Verlag New York Inc., 1969, pp. 419–428.

13. GALLIEN, L. G.: Genetic control of sexual differentiation in vertebrates. *In* Organogenesis (R. L. DeHaan and H. Ursprung, eds.), Holt, Rinehart and Winston, New York, pp. 583–610, 1965.

14. WITSCHI, E.: Biochemistry of sex differentiation in vertebrate embryos. *In* The Biochemistry of Animal Development (R. Weber, ed.), Academic Press, New York, Vol. II, pp. 193–225, 1967.

15. VOLPE, E. P. and S. DASGUPTA: Gynogenetic diploids of mutant leopard frogs. J. Exp. Zool. *151*:287–302, 1962.

16. ASHER, J.: personal communication.

17. LINDSLEY, D. L., G. FANKHAUSER and R. R. Humphrey: Mapping centromeres in the axolotl. Genetics *41*:58–64, 1956.

18. RAYMOND, W. B., D. NEWMEYER, D. D. PERKINS and L. GARNJOBST: Map construction in *Neurospora crassa*. *In* Advances in Genetics (M. Demerec, ed.), Academic Press, New York, Vol. VI, pp. 1–93, 1954.

19. RAFFERTY, K. A., JR.: Mass culture of amphibian cells: methods, and observations concerning stability of cell type. *In* Biology of Amphibian Tumors (M. Mizell, ed.), Springer-Verlag New York Inc., 1969, pp. 52–81.

20. WALLACE, R. A. and D. W. JARED: Estrogen induces lipophosphoprotein in serum of male *Xenopus laevis*. Science 160:91–92, 1968.

21. FOLLETT, B. K. and M. R. REDSHAW: The effects of oestrogen and gonadotrophins on lipid and protein metabolism in *Xenopus laevis Daudin*. J. Endocrinology 40:439–456, 1968.

Diseases in an Amphibian Colony[1]

GERALD D. ABRAMS

Department of Pathology and Unit for Laboratory Animal Medicine
The University of Michigan, Ann Arbor, Michigan

Although amphibia have long been the objects of detailed study in the field, and of experimental manipulation in the laboratory, relatively little attention has been devoted to the spontaneous diseases of these animals. In addition to the fact that the etiology and pathogenesis of most "naturally" occurring amphibian diseases are still poorly understood, the study of amphibian pathology has been further complicated by the recent introduction of methods of laboratory culture of a number of species; these methods, per se, creating new combinations of circumstances threatening the health of the animals.

As the experimental use of amphibia increases, and as these animals are maintained in laboratories in increasing numbers, the need for information concerning their health problems becomes more pressing. In this communication, therefore, the attempt is made to give, from the vantage point of the pathologist, a general perspective of the range of diseases encountered in amphibia maintained under laboratory conditions.

Materials and Methods

The animals used in this study were obtained from the Amphibian Facility of The University of Michigan, the operation of which has been described previously (1). *Rana pipiens* constitutes approximately 80–90% of the population of the facility, the remainder including a number of other anuran species and several species of urodeles. Most of the data collected in this study, therefore, relate to *R. pipiens*. However, the fragmentary information thus far available for other species in the colony suggests that comments concerning fundamental disease processes in *R. pipiens* are generally applicable to other amphibian species.

This report is based on approximately 100 detailed necropsies performed during the past 3 years on animals obtained from the Amphibian Facility. In addition to gross dissection and examination of each subject, necropsy often included, if allowed by the circumstances of death, bacteriological culture of the blood and of any apparently infectious lesions. In addition to samples of any grossly abnormal tissues, portions of heart, lungs, liver, spleen, kidney, and gastrointestinal tract were routinely prepared for histopathologic examination by formalin fixation, paraffin embedding, and staining of sections with hematoxylin and eosin.

[1] This investigation was supported in part by a NIH training grant, number GM 01067-04 and a Public Health Service grant 2PO6FR-00200-03.

The animals necropsied represent but a fraction of the total number of individuals found dead or identified as being ill during this time. Animals dying prior to metamorphosis were not included in this study. Metamorphosed individuals found dead generally were subjected only to simple gross examination of internal viscera unless deemed representative of a serious or unfamiliar problem. Thus, for instance, the study included only a few of the many individuals found to harbor the Lucké tumor. Similar criteria were used to select sick animals for euthanasia and necropsy.

Although for these reasons, precise quantitative conclusions relative to disease incidence cannot be drawn from the data, general impressions concerning the relative importance of various kinds of disease seen at necropsy correspond well to the overall clinical impressions of the staff.

Results

Infectious Diseases

Infectious diseases were, by far, the most important causes of morbidity and mortality among adult animals in the colony. In fully one-half of the necropsied cases, histologic and/or microbiological evidence indicated the presence of infection sufficiently severe to account for the observed clinical symptoms or death.

Of those animals with significant infection, approximately one-third had definite evidence of systemic, i.e., septicemic infection. Many of these individuals yielded positive bacteriological cultures of blood and/or internal organs, *Aeromonas* being the most commonly identified organism. Other isolates included gram negative organisms as yet unidentified, and *Staphylococcus epidermis* in one instance. Although some of the individuals with septicemia manifested signs and symptoms of the "red-leg" syndrome, some died with no perceptible premonitory signs. Gross examination of affected individuals was often unrewarding if the classic external signs of "red-leg" were absent. Microscopically, however, lesions were striking. Foci of necrosis were often evident in liver and spleen (Fig. 1) of animals with positive cultures. In some instances, the diagnosis of systemic infection was based on the histologic demonstration of myriads of organisms within various tissues (Figs. 2–4). Although the inflammatory reaction to bacteria in amphibian tissues was often slight, as compared to analogous reactions in mammals, areas of karyorrhexis and early leukocytic infiltrate around clumps of bacteria served to distinguish these examples from instances of artefact, i.e., postmortem bacterial growth so common in individuals "found" dead. In some animals necropsied immediately after euthanasia, large numbers of bacteria could be demonstrated in certain tissues, as shown in Fig. 2. In general, the precise portal of entry of these septicemic infections could not be determined.

In other animals harboring apparently infectious lesions, definite evidence of septicemia was lacking, although clinical circumstances often suggested strongly the likelihood of systemic spread from local lesions. The lesions recognized in this group included examples of conditions such as pneumonia, pyelonephritis, orbital cellulitis, brain abscess, infected compound fractures, infected injection sites, and a significant number of spontaneous cutaneous infections. A commonly observed clinical syndrome consisted of the appearance of cutaneous vesicles and pustules about the eyes

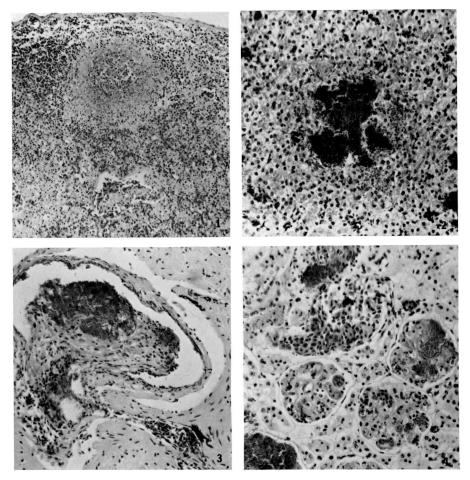

PLATE 1

Fig. 1. Focal splenic necrosis in septicemia. Only cellular debris remains in the light staining area. Hematoxylin and eosin. ×86.

Fig. 2. Clump of bacteria in liver. Note the surrounding zone of karyorrhexis and early leukocytic infiltrate. Hematoxylin and eosin. ×93.

Fig. 3. Clumps of bacteria within pulmonary blood vessel, apparently associated with organizing clot. Hematoxylin and eosin. ×79.

Fig. 4. Clumps of bacteria within renal glomeruli. Minimal evidence of karyorrhexis surrounding the dark clumps. Hematoxylin and eosin. ×120.

and ears. This syndrome seemed unrelated to "red-leg" but was occasionally associated with a high mortality rate in affected groups. An etiologic agent has not yet been identified, and the histologic appearance is non-specific (Fig. 5). In an occasional instance of isolated cutaneous ulcer it has been possible to demonstrate fungi in tissue sections with appropriate stains (Figs. 6–7).

Striking examples of apparently iatrogenic mycobacterial infection have been observed in the colony. Three years ago, 9 of a group of 21 *R. pipiens* in whom ovulation was being induced, and who had received progesterone-in-oil by injection into the dorsal lymph sac, developed indurated swellings at the site of injection. Three of these individuals were euthanized and found to have non-caseating granulomas in dorsal lymph sac, liver, and kidney (Fig. 8). Acid-fast bacilli were demonstrable in the lesions (Fig. 9) and group IV Mycobacteria were cultured from the lesions and from the water of the aquarium. It appeared that the mycobacteria had been intro-

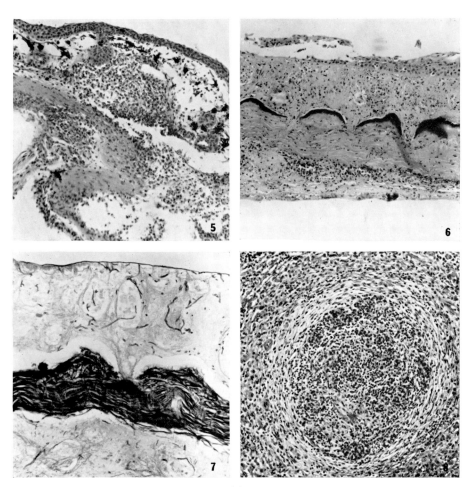

PLATE 2

Fig. 5. Pustular lesion in skin. Note the extent of the inflammatory infiltrate beneath the lesion itself. Hematoxylin and eosin. ×59.

Fig. 6. Histologically non-specific cutaneous ulcer. Note the diffuse inflammatory infiltrate throughout the section. Hematoxylin and eosin. ×59.

Fig. 7. The same lesion as in Fig. 6 stained with methenamine silver. Note the fungal hyphae throughout the section. ×90.

Fig. 8. Typical granuloma in liver of a frog with mycobacteriosis. Note the loose whorl of connective tissue about the central mass of lymphoid and mononuclear cells. Hematoxylin and eosin. ×76.

duced by the injection procedure. Subsequent investigation (2) indicated that these organisms are of a low order of virulence for the frog and that the oil in the inoculum potentiated the infection. More recently, only a few sporadic cases of mycobacteriosis have been observed, again usually in animals that have received percutaneous injections. Large outbreaks of the infection have not been observed since the original episode, probably because greater care has been used in maintaining the sterility of injected reagents now that ovulation is not induced as a terminal event.

Parasitic Infestation

Virtually all animals collected from the wild were found, regardless of the circumstances of their demise, to be infested with helminth parasites to some degree (Figs. 10–13). These infestations seemed generally inconsequential, and only in the rare instance, certainly less than 10% of the cases, did the assembled evidence suggest parasitism as a prime factor in the demise of the animal. In these latter cases, symptomatology seemed directly related to the density of infestation. Inflammatory reaction to the parasites was extremely unpredictable, often being imperceptible. The most commonly observed forms included *Hematoloechus* and *Rhabdias* in lung, and *Ophiotaenia* in coelomic cavity.

Laboratory-reared animals were generally easily distinguished from those collected in the field by the striking absence of helminth parasites from their tissues. Recently a few individuals reared in the laboratory have been found to harbor parasites, which have not as yet been specifically identified. *Rhabdias* and *Oswaldocruzia*, neither of which requires an intermediate host, seem to be likely candidates.

Nutritional Problems

Laboratory rearing of amphibia obviously introduces significant nutritional problems, some of which have been solved by elaborate diets (1). Continued poor survival of some species in the laboratory obviously reflects serious nutritional deficiency, although specific lesions often cannot be identified pathologically. Rickets constitutes the best example of a recognizable specific deficiency state seen in our necropsy material to date. Fig. 14 illustrates a typical lesion seen in *Rana sylvatica*. Rickets has also been recognized in *R. pipiens* and *R. japonica* in the facility, and therefore insects comprising the laboratory diets are now coated with multiple vitamins including D (1).

Neoplasms

Approximately one-sixth of the animals necropsied were found to harbor neoplasms. Because of the non-systematic exclusion of many grossly diagnosed examples of Lucké tumor from the necropsy series, this figure in no way reflects overall incidence of neoplasia. In keeping with other observations (3), renal adenocarcinoma was the most common neoplasm observed in our material: of 16 neoplasms observed microscopically, all but 3 were Lucké tumors. In 2 *R. pipiens* a small hepatoma (Fig. 15) was discovered incidentally. The third non-renal neoplasm, found also in *R. pipiens*, was considered to represent ovarian cystadenocarcinoma (Figs. 16–17).

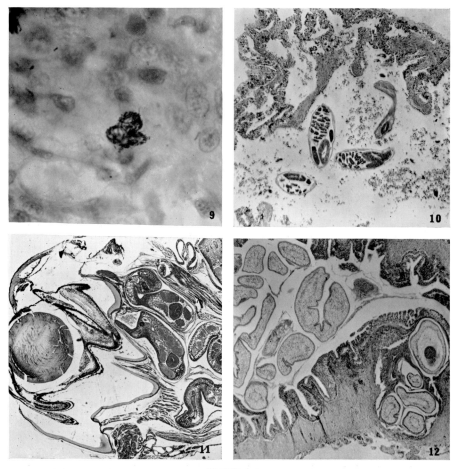

PLATE 3

Fig. 9. Acid-fast bacilli in a granuloma. Note the clump of organisms in the center. Ziehl-Neelsen. ×1230.

Fig. 10. Helminth parasites in lung. Hematoxylin and eosin. ×34.

Fig. 11. Massive infestation of retrobulbar tissues by helminth parasites. Hematoxylin and eosin. ×8.

Fig. 12. Helminth parasites within the lumen and the wall of the intestine. A slight inflammatory response surrounds the intramural parasites. Hematoxylin and eosin. ×13.

Miscellaneous Conditions

The cause of death remained indeterminate in approximately one-fifth of all animals in the series that had died spontaneously. Although clinical circumstances frequently suggested the likelihood of infection, often the tissues exhibited no lesions or were extensively autolyzed, and cultures, if taken at all, reflected only postmortem bacterial contamination.

Not infrequently, small granulomas were found in various organs microscopically.

It was not possible (with the exception of the case of mycobacteriosis) to relate these lesions to specific microbial agents. Some appear, by circumstantial evidence, to be associated with the passage of helminth parasites through the tissues.

At least one example has been encountered recently which illustrates that laboratory conditions can, per se, lead to striking anatomic findings (Dr. Christina Richards, personal communication). When egg-laden frogs are kept warm during the time they would ordinarily hibernate at low temperatures, the retained ova often degen-

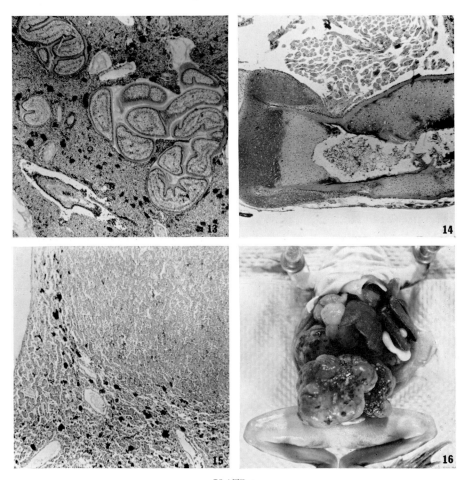

PLATE 4

Fig. 13. Heavy infestation of liver by helminth parasites. Hematoxylin and eosin. ×15.

Fig. 14. Rickets in *Rana sylvatica*. Note lack of calcification of portion of shaft of bone and irregular cartilaginous overgrowth with deformity. Hematoxylin and eosin. ×23.

Fig. 15. Hepatoma within liver. Note how the spherical tumor compresses adjacent parenchyma which contains numerous pigmented cells. Hematoxylin and eosin. ×24.

Fig. 16. Gross appearance of cystadenocarcinoma of ovary. The kidneys were free of neoplasm.

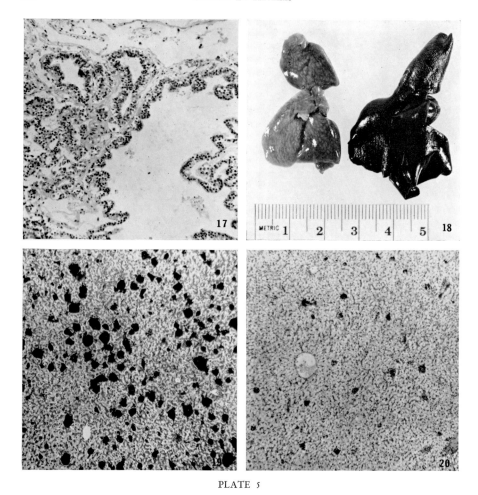

PLATE 5

Fig. 17. Microscopic appearance of neoplasm shown in Fig. 16. Hematoxylin and eosin. ×54.

Fig. 18. Gross appearance of liver from frog with resorbing ova. Compare the deeply pigmented liver on the right with the normal liver on the left.

Fig. 19. Photomicrograph of deeply pigmented liver in Fig. 18. Hematoxylin and eosin. ×37.

Fig. 20. Photomicrograph of normal liver in Fig. 18. Hematoxylin and eosin. ×37.

erate. Necropsy of these animals has revealed striking, jet black livers (Fig. 18), which microscopically are seen to contain abundant pigment, presumably liberated by the resorbing ova (Figs. 19–20).

Discussion

The results of this necropsy survey demonstrate, despite the limitations imposed by the sampling methods employed, that the most important diseases affecting laboratory populations of amphibia (at least beyond metamorphosis) are largely infectious. Observations of other colonies have led to similar conclusions (3).

The prominence of infectious disease in the laboratory situation is, given our present state of knowledge, not at all unexpected. Circumstances of crowding of animals and ready transmission of microbial agents on the one hand, conspire with subtle and poorly understood host resistance factors on the other, to produce devastating epizootics.

It is evident that even our descriptive information is incomplete, i.e., that the etiologic agents of many infectious diseases of amphibia have yet to be identified. The identification process is enormously hampered by the difficulty in detection of internal disease by clinical examination of living amphibians, and the difficulty in securing freshly-dead subjects for necropsy study. "Found" animals are too often unsuitable for microbiological and histologic study due to postmortem decomposition. Only by painstaking correlation of microbiological and histopathologic evidence accumulated at systematic necropsies of suitably selected cases can the details of etiology and pathogenesis be clarified. Certainly, identification of pathogens is the first step toward rational therapy of some of these diseases. However, given the difficulty of eliminating all potential pathogens from an aquatic environment, the satisfactory *control* and *prevention* of infectious disease in the laboratory environment ultimately will require an improved understanding of the factors affecting resistance of the amphibian host. At present, even with recognizable specific dietary deficiency states having been eliminated in certain species, the suspicion remains that laboratory amphibia may be abnormally susceptible animals.

The few diseases of amphibia that have been defined in studies such as this, obviously represent but a small segment of the whole of amphibian disease. The opportunity now available to study the diseases of these animals in the laboratory rather than the field should prove to be of great value despite the difficulties involved, if for no other reason than the fact that under field conditions sick and dying individuals are simply "lost" while in the laboratory they constitute a potential storehouse of valuable information.

Summary

Infectious diseases comprise a significant fraction of the conditions observed at necropsy of individuals in a colony of amphibians. Among these, apparently septicemic deaths (so-called "red-leg" syndrome) are common. Mycobacteriosis has been observed in a number of instances, often associated with certain injection procedures. Numerous other inflammatory lesions, presumably infectious, have been found but are difficult at present to associate with specific etiologic agents. Among individuals brought into the colony from the field, extensive visceral infestation with metazoan parasites is especially common. Nutritional problems are not infrequent under laboratory conditions, and striking examples of specific deficiency states such as rickets have been encountered. Spontaneous neoplasms other than the Lucké adenocarcinoma have been observed only rarely. At the present state of knowledge of amphibian medicine, many examples of disease and death in an amphibian colony continue to be of obscure etiology, even after careful pathological examination. In many instances these probably represent the results of subtle interaction between defects in host resistance and the presence of certain agents in the environment.

References

1. NACE, G. W.: The Amphibian Facility of The University of Michigan. Bioscience 18(8):767–775, 1968.
2. JOINER, G. N. and ABRAMS, G. D.: Experimental tuberculosis in the leopard frog. J. Amer. Vet. Assoc. 151:942–949, 1967.
3. GIBBS, E. L., GIBBS, T. J. and VAN DYCK, P. C.: *Rana pipiens:* health and disease. Lab. Animal Care 16:142–153, 1966.

Some Comparative Morphological Aspects of Renal Neoplasms in *Rana pipiens* and of Lymphosarcomas in Amphibia

Clyde J. Dawe

Laboratory of Pathology
National Cancer Institute [1]
Bethesda, Maryland

Those who first began to compare neoplasms of man with those of other animals had practical expectations in mind. One was that neoplasms resembling each other and arising from homologous organs and cells might have the same etiology, regardless of species differences among the hosts. While this hope springs eternal in the breast of the comparative oncologist, it has been learned from experience that such hope is not to be seized upon without a good deal of circumspection, though it ought not be abandoned.

Of the known causes of neoplasms in man, none was first detected as a direct result of studies showing it to be carcinogenic for other animals. Several agents, including a number of viruses and chemical substances that induce neoplasms in animals, remain good candidates to break this precedent. But it should be understood that, in the following discussion of some morphologically similar neoplasms and lesions, no etiologic interrelationships are implied. On the contrary, it will be evident that resemblances between neoplasms in different species correlate more closely with organ and cell type of origin than with inciting factors.

Renal Adenocarcinomas

Two groups of renal neoplasms in animals resemble rather closely the cortical adenomas and carcinomas in man. One of these groups is composed of the papillary adenomas and adenocarcinomas of the kidney in *Rana pipiens*. They have been known since the report of Smallwood in 1905 (1), and their morphology has been so well described by Lucké and others (2–4) that it need not be reviewed in detail here. Figs. 1 and 2 illustrate representative microscopic fields from a frog tumor and a human renal cortical neoplasm, respectively. The mesonephric origin of the frog kidney, as opposed to the metanephric origin of the human kidney, seems not to be reflected by any specific outstanding differences between these tumors, although cholesterol crystals have not, to my knowledge, been observed in the frog tumors whereas they may occur in renal adenomas and carcinomas in man. Also, the type A intranuclear inclusions characteristic of the tumors of frogs kept in the cold are not found

---

[1] National Institutes of Health, Public Health Service, U.S. Department of Health, Education, and Welfare.

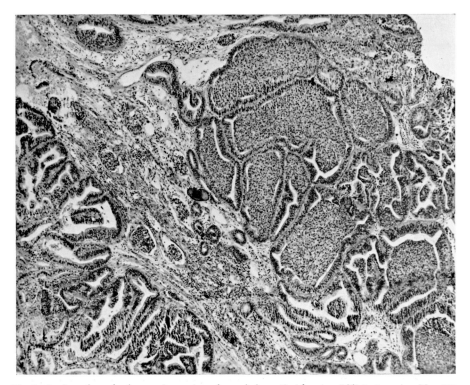

Fig. 1. Section of renal adenocarcinoma in a leopard frog (Smithsonian RTLA Accession No. 172, submitted by Gladys King). At left, the usual papillary structure is shown. On right, some papillae have solid central cores, suggestive of transition to solid carcinoma. ×62.

in human renal cortical adenomas or carcinomas. Still another difference can be found in the tendency of the human homologue to progress to a solid, "clear cell" neoplasm that is classically known as hypernephroma. However, traces of this type of change can sometimes be found in the frog tumors, as shown in Figs. 1 and 3. It deserves note that a sharp distinction between cortical adenomas and carcinomas in man is difficult to make. Many pathologists still follow the arbitrary rule suggested by Bell (5) of reserving the term carcinoma for those tumors exceeding 3 cm. in diameter. This rule was based on the practical consideration that only those cortical neoplasms larger than 3 cm. have (with rare exceptions) been observed to metastasize. A similar correlation between size and tendency to metastasize has been noted for the frog tumors (6). One can perhaps be most objectively impressed with the similarity between the frog and the human renal cortical tumors by going back to Smallwood's first report (1) of the frog neoplasm in 1905. With the collaboration of a clinical pathologist, Smallwood obtained a section of a human renal cortical tumor which showed a very comparable papillary and glandular structure. He included photomicrographs of the frog tumor and the human tumor in his report, but in that day it was believed that renal adenomas and hypernephromas (carcinomas) originated in adrenal cortical rests within the kidney. Therefore, in spite of the fact that he saw no anatomic connection between adrenal tissue and the tumors in each kidney of his specimen, Smallwood diagnosed the tumors as adrenal in origin, following the prevailing medical concept of his day. Ironically, in reward for this astuteness, his diagnosis drew the later criticism of Lucké (2).

A second group of renal neoplasms resembling cortical adenomas and carcinomas in man has been described in laboratory rats fed lead phosphate or lead acetete (7, 8). Similar tumors were observed by Kilham et al. (9) in feral rats presumably exposed to inhalation of lead fumes from burning refuse (storage batteries). In lead-treated rats intranuclear inclusion bodies are often present in the adjacent non-neoplastic renal tubular epithelium, but not in the neoplastic cells themselves (8). There is evidence that these inclusions actually contain lead (10). Electron microscopic studies have shown a characteristic structure of the extremely electron dense inclusion bodies (11, 12), and no virus particles have yet been found associated with either the neo plasms or the tubular epithelium containing the inclusions (8).

Many other renal neoplasms have been observed in wild, domesticated, and laboratory animals, but they are histologically distinct from the two types mentioned, and will not be commented on here.

A peculiar lesion of the renal cortical tubules in mice inoculated shortly after birth with polyoma virus is of interest, partly because it has sometimes been referred to as pre-neoplastic (13) and partly because the cytologic changes resemble those seen in cortical adenomas of frogs, rats, and man. However, these lesions do not at

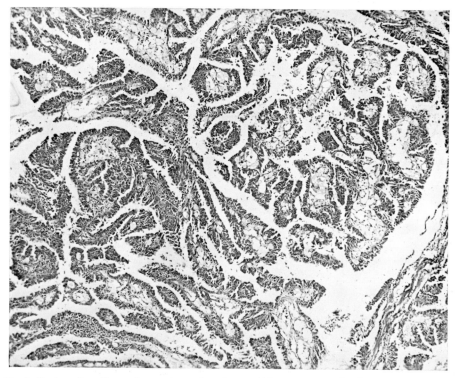

Fig. 2. Section of papillary adenocarcinoma in a human kidney. Some papillae have central cores of clear cells, but no typical areas of clear-cell carcinoma are present. ✕62.

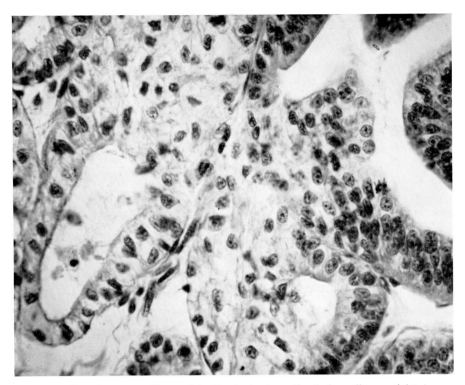

Fig. 3. Area from frog tumor illustrated in Fig. 1, showing cells of clear-cell type (left) in some of the neoplastic tubular structures. ×415.

this time merit the designation pre-neoplastic, since they have not been shown to progress to a continuously growing state. Some examples are illustrated in Figs. 5 to 7.

The lesions involve renal tubules in the outer portion of the cortex, usually just beneath the capsule. The tubules are moderately enlarged, have enlarged lumens, and their epithelium is heightened to a columnar form. The nuclei of these columnar cells are large, being about twice the diameter of normal nuclei in this region, and the cytoplasm is basophilic in contrast to the highly acidophilic cytoplasm of proximal convoluted tubules. Mitotic figures are numerous in some of the altered tubules, but absent in others, suggesting that the lesions go through a proliferative phase that is followed by a static one. Occasionally, intranuclear inclusion bodies of the type associated with polyoma virus infection elsewhere are found in nuclei of the altered cells.

More than anything else, the polyoma virus-induced tubular lesions resemble the early metanephric tubules seen in embryos shortly after tubulogenesis has been induced in the metanephric blastema by branches of the ureteric buds. This resemblance, together with the subcapsular location of the lesions and the knowledge that tubulogenesis continues for several days after birth in the outer cortex of the mouse kidney, suggests that the atypical tubules may result from tubulogenesis occurring in metanephric mesenchyme previously infected by polyoma virus. This concept is supported by the observation that adult mice made susceptible to tumor induction by total body X-irradiation do not exhibit these tubular lesions in the kidney (14). Having no remaining metanephric blastema, adult mice would not be able to develop atypical tubules from infected blastema. This concept is also consistent with the findings of Vainio *et al.* (15), in studies of polyoma-infected cultures of kidney rudiments. There it was shown that after the metanephric mesenchyme differentiates into tubular epithelium, it becomes refractory to infection by polyoma virus. The concept is also supported by the experimental results of Kirsten and Weil (16), who showed that rat metanephric blastema infected with polyoma virus goes on to develop neoplasms that are mixtures of epithelial and mesenchymal components.

The most difficult question remains as to why the tubular lesions in mice do not develop into neoplasms. Perhaps a lead to the answer lies in another characteristic of the lesions in mice. They are invariably associated with infiltrations of lymphocytes and plasma cells (Figs. 5 and 7). These infiltrates are particularly dense around the small cortical arterioles, but they are also found immediately adjacent to some of the altered tubules. Sometimes one can see plasma cells and lymphocytes in actual contact with the altered tubular epithelium. The possibility is therefore suggested that a cellular immune response occurs, preventing neoplastic "break-through."

This is merely an hypothesis that has not been subjected to test, however. Whether or not any similar considerations might be applied to genesis of the renal tumors in frogs is an open question. It is worth noting that Lucké, in his original histological

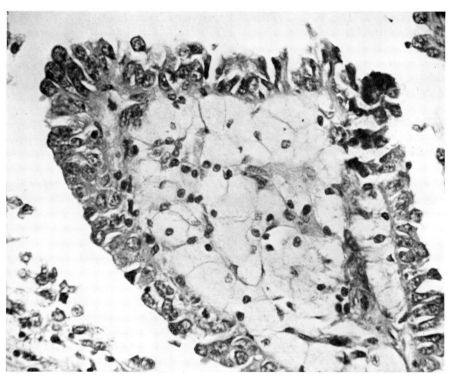

Fig. 4. A papilla from human tumor illustrated in Fig. 2. The clear cells composing the central, stromal portion of the papilla are probably not neoplastic. The neoplastic epithelium covering the papilla is more pleomorphic than that in the frog tumor in Figs. 1 and 3. ×415.

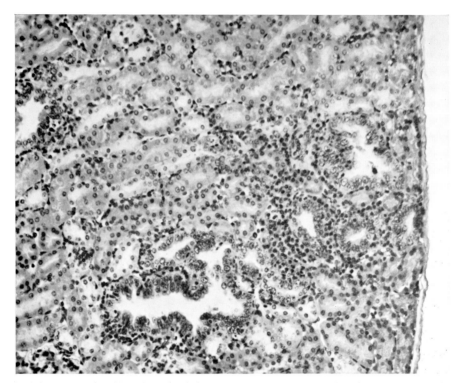

Fig. 5. Renal cortical lesions in a mouse bearing salivary gland tumors induced by polyoma virus. Note slight tendency toward papillarity in the epithelium of the tubule in lower center. Cells lining the abnormal tubules are columnar and have enlarged nuclei and basophilic cytoplasm. A mild infiltration of lymphocytes and plasma cells surrounds altered tubules on middle right. ×205.

study (2), illustrated an altered renal tubule surrounded by a dense collar of lymphoid cells (his figure 12). Such a situation may have been related coincidentally to some bacterial infection or parasitic infestation. It hardly need be said that transplantation resistance antigens should be looked for in the frog tumors, and that studies of tumor genesis in organ cultures of kidney rudiments might reveal much about their histogenesis.

Lymphosarcomas of Amphibians

The literature records five examples of transmissible or transplantable diseases of amphibians, classified as lymphoid tumors, lymphosarcomas, or sarcomas (see Balls and Ruben (17) for recent review). Each of these originated in different individuals of the species *Xenopus laevis* (17, 18) (the L-1 and L-2 diseases), *Triturus pyrrhogaster* (19), *Triturus cristatus* (20, 21), and *Siredon mexicanus* (22, 23). All except the disease of *S. mexicanus* have been transmitted allogeneically, xenogeneically, or even to species belonging to different orders (17).

This wide range of transmissibility makes it improbable that transmission of the first four diseases listed above has occurred through cellular transplantation, with the possible exception of allogeneic ocular grafts. Despite the accomplishment of some degree of inbreeding of X. *laevis* by Dr. Balls, the absence of a distinct and practi-cable morphological or histocompatibility marker within this species has so far pre-cluded positive proof of cellular propagation of the disease from one animal to another. It is unfortunate that the sex chromosomes of X. *laevis* are not morphologi-cally distinguishable (24), and that, as Dr. Ruben has stated, adult animals hetero-zygous for the anucleolar mutation (25) of X. *laevis* do not provide adequately marked cells. Nevertheless, as observed by Balls and Ruben (17), there is no ques-tion that transmission has been effected by subcellular materials.

For comparative purposes and for a more complete understanding of the nature of these diseases, it remains desirable to determine whether or not these conditions can be serially propagated by transfer of cell lineages as well as by transfer of sub-cellular materials. The murine leukemias and lymphomas though virally inducible, have long been characterized by their capability of propagation by cell transfer re-quiring, in some instances, only a single cell to establish the graft (26). Some virally-induced fowl leukoses (e.g., RPL-12 lymphoma) likewise have been shown to be propagated through continuity of cell lineages (27), although Pontén also (28, 29) obtained strong evidence that in apparent cellular transfers of Rous sarcoma and fowl erythroblastosis recruitment of newly-transformed cell populations from the suc-cessive hosts takes place and the original cell line is completely lost.

While the demonstration of cell transplantability of the diseases in X. *laevis, T.*

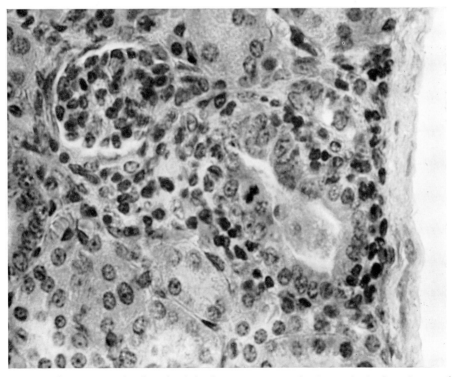

Fig. 6. A polyoma virus-induced renal tubular lesion in a mouse, showing a mitotic figure in one of the cells lining the tubule. Such lesions have not been shown to progress to frank neoplasia. ×660.

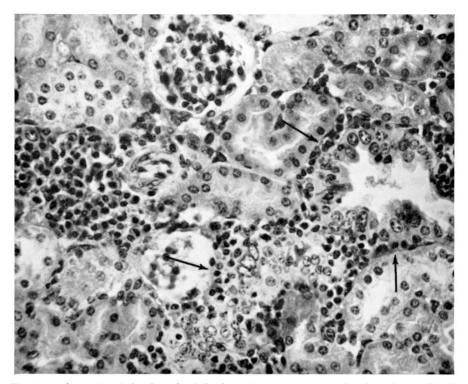

Fig. 7. A polyoma virus-induced renal tubular lesion in a mouse, associated with a plasma-cell infiltrate adjacent to the renal arteriole at middle left. Also note plasma cells (arrows) in contact with the atypical epithelium at several points. ×205.

pyrrhogaster, and *T. cristatus* seems to be technically out of reach for the moment, it is to be hoped that some useful cell marker will eventually be found that will make it possible to clarify this problem in cell kinetics. Meanwhile, it seems prudent to describe these conditions as transmissible, rather than transplantable.

Based on strictly morphological considerations, the question must be asked whether the transmissible diseases of *X. laevis, T. pyrrhogaster,* and *T. cristatus* should be regarded as infectious granulomas rather than neoplastic diseases. Many of the illustrations of the lesions (17, 18) show a nodular, or focal character, in which the central parts of the nodules are composed of cells with oval, lobulated, or reniform nuclei and relatively large amounts of pale-staining cytoplasm. These cells thus have the morphological characteristics of histiocytes and epithelioid cells, which are a definitive component of infectious granulomas. The presence of lymphoid aggregates on the peripheries of the epithelioid foci is also consistent with the classical picture of granuloma, although these need not be present.

The lesions of *X. laevis, T. pyrrhogaster,* and *T. cristatus* all seem to be basically similar, and in the L-1 and L-2 lesions of *X. laevis* (17, 30) as well as in those of *T. pyrrhogaster* (31), bacteria have been identified in the lesions and have been isolated in cultures on artificial media. Apparently bacteria have not been looked for in the transmissible disease of *T. cristatus*, and this should be done. In sections (Figs. 8 and 9) prepared from blocks of tissue from the L-2 lymphosarcoma, provided me by Dr. Ruben, acid-fast stains allowed recognition of occasional acid-fast bacilli in the cytoplasm of epithelioid cells forming the central parts of the lesions. Inoculation of bacteria (not specified as mycobacteria) grown from animals bearing the L-1 disease into immature *X. laevis* was not found to produce tumor formation (30). However, the acid-fast organism isolated by Inoue *et al.* from the tumors of *T. pyrrhogaster* was found able to reproduce similar lesions, not only in that species but also in *X. laevis* (31). The occurrence of central necrosis in the lesions of the L-1 disease is entirely consistent with the caseation that occurs in tuberculosis, concomitant with the development of delayed hypersensitivity to protein derivatives of the tubercle bacillus (32).

Mycobacterial and mycotic infections of amphibians are well known (33–36) and can produce massive lesions suggestive of neoplasia. Obviously, lethality of a disease is not an end-result limited to neoplasia. Visceral granuloma of trout (37) was originally thought to be a neoplasm (38), and a fungus-induced granuloma of mice is so exuberant that it was at first thought to be a neoplasm (39). Such considerations

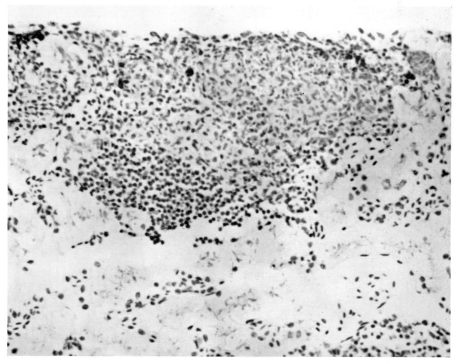

Fig. 8. A lesion in liver of a *Xenopus laevis*. Section from an animal bearing a transmissible disease in unpublished studies of L. N. Ruben (Smithsonian RTLA Accession No. 109). Nuclear stain only (methylene blue) was used, causing liver parenchyma in lower part of field to be largely unstained. The subcapsular lesion is composed of epithelioid cells forming a discrete granuloma, with aggregates of lymphocytes on the periphery. ×280.

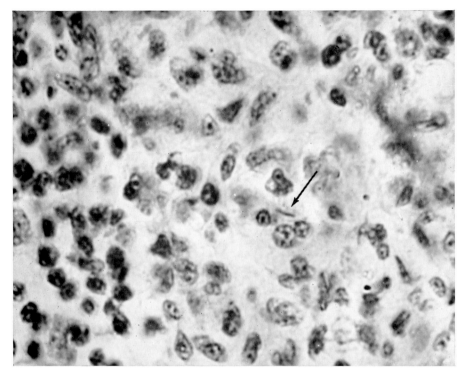

Fig. 9. A high magnification of acid-fast stain on a section of the same lesion shown in Fig. 8. Arrow indicates an acid-fast bacillus. ×1440.

urge caution in the interpretation of tumefactive lesions associated with bacteria or fungi.

On the other hand, it is certainly possible for neoplasms to become secondarily infected with a wide variety of micro-organisms, including viruses, that have no causal relationship to the neoplasms. It is furthermore known that in mice a neoplasm of histiocytic origin occurs [Type A reticulum cell sarcoma (40)] and may, because of its histiocytic composition, to some extent simulate granulomatous reaction. The distinction between neoplasia and granulomatous reaction, in view of our still imperfect definitions of neoplasia, may be an extremely fine one to resolve if the causal agent is a virus. The validity of the results of the filtration experiments conducted by Ruben and Balls (30) is therefore of critical importance. Until a viral agent is isolated, ultramicroscopically characterized, and shown able to induce the disease in the absence of other micro-organisms, we are confronted with a disorder that is transmissible, has the morphologic characteristics of a granuloma, and contains acid-fast bacilli within its lesions. It is not particularly important what name is applied to the disease, at this point of incomplete understanding. It *is* important that investigations continue until it becomes clear whether the disease is more closely related to tuberculosis, which in the past was often confused with lymphoid neoplasms (41), or to lymphoid neoplasms, which have often been complicated by bacterial and mycotic infections (42), but have not been shown to be caused by them.

Acknowledgments

For the use of histological specimens, the author thanks Dr. Louis B. Thomas of the Department of Pathologic Anatomy, the National Cancer Institute, and Dr. John C. Harshbarger of the Registry of Tumors of Lower Animals, at the Smithsonian Institution, Washington, D.C. Photomicrographs were prepared by Mr. Gebhard Gsell, Laboratory of Pathology, The National Cancer Institute.

References

1. SMALLWOOD, W. M.: Adrenal tumors in the kidney of the frog. Anat Anzeiger 26:652–658, 1905.

2. LUCKÉ, B.: A neoplastic disease in the leopard frog, *Rana pipiens*. Am. J. Cancer 20:352–379, 1934.

3. STEWART, H. L., SNELL, K. C., DUNHAM, L. J., and SCHLYEN, S. M.: Transplantable and transmissible tumors of animals. Atlas of Tumor Pathology, Section XII Fascicle 40, Armed Forces Institute of Pathology, 1959, pp. 208–217.

4. DURYEE, W. R.: Precancer cells in amphibian adenocarcinoma. Ann. N.Y. Acad. Sci. 63:1280–1302, 1956.

5. BELL, E. T.: A classification of renal tumors with observations on the frequency of the various types. J. Urol. 39:238–243, 1938.

6. LUCKÉ, B.: Kidney carcinoma in the frog: a virus tumor. *In*: Viruses as Causative Agents in Cancer. Ann. N.Y. Acad. Sci. 54:1093–1109, 1952.

7. ZOLLINGER, H. U.: Durch chronische Bleivergiftung erzeugte Nierenadenome und Carcinome bei Ratten und ihre Beziehungen zu den entsprechenden Neubildung des Menschen. Virch. Arch. Path. Anat. 323:694–710, 1953.

8. MAO, P., and MOLNAR, J. J.: The fine structure and histochemistry of lead-induced renal tumors in rats. Am. J. Path. 50:571–604, 1967.

9. KILHAM, L., LOW, R. J., CONTI, S. F. and DALLENBACH, F. D.: Intranuclear inclusions and neoplasms in the kidneys of wild rats. J. Nat. Cancer Inst. 29:863–885, 1962.

10. DALLENBACH, F. D.: Phenolrotausscheidung und trypanblauspeicherung bei der Bleinephropathie der Ratte. Virch. Arch. Path. Anat. 338:91–110, 1964.

11. BEAVER, D. L.: The ultrastructure of the kidney in lead intoxication with particular reference to intranuclear inclusions. Am. J. Path. 39:195–208, 1961.

12. GOYER, R. A.: The renal tubule in lead poisoning. I. Mitochondrial swelling and aminoaciduria. Lab. Invest. 19:71–77, 1968.

13. BUFFETT, R. F., COMMERFORD, S. L., FURTH, J. and HUNTER, M. J.: Agent in AK leukemic tissue, not sedimented at 105,000 g, causing neoplastic and non-neoplastic lesions. Proc. Soc. Exp. Biol. & Med. 99:401–407, 1958.

14. LAW, L. W. and DAWE, C. J.: Influence of total body X-irradiation on tumor induction by parotid tumor agent in adult mice. Proc. Soc. Exp. Biol. & Med. 105:414–419, 1960.

15. VAINIO, T., SAXEN, L. and TOIVONEN, S.: Acquisition of cellular resistance to polyoma virus during embryonic differentiation. Virology 20:380–385, 1963.

16. KIRSTEN, W. H. and WEISS, T. P.: The response of metanephric rudiments to polyoma virus in vitro. *In*: Recent Results in Cancer Research (W. H. Kirsten, ed.), pp. 34–43, Springer-Verlag New York Inc., 1966.

17. BALLS, M. and RUBEN, L. N.: Lymphoid tumors in *Amphibia*: a review. Progr. Exp. Tumor Res. 10: Karger, Basel/New York, pp. 238–260, 1968.

18. BALLS, M.: Spontaneous neoplasms in *Amphibia:* a review and descriptions of six new cases. Cancer Res. *22*:1142–1154, 1962.

19. INOUE, S. and SINGER, M.: Transmissibility and some histopathology of a spontaneously originated visceral tumor in the newt, *Triturus pyrrhogaster.* Cancer Res. *23*:1679–1684, 1963.

20. LEONE, V.: Tumori da meticolantrene in tritoni. Ist Lombardo Sci. Lett. Rendiconti Sci. (B) *92*:220–240, 1957.

21. LEONE, V. and T. ZAVANELLA: Some morphological and biological characteristics of a tumor of the newt, *Triturus cristatus* Laur. *In* Biology of Amphibian Tumors (M. Mizell, ed.), Springer-Verlag New York Inc., 1969, pp. 184–194.

22. DELANNEY, L. E., PRAHLAD, K. V. and MEIER, A. H.: A malignant tumor in the Mexican axolotl. Amer. Zool. *4*:279, (Abstr.), 1964.

23. DELANNEY, L. E. and K. BLACKLER: Acceptance and regression of a strain-specific lymphosarcoma in Mexican axolotls. *In* Biology of Amphibian Tumors (M. Mizell, ed.), Springer-Verlag New York Inc., 1969, pp. 399–408.

24. WICKBOM, T.: Cytological studies on Dipnoi, Urodela, Anura, and Emys. Hereditas *31*: 241–346, 1945.

25. ELSDALE, T. R., FISCHBERG, M. and SMITH, S.: A mutation that reduces nucleolar number in *Xenopus laevis.* Exptl. Cell Res. *14*:642–643, 1958.

26. FURTH, J. and KAHN, M. C.: The transmission of leukemia of mice with a single cell. Am. J. Cancer *31*:276–282, 1937.

27. PONTÉN, J.: Transplantation of chicken tumor RPL-12 in homologous hosts. J. Nat. Cancer Inst. *29*:1013–1021, 1962.

28. PONTÉN, J.: Homologous transfer of Rous sarcoma by cells. J. Nat. Cancer Inst. *29*:1147–1159, 1962.

29. PONTÉN, J.: Transmission *in vivo* of chicken erythroblastosis by intact cells. J. Cell Comp. Physiol. *60*:209–215, 1962.

30. BALLS, M. and RUBEN, L. N.: The transmission of lymphosarcoma in *Xenopus laevis,* the South African clawed toad. Cancer Res. *27*:654–659, 1967.

31. INOUE, S., SINGER, M. and HUTCHINSON, J.: Causative agent of a spontaneously originating visceral tumour in the newt, *Triturus pyrrhogaster.* Nature *205*:408–409, 1965.

32. RICH, A. R.: The Pathogenesis of Tuberculosis. Thomas, Springfield, pp. 358–387, 1951.

33. VOGEL, H.: Mycobacteria from cold-blooded animals. Am. Rev. Tuberc. Pulmonary Dis. *77*:823–838, 1958.

34. DARZINS, E.: The epizootic of tuberculosis among the Gias in Bahia. Acta Tub. *26*:170–174, 1952.

35. MACHICAO, N.: Lepra-like granulomas in frogs. Lab. Invest. *3*:219–227, 1954.

36. DHALIWAL, S. S. and GRIFFITHS, D. A.: Fungal disease in Malayan toads: an acute lethal inflammatory reaction. Nature *197*:467–469, 1963.

37. WOOD, E. M., YASUTAKE, W. T. and LEHMAN, W. L.: A mycosis-like granuloma of fish. J. Inf. Dis. *93*:262–267, 1955.

38. YOUNG, G. A. and OLAFSON, P.: Neurilemmomas in a family of brook trout. Am. J. Path. *20*:413–419, 1944.

39. SYMEONIDIS, A. and EMMONS, C. W.: Granulomatous growth induced in mice by *Absidia corymbifera.* AMA Arch. Path. *60*:251–258, 1955.

40. DUNN, T. B.: Normal and pathologic anatomy of the reticular tissue in laboratory mice, with a classification and discussion of neoplasms. J. Nat. Cancer Inst. *14*:1281–1433, 1954.

41. EWING, J.: Neoplastic Diseases. Saunders, Phila., pp. 429–433, 1940.

42. CASAZZA, A. R., DUVALL, C. P. and CARBONE, P. P.: Infection in lymphoma. Histology, treatment, and duration in relation to incidence and survival. JAMA *197*:710–716, 1966.

Immunological Approaches to the Study of Viral Antigens Associated with Neoplasms

Paul Gerber

Laboratory of Viral Immunology
Division of Biologics Standards
National Institutes of Health
Bethesda, Maryland

Advances in tumor virology and tumor immunology during the past 6 years or so have been characterized by 2 major achievements. One was the demonstration that in some SV_{40}-induced tumors the entire viral genome may persist in the transformed cells in a non-infectious and non-antigenic state (1). The other landmark was the discovery in most virus-induced tumors of 2 types of antigens—the transplantation antigens located on the cell surface and the intracellular T- or neoantigens. Both of these antigens are considered to be products specified by the viral genome, suggesting that most virus-induced tumors are characterized by the persistence of a portion of the viral genome as a heritable factor in the transformed cells (2).

Since both of these fundamental observations are of potential importance to this conference, I propose to digress briefly from the assigned topic to review some of the evidence that led to the demonstration of a virus-cell relationship in mammalian tumor cells which is analogous in some respects to the lysogenic state in bacteria.

About 6 years ago we began a study on the virus-cell relationship in SV_{40}-induced hamster tumors (1). Following intracerebral inoculation of newborn hamsters with SV_{40}, the virus disappeared rapidly from the brain and other organs. The animals remained free of detectable virus and developed signs of neurologic dysfunction about 100 days post-inoculation. When the animals were sacrificed we found ependymal tumors in the lateral ventricles of the brain. All attempts to detect infectious SV_{40} in tumor extracts were consistently unsuccessful. Experiments designed to "unmask" the virus also gave negative results. However, when intact tumor cells were seeded directly on sensitive indicator cells, infectious virus could be demonstrated regularly. Most of the tumor bearing hamsters were free of detectable antiviral antibodies and we could not detect viral antigens in the tumor cells. The consistent failure to detect infectious virus in tumor extracts in contrast to the recovery of virus from mixed cultures of intact tumor cells and indicator cells, suggested 2 possibilities: 1. A virus carrier state in which a small fraction of the tumor cells is infected and releases trace amounts of virus. This in turn, may lead to the production of an interferon which prevents the spread of infection to other cells; or 2. The virus may persist in an altered state, presumably viral DNA, which is intimately associated with the cell genome and transmitted to the daughter cells.

The results of extensive experiments strongly supported the second hypothesis.

Cloning studies revealed that every cell of these hamster tumors contained the SV$_{40}$ genome after many generations of *in vitro* culture. Recovery of virus from virogenic tumor cells required direct contact of viable, intact tumor cells with indicator cells. It was found that subviral material was transferred from the tumor to the indicator cell during a process of cell fusion, resulting in the formation of heterokaryons (3). This process could be greatly enhanced by the addition of inactivated Sendai virus which contains a cell fusion factor (4). A similar activation of the viral genome in a non-infectious Rous sarcoma virus-induced rat tumor has also been reported (5).

Application of these techniques may be of potential value in studies on the viral etiology of amphibian tumors. From the immunologic viewpoint it is convenient to divide tumors of higher vertebrates into 2 groups: those induced by DNA viruses (SV$_{40}$, polyoma and adenoviruses) and tumors and leukemias induced by RNA viruses of the avian leukosis and murine leukemia complexes. The separation into these 2 categories is based on the fundamental differences in the virus-cell relationships in tumors caused by these viruses. Table 1 shows a comparison of the properties of oncogenic DNA and RNA viruses. Virions of the DNA group of viruses are non-enveloped and have a capsid of cubic, icosahedral symmetry. Viral synthesis and maturation take place in the cell nucleus. When an oncogenic DNA virus infects a cell, it may either multiply and destroy it in the process of producing more infectious virus or it may transform the cell without subsequent virus release. By contrast, RNA tumor viruses structurally resemble the myxoviruses and are surrounded by a lipoprotein envelope, which is formed of the cell membrane during the process of maturation and budding. Leukemic cells transformed by RNA viruses continue to release infectious virus. Since DNA virus-induced tumors are generally free of structural viral antigens they lend themselves particularly well to analysis of virus-induced antigens.

In 1961 Habel (6) and Sjögren (7) demonstrated for the first time the existence of a virus specific transplantation antigen at the surface of polyoma tumor cells. Adult mice inoculated with polyoma virus failed to develop tumors but developed an antiviral immune response. These immunized animals were found to be resistant to challenge with virus-free, isologous polyoma tumor cells. Habel explained this phenomenon by postulating the appearance of this new antigen in a few cells that became transformed *in vivo* after inoculation of virus. The immunologically competent adult mouse develops antibodies against this foreign antigen and rejects its own trans-

TABLE 1

VIRUS-CELL RELATIONSHIPS IN TUMORS INDUCED BY DNA AND RNA VIRUSES

DNA viruses SV$_{40}$, polyoma, adenoviruses	RNA viruses avian and murine leukemias
Virions nonenveloped, cubic symmetry, maturation in nucleus.	Enveloped, myxovirus-like, maturation by budding at cell membrane.
Infectious virus usually absent in tumors.	Infectious virus present in tumors.

formed cells. When challenged a few weeks later with transplantable, isologous polyoma tumor cells, these sensitized animals reject the tumor graft. On the other hand, newborn animals being immunologically incompetent, fail to recognize the new transplantation antigen in its developing tumor cells, which can continue to multiply and form tumor masses. This new transplantation antigen in tumor cells is virus specific, since animals resistant to challenge with polyoma tumor cells are completely susceptible to challenge with SV_{40} tumors and vice versa.

The experimental model developed in the polyoma system has been extended to other tumors induced by DNA and RNA viruses. Resistance to tumor challenge following inoculation of virus into adult animals has been demonstrated in SV_{40} (8), adenovirus (9) and Moloney leukemia (10). Several virus-specific surface antigens have been demonstrated in murine leukemia cells by means of fluorescent antibody and cytotoxic tests on living cells. Klein and his associates (11) claim to have identified a new virus-specific surface antigen in cells of Burkitt's lymphoma persistently infected with a herpes-like virus. According to their recent findings (12) this surface antigen is also present in lymphoblastoid cells obtained from patients with infectious mononucleosis. These patients appear to develop antibodies to these antigens during the course of illness. If confirmed, this would be the first demonstration of a virus specific tumor antigen in man.

A second class of antigens associated with cells transformed by oncogenic DNA viruses are the so-called T-antigens or neo-antigens (2). They are present in the nucleus of tumor cells and can be detected by fluorescent antibody or complement-fixation tests with the serum of tumor bearing animals. The T-antigens are immunologically distinct from the structural viral antigens; they are specific for tumors induced by a given virus and are identical in all species transformed by the same virus.

Thus the detection of specific antigens in virus-free tumors specified by the persisting viral genome provides a method for determining the etiology of a tumor by immunological approaches.

References

1. GERBER, P. and KIRSCHSTEIN, R. L.: SV_{40}-induced ependymomas in newborn hamsters. Virology 18:582, 1962.
2. HUEBNER, R. J., ROWE, W. P., TURNER, H. C. and LANE, W. T.: Specific adenovirus complement-fixing antigens in virus-free hamster and rat tumors. Proc. Nat. Acad. Sc. (US) 50:379, 1963.
3. WATKINS, J. F. and DULBECCO, R.: Production of SV_{40} virus in heterokaryons of transformed and susceptible cells. Proc. Nat. Acad. Sc. (US) 58:1396, 1967.
4. GERBER, P.: Studies on the transfer of subviral infectivity from SV_{40}-induced hamster tumor cells to indicator cells. Virology 28:501, 1966.
5. SVOBODA, J., CHYLE, P. and SIMKOVIC, D.: Demonstration of the absence of infectious Rous virus in rat tumor XC whose structurally intact cells produce Rous sarcoma when transferred to chick. Folia Biol. 9:77, 1963.
6. HABEL, K.: Resistance of polyoma virus immune animals to transplanted polyoma tumors. Proc. Soc. Exp. Biol. & Med. 106:722, 1961.
7. SJÖGREN, H. O., HELLSTRÖM, I. and KLEIN, G.: Transplantation of polyoma virus-induced tumors in mice. Canc. Res. 21:329, 1961.

8. DEFENDI, V.: Effect of SV_{40} immunization on growth of transplantation SV_{40} and polyoma tumors in hamsters. Proc. Soc. Exp. Biol. & Med. *113*:12, 1963.

9. TRENTIN, J. J. and BRYAN, E.: Immunization of hamsters and histoisogenic mice against transplantation of tumors induced by human adenovirus type 12. Proc. Am. Assoc. Canc. Res. *5*:64, 1964.

10. SACHS, L.: Transplantability of an X-ray-induced and virus-induced leukemia in isologous mice inoculated with leukemia virus. J. Nat. Canc. Inst. *29*:759, 1962.

11. KLEIN, G., CLIFFORD, P., KLEIN, G. and STJERNSWARD, J.: Search for tumor-specific immune reactions in Burkitt lymphoma patients by the membrane immunofluorescence reaction. Proc. Nat. Acad. Sc. (US) *55*:1628, 1966.

12. KLEIN, G., PEARSON, G., HENLE, G., HENLE, W., DIEHL, V. and NIEDERMAN, J. C.: Relation between EB virus and cell membrane immunofluorescence in Burkitt tumor cells. J. Exp. Med. *128*:1021–1030, 1968.

Nucleic Acid Homology as Applied to Investigations on the Relationship of Viruses to Neoplastic Diseases

MAURICE GREEN

Institute for Molecular Virology
Saint Louis University School of Medicine
St. Louis, Missouri

Introduction

It is of both fundamental and practical importance to determine whether the Lucké renal carcinoma of the frog is induced by a herpes-like virus. Definitive evidence that a member of the herpesvirus group induces a tumor in any species would spur efforts to determine whether human neoplasms such as Burkitt's lymphoma and cervical cancer are induced by similar viral agents. An evaluation of the evidence required to indict a virus as a causative agent of neoplastic disease is appropriate at this time. For this purpose I will review the recent results of studies on adenovirus transformed cells and adenovirus induced tumors of hamsters, rats, and mice in which the concepts and methodology of molecular biology have been successfully employed to detect viral gene activity in adenovirus tumor and transformed cells, to investigate the mechanism of viral oncogenesis, and to analyze human tumors for adenovirus genetic information.

Properties of Human Adenoviruses

Milligram amounts of the 31 human adenoviruses have been grown and isolated in highly purified form [(12); Green and Piña, unpublished data]. Fig. 1 shows a band of pure human adenovirus (Ad) type 12 after centrifugation to equilibrium in a cesium chloride gradient. The human adenoviruses contain only protein and 12–13% DNA (12). The viral DNA's are linear duplex molecules ranging in G + C content from 48 to 61% [(12); Green et al., unpublished data]. Three groups of oncogenic and transforming human adenoviruses are recognized, the A, B, and C groups (Table 1). Group A includes highly oncogenic Ad 12, 18, and 31, viruses which induce lethal sarcomas in virtually all inoculated newborn hamsters. Group B includes Ad 3, 7, 11, 14, 16, and 21, common respiratory viruses in the human population; of these, five are "weakly" oncogenic, producing tumors in a small fraction of newborn hamsters. Group C includes Ad 1, 2, 5, and 6, adenoviruses commonly infecting young children. Group C adenoviruses do not induce tumors in newborn animals but transform rat embryo cells morphologically *in vitro*. The mechanisms of cell transformation by group A, B, and C adenoviruses have been studied in detail, the results of some of these studies are described below briefly (2, 3, 4, 5, 6).

445

Fig. 1. Visible band of "pure" adenovirus type 12, containing about 2 mg. of virus in 5 ml of rubidium chloride solution after density gradient centrifugation. (Green, 1965.)

TABLE 1

ONCOGENIC AND TRANSFORMING HUMAN ADENOVIRUSES

Group	Adenovirus Members	Oncogenicity	Viral DNA % G + C[a]
A	Ad 12, 18, and 31	"Highly oncogenic"[b] in newborn hamsters	48–49
B	Ad 3, 7, 11, 14, 16, and 21	"Weakly oncogenic"[b] in newborn hamsters (all but Ad 11)	49–52
C	Ad 1, 2, 5, and 6	"Nononcogenic" in newborn hamsters but morphologically transforms rat embryo cells *in vitro*[c]	57–59
	Ad 4, 8, 9, 10, 13, 15, 17, 19, 20, and 22–30	"Nononcogenic"	55–61

[a] Piña and Green (12).

[b] Highly oncogenic adenoviruses induce tumors in a large proportion of newborn hamsters within two months after injection with purified virus; "weakly oncogenic" in a small proportion after 4–18 months.

[c] Freeman *et al.* (1).

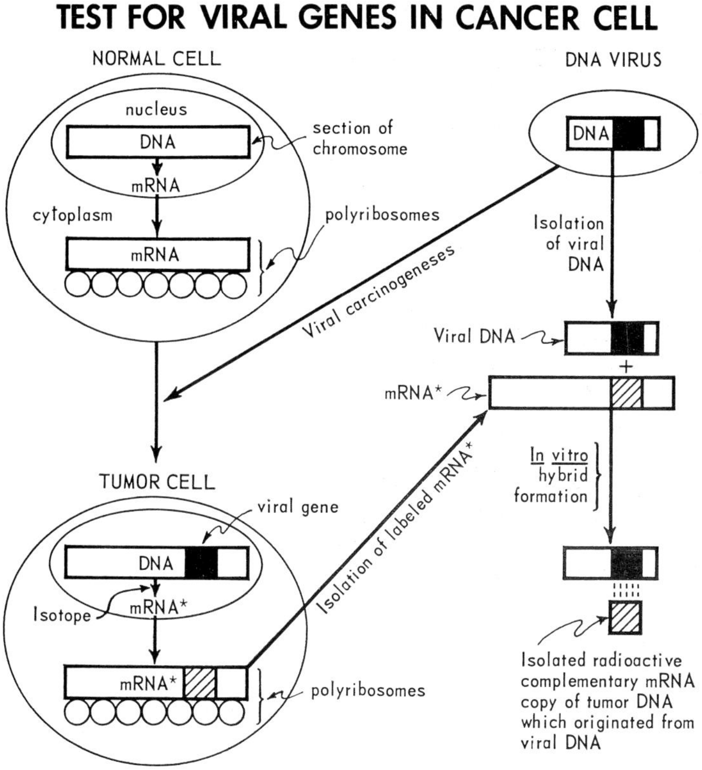

TEST FOR VIRAL GENES IN CANCER CELL

Fig. 2. Tests for viral genes in cancer cell. This scheme depicts the incorporation and transcription of viral genes in cells neoplastically transformed by virus infection. Viral mRNA synthesized in the cell nucleus is subsequently transported to the cytoplasm to form viral polyribosomes. Transformed cells are grown in media containing radioactive precursors of RNA and labeled RNA is isolated from the nucleus and polyribosomes and annealed with viral DNA. The formation of viral DNA-labeled RNA hybrids provides direct evidence for the presence of functioning viral genes in the cancer cell. (Green, in press.)

Mechanism of Oncogenesis by Human Adenoviruses

Adenovirus tumor and transformed cells possess no detectable infectious virus; thus the presence and synthesis of infectious viruses is not required for oncogenicity. Huebner et al. (11) showed that adenovirus tumor and transformed cells synthesize virus-specific T antigens, evidence that functional viral genes are present in adenovirus transformed cells.

The direct demonstration that viral genetic information resides in adenovirus transformed cells has been accomplished by nucleic acid homology measurements. The rationale behind this approach is shown in Fig. 2. It is hypothesized that during cell transformation viral genes are incorporated into the cell nucleus; these viral genes should be transcribed to virus-specific mRNA molecules, which would be transported subsequentially to the cytoplasm forming viral polyribosomes. To test cells for the presence of functional viral genes, the RNA of transformed cells was labeled by incorporation of tritiated uridine. Radioactive RNA was isolated from the cell nucleus and cytoplasmic polyribosomes and annealed with viral DNA by the DNA-RNA

TABLE 2

IDENTIFICATION AND QUANTITATION OF VIRUS-
SPECIFIC RNA—DNA-RNA * HYBRIDIZATION

Viral DNA + RNA* →   DNA-RNA* Hybrid
(excess)

* Radioactive molecules.

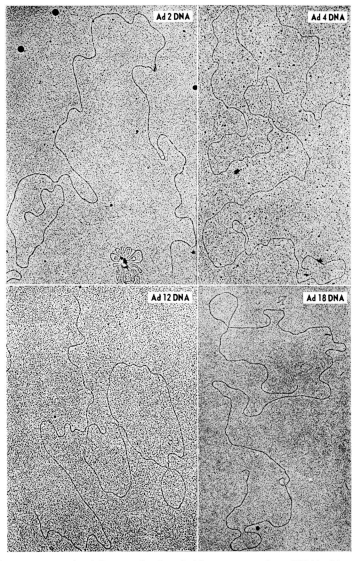

Fig. 3. Electron micrograph of linear molecules of Ad 2, 4, 12, and 18 DNA's. Magnification to photographic plate, ×7000. (Green *et al.*, 1967.)

TABLE 3

Hybridization of RNA from Polyribosomes and Nuclei of AD 12
Transformed Cells with Viral DNA [a]

RNA from	Input RNA (cpm)	Ad 12 DNA μg/filter	Bound RNA (cpm)	Bound % (background not subtracted)
Polyribosomes[b]	52,400	3	146	0.28
"	"	3	134	0.26
"	"	None	2	0.004
Nuclei[b]	214,000	3	438	0.20
"	"	3	423	0.20
"	"	None	26	0.01
	42,450	3	97	0.23
"	"	3	114	0.27
"	"	None	12	0.03
Whole cell[b]	283,100	3	356	0.13
"	"	3	406	0.14
"	"	None	60	0.02
	59,600	3	113	0.19
"	"	3	103	0.17
"	"	None	14	0.02

[a] Fujinaga and Green (4).
[b] Labeled during 180 min. period with [^{3}H]-uridine (4 μc/ml).

hybridization reaction shown in Table 2. The presence of virus-specific RNA, complementary to the viral DNA, would be detected by the formation of specific radioactive DNA-RNA hybrids.

The reagent for this DNA-RNA hybrid test for viral genetic information is the viral chromosomes, viral DNA, shown by electron microscopy to consist of a linear-double-stranded duplex molecule 11 to 13 microns in length (Fig. 3). In the DNA-RNA hybridization test, viral DNA is denatured and immobilized on a nitrocellulose membrane, as described by Gillespie and Spiegelman (7), and annealed with labeled RNA. A typical result of this analysis is shown in Table 3. Virus-specific RNA was detected in the nucleus and polyribosomes of Ad 12 transformed hamster embryo cells (Table 3). When 52,000 cpm of polyribosomal RNA was annealed with viral DNA, 146 and 134 cpm were bound specifically; only two counts were bound to DNA-free membranes. When 214,000 cpm of nuclear RNA were annealed with Ad 12 DNA, 438 and 423 cpm were bound (Table 3). Labeled RNA from "normal" cells or cells transformed by SV40 and polyoma virus did not anneal with Ad 12 (3, 4).

The synthesis of virus-specific RNA occurs in all human adenovirus tumor and transformed cells thus far examined (2, 3, 4, 5). As shown in Table 4, tumor and transformed cells induced by 10 different human adenoviruses possess 6 to 27 parts of labeled virus-specific RNA in 10,000 parts of total labeled RNA, amounts of virus-specific RNA readily detected. The relationships between virus-specific RNA molecules induced by different adenovirus tumor and transformed cells was determined by annealing labeled virus-specific RNA's with different adenovirus DNA's (Table 5). These results show that three different populations of virus-specific RNA molecules are synthesized by adenovirus tumor and transformed cells, one specific for group A adenoviruses, the second for group B adenoviruses, and the third for group C adenoviruses. No viral genes in common were transcribed by cells transformed by members of the different A, B, and C groups.

Adenovirus DNA's possess sufficient genetic information to code for 23 to 46 genes. By new hybridization procedures [(6); Fujinaga and Green, in manuscript], we estimated the number of viral genes transcribed "early" and "late" after productive infection with Ad 2 and those transcribed in cells transformed by Ad 2. During the infectious process, 20 to 46 genes are transcribed, representing 80 to 100% of the total genetic information of the virion (Table 6). Early after infection, i.e., before viral DNA synthesis commences, from 2 to 10 genes are transcribed. Most surprising, only 1 to 5 genes are transcribed in Ad 2 transformed cells. Thus, only several viral genes are required to maintain an Ad 2 cell in the transformed state. Adenovirus

TABLE 4

PRESENCE OF VIRUS-SPECIFIC RNA'S IN TUMOR AND TRANSFORMED CELLS
INDUCED BY HUMAN ADENOVIRUSES [a]

Inducing virus	Oncogenicity	Fraction bound ($\times 10^4$)[b]					
		Polyribosomal RNA[c]		Nuclear RNA[c]		Total cell RNA[c]	
		Viral DNA	None[d]	Viral DNA	None[d]	Viral DNA	None[d]
Ad 12	Highly	27.0	0.4	16.2	0.6		
Ad 18	"	6.6	1.5	8.0	0.7		
Ad 31	"	7.7	1.7	8.1	1.4		
Ad 3	Weakly	8.6	1.8	6.3	1.5		
Ad 7	"	9.4	1.2	10.8	0.7		
Ad 14	"	12.8	1.2	6.6	0.8		
Ad 16	"	8.0	1.2	14.4	0.9		
Ad 2	Nononcogenic					7.1	0.2
Ad 5	"					18.8	1.1
Ad 6	"					22.8	0.8

[a] Fujinaga and Green (2, 3, 4, 5).

[b] Average of duplicate hybridization reactions.

[c] RNA from tumor or transformed cells labeled for 180 min. with [³H]-uridine (4 μc/ml).

[d] Fraction bound to empty membrane.

TABLE 5

RELATIONSHIP BETWEEN VIRAL-SPECIFIC RNA'S IN TUMOR AND TRANSFORMED CELLS
INDUCED BY HIGHLY ONCOGENIC AND WEAKLY ONCOGENIC
HUMAN ADENOVIRUSES [a]

	RNA bound % relatedness [b] RNA from tumor or transformed cells induced by									
DNA from	Ad 12	Ad 18	Ad 31	Ad 3	Ad 7	Ad 14	Ad 16	Ad 2	Ad 5	Ad 6
Ad 12	100	29	62	<15[c]	<10[c]	<10[c]	<10[c]	<10	<10	<20[c]
Ad 18	34	100	62	<15[c]	<10[c]	<10[c]	<10[c]	—	—	—
Ad 31	61	30	100	—	—	—	—	—	—	—
Ad 3	<10[c]	<5[c]	<10[c]	100	69	74	100	—	—	—
Ad 7	<10[c]	<5[c]	<10[c]	100	100	88	81	<10	<10	<20[c]
Ad 11	<10[c]	<5[c]	<10[c]	62	35(?)	107	93	—	—	—
Ad 14	<10[c]	<5[c]	<10[c]	100	69	100	89	—	—	—
Ad 16	<10[c]	<5[c]	<10[c]	95	82	83	100	—	—	—
Ad 21	<10	<5	<10	100	78	93	92	—	—	—
Ad 1	—	—	—	—	—	—	—	102	105	110
Ad 2	<10[c]	<5[c]	<10[c]	<15[c]	<10[c]	<10[c]	<10[c]	100	95	105
Ad 4	<10[c]	<5[c]	<10[c]	<17[c]	<19	<15[c]	<18[c]	<10[c]	<10[c]	<20[c]
Ad 5	—	—	—	—	—	—	—	94	100	101
Ad 6	—	—	—	—	—	—	—	100	104	100

[a] Fujinaga and Green [(2, 3, 4); unpublished data].

[b] Average of duplicate experiments. Binding to homologous DNA was normalized to 100%.

[c] The % relatedness cannot be evaluated since too few counts were bound (less than 25 cpm above that bound to a DNA-free membrane).

TABLE 6

FRACTION OF VIRAL GENOME TRANSCRIBED IN ADENOVIRUS TYPE 2
INFECTED AND TRANSFORMED CELLS

Source of virus-specific RNA	Fraction of genome transcribed	Estimated No. of viral genes
"Early" plus "late" (2–18 hours)	80–100%	18–46
"Early" (2–6 hours)	8–20%	2–10
"Transformed"	4–10%	1–5

TABLE 7

DNA-RNA HYBRIDIZATION TEST FOR VIRAL GENETIC
INFORMATION IN HUMAN CANCER

$$\text{Viral DNA + human cancer RNA } * \xrightarrow[\text{20 hrs}]{66°} \text{ DNA-RNA hybrid } *$$

* Radioactive molecules. Positive reaction = hybrid formation.
Negative reaction = no hybrid formation.

genes transcribed in transformed cells have a G + C content of 47 to 51% (Fujinaga
and Green, 1968, unpublished data). These genes predictably have important roles
in viral oncogenesis.

Application of Nucleic Acid Homology Procedures to the Detection of Virus-Specific Molecules in Tumors

The DNA-RNA hybridization technique is being applied directly to the study of
possible viral etiology of human cancer as shown in Table 7. Viral DNA is annealed
with radioactive human tumor RNA. The formation of a labeled DNA-RNA hybrid
would demonstrate the presence of adenovirus-specific nucleotide sequences in the
cancer cell, data providing presumptive evidence for the adenovirus etiology of the
cancer. In model systems, i.e., hamster tumors induced by Ad 12, this procedure is

TABLE 8 *

DETECTION OF VIRAL-SPECIFIC RNA IN AD 12 HAMSTER TUMOR TISSUE

Exp. No.	Input RNA[a] (cpm)	DNA (3 µg/filter)	RNA bound (cpm)	% of RNA bound (background not subtracted)
E004A[b]	185,800	Ad 12	101	0.054
		Ad 12	100	0.054
		None	6	0.003
E004B[c]	138,000	Ad 12	111	0.081
		Ad 12	144	0.104
		None	6	0.004

* Fujinaga and Green (3).

[a] Whole cell RNA was isolated by the hot phenol-SDS method, followed by
a DNase treatment (see "Experimental Methods"), a repeated hot phenol-SDS
extraction, and removal of phenol as described in the text.

[b] Minced hamster tumor tissue (1.0 ml wet volume) suspended in 40 ml of
media was labeled with H^3-uridine (4 µc/ml; 20 C/mM) for 8 hours.

[c] About 0.25 ml of cells derived by trypsinization of hamster tumor tissue
was labeled for 6 hours in 10 ml of media as in footnote b.

TABLE 9

HYBRIDIZATION-INHIBITION TEST FOR VIRAL GENETIC
INFORMATION IN HUMAN CANCER

Step 1

$$\text{Viral DNA} + \text{human cancer RNA} \xrightarrow[20\ \text{hrs}]{66°} \text{DNA-RNA hybrid}$$

Step 2

$$+ \text{virus-specific RNA} * \xrightarrow[20\ \text{hrs}]{66°} \text{DNA-RNA hybrid} *$$

* Radioactive molecules. Positive reaction = inhibition of radioactive hybrid formation. Negative reaction = no inhibition of radioactive hybrid formation.

successful (Table 8). Labeled RNA from Ad 12 hamster tumors, minced, trypsinized, and labeled with tritiated uridine *in vitro,* was isolated and annealed with Ad 12. The specific binding of 100 to 150 counts to Ad 12 DNA was readily detected (Table 8). This procedure is now being applied to human tumors, labeled *in vitro* with radioactive RNA precursors.

An additional nucleic acid homology procedure of more general use is the hybridization-inhibition technique described in Table 9. Viral DNA, immobilized on a nitrocellulose membrane, is annealed first with unlabeled RNA derived from human cancer tissue. Unreacted DNA is annealed in a second reaction with radioactive virus-specific RNA isolated from adenovirus transformed cells. If virus-specific RNA is present in the human tumor RNA preparation, it will bind to viral DNA and inhibit the second annealing reaction with radioactive virus-specific RNA. This procedure has been successfully applied to primary hamster tumors induced by members of the adenovirus A, B, and C groups and is being applied presently to large numbers of human cancers.

Criteria for Identifying a Herpes-Like Agent
as the Etiological Agent of Lucké Carcinoma

It is essential first to isolate milligram quantities of the virus in highly purified form. Viral nucleic acid can then be extracted from the virion and used in DNA-RNA hybridization procedures as described above. The formation of a DNA-RNA hybrid between RNA derived from a large number of tumors and viral DNA would provide direct evidence for functioning viral genes in the tumor cell. If the herpes-like agent is the causative agent, one would expect all tumors to contain virus-specific RNA. It is difficult to conceive of a passenger virus which would be present in all Lucké carcinomas. Especially important is the examination of the summer tumors which are free of virus detectable by electron microscopy. The detection of RNA specific for herpes-like agents in summer tumor by DNA-RNA hybridization would provide quite strong proof of the viral etiology of the Lucké carcinoma.

Acknowledgments

This investigation was supported by Public Health Service grant AI-01725, contract PH43-64-928 from the National Institute of Allergy and Infectious Diseases, Vaccina Development Branch, National Institutes of Health, and contract PH43-67-692 from the National Cancer Institute, Viral Carcinogenesis Branch, Etiology Area, National Institutes of Health, U.S. Public Health Service, Bethesda, Maryland. Dr. Green has a Research Career Award (5-K6-AI-4739), National Institutes of Health, Public Health Service.

References

1. FREEMAN, A. E., BLACK, P. H., VANDERPOOL, E. A., HENRY, P. H., AUSTIN, J. B. and HUEBNER, R. J.: Transformation of primary rat embryo cells by adenovirus type 2. Proc. Natl. Acad. Sci. U.S. 58:1205–1212, 1967.

2. FUJINAGA, K., and GREEN, M.: The mechanism of viral carcinogenesis by DNA mammalian viruses. I. Viral specific RNA in polyribosomes of adenovirus tumor and transformed cells. Proc. Natl. Acad. Sci. U.S. 55:1567–1574, 1966.

3. FUJINAGA, K. and GREEN, M.: The mechanism of viral carcinogenesis by DNA mammalian viruses. II. Viral specific RNA in tumor cells induced by "weakly" oncogenic human adenoviruses. Proc. Natl. Acad. Sci. U.S. 57:806–812, 1967.

4. FUJINAGA, K. and GREEN, M.: Mechanism of viral carcinogenesis by DNA mammalian viruses. IV. Related virus-specific RNA in tumor cells induced by "highly" oncogenic adenovirus types 12, 18, and 31. J. Virol. 1:576–582, 1967.

5. FUJINAGA, K. and GREEN, M.: The mechanism of viral carcinogenesis by DNA mammalian viruses. V. Properties of purified viral-specific RNA from human adenovirus induced tumor cells. J. Mol. Biol. 31:63–73, 1968.

6. FUJINAGA, K., Mak, S. and GREEN, M.: A method for determining the fraction of the viral genome transcribed during infection and its application to adenovirus-infected cells. Proc. Natl. Acad. Sci. U.S. 60:959–966, 1968.

7. GILLESPIE, D. and SPIEGELMAN, S.: A quantitative assay for DNA-RNA hybrids with DNA immobilized on a membrane. J. Mol. Biol. 12:829–842, 1965.

8. GREEN, M.: Chemistry and structure of animal virus particles. Am. J. Med. 38:651–668, 1965.

9. GREEN, M.: Detection of "viral latency" by biochemical methods. Proc. of Conference on Cell Cultures for Virus Vaccine Production (National Cancer Institute Monograph No. 29). In press.

10. GREEN, M., PIÑA, M., KIMES, R., WENSINK, P. C., MacHATTIE, L. A. and THOMAS, C. A., JR.: Adenovirus DNA. I. Molecular weight and conformation. Proc. Natl. Acad. Sci. U.S. 57:1302–1309, 1967.

11. HUEBNER, R. J., CASEY, M. J., CHANOCK, R. M. and SCHELL, K.: Tumors induced in hamsters by a strain of adenovirus 3: sharing of tumor antigens and "neoantigens" with those produced by adenovirus type 7 tumors. Proc. Natl. Acad. Sci. U.S. 54:381–388, 1965.

12. PIÑA, M. and GREEN, M.: Biochemical studies on adenovirus multiplication. IX. Chemical and base composition analysis of 28 human adenoviruses. Proc. Natl. Acad. Sci. U.S. 54:547–551, 1965.

Viruses Associated with Burkitt's Lymphoma

Robert A. Manaker

Microbiology Section
Viral Biology Branch
National Cancer Institute [1]
Bethesda, Maryland

A lymphoma of African children, described as a distinct clinical entity by Burkitt in 1958 (1), has aroused considerable interest because epidemiological evidence strongly suggests that an external environmental factor is involved, possibly a vector-borne virus disease. Burkitt's tumor occurs in high incidence in those regions of Africa where climatic conditions are favorable for the dissemination of arthropod-vectored agents (2, 3). A high incidence of the tumor, but not the geographic and climatic limitations noted in Africa, has also been observed in New Guinea (4). Cases in Africa are infrequent among adults residing in endemic areas. However, among immigrants from regions where the tumor is rare, nearly 50 percent were over 15 years of age. Racial and tribal characteristics have been said to be of no significance in susceptibility to tumor development. These observations suggest that immunity develops in most persons exposed to the inciting agent and may be a factor in the response of patients to therapy (5).

Childhood lymphomas resembling Burkitt's tumor have been reported to occur in the United States (6, 7) and in Great Britain (8). Transmission in these instances by an insect vector would be unlikely. Lymphomas histologically resembling the Burkitt lymphoma have been described in the dog (9) and the cat (10). These observations support the view that Burkitt's lymphoma represents a disease manifestation peculiar to childhood rather than a specific entity confined to certain geographic areas or associated with specific etiologic factors.

Among a number of viruses found in association with Burkitt's tumor, reovirus type 3 has been isolated with sufficient regularity (29% of cases) to attract attention. Reovirus infections of man and most animals are common, but serological tests showed the presence of neutralizing antibodies to the type 3 virus in 73% of patients' sera in comparison to 18% of control children's sera (11). This virus can be mechanically transmitted by mosquitoes, but since the possibility for such transmission occurs where the neoplasm is rare, this route of infection is probably not significant.

Stanley and his colleagues (12) observed the development of lymphoma in mice inoculated with spleen cells from a mouse which survived oral infection with reovirus type 3. The tumor could be carried in serial transplant passage. Although in-

[1] National Institutes of Health, Public Health Service, U.S. Department of Health, Education and Welfare.

fectious virus was not released, reovirus type 3 complement-fixing antigen was contained in the tumor, suggesting that a non-infectious genome is carried by the cells.

Recently, the development of a multifocal, malignant lymphoma in a 2-year-old rabbit was described by Bell, Munube and Wright (13). The tumor developed 7 months after the animal had been given serial intravenous injections of a strain of reovirus isolated from the jaw of a case of Burkitt's lymphoma. Since lymphoma is rare in the rabbit, this is a significant observation. Although the results obtained in animals do not provide evidence of direct oncogenic activity, an indirect association is possible.

Epstein, Achong and Barr were the first to observe a herpes-type virus in cultured lymphoblasts from a Burkitt's tumor (14). Observations made electron microscopically on other cell lines originated from African lymphomas showed the presence of the virus, now termed EB virus, in nearly all those thoroughly examined. Relatively few cells contained the agent, and these cells were in various stages of degeneration. A considerable research effort to determine the significance of EB virus in the etiology of the lymphoma was initiated under the Special Virus Cancer Program of the National Cancer Institute. Two cell lines of Nigerian origin were selected from a number of cultures provided by Professor R. J. V. Pulvertaft and Dr. B. O. Osunkoya. The Raji line was virus-free and has served control purposes. The Jijoye line, designated P3-J in our laboratory, consistently produced good yields of virus and has been used for production purposes.

The indirect immunofluorescence test was successfully applied to detect cells containing virus in Burkitt tumor cell cultures (15). The reaction was not restricted to sera from patients with Burkitt's tumor, for many sera from normal American donors were positive for antibody. A high incidence of reactive sera (60%) was observed in newborn children. Between the ages of 4 to 24 months, the incidence was low but rose rapidly after the second year of life to plateau at about 50% between 4 and 16 years of age. About 90% of adult sera tested had positive antibody titers. The mean serum titers observed with Burkitt's tumor patient's sera were higher than those in the American sera studied. Present information indicates that EB virus is not antigenically related to the common herpes viruses infecting man. The agent could also not be identified with a number of animal herpes viruses tested.

About 59% of Burkitt's lymphoma patients' sera contained precipitating antibody to an antigen prepared from the Burkitt P3-J cell line. Similar tests showed antibody in 87% of sera from African patients with nasopharyngeal carcinoma, in comparison to 1% of sera from Africans with other malignant diseases and 5% of sera from non-malignant disorders (16). A high incidence of precipitating antibody was also detected in sera from Americans with carcinoma of the nasopharynx.

Lymphoblastoid cell lines were established from the peripheral blood of normal Americans (17) as well as from individuals with neoplastic diseases (18). Many of the lines contained EB virus, and the question arose whether the virus was responsible for the ability of these cells to continue growth *in vitro*. Henle and his colleagues (19) prepared duplicate cultures from female infants. Cells not exposed to EB virus failed to survive. Cells mixed with irradiated male Burkitt tumor cells of the P3-J line containing EB virus continued to grow and were maintained for 3 to 8 months. Virus was detected in the female cells. Secondary constrictions in the long arms of the no. 10 chromosomes similar to those detected in cultured Burkitt's lymphoma cells were present. The mechanism, direct or indirect, whereby the virus influenced cell growth characteristics is unknown.

Cultures similar to those from the African lymphoma were established from the peripheral blood leukocytes of young chimpanzees. A herpes-type virus similar to EB virus was detected in these cells (20). In our laboratories a herpes-type virus was observed in cultured lymphoblastoid cells originated from a rhesus monkey which developed myeloid leukemia after exposure to a chemical carcinogen, but the culture was lost due to a contaminant before identity to EB virus was firmly established. The complement-fixation test, applied to the determination of antibodies to EB virus in human sera, yielded results comparable to those achieved by immunofluorescence (21, 22). Sera from chimpanzees, cynomologous, rhesus and African green monkeys, and baboons were examined and found to contain CF antibodies. Only in the baboon was the incidence of positive reaction low. It is evident that the EB virus or closely related agents have a broad distribution in lower primates as well as in the human population.

The development of antibodies to EB virus in individuals with infectious mononucleosis suggested a relationship of the agent to this disease (23). It is possible that an agent capable of eliciting so profound an effect on blood elements may under certain conditions induce malignant change. The continued insults to the reticulo-endothelial system from parasitic and viral infections suffered by children in areas where the tumor is endemic may provide the foundation for neoplastic tranformation.

The EB virus produced in cell cultures is poorly infective although the incidence of exposure apparent from serological tests suggests a high order of infectivity under natural conditions. Horoszewicz (24) successfully infected virus-free cultured lymphoblastoid cells with high multiplicities of free virus from the HR1K clone of the P3-J cell line. The virus has not been shown to be infective for other cell types. Rapidly growing cell cultures may lose the virus while cultural conditions which retard cell growth favor the virus. Apparently the virus exists as a chronic infection and is transmitted from cell to cell, largely by close cell contact. It grows poorly in agitated cultures whereas static cultures in which cells form suspended clusters are optimum for its production. Cell lines initiated in African laboratories with media containing human serum retain the virus though it is highly probable that antibody is consistently present. This suggests slow cell-to-cell transmission by close contact in these cultures.

Benyesh-Melnick studied lymphoblastoid cell lines originated from patients with infectious mononucleosis (25). Three lines which appeared free of EB virus were co-cultivated with embryonic bone marrow fibroblasts, also free of virus. EB virus was detected in the mixed cultures (26). These results indicate that occult infection is possible.

Studies on the relationship of viruses to human neoplasias are considerably more difficult than in animals where the availability of tissue materials and susceptible hosts permit active investigation. The lower primates have been used in the investigations on the EB virus. No response to the inoculations of virus has been observed to date. However, the keen interest of many investigators in the Burkitt lymphoma and in associated viral agents promises elucidation of the problems of the moment.

Summary

In summary, two viruses, reovirus type 3 and EB virus have been found frequently in association with Burkitt's lymphoma. However, the distribution of each is as broad as that of leukemia viruses in laboratory mice. The tumor occurs most frequently in areas where transmission of viral agents by arthropod vectors is common, and the apparent resistance of older residents in these regions suggests development of immunity to tumor development. Since all lymphoma patients have antibody to the EB virus, it is a prime suspect as a contributing factor in the development of the neoplasm. Although the EB virus is poorly infective in *in vitro* systems, it apparently is highly infectious under natural conditions. This agent has a predilection for lymphoid cells, and may have a profound effect upon them as evidenced by the conferment of ability of sustained growth *in vitro* and by an apparent relationship to infectious mononucleosis *in vivo*. Although the evidence does not support a direct cause and effect relationship to the tumor, strain differences may exist, and in conjunction with other factors affecting the susceptibility of the host and perhaps in conjunction with other agents such as reovirus type 3, it may be a significant factor in promoting malignancy in lymphoreticular cells.

References

1. BURKITT, D. P.: A sarcoma involving the jaws in African children. Brit. J. Surg. 46:218–223, 1958.
2. BURKITT, D. P. and DAVIES, J. N. P.: Lymphoma syndrome in Uganda and tropical Africa. Med. Press 245:367–369, 1961.
3. HADDOW, A. J.: An improved map for the study of Burkitt's lymphoma syndrome in Africa. E. Afr. Med. J. 40:429–432, 1963.
4. TEN SELDAM, R. E. J., COOKE, R. A. and ANDERSON, L.: Childhood lymphoma in the territories of Papua and New Guinea. Cancer 19:437–446, 1966.
5. BURKITT, D. P. and WRIGHT, D. H.: Geographical and tribal distribution of the African lymphoma in Uganda. Brit. Med. J. 1:569–573, 1966.
6. O'CONOR, G. T., RAPPAPORT, H. and SMITH, E. B.: Childhood lymphoma resembling "Burkitt tumor" in the United States. Cancer 18:411–417, 1965.
7. DORFMAN, R. F.: Childhood lymphosarcoma in St. Louis, Missouri clinically and histologically resembling Burkitt's tumor. Cancer 18:418–430, 1965.
8. BASKERVILLE, A., HUNT, A. C. and LUCKÉ, M. V.: Burkitt's lymphoma in Great Britain. Lancet 2:547, 1966.
9. LUKES, R. J., PARKER, J. W., BELL, R. E., McFRIDE, N. L. and MADILL, K. R.: Canine lymphomas histologically indistinguishable from Burkitt's lymphoma. Lancet 2:389–390, 1966.
10. SQUIRE, R. A.: Feline lymphoma. A comparison with the Burkitt tumor of children. Cancer 19:447–453, 1966.
11. BELL, T. M.: Viruses associated with Burkitt's tumor. Prog. Med. Virol. 9:1–34, 1967.
12. STANLEY, N. F., WALTERS, M. N. I., LEAK, P. J. and KEAST, D.: The association of a murine lymphoma with reovirus type 3 infection. Proc. Soc. Exp. Biol. Med. 121:90–94, 1966.
13. BELL, T. M., MUNUBE, G. M. R. and WRIGHT, D. H.: Malignant lymphoma in a rabbit inoculated with reovirus. Lancet 1:955–957, 1968.

14. EPSTEIN, M. A., ACHONG, B. G. and BARR, Y. M.: Virus particles in cultured lymphoblasts from Burkitt's lymphoma. Lancet *1*:702–703, 1964.

15. HENLE, G. and HENLE, W.: Immunofluorescence in cells derived from Burkitt's lymphoma. J. Bact. *91*:1248–1256, 1966.

16. OLD, L. J., BOYSE, E. A., OETTGEN, H. F., DEHARVEN, E., GEERING, G., WILLIAMSON, B. and CLIFFORD, P.: Precipitating antibody in human serum to an antigen present in cultured Burkitt's lymphoma cells. Proc. Nat. Acad. Sci. USA *56*:1699–1704, 1966.

17. MOORE, G. E., GERNER, R. E. and FRANKLIN, H. A.: Culture of normal human leukocytes. J. Amer. Med. Ass. *199*:519–524, 1967.

18. MOORE, G. E., ITO, E., ULRICH, K., and SANDBERG, A. A.: Culture of human leukemia cells. Cancer *19*:713–723, 1966.

19. HENLE, W., DIEHL, V., KOHN, G. and HENLE, G.: Herpes-type virus and chromosome marker in normal leukocytes after growth with irradiated Burkitt cells. Science *157*: 1064–1065, 1967.

20. LANDON, J. C., ELLIS, L. B., ZEVE, V. H. and FABRIZIO, D. P. A.: Herpes-type virus in cultured leukocytes from chimpanzees. J. Nat. Cancer Inst. *40*:181–192, 1968.

21. ARMSTRONG, D., HENLE, G. and HENLE, W.: Complement-fixation tests with cell lines derived from Burkitt's lymphoma and acute leukemia. J. Bact. *91*:1257–1262, 1966.

22. GERBER, P. and BIRCH, S. M.: Complement-fixing antibodies in sera of human and non-human primates to viral antigens derived from Burkitt's lymphoma cells. Proc. Natl. Acad. Sci. USA *58*:478–484, 1967.

23. HENLE, W., HENLE, G. and DIEHL, V.: Relation of Burkitt's tumor-associated herpes-type virus to infectious mononucleosis. Proc. Nat. Acad. Sci. USA *59*:94–101, 1968.

24. HOROSZEWICZ, J. Unpublished results.

25. BENYESH-MELNICK, M., PHILIPS, C. F., LEWIS, R. T. and SEIDEL, E. H.: Studies on acute leukemia and infectious mononucleosis of childhood. IV. Continuous propagation of lymphoblastoid cells from spontaneously transformed bone marrow cultures. J. Nat. Cancer Inst. *40*:123–134, 1968.

26. BENYESH-MELNICK, M.: Personal communication.

A Herpes Virus as a Cause of
Marek's Disease in Chickens

B. R. BURMESTER, R. L. WITTER, K. NAZERIAN and H. G. PURCHASE

United States Department of Agriculture *

Marek's disease (MD), first described by Marek in 1907 (1), is a common infectious disease of the domestic chicken in which there is both an inflammatory and neoplastic response of the lymphoid system. Tumorous lesions commonly occur in the nervous system and the visceral organs and sometimes in the iris and ciliary body, the skeletal muscle, and feather follicles. Formerly, reference to this disease was included under the term lymphomatosis; however, since MD and lymphoid leukosis are known to be caused by different viruses, distinctive terms for each are now employed.

Experimental transmission of MD was only sporadically successful until it was realized that transmission occurred only when viable cells were present in the inoculum. Attempts to obtain infectious cell-free filtrates have thus far been generally unsuccessful (2).

Extensive examination of tumors and other tissues of MD infected birds has failed to reveal virus-like particles which appear definitely related to the disease. Particles of "C" type have been observed in some cases of MD (3, 4); however, such particles could not be distinguished from those of the leukosis/sarcoma group of viruses which are ubiquitous in chickens. Herpes-like particles were occasionally observed in gonad tumors and nerve lesions of MD infected birds (K. Nazerian, unpublished data). Since particles were not consistently associated with MD lesions, the significance of these findings in the etiology of the disease could not be evaluated.

Marek's disease is highly contagious. The virus is present in oral and tracheal washings and in droppings and is easily disseminated by the air-borne route (5, 6, 7, 8). The virus survives for various periods in droppings, in beetles, and in chicken embryos (2, 9, 10), and there is some evidence for transovarian transmission (M. Sevoian, personal communication).

Preliminary data (11, 12) indicate that the infection is present in practically all commercial flocks, that the rate of infection within flocks is high and that most infections do not result in clinical disease. Progeny from infected flocks have maternal antibody for at least the first three weeks of life. Under normal conditions, infection occurs relatively early and antibodies appear in about one month and persist for long periods.

---

* Poultry Research Branch, Animal husbandry Research Division, ARS, Regional Poultry Research Laboratory, East Lansing, Michigan.

Virus Isolation and Identification

Recently, a cell associated herpes virus was isolated from the tissues of chickens with MD. Isolations were obtained in chicken kidney cultures (13) and in duck embryo fibroblast cultures (14, 15), and the virus was also propagated in chicken embryo fibroblasts (17). Infected cell cultures developed discrete focal lesions (plaques) in 10 to 25 days (Fig. 1). The plaques had many highly refractile round cells which were vacuolated and frequently multinucleated. Some of these possessed intranuclear inclusion bodies containing DNA (13, 15, 16). Changes in the cytoplasm of the infected cell include extensive vacuolization and formation of lysozyme-like structures. Nuclear membrane ruptures occur, resulting in a transfer of nuclear material into the cytoplasm (18).

Studies of cell cultures infected with the MD agent have led to the identification of the causative virus. Herpes-type virus particles have been consistently observed in infected cultures of chicken kidney cells (13) and duck and chicken embryo fibroblasts (15, 17, 18). The virus, however, was found to be closely associated with infected cells and, with the exception of certain chicken embryo fibroblast cultures, infection could not be transmitted by inoculation of cell-free material (17). The proportion of cells containing virus particles was found to vary widely. In monolayer cultures, 1 to 10% of the cells contained particles and in the aggregated cells of suspension cultures, up to 83% had herpes-like particles (18).

Three morphologically distinct types of particles were seen in the nuclei of infected cells, i.e., naked particles, enveloped particles, and small amorphous particles. The naked particles were 95–100 mμ in diameter and some of these had electron dense nucleoids (Fig. 2). Enveloped particles were found in nuclear vesicles and free in the nucleoplasm (Fig. 3). They were 150–170 mμ in diameter and appeared to obtain their second membrane in the process of budding from the nuclear membrane. The third particles were 30–40 mμ in diameter, had a poorly defined structure and were only seen in association with the herpes virus like particles (Fig. 4). Many naked particles were found in the growth fluid of infected cultures (Fig. 5). Negatively stained preparations showed the nucleocapsid to consist of hollow capsomeres, 5 on each edge of a triangle; thus, there are a total of 162 capsomeres per virion (Fig. 6).

On the basis of the morphology and morphogenesis of the virus, its DNA content, its sensitivity to DNA analogs, and its close association with infected cells, the virus was identified as a member of the B group of herpes viruses (13, 15, 17, 18, 19). It will be referred to as Marek's disease herpes virus (MDHV).

Etiologic Evidence

Initial reports (13, 14, 15) presented data which showed that there was an excellent correlation between the presence of the herpes-like virus in cell cultures, the presence of plaques, and the ability of such cultures to produce the disease in susceptible chickens, thus providing suggestive evidence that a herpes virus was the cause of Marek's disease.

Since the requirement of intact cells precluded the use of purified virus in critical infectivity experiments, further studies were conducted to obtain additional circum-

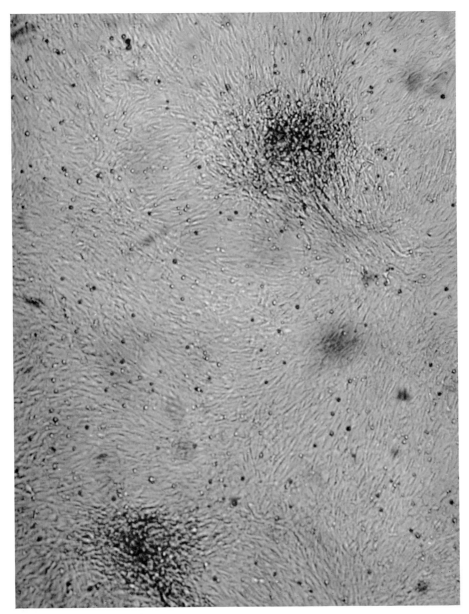

Fig. 1. Focal areas of CPE in a DEF monolayer culture inoculated with JM strain of Marek's disease virus. ✕43. (*Note:* All micrographs are from JM strain of MD virus inoculated duck embryo fibroblast cell cultures.)

stantial evidence that this MD-associated herpes virus is the cause of MD. Some of the results follow (11):

1. MDHV has been isolated from all strains of MD examined. This included two strains propagated at the East Lansing Laboratory and six strains obtained directly from as many other laboratories. At the same time, attempts to isolate a similar virus

from kidney and blood from many chickens reared in isolation have been unsuccessful.

2. MDHV was isolated from 27 of 28 field flocks located in four states. Of 134 chickens tested, 68% were found to be infected. Some of these flocks had no clinical history of MD, yet there was a distinct positive correlation between the rate of virus isolation and extent of clinical disease. Within 18 flocks having clinical MD, MDHV was isolated from 72 of 86 or 84%; whereas, within 10 flocks without clinical MD, isolations were obtained from 20 of 48 chickens or 42%.

3. Further correlative studies were conducted with 187 individual chickens of

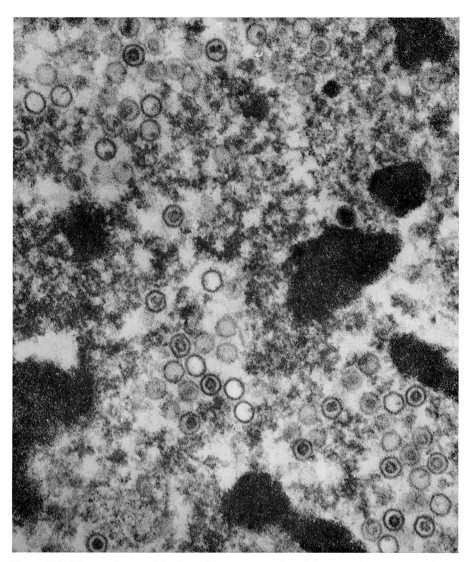

Fig. 2. Naked herpes virus particles in a disintegrating nucleus. These particles are seen with and without central nucleoid. $\times 56,000$.

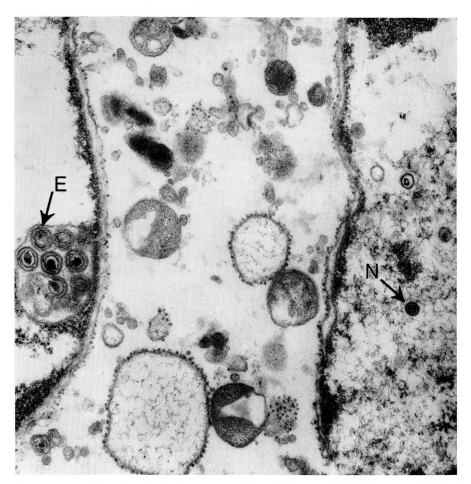

Fig. 3. Portion of an infected cell showing parts of two different nuclei in the same cell. Naked particles (N) are seen in one nucleus while enveloped particles (E) are seen in a nuclear vesicle in the other nucleus. Cytoplasm shows generalized degeneration. ×36,000.

which 99 were from the field and 45 were laboratory reared. MDHV was isolated from 85 of 86 chickens with MD lesions and from 20 of 58 chickens presumably exposed but which did not have lesions. In contrast, no virus and no lesions were detected in all of 43 chickens reared in isolation. All in all, agreement between virus isolation and presence of lesions was obtained in 89% of the 187 cases.

4. A total of 70 samples were tested for virus by two methods, the usual chicken inoculation assay and CPE induction in cell culture. Agreement was obtained in 92% of the 70 samples tested. Six samples which induced MD *in vivo* were negative by the tissue culture test. This is consistent with previous findings that the chick inoculation test is 6 to 200 times more sensitive than the cell culture assay (16).

5. In studies of the relationship between the occurrence of typical herpes virus CPE in cell culture and the induction of MD in chickens, it was found that when test chickens were inoculated with 57 cultures having CPE and 74 cultures without

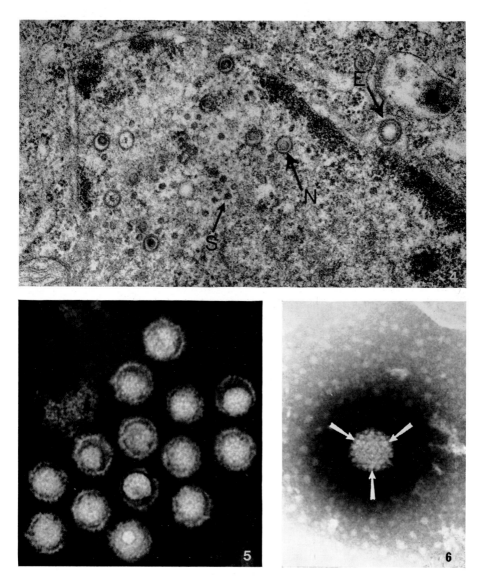

Fig. 4. Portion of an infected cell showing part of the nucleus and the cytoplasm. Naked particles (N) and small particles (S) are seen in the nucleus. Two enveloped particles (E) are seen in the cytoplasm. ✕36,000.

Fig. 5. A number of naked particles are seen in negatively stained preparation of the virus in the growth media of infected cultures. ✕96,000.

Fig. 6. Individual capsomeres of this naked particle are quite distinguishable. Five capsomeres can be seen on each edge of one of the triangular facets (arrows) of the capsid. ✕120,000.

CPE, agreement between the presence of CPE and induction of MD in chickens was obtained in 87% of the pairs. Discrepancy was no doubt largely due to the greater sensitivity of the chicken test than the cell culture test. The *in vivo* work was done with progeny of a highly susceptible inbred cross.

Other laboratories have confirmed the isolation from MD chicken tissue of a herpes-type virus in cell cultures, induction of typical CPE and reproduction of the disease with such cultures [(20); J. L. Spencer and S. G. Kenzy, personal communications].

Various treatments which disrupt or remove the cells, such as ultrasonic disintegration, homogenization, and low speed centrifugation, destroy the infectivity of an inoculum for birds and also destroy infectivity for cell cultures (13).

Using the agar gel diffusion technic, a precipitation reaction has been obtained between serums from MD infected birds and an antigen from cultures with CPE induced by MDHV (12). Precipitin lines of identity were found between 5 MD isolates but not with infectious laryngotracheitis virus and pigeon herpes virus. Various treatments which prevented CPE also prevented formation of reactive levels of antigen. Precipitin lines were not obtained with tumor homogenates. This is probably related to the scarcity of virus particles as revealed by electron microscopy (K. Nazerian, unpublished data).

Other investigators using rabbit antiserum obtained double precipitin lines with plasma and bone marrow antigen of MD chickens and only one line with bone marrow from uninfected chickens (21).

Serums obtained from birds immunized with the MD agent and from recovered birds contain antibody which attaches MD antigen in cell culture. This antigen-antibody complex can be detected by the indirect fluorescent antibody (FA) test. Quantitative studies indicate that the fluorescent staining areas and the areas with cytopathology are caused by the same agent. There is no evidence of other antigens in cell cultures which induce MD. Also, the serum from recovered birds does not contain antibody to other agents which might grow in these cultures. The indirect FA test has been used extensively to detect antibody to the MD tissue culture antigen in the sera of birds. Only young chickens from dams with antibody and older chickens known to be exposed to the MD agent show antibody. Isolated controls remain free of antibody (22).

The foregoing data provide strong circumstantial evidence for the conclusion that this cell-associated herpes virus is an etiologic agent of MD. They do not entirely exclude the possibility that other agents unrelated to the herpes virus might also induce lesions which currently are classified as MD.

Summary

A cytopathic virus has been isolated in avian embryo fibroblasts and kidney epithelial cultures from chickens with MD. Based on morphology, morphogenesis, nucleic acid type and cell-associated infectivity, the virus has been identified as a member of the B group of herpes viruses. Although herpes virus particles have seldom been seen in the MD lesions, extensive correlative data on the occurrence of CPE and of typical virus particles in MD cell cultures and the induction of MD in chickens with such cultures, together with critical data from agar gel precipitin and fluorescent antibody tests, provide conclusive evidence that a cell-associated herpes virus is a primary cause of this disease. Preliminary data provided by virus isolation, precipitin and fluorescent antibody tests indicate that infection is present in all flocks at a relatively high rate and most infections occur early, remain inapparent, and persist for long periods.

Addendum

Studies on susceptibility of other species to Marek's disease herpes virus (MDHV) infections are very limited. Although there is some indication that infections with this virus may occur in other avian species [(23); Witter, unpublished data], mammalian cells appear to be refractory. In one study, 21 cell culture lines from 15 different mammalian species were tested for growth of MDHV. None of the lines showed evidence of cell alteration at 14 to 23 days or infectiousness at 9 to 19 days post inoculation (24). In a limited survey, precipitin antibodies were not found in sera of 16 laboratory workers having close and continuing contact with infectious material (Burgoyne, unpublished data).

References

1. MAREK, J.: Multiple Nervenentzündung (Polyneuritis) bei Hühnern. Deutsch. tierarztl. Wochenschr. 15:417–421, 1907.
2. BIGGS, P. M. and PAYNE, L. N.: Studies on Marek's disease. I. Experimental transmission. J. Nat. Cancer Inst. 39:267–280, 1967.
3. DiSTEFANO, H. S. and DOUGHERTY, R. M.: Virus particles in the nerve of Remak of chick embryos. J. Nat. Cancer Inst. 33:921–934, 1964.
4. WIGHT, P. A., WILSON, J. E., CAMPBELL, J. G. and FRASER, E.: Virus-like particles in blood lymphocytes in acute Marek's disease. Nature 216:804–805, 1967.
5. SEVOIAN, M., CHAMBERLAIN, D. M. and LaROSE, R. N.: Avian lymphomatosis. V. Airborne transmission. Avian Dis. 7:102–105, 1963.
6. WITTER, R. L. and BURMESTER, B. R.: Transmission of Marek's disease with oral washings and feces from infected chickens. Proc. Soc. Exp. Biol. Med. 124:59–62, 1967.
7. KENZY, S. G. and BIGGS, P. M.: Excretion of Marek's disease agent by infected chickens. Vet. Rec. 80:565–568, 1967.
8. EIDSON, C. S. and SCHMITTLE, S. C.: Studies on acute Marek's disease. V. Attempted transmission of isolate GA with feces and nasal washings. Avian Dis. 12:549–553, 1968.
9. WITTER, R. L., BURGOYNE, G. H. and BURMESTER, B. R.: Survival of Marek's disease agent in litter and droppings. Avian Dis. 12:522–530, 1968.
10. EIDSON, C. S., SCHMITTLE, S. C., GOODE, R. B. and LAL, J. B.: Induction of leukosis tumors with the beetle Alphitobius diaperinus. Amer. J. Vet. Res. 27:1053–1057, 1966.
11. WITTER, R. L., BURGOYNE, G. H. and SOLOMON, J. J.: Evidence for a herpesvirus as an etiologic agent of Marek's disease. Avian Dis. 13:171–184, 1969.
12. CHUBB, R. C. and CHURCHILL, A. E.: Precipitating antibodies associated with Marek's disease. Vet. Rec. 83:4–7, 1968.
13. CHURCHILL, A. E. and BIGGS, P. M.: Agent of Marek's disease in tissue culture. Nature 215:528–530, 1967.

14. Solomon, J. J., Witter, R. L., Nazerian, K. and Burmester, B. R.: Studies on the etiology of Marek's disease. I. Propagation of the agent in cell culture. Proc. Soc. Exp. Biol. Med. *127*:173–177, 1968.

15. Nazerian, K., Solomon, J. J., Witter, R. L. and Burmester, B. R.: Studies on the etiology of Marek's disease. II. Finding of a herpesvirus in cell culture. Proc. Soc. Exp. Biol. Med. *127*:177–182, 1968.

16. Witter, R. L., Solomon, J. J. and Burgoyne, G. H.: Cell culture technics for the primary isolation of Marek's disease-associated herpesvirus. Avian Dis. *13*:101–118, 1969.

17. Nazeria, K.: Electron microscopy of a herpesvirus isolated from Marek's disease in duck and chicken embryo fibroblast cultures. Proc. Electron Micro. Soc. Amer. 26th Ann. Mtg.: 222–223, 1968.

18. Nazerian, K. and Burmester, B. R.: Electron microscopy of a herpesvirus associated with the agent of Marek's disease in cell culture. Cancer Res. *28*:2454–2462, 1968.

19. Epstein, M. A., Achong, B. G., Churchill, A. E. and Biggs, P. M.: Structure and development of the herpes-type virus of Marek's disease. J. Nat. Cancer Inst. *41*:805–820, 1968.

20. Eidson, C. S. and Schmittle, S. C.: Studies on acute Marek's disease: Propagation of isolate GA in tissue culture. J. Amer. Vet. Med. Assoc. *152*:1351, 1968.

21. Kottaridis, S. D., Luginbuhl, R. E. and Chomiak, T. W.: Marek's disease. IV. Antigenic components demonstrated by immunodiffusion test. Avian Dis. *12*:394–400, 1968.

22. Purchase, H. G.: Application of immunofluorescence to the detection of Marek's disease antigen and antibody. Program, 105th Ann. Mtg. Amer. Vet. Med. Assoc.: p. 141, 1968.

23. Kenzy, S. G. and Cho, B. R.: Transmission of classical Marek's disease by affected and carrier birds. J. Amer. Vet. Med. Assoc. *152*:1354, 1968.

24. Calnek, B. W., Stewart, H. M. and Kniazeff, A. J.: Susceptibility of cultured mammalian cells to infection with a herpesvirus from Marek's disease and T-virus from reticuloendotheliosis of chickens. Amer. J. Vet. Res., in press.

Studies on the Viral Etiology
of Marek's Disease of Fowl*

Dale J. Richey

Poultry Disease Research Center
University of Georgia
Athens, Georgia

Introduction

The diseases of the avian leukosis complex include a variety of disorders of practical, scientific and academic interest to those connected with poultry disease research.

Recent advances in this field have added greatly to our knowledge of neoplasms in general. A general description of two important diseases of the avian leukosis complex is included to assist those not involved in this work.

Incidence of Marek's Disease

During the last 10 years there has been a continuing increase in the incidence of "avian leukosis" outbreaks, especially in heavily concentrated poultry producing areas of the United States and some foreign countries. A decade ago this disorder accounted for less than 10 percent of the poultry disease diagnosis, while today approximately 50 percent of the total cases examined are reported as "avian leukosis complex." Poultry inspection condemnation records show similar data (Fig. 1). The monetary loss to the poultry industry is conservatively estimated at 200 million dollars annually and increasing.

Two distinct types of neoplastic disorders are now observed to comprise the majority of avian leukosis complex outbreaks (1). Viral characteristics and etiology of the so-called "big liver disease" or "visceral leukosis" but now referred to as lymphoid or Type I lymphoid leukosis has been studied extensively since a specific strain (RPL-12) was originally described and propagated by Olson (2, 3). This viral strain is among a group considered RNA type, transmitted readily by way of the egg, antigenic and having an inhibitory effect upon the growth of Rous virus in cultured fibroblasts (resistance-inducing factor, or RIF) (4). An extensive bibliography of this disease is available (5).

A second disease of the leukosis complex, although similar in pathology to Type I

---

* University of Georgia, College of Agriculture Experiment Stations Journal Series Paper number 414, College Station, Athens.

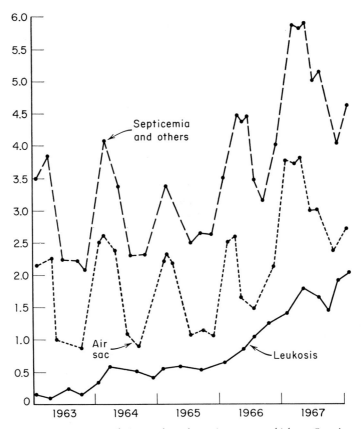

Fig. 1. Percent accumulative total condemnations, young chickens, Georgia.

infection mentioned above, is generally described as "acute leukosis," Type II lymph-oid leukosis or Marek's disease (MD) (1). The classical form of MD, where symptoms are characterized by various degrees of paralysis, was originally described by Marek (6) and later by Pappenheimer *et al.* (7), who also observed the occurrence of lymphoid tumors in the visceral organs of affected birds. The acute form of MD is often arbitrarily differentiated from the classical form by its explosive nature, high incidence of lymphoid tumors most often involving the gonads, and high mortality. Tumors may be observed in any organ or tissue of the bird, including the skin. This form of the disease has become of major concern to broiler and egg production stock since birds 4–16 weeks of age usually succumb to the disease. The isolates associated with acute MD are extremely contagious, not RIF positive, highly cell-associated and transmitted environmentally in the air or by direct bird-to-bird contact. Studies independently conducted at laboratories in England and the United States suggest the etiological agent of MD is a DNA virus belonging to the herpes-type group (8, 9).

Information regarding other diseases of the avian leukosis complex has been outlined by Burmester and Witter (10).

Pathogenesis

A study on the pathogenesis of the classical form of MD following infection of young chickens with the Houghton Poultry Research Station (HPRS-B14) isolate by Payne and Biggs (11) initiated a classification for the pathological changes occurring in the nerves. It is interesting to note from this study that lymphoid tumors in other organs occurred mainly in birds with a proliferative A-type or mixed A- and B-types of nerve lesions, as compared to the less proliferative B- and C-type lesions. Cytologically, the proliferative nerve lesions and the lymphoid tumors in other organs were identical, suggesting they represented the same pathological process. The HPRS-B14 isolate is, therefore, an example of a MD isolate producing the classical form of the disease. The above authors reported 62 percent of 21 birds having nerve lesions and 24 percent lymphoid tumors associated with A-type nerve lesions when examined 11–30 days post infection.

Other MD isolates such as JM, GA, HPRS-16 and CONN-A produce variable lesions in the central nervous system and peripheral nerves and visceral tumors, especially in the gonads, kidneys, spleen, liver, proventriculus and lungs. It is thought that the difference in host response to the different isolates is due to "viral strain" and also the host chicken used in the experiments.

Marek's disease is characterized by an abnormal (multicentric) aggregation of lymphoid cells which may be observed in any tissue or organ of the growing bird. A wide variability of cell types ranging from undifferentiated mesenchymal forms to small mature lymphocytes comprise the usual cytological picture. The pleomorphic reaction suggests an inflammatory reaction.

In contrast, lymphoid leukosis originates in the bursa of Fabricius (12) and the tumors consist primarily of uniform-appearing hemocytoblasts or immature lymphocytes.

The pathological nature of MD has not been resolved: the question of neoplasia or inflamamtion is presently a matter of opinion. Detailed information on this subject may be studied in the publications of Payne and Biggs (9), Sevoian (13), Purchase, Chubb and Biggs (14), and Foster and Moll (15).

Body Temperature and MD Infection

Fluctuations in body temperature are often characteristic of infectious diseases of man and domestic animals. Colwell and Schmittle (16) compared the daily body temperatures of 80 chicks which were exposed to MD at one day of age to the body temperatures of 90 hatchmates held in isolation for the first three weeks of life. Exposure of susceptible chicks to the MD agent resulted in a temperature pattern which differed markedly from the normal. The pattern is easily discernible in Fig. 2, which compares the mean daily rectal temperature of the 90 MD-infected birds to the mean and range of the 90 control birds. Body temperatures of exposed birds tended to be lower than temperatures of control birds during the first 13 days with an abrupt drop around the eighth day post-exposure. Temperatures fluctuated widely but averaged

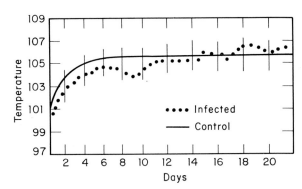

Fig. 2. Mean daily rectal temperature of 80 Marek's-infected birds superimposed on the mean and range of 90 control birds.

above normal during days 13–21. Fig. 3 illustrates the actual daily temperature readings of a typical individual bird from the exposed group along with the mean and range of the 90 controls.

Transmission

Sevoian *et al.* (17) and Colwell and Schmittle (18) have shown that the MD isolates JM and GA may pass with the exhaust air from an isolation cage containing infected chickens to other isolation cages and infect susceptible day-old chicks. In the latter study, transmission of infection from donor birds began during the first week postinoculation and continued during the three-week period of observation. The number of birds with MD lesions in the recipient group when the donor birds were three weeks of age was equal to that of the tumor-injected hatchmates. Airborne transmission of the MD agent occurred in three successive weekly groups of susceptible chicks exposed to the exhaust from the donor isolation unit after the chicks were removed. Some chicks exposed during the third week after the unit had been emptied developed MD.

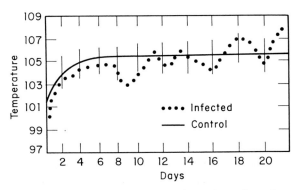

Fig. 3. Daily rectal temperature chart of an infected bird superimposed on the mean and range of 90 control birds.

TABLE 1

TRANSMISSION OF THE GA ISOLATE OF MAREK'S DISEASE (MD)
IN EXHAUST AIR FROM AN ISOLATION UNIT OF INFECTED CHICKS
DIVERTED TO TWO UNITS CONTAINING SUSCEPTIBLE CHICKS

Isolation unit	No. of chicks	Treatment of chicks	Treatment of incoming air	Incidence of MD *
1	12	MD infected	Normal †	5
2	12	None	None	4
3	12	None	Filtered	0

* Four-week isolation period.
† All units normally under positive filtered air pressure.

Richey (19) observed that use of the G-50 biological filter medium * to filter exhaust air from an isolation unit containing MD-infected chicks prevented transmission of the agent during a four-week trial period (Table 1).

Witter and Burmester (20) have shown that the JM isolate of MD may readily be transmitted by way of nasal washings and feces from infected birds and from contaminated litter. Kenzy and Biggs (21) were unable to transmit the B16 isolate with feces but did so with oral washings from infected birds. The GA isolate was transmitted in nasal washings from 3-week-old donor birds to one-day-old susceptible chicks (22). Feces taken directly from GA-infected birds were not infective when injected into day-old chicks. Richey (23) observed transmission of MD with the GA isolate by chick or tissue culture assay when susceptible chicks were placed in isolation for eight weeks on litter obtained directly from a heavily contaminated poultry house.

A considerable amount of work has been accomplished in determining the role of external parasites in the transmission of MD. Eidson et al. (24) observed that chickens dead of MD had larvae and adults of the beetle Alphitobius diaperinus in the subcutis. A prepared suspension of larvae or adult beetles collected from litter in a poultry house where infected birds were maintained was inoculated into day-old chicks orally and also intra-abdominally. Twenty-five to 83 percent of the chicks had tumors typical of MD by four weeks of age. Sterilization of larvae or beetle suspension inactivated the tumor-producing properties.

Brewer et al. (25) were not successful in transmitting MD by coccidial oocysts harvested from the litter of contaminated poultry houses or by oocysts taken directly from the intestinal tract of MD-infected birds. Birds inoculated with one or more species of coccidia at various times before or after exposure to the MD isolate also failed to have an increase in MD rate over those birds inoculated with the isolate only.

No evidence of biological transmission of MD was observed by the bite of Culex quinquefasciatus or Culex pipiens mosquitoes which had fed on Marek's-infected

---

* American Air Filter Co., Inc., Louisville, Kentucky, USA.

chickens (26). When recently engorged mosquitoes were ground and injected into susceptible day-old chicks, 10 of 30 had MD lesions four weeks later. Litter mites were not considered a hazard in the transmission of the disease when suspensions were given orally or intraabdominally to susceptible chicks (27).

Sevoian (28) has reported egg transmission of the JM isolate. Transmission of the GA isolate in chicks by way of the egg was not observed when trap-nested eggs from MD-infected hens were hatched under gnotobiotic environment (29). Whole blood from some of the hens remained infectious by chick assay for two weeks post-inoculation.

Cell-Association of Marek's Disease Isolates

The nature of the causative agent of MD is not clear although most workers doing tissue culture studies of infected organs or tissues observe a herpes-type virus particle when cultured material is examined with the electron microscope (8, 9). Cultures of chick kidney cells exhibiting the "rounded-cell" cytopathogenicity and containing a herpes-type virus produce MD when inoculated into susceptible chicks. The herpes-type virus has not been observed in numerous samples of visceral tumor tissue, skin lesions, plasma, serum or whole blood submitted for electron microscopic examination although the samples were highly infectious (30). (See Addendum.)

An additional difficulty in studying the herpes-type virus as the etiologic agent of MD is its high degree of cell-association typical of the B group of herpes-viruses (varicella-zoster and cytomegaloviruses). A series of Millipore membrane filtrations of infectious plasma resulted in retention of the GA agent by the first membrane which had a pore diameter of 5 μ (Table 2). A second trial of this type resulted in passage of the GA ioslate through an 8 μ pore diameter membrane but not the 5 μ. Infectivity was present on both membranes and the first filtrate (8 μ) when assayed by check inoculation.

TABLE 2

EFFECT OF MILLIPORE MEMBRANE
FILTRATION ON THE INFECTIVITY OF MAREK'S
DISEASE (MD) INFECTIVE PLASMA

Membrane pore size in μ	No. chicks inoculated	Incidence of MD *
5	12	0
3	12	0
1.2	12	0
0.8	12	0
0.45	12	0
None	12	9

* Four-week isolation period.

TABLE 3
RELEASE OF GA ISOLATE OF MAREK'S DISEASE (MD)
FROM CULTURED CHICK KIDNEY CELLS BY FREEZING
AND THAWING

Treatment	No. chicks inoculated	Incidence of MD *
None	20	17
Freeze and thaw (3 times)	10	4
Freeze, thaw and filter †	10	4
Control (uninoculated)	10	0

* Four-week isolation period.

† Filter membrane pore size, 0.45 μ.

Release of the GA Isolate from Chick Kidney Cell Cultures

Eidson (31) has prepared cell-free infectious material of the GA isolate by freezing, thawing and filtration. The infected kidney cells were cultured with frequent changes of the medium until "rounded-cell" formation was prominent in the monolayer. Monolayers of several dishes were combined, centrifuged, reconstituted in Medium 199 plus 10 percent calf serum and frozen and thawed three times at 30 minute intervals. Susceptible chicks were inoculated with portions of the reconstituted material before freezing, after freezing and thawing and following filtration of the frozen and thawed material (Table 3). Normal laboratory techniques used to determine characteristics of avian viruses often reduce or destroy infectivity of MD isolates. Freezing and thawing of the infectious material did reduce infectivity but there was sufficient MD agent to infect 40 percent of the inoculated chicks after filtration of the released isolate. This trial has been repeated with similar results.

The Etiologic Agent of Marek's Disease

The GA isolate of MD consistently induces a characteristic cytopathic effect in chick kidney monolayers. When cell material was concentrated by centrifugation and inoculated into isolated day-old chicks, typical MD developed in the majority of birds depending on the dose injected. Electron micrographs of the pelleted cell material revealed herpes-type virus present in the nucleus (32). When cell cultures were frozen and thawed and then filtered and the filtrate inoculated onto monolayers of normal chick kidney cells, the cytopathic effect previously mentioned developed after five to eight days incubation.

Additional evidence of the herpes-virus association with MD was obtained when infected chick kidney monolayers were stained with acridine orange. Cells exhibiting the cytopathic effect mentioned above stained a brilliant yellow-orange indicating the presence of double stranded DNA. Cells not infected had a diffuse reddish color in the cytoplasm and the nuclei stained green.

Witter *et al.* (33) observed herpes-type virus to be present in cultured cell-material containing isolates JM, GA, CONN-A, CR64, MSD-1 and C-1 obtained from various laboratories in the U.S. The virus was not observed in tissues from lesion-free, isolation-reared control birds. In electron microscopy studies of blood from cases of MD-infected chickens, Wight *et al.* (34) observed virus-like particles within cytoplasmic vesicles of lymphocytes. The particles were morphologically similar to the RNA viruses associated with the avian leukosis/sarcoma diseases. Such particles were not found in nerves, gonad or renal tumors of affected birds.

Available information concerning the etiology of MD strongly indicates a herpes-virus as the causative agent. Additional studies need to be completed to determine the exact host-parasite relationship before this question is resolved.

Addendum

Schidlovsky *et al.* recently observed intranuclear and cytoplasmic virus particles of the herpes type in cells that lined the kidney collecting tubules obtained from a Marek's disease infected chick (Schidlovsky, G., Ahmed, M. and Jensen, K. E.: Herpes-virus in Marek's disease tumors. Science *164:959–961,* 1969).

References

1. BIGGS, P. M.: Avian leukosis and Marek's disease. In XIIIth World's Poultry Congress symposium papers. Kiev, USSR, 1966, pp. 91–118.
2. OLSON, C., JR.: A transmissible lymphoid tumor of the chicken. Cancer Res. *1:*384–392, 1941.
3. OLSON, C., JR.: The serial passage of an avian lymphoid tumor of the chicken. Cancer Res. *4:*707–712, 1944.
4. RUBIN, H.: A virus in chick embryos which induces resistance *in vitro* to infection with Rous sarcoma virus. Proc. Nat. Acad. Sci. *46:*1105–1119, 1960.
5. JUNGHERR, E. and HUGHES, W. F.: The avian leukosis complex. *In* Diseases of Poultry (Biester and Schwarte, ed.). Ames, Iowa, USA, Iowa State University Press, 1965, pp. 512–567.
6. MAREK, J.: Multiple Nervenentzundung (Polyneuritis) bei Huhnern. Deutsch. Tierarztl. Wschr. *15:*417–421, 1907.
7. PAPPENHEIMER, A. M., DUNN, L. C. and CONE, V.: A study of fowl paralysis (neuro-lymphomatosis gallinarum). Storrs Agric. Exp. Sta. Bull. No. *143:*186–290, 1926.
8. CHURCHILL, A. E., and BIGGS, P. M.: Agent of Marek's disease in tissue culture. Nature *215:*528–530, 1967.
9. NAZERIAN, K., SOLOMON, J. J., WITTER, R. L. and BURMESTER, B. R.: Studies on the etiology of Marek's disease. II. Finding of a herpes virus in cell culture. Proc. Soc. Exp. Biol. Med. *127:*116–119, 1968.
10. BURMESTER, B. R. and WITTER, R. S.: An outline of the diseases of the avian leukosis complex. United States Department of Agriculture, Agricultural Research Service, Production Research Report No. 94, Washington, D.C., 1966, pp. 2–8.
11. PAYNE, L. N. and BIGGS, P. M.: Studies on Marek's disease. II. Pathogenesis. J. Nat. Cancer Inst. *39:*281–302, 1967.
12. DENT, P. B., COOPER, M. D., PAYNE, L. N., GOOD, R. A. and BURMESTER, B. R.: Characterization of avian lymphoid leukosis as a malignancy of the bursal lymphoid system. *In*

Perspectives in Virology V (Pollard, M., ed.). New York, London, Academic Press, Inc., pp. 251–265, 1967.

13. SEVOIAN, M.: On the terminology and classification of the avian leukosis complex. Avian Dis. *11*:98–103, 1967.

14. PURCHASE, H. G., CHUBB, R. C. and BIGGS, P. M.: Effect of lymphoid leukosis and Marek's disease on the immunological responsiveness of the chicken. J. Nat. Cancer Inst. *40*:583–592, 1968.

15. FOSTER, A. G. and MOLL, T.: Effect of immunosuppression on clinical and pathologic manifestations of Marek's disease in chickens. Am. J. Vet. Res. *29*:1831–1835, 1968.

16. COLWELL, W. M. and SCHMITTLE, S. C.: Studies on acute Marek's disease. VI. Body temperatures of infected chickens. Avian Dis. *12*:716–723, 1968.

17. SEVOIAN, M., CHAMBERLAIN, D. M. and LAROSE, R. N.: V. Airborne transmission. Avian Dis. *7*:102–105, 1963.

18. COLWELL, W. M. and SCHMITTLE, S. C.: Studies on acute Marek's disease. VII. Airborne transmission of the GA isolate. Avian Dis. *12*:724–729, 1968.

19. RICHEY, DALE J.: Unpublished data, 1968.

20. WITTER, R. L. and BURMESTER, B. R.: Transmission of Marek's disease with oral washings and feces from infected birds. Proc. Soc. Exp. Biol. Med. *124*:59–62, 1967.

21. KENZY, S. G. and BIGGS, P. M.: Excretion of the Marek's agent by infected chickens. Vet. Rec. *80*:565–568, 1967.

22. EIDSON, C. S. and SCHMITTLE, S. C.: Studies on acute Marek's disease. V. Attempted transmission of isolate GA with feces and nasal washings. Avian Dis. *12*:549–553, 1968.

23. RICHEY, DALE J.: Unpublished data, 1968.

24. EIDSON, C. S., SCHMITTLE, S. C., GOODE, R. B. and LAL, J. B.: Induction of leukosis tumors with the beetle *Alphitobius diaperinus*. Amer. J. Vet. Res. *27*:1053–1057, 1966.

25. BREWER, R. N., REID, W. M., BOTERO, H. and SCHMITTLE, S. C.: Studies on acute Marek's disease. II. The role of coccidia in transmission and induction. Poultry Sci. *47*: 2003–2012, 1968.

26. BREWER, R. N., REID, W. M., JOHNSON, J. and SCHMITTLE, S. C.: Studies on acute Marek's disease. VIII. The role of mosquitoes in transmission of the disease under experimental conditions. Avian Dis. *13*:83–88, 1969.

27. AIGSTER, F. G.: The role of free living mites in transmission of Marek's disease. Unpublished data, 1968.

28. SEVOIAN, M.: Current status of avian leukosis. 105th Annual Meeting AVMA, July 21–25, 1968, Boston, p. 159 (Abstr.).

29. RICHEY, DALE J.: Unpublished data, 1968.

30. RICHEY, DALE J.: Unpublished data, 1968.

31. EIDSON, C. S.: Unpublished data, 1968.

32. EIDSON, C. S., RICHEY, D. J. and SCHMITTLE, S. C.: Studies on acute Marek's disease. XI. Tissue culture propagation of the GA isolate of Marek's disease. Avian Dis., in press.

33. WITTER, R. L., BURGOYNE, G. H. and SOLOMON, J. J.: Evidence for a herpesvirus as the etiologic agent of Marek's disease. 105th Annual Meeting AVMA, July 21–25, 1968, Boston, p. 150 (Abstr.).

34. WIGHT, P. A. L., WILSON, J. E., CAMPBELL, J. G. and FRASER, E.: Virus-like particles in blood lymphocytes in acute Marek's disease. Nature *216*:804–805, 1967.

Herpes Simplex Viruses and Human Cancer: Current Status of the Problem

BERNARD ROIZMAN

Department of Microbiology
University of Chicago
Chicago, Illinois

The notion that herpesviruses cause cancer in man is based solidly on the historical principle that where there is smoke there must be fire. There is in fact a lot of smoke. The clues pointing to the oncogenicity of herpes simplex fall into 4 categories as follows. First, it has been reported that patients with severe and frequently recurring labial infections develop squamous cell carcinoma (1). Second, it has been demonstrated now quite conclusively that there are at least two types of herpes simplex viruses infecting man. The viruses differ with respect to physical, immunologic, and certain biologic properties (2, 3, 4, 5, 6). One of the two types causes predominantly infection of the genitalia transmitted by sexual contact (7, 8, 9). On epidemiologic grounds at least two laboratories have suggested that the genital strain might be responsible for cervical cancer in women (10, 11, 12). Into the third category fall numerous studies with cells in culture. Even though the data published so far (13) do not indicate that herpes simplex viruses "transform" cells *in vitro* in a manner of oncogenic viruses, there are nevertheless many reports that the viruses cause chromosome breakage in nonpermissive cells (14, 15, 16, 17, 18, 19, 20, 21, 22). It has been reported that cells infected with herpes simplex virus acquire the capacity to synthesize an antigen (designated as G) characteristic of some tumors (23). Lastly, there is guilt by association. The recurrent theme of this symposium is the association of herpes-type particles with renal adenocarcinoma of the frog. Herpes-type particles have been found associated with Marek's disease of chickens (24) and with human lymphoma (25), described by Burkitt (26). Considering the rich variety of herpes-type viruses which persist and thrive in human cells, it seems a safe bet that at least one and possibly all are inherently oncogenic.

It should be pointed out, however, that the observations and data cited so far are not compelling evidence that herpes simplex viruses are oncogenic. The association between recurrent herpetic infection and squamous carcinoma of the lip has been reported by two investigators i.e., by Wyburn-Mason (1) and by Kvasnicka (27, 28). The first reported a series of case histories. The other reported studies involving many patients. The implication is that frequent recurrence of lesions over a long time at one site ultimately causes malignancy in a manner as yet unknown. Alas, my colleagues specializing in dermatology are rather skeptical. Squamous cell carcinoma of the lip is rather rare and consequently it would be very difficult to reproduce the studies of Dr. Kvasnicka in the United States. Perhaps more interesting and relevant

478

is that in the afflicted individual the fever blister recurs on the same area of the face, but not in exactly the same place.

The epidemiologic studies relating cervical cancer with genital herpes infection must also be taken with a grain of salt. Cervical cancer occurs most frequently in a population characterized by sexual permissiveness, promiscuity, and poor personal hygiene. It is well known that the same population harbors preferentially (but not by choice) selected bacteria and parasites as well as the genital strain of herpes simplex virus. Obviously it remains to be seen whether the virus alone, to the exclusion of all other vaginal inhabitants, is the oncogenic agent. In a similar vein, the significance of chromosome breakage caused by herpesvirus infection remains obscure. It could be argued, for example, that the site of fragmentation is particularly labile and that similar breakage could probably be caused by other agents (17, 29). To pursue this further, one could argue that there are reasonable grounds for further study but there is in fact no sufficient and adequate evidence that any herpes-type viruses cause cancer. One obvious question before us is what would constitute sufficient and adequate evidence.

It seems clear that in this era of the art of experimentation only two types of evidence are truly significant. The first is a controlled experimental demonstration that herpesviruses cause tumors. In experimental animals herpes simplex viruses have been shown to produce tumors but only in conjunction with a known chemical carcinogen (30, 31). Studies in man are wrought with obvious difficulties. For example the maximum rate of cervical cancer in highly selected populations is about .5%. Meaningful studies cannot be done with a few volunteers. The availability of female volunteers in numbers, in age and other characteristics suitable for a controlled study is outside the realm of probable events. What we may hope for is a long term epidemiologic surveillance of several thousand women, but even that would be very costly. There remains then the second approach, namely to determine whether human cancer cells or their parentage were ever infected with herpesviruses.

A debatable rationale for the attempts to determine whether human cancer cells were ever infected with herpesviruses is based on the observation that in experimental animals the cells transformed from normal to malignant by oncogenic viruses continue to make products specified by the virus. A major part of these products identifiable by immunochemical methods consists of viral proteins which are not structural components of the virus. It has also been shown (32) in hybridization tests with viral DNA that tumor cells contain viral RNA which probably functions as an intermediary in the synthesis of proteins. To date however, analysis of human cancer cells for evidence of infection with herpes simplex viruses has not been very productive. There are probably two major reasons for this. First of all, the two types of human cancer suspected of being induced by herpesviruses are highly invasive but do not produce useful quantities of localized masses of cancer cells. Moreover, because of the invasive nature of the cancer the pathologist is frequently reluctant to part with much more than the tiniest sliver of material. We have on several occasions stared at a nearly transparent slice of tissue wondering which of the many plans we had for the specimen could be salvaged. The second reason for the lack of data is inherently the lack of suitable reagents with which to test the sera and the tissue containing the neoplastic cells. As I mentioned earlier, non-structural viral proteins appear to be the predominant antigens in tumor induced by viruses in experimental animals. Ideally, the sera and the cells from the cancer patients should be tested, respectively, with non-structural viral antigens and sera known to contain only antibody against these antigens. Preparations containing nonstructural viral proteins exclusively have been difficult to prepare and only recently have such preparations been reported (32). I should like to point out, however, that the whole rationale for this approach is debatable; the conclusion that structural viral antigens are not present in tumors induced by DNA viruses is based on work with just two virus groups. This point of view ignores two facts: first, that virus particles are present in Burkitt lymphoma and in amphibian renal tumors and no one has conclusively proven that these are passenger viruses, and second that viral particles are present in tumors induced by RNA viruses.

In summary, an "association" between herpes simplex viruses and the two types of malignancy in man has been suspected for many years. However, sufficient and adequate evidence of the type obtained with oncogenic viruses in experimental animals has not been furnished. It remains to be seen whether herpes simplex viruses are truly oncogenic.

References

1. WYBURN-MASON, R.: Malignant change following herpes simplex. Brit. Med. J. 2:615–616, 1957.
2. SCHNEWEISS, K. E.: Serologische untersuchungen zur type differzierund des herpes virus hominis. Z. Immunoforsch. 124:24–48, 1962.
3. PLUMMER, G.: Serological comparison of the herpes viruses. B. J. Exp. Path. 45:135–141, 1964.
4. DOWDLE, W. R., NAHMIAS, A. J., HARWELL, R. W. and PAULS, F. P.: Association of antigenic type of herpesvirus hominis with site of viral recovery. J. Immunol. 99:974–980, 1967.
5. PLUMMER, G., WANER, J. L. and BOWLING, C. P.: Comparative studies of type 1 and type 2 "herpes simplex" viruses. Brit. J. Exptl. Path. 49:202–208, 1968.
6. EJERCITO, P. et al.: Characterization of herpes simplex virus strains differing in their effect on social behavior of infected cells. J. Gen. Virology 3:357–364, 1968.
7. NAHMIAS, A. J., ZUHER, M., NAIB, Z. M., JOSEY, W. E. and CLEPPER, A. C.: Genital herpes simplex infection: virologic and cytologic studies. Obstetrics and Gynecology 29: 395–400, 1967.
8. DUXBURY, A. E. and LAWRENCE, J. R.: Primary venereal herpes simplex infection in male. Med. J. Australia 46:250–252, 1959.
9. BEILBY, J. O. W., CAMERON, C. H., CATTERALL, R. D. and DAVIDSON, D.: Herpesvirus hominis infection of cervix associated with gonorrhea. Lancet 1:1065–1066, 1968.
10. JOSEY, W. E., NAHMIAS, A. J. and NAIB, Z. M.: Genital infection with type 2 herpesvirus hominis—present knowledge and possible relation to cervical cancer. Am. J. Obst. G. 101: 718–729, 1968.
11. NAHMIAS, A.: First International Congress for Virology, Helsinki, Finland, in press, 1968.
12. RAWLS, W. E., TOMPKINS, W. A. F., FIGUEROA, M. E. and MELNICK, J. L.: Herpesvirus type 2: association with carcinoma of the cervix. Science 161:1255–1256, 1968.
13. HINZE, H. C. and WALKER, D. L.: Occurrence of focal three dimensional proliferation in cultured human cells after prolonged infection with herpes simplex virus. J. Exptl. Med. 113:885–898, 1961.

14. HAMPAR, B. and ELLISON, S. A.: Chromosomal aberrations induced by an animal virus. Nature *192*:145–147, 1961.

15. HAMPAR, B. and ELLISON, S. A.: Cellular alterations in the MCH line of chinese hamster cells following infection with herpes simplex virus. Proc. Natl. Acad. Sci. *49*:474–480, 1963.

16. TANZER, J., THOMAS, M., STOITCHKOV, Y., BOIRON, M. and BERNARD, J.: Alterations chromosomiques observées dans des cellules de reine de singe infectées *in vitro* par le virus de l'herpes. Ann. Inst. Pasteur *107*:366–373, 1964.

17. STICH, H. F., HSU, T. C. and RAPP, F.: Viruses and mammalian chromosomes. I. Localization of chromosome aberrations after infection with herpes simplex virus. Virology *22*: 439–445, 1964.

18. BENYESH-MELNICK, M., STICH, H. F., RAPP, F. and HSU, T. C.: Viruses and mammalian chromosomes. III. Effect of herpes zoster virus on human embryonal lung cultures. Proc. Soc. Exptl. Biol. Med. *117*:546–549, 1964.

19. BOIRON, M., TANZER, J., THOMAS, M. and HAMPE, A.: Early diffuse chromosome alterations in monkey kidney cells infected *in vitro* with herpes simplex virus. Nature *209*: 737–738, 1966.

20. AYA, T. *et al.*: Chromosome aberrations induced in cultured human leucocytes. HSV infection. Proc. Jap. Acad. *43*:239–244, 1967.

21. NICHOLS, W. W.: One role of viruses in the etiology of chromosomal abnormalies. Amer. J. Human Genet. *18*:81–92, 1966.

22. MIKHARLOVA, G. R.: Action on the karyotype of man and animals. Genetika *7*:129–137, 1967.

23. McKENNA, J. M., DAVIS, F. E., PRIER, J. E. and KLEGER, B.: Induction of neoantigen (G) in human amnion ("wish") cells by herpes virus A. Nature *212*:1602–1603, 1966.

24. WIGHT, P. A. L., WILSON, J. E., CAMPBELL, J. G. and FRASER, E.: Virus-like particles in blood lymphocytes in acute Marek's disease. Nature *216*:804–805, 1967.

25. EPSTEIN, M. A., ACHONG, B. G. and BARR, Y. M.: Virus particles in cultured lymphoblasts from Burkitt's lymphoma. Lancet *2*:702–703, 1964.

26. BURKITT, D.: A sarcoma involving the jaws in African children. Brit. J. Surg. *46*:218–223, 1958.

27. KVASNICKA, A.: Relationship between herpes simplex and lip carcinoma. III. Neoplasma (Bratislava) *10*:199–203, 1963.

28. KVASNICKA, A.: Relationship between herpes simplex and lip carcinoma. IV. Selected cases. Neoplasma (Bratislava) *12*:61–70, 1965.

29. HUANG, C. C.: Induction of a high incidence of damage to x chromosomes of rattus (mastomys) natalensis by base analogues, viruses and carcinogens. Chromosoma *23*:162–179, 1967.

30. TANAKA, S. and SOUTHAM, C. M.: Joint action of herpes simplex virus and 3-methylcholanthrene in production of papillomas in mice. J. Nat. Cancer Inst. *34*:441–451, 1965.

31. RAPP, F. and FALK, L. A.: Study of virulence and tumorigenicity of variants of herpes simplex virus. Proc. Soc. Exptl. Biol. & Med. *116*:361–365, 1964.

32. FUJINAGA, K. and GREEN, M.: Mechanism of viral carcinogenesis by DNA mammalian viruses. V. Properties of purified viral-specific RNA from human adenovirus-induced tumor cells. J. Mol. Biol. *31*:63–73, 1968.

33. SABIN, A. B.: Proc. First International Congress for Virology, Helsinki, Finland, in press, 1968.

Summary and Perspectives

KARL HABEL

Department of Experimental Pathology
Scripps Clinic and Research Foundation
La Jolla, California

Obviously it would be foolish for me to try to summarize all that has been presented at this symposium, especially the important part on the general biology of Amphibia. Therefore, most of my comments will be related to the sessions on amphibian tumors and viruses. Certainly after these two and one half days of exposure to your experimental results, I find that all the elements appear to be present in amphibian hosts to indicate that tumor-virus systems are indeed operative.

1. Tumors do occur under natural conditions, indeed they transplant and metastasize.
2. Epidemiological factors suggest an infectious element.
3. Perfectly good viral type inclusions are seen in Lucké tumor cells.
4. Viral particles are seen by electron microscopic examination of tumors.
5. Subcellular material extracted from tumors can produce the same type of tumors on inoculation of proper hosts.

The important current questions are first whether the subcellular inducer is a virus and secondly, if so, which one of the four or five apparently different viruses already isolated, if any, is the etiological agent.

Certainly it is not surprising that amphibian as well as mammalian species are infected by a number of viruses if even plants, insects and bacteria are. The interesting finding in kidney adenocarcinoma studies is that they are all DNA viruses, since in mammalian systems the RNA viruses far outnumber those with DNA as their genetic material. This may well be due to the nature of the tissue which has been examined. Major emphasis has been on tumors whereas the larger variety of mammalian viruses, particularly of the RNA type, have come from examining the intestinal and respiratory mucous membranes. I would wager that when as much effort is put on isolation attempts with stool and respiratory tract secretions of Amphibia, the list will get much longer and more RNA type viruses will be found. Since these frog kidney tumor agents are DNA viruses, it is important to recall some of the facts concerning DNA virus-induced mammalian tumors which I believe may be pertinent. Of all the DNA viruses well proven to be oncogenic, only one class—the virus causing papillomas, which are benign tumors—produces tumors under natural conditions of infection in its natural host as far as we now know. At least you people are starting with a tumor which exists in nature and is not a product of the laboratory.

Furthermore, all the DNA tumor viruses, except again the papilloma virus, usually can not be demonstrated as infectious entities in the tumors they induce. When infectious virus production is induced by some laboratory trick in tissue culture or perhaps spontaneously in tumors on rare occasions, the virus-producing cell dies. There is some evidence that this may be true also in the Lucké tumor.

Although the obvious analogies (and even possible specific relationships as reported by Dr. Fink) between the herpes-like virus which has a possible etiological role in Lucké frog tumors and the herpes-like agents in Burkitt lymphomas and Marek's Disease are exciting, I would prefer to compare the frog herpes virus situation to that with the Shope papilloma virus, since here is a system in which there is no question as to the etiological relationship of virus to tumor.

Here, as with summer frog tumors, not all papillomas contain demonstrable infectious virus. Inoculated domestic rabbits get papillomas which are virus-free; but DNA extracted from them is infectious, producing virus yielding tumors when inoculated into cottontail rabbits. Even in the cottontail, virus is not demonstrable in the rapidly dividing tumor cells in the dermis, but only in the superficial keratinized "cool" cells, which have died.

Recently Ito has cultured papilloma cells and has infected normal cells in culture with virus. The appearance of FA staining with antiviral antiserum was demonstrated only by lowering the temperature of his cultures. Likewise Marguerite Vogt working in Dulbecco's laboratory, has recently found a temperature-sensitive mutant of polyoma virus which transforms cells *in vitro* and these cells can be induced to produce whole infectious virus when cultivated at a reduced temperature.

The differential temperature sensitivity of cellular enzymes versus those involved in completion of virus replication may very well be operative in all DNA tumor virus systems. Even though the DNA viruses may be masked as infectious entities in most of the tumors they induce, they obviously have to multiply somewhere in nature otherwise a lot of us wouldn't be making a living and having fun working with them. However, the virus replication cycle probably occurs at a time greatly in advance of the appearance of tumors and may well be in cells of organs never involved in gross tumor formation.

In mammalian and avian systems, and I suspect also in amphibian hosts, the tumor viruses are ubiquitous in nature. Not all infected animals develop tumors, so there are other factors involved. At least in the polyoma-mouse system the evidence is quite strong that all infected animals have their normal cells transformed to tumor cells, but that the immunologically competent adult animal rejects his own tumor cells on the basis of the new, foreign, transplantation-type antigen on their surface. The high incidence of naturally occurring frog kidney tumors may be a reflection of the inefficient immuno-rejection mechanism mentioned by Dr. Cohen or perhaps due to immunological tolerance if oncogenesis is initiated during embryonic development.

But enough of analogies and back to the Amphibia. What are the prospects for future developments in virus-induced tumors and what are the priorities which should be considered in future work? It seems to me that all the necessary tools are now available as the result of hard pioneering work by you people already in the field.

Sources of virus in the form of primary and particularly transplant tumors should be no problem as shown by Dr. Mizell and his associates. Drs. Rafferty, Granoff and Clark, have gotten a good start on replication of some of these agents in tissue cul-

KARL HABEL

ture systems. Modern physical chemical methods are already being used for concentration and purification of particles. Dr. Tweedell has an *in vivo* virus assay system. It has been shown that Amphibia have all the important immunological systems operative in cellular and humoral reactions involved in oncogenesis and tumor development. There is some evidence, and it certainly is to be expected, that amphibian tumors, like their avian and mammalian counterparts, will contain new foreign antigens. Drs. Balls and Ruben have already shown that many of the biological characteristics of avian and murine virus-induced lymphosarcomas are present in the amphibian counterpart. The most pertinent problem at the moment is the firm establishment of etiological relationship. There are several direct and indirect methods for establishing the virus etiology of a tumor but for most of them to be used in a meaningful way it is essential that purified, concentrated, whole, intact virus be available in workable amounts.

The old, more standard biological method of direct production of tumors by virus inoculation is still convincing evidence if purified virus is used and especially if inactivation by physical and chemical treatments or exposure to specific antibody prevents the oncogenicity. The availability of genetically defined strains of animals and those known to be virus-free would greatly help this effort and would also be important in any immunological approach. Obviously the manipulation of age and environmental factors as well as immunosuppression should be considered in these oncogenicity experiments.

In vitro transformation with test back into the anterior chamber of the eye of the proper host animal represents a direct approach to oncogenicity studies in tissue culture systems. The direct biochemical approach using the elegant nucleic acid hybridization techniques discussed by Dr. Green are of course impossible without purified virus, but certainly are now applicable here. It would be especially interesting to apply them to the summer kidney tumors.

It appears to me that the immunological approach to establishing etiological relationship has been especially neglected in the amphibian tumor-virus field. All the elements appear to be on hand and the techniques do not so strictly require purified virus or even tissue culture systems. More work is indicated on nonstructural virus-coded antigens demonstrated by serological and cellular techniques.

Finally, I would like to emphasize that the work in this field should not be approached from the standpoint of merely showing that viruses can produce tumors in yet another taxonomic group. Rather the amphibian systems should be exploited for their special advantages to help provide answers to basic questions difficult to answer in other oncogenic systems. The special ability of epithelial cells to grow in culture with long persistence of normal karyotype and culture of haploid cells, the important effects of temperature, the ability to work at the egg and embryo level and the availability of usable microsurgical techniques, all make new and exciting experiments possible in basic research on oncogenesis using amphibian systems.

In conclusion, I would say that the field of oncogenesis and tumor viruses in amphibians is a very healthy organism, about to undergo metamorphosis and all it now requires is a stimulating environment and good nourishment in the form of that kind of lettuce known as the "green stuff."